Mastering the Reimbursement Process

Fourth Edition

Joanne M. Waters

American Medical Association
Executive Vice President, Chief Executive Officer: Michael D. Maves, MD, MBA
Chief Operating Officer: Bernard L. Hengesbaugh
Senior Vice President, Publishing and Business Services: Robert A. Musacchio, PhD
Vice President, Business Products: Anthony J. Frankos
Director, Editorial and Operations: Mary Lou White
Senior Acquisitions Editor: Marsha Mildred
Director, Production and Manufacturing: Jean Roberts
Director, Business Marketing and Communication: Pam Palmersheim
Director, Sales and Strategic Partnerships: J. D. Kinney
Senior Production Specialist: Rosalyn Carlton
Senior Print Production Specialist: Ronnie Summers
Marketing Manager: Erica Duke

Mastering the Reimbursement Process
Fourth Edition

©2008 by the American Medical Association
All rights reserved
Printed in the United States of America

Internet address: www.ama-assn.org

This book is for informational purposes only. It is not intended to constitute legal or financial advice. If legal, financial, or other professional advice is required, the services of a competent professional should be sought.

No part of this publication may be reproduced, stored in a retrieval system, or transmitted, in any form or by any means electronic, mechanical, photocopying, recording, or otherwise, without the prior written permission of the publisher.

Current Procedural Terminology (CPT®) © 1966, 1970, 1973, 1977, 1981, 1983–2007 American Medical Association. All rights reserved.

CPT is a registered trademark of the American Medical Association.

Advanced Healthcare Solutions (AHS) and SecureSelect provide services and technical support in the areas of health care reimbursement, operations management, outsourcing, practice improvement, compliance, education, and coding and billing for physicians, hospitals, and other health care providers. Advanced Healthcare Solutions and SecureSelect can be reached at 813 261-5001 or www.secureselect.us or my-ahs.com.

Additional copies of this book may be ordered by calling 800 621-8335.
Secure online orders can be taken at www.amabookstore.com.
Mention product number OP080003.

ISBN 978-1-57947-351-8
BP48:05-P-028:12/07

Library of Congress Cataloging-in-Publication Data

Waters, Joanne M.
　　Mastering the reimbursement process / Joanne M. Waters.—4th ed.
　　　p. ; cm.
　　Rev. ed. of: Mastering the reimbursement process / L. Lamar Blount. 3rd ed. c2001.
　　Includes bibliographical references and index.
　　Summary: "Up-to-date information on proper medical billing reimbursement and the codes, third party payers, and laws that affect it"—Provided by publisher.
　　ISBN-13: 978-1-57947-351-8 (alk. paper)
　　ISBN-10: 1-57947-351-2 (alk. paper)
　　1. Hospitals—Prospective payment—United States. I. Blount, L. Lamar. Mastering the reimbursement process. II. American Medical Association. III. Title.
　　[DNLM: 1. Insurance, Health, Reimbursement—United States. 2. Forms and Records Control—United States. 3. Insurance Claim Reporting—United States. 4. Insurance Claim Review—United States. 5. Patient Credit and Collection—United States.　　W 275 AA1 W29m 2006]
　RA981.A2U34 2006
　362.11068'1—dc22

2005031891

Contents

List of Illustrations   vii
Preface   xi
About the Author   xiii
About the Contributing Authors   xiv
Acknowledgments   xv

1 Understanding Insurance Basics   01

Individual Insurance vs Group Insurance   02
Types of Insurance   02
Methods of Insurance Reimbursement   04
Processing Claims   08
Summary   19
Endnote   19

2 Types of Insurance and Third-Party Payers   21

Commercial Carriers: Background Information   21
Medicare   54
Medicaid   77
TRICARE and CHAMPVA   86
Alternate Health Plans   107
Workers' Compensation and Disability   112
Summary   113

3 Electronic Claims Processing   115

Advantages of EDI   116
Options for Putting EDI Into the Practice   121
Medical Billing Software   121
Shortcomings of EDI   122
Pre-Claim Submission Operations   123
Privacy and Medical Records   124
HIPAA and EDI   124
The American Medical Association and EDI   125
Provider Enrollment Chain and Ownership System   129
Conclusion   130

4 The Coding Systems   131

CPT Procedure Coding   132
HCPCS Procedure Coding   151
ICD-9-CM Coding   153
Summary   170

5 Billing for Ancillary Services 171

Durable Medical Equipment 171
Nursing Home Facility 180
Alternatives to Nursing Home Care 188
Home Health Care 190
Ambulance Services 197
Hospice Care 201
Dietary and Nutritional Services 205
Summary 207

6 Insurance Processing: Managing Insurance and Patient Accounts 209

National Provider Identification (NPI) 210
Employee Job Description 213
Pre-Claim Submission Operations 213
Appointments and Preregistration 213
Information Verification 217
Patient Education and Preauthorizations 228
Insurance Claims Processing and Submission 238
Handling Bad Debts 260
Summary 266
Endnote 266

7 After Submission of Claims 267

Understanding Third-Party Reimbursements 267
Interpreting Explanation of Benefits and Payment Posting 269
Conclusion 273

8 Managing Insurance Accounts Receivable 275

A/R Report Preparation 275
Follow-up of Unpaid Insurance Claims 277
Insurance A/R Process Overview 291
Conclusion 294

9 Requests for Appeals and Review 295

Requests for Review 297
Medicare Part B Appeal Rights 297
Conclusion 304

10 Compliance Programs and the Office of the Inspector General 305

The Quality of Care Standard 306
Seven Basic Elements of an Effective Compliance Program 310
Compliance and Internal Controls 316

The Value a Compliance Program Brings to the Provider   316
Conclusion   320

11 Health Insurance Portability and Accountability Act: Administrative Simplification   321

Administrative Simplification Objectives   321
HIPAA Standards   322
HIPAA Privacy Rule   323
HIPAA Security Rule   330
Transactions and Code Sets   335
Conclusion   341
References   341

Appendix A   Internet Resources   345

Appendix B   Office of the Inspector General Compliance Program for Individual and Small Group Physician Practices   355

Appendix C   Medicare Modernization Act   375

Appendix D   Medicare Secondary Payer Guide   383

Appendix E   MSP Recoveries/Debt-Related Issues   397

Appendix F   Medicare Part B EDI Helpline   405

Glossary   409

Index   419

ILLUSTRATIONS

Figures

Figure 1-1: CMS-1500 Form   9
Figure 1-2: Sample Encounter Form (Superbill)   11
Figure 2-1: Blue Cross Blue Shield Identification Card   40
Figure 2-2: Medicare Beneficiary Health Insurance Identification Card   62
Figure 2-3: County Benchmarks for MA Plans, 2006   66
Figure 2-4: Counties With MA Plans, 2006   67
Figure 2-5: Role of Federal Government in Medicare   72
Figure 2-6: Benefits Example for Billing Medicare Coinsurance and Lifetime Reserve Days   73
Figure 2-7: Election Not to Use Lifetime Reserve Days   75
Figure 2-8: Revocation of Election Not to Use Lifetime Reserve Days   75
Figure 2-9: Billing Tips to Bill Medicare Blood Deductible   76
Figure 2-10: Total Annual Medicaid Population Distribution by Year: Managed Care v Other as of June 30, 2005   86
Figure 2-11: Form DD2642-CHAMPUS   91
Figure 2-12: CHAMPVA Identification Card   105
Figure 2-13: PPO and HMO Enrollment   109
Figure 2-14: Medicare HMO Enrollment Growth Rate   110
Figure 2-15: PPO Eligible Employees   110
Figure 2-16: Breakout of All PPOs by Type, 1999 v 2006   111
Figure 4-1: Comprehensive, Component and Mutually Exclusive Codes   137
Figure 4-2: CPT Modifiers Found in the 2005 Codebook   147
Figure 4-3: UB-92   163
Figure 5-1: Spending for Post-Acute Care   182
Figure 5-2: Medicare Spending for Skilled Nursing Facility Services   183
Figure 5-3: Medicare Costs per Day in Freestanding Skilled Nursing Facilities   184
Figure 5-4: Spending for Home Health Care, 1992–2005   191
Figure 6-1: Reporting of NPIs on Claims Sent to Medicare   211
Figure 6-2: New Patient Information Sheet   216
Figure 6-3: Employer-Insurance Verification Information Form   219
Figure 6-4: Patient-Insurance Coverage Verification Form   220
Figure 6-5: Sample Sign-in Sheet   224
Figure 6-6: Assignment and Instruction for Direct Payment to Medical Providers   226
Figure 6-7: Authorization for Release of Medical-Related Information   227
Figure 6-8: Signature-on-File Form   227
Figure 6-9: Sample Welcome Letter   229
Figure 6-10: Insurance Fact Sheet   231
Figure 6-11: Medical Cost Estimate Form   232
Figure 6-12: Advance Notice Form for Elective Surgery Greater Than $500   233
Figure 6-13: Medicare Advanced Notice Service Waiver   234
Figure 6-14: Insurance Coverage Advanced Notice Service Waiver   235

Figure 6-15:   Explanation of Benefits   257
Figure 6-16:   Sample Letter for Billing a Supplemental Claim: Practice Will File   259
Figure 6-17:   Sample Letter for Billing a Supplemental Claim: Patient Will File   259
Figure 6-18:   Sample Deductible Letter   260
Figure 6-19:   Sample Collection Policy   262
Figure 6-20:   Sample Overdue Letter   264
Figure 7-1:   TRICARE Explanation of Benefits   271
Figure 8-1:   Sample Letter for Claim Inquiry on Assigned Claims   292
Figure 8-2:   Sample Letter for Claim Inquiry on Unassigned Claims   293
Figure 8-3:   Sample Letter to Send to the Insurance Commissioner   294
Figure 9-1:   Sample Letter for Requesting a Review   296
Figure 9-2:   Comparison of Former and Current 1869 Fee-for-Service Appeals   298
Figure 9-3:   Form CMS-1964   299
Figure 10-1:   National Error Rates by Category, 2004 vs 2005   307
Figure 10-2:   The Quality of Care Standard   309
Figure 10-3:   Sample Compliance Training and Education Tool   313
Figure 10-4:   Physician Benchmarking: Evaluation and Management Distribution   314
Figure 10-5:   Physician Benchmarking: Variance From National Peers   315
Figure 11-1:   Sample Risk Analysis   331
Figure 11-2:   Structure of the Security Rule   332

Tables

Table 1-1:   Sources of US Provider Payments for 2002 and 2003   2
Table 1-2:   Medicare Conversion Factors, 1997-2005   6
Table 2-1:   National Health Care Expenditures Projections: 2005–2015   22
Table 2-2:   BCBS 2006 Standard Option Benefits at a Glance: What You Pay   41
Table 2-3:   BCBS 2006 Basic Option Benefits at a Glance: What You Pay   44
Table 2-4:   BCBS Overseas and Local Plans Customer Service Contact   47
Table 2-5:   Examples of Items Not Covered Under Medicare Part B   57
Table 2-6:   Medicare-Covered Preventive Services   58
Table 2-7:   Common Health Insurance Claim Number (HICN) Suffix Modifiers   63
Table 2-8:   Most Common Prefixes for Railroad Retirement Beneficiaries   63
Table 2-9:   Percentage of Medicare Beneficiaries With Access to MA Plans   65
Table 2-10:   Benefits Available in MA Plans   66
Table 2-11:   Method 1 and Method 2 Payment Chart for Home Dialysis Equipment, Supplies, and Support Servives   71
Table 2-12:   Sample Bill Types   77
Table 2-13:   Federal Medical Assistance Percentage by State   79
Table 2-14:   States With Comprehensive Health Care Reform Demonstrations as of December 31, 2005   84
Table 2-15:   Managed Care Trends, 1996–2005   85
Table 2-16:   National Breakout of Managed Care Entities and Enrollment as of June 30, 2005   85
Table 2-17:   Medicaid Managed Care Enrollment as of December 31, 2005   87
Table 2-18:   Tier Eligibility   97
Table 2-19:   2006 Premiums   97

Table 2-20:	TRICARE Deductibles and Coinsurance	99
Table 2-21:	TFL Costs for 2006 Health Care Coverage	102
Table 2-22:	Enrollment by Type of HMO Plan	109
Table 3-1:	Advantages of Using Medicare EDI	116
Table 4-1:	Levels of Medical Decision-Making	141
Table 4-2:	New Patient Evaluations	142
Table 4-3:	Established Patient Evaluations	143
Table 4-4:	Side-by-side Comparison of E/M Documentation Guidelines	143
Table 4-5:	HCPCS Level II (National) Modifiers for Hospital Outpatient Use	152
Table 4-6:	Diagnosis Codes for Terrorism	159
Table 4-7:	Sample Table of V Codes	166
Table 4-8:	Anthrax-Related Diagnosis Codes	170
Table 5-1:	Regional Carriers of Durable Medical Equipment	172
Table 5-2:	Covered and Noncovered Durable Medical Equipment	173
Table 5-3:	Claims Accepted During Transition Period	178
Table 5-4:	Newly Revised CMNs Accepted During Transition Period	179
Table 5-5:	CMNs Eliminated	179
Table 5-6:	The Number of Post-Acute Care Providers	181
Table 5-7:	Medicare Skilled Nursing Facility Use	183
Table 5-8:	Characteristics of Skilled Nursing Facilities, 2003	184
Table 5-9:	Freestanding Skilled Nursing Facility Medicare Margin, by Facility Group, 2004	185
Table 5-10:	SNF Care Paid for by Medicare	188
Table 5-11:	Medicare Home Health Care Use, 1992–2003	191
Table 5-12:	Aggregate Medicare Margins for All Freestanding Home Health Agencies, 2004	192
Table 5-13:	Changes to the Home Health Product After the Prospective Payment System Started	193
Table 5-14:	Origin and Destination Modifiers	197
Table 5-15:	Ambulance Fee Schedule	201
Table 5-16:	Medicare Hospice Payment Categories and Rates, FY 2006	202
Table 5-17:	Levels of Care	204
Table 5-18:	Codes Used to Determine Type of Service Location for Hospice Services	204
Table 5-19:	HCPCS and CPT Codes for the Reporting of MNT Services	206
Table 5-20:	Applicable FI Claim Bill Types and Associated Revenue Codes for MNT	207
Table 6-1:	Office Manager Job Responsibilities	214
Table 6-2:	Billing and Collection Staff Job Responsibilities	215
Table 6-3:	Reception and Patient Registration Job Responsibilities	215
Table 6-4:	Place of Service Codes	252
Table 8-1:	Insurance Responses and Explanations to Unpaid Insurance Claims	277
Table 8-2:	Follow-Up Procedures for Unpaid Claims	279
Table 8-3:	State Prompt Payment Laws, as of October 2003	280
Table 8-4:	Health Care Appeal Process	288
Table 8-5:	Health Care Appeals Statistics	289
Table 10-1:	National Error Rates by Year	306
Table 10-2:	Summary of Error Rates by Category	306
Table 10-3:	Qui Tam Explosion Since 1987	308

Table 10-4: OIG Projects for Medicare Physicians and Other Health Professionals   316
Table 10-5: Other OIG Medicare Projects   317
Table 10-6: Internal Control Checklist   319
Table 11-1: HIPAA Timeline   323
Table 11-2: Permissions & Special Requirements for Disclosing PHI   324
Table 11-3: How to Designate a Privacy Official   326
Table 11-4: HIPAA Privacy Administrative Tasks and How to Do Them   328
Table 11-5: Technical Safeguard Issues   329
Table 11-6: Technical Safeguard Terms   329
Table 11-7: Leverage Privacy to Meet Security   334
Table 11-8: Administrative Safeguards   334
Table 11-9: Physical Safeguards   335
Table 11-10: Technical Safeguards   335

PREFACE

This fourth edition of *Mastering the Reimbursement Process* includes many new and updated pages, reflecting the fact that the US health care system continues to become more complex and demanding. Despite the Health Insurance Portability and Accountability Act (HIPAA) Administrative Simplification provisions passed by Congress in 1996, dealing with reimbursement issues continues to become more and more complicated for physicians and their staff members. Comprehensive regulatory changes have taken place in the health care industry during the past few years.
The Medicare Prescription Drug Improvement and Modernization Act was signed into law on December 8, 2003. Appendix C in this book provides an overview of these changes. The National Provider Identifier mandated under HIPAA regulations is being implemented. The UB-04 replaced the UB-92 in May 2007. The CMS-1500 form is being updated also.

In 2004, total national health care expenditures in the United States reached $1.9 trillion, 16% of gross domestic product (GDP). The United States spends more on health care than other industrialized nations, although over 46 million Americans are uninsured. Total health care expenditures rose 7.9%, more than three times the rate of inflation in 2004. According to a forecast by the Centers for Medicare and Medicaid Services, health care spending was expected to grow 7.4% and surpass $2 trillion in 2005. Health care spending is expected to reach $4.0 trillion and 20% of GDP by 2015. In 2005, actual health care spending in the United States reached $2.0 trillion, rising 6.9%.

The Office of Inspector General (OIG) admits that the complexity of Medicare's rules results in some billing errors. Significant improvements and efforts have brought the error rates down in recent years. Physician services accounted for the third largest category with common errors being related to the adequacy of documentation and appropriate coding of services.

Several agencies now investigate physicians and other providers who have questionable billings. Private whistleblower cases are filed against physicians and other health care providers, and Medicare contractor fraud control units have referred civil and criminal cases. In addition, every state Medicaid agency and most insurance companies also have their own fraud control units, all staffed with investigators, analysts, and attorneys seeking to find improper claims.

Because of the increasing allegations of improper claims, it is only prudent that physicians, practice managers, and other health care providers learn as much as possible about the reimbursement process. Failure to understand and follow specific billing requirements could be considered "reckless disregard," exposing physicians and other health care providers to federal False Claim Act charges. Additionally, with a better understanding of the reimbursement process, physicians and other health care providers will be able to obtain the full reimbursement to which they are legitimately entitled for their services.

This fourth edition of *Mastering the Reimbursement Process* contains significant new material. A new chapter presents ancillary services: durable medical equipment, ambulance services, home health care, hospice, skilled nursing facility services, and dietary services. Numerous statistics and informative information have been added to each of the new chapters in addition to regulatory changes that have taken place. This edition also contains six appendices and a glossary with extensive new material. This material will help readers familiarize themselves with the unique terminology of health care reimbursement as well as help them access many other resources.

ABOUT THE AUTHOR

Joanne M. Waters, FHFMA, CHFP, is the founder and Chief Executive Officer for Advanced Healthcare Solutions (AHS), a firm providing consulting and outsourcing solutions for providers nationwide. AHS provides comprehensive reimbursement consulting and outsourcing services including education and training services. The firm also provides medical record coding and billing services on both an interim basis as well as a full service outsourcing basis. Joanne has served the health care industry for more than 25 years.

Joanne uses her many years of experience in health care to consult on matters that include patient financial services; diverse financial management of integrated delivery systems; medical facilities and multiphysician practice management; external and internal financial reporting; capital and operational budgeting; third-party reimbursement; managed care; and general accounting.

Prior to founding AHS, Joanne served as president of a consulting firm in Atlanta, Georgia, which provided extensive clinical data, compliance, and financial expertise to providers nationwide. Previous to that position, Joanne was director of patient financial services at Southwest Hospital and Medical Center in Atlanta. Additionally, she worked for more than 10 years in the finance division of South Fulton Medical Center, where she had responsibilities in both the accounting and patient financial services departments. Prior to moving to the Atlanta area, she was an office manager for a specialty surgeon's practice in Tampa, Florida, and was with the University of South Florida College of Medicine.

Joanne is an active member of the Healthcare Financial Management Association (HFMA) and the Health Care Compliance Association. She is a fellow of the Healthcare Financial Management Association (FHFMA) as well as a Certified Healthcare Financial Professional (CHFP) with a specialty area in patient financial services. She is also an advanced member of HFMA. Joanne previously served as co-chairperson of the Managed Care Education Committee for the Georgia Chapter of Healthcare Financial Management Association and chairperson of the Georgia HFMA Chapter Web Committee. She graduated from Georgia State University with a Bachelor of Business Administration in accounting. Joanne has completed the managed care certificate program conducted by the Georgia Healthcare Financial Management Association and Mercer University. She is presently an active member of the Florida chapter of HFMA.

Joanne has written articles for the Healthcare Financial Management Association on compliance issues in patient financial management and she coauthored previous editions of this book.

ABOUT THE CONTRIBUTING AUTHORS

Michelle Niski, CPC, is Senior Manager of Coding and Consulting Services for Advanced Healthcare Solutions and has more than 15 years experience in health care coding and management. Michelle has performed numerous compliance risk assessments and reviews. She has developed and presented several training and education programs for both compliance and coding services. Previously she worked at the University of South Florida College of Medicine for more than 10 years. She is an active member of the American Academy of Professional Coders (AAPC). Michelle has provided significant assistance throughout the book, including material contributions as well as reviewing and editing.

Barbara Pankau, Esquire, is a partner in the health law practice of Shumaker, Loop and Kendrick, LLP. She provided significant material to Chapter 11 on HIPAA. Her principal area of practice is health care provider representation. Ms Pankau has extensive experience representing physicans, hospitals, IPAs, HMOs, home health agencies, rehabilitation agencies, and other providers and payers. She has substantial experience in managed care and integrated delivery systems, antireferral legislation, health information privacy issues (HIPAA), state licensure and regulations, provider operational issues such as employment and other contractual arrangements, Medicare and Medicaid certification and reimbursement, medical staff matters (including staff privileges), and various administrative and corporate matters.

In the health law category, Ms Pankau has been selected as one of the *Best Lawyers in America* and one of the Leading Florida Attorneys. She has also been recognized as a 2006 and 2007 *Florida Super Lawyer* in the health law practice area.

Ms Pankau is certified as a Health Care Law Specialist under the Florida certification rules.

ACKNOWLEDGMENTS

Several individuals assisted in the preparation and review of this latest edition of *Mastering the Reimbursement Process*. I would like to thank the following individuals for reviewing, editing, and providing contributions to the text:

Michelle Niski, CPC

Melora Jones, RHIA, CCS

Diana Juhl, CPC

Barbara R. Pankau, Esquire

Peter Keohane, JD, MPH, CPC

Dane Cuter, CPA,

Dr. Michael A. LoGuidice, Sr, Board Certified Emergency Medicine Physician

Peter provided assistance, editing, and contributions to Chapter 9. He is a founder and senior partner of the CMC Group, LLC. Barbara, a partner in the health law practice of Shumaker, Loop & Kendrick LLP, provided significant contributions to Chapter 11. Dane Cutler, CPA, provided and reviewed material; and Dr Michael LoGuidice, Sr, provided reviews of material. Dane is founder and President of Cornerstone Health Care Services, Inc. Dr Michael A. LoGuidice, Sr, is a Board Certified Emergency Medicine Physician and author of *Open Up and Say Aaaggghhh!* and *The Emergency Department: A Patient's Practical Guide*. Michelle, Melora, and Diana reviewed and edited material in the coding and insurance areas. They are certified coders and consultants and have worked with me during the past several years. I would especially like to thank and acknowledge Michelle Niski for her significant contributions and dedication in the course of this project.

In addition to the contributors and reviewers listed, a special thanks goes to the editorial and production staff at the American Medical Association for its guidance and support, as well as extraordinary job in format, design, and editorial review.

chapter 1

Understanding Insurance Basics

OBJECTIVES

- Explain the difference between group insurance plans and individual insurance plans.
- Understand the methods of reimbursement.
- Understand the resource-based relative value scale (RBRVS) fee schedule.
- Explain the difference between contracted rates and capitated rates.
- Understand the claims process.
- Understand the significance of prompt payment legislation.

Traditionally, health insurance has been made available to help offset the costs of treating illness or injury. At its most basic, an indemnity health insurance plan pays for hospital stays and services provided by physicians and other health care providers. The purchaser of the health insurance (often the patient's employer) pays the insurance company a fixed amount, referred to as the *premium*, every month. In return for premiums paid, the health insurance company or carrier promises, according to terms set out in the insurance policy, to pay for the medical services provided to those covered under the insurance policy, often called *beneficiaries*.

With the meteoric expansion of managed care, traditional indemnity health insurance is no longer the norm for most beneficiaries. However, the basic concept of health insurance has not changed, ie, a premium is paid by a beneficiary or another on behalf of a beneficiary (such as an employer) in return for which the insurance company agrees to pay for defined medical services provided to the beneficiary. Managed care organizations (MCOs) and plans now offer different types of health plans that vary in terms of coverage and level of patient financial responsibility or shared payments such as copayments and deductibles.

According to the US Census Bureau Population Survey, 2004 and 2005 Annual Social and Economic Supplements, 84.4% of Americans, or 243.3 million people, had some type of health insurance in calendar year 2003. In 2004, the number of people with health insurance coverage increased by 20 million to 245.3 million, or 84.3% of the population. Table 1-1 illustrates the payer-mix sources from 2003 and 2004.

It is important to note that these percentages constantly change. Private and public insurance programs redesign their products and offer more options for health care delivery. For example, both Medicare and many state Medicaid programs have designed and implemented—with varying degrees of success—managed care options to replace the traditional fee-for-service programs. Furthermore, other types of programs, such as provider-sponsored organizations (PSOs), are themselves becoming insurance plans. In the future, the traditional separations between insurance plans and providers will continue to narrow.

TABLE 1-1

Sources of US Provider Payments for 2002, 2003, and 2004

Type of Health Insurance	Year 2002 (%)	Year 2003 (%)	Year 2004 (%)
Private insurance plan	69.6	68.6	68.1
Medicare	13.4	13.7	13.7
Medicaid	11.6	12.4	12.9
Military health care	3.5	3.5	3.7
No insurance coverage	15.2	15.6	15.7

Source: US Census Bureau. Population Survey, 2003 and 2004 Annual Social and Economic Supplements. Because some individuals have insurance from both private and government sources, these figures exceed 100%.

INDIVIDUAL INSURANCE VS GROUP INSURANCE

Both individuals and groups purchase different types of insurance that can be broadly grouped into indemnity insurance and managed care. Within managed care, in particular, there are a number of differences among and between the types of plans.

Individual insurance is purchased by the individual on his or her own behalf. Generally, the purchaser is also entitled to insure his or her primary family members under this coverage. Individual insurance plans are often more expensive than policies purchased through a group because of the concept of risk sharing: when an individual purchases insurance, the risk is not spread among many people and, thus, each individual assumes the full risk of his or her health status without benefit of pooling individuals or a large group, which can spread the risk over many people.

Group insurance is purchased through a group that can include employers, trade associations, and professional associations. The insurance is purchased by the group itself and is then offered to that group's members. Group insurance, similar to individual policies, generally also permits coverage of primary family members. Group policies are generally less expensive than individual coverage because the risk of adverse claims is spread across a larger number of people.

TYPES OF INSURANCE

Notwithstanding the method by which the insurance is purchased, alternative types of insurance are available. The types are broadly distinguished between indemnity and managed care.

Indemnity Insurance

Indemnity insurance is also known as *fee-for-service (FFS)*. Under traditional indemnity insurance, there are no restrictions as to the physician, hospital, or other health care provider the beneficiary can use. There is no requirement for preapproval for medical visits. After receiving medical care, the beneficiary submits a bill to his or her indemnity insurance carrier. The carrier then pays the charges. Each year, the beneficiary must meet his or her deductible, which is the amount the beneficiary must pay out of pocket before the insurance company begins paying for medical services. After the deductible is met, the indemnity insurance carrier pays the entire cost of medical services except for the following points:

- There is generally a copayment or coinsurance for each service. An example of coinsuring is an 80/20 coverage that would require the beneficiary to pay 20% of each dollar of medical care provided.

- Instances in which the physician's fee (also known as the physician's *usual* fee) is greater than considered customary or reasonable. (A fee is "customary" when it is within the range of usual fees currently charged by physicians of similar training and experience for the same service within the same specific and limited geographic area. A fee is "reasonable" when, after any special circumstances of the particular case are taken into account, it is no more than the customary fee, without regard to payments that have been discounted under governmental or private plans.)
- Limitations may exist on the type of care that is covered. For example, previously chiropractic care was often excluded from coverage.
- Coverage may not include preventive care, such as mammograms and well-baby checkups.
- Other restrictions may exist in the insurance coverage.

Managed Care Organizations

MCOs enter into contracts with physicians, hospitals, and other health care providers. In each contract, the physician or other health care provider agrees to provide defined medical services to beneficiary members who have purchased insurance from the MCO. The physicians and providers agree to discount their normal charges in exchange for being included by the MCO on its list of approved providers. MCOs tend to be less costly to the beneficiaries in exchange for certain limitations of beneficiary access to physicians, providers, or services. Types of MCOs include health maintenance organizations (HMOs), preferred provider organizations (PPOs), and point of service (POS) plans.

Health Maintenance Organization

An HMO is the most restrictive health plan, yet it is generally the least costly for the beneficiary. In an HMO, a beneficiary pays a premium for health care. Services available to beneficiaries may be quite broad and may include benefits such as preventive care and prescriptions. The beneficiary is restricted as to which physician he or she may see for care. Most HMOs require the beneficiary to initially visit a primary care physician for all care; this is referred to as a "gatekeeper" arrangement. Only if the primary care physician refers the beneficiary to another physician or prescribes other medical services will the HMO be responsible to pay for such services. An open access HMO allows the beneficiary to see specialists without a primary care physician "gatekeeper" referral.

Staff model HMOs restrict the beneficiary to HMO-employed physicians who are located in medical offices or clinics owned and managed by the HMO. HMOs based on independent practice associations (IPAs) or other networks will permit a beneficiary to use physicians in private practice who are not employed by the HMO but are under contract with the HMO. These private physicians will also see patients from other MCOs and indemnity plans and also self-pay patients. For each patient, the type of coverage they have purchased (eg, HMO, indemnity, preferred provider organization [PPO]) will determine the type and, perhaps, amount of charges the physician will submit. Nearly all insurance carriers accept the standard CMS-1500 form. The CMS-1500 form is used by noninstitutional providers and suppliers to bill Medicare Part B covered services. As stated, most health insurers and carriers accept the CMS-1500 form. The form has been adopted by TRICARE and has received the approval of the American Medical Association (AMA) Council on Medical Services.

Out-of-pocket costs to the beneficiary for health care services typically range from $15 to $35 per physician visit, and may also have a prescription benefit that limits the out-of-pocket costs for approved drugs. If a beneficiary goes to a physician without the approval of his or her primary care physician or if the beneficiary visits a physician who is not under contract with the HMO, the beneficiary may be responsible for all costs for that care.

Preferred Provider Organization

As in an HMO, physicians and other health care providers enter into contracts with managed care plans to provide health care services to the beneficiaries of the PPO. However, unlike the HMO, PPOs are generally more flexible and give more options to the beneficiary. For this flexibility and options, the beneficiary pays a higher premium than for an HMO. Under a PPO, the physician and other providers agree to a reduction in their normal fees and charges in exchange for being listed by the PPO as a provider who has a contract with that PPO. This provider may be called an "in-network" physician. PPOs do not use primary care physicians, thus allowing the beneficiary to choose a health care provider so long as the physician or other providers are in-network. PPOs generally require a yearly deductible and copayment or coinsurance for each visit. However, if the beneficiary visits a physician or provider who is not in the PPO network, the beneficiary may be responsible for all costs associated with that physician's services and charges.

Point of Service

The POS managed care plan has been called a leaky HMO or gatekeeper PPO. If the beneficiary receives medical care from in-network physicians, he or she will receive benefits similar to those in an HMO, ie, if the beneficiary first goes to the primary care physician, does not self-refer him- or herself to other specialists, and only seeks care that has been approved by the primary care physician, all care is covered under the terms of the POS agreement between the beneficiary and POS. However, if the beneficiary sees a physician who is not in-network, unlike a PPO or HMO, the POS plan will pay the physician or other provider but at a rate usually significantly less than that for care provided by physicians within the POS network. The difference between the POS plan payment and the billed charges is the beneficiary's responsibility. Unique to POS plans, the beneficiary may decide each time he or she seeks care whether to stay within the POS network for maximum benefits or go outside the POS network for greater options but reduced benefits.

As health insurance plans mature, the distinction between and among the various plans are becoming less distinct and the features that characterize a plan may not accurately reflect the plan and its coverage.

METHODS OF INSURANCE REIMBURSEMENT

Payments to physicians and other providers differ depending on whether the patient has insurance and, if so, on the type and extent of coverage. The provider's being in or out of network is also a factor. Most commonly, the provider bills a standard fee to the patient and/or files a claim with the patient's insurance carrier. With the advent of managed care, payments may be determined by a contracted discount rate, a fee schedule, a case rate, or a capitated rate. For example, Medicare payments are determined on the basis of a national fee schedule.

Usual, Customary, and Reasonable Method

The patient is responsible for payment of the physician's full fee schedule. Historically, however, some commercial plans have based provider payments on the lowest of the following:

- The fee usually charged for a given service by an individual physician to his or her private patient (i.e., that doctor's usual fee): *usual*
- A fee that is within the range of usual fees currently charged by physicians of similar training and experience for the same service within the same specific and limited geographic area: *customary*
- A fee that meets the above two criteria and is justifiable, considering the special circumstances of the particular case in question, without regard to payments that have been discounted under governmental or private plans: *reasonable*

This method of determining payment is referred to as the usual, customary, and reasonable (UCR) method. Each component amount is calculated based on previous charges submitted to the insurer. For individual providers, a profile of all charges submitted is maintained and the most frequent charge is identified to determine the *usual* charge. All provider charges within a specified area are collated and averaged to determine a *customary* charge. To arrive at a payment amount for a claim, the carrier then compares the physician's most frequent charge (the usual), the average charge of all providers in the area (the customary), and the actual charge submitted on the claim (which, if submitted by a provider, must be *reasonable* to that provider). The lowest amount is used as the basis for payment (the allowable charge).

For example, a physician usually charges $100 for a procedure and the average charge of providers in the geographic area is $105. The physician submits a charge of $120 on a particular claim. Payment for that claim will be based on $100, which is the lowest of the usual ($100), customary ($105), and actual ($120) charges.

Relative Value Payment Schedules Method

Another method used by insurance plans to develop payment schedules for provider services involves the use of relative value scales. The Medicare resource-based relative value scale (RBRVS) is the most well-known relative value scale. Another relative value scale is the St Anthony's Relative Value for Physicians (RVP), formerly known as the McGraw-Hill's Relative Values for Physicians.

Formerly, practice expense relative values were based on a formula that used average Medicare-approved changes from 1991 (the year before the RBRVS was implemented) and the proportion of each specialty's revenue attributable to practice expenses. However, effective January 1999, the Centers for Medicare and Medicaid Services (CMS) began a transition to resource-based practice expense relative values for each Current Procedural Terminology (CPT®) code that differed based on the site of service. Effective January 1, 2002, the resource-based practice expenses were fully transitioned.

On January 1, 2000, CMS implemented the resource-based professional liability insurance (PLI) relative value units (RVUs). With this implementation and final transition of the resource-based practice expense relative units on January 1, 2002, all components of the RBRVS are resource based. In 2004, the AMA/Specialty Society RVS Update Committee (RUC) began reviewing appropriate PLI relative value crosswalks.

Relative value scales assign a relative weight to individual services according to the basis for the scale. Some relative value scales are based on the cost of resources used or on the physician's effort and intensity. Some are based on a combination of both, as in the case of Medicare's RBRVS. Services that are more difficult, time consuming, or resource intensive to perform typically have higher relative values than other services. Payments are determined by multiplying a code's relative value by a constant dollar amount called the conversion factor or multiplier. For example, if a procedure has a relative value of 10 and the conversion factor is $20, the fee for the service would be $200 (ie, 10 × $20). Third-party payers using relative value systems often apply additional methodologies, such as UCR, to determine payment limits.

Medicare's RBRVS Payment Schedule

On January 1, 1992, Medicare began implementation of a national provider payment schedule using the RBRVS. The RBRVS was developed for the CMS under contract by researchers at Harvard University and continues to be refined. Under RBRVS, a procedure's RVU total is the sum of the following three elements:

RVU WK: The provider's work (time and intensity)

RVU PE: The practice expense related to performing the service

RVU MP: Malpractice costs associated with the service

To account for economic variation across different areas of the country, the Medicare RBRVS applies a geographic component called the geographic practice cost index (GPCI).

GPCIs were developed for each of the 210 Medicare payment localities. These localities were established in the early 1960s and are based on historical circumstances. CMS plans to review the current payment localities for further refinements.

Medicare conversion factors (CFs) used to calculate annual payment amounts are determined annually by CMS in cooperation with Congress. Previous values as well as current values are shown in Table 1-2. To calculate payment for a CPT code, the conversion factor is multiplied by the sum of the RVU for physician work, practice costs, and malpractice insurance. The formula is:

$$\text{Work RVU} \times \text{Work GPCI} + \text{Practice Expense (PE) RVU} \times \text{PE GPCI}$$
$$+ \text{Malpractice (PLI) RVU} \times \text{PLI GPCI} - \text{Total RVU} \times \$37.8975$$
$$(2006 \text{ Medicare Payment Schedule Conversion Factor}) = \text{Payment}$$

Elements of the Medicare RBRVS payment schedule formula—the CFs, RVUs, and geographic adjustment factors—are continually reviewed for refinements. For example, Congress and the Physician Payment Review Commission (PPRC) make recommendations for the annual update of CFs, and the American Medical Association (AMA)/Specialty Society RVS Update Committee and CMS suggest refinements in service RVUs. The RVU updates are published in an issue of the *Federal Register* in late October or early November and go into effect the following January 1. Local Medicare carriers annually publish this calculated fee schedule and distribute it with their Medicare participation agreements.

In the November 21, 2005, Final Rule, CMS reported that the physician fee schedule conversion factor for 2006 would be $36.1770, that the physician fee schedule update would be −4.4%, and the initial estimate for the sustainable growth rate for 2006 would be 1.7%. The AMA waged an aggressive campaign against the reduction. CMS halted the 4.4% cut. Legislation was signed into law on February 9, 2006, reverting the conversion factor back to the 2005 conversion factor of $37.8975.

Relative Value for Physicians

The St Anthony Relative Value for Physicians (RVP) was formerly known as the McGraw-Hill RVP. In many respects, the RVP is simpler than the RBRVS. It has no geographic adjustment factors or individual RVU components to calculate. The relative value given by RVP is the number used to decide both fees and CFs. A drawback of the RVP is that for each major category of procedures, a separate CF needs to be developed. For example, the CF developed for surgical procedures (CPT codes 10000 through 69999) cannot be used with the pathology codes (80000 through 89999).

The fee amount for the RVP is calculated using the same basic principles as those used in the RBRVS, with the exception of the location and component characteristics. For example, procedure code 99204 has an RVU of 20. When divided by the RVU (20), the $80 fee for this procedure results in a CF of $4. To establish the fee for other procedures in the category (those from 90000 to 99999), the procedure-specific RVU is multiplied by the CF of $4.

TABLE 1-2

Medicare Conversion Factors, 1997–2006

Conversion Factors	1997*	1998	1999	2000	2001	2002	2003	2004	2005	2006
Primary care	$35.77	$36.69	$34.73	$36.61	$38.26	$36.20	$36.79	$37.34	$37.90	$37.90
Surgical	$40.96	$36.69	$34.73	$36.61	$38.26	$36.20	$36.79	$37.34	$37.90	$37.90
Nonsurgical	$33.85	$36.69	$34.73	$36.61	$38.26	$36.20	$36.79	$37.34	$37.90	$37.90

*Initially, the Medicare Physician Payment Schedule included distinct conversion factors for various categories of services. In 1998, a single conversion factor was implemented.

Use of Relative Value by Other Payers

Relative value scales are important not only for programs like Medicare but also for managing reimbursements from Medicaid, Blue Cross Blue Shield, and other commercial payers. Studies have shown that several insurers have implemented a payment system similar to RBRVS.

Contracted Rates With Managed Care Organizations

A major tool in managed care is the ability to negotiate with physicians and other providers for reduced fees in exchange for the promise of patient volume. A physician may agree to provide services at a discount of his or her normal fee with the understanding that the MCO will refer patients to the provider or will provide the provider with a pool of existing patients. The physician or practice may also accept a capitated rate and elect to take financial risk to improve patient volume or practice profitability.

Capitated Rates

A common payment arrangement between physicians and MCOs is a capitation plan. Capitated health plans contract with select physicians, usually primary health care providers, who are charged with managing the health care delivery of their members. Under capitation, the physician provides the full range of contracted services to covered patients for a fixed amount on a periodic basis. For instance, the physician will be paid an amount per member per month (PM/PM). As an example, if an MCO has 300 patients who select Dr Smith as their primary provider and the plan agrees to pay Dr Smith $12 per patient per month, Dr Smith will be paid $3600 each month regardless of the number of patients seen or treatments provided. Although guaranteed a fixed amount each month, Dr Smith assumes the risk that the cost of providing care to these patients may exceed the payment amount, for which Dr Smith will not receive additional reimbursement. The physician's only additional charge may be a predetermined copayment and/or deductible coinsurance payment.

The positive aspects of a capitation arrangement are a guaranteed fixed payment, no bad debt, and an ensured cash flow; however, the provider can lose money if his or her services are used heavily. To succeed under capitation, a physician must fully understand the contract before it is signed. Capitation agreements range from risk for services performed only in the physician's office to assumption of risk for all health care services provided to the patient.

The MCO will set the capitation rate after a detailed evaluation of the number and type of services likely to be provided to patients covered by the plan. The physician must know in detail the costs for services, provided by CPT code, to ensure that the capitation amount is adequate. If the physician is at risk for out-of-office services, he or she may also be required to negotiate with a hospital or specialist for a rate for the services that may be needed by a patient. Since capitation contracts are variable, the services of an experienced health care attorney and practice manager should be utilized for the physician's negotiations to be successful.

Physicians must manage their costs through controlled service utilization with an emphasis on preventive health care and use of cost-effective tests, supplies, and allied health personnel, such as nurse practitioners and physician assistants. Primary care providers are encouraged to avoid excessive use of ancillaries (eg, radiology and laboratory) or high-cost procedures that have limited positive clinical outcomes. Outside costs are managed by prudent selection of consultants, facilities, and clinical services.

Accounting controls are vital. For example, if a test or procedure that could put a patient at risk is ordered and the physician is financially responsible for payment in the next accounting period, the test or procedure must be recorded as an *incurred but not reported* (IBNR) item. If it is not, the accounting at the end of the period may show a false profit. Costs for compliance with utilization review and quality assurance must be taken into account. Close monitoring of these reports is vital.

A physician must ask these two important questions: How much do I get? and What services am I required by the contract to provide to the patient?

PROCESSING CLAIMS

Provider insurance claims are sent in two ways: (1) paper claims are mailed or faxed to the plan and (2) electronic claims are stored on computer media (disks, tapes, or CDs) and transmitted via modem.

Paper Claims

The paper claim has been the traditional method for physicians and other health care providers to submit their charges to insurance companies. The universal claim form, CMS-1500 (see Figure 1-1), is the most common form used, although individual companies may have their own forms. Some health plans may still accept a physician's charge ticket (often termed a *superbill* or *encounter form*) as a billing record for services provided to a patient. All claim forms must provide information that is essential to processing the claim, such as the name of the payer, patient, and provider; place and date of service; description of the service provided (ie, diagnostic codes and procedure codes); and the charges.

Each practice must create its own encounter form (see Figure 1-2) that lists information and codes relevant to its needs. A trained practice administrator or consultant who is familiar with coding issues and payer requirements along with a printer who is familiar with the needs of the physician will facilitate the effective design of an encounter form. At a minimum, all encounter forms must include the information requested on the CMS-1500 form. Because coding requirements change at least annually, all encounter forms must be periodically updated. A poorly designed encounter form can adversely affect the physician's reimbursement by payers.

Medicare will only accept paper claims on the CMS-1500 form and will not accept encounter forms. CMS discourages the use of paper claims, strongly preferring electronic claims. According to a study by the America's Health Insurance Plans (AHIP) Center for Policy and Research, electronic submission of health insurance claims more than tripled in the last decade, reducing administrative costs and allowing 98% of claims to be processed within 30 days of receipt. It shows that the percentage of claims filed electronically rose substantially between 2002 and 2006, from 44% and 75%, while during the same period the percentage of claims submitted on paper dropped from 56% in 2002 to 25% in 2006. This study is shown in its entirely in Chapter 3. Because virtually all third-party payers accept the CMS-1500 form, thorough knowledge of this form is necessary for proper billing operations. (Directions on how to complete a CMS-1500 form are provided in Chapter 6.)

Processing a paper claim involves the following fundamental steps:

1. The paper claim is received through the mail and scanned by the payer into its administrative system. Any attachments accompanying the claim are separated for scanning. Since the payer may receive and scan thousands of claims each day, the payer may be unable to match attachments to their associated claims if the following information is not provided on the attachments:
    a. Physician name
    b. Physician identification number
    c. Patient name
    d. Patient identification number
    e. Patient policy number
    f. Date of service

    Failure to include this information on attachments may result in claim delays, requests for additional information from the payer, or claim denials.

2. After the claim has been scanned or microfilmed, it is sent to the claims processing department. Some payers may first screen the claim. Screeners review basic claim data to verify that:
    a. The patient or provider is eligible
    b. The policy is in effect

FIGURE 1-1

CMS-1500 Form

Source: Centers for Medicare and Medicaid Services. Available at: http://cms.hhs.gov/cmsforms/downloads/CMS1500.pdf.

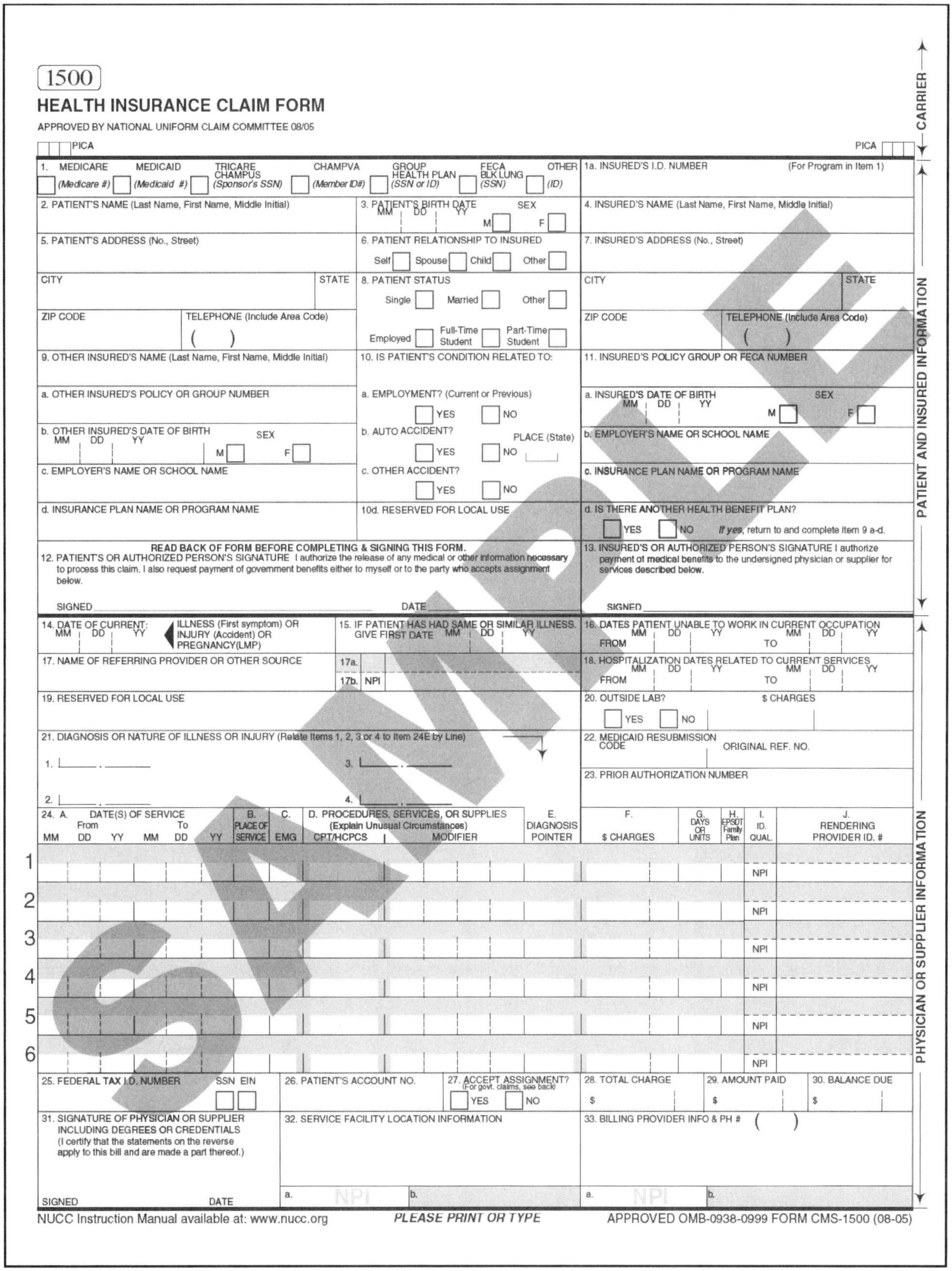

1500

HEALTH INSURANCE CLAIM FORM

APPROVED BY NATIONAL UNIFORM CLAIM COMMITTEE 08/05

PICA   PICA   CARRIER

1. MEDICARE (Medicare #) MEDICAID (Medicaid #) TRICARE CHAMPUS (Sponsor's SSN) CHAMPVA (Member ID#) GROUP HEALTH PLAN (SSN or ID) FECA BLK LUNG (SSN) OTHER (ID)

1a. INSURED'S I.D. NUMBER (For Program in Item 1)

2. PATIENT'S NAME (Last Name, First Name, Middle Initial)

3. PATIENT'S BIRTH DATE MM DD YY SEX M F

4. INSURED'S NAME (Last Name, First Name, Middle Initial)

5. PATIENT'S ADDRESS (No., Street)

6. PATIENT RELATIONSHIP TO INSURED Self Spouse Child Other

7. INSURED'S ADDRESS (No., Street)

CITY STATE

8. PATIENT STATUS Single Married Other

CITY STATE

ZIP CODE TELEPHONE (Include Area Code) ( )

Employed Full-Time Student Part-Time Student

ZIP CODE TELEPHONE (Include Area Code) ( )

9. OTHER INSURED'S NAME (Last Name, First Name, Middle Initial)

10. IS PATIENT'S CONDITION RELATED TO:

11. INSURED'S POLICY GROUP OR FECA NUMBER

a. OTHER INSURED'S POLICY OR GROUP NUMBER

a. EMPLOYMENT? (Current or Previous) YES NO

a. INSURED'S DATE OF BIRTH MM DD YY SEX M F

b. OTHER INSURED'S DATE OF BIRTH MM DD YY SEX M F

b. AUTO ACCIDENT? YES NO PLACE (State)

b. EMPLOYER'S NAME OR SCHOOL NAME

c. EMPLOYER'S NAME OR SCHOOL NAME

c. OTHER ACCIDENT? YES NO

c. INSURANCE PLAN NAME OR PROGRAM NAME

d. INSURANCE PLAN NAME OR PROGRAM NAME

10d. RESERVED FOR LOCAL USE

d. IS THERE ANOTHER HEALTH BENEFIT PLAN? YES NO *If yes,* return to and complete item 9 a-d.

READ BACK OF FORM BEFORE COMPLETING & SIGNING THIS FORM.

12. PATIENT'S OR AUTHORIZED PERSON'S SIGNATURE I authorize the release of any medical or other information necessary to process this claim. I also request payment of government benefits either to myself or to the party who accepts assignment below.

SIGNED DATE

13. INSURED'S OR AUTHORIZED PERSON'S SIGNATURE I authorize payment of medical benefits to the undersigned physician or supplier for services described below.

SIGNED

PATIENT AND INSURED INFORMATION

14. DATE OF CURRENT: MM DD YY ILLNESS (First symptom) OR INJURY (Accident) OR PREGNANCY(LMP)

15. IF PATIENT HAS HAD SAME OR SIMILAR ILLNESS. GIVE FIRST DATE MM DD YY

16. DATES PATIENT UNABLE TO WORK IN CURRENT OCCUPATION FROM MM DD YY TO MM DD YY

17. NAME OF REFERRING PROVIDER OR OTHER SOURCE 17a. 17b. NPI

18. HOSPITALIZATION DATES RELATED TO CURRENT SERVICES FROM MM DD YY TO MM DD YY

19. RESERVED FOR LOCAL USE

20. OUTSIDE LAB? YES NO $ CHARGES

21. DIAGNOSIS OR NATURE OF ILLNESS OR INJURY (Relate Items 1, 2, 3 or 4 to Item 24E by Line)

1. ___ . ___ 3. ___ . ___

2. ___ . ___ 4. ___ . ___

22. MEDICAID RESUBMISSION CODE ORIGINAL REF. NO.

23. PRIOR AUTHORIZATION NUMBER

24. A. DATE(S) OF SERVICE From MM DD YY To MM DD YY	B. PLACE OF SERVICE	C. EMG	D. PROCEDURES, SERVICES, OR SUPPLIES (Explain Unusual Circumstances) CPT/HCPCS MODIFIER	E. DIAGNOSIS POINTER	F. $ CHARGES	G. DAYS OR UNITS	H. EPSDT Family Plan	I. ID. QUAL.	J. RENDERING PROVIDER ID. #
1								NPI	
2								NPI	
3								NPI	
4								NPI	
5								NPI	
6								NPI	

25. FEDERAL TAX I.D. NUMBER SSN EIN

26. PATIENT'S ACCOUNT NO.

27. ACCEPT ASSIGNMENT? (For govt. claims, see back) YES NO

28. TOTAL CHARGE $

29. AMOUNT PAID $

30. BALANCE DUE $

31. SIGNATURE OF PHYSICIAN OR SUPPLIER INCLUDING DEGREES OR CREDENTIALS (I certify that the statements on the reverse apply to this bill and are made a part thereof.)

SIGNED DATE

32. SERVICE FACILITY LOCATION INFORMATION a. NPI b.

33. BILLING PROVIDER INFO & PH # ( ) a. NPI b.

PHYSICIAN OR SUPPLIER INFORMATION

NUCC Instruction Manual available at: www.nucc.org *PLEASE PRINT OR TYPE* APPROVED OMB-0938-0999 FORM CMS-1500 (08-05)

F I G U R E 1-1 (*continued*)

BECAUSE THIS FORM IS USED BY VARIOUS GOVERNMENT AND PRIVATE HEALTH PROGRAMS, SEE SEPARATE INSTRUCTIONS ISSUED BY APPLICABLE PROGRAMS.

NOTICE: Any person who knowingly files a statement of claim containing any misrepresentation or any false, incomplete or misleading information may be guilty of a criminal act punishable under law and may be subject to civil penalties.

REFERS TO GOVERNMENT PROGRAMS ONLY

MEDICARE AND CHAMPUS PAYMENTS: A patient's signature requests that payment be made and authorizes release of any information necessary to process the claim and certifies that the information provided in Blocks 1 through 12 is true, accurate and complete. In the case of a Medicare claim, the patient's signature authorizes any entity to release to Medicare medical and nonmedical information, including employment status, and whether the person has employer group health insurance, liability, no-fault, worker's compensation or other insurance which is responsible to pay for the services for which the Medicare claim is made. See 42 CFR 411.24(a). If item 9 is completed, the patient's signature authorizes release of the information to the health plan or agency shown. In Medicare assigned or CHAMPUS participation cases, the physician agrees to accept the charge determination of the Medicare carrier or CHAMPUS fiscal intermediary as the full charge, and the patient is responsible only for the deductible, coinsurance and noncovered services. Coinsurance and the deductible are based upon the charge determination of the Medicare carrier or CHAMPUS fiscal intermediary if this is less than the charge submitted. CHAMPUS is not a health insurance program but makes payment for health benefits provided through certain affiliations with the Uniformed Services. Information on the patient's sponsor should be provided in those items captioned in "Insured"; i.e., items 1a, 4, 6, 7, 9, and 11.

BLACK LUNG AND FECA CLAIMS

The provider agrees to accept the amount paid by the Government as payment in full. See Black Lung and FECA instructions regarding required procedure and diagnosis coding systems.

SIGNATURE OF PHYSICIAN OR SUPPLIER (MEDICARE, CHAMPUS, FECA AND BLACK LUNG)

I certify that the services shown on this form were medically indicated and necessary for the health of the patient and were personally furnished by me or were furnished incident to my professional service by my employee under my immediate personal supervision, except as otherwise expressly permitted by Medicare or CHAMPUS regulations.

For services to be considered as "incident" to a physician's professional service, 1) they must be rendered under the physician's immediate personal supervision by his/her employee, 2) they must be an integral, although incidental part of a covered physician's service, 3) they must be of kinds commonly furnished in physician's offices, and 4) the services of nonphysicians must be included on the physician's bills.

For CHAMPUS claims, I further certify that I (or any employee) who rendered services am not an active duty member of the Uniformed Services or a civilian employee of the United States Government or a contract employee of the United States Government, either civilian or military (refer to 5 USC 5536). For Black-Lung claims, I further certify that the services performed were for a Black Lung-related disorder.

No Part B Medicare benefits may be paid unless this form is received as required by existing law and regulations (42 CFR 424.32).

NOTICE: Any one who misrepresents or falsifies essential information to receive payment from Federal funds requested by this form may upon conviction be subject to fine and imprisonment under applicable Federal laws.

NOTICE TO PATIENT ABOUT THE COLLECTION AND USE OF MEDICARE, CHAMPUS, FECA, AND BLACK LUNG INFORMATION
(PRIVACY ACT STATEMENT)

We are authorized by CMS, CHAMPUS and OWCP to ask you for information needed in the administration of the Medicare, CHAMPUS, FECA, and Black Lung programs. Authority to collect information is in section 205(a), 1862, 1872 and 1874 of the Social Security Act as amended, 42 CFR 411.24(a) and 424.5(a) (6), and 44 USC 3101;41 CFR 101 et seq and 10 USC 1079 and 1086; 5 USC 8101 et seq; and 30 USC 901 et seq; 38 USC 613; E.O. 9397.

The information we obtain to complete claims under these programs is used to identify you and to determine your eligibility. It is also used to decide if the services and supplies you received are covered by these programs and to insure that proper payment is made.

The information may also be given to other providers of services, carriers, intermediaries, medical review boards, health plans, and other organizations or Federal agencies, for the effective administration of Federal provisions that require other third parties payers to pay primary to Federal program, and as otherwise necessary to administer these programs. For example, it may be necessary to disclose information about the benefits you have used to a hospital or doctor. Additional disclosures are made through routine uses for information contained in systems of records.

FOR MEDICARE CLAIMS: See the notice modifying system No. 09-70-0501, titled, 'Carrier Medicare Claims Record,' published in the <u>Federal Register</u>, Vol. 55 No. 177, page 37549, Wed. Sept. 12, 1990, or as updated and republished.

FOR OWCP CLAIMS: Department of Labor, Privacy Act of 1974, "Republication of Notice of Systems of Records," <u>Federal Register</u> Vol. 55 No. 40, Wed Feb. 28, 1990, See ESA-5, ESA-6, ESA-12, ESA-13, ESA-30, or as updated and republished.

FOR CHAMPUS CLAIMS: <u>PRINCIPLE PURPOSE(S):</u> To evaluate eligibility for medical care provided by civilian sources and to issue payment upon establishment of eligibility and determination that the services/supplies received are authorized by law.

<u>ROUTINE USE(S):</u> Information from claims and related documents may be given to the Dept. of Veterans Affairs, the Dept. of Health and Human Services and/or the Dept. of Transportation consistent with their statutory administrative responsibilities under CHAMPUS/CHAMPVA; to the Dept. of Justice for representation of the Secretary of Defense in civil actions; to the Internal Revenue Service, private collection agencies, and consumer reporting agencies in connection with recoupment claims; and to Congressional Offices in response to inquiries made at the request of the person to whom a record pertains. Appropriate disclosures may be made to other federal, state, local, foreign government agencies, private business entities, and individual providers of care, on matters relating to entitlement, claims adjudication, fraud, program abuse, utilization review, quality assurance, peer review, program integrity, third-party liability, coordination of benefits, and civil and criminal litigation related to the operation of CHAMPUS.

<u>DISCLOSURES:</u> Voluntary; however, failure to provide information will result in delay in payment or may result in denial of claim. With the one exception discussed below, there are no penalties under these programs for refusing to supply information. However, failure to furnish information regarding the medical services rendered or the amount charged would prevent payment of claims under these programs. Failure to furnish any other information, such as name or claim number, would delay payment of the claim. Failure to provide medical information under FECA could be deemed an obstruction.

It is mandatory that you tell us if you know that another party is responsible for paying for your treatment. Section 1128B of the Social Security Act and 31 USC 3801-3812 provide penalties for withholding this information.

You should be aware that P.L. 100-503, the "Computer Matching and Privacy Protection Act of 1988", permits the government to verify information by way of computer matches.

MEDICAID PAYMENTS (PROVIDER CERTIFICATION)

I hereby agree to keep such records as are necessary to disclose fully the extent of services provided to individuals under the State's Title XIX plan and to furnish information regarding any payments claimed for providing such services as the State Agency or Dept. of Health and Human Services may request.

I further agree to accept, as payment in full, the amount paid by the Medicaid program for those claims submitted for payment under that program, with the exception of authorized deductible, coinsurance, co-payment or similar cost-sharing charge.

SIGNATURE OF PHYSICIAN (OR SUPPLIER): I certify that the services listed above were medically indicated and necessary to the health of this patient and were personally furnished by me or my employee under my personal direction.

NOTICE: This is to certify that the foregoing information is true, accurate and complete. I understand that payment and satisfaction of this claim will be from Federal and State funds, and that any false claims, statements, or documents, or concealment of a material fact, may be prosecuted under applicable Federal or State laws.

According to the Paperwork Reduction Act of 1995, no persons are required to respond to a collection of information unless it displays a valid OMB control number. The valid OMB control number for this information collection is 0938-0999. The time required to complete this information collection is estimated to average 10 minutes per response, including the time to review instructions, search existing data resources, gather the data needed, and complete and review the information collection. If you have any comments concerning the accuracy of the time estimate(s) or suggestions for improving this form, please write to: CMS, Attn: PRA Reports Clearance Officer, 7500 Security Boulevard, Baltimore, Maryland 21244-1850. This address is for comments and/or suggestions only. DO NOT MAIL COMPLETED CLAIM FORMS TO THIS ADDRESS.

FIGURE 1-2

Sample Encounter Form (Superbill)

Jane Doe, M.D.
Internal Medicine
300 Practitioner Road
Smallville, State 99999

Telephone: (555) 555-1212

DATE:

LAST NAME	FIRST	ACCOUNT#	DOB	☐ Male ☐ Female
INSURANCE		PLAN#	SUBSCRIBER#	GROUP#

OFFICE CARE

✓	DESCRIPTION	CPT-MOD		
	NEW PATIENT			
	Focused	99201		
	Expanded	99202		
	Detailed	99203		
	Comprehensive-Mod.	99204		
	Comprehensive-High	99205		
	ESTABLISHED PATIENT			
	Minimal	99211		
	Focused	99212		
	Expanded	99213		
	Detailed	99214		
	Comprehensive-Mod.	99215		
	Comprehensive-High	99216		
	CONSULTATION OFFICE			
	Focused	99241		
	Expanded	99242		
	Detailed	99243		
	Comprehensive-Mod.	99254		
	Comprehensive-High	99265		
	Dr.			
	Post-op Exam	99024		
	EVALUATION/MANAGEMENT			
	Brief - 30 minutes	99361		
	Intermediate - 60	99362		
	Telephone-Brief	99371		
	Telephone-Intermed.	99372		
	Telephone-Complex	99373		

PROCEDURES

✓	DESCRIPTION	CPT-MOD		
	Treadmill	93015		
	24 Hour Holter	93224		
	Recording only	93225		
	Interp. & Report	93227		
	EKG and interp.	93000		
	EKG (Medicare)	93005		
	Sigmoidoscopy	45300		
	Sigmoidoscopy (flex)	45330		
	Sigmoid (flex) w/bx	45331		

DIAGNOSIS

052.9	Chickenpox, NOS	266.2	B12 deficiency w/o anemia	309.9	Adjustment reaction, unspecified
111.9	Dermatomycosis, unspecified	276.5	Dehydration	305.00	Alcohol abuse, unspecified
009.1	Gastroenteritis, infectious	250.91	Diabetes mellitus, I, compl	303.90	Alcoholism, unspecified
007.1	Giardiasis	250.01	Diabetes mellitus, I, uncompl	331.0	Alzheimers
098.0	Gonorrhea, acute, lower GU	250.90	Diabetes mellitus, II, compl	307.1	Anorexia nervosa
054.9	Herpes simplex, any site	250.00	Diabetes mellitus, II, uncompl	300.00	Anxiety state, unspecified
053.9	Herpes zoster, NOS	250.13	Diabetic ketoacidosis	314.01	Attention deficit, w/ hyperactivity
042	HIV Disease	271.9	Glucose intolerance		
V08	HIV positive, asymp	240.9	Goiter, unspecified	314.00	Attention deficit, w/o hyperactivity
136.9	Infectious/parasitic dis unspec	274.9	Gout, unspecified		
487.1	Influenza w/ upper resp sx	275.42	Hypercalcemia	307.51	Bulimia
007.9	Intestinal protozoa, NOS	276.7	Hyperkalemia	312.90	Conduct disorder, unspecified
088.81	Lyme disease	276.0	Hypernatremia	311	Depressive disorder, NOS
055.9	Measles, NOS	252.0	Hyperparathyroidism	305.90	Drug abuse, unspecified

DIAGNOSIS		
RETURN APPT	REFERRING MD	SIGNATURE

☐ Cash
☐ Check
☐ Credit

c. Services provided are covered by the patient's contract
   d. Required preoperative clearances were obtained
   e. Any other information determined pertinent by the payer is included

   Increasingly, computers handle the screening functions at the time the claim is entered. Some payers use optical scanners to process CMS-1500 forms. The scanners digitize the data on the claim form into their claims processing system for adjudication.

3. Claims processors enter the information on the claim into the payer's computer system. Due to the vast number of claims the payer must process each day, the claim may be with the processor only 2 or 3 minutes. If the physician has provided incomplete or illegible information, the claim may be delayed, suspended for manual review, or denied. Paper claims have a significantly higher data error entry rate than electronic claims.

   If there are unusual facts surrounding the claim, it is important to include any supporting documentation at the time the claim is submitted. A processor may then send the claim to a supervisor who will make a payment decision or forward the claim to the payer's medical review staff. Because claims processors and their immediate supervisors may have limited training in medical terminology, they may not fully understand operative reports and other supporting documentation. The physician may then be required to submit additional documentation to explain or justify the services, including a brief cover letter describing what was done, why it was done, and the unusual facts that affected the physician's services.

A study published by the *American Journal of Roentgenology*[1] analyzed all February and June 2000 claims submitted to six major payers by a common third-party billing company on behalf of 11 radiology practices of various sizes, settings, and locations in New Jersey. A total of 33,537 claims were submitted. The study found that the overall percentage of claims paid within 40 days was only 70%. The overall percentage of claims paid after 170 days was 93%. The annualized interest lost by the practices in the study totaled $23,939. Late payments cause threats to cash flow, network stability, and enrollee access; threats of bankruptcy; and a significant threat to the practice's earnings.

The AMA Private Sector Advocacy Unit has reported that in the past several years level prompt payment fines, interest, and restitution have totaled more than $70 million in aggregate.

A report published in the *Dallas Medical Journal* in 2002, states that more than 95% of claims filed by physicians in Texas do not meet the clean claim standard defined by Texas Department of Insurance. Even though, 50 states as well as the District of Columbia have enacted prompt-payment laws as of August 2006, claims may still be delayed and denied as a result of improper, incomplete, or inaccurate information on claims. Many state prompt-payment laws do not address clean claim requirements. Numerous definitions of a clean claim can be found. At this time, there is not a universal definition of clean claim in place. Some definitions of a *clean claim* follow:

- **Medicare.** A clean claim "has no defect, impropriety (including any lack of any substantial documentation) or particular circumstance requiring special treatment that prevents timely payment from being made." (See 42.U.S.C. 139 h[c].) The Medicare manual provides the following definition and examples of a clean claim.
- **Alabama.** Ala. Code § 27-1-17(b).
  "(1) Clean electronic claim. The transmission of data for purposes of payment of covered health care expenses that is submitted to an insurer, health service corporation, or health benefit plan which contains substantially all of the required data elements necessary for accurate adjudication, without obtaining additional information from the provider of the service or from a third party, in an electronic data format specified by the insurer's, health service corporation's, or health benefit plan's published filing requirements. In no event shall an insurer, health service corporation, or health benefit plan require that the health care provider submit data elements in excess of

those required on the standard electronic health insurance claim format designated by Section 27-1-16 as a condition to the acceptance and processing of an initial claim as a clean claim. "(2) Clean written claim. A claim for payment of covered health care expenses that is submitted to an insurer, health service corporation, or health benefit plan on the claim form of the insurer, health service corporation, or health benefits plan which contains substantially all of the required data elements necessary for accurate adjudication, without obtaining additional information from the provider of the service or from a third party. In no event shall an insurer, health service corporation, or health benefit plan require that the health care provider submit information or data elements in excess of those required on the standard health insurance claim form designated by Section 27-1-16 as a condition to the acceptance and processing of an initial claim as a clean claim."

- **Alaska.** Alaska Stat. § 21.54.020.

"'Clean claim' means a claim that does not have a defect, impropriety, or circumstance requiring special treatment that precludes timely payment on the claim."

- **Arizona.** Ariz. Rev. Stat. Ann. § 20-3101.

"'Clean claim' means a written or electronic claim for health care services or benefits that may be processed without obtaining additional information, including coordination of benefits information, from the health care provider, the enrollee or a third party, except in cases of fraud."

- **Arkansas.** Ark. Reg. 43 § 5(q).

"'Clean claim' means a claim for payment of health care expenses that is submitted on a HCFA 1500, on a UB92, in a format required by the Health Insurance Portability and Accountability Act of 1996 ('HIPAA'), or on the carrier's standard claim form with all required fields completed in accordance with the Health Carrier's published claim filing requirements. A Clean Claim shall not include a claim (1) for payment of expenses incurred during a period of time for which premiums are delinquent, (2) for benefits under a Medicare supplement policy if the claim is not accompanied by an explanation of Medicare benefits or the Explanation of Medicare Benefits ('EOMB') has not been otherwise received by the Health Carrier, or (3) for which the Health Carrier needs additional information in order to resolve one or more of the issues listed in Subsection 13(b) of this rule."

- **Colorado.** Colo. Rev. Stat. § 10-16-106.5.

"'Clean claim' means a claim for payment of health care expenses that is submitted to a carrier on the uniform claim form adopted pursuant to section 1016-106.3 with all required fields completed with correct and complete information, including all required documents. A claim requiring additional information shall not be considered a clean claim and shall be paid, denied, or settled as set forth in paragraph (b) of subsection (4) of this section. 'Clean claim' does not include a claim for payment of expenses incurred during a period of time for which premiums are delinquent, except to the extent otherwise required by law."

- **Delaware.** Del. Dept. of Insurance, Reg. 310.

"... a claim that has no defect or impropriety (including any lack of any required substantiating documentation) or particular circumstance requiring special treatment that substantially prevents timely payments from being made on the claim."

- **District of Columbia.** D.C. Code Ann. § 31-3131.

"'Clean claim' means a claim that has no material defect or impropriety, including any lack of reasonably required substantiating documentation, which substantially prevents timely payment from being made on the claim or with respect to a health insurer that has failed timely to notify the person submitting the claim for any such defect or impropriety in accordance with § 31-3132. For the purposes of this paragraph, the term 'material defect' means an imperfection in the submission of a claim consisting in the omission of information that is essential to process the claim in accordance with the health plan's published claim filing requirements. The requirements for electronic claim submissions shall be consistent with regulations promulgated by Secretary of Health and Human Services pursuant to section 1173 of the Social Security Act, approved August 14, 1935 (110 Stat. 2024; 42 U.S.C.S. § 1320d-2)."

- **Hawaii.** Haw. Rev. Stat. § 431:13-108.

"'Clean claim' means a claim in which the information in the possession of an entity adequately indicates that: (1) The claim is for a covered health care service provided by an eligible health care provider to a covered person under the contract; (2) The claim has no material defect or impropriety; (3) There is no dispute regarding the amount claimed; and (4) The payer has no reason to believe that the claim was submitted fraudulently. The term does not include: (1) Claims for payment of expenses incurred during a period of time when premiums were delinquent; (2) Claims that are submitted fraudulently or that are based upon material misrepresentations; (3) Medicaid or Medigap claims; and (4) Claims that require a coordination of benefits, subrogation, or preexisting condition investigations, or that involve third-party liability."

- **Indiana.** Ind. Code § 5-10-8.1-2.

"'Clean claim' means a claim submitted by a provider for payment under a health benefit plan that has no defect, impropriety, or particular circumstance requiring special treatment preventing payment."

- **Iowa.** Iowa Code § 507B.4A.

"'Clean claim' means a properly completed paper or electronic billing instrument containing all reasonably necessary information, that does not involve coordination of benefits for third-party liability, preexisting condition investigations, or subrogation, and that does not involve the existence of particular circumstances requiring special treatment that prevents a prompt payment from being made."

- **Kansas.** Kan. Stat. Ann. § 40-2441.

"'Clean claim' means a claim that has no defect or impropriety, including any lack of required substantiating documentation, or particular circumstance requiring special treatment that prevents timely payment from being made on the claim under the Kansas health care prompt payment act."

- **Kentucky.** Ky. Rev. Stat. Ann. § 304.17A-700.

"'Clean claim' means a properly completed billing instrument, paper or electronic, including the required health claim attachments, submitted in the following applicable form. . . . (c) A clean claim for all other providers shall consist of the HCFA 1500 data set or its successor submitted on the designated paper or electronic format as adopted by the National Uniform Claims Committee. . ."

- **Louisiana.** La. Rev. Stat. Ann. 22 § 250.31(3).

"'Clean claim' means an accepted claim that has no defect or impropriety including any lack of required substantiating documentation or other particular circumstance requiring special treatment that prevents timely payment from being made on the claim under this Part."

La. Rev. Stat. Ann. 22 § 250.31(1). "'Accepted claim' means either of the following: (a) A nonelectronic claim on a HCFA 1500 form or Uniform Billing Form 92 (UB92), properly completed according to Medicare guidelines. (b) An electronic claim in an 837 (ASC X12N 837) format or its successor adopted by the United States Department of Health and Human Services or its successor, in compliance with the provisions of the Health Insurance Portability and Accountability Act (42 USC 1302d et seq. and 45 C.F.R. Parts 160 and 162), that includes all of the following: (i) Data that is required according to the United States Department of Health and Human Services standards for electronic transactions. (ii) Data that becomes required due to the situation according to the United States Department of Health and Human Services standards for electronic transactions. (iii) Data that is required according to notice by the health insurance issuer or its agent to the health care provider or its agent. Such data shall be as described in the Payer's Companion Guide in accordance with the United States Department of Health and Human Services standards for electronic transactions."

- **Maine.** Me. Rev. Stat. Ann. tit. 24-A, §2436, sub-§2-A.

"For purposes of this section, an 'undisputed claim' means a timely claim for payment of covered health care expenses under a policy or certificate providing health care coverage that is submitted to an insurer on the insurer's standard claim form using the most current published procedural codes with all the required fields completed with correct and complete information in accordance with the insurer's published claims filing requirements . . ."

- **Maryland.** Md. Code Ann., Ins. §15-1003.

"The Commissioner shall adopt by regulation . . . a definition of clean claim, including: 1. the essential data elements that must be completed on the uniform claims form; and 2. uniform standards for attachments to the uniform claims form."

- **Michigan.** Mich. Comp. Laws § 500.2006(14)(a).

"'Clean claim' means a claim that does all of the following: (1) Identifies the health professional or health facility that provided service sufficiently to verify, if necessary, affiliation status and includes any identifying numbers. (2) Sufficiently identifies the patient and health plan subscriber. (3) Lists the date and place of service. (4) Is a claim for covered services for an eligible individual. (5) If necessary, substantiates the medical necessity and appropriateness of the service provided. (6) If prior authorization is required for certain patient services, contains information sufficient to establish that prior authorization was obtained. (7) Identifies the service rendered using a generally accepted system of procedure or service coding. (8) Includes additional documentation based upon services rendered as reasonably required by the health plan."

- **Minnesota.** Minn. Stat. § 62Q.75.

"'Clean claim' means a claim that has no defect or impropriety, including any lack of any required substantiating documentation, including but not limited to, coordination of benefits information, or particular circumstance requiring special treatment that prevents timely payment from being made on a claim under this section. Nothing in this section alters an enrollee's obligation to disclose information as required by law."

- **Mississippi.** Miss. Code Ann. § 83-9-5(1)(h).

"A 'clean claim' means a claim received by an insurer for adjudication and which requires no further information, adjustment or alteration by the provider of the services or the insured in order to be processed and paid by the insurer. A claim is clean if it has no defect or impropriety, including any lack of substantiating documentation, or particular circumstance requiring special treatment that prevents timely payment from being made on the claim under this provision. A clean claim includes resubmitted claims with previously identified deficiencies corrected.

A clean claim does not include any of the following: (a) A duplicate claim, which means an original claim and its duplicate when the duplicate is filed within thirty (30) days of the original claim; (b) Claims which are submitted fraudulently or that are based upon material misrepresentations; (c) Claims that require information essential for the insurer to administer preexisting condition, coordination of benefits or subrogation provisions; or (d) Claims submitted by a provider more than thirty (30) days after the date of service; if the provider does not submit the claim on behalf of the insured, then a claim is not clean when submitted more than (30) days after the date of billing by the provider to the insured."

- **New Hampshire.** N.H. Rev. Stat. Ann. §§ 415:18-k, 415:6-h.

"'Clean claim' means a claim for payment of covered health care expenses that is submitted to an insurer on the insurer's standard claim form using the most current published procedural codes, with all the required fields completed with correct and complete information in accordance with the insurer's published filing requirements."

- **New Mexico.** N.M. Stat. Ann. § 59A-2-9.2(A)

    (1). "'Clean claim' means a manually or electronically submitted claim from a participating provider that: (a) contains substantially all the required data elements necessary for accurate adjudication without the need for additional information from outside of the health plan's system; (b) is not materially deficient or improper, including lacking substantiating documentation currently required by the health plan; or (c) has no particular or unusual circumstances requiring special treatment that prevent payment from being made by the health plan within thirty days of the date of receipt if submitted electronically or forty-five days if submitted manually."

- **New York.** N.Y.C.R.R. 217, § 217.2(a) & (b).

    "(a) A claim for payment of medical or hospital services submitted on paper shall be deemed complete if it contains the minimum data elements set forth in this Part. If the minimum data elements set forth are not present or accurate, the payer may, but need not, adjudicate the claim if the payer can determine, based on the information submitted, whether such claim should be paid or denied. Even if the claim is deemed complete, a payer may, pursuant to the provision of Section 3224-a(b) of the New York Insurance Law, request specific additional information, distinct from information on the claim form, necessary to make a determination as to its obligation to pay such claim. (b)(1) In the case of a medical claim submitted on the national standard form known as a CMS 1500 (previously known as HCFA 1500 (New York State), attached as an appendix (Appendix 26), the claim shall contain at least the items in the following fields of the claim form, except as provided in paragraph (2) of this subdivision: (1a) Insured's I.D. Number; (2) Patient's Name; (3) Patient's Date of Birth and Gender; (4) Insured's Name (Last Name, First Name); (5) Patient's Address; (9) Other Insured's Name (if appropriate); (9a) Other Insured's Policy or Group Number (if appropriate); (9b) Other Insured's Date of Birth and Gender (if appropriate); (9c) Employer's Name or School Name (if appropriate); (9d) Insurance Plan Name or Program Name (if appropriate); (10a) Is Patient's Condition Related to Employment?; (10b) Is Patient's Condition Related to Auto Accident?; (10c) Is Patient's Condition Related to Other Accident?; (11) Insured's Policy, Group or FECA Number (if provided on ID Card); (11d) Is There Another Health Benefit Plan?; (12) Patient's or Authorized Person's Signature (Can be completed by writing "signature on file" where appropriate); (13) Insured's or Authorized Person's Signature (if appropriate); (17) Name of Referring Physician or Other Source; (17a) I.D. Number of Referring Physician (if appropriate); (18) Hospitalization Dates Related to Current Services (if appropriate); (21) Diagnosis or Nature of Illness or Injury; (24A) Dates of Service; (24B) Place of Service; (24D) Procedures, Services, or Supplies; (24E) Diagnosis Code (refer to item 21); (24F) $ Charges; (24G) Days or Units (for Durable Medical Equipment) (if appropriate); (25) Federal Tax I.D. Number; (28) Total Charge; (29) Amount Paid (if appropriate); (30) Balance Due; (31) Signature of Physician or Supplier Including Degrees or Credentials (if not already on file, except as required by applicable Federal and State laws); (33) Personal Identifying Number of the particular practitioner rendering the care plus, if practicing in a group, the Identifying Number of the group as well. (2) For items listed in paragraph (1) of this subdivision with the notation "(if appropriate)", the generic nature of the standard claim form produces some instances when the information is not relevant in a particular instance. In those cases, the payer shall not insist upon completion of that item if the information is not relevant to the situation of that particular practitioner or patient or the information will not be used by the payer. If an item is not applicable at all, it should be left blank rather than inserting a notation that it is not applicable.

- **Oklahoma.** Okla. Stat. tit. 36, § 2514.

    "'Clean claim' means a claim that has no defect or impropriety, including a lack of any required substantiating documentation, or particular circumstance requiring special treatment that impedes prompt payment."

- **Oregon.** Or. Rev. Stat. § 743.866(6).

  "The director [of the Department of Consumer and Business Services] shall adopt by rule a definition of 'clean claim' and shall consider the definition of 'clean claim' used by the federal Department of Health and Human Services for the payment of Medicare claims."

- **Pennsylvania.** 40 Pa. Cons. Stat. § 991.2102.

  "A claim for payment for a health care service which has no defect or impropriety. A defect or impropriety shall include lack of required substantiating documentation or a particular circumstance requiring special treatment which prevents timely payment from being made on the claim. The term shall not include a claim from a health care provider who is under investigation for fraud or abuse regarding that claim."

- **Rhode Island.** R.I. Gen. Laws § 27-18-61(a).

  ". . . Each health plan shall establish a written standard defining what constitutes a complete claim and shall distribute this standard to all participating providers."

- **South Dakota.** S.D. Codified Laws Ann. § 58-12-19.

  "As used in §§ 58-12-19 to 58-12-21, inclusive, the term, clean claim, means a claim for which there is no need for additional information to determine eligibility or adjudicate the claim. The term, clean claim, does not include a claim for payment of expenses incurred during a period of time for which premiums are delinquent, except to the extent otherwise required by law or a claim for which fraud is suspected."

- **Tennessee.** Tenn. Code Ann. § 56-7-109(1).

  "(A) 'Clean claim' means a claim received by a health insurance entity for adjudication, and which requires no further information, adjustment or alteration by the provider of the services in order to be processed and paid by the health insurer. A claim is clean if it has no defect or impropriety (including any lack of any required substantiating documentation) or particular circumstance requiring special treatment that prevents timely payment from being made on the claim under this section; (B) A clean claim does not include a duplicate claim. 'Duplicate claim' means an original claim and its duplicate when the duplicate is filed within 30 days of the original claim; (C) A clean claim does not include any claim submitted more than 90 days after the date of service; (D) The definition of 'clean claim' includes resubmitted paper claims with previously identified deficiencies corrected."

- **Texas.** Tex. Ins. Code Ann. § 3.70-3C, Sec. 3A.

  "In this section, 'clean claim' means a claim that complies with Section 3C of this article." Tex. Ins. Code Ann. § 3.70-3C, Sec. 3C. "(A) A nonelectronic claim by a physician or provider, other than an institutional provider, is a 'clean claim' if the claim is submitted using the Centers for Medicare and Medicaid Services Form 1500 or, if adopted by the Commissioner by rule, a successor to that form developed by the National Uniform Claim Committee or its successor. An electronic claim by a physician or provider, other than an institutional provider, is a 'clean claim' if the claim is submitted using the professional 837 (ASC X 12N 837) format or, if adopted by the Commissioner by rule, a successor to that format adopted by the Centers for Medicare and Medicaid Services or its successor. (B) A nonelectronic claim by an institutional provider is a 'clean claim' if the claim is submitted using the Centers for Medicare and Medicaid Services Form UB-92 or, if adopted by the Commissioner by rule, a successor to that form developed by the National Uniform Billing Committee or its successor. An electronic claim by an institutional provider is a 'clean claim' if the claim is submitted using the institutional 837 (ASC X 12N 837) format or, if adopted by the Commissioner by rule, a successor to that format adopted by the Centers for Medicare and Medicaid Services or its successor . . ."

- **Virginia.** Va. Code Ann. § 38.2-3407.15(A).

  "'Clean claim' means a claim (i) that has no material defect or impropriety (including any lack of any reasonably required substantiation documentation) which substantially prevents timely payment from being made on the claim or (ii) with respect to which a carrier has failed timely to notify the person submitting the claim of any such defect or impropriety in accordance with this section."

- **Washington.** Wash. Admin. Code § 284-43-321(3).

    "For purposes of this section, 'clean claim' means a claim that has no defect or impropriety, including any lack of any required substantiating documentation, or particular circumstances requiring special treatment that prevents timely payments from being made on the claim under this section."

- **West Virginia.** W. Va. Code § 33-45-1(2).

    "'Clean claim' means a claim: (A) That has no material defect or impropriety, including all reasonably required information and substantiating documentation, to determine eligibility or to adjudicate the claim; or (B) with respect to which an insurer has failed timely to notify the person submitting the claim of any such defect or impropriety in accordance with section two of this article."

Claim delays and denials may result from improper, incomplete, or inaccurate information on claims. These are sometimes called "dirty claims." The following issues may result in "dirty claims":

- Illegible handwriting
- Lack of provider name, identification, or signature
- Lack of patient name or policy number (The name of the patient submitted for Medicare must be identical to the patient's Medicare card, including middle initials.)
- Out-of-date patient information
- Outdated codes (CPT, Healthcare Common Procedure Coding System [HCPCS], and *International Classification of Diseases, Ninth Edition, Clinical Modification* [ICD-9-CM])
- Improper place-of-service code
- Lack of name or identification of any referring provider
- Illogical relationships between patient diagnoses and services provided
- Service that does not match Medicare utilization screening criteria
- Lack of necessary provider identification numbers (national provider identifier [NPI], personal identification number [PIN], or universal physician identification number [UPIN])

Many practice management computer systems and electronic claims submission (ECS) programs facilitate submission of cleaner claims by requiring that basic claim information be included. A basic office policy should require that all claims submitted have complete, correct, and current information.

Electronic Claims

An alternative to a paper claim is an electronic claim submitted to the payer either directly by the physician or through a claims clearinghouse. The electronic process requires a computer, modem, and special software. Many firms offer simple terminals or data entry devices specifically for the purpose of submitting claims. Most provider practice management computer systems have capabilities for ECS. Computer vendors, Blue Cross and Blue Shield, Medicare, and other organizations can provide information about setting up an ECS system.

ECS has several advantages over paper claims submission. On average, ECS claims are paid more quickly than paper claims. Medicare, for example, is mandated to pay ECS claims within 14 days, while the paper claim threshold is 27 days. ECS claims are less likely to be rejected by payers. Most ECS software contains claim-editing features that detect and report incomplete claims, invalid codes, and other problems that will cause a claim to be rejected. These are basic edits that flag or reject claims, eg, a prostatectomy being reported for a female or a Pap smear being reported for a male. This edit feature forces the practice to file cleaner claims. Most practices have found that ECS is less expensive than processing paper claims. A study displayed in its entirety in Chapter 3 shows that a "clean claim" received electronically costs $0.85 per claim while a "clean claim" on paper costs $1.58 per claim to process. A *clean claim* is defined in the study as one "for when no additional information is needed." Third-party payers also realize cost savings through the receipt of electronic claims. Payment posting and reconciliation of claims is far superior using ECS. In summary, electronic claims are easier to submit and are more likely to be paid.

However, ECS does have some shortcomings that should be noted. Claims that require documentation are still filed using the paper claim method. As ECS systems begin to accommodate the electronic transmission of reports, radiographs, and related information, claims may be generated from an electronic medical record, which will enhance proper documentation. In addition, start-up costs for ECS can be significant.

When evaluating ECS, the following three methods or a combination of these methods for submitting claims electronically may be considered:

- Using software that allows the submission of claims directly to major third-party payers, such as Medicare and Blue Cross and Blue Shield
- Using software to submit claims electronically to a clearinghouse that in turn routes the claims electronically to various third-party payers
- Sending paper claims to a service bureau that enters the claims in its computer and submits them electronically on behalf of the physician

Because not all third-party payers accept electronic claims, even the most automated practices, clearinghouses, and service bureaus must still produce and mail a large number of paper claims. In most systems, a paper claim may be produced from the electronically stored data.

SUMMARY

Chapter 1 reviews the basics of insurance and claim processing. Methods of reimbursement and types of insurance are discussed. It is necessary for practice managers to understand these topics. A solid understanding of these basics will help practice staff members as they progress in learning more complex reimbursement issues. Both electronic and paper claim processing are also addressed, including a discussion of the advantages and shortcomings of each. Clean claim processing as well as a brief discussion of prompt payment laws is presented. Prompt payment laws are discussed further in Chapter 8, and detailed examples and contact information for each state are provided. Chapter 1 also provides a brief discussion of the CMS-1500 form. A detailed discussion of the CMS-1500 form and review of fields is provided in Chapter 6. A sample encounter form as well as a CMS-1500 form are displayed in the chapter for reference.

ENDNOTE

1. Swayne LC, Fask A, Crewson PE, Stelletell HD, Fanburg JD, Williams G. Compliance with prompt payment legislation: the initial experiences of New Jersey radiologists. *Am J Roentgenology.* January 2002. Available at: www.ajronline.org/cgi/content/full/179/1/21. Accessed September 19, 2005.

chapter 2

Types of Insurance and Third-Party Payers

OBJECTIVES

- Understand what distinguishes Blue Cross Blue Shield plans from other commercial insurance carriers.
- Be able to identify the services covered under Medicare Parts A and B and be able to file claims with Medicare.
- Understand the basics of the Medicare Advantage program.
- Gain a basic knowledge of the Medicaid program including eligibility and scope of services.
- Understand the basics of the Civilian Health and Medical Program of the Veterans Affairs (CHAMPVA) and TRICARE programs.
- Be able to identify alternative health plans including health maintenance organizations (HMOs) and preferred provider organizations (PPOs).
- Understand workers' compensation insurance program basics and coverage guidelines.

Thousands of organizations in the United States may be classified as third-party payers, each offering a variety of health care benefit packages. The packages range from small corporate self-funded plans to Medicare. This chapter describes the different types of third-party payers, both public and private. Health care spending is at an all time high in the United States. Table 2-1 shows a forecast summary and national health care expenditures projections from 2005 through 2015. Health care expenditures in 2004 were $1.9 trillion or $6,280 per person. Total health care spending represented 16% of the gross domestic product (GDP). In 2005, employer health insurance premiums increased by 9.2%. According to a report by the National Coalition on Health Care, the annual premium that a health insurer charged an employer for a health plan covering a family of four averaged $10,800 in 2005.

COMMERCIAL CARRIERS: BACKGROUND INFORMATION

Commercial carriers are private, for-profit organizations that sell health insurance policies to groups (usually employers) and/or individuals. In return for premiums paid by employers or employees, the organizations determine a defined set of health benefits, which may vary on a company-by-company or individual-by-individual basis. Major insurance companies such as Aetna, Cigna, Health Net, Humana, and United Healthcare are examples of commercial carriers.

T A B L E 2-1

National Health Care Expenditures Projections: 2005–2015

Forecast Summary

Health care spending in the United States is projected to grow 7.4 percent and surpass $2 trillion in 2005, down from the 7.9 percent growth experienced in 2004. This rate is 0.5 percentage points less than the 7.9 percent growth observed in 2004 and represents the third consecutive year of decelerating growth, following six years of acceleration from 1996 through 2002.

As a percentage of Gross Domestic Product (GDP), health care spending is expected to continue to grow, reaching 16.2 percent in 2005, up from 16.0 percent in 2004. By 2015, health care spending in the United States is projected to reach $4.0 trillion and 20.0 percent of GDP.

From 2004 to 2015, health care spending is projected to remain relatively stable and to grow 7.2 percent per year on average. Despite substantive revisions to the historical National Health Expenditures data and a new model for private personal health care spending, aggregate growth calculated in this year's projection stands a negligible 0.2 percentage points higher than in last year's projection.

Spending growth on personal health care is projected to fall to 7.0 percent in 2007, due largely to legislated Medicare payment adjustments that are to be implemented that year. In 2008, growth is expected to rebound to 7.5 percent, but then gradually slow over the remainder of the 10-year projection.

Public personal health care spending is projected to slightly decelerate in 2005 to 8.0 percent from 8.2 percent in 2004. This continued strong growth occurs predominantly due to Medicare spending growth, reflecting changes associated with the Medicare Prescription Drug, Improvement, and Modernization Act of 2003 (MMA) distinct from the new Medicare Part D prescription drug benefit. In 2006, with the introduction of prescription drug coverage in Medicare (Part D), public spending growth is projected to escalate to 11.8 percent while private spending growth slows to 3.9 percent. Over the remainder of the period, growth is expected to range between 6.5 and 7.8 percent.

Private personal health care, already outpaced by public personal health care spending, will decelerate from 7.5 percent in 2004 to 7.2 percent in 2005 due to the anticipated slowdown in medical price inflation. A shift in payments due to the start of Medicare part D will lead growth to decelerate sharply to 3.9 percent in 2006, but growth will rebound and peak at 7.7 percent by 2008, then decelerate through 2015.

Growth in private health insurance premiums are expected to slow for the third consecutive year are expected to grow at 6.8 percent in 2005, a deceleration of 1.6 percentage points from 2004. This trend is driven by the underwriting cycle and slower growth in projected medical benefits per enrollee.

Out of pocket spending growth is expected to remain essentially flat in 2005, and then decrease substantially due to Medicare Part D coverage in 2006. While growth in out of pocket spending has remained slower than that of private health insurance spending and we expect these growth rates to converge over the next decade, the out of pocket share of health care spending is expected to decline from 15.1 percent in 2004 to 12.6 percent by 2015.

Due to significantly lower spending growth in 2004, prescription drug spending is projected at 8.0 percent in 2005, significantly lower than in last year's projection. This deceleration is driven by a slowdown in drug utilization. While the Medicare Part D prescription drug benefit is expected to slightly lower growth in drug spending, the benefit will result in a substantial shift in funding from the private sector and Medicaid to Medicare. For 2007 through 2015, drug spending growth is projected to remain in the range of 8.0 to 8.4 percent, as upward and downward pressures on growth essentially offset each other.

Medicare spending is expected to slow slightly in 2005, then spike in 2006 at 25.2 percent, due to the implementation of the Medicare Part D benefit. In 2007, however, growth is expected to decelerate to 5.9 percent, and then accelerate to an average of 7.6 percent growth for the remainder of the forecast. The expected expiration of cuts in Medicare physician payments mandated by the Sustainable Growth Rate (SGR) system drives this end of period acceleration, while the short-run deceleration is due to an expected enrollment shift from traditional fee-for-service Medicare to managed care due to MMA-mandated increases in payments to managed care plans in 2004 and 2005.

Combined federal and state Medicaid spending growth is expected to slow for the fourth consecutive year to 7.7 percent. While Medicaid enrollment growth is expected to decelerate in 2005 to 2.1 percent from 4.2 percent in 2004 due to the improved economy, per enrollee spending is expected to increase 1.8 percentage points to 2.8 percent in 2005. Medicaid spending is expected to remain a strain on state budgets, and every state is pursuing at least one cost-containment measure for 2005 and 2006.

Hospital spending growth for 2005 is projected at 7.9 percent, marking the second consecutive year hospital spending is expected to outpace in total personal health care. Private payer spending growth is expected to slow 1.1 percentage points to 8.5 percent in 2005, then grow to 9.0 percent in 2006, then moderate to an average of 7.9 percent for the remainder of the period. Public payer spending growth, on the other hand, is expected to slow in 2005 to 7.5 percent, 6.4 percent in 2006 due to decreased Medicaid enrollment, and 5.5 percent in 2007 due to legislative adjustments to managed care payments, and then accelerate to 6.8 percent by 2015.

Home Health spending growth is expected to remain strong in 2005 at 13.2 percent, following 13.3 percent growth in 2004. Public payers, particularly Medicare, drive this trend. While growth of 15.3 percent for Medicare home health services in 2005 would mark the fifth consecutive year of double digit growth, we expect that trend to moderate and settle to 6.9 percent from 2007–2015. Growth in home health services provided by Medicaid, on the other hand, is expected to grow to 18.6 percent in 2005, and by 2007–2015 settle to an average growth rate of 10.9 percent.

Table 1
National Health Expenditures and Selected Economic Indicators, Levels and Annual Percent Change: Selected Calendar Years 1999-2015 [1]

Item	1999	2000	2001	2002	2003	2004	2005	2006	2007	2008	2009	2010	2011	2012	2013	2014	2015
							Projected										
National Health Expenditures (billions)	$1,270.3	$1,358.5	$1,474.2	$1,607.9	$1,740.6	$1,877.6	$2,016.0	$2,169.5	$2,325.7	$2,504.7	$2,696.2	$2,887.3	$3,086.7	$3,307.0	$3,543.3	$3,787.2	$4,043.6
National Health Expenditures as a Percent of Gross Domestic Product	13.7%	13.8%	14.6%	15.4%	15.9%	16.0%	16.2%	16.5%	16.8%	17.2%	17.7%	18.0%	18.4%	18.8%	19.2%	19.6%	20.0%
National Health Expenditures Per Capita	$4,471	$4,729	$5,079	$5,485	$5,879	$6,280	$6,683	$7,129	$7,576	$8,090	$8,636	$9,173	$9,727	$10,339	$10,992	$11,660	$12,357
Gross Domestic Product (billions)	$9,268.4	$9,817.0	$10,128.0	$10,469.6	$10,971.2	$11,734.3	$12,450.1	$13,134.8	$13,831.0	$14,536.4	$15,263.2	$16,026.4	$16,811.6	$17,618.6	$18,446.7	$19,295.2	$20,197.9
Gross Domestic Product (billions of 2000 $)	9,470.3	9,817.0	9,890.7	10,048.8	10,320.6	10,755.7	11,132.1	11,488.4	11,833.0	12,152.5	12,456.3	12,767.7	13,074.2	13,374.9	13,669.1	13,956.2	14,249.3
Gross Domestic Product Implicit Price Deflator (chain weighted 2000 base year)	0.979	1.000	1.024	1.042	1.063	1.091	1.119	1.145	1.171	1.200	1.230	1.260	1.292	1.324	1.357	1.391	1.426
Consumer Price Index (CPI-W) - 1982-1984 base	1.666	1.722	1.771	1.799	1.840	1.889	1.934	1.981	2.028	2.085	2.143	2.203	2.265	2.329	2.394	2.461	2.530
HCFA Implicit Medical Price Deflator [2]	0.967	1.000	1.038	1.078	1.118	1.163	1.205	1.250	1.298	1.348	1.400	1.453	1.508	1.565	1.625	1.687	1.752
U.S. Population[3]	284.1	287.3	290.3	293.2	296.1	299.0	301.7	304.3	307.0	309.6	312.2	314.8	317.3	319.8	322.3	324.8	327.2
Population age less than 65 years	249.0	251.9	254.6	257.2	259.8	262.3	264.7	266.9	269.1	271.1	272.9	274.6	276.1	277.4	278.7	279.8	280.8
Population age 65 years and older	35.1	35.4	35.7	35.9	36.3	36.6	37.0	37.4	37.9	38.5	39.3	40.2	41.2	42.4	43.7	45.0	46.4
Private Health Insurance - NHE (billions)	$417.8	$454.8	$497.7	$552.2	$606.3	$658.5	$706.4	$745.0	$806.2	$875.5	$950.5	$1,017.7	$1,086.9	$1,162.6	$1,242.1	$1,320.2	$1,397.1
Private Health Insurance - PHC (billions)	371.8	402.7	441.0	481.8	519.9	563.5	608.1	641.7	693.3	749.6	808.8	870.3	934.2	997.4	1,061.2	1,127.6	1,196.4
							Annual Percent Change From Previous Year Shown										
National Health Expenditures (billions)	--	6.9	8.5	9.1	8.2	7.9	7.4	7.6	7.2	7.7	7.6	7.1	6.9	7.1	7.1	6.9	6.8
National Health Expenditures as a Percent of Gross Domestic Product	--	1.0	5.2	5.5	3.3	0.9	1.2	2.0	1.8	2.5	2.5	2.0	1.9	2.2	2.3	2.2	2.0
National Health Expenditures Per Capita	--	5.7	7.4	8.0	7.2	6.8	6.4	6.7	6.3	6.8	6.7	6.2	6.0	6.3	6.3	6.1	6.0
Gross Domestic Product (billions)	--	5.9	3.2	3.4	4.8	7.0	6.1	5.5	5.3	5.1	5.0	5.0	4.9	4.8	4.7	4.6	4.7
Gross Domestic Product (billions of 2000 $)	--	3.7	0.8	1.6	2.7	4.2	3.5	3.2	3.0	2.7	2.5	2.5	2.4	2.3	2.2	2.1	2.1
Gross Domestic Product Implicit Price Deflator (chain weighted 2000 base year)	--	2.2	2.4	1.7	2.0	2.6	2.6	2.3	2.3	2.4	2.5	2.5	2.5	2.5	2.5	2.5	2.5
Consumer Price Index (CPI-W) - 1982-1984 base	--	3.4	2.8	1.6	2.3	2.7	2.4	2.4	2.4	2.8	2.8	2.8	2.8	2.8	2.8	2.8	2.8
HCFA Implicit Medical Price Deflator [2]	--	3.4	3.8	3.8	3.7	4.1	3.5	3.8	3.8	3.9	3.8	3.8	3.8	3.8	3.8	3.8	3.9
U.S. Population[3]	--	1.1	1.0	1.0	1.0	1.0	0.9	0.9	0.9	0.9	0.8	0.8	0.8	0.8	0.8	0.8	0.8
Population age less than 65 years	--	1.2	1.1	1.0	1.0	1.0	0.9	0.8	0.8	0.7	0.7	0.6	0.5	0.5	0.4	0.4	0.4
Population age 65 years and older	--	0.8	0.7	0.7	1.0	1.0	1.0	1.2	1.4	1.6	2.0	2.3	2.6	2.9	3.0	3.1	3.1
Private Health Insurance - NHE	--	8.9	9.4	11.0	9.8	8.6	7.3	5.5	8.2	8.6	8.6	7.1	6.8	7.0	6.8	6.3	5.8
Private Health Insurance - PHC	--	8.3	9.5	9.3	7.9	8.4	7.9	5.5	8.0	8.1	7.9	7.6	7.3	6.8	6.4	6.3	6.1

[1] The health spending projections were based on the 2004 version of the National Health Expenditures released in January 2006.
[2] 2000 base year. Calculated as the difference between nominal personal health care spending and real personal health care spending. Real personal health care spending is produced by deflating spending on each service type by the appropriate deflator (PPI, CPI, etc.) and adding real spending by service type.
[3] July 1 Census resident based population estimates.
NOTE: Numbers and percents may not add to totals because of rounding.
SOURCE: Centers for Medicare & Medicaid Services, Office of the Actuary.

Table 2
National Health Expenditure Amounts, and Annual Percent Change by Type of Expenditure: Selected Calendar Years 1999-2015[1]

Type of Expenditure	1999	2000	2001	2002	2003	2004	2005	2006	2007	2008	2009	2010	2011	2012	2013	2014	2015
							Projected										
National Health Expenditures	$1,270.3	$1,358.5	$1,474.2	$1,607.9	$1,740.6	$1,877.6	$2,016.0	$2,169.5	$2,325.7	$2,504.7	$2,696.2	$2,887.3	$3,086.7	$3,307.0	$3,543.3	$3,787.2	$4,043.6
Health Services and Supplies	1,180.0	1,264.5	1,375.5	1,499.2	1,624.5	1,753.0	1,882.2	2,026.0	2,171.3	2,338.8	2,517.8	2,696.0	2,881.6	3,087.3	3,308.2	3,535.7	3,774.8
Personal Health Care	1,068.3	1,139.9	1,239.1	1,341.4	1,445.7	1,560.2	1,677.8	1,801.9	1,928.7	2,073.4	2,225.9	2,386.9	2,555.2	2,735.1	2,926.3	3,127.3	3,342.1
Hospital Care	395.0	417.0	451.4	488.6	525.5	570.8	616.1	662.5	709.1	763.2	821.0	882.4	946.5	1,012.9	1,081.6	1,153.7	1,230.9
Professional Services	397.9	426.7	465.4	503.2	543.3	587.4	631.3	680.0	729.6	785.8	843.6	903.4	964.9	1,032.6	1,105.4	1,181.1	1,261.4
Physician and Clinical Services	269.6	288.6	313.1	337.9	367.0	399.9	429.9	463.3	496.5	533.8	571.7	610.7	650.6	695.5	744.6	795.5	849.8
Other Professional Services	37.1	39.1	42.8	45.7	49.1	52.7	55.8	59.7	64.0	68.7	73.5	78.5	83.9	89.7	95.9	102.5	109.4
Dental Services	57.1	62.0	67.5	73.3	76.9	81.5	87.4	94.3	101.3	109.0	116.9	124.9	133.2	141.7	150.1	158.6	167.3
Other Personal Health Care	34.0	37.1	41.9	46.3	50.4	53.3	58.1	62.7	67.8	74.3	81.5	89.2	97.3	105.8	114.8	124.5	134.8
Nursing Home and Home Health	122.1	125.8	133.8	140.0	148.6	158.4	170.6	181.5	192.2	204.7	218.3	232.8	248.1	264.5	281.9	300.5	320.5
Home Health Care	31.6	30.6	32.2	34.3	38.1	43.2	48.9	53.1	57.3	62.1	67.0	72.3	77.9	83.8	90.0	96.6	103.7
Nursing Home Care	90.5	95.3	101.5	105.7	110.4	115.2	121.7	128.4	134.8	142.7	151.2	160.5	170.3	180.7	191.9	203.9	216.8
Retail Outlet Sales of Medical Products	153.4	170.3	188.5	209.5	228.3	243.7	259.8	277.9	297.8	319.7	343.0	368.4	395.7	425.2	457.4	491.9	529.3
Prescription Drugs	104.7	120.8	138.6	157.9	174.1	188.5	203.5	219.2	236.8	255.8	276.6	299.2	323.8	350.5	379.9	411.7	446.2
Other Medical Products	48.8	49.5	49.9	51.6	54.2	55.2	56.3	58.7	61.1	63.9	66.4	69.1	71.9	74.7	77.5	80.3	83.1
Durable Medical Equipment	19.0	19.3	19.6	20.8	22.1	23.0	23.7	24.9	26.0	27.3	28.2	29.5	30.8	32.1	33.5	34.8	36.2
Other Non-Durable Medical Products	29.8	30.2	30.3	30.9	32.1	32.3	32.6	33.8	35.1	36.6	38.2	39.6	41.1	42.6	44.0	45.5	46.9
Government Administration and Net Cost of Private Health Insurance	70.9	81.2	89.6	106.1	124.9	136.7	142.4	157.1	170.3	187.4	207.8	218.5	228.7	246.9	268.7	286.7	301.8
Government Public Health Activities	40.7	43.4	46.8	51.7	54.0	56.1	62.0	67.0	72.3	78.0	84.1	90.7	97.7	105.2	113.2	121.7	130.9
Investment	90.3	94.0	98.7	108.8	116.1	124.6	133.8	143.6	154.4	165.9	178.4	191.3	205.1	219.7	235.2	251.5	268.9
Research[2]	23.4	25.6	28.8	32.5	35.6	39.0	42.0	45.2	48.9	52.6	56.4	60.2	64.1	68.1	72.3	76.6	81.0
Structures & Equipment	66.8	68.4	69.9	76.2	80.5	85.7	91.8	98.4	105.5	113.3	122.0	131.1	141.0	151.6	162.9	175.0	187.9
							Annual Percent Change From Previous Year Shown										
National Health Expenditures	--	6.9	8.5	9.1	8.2	7.9	7.4	7.6	7.2	7.7	7.6	7.1	6.9	7.1	7.1	6.9	6.8
Health Services and Supplies	--	7.2	8.8	9.0	8.4	7.9	7.4	7.6	7.2	7.7	7.7	7.1	6.9	7.1	7.2	6.9	6.8
Personal Health Care	--	6.7	8.7	8.3	7.8	7.9	7.5	7.4	7.0	7.5	7.4	7.2	7.1	7.0	7.0	6.9	6.9
Hospital Care	--	5.6	8.2	8.2	7.5	8.6	7.9	7.5	7.0	7.6	7.6	7.5	7.3	7.0	6.8	6.7	6.7
Professional Services	--	7.3	9.0	8.1	8.0	8.1	7.5	7.7	7.3	7.7	7.4	7.1	6.8	7.0	7.0	6.9	6.8
Physician and Clinical Services	--	7.0	8.5	7.9	8.6	9.0	7.5	7.8	7.2	7.5	7.1	6.8	6.5	6.9	7.1	6.8	6.8
Other Professional Services	--	5.4	9.5	6.7	7.5	7.4	5.9	6.9	7.1	7.5	6.9	6.9	6.8	6.3	5.9	5.7	6.8
Dental Services	--	8.5	9.0	8.6	4.8	6.1	7.2	7.9	7.4	7.5	7.3	6.9	6.6	6.3	5.9	5.7	5.5
Other Personal Health Care	--	9.0	13.0	10.6	8.7	5.8	9.1	7.9	8.1	9.6	9.7	9.4	9.1	8.7	8.5	8.4	8.3
Nursing Home and Home Health	--	3.1	6.3	4.7	6.1	6.6	7.7	6.4	5.9	6.6	6.6	6.6	6.6	6.6	6.6	6.6	6.6
Home Health Care	--	-3.1	5.5	6.4	11.1	13.3	13.2	8.6	7.9	8.3	8.0	7.8	7.7	7.6	7.5	7.3	7.3
Nursing Home Care	--	5.3	6.6	4.1	4.5	4.3	5.6	5.5	5.0	5.8	6.0	6.1	6.1	6.1	6.2	6.3	6.3
Retail Outlet Sales of Medical Products	--	11.0	10.7	11.2	9.0	6.7	6.6	7.0	7.2	7.3	7.3	7.4	7.4	7.5	7.6	7.6	7.6
Prescription Drugs	--	15.4	14.7	14.0	10.2	8.2	8.0	7.7	8.0	8.1	8.1	8.2	8.2	8.3	8.4	8.4	8.4
Other Medical Products	--	1.5	0.9	3.3	5.1	1.9	2.0	4.2	4.0	4.6	3.9	4.1	3.9	3.9	3.7	3.6	3.5
Durable Medical Equipment	--	1.8	1.6	5.7	6.4	4.0	3.3	5.1	4.4	4.8	3.6	4.5	4.3	4.3	4.1	4.0	3.9
Other Non-Durable Medical Products	--	1.4	0.5	1.8	4.2	0.4	1.1	3.5	3.8	4.5	4.2	3.8	3.6	3.6	3.4	3.3	3.2
Government Administration and Net Cost of Private Health Insurance	--	14.5	10.3	18.4	17.7	9.4	4.2	10.3	8.4	10.0	10.9	5.2	4.7	8.0	8.8	6.7	5.3
Government Public Health Activities	--	6.5	7.9	10.4	4.4	4.0	10.5	8.0	7.9	7.9	7.9	7.7	7.7	7.7	7.6	7.5	7.5
Investment	--	4.1	5.0	10.3	6.7	7.3	7.4	7.3	7.5	7.4	7.5	7.3	7.2	7.1	7.0	7.0	6.9
Research[2]	--	9.2	12.3	13.2	9.5	9.3	7.9	7.7	8.1	7.6	7.2	6.8	6.5	6.3	6.1	5.9	5.8
Structures & Equipment	--	2.3	2.2	9.1	5.5	6.5	7.1	7.2	7.3	7.4	7.7	7.5	7.5	7.5	7.4	7.4	7.4

[1] The health spending projections were based on the 2004 version of the National Health Expenditures (NHE) released in January 2006.
[2] Research and development expenditures of drug companies and other manufacturers and providers of medical equipment and supplies are excluded from research expenditures. These research expenditures are implicitly included in the expenditure class in which the product falls, in that they are covered by the payment received for that product.
NOTE: Numbers may not add to totals because of rounding.
SOURCE: Centers for Medicare & Medicaid Services, Office of the Actuary.

Table 3
National Health Expenditures; Aggregate and per Capita Amounts, Percent Distribution and Annual Percent Change by Source of Funds: Selected Calendar Years 1999-2015[1]

Year	Total	Out-of-Pocket Payments	Third-Party Payments Total	Private Health Insurance	Other Private Funds	Public Total	Federal[2]	State and Local[2]	Medicare[3]	Medicaid[4]
Historical Estimates					Amount in Billions					
1999	$1,270.3	$183.9	$1,086.4	$417.8	$108.6	$560.1	$390.0	$170.1	$213.2	$184.2
2000	1,358.5	192.6	1,165.9	454.8	108.9	602.2	418.4	183.8	225.2	201.6
2001	1,474.2	199.8	1,274.3	497.7	109.7	667.0	465.0	202.0	248.3	225.3
2002	1,607.9	210.8	1,397.2	552.2	118.4	726.5	509.5	217.1	266.3	249.0
2003	1,740.6	223.5	1,517.1	606.3	127.5	783.4	554.4	229.0	283.8	271.2
2004	1,877.6	235.7	1,641.9	658.5	136.1	847.3	600.0	247.3	309.0	292.7
Projected										
2005	2,016.0	248.8	1,767.2	706.4	146.2	914.6	645.9	268.7	335.5	315.2
2006	2,169.5	246.2	1,923.3	745.0	157.1	1,021.2	742.0	279.2	420.1	320.0
2007	2,325.7	261.9	2,063.8	806.2	169.0	1,088.7	789.5	299.2	442.7	347.3
2008	2,504.7	279.1	2,225.7	875.5	181.8	1,168.4	846.7	321.6	472.6	378.6
2009	2,696.2	297.5	2,398.7	950.5	195.9	1,252.3	906.5	345.8	502.5	413.3
2010	2,887.3	316.3	2,571.0	1,017.7	210.6	1,342.6	971.4	371.2	536.0	450.4
2011	3,086.7	335.8	2,750.9	1,086.9	226.1	1,437.9	1,040.0	397.9	572.1	489.5
2012	3,307.0	356.3	2,950.6	1,162.6	242.7	1,545.3	1,119.5	425.8	617.6	530.3
2013	3,543.3	376.8	3,166.5	1,242.1	260.1	1,664.3	1,209.1	455.2	671.4	573.7
2014	3,787.2	398.3	3,388.9	1,320.2	278.6	1,790.1	1,303.8	486.3	728.2	620.1
2015	4,043.6	421.0	3,622.6	1,397.1	298.3	1,927.2	1,407.8	519.4	792.0	669.8
Historical Estimates					Per Capita Amount					
1999	$4,471	$647	$3,824	$1,471	$382	$1,971	$1,373	$599	(5)	(5)
2000	4,729	670	4,058	1,583	379	2,096	1,456	640	(5)	(5)
2001	5,079	688	4,390	1,715	378	2,298	1,602	696	(5)	(5)
2002	5,485	719	4,766	1,884	404	2,478	1,738	740	(5)	(5)
2003	5,879	755	5,125	2,048	431	2,646	1,873	774	(5)	(5)
2004	6,280	788	5,492	2,202	455	2,834	2,007	827	(5)	(5)
Projected										
2005	6,683	825	5,858	2,342	485	3,032	2,141	891	(5)	(5)
2006	7,129	809	6,320	2,448	516	3,355	2,438	917	(5)	(5)
2007	7,576	853	6,723	2,626	550	3,546	2,572	975	(5)	(5)
2008	8,090	901	7,189	2,828	587	3,774	2,735	1,039	(5)	(5)
2009	8,636	953	7,683	3,045	628	4,011	2,904	1,108	(5)	(5)
2010	9,173	1,005	8,168	3,233	669	4,265	3,086	1,179	(5)	(5)
2011	9,727	1,058	8,669	3,425	712	4,531	3,277	1,254	(5)	(5)
2012	10,339	1,114	9,225	3,635	759	4,831	3,500	1,331	(5)	(5)
2013	10,992	1,169	9,823	3,853	807	5,163	3,751	1,412	(5)	(5)
2014	11,660	1,226	10,434	4,065	858	5,511	4,014	1,497	(5)	(5)
2015	12,357	1,287	11,070	4,269	912	5,889	4,302	1,587	(5)	(5)
Historical Estimates					Percent Distribution					
1999	100.0	14.5	85.5	32.9	8.5	44.1	30.7	13.4	16.8	14.5
2000	100.0	14.2	85.8	33.5	8.0	44.3	30.8	13.5	16.6	14.8
2001	100.0	13.6	86.4	33.8	7.4	45.2	31.5	13.7	16.8	15.3
2002	100.0	13.1	86.9	34.3	7.4	45.2	31.7	13.5	16.6	15.5
2003	100.0	12.8	87.2	34.8	7.3	45.0	31.9	13.2	16.3	15.6
2004	100.0	12.6	87.4	35.1	7.3	45.1	32.0	13.2	16.5	15.6
Projected										
2005	100.0	12.3	87.7	35.0	7.3	45.4	32.0	13.3	16.6	15.6
2006	100.0	11.3	88.7	34.3	7.2	47.1	34.2	12.9	19.4	14.8
2007	100.0	11.3	88.7	34.7	7.3	46.8	33.9	12.9	19.0	14.9
2008	100.0	11.1	88.9	35.0	7.3	46.6	33.8	12.8	18.9	15.1
2009	100.0	11.0	89.0	35.3	7.3	46.4	33.6	12.8	18.6	15.3
2010	100.0	11.0	89.0	35.2	7.3	46.5	33.6	12.9	18.6	15.6
2011	100.0	10.9	89.1	35.2	7.3	46.6	33.7	12.9	18.5	15.9
2012	100.0	10.8	89.2	35.2	7.3	46.7	33.9	12.9	18.7	16.0
2013	100.0	10.6	89.4	35.1	7.3	47.0	34.1	12.8	18.9	16.2
2014	100.0	10.5	89.5	34.9	7.4	47.3	34.4	12.8	19.2	16.4
2015	100.0	10.4	89.6	34.6	7.4	47.7	34.8	12.8	19.6	16.6
Historical Estimates					Annual Percent Change from Previous Year Shown					
1999	--	--	--	--	--	--	--	--	--	--
2000	6.9	4.8	7.3	8.9	0.3	7.5	7.3	8.1	5.7	9.5
2001	8.5	3.7	9.3	9.4	0.7	10.8	11.1	9.9	10.3	11.8
2002	9.1	5.5	9.6	11.0	7.9	8.9	9.6	7.4	7.2	10.5
2003	8.2	6.0	8.6	9.8	7.7	7.8	8.8	5.5	6.6	8.9
2004	7.9	5.5	8.2	8.6	6.8	8.2	8.2	8.0	8.9	7.9
Projected										
2005	7.4	5.6	7.6	7.3	7.4	7.9	7.7	8.7	8.6	7.7
2006	7.6	-1.0	8.8	5.5	7.5	11.6	14.9	3.9	25.2	1.5
2007	7.2	6.4	7.3	8.2	7.5	6.6	6.4	7.2	5.4	8.5
2008	7.7	6.6	7.8	8.6	7.6	7.3	7.3	7.5	6.7	9.0
2009	7.6	6.6	7.8	8.6	7.7	7.2	7.1	7.5	6.3	9.2
2010	7.1	6.3	7.2	7.1	7.5	7.2	7.2	7.3	6.7	9.0
2011	6.9	6.2	7.0	6.8	7.3	7.1	7.1	7.2	6.7	8.7
2012	7.1	6.1	7.3	7.0	7.4	7.5	7.6	7.0	8.0	8.3
2013	7.1	5.7	7.3	6.8	7.2	7.7	8.0	6.9	8.7	8.2
2014	6.9	5.7	7.0	6.3	7.1	7.6	7.8	6.8	8.5	8.1
2015	6.8	5.7	6.9	5.8	7.1	7.7	8.0	6.8	8.8	8.0

[1] The health spending projections were based on the 2004 version of the National Health Expenditures (NHE) released in January 2006.
[2] Includes Medicaid SCHIP Expansion and SCHIP.
[3] Subset of Federal funds.
[4] Subset of Federal and State and local funds. Includes Medicaid SCHIP Expansion.
[5] Calculation of per capita estimates is inappropriate.
NOTES: Per capita amounts based on July 1 Census resident based population estimates. Numbers and percents may not add to totals because of rounding
SOURCE: Centers for Medicare & Medicaid Services, Office of the Actuary.

Table 4
Health Services and Supplies Expenditures; Aggregate and per Capita Amounts, Percent Distribution and Annual Percent Change by Source of Funds: Selected Calendar Years 1999-2015[1]

| | | | Third-Party Payments | | | | | | | |
| | | | | | | | Public | | | |
Year	Total	Out-of-Pocket Payments	Total	Private Health Insurance	Other Private Funds	Total	Federal[2]	State and Local[2]	Medicare[3]	Medicaid[4]
Historical Estimates					Amount in Billions					
1999	$1,180.0	$183.9	$996.1	$417.8	$58.4	$519.9	$365.9	$154.0	$213.2	$184.2
2000	1,264.5	192.6	1,071.9	454.8	57.9	559.2	392.6	166.6	225.2	201.6
2001	1,375.5	199.8	1,175.7	497.7	57.5	620.5	436.3	184.2	248.3	225.3
2002	1,499.2	210.8	1,288.4	552.2	59.5	676.7	477.5	199.2	266.3	249.0
2003	1,624.5	223.5	1,401.1	606.3	65.0	729.8	519.1	210.7	283.8	271.2
2004	1,753.0	235.7	1,517.3	658.5	70.0	788.8	561.7	227.2	309.0	292.7
Projected										
2005	1,882.2	248.8	1,633.4	706.4	74.8	852.2	604.6	247.6	335.5	315.2
2006	2,026.0	246.2	1,779.7	745.0	80.1	954.6	697.5	257.1	420.1	320.0
2007	2,171.3	261.9	1,909.4	806.2	85.8	1,017.5	741.5	275.9	442.7	347.3
2008	2,338.8	279.1	2,059.8	875.5	91.9	1,092.4	795.2	297.2	472.6	378.6
2009	2,517.8	297.5	2,220.4	950.5	98.5	1,171.4	851.3	320.1	502.5	413.3
2010	2,696.0	316.3	2,379.7	1,017.7	105.3	1,256.6	912.5	344.2	536.0	450.4
2011	2,881.6	335.8	2,545.8	1,086.9	112.2	1,346.7	977.2	369.5	572.1	489.5
2012	3,087.3	356.3	2,730.9	1,162.6	119.5	1,448.8	1,052.8	395.9	617.6	530.3
2013	3,308.2	376.8	2,931.4	1,242.1	127.0	1,562.2	1,138.4	423.8	671.4	573.7
2014	3,535.7	398.3	3,137.4	1,320.2	134.8	1,682.4	1,228.9	453.5	728.2	620.1
2015	3,774.8	421.0	3,353.8	1,397.1	143.1	1,813.6	1,328.6	485.0	792.0	669.8
Historical Estimates					Per Capita Amount					
1999	$4,154	$647	$3,506	$1,471	$206	$1,830	$1,288	$542	(5)	(5)
2000	4,401	670	3,731	1,583	202	1,946	1,366	580	(5)	(5)
2001	4,739	688	4,050	1,715	198	2,138	1,503	635	(5)	(5)
2002	5,114	719	4,395	1,884	203	2,308	1,629	679	(5)	(5)
2003	5,487	755	4,732	2,048	220	2,465	1,753	712	(5)	(5)
2004	5,864	788	5,075	2,202	234	2,638	1,879	760	(5)	(5)
Projected										
2005	6,239	825	5,415	2,342	248	2,825	2,004	821	(5)	(5)
2006	6,657	809	5,848	2,448	263	3,137	2,292	845	(5)	(5)
2007	7,073	853	6,220	2,626	279	3,314	2,416	899	(5)	(5)
2008	7,554	901	6,653	2,828	297	3,528	2,568	960	(5)	(5)
2009	8,065	953	7,112	3,045	316	3,752	2,727	1,025	(5)	(5)
2010	8,565	1,005	7,560	3,233	335	3,992	2,899	1,093	(5)	(5)
2011	9,081	1,058	8,023	3,425	354	4,244	3,080	1,164	(5)	(5)
2012	9,652	1,114	8,538	3,635	374	4,530	3,292	1,238	(5)	(5)
2013	10,263	1,169	9,094	3,853	394	4,846	3,532	1,315	(5)	(5)
2014	10,886	1,226	9,660	4,065	415	5,180	3,784	1,396	(5)	(5)
2015	11,535	1,287	10,249	4,269	437	5,542	4,060	1,482	(5)	(5)
Historical Estimates					Percent Distribution					
1999	100.0	15.6	84.4	35.4	5.0	44.1	31.0	13.0	18.1	15.6
2000	100.0	15.2	84.8	36.0	4.6	44.2	31.0	13.2	17.8	15.9
2001	100.0	14.5	85.5	36.2	4.2	45.1	31.7	13.4	18.1	16.4
2002	100.0	14.1	85.9	36.8	4.0	45.1	31.9	13.3	17.8	16.6
2003	100.0	13.8	86.2	37.3	4.0	44.9	32.0	13.0	17.5	16.7
2004	100.0	13.4	86.6	37.6	4.0	45.0	32.0	13.0	17.6	16.7
Projected										
2005	100.0	13.2	86.8	37.5	4.0	45.3	32.1	13.2	17.8	16.7
2006	100.0	12.2	87.8	36.8	4.0	47.1	34.4	12.7	20.7	15.8
2007	100.0	12.1	87.9	37.1	3.9	46.9	34.2	12.7	20.4	16.0
2008	100.0	11.9	88.1	37.4	3.9	46.7	34.0	12.7	20.2	16.2
2009	100.0	11.8	88.2	37.8	3.9	46.5	33.8	12.7	20.0	16.4
2010	100.0	11.7	88.3	37.7	3.9	46.6	33.8	12.8	19.9	16.7
2011	100.0	11.7	88.3	37.7	3.9	46.7	33.9	12.8	19.9	17.0
2012	100.0	11.5	88.5	37.7	3.9	46.9	34.1	12.8	20.0	17.2
2013	100.0	11.4	88.6	37.5	3.8	47.2	34.4	12.8	20.3	17.3
2014	100.0	11.3	88.7	37.3	3.8	47.6	34.8	12.8	20.6	17.5
2015	100.0	11.2	88.8	37.0	3.8	48.0	35.2	12.8	21.0	17.7
Historical Estimates					Annual Percent Change from Previous Year Shown					
1999	--	--	--	--	--	--	--	--	--	--
2000	7.2	4.8	7.6	8.9	-0.9	7.6	7.3	8.2	5.7	9.5
2001	8.8	3.7	9.7	9.4	-0.7	11.0	11.1	10.6	10.3	11.8
2002	9.0	5.5	9.6	11.0	3.4	9.1	9.5	8.1	7.2	10.5
2003	8.4	6.0	8.7	9.8	9.4	7.8	8.7	5.8	6.6	8.9
2004	7.9	5.5	8.3	8.6	7.6	8.1	8.2	7.8	8.9	7.9
Projected										
2005	7.4	5.6	7.7	7.3	6.9	8.0	7.6	9.0	8.6	7.7
2006	7.6	-1.0	9.0	5.5	7.1	12.0	15.4	3.8	25.2	1.5
2007	7.2	6.4	7.3	8.2	7.0	6.6	6.3	7.3	5.4	8.5
2008	7.7	6.6	7.9	8.6	7.2	7.4	7.2	7.7	6.7	9.0
2009	7.7	6.6	7.8	8.6	7.2	7.2	7.1	7.7	6.3	9.2
2010	7.1	6.3	7.2	7.1	6.9	7.3	7.2	7.5	6.7	9.0
2011	6.9	6.2	7.0	6.8	6.5	7.2	7.1	7.4	6.7	8.7
2012	7.1	6.1	7.3	7.0	6.5	7.6	7.7	7.2	8.0	8.3
2013	7.2	5.7	7.3	6.8	6.3	7.8	8.1	7.0	8.7	8.2
2014	6.9	5.7	7.0	6.3	6.2	7.7	8.0	7.0	8.5	8.1
2015	6.8	5.7	6.9	5.8	6.1	7.8	8.1	7.0	8.8	8.0

[1] The health spending projections were based on the 2004 version of the National Health Expenditures (NHE) released in January 2006.
[2] Includes Medicaid SCHIP Expansion and SCHIP.
[3] Subset of Federal funds.
[4] Subset of Federal and State and local funds. Includes Medicaid SCHIP Expansion.
[5] Calculation of per capita estimates is inappropriate.
NOTES: Per capita amounts based on July 1 Census resident based population estimates. Numbers and percents may not add to totals because of rounding
SOURCE: Centers for Medicare & Medicaid Services, Office of the Actuary.

Table 5
Personal Health Care Expenditures; Aggregate and per Capita Amounts, Percent Distribution and Annual Percent Change by Source of Funds: Selected Calendar Years 1999-2015[1]

			Third-Party Payments							
						Public				
Year	Total	Out-of-Pocket Payments	Total	Private Health Insurance	Other Private Funds	Total	Federal[2]	State and Local[2]	Medicare[3]	Medicaid[4]
Historical Estimates					Amount in Billions					
1999	$1,068.3	$183.9	$884.5	$371.8	$57.5	$455.3	$347.0	$108.3	$206.4	$171.9
2000	1,139.9	192.6	947.3	402.7	56.8	487.7	371.1	116.6	217.4	187.9
2001	1,239.1	199.8	1,039.3	441.0	56.3	542.0	413.3	128.7	240.5	210.0
2002	1,341.4	210.8	1,130.6	481.8	58.2	590.6	450.4	140.2	258.2	231.9
2003	1,445.7	223.5	1,222.2	519.9	63.8	638.6	489.4	149.1	275.9	251.9
2004	1,560.2	235.7	1,324.5	563.5	68.6	692.4	529.2	163.2	299.6	272.6
Projected										
2005	1,677.8	248.8	1,429.0	608.1	73.4	747.4	568.5	179.0	325.4	293.5
2006	1,801.9	246.2	1,555.7	641.7	78.7	835.3	651.3	184.0	402.6	296.6
2007	1,928.7	261.9	1,666.8	693.3	84.2	889.3	691.2	198.1	423.9	321.8
2008	2,073.4	279.1	1,794.4	749.6	90.3	954.4	740.3	214.2	452.2	350.8
2009	2,225.9	297.5	1,928.5	808.8	96.8	1,022.8	791.3	231.5	480.5	383.0
2010	2,386.9	316.3	2,070.5	870.3	103.6	1,096.7	847.0	249.7	512.1	417.4
2011	2,555.2	335.8	2,219.4	934.2	110.4	1,174.8	906.1	268.7	546.3	453.7
2012	2,735.1	356.3	2,378.8	997.4	117.7	1,263.7	975.2	288.5	589.6	491.5
2013	2,926.3	376.8	2,549.5	1,061.2	125.1	1,363.1	1,053.9	309.3	640.9	531.8
2014	3,127.3	398.3	2,729.0	1,127.6	132.9	1,468.5	1,137.1	331.4	695.2	574.7
2015	3,342.1	421.0	2,921.1	1,196.4	141.1	1,583.6	1,228.8	354.8	756.0	620.8
Historical Estimates					Per Capita Amount					
1999	$3,761	$647	$3,113	$1,309	$202	$1,603	$1,221	$381	(5)	(5)
2000	3,968	670	3,297	1,402	198	1,698	1,292	406	(5)	(5)
2001	4,269	688	3,580	1,519	194	1,867	1,424	443	(5)	(5)
2002	4,576	719	3,857	1,644	198	2,015	1,536	478	(5)	(5)
2003	4,883	755	4,128	1,756	215	2,157	1,653	504	(5)	(5)
2004	5,219	788	4,430	1,885	230	2,316	1,770	546	(5)	(5)
Projected										
2005	5,562	825	4,737	2,016	243	2,478	1,884	593	(5)	(5)
2006	5,921	809	5,112	2,109	258	2,745	2,140	604	(5)	(5)
2007	6,283	853	5,430	2,258	274	2,897	2,252	645	(5)	(5)
2008	6,697	901	5,796	2,421	292	3,083	2,391	692	(5)	(5)
2009	7,130	953	6,177	2,591	310	3,276	2,535	742	(5)	(5)
2010	7,583	1,005	6,578	2,765	329	3,484	2,691	793	(5)	(5)
2011	8,053	1,058	6,994	2,944	348	3,702	2,855	847	(5)	(5)
2012	8,551	1,114	7,437	3,118	368	3,951	3,049	902	(5)	(5)
2013	9,078	1,169	7,909	3,292	388	4,229	3,269	959	(5)	(5)
2014	9,628	1,226	8,402	3,472	409	4,521	3,501	1,020	(5)	(5)
2015	10,213	1,287	8,927	3,656	431	4,839	3,755	1,084	(5)	(5)
Historical Estimates					Percent Distribution					
1999	100.0	17.2	82.8	34.8	5.4	42.6	32.5	10.1	19.3	16.1
2000	100.0	16.9	83.1	35.3	5.0	42.8	32.6	10.2	19.1	16.5
2001	100.0	16.1	83.9	35.6	4.5	43.7	33.4	10.4	19.4	16.9
2002	100.0	15.7	84.3	35.9	4.3	44.0	33.6	10.5	19.3	17.3
2003	100.0	15.5	84.5	36.0	4.4	44.2	33.9	10.3	19.1	17.4
2004	100.0	15.1	84.9	36.1	4.4	44.4	33.9	10.5	19.2	17.5
Projected										
2005	100.0	14.8	85.2	36.2	4.4	44.5	33.9	10.7	19.4	17.5
2006	100.0	13.7	86.3	35.6	4.4	46.4	36.1	10.2	22.3	16.5
2007	100.0	13.6	86.4	35.9	4.4	46.1	35.8	10.3	22.0	16.7
2008	100.0	13.5	86.5	36.2	4.4	46.0	35.7	10.3	21.8	16.9
2009	100.0	13.4	86.6	36.3	4.4	46.0	35.6	10.4	21.6	17.2
2010	100.0	13.3	86.7	36.5	4.3	45.9	35.5	10.5	21.5	17.5
2011	100.0	13.1	86.9	36.6	4.3	46.0	35.5	10.5	21.4	17.8
2012	100.0	13.0	87.0	36.5	4.3	46.2	35.7	10.5	21.6	18.0
2013	100.0	12.9	87.1	36.3	4.3	46.6	36.0	10.6	21.9	18.2
2014	100.0	12.7	87.3	36.1	4.3	47.0	36.4	10.6	22.2	18.4
2015	100.0	12.6	87.4	35.8	4.2	47.4	36.8	10.6	22.6	18.6
Historical Estimates					Annual Percent Change from Previous Year Shown					
1999	--	--	--	--	--	--	--	--	--	--
2000	6.7	4.8	7.1	8.3	-1.1	7.1	7.0	7.7	5.3	9.3
2001	8.7	3.7	9.7	9.5	-1.0	11.1	11.4	10.3	10.6	11.8
2002	8.3	5.5	8.8	9.3	3.3	9.0	9.0	8.9	7.3	10.4
2003	7.8	6.0	8.1	7.9	9.6	8.1	8.7	6.4	6.8	8.6
2004	7.9	5.5	8.4	8.4	7.7	8.4	8.1	9.4	8.6	8.2
Projected										
2005	7.5	5.6	7.9	7.9	6.9	8.0	7.4	9.7	8.6	7.7
2006	7.4	-1.0	8.9	5.5	7.1	11.8	14.6	2.8	23.7	1.0
2007	7.0	6.4	7.1	8.0	7.1	6.5	6.1	7.7	5.3	8.5
2008	7.5	6.6	7.7	8.1	7.2	7.3	7.1	8.1	6.7	9.0
2009	7.4	6.6	7.5	7.9	7.2	7.2	6.9	8.1	6.3	9.2
2010	7.2	6.3	7.4	7.6	7.0	7.2	7.0	7.8	6.6	9.0
2011	7.1	6.2	7.2	7.3	6.6	7.1	7.0	7.6	6.7	8.7
2012	7.0	6.1	7.2	6.8	6.6	7.6	7.6	7.4	7.9	8.3
2013	7.0	5.7	7.2	6.4	6.3	7.9	8.1	7.2	8.7	8.2
2014	6.9	5.7	7.0	6.3	6.2	7.7	7.9	7.1	8.5	8.1
2015	6.9	5.7	7.0	6.1	6.2	7.8	8.1	7.1	8.7	8.0

[1] The health spending projections were based on the 2004 version of the National Health Expenditures (NHE) released in January 2006.
[2] Includes Medicaid SCHIP Expansion and SCHIP.
[3] Subset of Federal funds.
[4] Subset of Federal and State and local funds. Includes Medicaid SCHIP Expansion.
[5] Calculation of per capita estimates is inappropriate.
NOTES: Per capita amounts based on July 1 Census resident based population estimates. Numbers and percents may not add to totals because of rounding.
SOURCE: Centers for Medicare & Medicaid Services, Office of the Actuary.

Table 6
Hospital Care Expenditures; Aggregate and per Capita Amounts, Percent Distribution and Annual Percent Change by Source of Funds: Selected Calendar Years 1999-2015[1]

			Third-Party Payments							
							Public			
Year	Total	Out-of-Pocket Payments	Total	Private Health Insurance	Other Private Funds	Total	Federal[2]	State and Local[2]	Medicare[3]	Medicaid[4]
Historical Estimates					Amount in Billions					
1999	$395.0	$12.8	$382.2	$131.6	$21.1	$229.4	$186.6	$42.8	$122.5	$66.8
2000	417.0	13.6	403.5	143.6	21.8	238.1	192.9	45.2	125.5	71.4
2001	451.4	14.2	437.2	156.7	20.8	259.7	210.9	48.9	137.6	76.9
2002	488.6	15.5	473.1	171.3	21.4	280.3	227.2	53.2	146.7	84.8
2003	525.5	17.0	508.5	186.0	24.9	297.6	242.3	55.4	154.0	90.2
2004	570.8	18.6	552.2	203.4	27.7	321.1	258.7	62.4	163.4	99.1
Projected										
2005	616.1	20.1	596.0	220.2	30.5	345.3	277.5	67.8	177.4	105.8
2006	662.5	21.7	640.8	240.3	33.2	367.3	295.3	71.9	189.7	112.5
2007	709.1	23.7	685.4	262.0	36.1	387.4	310.7	76.7	198.6	121.1
2008	763.2	25.8	737.4	285.3	39.2	412.9	331.2	81.7	211.8	130.6
2009	821.0	28.2	792.8	310.3	42.8	439.7	352.8	87.0	225.7	141.1
2010	882.4	30.6	851.8	337.0	46.6	468.1	375.6	92.5	240.6	152.1
2011	946.5	33.0	913.5	365.0	50.5	498.0	400.0	98.1	256.7	163.8
2012	1,012.9	35.3	977.6	392.0	54.7	530.9	427.1	103.8	275.4	175.8
2013	1,081.6	37.4	1,044.1	418.4	59.0	566.7	456.9	109.8	296.4	188.6
2014	1,153.7	39.7	1,114.1	446.0	63.7	604.4	488.3	116.1	318.5	202.2
2015	1,230.9	42.0	1,188.9	474.9	68.7	645.3	522.6	122.7	343.1	216.6
Historical Estimates					Per Capita Amount					
1999	$1,390	$45	$1,345	$463	$74	$808	$657	$151	(5)	(5)
2000	1,452	47	1,404	500	76	829	671	157	(5)	(5)
2001	1,555	49	1,506	540	72	895	726	168	(5)	(5)
2002	1,667	53	1,614	584	73	956	775	181	(5)	(5)
2003	1,775	57	1,718	628	84	1,005	818	187	(5)	(5)
2004	1,909	62	1,847	680	93	1,074	865	209	(5)	(5)
Projected										
2005	2,042	67	1,976	730	101	1,145	920	225	(5)	(5)
2006	2,177	71	2,105	790	109	1,207	970	236	(5)	(5)
2007	2,310	77	2,233	853	118	1,262	1,012	250	(5)	(5)
2008	2,465	83	2,382	922	127	1,334	1,070	264	(5)	(5)
2009	2,630	90	2,540	994	137	1,409	1,130	279	(5)	(5)
2010	2,803	97	2,706	1,071	148	1,487	1,193	294	(5)	(5)
2011	2,983	104	2,879	1,150	159	1,569	1,260	309	(5)	(5)
2012	3,167	110	3,056	1,226	171	1,660	1,335	325	(5)	(5)
2013	3,355	116	3,239	1,298	183	1,758	1,418	341	(5)	(5)
2014	3,552	122	3,430	1,373	196	1,861	1,503	357	(5)	(5)
2015	3,762	128	3,633	1,451	210	1,972	1,597	375	(5)	(5)
Historical Estimates					Percent Distribution					
1999	100.0	3.2	96.8	33.3	5.3	58.1	47.2	10.8	31.0	16.9
2000	100.0	3.3	96.7	34.4	5.2	57.1	46.2	10.8	30.1	17.1
2001	100.0	3.1	96.9	34.7	4.6	57.5	46.7	10.8	30.5	17.0
2002	100.0	3.2	96.8	35.1	4.4	57.4	46.5	10.9	30.0	17.4
2003	100.0	3.2	96.8	35.4	4.7	56.6	46.1	10.5	29.3	17.2
2004	100.0	3.3	96.7	35.6	4.9	56.3	45.3	10.9	28.6	17.4
Projected										
2005	100.0	3.3	96.7	35.7	4.9	56.0	45.0	11.0	28.8	17.2
2006	100.0	3.3	96.7	36.3	5.0	55.4	44.6	10.9	28.6	17.0
2007	100.0	3.3	96.7	36.9	5.1	54.6	43.8	10.8	28.0	17.1
2008	100.0	3.4	96.6	37.4	5.1	54.1	43.4	10.7	27.8	17.1
2009	100.0	3.4	96.6	37.8	5.2	53.6	43.0	10.6	27.5	17.2
2010	100.0	3.5	96.5	38.2	5.3	53.0	42.6	10.5	27.3	17.2
2011	100.0	3.5	96.5	38.6	5.3	52.6	42.3	10.4	27.1	17.3
2012	100.0	3.5	96.5	38.7	5.4	52.4	42.2	10.2	27.2	17.4
2013	100.0	3.5	96.5	38.7	5.5	52.4	42.2	10.2	27.4	17.4
2014	100.0	3.4	96.6	38.7	5.5	52.4	42.3	10.1	27.6	17.5
2015	100.0	3.4	96.6	38.6	5.6	52.4	42.5	10.0	27.9	17.6
Historical Estimates					Annual Percent Change from Previous Year Shown					
1999	--	--	--	--	--	--	--	--	--	--
2000	5.6	6.0	5.6	9.1	3.2	3.8	3.4	5.6	2.4	6.9
2001	8.2	4.7	8.4	9.1	-4.4	9.1	9.3	8.1	9.7	7.6
2002	8.2	9.4	8.2	9.3	3.1	7.9	7.7	8.7	6.6	10.3
2003	7.5	9.3	7.5	8.6	16.0	6.2	6.6	4.1	5.0	6.4
2004	8.6	9.6	8.6	9.3	11.4	7.9	6.8	12.7	6.1	9.9
Projected										
2005	7.9	8.0	7.9	8.3	10.1	7.5	7.3	8.7	8.5	6.7
2006	7.5	8.2	7.5	9.1	8.9	6.4	6.4	6.1	6.9	6.3
2007	7.0	9.0	7.0	9.0	8.7	5.5	5.2	6.6	4.7	7.6
2008	7.6	9.0	7.6	8.9	8.7	6.6	6.6	6.5	6.7	7.9
2009	7.6	9.2	7.5	8.8	9.2	6.5	6.5	6.5	6.5	8.0
2010	7.5	8.5	7.4	8.6	8.9	6.4	6.5	6.3	6.6	7.8
2011	7.3	7.9	7.2	8.3	8.2	6.4	6.5	6.1	6.7	7.7
2012	7.0	6.9	7.0	7.4	8.3	6.6	6.8	5.8	7.3	7.4
2013	6.8	6.1	6.8	6.7	8.0	6.7	7.0	5.8	7.6	7.3
2014	6.7	5.9	6.7	6.6	7.9	6.6	6.9	5.7	7.5	7.2
2015	6.7	6.0	6.7	6.5	7.9	6.8	7.0	5.6	7.7	7.1

[1] The health spending projections were based on the 2004 version of the National Health Expenditures (NHE) released in January 2006.
[2] Includes Medicaid SCHIP Expansion and SCHIP.
[3] Subset of Federal funds.
[4] Subset of Federal and State and local funds. Includes Medicaid SCHIP Expansion.
[5] Calculation of per capita estimates is inappropriate.
NOTES: Per capita amounts based on July 1 Census resident based population estimates. Numbers and percents may not add to totals because of rounding.
SOURCE: Centers for Medicare & Medicaid Services, Office of the Actuary.

Table 7
Physician and Clinical Services Expenditures; Aggregate and per Capita Amounts, Percent Distribution and Annual Percent Change by Source of Funds: Selected Calendar Years 1999-2015[1]

Year	Total	Out-of-Pocket Payments	Third-Party Payments Total	Private Health Insurance	Other Private Funds	Public Total	Federal[2]	State and Local[2]	Medicare[3]	Medicaid[4]
Historical Estimates					Amount in Billions					
1999	$269.6	$30.7	$238.9	$127.9	$22.9	$88.1	$71.3	$16.8	$53.2	$17.5
2000	288.6	32.2	256.4	136.8	22.2	97.4	79.0	18.4	58.3	19.3
2001	313.1	33.5	279.6	149.1	23.2	107.3	86.9	20.4	63.6	21.8
2002	337.9	35.2	302.7	162.7	24.4	115.6	93.9	21.6	67.7	24.0
2003	367.0	37.5	329.5	177.5	26.1	125.9	102.9	23.0	73.7	25.7
2004	399.9	40.0	359.9	194.0	27.6	138.3	113.8	24.4	81.8	27.8
Projected										
2005	429.9	41.9	388.0	209.6	28.8	149.7	123.2	26.5	88.7	30.1
2006	463.3	44.6	418.7	227.2	30.3	161.1	132.6	28.6	95.5	32.5
2007	496.5	47.6	448.9	246.6	32.1	170.2	139.1	31.1	99.3	35.8
2008	533.8	51.0	482.8	268.3	34.0	180.4	146.5	33.9	103.8	39.3
2009	571.7	54.7	517.0	290.7	35.9	190.4	153.6	36.8	107.7	43.1
2010	610.7	58.7	552.0	313.5	37.8	200.8	161.2	39.5	111.9	47.2
2011	650.6	62.9	587.7	336.4	39.8	211.5	169.1	42.5	116.4	51.6
2012	695.5	67.5	627.9	359.3	41.8	226.8	181.3	45.5	125.1	56.2
2013	744.6	72.2	672.4	382.3	43.9	246.2	197.6	48.6	137.6	61.1
2014	795.5	77.2	718.3	405.9	46.0	266.5	214.6	51.8	150.8	66.3
2015	849.8	82.5	767.3	430.3	48.1	288.9	233.7	55.3	165.7	72.0
Historical Estimates					Per Capita Amount					
1999	$949	$108	$841	$450	$80	$310	$251	$59	(5)	(5)
2000	1,004	112	892	476	77	339	275	64	(5)	(5)
2001	1,079	116	963	514	80	370	300	70	(5)	(5)
2002	1,152	120	1,032	555	83	394	320	74	(5)	(5)
2003	1,240	127	1,113	600	88	425	348	78	(5)	(5)
2004	1,338	134	1,204	649	92	463	381	82	(5)	(5)
Projected										
2005	1,425	139	1,286	695	95	496	408	88	(5)	(5)
2006	1,522	147	1,376	747	100	529	436	94	(5)	(5)
2007	1,617	155	1,462	803	104	554	453	101	(5)	(5)
2008	1,724	165	1,559	867	110	583	473	110	(5)	(5)
2009	1,831	175	1,656	931	115	610	492	118	(5)	(5)
2010	1,940	187	1,754	996	120	638	512	126	(5)	(5)
2011	2,050	198	1,852	1,060	125	667	533	134	(5)	(5)
2012	2,174	211	1,963	1,123	131	709	567	142	(5)	(5)
2013	2,310	224	2,086	1,186	136	764	613	151	(5)	(5)
2014	2,449	238	2,212	1,250	142	820	661	160	(5)	(5)
2015	2,597	252	2,345	1,315	147	883	714	169	(5)	(5)
Historical Estimates					Percent Distribution					
1999	100.0	11.4	88.6	47.4	8.5	32.7	26.5	6.2	19.7	6.5
2000	100.0	11.2	88.8	47.4	7.7	33.8	27.4	6.4	20.2	6.7
2001	100.0	10.7	89.3	47.6	7.4	34.3	27.8	6.5	20.3	7.0
2002	100.0	10.4	89.6	48.2	7.2	34.2	27.8	6.4	20.0	7.1
2003	100.0	10.2	89.8	48.4	7.1	34.3	28.0	6.3	20.1	7.0
2004	100.0	10.0	90.0	48.5	6.9	34.6	28.5	6.1	20.5	6.9
Projected										
2005	100.0	9.7	90.3	48.7	6.7	34.8	28.7	6.2	20.6	7.0
2006	100.0	9.6	90.4	49.0	6.5	34.8	28.6	6.2	20.6	7.0
2007	100.0	9.6	90.4	49.7	6.5	34.3	28.0	6.3	20.0	7.2
2008	100.0	9.6	90.4	50.3	6.4	33.8	27.4	6.4	19.4	7.4
2009	100.0	9.6	90.4	50.8	6.3	33.3	26.9	6.4	18.8	7.5
2010	100.0	9.6	90.4	51.3	6.2	32.9	26.4	6.5	18.3	7.7
2011	100.0	9.7	90.3	51.7	6.1	32.5	26.0	6.5	17.9	7.9
2012	100.0	9.7	90.3	51.7	6.0	32.6	26.1	6.5	18.0	8.1
2013	100.0	9.7	90.3	51.3	5.9	33.1	26.5	6.5	18.5	8.2
2014	100.0	9.7	90.3	51.0	5.8	33.5	27.0	6.5	19.0	8.3
2015	100.0	9.7	90.3	50.6	5.7	34.0	27.5	6.5	19.5	8.5
Historical Estimates					Annual Percent Change from Previous Year Shown					
1999	--	--	--	--	--	--	--	--	--	--
2000	7.0	4.7	7.3	6.9	-2.9	10.5	10.8	9.5	9.8	10.4
2001	8.5	4.2	9.1	9.0	4.4	10.2	10.0	10.9	9.0	13.2
2002	7.9	4.9	8.3	9.1	5.1	7.7	8.1	6.1	6.4	10.1
2003	8.6	6.6	8.9	9.1	7.2	8.9	9.5	6.3	8.8	7.2
2004	9.0	6.6	9.2	9.3	5.7	9.9	10.6	6.3	11.1	7.9
Projected										
2005	7.5	4.8	7.8	8.0	4.3	8.2	8.2	8.3	8.3	8.4
2006	7.8	6.5	7.9	8.4	5.4	7.7	7.6	7.9	7.7	8.1
2007	7.2	6.7	7.2	8.5	5.7	5.6	4.9	8.9	3.9	9.9
2008	7.5	7.2	7.5	8.8	6.1	6.0	5.3	9.2	4.6	9.8
2009	7.1	7.2	7.1	8.3	5.6	5.5	4.9	8.3	3.8	9.9
2010	6.8	7.3	6.8	7.8	5.3	5.5	4.9	7.6	3.9	9.5
2011	6.5	7.1	6.5	7.3	5.2	5.4	4.9	7.5	4.0	9.2
2012	6.9	7.4	6.9	6.8	5.1	7.2	7.2	7.1	7.5	8.9
2013	7.1	7.0	7.1	6.4	4.9	8.5	9.0	6.8	10.0	8.7
2014	6.8	6.8	6.8	6.2	4.8	8.3	8.6	6.7	9.6	8.6
2015	6.8	6.9	6.8	6.0	4.7	8.4	8.9	6.6	9.9	8.6

[1] The health spending projections were based on the 2004 version of the National Health Expenditures (NHE) released in January 2006.
[2] Includes Medicaid SCHIP Expansion and SCHIP.
[3] Subset of Federal funds.
[4] Subset of Federal and State and local funds. Includes Medicaid SCHIP Expansion.
[5] Calculation of per capita estimates is inappropriate.
NOTES: Per capita amounts based on July 1 Census resident based population estimates. Numbers and percents may not add to totals because of rounding
SOURCE: Centers for Medicare & Medicaid Services, Office of the Actuary.

Table 8
Dental Services Expenditures; Aggregate and per Capita Amounts, Percent Distribution and Annual Percent Change by Source of Funds: Selected Calendar Years 1999-2015[1]

Year	Total	Out-of-Pocket Payments	Third-Party Payments Total	Private Health Insurance	Other Private Funds	Public Total	Federal[2]	State and Local[2]	Medicare[3]	Medicaid[4]
Historical Estimates					Amount in Billions					
1999	$57.1	$25.2	$31.9	$29.2	$0.1	$2.5	$1.5	$1.0	$0.1	$2.2
2000	62.0	27.7	34.3	31.3	0.2	2.8	1.7	1.1	0.1	2.4
2001	67.5	29.3	38.2	34.3	0.1	3.8	2.3	1.6	0.1	3.2
2002	73.3	32.4	41.0	36.6	0.1	4.3	2.6	1.7	0.1	3.6
2003	76.9	34.3	42.6	38.0	0.0	4.6	2.8	1.8	0.1	4.0
2004	81.5	36.1	45.5	40.5	0.0	4.9	3.0	1.9	0.1	4.2
Projected										
2005	87.4	38.7	48.7	43.3	0.1	5.4	3.2	2.1	0.1	4.6
2006	94.3	42.1	52.3	46.4	0.1	5.8	3.5	2.3	0.2	5.0
2007	101.3	45.1	56.2	49.7	0.1	6.4	3.9	2.6	0.2	5.6
2008	109.0	48.3	60.7	53.4	0.1	7.2	4.3	2.9	0.3	6.3
2009	116.9	51.5	65.3	57.2	0.1	8.1	4.8	3.2	0.3	7.1
2010	124.9	54.7	70.2	61.1	0.1	9.0	5.4	3.6	0.3	8.0
2011	133.2	57.9	75.3	65.2	0.1	10.0	6.0	4.0	0.4	9.0
2012	141.7	61.2	80.4	69.1	0.1	11.2	6.6	4.5	0.4	10.1
2013	150.1	64.4	85.7	73.1	0.2	12.4	7.4	5.0	0.4	11.3
2014	158.6	67.5	91.1	77.1	0.2	13.8	8.2	5.6	0.5	12.6
2015	167.3	70.9	96.4	80.9	0.2	15.3	9.1	6.3	0.6	14.0
Historical Estimates					Per Capita Amount					
1999	$201	$89	$112	$103	$0	$9	$5	$4	(5)	(5)
2000	216	96	119	109	1	10	6	4	(5)	(5)
2001	233	101	132	118	0	13	8	5	(5)	(5)
2002	250	110	140	125	0	15	9	6	(5)	(5)
2003	260	116	144	128	0	15	10	6	(5)	(5)
2004	273	121	152	136	0	16	10	6	(5)	(5)
Projected										
2005	290	128	162	144	0	18	11	7	(5)	(5)
2006	310	138	172	152	0	19	12	8	(5)	(5)
2007	330	147	183	162	0	21	13	8	(5)	(5)
2008	352	156	196	172	0	23	14	9	(5)	(5)
2009	374	165	209	183	0	26	16	10	(5)	(5)
2010	397	174	223	194	0	29	17	12	(5)	(5)
2011	420	182	237	205	0	32	19	13	(5)	(5)
2012	443	191	251	216	0	35	21	14	(5)	(5)
2013	466	200	266	227	1	38	23	16	(5)	(5)
2014	488	208	280	237	1	42	25	17	(5)	(5)
2015	511	217	295	247	1	47	28	19	(5)	(5)
Historical Estimates					Percent Distribution					
1999	100.0	44.2	55.8	51.2	0.2	4.4	2.6	1.8	0.1	3.8
2000	100.0	44.6	55.4	50.5	0.3	4.6	2.7	1.8	0.1	3.9
2001	100.0	43.4	56.6	50.8	0.2	5.7	3.4	2.3	0.1	4.8
2002	100.0	44.1	55.9	49.9	0.1	5.9	3.5	2.4	0.1	5.0
2003	100.0	44.6	55.4	49.4	0.1	6.0	3.7	2.3	0.1	5.1
2004	100.0	44.3	55.7	49.7	0.1	6.0	3.7	2.3	0.1	5.2
Projected										
2005	100.0	44.3	55.7	49.5	0.1	6.1	3.7	2.4	0.2	5.3
2006	100.0	44.6	55.4	49.2	0.1	6.1	3.7	2.4	0.2	5.3
2007	100.0	44.5	55.5	49.0	0.1	6.4	3.8	2.5	0.2	5.5
2008	100.0	44.3	55.7	49.0	0.1	6.6	4.0	2.6	0.2	5.8
2009	100.0	44.1	55.9	48.9	0.1	6.9	4.1	2.8	0.2	6.1
2010	100.0	43.8	56.2	48.9	0.1	7.2	4.3	2.9	0.3	6.4
2011	100.0	43.5	56.5	48.9	0.1	7.5	4.5	3.0	0.3	6.8
2012	100.0	43.2	56.8	48.8	0.1	7.9	4.7	3.2	0.3	7.1
2013	100.0	42.9	57.1	48.7	0.1	8.3	4.9	3.4	0.3	7.5
2014	100.0	42.6	57.4	48.6	0.1	8.7	5.1	3.5	0.3	7.9
2015	100.0	42.4	57.6	48.3	0.1	9.2	5.4	3.7	0.3	8.4
Historical Estimates					Annual Percent Change from Previous Year Shown					
1999	--	--	--	--	--	--	--	--	--	--
2000	8.5	9.7	7.5	7.1	22.0	12.2	13.5	10.3	4.8	9.8
2001	9.0	5.8	11.5	9.4	-18.8	35.9	34.7	37.7	6.3	35.2
2002	8.6	10.5	7.1	6.9	-50.0	11.9	13.1	10.1	-9.9	12.3
2003	4.8	5.9	3.9	3.7	-38.3	6.8	10.5	1.3	-9.1	8.8
2004	6.1	5.3	6.7	6.7	13.6	6.5	5.5	8.1	3.2	7.2
Projected										
2005	7.2	7.2	7.3	6.9	16.0	9.9	8.5	12.0	78.5	8.8
2006	7.9	8.7	7.2	7.1	16.4	8.1	8.1	8.0	42.7	7.9
2007	7.4	7.2	7.6	7.1	16.2	11.3	11.0	11.6	20.7	12.2
2008	7.5	7.1	7.9	7.4	15.1	11.8	11.4	12.3	12.8	12.9
2009	7.3	6.7	7.7	7.1	13.8	12.0	11.7	12.5	12.0	13.0
2010	6.9	6.1	7.5	6.9	13.7	11.7	11.4	12.2	12.0	12.7
2011	6.6	5.8	7.2	6.6	14.3	11.2	10.8	11.8	10.1	12.2
2012	6.3	5.8	6.8	6.1	13.8	11.2	11.0	11.6	12.1	11.9
2013	5.9	5.1	6.6	5.8	13.2	11.2	11.0	11.5	13.0	11.8
2014	5.7	5.0	6.3	5.5	12.2	11.1	10.9	11.4	11.2	11.7
2015	5.5	5.0	5.8	4.9	10.3	11.2	11.0	11.4	12.9	11.6

[1] The health spending projections were based on the 2004 version of the National Health Expenditures (NHE) released in January 2006.
[2] Includes Medicaid SCHIP Expansion and SCHIP.
[3] Subset of Federal funds.
[4] Subset of Federal and State and local funds. Includes Medicaid SCHIP Expansion.
[5] Calculation of per capita estimates is inappropriate.

NOTES: Per capita amounts based on July 1 Census resident based population estimates. 0.0 denotes less than $50 million for aggregate amounts, and 0 denotes less than $.50 for per capita amounts. Numbers and percents may not add to totals because of rounding.
SOURCE: Centers for Medicare & Medicaid Services, Office of the Actuary.

Table 9
Other Professional Services Expenditures; Aggregate and per Capita Amounts, Percent Distribution and Annual Percent Change by Source of Funds: Selected Calendar Years 1999-2015[1]

Year	Total	Out-of-Pocket Payments	Third-Party Payments Total	Private Health Insurance	Other Private Funds	Public Total	Federal[2]	State and Local[2]	Medicare[3]	Medicaid[4]
Historical Estimates					Amount in Billions					
1999	$37.1	$10.5	$26.6	$13.2	$2.8	$10.6	$7.3	$3.3	$6.3	$1.4
2000	39.1	11.0	28.1	13.9	2.7	11.6	8.1	3.5	6.9	1.5
2001	42.8	11.6	31.2	15.2	2.7	13.4	9.4	3.9	8.1	1.8
2002	45.7	11.9	33.8	16.1	2.7	14.9	10.3	4.6	8.6	2.5
2003	49.1	12.7	36.3	17.6	2.9	15.9	10.9	4.9	9.1	2.7
2004	52.7	13.8	38.9	18.8	2.9	17.2	12.3	4.9	10.1	3.2
Projected										
2005	55.8	14.6	41.2	20.0	3.1	18.1	12.9	5.2	10.6	3.4
2006	59.7	15.6	44.1	21.6	3.3	19.1	13.6	5.5	11.3	3.4
2007	64.0	16.7	47.2	23.4	3.5	20.3	14.3	6.0	11.8	3.8
2008	68.7	18.0	50.7	25.2	3.8	21.7	15.2	6.5	12.4	4.2
2009	73.5	19.4	54.1	27.0	4.0	23.0	16.0	7.1	12.9	4.6
2010	78.5	20.6	57.9	28.9	4.3	24.7	17.0	7.7	13.6	5.1
2011	83.9	22.0	61.9	30.8	4.6	26.5	18.1	8.4	14.4	5.6
2012	89.7	23.4	66.3	32.7	4.8	28.7	19.6	9.1	15.6	6.1
2013	95.9	24.9	71.0	34.6	5.1	31.4	21.5	9.8	17.1	6.7
2014	102.5	26.4	76.0	36.5	5.3	34.2	23.5	10.7	18.7	7.4
2015	109.4	28.1	81.3	38.5	5.6	37.3	25.8	11.5	20.5	8.1
Historical Estimates					Per Capita Amount					
1999	$131	$37	$94	$46	$10	$37	$26	$12	(5)	(5)
2000	136	38	98	48	9	40	28	12	(5)	(5)
2001	147	40	108	52	9	46	32	14	(5)	(5)
2002	156	40	115	55	9	51	35	16	(5)	(5)
2003	166	43	123	59	10	54	37	17	(5)	(5)
2004	176	46	130	63	10	58	41	16	(5)	(5)
Projected										
2005	185	48	137	66	10	60	43	17	(5)	(5)
2006	196	51	145	71	11	63	45	18	(5)	(5)
2007	208	55	154	76	11	66	47	19	(5)	(5)
2008	222	58	164	81	12	70	49	21	(5)	(5)
2009	235	62	173	87	13	74	51	23	(5)	(5)
2010	249	66	184	92	14	79	54	25	(5)	(5)
2011	264	69	195	97	14	83	57	26	(5)	(5)
2012	280	73	207	102	15	90	61	28	(5)	(5)
2013	297	77	220	107	16	97	67	31	(5)	(5)
2014	315	81	234	112	16	105	72	33	(5)	(5)
2015	334	86	249	118	17	114	79	35	(5)	(5)
Historical Estimates					Percent Distribution					
1999	100.0	28.3	71.7	35.6	7.4	28.7	19.7	9.0	16.9	3.8
2000	100.0	28.1	71.9	35.5	6.8	29.7	20.6	9.0	17.7	3.9
2001	100.0	27.1	72.9	35.5	6.2	31.2	22.0	9.2	18.9	4.3
2002	100.0	26.0	74.0	35.3	6.0	32.7	22.6	10.2	18.8	5.4
2003	100.0	26.0	74.0	35.9	5.9	32.3	22.3	10.0	18.5	5.5
2004	100.0	26.1	73.9	35.7	5.5	32.6	23.3	9.4	19.1	6.1
Projected										
2005	100.0	26.2	73.8	35.9	5.5	32.4	23.1	9.3	19.0	6.0
2006	100.0	26.1	73.9	36.3	5.5	32.1	22.9	9.2	19.0	5.7
2007	100.0	26.2	73.8	36.5	5.5	31.8	22.4	9.3	18.5	5.9
2008	100.0	26.2	73.8	36.7	5.5	31.6	22.2	9.5	18.1	6.1
2009	100.0	26.3	73.7	36.8	5.5	31.4	21.7	9.7	17.5	6.3
2010	100.0	26.3	73.7	36.8	5.5	31.5	21.6	9.8	17.4	6.5
2011	100.0	26.2	73.8	36.8	5.4	31.6	21.6	10.0	17.2	6.7
2012	100.0	26.1	73.9	36.5	5.4	32.0	21.9	10.1	17.4	6.9
2013	100.0	25.9	74.1	36.1	5.3	32.7	22.4	10.3	17.9	7.0
2014	100.0	25.8	74.2	35.6	5.2	33.3	22.9	10.4	18.3	7.2
2015	100.0	25.7	74.3	35.2	5.1	34.1	23.5	10.5	18.8	7.4
Historical Estimates					Annual Percent Change from Previous Year Shown					
1999	--	--	--	--	--	--	--	--	--	--
2000	5.4	4.5	5.8	5.1	-3.7	9.0	10.5	5.7	10.7	10.7
2001	9.5	5.6	11.0	9.5	-0.1	15.3	16.9	11.6	17.0	18.9
2002	6.7	2.4	8.2	6.0	3.3	11.7	9.2	17.7	5.9	34.0
2003	7.5	7.4	7.5	9.3	5.1	6.1	6.1	6.0	5.7	9.2
2004	7.4	8.1	7.1	7.0	0.6	8.5	12.3	0.1	11.0	18.7
Projected										
2005	5.9	6.0	5.8	6.3	6.1	5.2	5.0	5.5	5.2	5.8
2006	6.9	6.7	7.0	8.0	7.2	5.9	6.0	5.7	7.0	1.1
2007	7.1	7.2	7.1	8.0	7.0	6.1	5.2	8.6	4.2	10.5
2008	7.5	7.7	7.4	7.8	7.3	7.0	6.1	8.9	5.3	10.6
2009	6.9	7.4	6.8	7.4	6.9	6.0	4.8	9.0	3.6	10.7
2010	6.8	6.6	6.9	6.7	6.3	7.3	6.6	8.8	5.8	10.4
2011	6.8	6.5	6.9	6.8	6.1	7.2	6.5	8.6	5.8	10.0
2012	6.9	6.3	7.1	6.2	5.9	8.4	8.4	8.5	8.2	9.7
2013	7.0	6.4	7.2	5.6	5.2	9.2	9.6	8.3	9.8	9.6
2014	6.9	6.4	7.0	5.6	5.0	8.9	9.2	8.2	9.3	9.5
2015	6.8	6.2	7.0	5.4	4.6	9.1	9.6	8.1	9.7	9.5

[1] The health spending projections were based on the 2004 version of the National Health Expenditures (NHE) released in January 2006.
[2] Includes Medicaid SCHIP Expansion and SCHIP.
[3] Subset of Federal funds.
[4] Subset of Federal and State and local funds. Includes Medicaid SCHIP Expansion.
[5] Calculation of per capita estimates is inappropriate.

NOTES: Per capita amounts based on July 1 Census resident based population estimates. Numbers and percents may not add to totals because of rounding.
SOURCE: Centers for Medicare & Medicaid Services, Office of the Actuary.

Table 10
Home Health Care Expenditures; Aggregate and per Capita Amounts, Percent Distribution and Annual Percent Change by Source of Funds: Selected Calendar Years 1999-2015[1]

Year	Total	Out-of-Pocket Payments	Third-Party Payments						Medicare[3]	Medicaid[4]
			Total	Private Health Insurance	Other Private Funds	Public				
						Total	Federal[2]	State and Local[2]		
Historical Estimates					Amount in Billions					
1999	$31.6	$6.1	$25.4	$7.9	$1.6	$15.9	$11.6	$4.3	$8.3	$5.9
2000	30.6	5.3	25.3	7.0	1.2	17.0	12.4	4.6	8.7	6.8
2001	32.2	5.4	26.9	5.8	1.0	20.1	14.6	5.5	10.0	8.4
2002	34.3	4.9	29.4	5.1	0.8	23.5	17.3	6.2	11.7	10.0
2003	38.1	4.8	33.4	5.2	0.9	27.3	20.6	6.7	13.8	11.8
2004	43.2	4.9	38.2	5.2	0.9	32.1	24.2	7.9	16.4	13.7
Projected										
2005	48.9	5.2	43.7	5.4	1.0	37.3	27.8	9.5	18.9	16.3
2006	53.1	5.5	47.6	5.6	1.1	40.8	30.6	10.3	20.8	17.7
2007	57.3	5.8	51.5	5.9	1.2	44.4	33.1	11.3	22.3	19.7
2008	62.1	6.2	55.9	6.2	1.2	48.5	36.1	12.4	24.0	22.0
2009	67.0	6.5	60.6	6.5	1.3	52.8	39.1	13.7	25.6	24.5
2010	72.3	6.8	65.5	6.8	1.3	57.4	42.3	15.1	27.3	27.2
2011	77.9	7.1	70.8	7.2	1.4	62.3	45.7	16.5	29.1	30.2
2012	83.8	7.4	76.4	7.5	1.4	67.5	49.4	18.1	31.1	33.3
2013	90.0	7.6	82.4	7.7	1.5	73.2	53.4	19.8	33.3	36.6
2014	96.6	7.9	88.7	8.0	1.5	79.2	57.7	21.6	35.6	40.2
2015	103.7	8.1	95.5	8.3	1.5	85.7	62.2	23.5	38.0	44.1
Historical Estimates					Per Capita Amount					
1999	$111	$22	$90	$28	$6	$56	$41	$15	(5)	(5)
2000	106	18	88	24	4	59	43	16	(5)	(5)
2001	111	18	93	20	3	69	50	19	(5)	(5)
2002	117	17	100	18	3	80	59	21	(5)	(5)
2003	129	16	113	17	3	92	70	23	(5)	(5)
2004	144	17	128	17	3	107	81	26	(5)	(5)
Projected										
2005	162	17	145	18	3	124	92	31	(5)	(5)
2006	174	18	156	19	4	134	100	34	(5)	(5)
2007	187	19	168	19	4	145	108	37	(5)	(5)
2008	200	20	181	20	4	157	116	40	(5)	(5)
2009	215	21	194	21	4	169	125	44	(5)	(5)
2010	230	21	208	22	4	182	134	48	(5)	(5)
2011	245	22	223	23	4	196	144	52	(5)	(5)
2012	262	23	239	23	4	211	155	57	(5)	(5)
2013	279	24	256	24	5	227	166	61	(5)	(5)
2014	297	24	273	25	5	244	177	66	(5)	(5)
2015	317	25	292	25	5	262	190	72	(5)	(5)
Historical Estimates					Percent Distribution					
1999	100.0	19.4	80.6	25.1	5.2	50.4	36.7	13.7	26.1	18.8
2000	100.0	17.2	82.8	23.0	4.1	55.7	40.7	15.0	28.4	22.1
2001	100.0	16.6	83.4	17.9	3.1	62.4	45.3	17.0	30.9	26.0
2002	100.0	14.2	85.8	15.0	2.4	68.4	50.4	18.0	34.0	29.3
2003	100.0	12.5	87.5	13.6	2.4	71.6	54.1	17.5	36.2	30.9
2004	100.0	11.5	88.5	12.0	2.2	74.3	56.0	18.3	38.0	31.7
Projected										
2005	100.0	10.6	89.4	11.0	2.1	76.3	57.0	19.4	38.7	33.3
2006	100.0	10.4	89.6	10.6	2.1	76.9	57.6	19.3	39.3	33.3
2007	100.0	10.2	89.8	10.3	2.0	77.4	57.8	19.7	38.9	34.4
2008	100.0	9.9	90.1	10.0	2.0	78.1	58.1	20.0	38.6	35.4
2009	100.0	9.7	90.3	9.7	1.9	78.7	58.3	20.4	38.2	36.5
2010	100.0	9.4	90.6	9.5	1.8	79.3	58.5	20.8	37.8	37.7
2011	100.0	9.1	90.9	9.2	1.8	80.0	58.7	21.2	37.4	38.7
2012	100.0	8.8	91.2	8.9	1.7	80.6	59.0	21.6	37.2	39.7
2013	100.0	8.5	91.5	8.6	1.6	81.3	59.4	22.0	37.0	40.6
2014	100.0	8.2	91.8	8.3	1.6	82.0	59.7	22.3	36.8	41.6
2015	100.0	7.8	92.2	8.0	1.5	82.7	60.0	22.7	36.7	42.6
Historical Estimates					Annual Percent Change from Previous Year Shown					
1999	--	--	--	--	--	--	--	--	--	--
2000	-3.1	-14.0	-0.5	-11.1	-23.7	7.1	7.4	6.4	5.1	13.7
2001	5.5	2.0	6.2	-17.9	-19.6	18.1	17.4	19.9	15.0	23.9
2002	6.4	-9.3	9.5	-11.0	-16.8	16.7	18.3	12.4	17.0	20.0
2003	11.1	-2.2	13.3	0.6	7.9	16.3	19.3	8.1	18.3	17.4
2004	13.3	4.0	14.6	0.5	5.2	17.6	17.4	18.1	19.0	16.2
Projected										
2005	13.2	4.9	14.3	3.1	6.8	16.3	15.1	20.1	15.3	18.6
2006	8.6	6.5	8.9	5.1	8.6	9.4	9.8	8.3	10.1	8.9
2007	7.9	5.7	8.2	5.1	6.0	8.7	8.3	9.8	6.8	11.3
2008	8.3	5.3	8.6	5.0	5.0	9.2	8.9	10.2	7.6	11.5
2009	8.0	5.2	8.3	5.1	4.2	8.9	8.4	10.3	6.8	11.5
2010	7.8	4.5	8.2	4.8	4.0	8.7	8.2	10.1	6.7	11.2
2011	7.7	4.5	8.1	4.5	3.7	8.6	8.1	9.8	6.7	10.7
2012	7.6	4.1	7.9	4.3	3.6	8.4	8.1	9.4	6.9	10.3
2013	7.5	3.7	7.9	3.7	3.2	8.4	8.1	9.2	7.0	10.0
2014	7.3	3.4	7.7	3.5	2.8	8.2	7.9	9.1	6.7	9.9
2015	7.3	3.0	7.7	3.2	2.5	8.2	7.9	9.1	6.8	9.7

[1] The health spending projections were based on the 2004 version of the National Health Expenditures (NHE) released in January 2006.
[2] Includes Medicaid SCHIP Expansion and SCHIP.
[3] Subset of Federal funds.
[4] Subset of Federal and State and local funds. Includes Medicaid SCHIP Expansion.
[5] Calculation of per capita estimates is inappropriate.

NOTES: Per capita amounts based on July 1 Census resident based population estimates. Numbers and percents may not add to totals because of rounding.
SOURCE: Centers for Medicare & Medicaid Services, Office of the Actuary.

Table 11
Prescription Drug Expenditures; Aggregate and per Capita Amounts, Percent Distribution and Annual Percent Change by Source of Funds: Selected Calendar Years 1999-2015[1]

Year	Total	Out-of-Pocket Payments	Third-Party Payments Total	Private Health Insurance	Other Private Funds	Public Total	Federal[2]	State and Local[2]	Medicare[3]	Medicaid[4]
Historical Estimates					Amount in Billions					
1999	$104.7	$30.4	$74.3	$51.2	--	$23.1	$13.2	$9.9	$1.9	$17.1
2000	120.8	33.4	87.4	59.7	--	27.6	15.8	11.8	2.1	20.3
2001	138.6	36.2	102.4	69.3	--	33.0	19.2	13.8	2.4	24.0
2002	157.9	40.0	117.9	78.7	--	39.2	23.1	16.2	2.4	28.0
2003	174.1	43.7	130.4	84.2	--	46.1	28.1	18.1	2.4	32.9
2004	188.5	46.9	141.6	89.7	--	51.9	31.9	20.0	3.4	36.6
Projected										
2005	203.5	50.6	152.9	97.4	--	55.5	33.5	22.0	3.5	38.9
2006	219.2	35.6	183.6	87.6	--	96.0	80.2	15.8	58.3	23.5
2007	236.8	38.2	198.6	92.1	--	106.5	88.9	17.6	64.1	27.1
2008	255.8	41.0	214.8	96.8	--	118.0	98.5	19.5	71.1	30.3
2009	276.6	44.3	232.4	102.1	--	130.3	108.8	21.5	78.5	33.9
2010	299.2	47.9	251.4	107.5	--	143.9	120.2	23.7	86.8	37.7
2011	323.8	51.8	272.0	113.7	--	158.3	132.3	25.9	95.9	41.5
2012	350.5	56.2	294.3	120.3	--	174.1	145.9	28.2	106.3	45.3
2013	379.9	60.8	319.1	128.1	--	191.0	160.5	30.5	117.7	49.0
2014	411.7	65.9	345.8	136.6	--	209.2	176.3	32.9	130.3	52.7
2015	446.2	71.4	374.8	145.8	--	229.0	193.6	35.3	144.2	56.4
Historical Estimates					Per Capita Amount					
1999	$368	$107	$261	$180	--	$81	$46	$35	(5)	(5)
2000	420	116	304	208	--	96	55	41	(5)	(5)
2001	477	125	353	239	--	114	66	48	(5)	(5)
2002	539	136	402	268	--	134	79	55	(5)	(5)
2003	588	148	440	285	--	156	95	61	(5)	(5)
2004	630	157	474	300	--	173	107	67	(5)	(5)
Projected										
2005	675	168	507	323	--	184	111	73	(5)	(5)
2006	720	117	603	288	--	315	263	52	(5)	(5)
2007	771	124	647	300	--	347	290	57	(5)	(5)
2008	826	132	694	313	--	381	318	63	(5)	(5)
2009	886	142	744	327	--	417	348	69	(5)	(5)
2010	951	152	799	341	--	457	382	75	(5)	(5)
2011	1,021	163	857	358	--	499	417	82	(5)	(5)
2012	1,096	176	920	376	--	544	456	88	(5)	(5)
2013	1,179	189	990	397	--	593	498	95	(5)	(5)
2014	1,267	203	1,065	421	--	644	543	101	(5)	(5)
2015	1,364	218	1,145	446	--	700	592	108	(5)	(5)
Historical Estimates					Percent Distribution					
1999	100.0	29.0	71.0	48.9	--	22.1	12.6	9.5	1.8	16.3
2000	100.0	27.7	72.3	49.4	--	22.9	13.1	9.8	1.7	16.8
2001	100.0	26.1	73.9	50.0	--	23.8	13.9	10.0	1.7	17.3
2002	100.0	25.3	74.7	49.8	--	24.8	14.6	10.2	1.5	17.7
2003	100.0	25.1	74.9	48.4	--	26.5	16.1	10.4	1.4	18.9
2004	100.0	24.9	75.1	47.6	--	27.5	16.9	10.6	1.8	19.4
Projected										
2005	100.0	24.9	75.1	47.9	--	27.3	16.5	10.8	1.7	19.1
2006	100.0	16.2	83.8	40.0	--	43.8	36.6	7.2	26.6	10.7
2007	100.0	16.1	83.9	38.9	--	45.0	37.5	7.4	27.1	11.5
2008	100.0	16.0	84.0	37.9	--	46.1	38.5	7.6	27.8	11.8
2009	100.0	16.0	84.0	36.9	--	47.1	39.3	7.8	28.4	12.2
2010	100.0	16.0	84.0	35.9	--	48.1	40.2	7.9	29.0	12.6
2011	100.0	16.0	84.0	35.1	--	48.9	40.9	8.0	29.6	12.8
2012	100.0	16.0	84.0	34.3	--	49.7	41.6	8.0	30.3	12.9
2013	100.0	16.0	84.0	33.7	--	50.3	42.2	8.0	31.0	12.9
2014	100.0	16.0	84.0	33.2	--	50.8	42.8	8.0	31.6	12.8
2015	100.0	16.0	84.0	32.7	--	51.3	43.4	7.9	32.3	12.6
Historical Estimates					Annual Percent Change from Previous Year Shown					
1999	--	--	--	--	--	--	--	--	--	--
2000	15.4	10.0	17.6	16.7	--	19.7	20.4	18.8	10.1	19.0
2001	14.7	8.3	17.2	16.1	--	19.5	21.1	17.3	17.6	18.2
2002	14.0	10.5	15.2	13.5	--	18.8	20.2	16.9	0.0	16.7
2003	10.2	9.4	10.5	7.0	--	17.6	21.7	11.7	-2.1	17.6
2004	8.2	7.1	8.6	6.5	--	12.5	13.6	10.7	42.6	11.1
Projected										
2005	8.0	8.0	8.0	8.6	--	6.9	5.1	9.9	3.1	6.4
2006	7.7	-29.7	20.1	-10.1	--	73.1	139.4	-28.1	1,576.3	-39.6
2007	8.0	7.3	8.2	5.1	--	11.0	10.9	11.6	9.9	15.2
2008	8.0	7.4	8.2	5.2	--	10.7	10.8	10.4	10.9	11.7
2009	8.1	8.0	8.2	5.4	--	10.5	10.4	10.5	10.4	11.8
2010	8.2	8.1	8.2	5.3	--	10.4	10.5	10.1	10.7	11.2
2011	8.2	8.3	8.2	5.8	--	10.0	10.1	9.5	10.4	10.2
2012	8.3	8.5	8.2	5.7	--	10.0	10.2	8.7	10.9	9.0
2013	8.4	8.2	8.4	6.5	--	9.7	10.0	8.2	10.8	8.2
2014	8.4	8.4	8.4	6.6	--	9.5	9.8	7.7	10.7	7.5
2015	8.4	8.4	8.4	6.8	--	9.5	9.8	7.5	10.7	7.1

[1] The health spending projections were based on the 2004 version of the National Health Expenditures (NHE) released in January 2006.
[2] Includes Medicaid SCHIP Expansion and SCHIP.
[3] Subset of Federal funds.
[4] Subset of Federal and State and local funds. Includes Medicaid SCHIP Expansion.
[5] Calculation of per capita estimates is inappropriate.
NOTES: Per capita amounts based on July 1 Census resident based population estimates. Numbers and percents may not add to totals because of rounding.
SOURCE: Centers for Medicare & Medicaid Services, Office of the Actuary.

Table 12
Other Non Durable Medical Products Expenditures Aggregate and per Capita Amounts, Percent Distribution and Annual Percent Change by Source of Funds: Selected Calendar Years 1999-2015[1]

			Third-Party Payments							
						Public				
Year	Total	Out-of-Pocket Payments	Total	Private Health Insurance	Other Private Funds	Total	Federal[2]	State and Local[2]	Medicare[3]	Medicaid[4]
Historical Estimates					Amount in Billions					
1999	$29.8	$28.6	$1.2	--	--	$1.2	$1.2	--	$1.2	--
2000	30.2	28.8	1.3	--	--	1.3	1.3	--	1.3	--
2001	30.3	28.8	1.5	--	--	1.5	1.5	--	1.5	--
2002	30.9	29.3	1.6	--	--	1.6	1.6	--	1.6	--
2003	32.1	30.4	1.7	--	--	1.7	1.7	--	1.7	--
2004	32.3	30.3	1.9	--	--	1.9	1.9	--	1.9	--
Projected										
2005	32.6	30.7	2.0	--	--	2.0	2.0	--	2.0	--
2006	33.8	31.8	1.9	--	--	1.9	1.9	--	1.9	--
2007	35.1	33.1	1.9	--	--	1.9	1.9	--	1.9	--
2008	36.6	34.6	2.0	--	--	2.0	2.0	--	2.0	--
2009	38.2	36.2	2.0	--	--	2.0	2.0	--	2.0	--
2010	39.6	37.6	2.0	--	--	2.0	2.0	--	2.0	--
2011	41.1	39.0	2.1	--	--	2.1	2.1	--	2.1	--
2012	42.6	40.3	2.2	--	--	2.2	2.2	--	2.2	--
2013	44.0	41.6	2.4	--	--	2.4	2.4	--	2.4	--
2014	45.5	42.9	2.6	--	--	2.6	2.6	--	2.6	--
2015	46.9	44.1	2.8	--	--	2.8	2.8	--	2.8	--
Historical Estimates					Per Capita Amount					
1999	$105	$101	$4	--	--	$4	$4	--	(5)	(5)
2000	105	100	5	--	--	5	5	--	(5)	(5)
2001	104	99	5	--	--	5	5	--	(5)	(5)
2002	105	100	5	--	--	5	5	--	(5)	(5)
2003	109	103	6	--	--	6	6	--	(5)	(5)
2004	108	102	6	--	--	6	6	--	(5)	(5)
Projected										
2005	108	102	7	--	--	7	7	--	(5)	(5)
2006	111	105	6	--	--	6	6	--	(5)	(5)
2007	114	108	6	--	--	6	6	--	(5)	(5)
2008	118	112	6	--	--	6	6	--	(5)	(5)
2009	122	116	6	--	--	6	6	--	(5)	(5)
2010	126	119	6	--	--	6	6	--	(5)	(5)
2011	129	123	7	--	--	7	7	--	(5)	(5)
2012	133	126	7	--	--	7	7	--	(5)	(5)
2013	137	129	7	--	--	7	7	--	(5)	(5)
2014	140	132	8	--	--	8	8	--	(5)	(5)
2015	143	135	9	--	--	9	9	--	(5)	(5)
Historical Estimates					Percent Distribution					
1999	100.0	96.0	4.0	--	--	4.0	4.0	--	4.0	--
2000	100.0	95.6	4.4	--	--	4.4	4.4	--	4.4	--
2001	100.0	95.1	4.9	--	--	4.9	4.9	--	4.9	--
2002	100.0	94.9	5.1	--	--	5.1	5.1	--	5.1	--
2003	100.0	94.7	5.3	--	--	5.3	5.3	--	5.3	--
2004	100.0	94.0	6.0	--	--	6.0	6.0	--	6.0	--
Projected										
2005	100.0	94.0	6.0	--	--	6.0	6.0	--	6.0	--
2006	100.0	94.3	5.7	--	--	5.7	5.7	--	5.7	--
2007	100.0	94.5	5.5	--	--	5.5	5.5	--	5.5	--
2008	100.0	94.6	5.4	--	--	5.4	5.4	--	5.4	--
2009	100.0	94.8	5.2	--	--	5.2	5.2	--	5.2	--
2010	100.0	94.9	5.1	--	--	5.1	5.1	--	5.1	--
2011	100.0	94.9	5.1	--	--	5.1	5.1	--	5.1	--
2012	100.0	94.8	5.2	--	--	5.2	5.2	--	5.2	--
2013	100.0	94.5	5.5	--	--	5.5	5.5	--	5.5	--
2014	100.0	94.3	5.7	--	--	5.7	5.7	--	5.7	--
2015	100.0	94.0	6.0	--	--	6.0	6.0	--	6.0	--
Historical Estimates					Annual Percent Change from Previous Year Shown					
1999	--	--	--	--	--	--	--	--	--	--
2000	1.4	1.0	10.5	--	--	10.5	10.5	--	10.5	--
2001	0.5	-0.1	11.9	--	--	11.9	11.9	--	11.9	--
2002	1.8	1.6	5.8	--	--	5.8	5.8	--	5.8	--
2003	4.2	3.9	9.4	--	--	9.4	9.4	--	9.4	--
2004	0.4	-0.3	13.0	--	--	13.0	13.0	--	13.0	--
Projected										
2005	1.1	1.0	1.2	--	--	1.2	1.2	--	1.2	--
2006	3.5	3.8	-1.2	--	--	-1.2	-1.2	--	-1.2	--
2007	3.8	4.1	-0.8	--	--	-0.8	-0.8	--	-0.8	--
2008	4.5	4.6	2.8	--	--	2.8	2.8	--	2.8	--
2009	4.2	4.4	0.0	--	--	0.0	0.0	--	0.0	--
2010	3.8	3.9	2.8	--	--	2.8	2.8	--	2.8	--
2011	3.6	3.7	3.6	--	--	3.6	3.6	--	3.6	--
2012	3.6	3.5	5.9	--	--	5.9	5.9	--	5.9	--
2013	3.4	3.2	7.8	--	--	7.8	7.8	--	7.8	--
2014	3.3	3.0	8.0	--	--	8.0	8.0	--	8.0	--
2015	3.2	2.9	7.6	--	--	7.6	7.6	--	7.6	--

[1] The health spending projections were based on the 2004 version of the National Health Expenditures (NHE) released in January 2006.
[2] Includes Medicaid SCHIP Expansion and SCHIP.
[3] Subset of Federal funds.
[4] Subset of Federal and State and local funds. Includes Medicaid SCHIP Expansion.
[5] Calculation of per capita estimates is inappropriate.
NOTES: Per capita amounts based on July 1 Census resident based population estimates. Numbers and percents may not add to totals because of rounding.
SOURCE: Centers for Medicare & Medicaid Services, Office of the Actuary.

Table 13
Nursing Home Care Expenditures; Aggregate and per Capita Amounts, Percent Distribution and Annual Percent Change by Source of Funds: Selected Calendar Years 1999-2015[1]

Year	Total	Out-of-Pocket Payments	Third-Party Payments						Medicare[3]	Medicaid[4]
			Total	Private Health Insurance	Other Private Funds	Public				
						Total	Federal[2]	State and Local[2]		

Historical Estimates — Amount in Billions
Year	Total	Out-of-Pocket	Total	PHI	Other Priv	Public Total	Federal	State/Local	Medicare	Medicaid
1999	$90.5	$27.4	$63.1	$8.2	$5.0	$50.0	$33.0	$17.0	$9.1	$38.9
2000	95.3	28.6	66.7	7.9	4.5	54.3	36.5	17.8	10.3	42.0
2001	101.5	28.8	72.7	8.1	4.0	60.6	42.2	18.4	12.6	45.8
2002	105.7	29.5	76.2	8.6	4.0	63.6	44.6	18.9	14.1	47.1
2003	110.4	30.5	80.0	8.7	4.0	67.2	46.5	20.7	14.9	49.6
2004	115.2	31.9	83.3	9.0	4.2	70.0	48.4	21.6	16.0	51.1

Projected
Year	Total	Out-of-Pocket	Total	PHI	Other Priv	Public Total	Federal	State/Local	Medicare	Medicaid
2005	121.7	33.4	88.3	9.3	4.4	74.6	51.0	23.6	17.7	53.7
2006	128.4	34.9	93.5	9.8	4.6	79.1	53.6	25.5	18.0	57.8
2007	134.8	36.7	98.1	10.2	4.8	83.1	56.2	26.9	18.7	60.9
2008	142.7	38.7	104.0	10.7	5.0	88.3	59.5	28.8	19.3	65.2
2009	151.2	40.8	110.4	11.1	5.2	94.1	63.2	30.9	20.1	69.9
2010	160.5	43.0	117.5	11.5	5.4	100.6	67.5	33.2	21.2	75.1
2011	170.3	45.3	125.0	11.8	5.6	107.6	72.0	35.6	22.4	80.6
2012	180.7	47.6	133.0	12.1	5.8	115.1	76.9	38.2	23.8	86.4
2013	191.9	50.1	141.8	12.4	6.1	123.3	82.3	41.0	25.4	92.7
2014	203.9	52.8	151.1	12.7	6.3	132.1	88.1	44.0	27.0	99.7
2015	216.8	55.5	161.4	13.1	6.5	141.8	94.5	47.4	28.8	107.2

Historical Estimates — Per Capita Amount
Year	Total	Out-of-Pocket	Total	PHI	Other Priv	Public Total	Federal	State/Local	Medicare	Medicaid
1999	$319	$97	$222	$29	$17	$176	$116	$60	(5)	(5)
2000	332	100	232	27	16	189	127	62	(5)	(5)
2001	350	99	250	28	14	209	145	63	(5)	(5)
2002	361	101	260	29	14	217	152	65	(5)	(5)
2003	373	103	270	29	14	227	157	70	(5)	(5)
2004	385	107	278	30	14	234	162	72	(5)	(5)

Projected
Year	Total	Out-of-Pocket	Total	PHI	Other Priv	Public Total	Federal	State/Local	Medicare	Medicaid
2005	403	111	293	31	15	247	169	78	(5)	(5)
2006	422	115	307	32	15	260	176	84	(5)	(5)
2007	439	120	320	33	16	271	183	88	(5)	(5)
2008	461	125	336	35	16	285	192	93	(5)	(5)
2009	484	131	354	36	17	301	203	99	(5)	(5)
2010	510	137	373	36	17	320	214	105	(5)	(5)
2011	537	143	394	37	18	339	227	112	(5)	(5)
2012	565	149	416	38	18	360	241	119	(5)	(5)
2013	595	156	440	39	19	382	255	127	(5)	(5)
2014	628	162	465	39	19	407	271	136	(5)	(5)
2015	663	169	493	40	20	433	289	145	(5)	(5)

Historical Estimates — Percent Distribution
Year	Total	Out-of-Pocket	Total	PHI	Other Priv	Public Total	Federal	State/Local	Medicare	Medicaid
1999	100.0	30.3	69.7	9.0	5.5	55.2	36.5	18.7	10.1	43.0
2000	100.0	30.0	70.0	8.2	4.7	57.0	38.4	18.6	10.8	44.1
2001	100.0	28.4	71.6	8.0	3.9	59.7	41.5	18.1	12.4	45.1
2002	100.0	27.9	72.1	8.2	3.8	60.1	42.2	17.9	13.3	44.6
2003	100.0	27.6	72.4	7.9	3.6	60.9	42.1	18.8	13.5	44.9
2004	100.0	27.7	72.3	7.8	3.6	60.8	42.0	18.8	13.9	44.3

Projected
Year	Total	Out-of-Pocket	Total	PHI	Other Priv	Public Total	Federal	State/Local	Medicare	Medicaid
2005	100.0	27.4	72.6	7.6	3.6	61.3	41.9	19.4	14.6	44.1
2006	100.0	27.2	72.8	7.6	3.6	61.6	41.8	19.9	14.0	45.0
2007	100.0	27.2	72.8	7.6	3.6	61.6	41.7	19.9	13.8	45.2
2008	100.0	27.1	72.9	7.5	3.5	61.9	41.7	20.2	13.5	45.7
2009	100.0	27.0	73.0	7.3	3.4	62.2	41.8	20.4	13.3	46.2
2010	100.0	26.8	73.2	7.1	3.4	62.7	42.0	20.7	13.2	46.8
2011	100.0	26.6	73.4	6.9	3.3	63.2	42.3	20.9	13.2	47.3
2012	100.0	26.4	73.6	6.7	3.2	63.7	42.6	21.1	13.2	47.8
2013	100.0	26.1	73.9	6.5	3.2	64.2	42.9	21.3	13.2	48.3
2014	100.0	25.9	74.1	6.3	3.1	64.8	43.2	21.6	13.2	48.9
2015	100.0	25.6	74.4	6.0	3.0	65.4	43.6	21.8	13.3	49.4

Historical Estimates — Annual Percent Change from Previous Year Shown
Year	Total	Out-of-Pocket	Total	PHI	Other Priv	Public Total	Federal	State/Local	Medicare	Medicaid
1999	--	--	--	--	--	--	--	--	--	--
2000	5.3	4.3	5.7	-3.6	-9.1	8.7	10.7	4.8	12.5	7.9
2001	6.6	0.9	9.0	2.8	-11.3	11.6	15.4	3.7	23.0	8.9
2002	4.1	2.3	4.9	6.9	0.2	4.9	5.8	2.8	11.6	3.0
2003	4.5	3.2	4.9	1.0	0.1	5.8	4.2	9.6	5.7	5.3
2004	4.3	4.9	4.1	3.5	4.6	4.2	4.1	4.3	7.4	3.0

Projected
Year	Total	Out-of-Pocket	Total	PHI	Other Priv	Public Total	Federal	State/Local	Medicare	Medicaid
2005	5.6	4.5	6.1	2.7	4.4	6.6	5.4	9.2	10.9	5.1
2006	5.5	4.6	5.9	5.2	5.0	6.0	5.1	7.9	1.2	7.5
2007	5.0	5.2	5.0	4.8	4.1	5.0	4.8	5.4	3.8	5.4
2008	5.8	5.3	6.0	4.8	4.4	6.3	5.9	7.1	3.6	7.0
2009	6.0	5.5	6.2	3.5	4.1	6.6	6.2	7.3	4.1	7.3
2010	6.1	5.4	6.4	3.2	3.9	6.9	6.7	7.4	5.5	7.3
2011	6.1	5.2	6.4	2.8	3.8	6.9	6.8	7.3	5.7	7.3
2012	6.1	5.3	6.4	2.8	3.8	7.0	6.8	7.3	6.2	7.2
2013	6.2	5.2	6.5	2.7	3.7	7.1	7.0	7.3	6.5	7.3
2014	6.3	5.2	6.6	2.6	3.7	7.2	7.0	7.5	6.4	7.5
2015	6.3	5.1	6.8	2.5	3.6	7.3	7.2	7.6	6.8	7.6

[1] The health spending projections were based on the 2004 version of the National Health Expenditures (NHE) released in January 2006.
[2] Includes Medicaid SCHIP Expansion and SCHIP.
[3] Subset of Federal funds.
[4] Subset of Federal and State and local funds. Includes Medicaid SCHIP Expansion.
[5] Calculation of per capita estimates is inappropriate.
NOTES: Per capita amounts based on July 1 Census resident based population estimates. Numbers and percents may not add to totals because of rounding.
SOURCE: Centers for Medicare & Medicaid Services, Office of the Actuary.

Table 14
Other Personal Health Care Expenditures; Aggregate and per Capita Amounts, Percent Distribution and Annual Percent Change by Source of Funds: Selected Calendar Years 1999-2015[1]

Year	Total	Out-of-Pocket Payments	Third-Party Payments Total	Private Health Insurance	Other Private Funds	Public Total	Federal[2]	State and Local[2]	Medicare[3]	Medicaid[4]
Historical Estimates					Amount in Billions					
1999	$34.0	--	$34.0	--	$4.0	$30.0	$17.3	$12.7	--	$22.1
2000	37.1	--	37.1	--	4.3	32.8	19.0	13.8	--	24.2
2001	41.9	--	41.9	--	4.5	37.4	21.6	15.8	--	28.1
2002	46.3	--	46.3	--	4.7	41.6	24.3	17.4	--	31.8
2003	50.4	--	50.4	--	4.9	45.4	27.2	18.3	--	34.9
2004	53.3	--	53.3	--	5.3	48.0	28.4	19.6	--	36.8
Projected										
2005	58.1	--	58.1	--	5.6	52.5	30.6	21.9	--	40.7
2006	62.7	--	62.7	--	6.1	56.7	33.0	23.7	--	44.1
2007	67.8	--	67.8	--	6.5	61.3	35.7	25.6	--	47.9
2008	74.3	--	74.3	--	7.0	67.3	39.2	28.1	--	53.0
2009	81.5	--	81.5	--	7.5	74.0	43.1	30.9	--	58.8
2010	89.2	--	89.2	--	8.0	81.2	47.3	33.9	--	64.9
2011	97.3	--	97.3	--	8.5	88.8	51.7	37.1	--	71.5
2012	105.8	--	105.8	--	9.0	96.8	56.2	40.6	--	78.4
2013	114.8	--	114.8	--	9.5	105.3	61.1	44.2	--	85.8
2014	124.5	--	124.5	--	10.0	114.5	66.4	48.1	--	93.7
2015	134.8	--	134.8	--	10.5	124.3	72.0	52.3	--	102.3
Historical Estimates					Per Capita Amount					
1999	$120	--	$120	--	$14	$106	$61	$45	(5)	(5)
2000	129	--	129	--	15	114	66	48	(5)	(5)
2001	144	--	144	--	15	129	74	54	(5)	(5)
2002	158	--	158	--	16	142	83	59	(5)	(5)
2003	170	--	170	--	17	153	92	62	(5)	(5)
2004	178	--	178	--	18	161	95	66	(5)	(5)
Projected										
2005	193	--	193	--	19	174	101	73	(5)	(5)
2006	206	--	206	--	20	186	108	78	(5)	(5)
2007	221	--	221	--	21	200	116	83	(5)	(5)
2008	240	--	240	--	23	217	127	91	(5)	(5)
2009	261	--	261	--	24	237	138	99	(5)	(5)
2010	283	--	283	--	25	258	150	108	(5)	(5)
2011	307	--	307	--	27	280	163	117	(5)	(5)
2012	331	--	331	--	28	303	176	127	(5)	(5)
2013	356	--	356	--	29	327	190	137	(5)	(5)
2014	383	--	383	--	31	353	204	148	(5)	(5)
2015	412	--	412	--	32	380	220	160	(5)	(5)
Historical Estimates					Percent Distribution					
1999	100.0	--	100.0	--	11.8	88.2	50.8	37.5	--	65.0
2000	100.0	--	100.0	--	11.5	88.5	51.2	37.3	--	65.2
2001	100.0	--	100.0	--	10.7	89.3	51.6	37.7	--	67.0
2002	100.0	--	100.0	--	10.1	89.9	52.4	37.5	--	68.6
2003	100.0	--	100.0	--	9.8	90.2	53.9	36.2	--	69.3
2004	100.0	--	100.0	--	9.9	90.1	53.3	36.8	--	69.1
Projected										
2005	100.0	--	100.0	--	9.6	90.4	52.7	37.7	--	70.0
2006	100.0	--	100.0	--	9.7	90.3	52.6	37.8	--	70.3
2007	100.0	--	100.0	--	9.6	90.4	52.6	37.8	--	70.6
2008	100.0	--	100.0	--	9.4	90.6	52.8	37.8	--	71.4
2009	100.0	--	100.0	--	9.2	90.8	52.9	37.9	--	72.1
2010	100.0	--	100.0	--	8.9	91.1	53.0	38.0	--	72.8
2011	100.0	--	100.0	--	8.7	91.3	53.1	38.2	--	73.5
2012	100.0	--	100.0	--	8.5	91.5	53.2	38.3	--	74.1
2013	100.0	--	100.0	--	8.3	91.7	53.2	38.5	--	74.7
2014	100.0	--	100.0	--	8.0	92.0	53.3	38.7	--	75.3
2015	100.0	--	100.0	--	7.8	92.2	53.4	38.8	--	75.9
Historical Estimates					Annual Percent Change from Previous Year Shown					
1999	--	--	--	--	--	--	--	--	--	--
2000	9.0	--	9.0	--	6.9	9.3	9.9	8.6	--	9.4
2001	13.0	--	13.0	--	4.8	14.0	13.9	14.2	--	16.1
2002	10.6	--	10.6	--	4.7	11.3	12.3	10.0	--	13.2
2003	8.7	--	8.7	--	5.4	9.1	12.0	5.0	--	9.7
2004	5.8	--	5.8	--	6.2	5.7	4.5	7.5	--	5.6
Projected										
2005	9.1	--	9.1	--	6.7	9.4	7.9	11.6	--	10.4
2006	7.9	--	7.9	--	8.1	7.9	7.7	8.1	--	8.4
2007	8.1	--	8.1	--	7.4	8.2	8.2	8.1	--	8.6
2008	9.6	--	9.6	--	7.3	9.8	9.9	9.8	--	10.7
2009	9.7	--	9.7	--	7.0	9.9	10.0	9.9	--	10.8
2010	9.4	--	9.4	--	6.6	9.7	9.6	9.8	--	10.5
2011	9.1	--	9.1	--	6.3	9.4	9.3	9.5	--	10.1
2012	8.7	--	8.7	--	6.0	9.0	8.9	9.2	--	9.6
2013	8.5	--	8.5	--	5.5	8.8	8.7	9.0	--	9.4
2014	8.4	--	8.4	--	5.2	8.7	8.6	8.8	--	9.3
2015	8.3	--	8.3	--	4.9	8.6	8.5	8.7	--	9.1

[1] The health spending projections were based on the 2004 version of the National Health Expenditures (NHE) released in January 2006.
[2] Includes Medicaid SCHIP Expansion and SCHIP.
[3] Subset of Federal funds.
[4] Subset of Federal and State and local funds. Includes Medicaid SCHIP Expansion.
[5] Calculation of per capita estimates is inappropriate.
NOTES: Per capita amounts based on July 1 Census resident based population estimates. Numbers and percents may not add to totals because of rounding.
SOURCE: Centers for Medicare & Medicaid Services, Office of the Actuary.

Table 15
Durable Medical Equipment Expenditures; Aggregate and per Capita Amounts, Percent Distribution and Annual Percent Change by Source of Funds: Selected Calendar Years 1999-2015[1]

			Third-Party Payments							
				Private			Public			
Year	Total	Out-of-Pocket Payments	Total	Private Health Insurance	Other Private Funds	Total	Federal[2]	State and Local[2]	Medicare[3]	Medicaid[4]
Historical Estimates				Amount in Billions						
1999	$19.0	$12.1	$6.9	$2.5	--	$4.4	$4.1	$0.3	$4.0	$0.0
2000	19.3	12.1	7.3	2.6	--	4.7	4.4	0.4	4.2	0.0
2001	19.6	12.0	7.7	2.5	--	5.1	4.8	0.4	4.6	0.0
2002	20.8	12.2	8.6	2.6	--	6.0	5.6	0.4	5.5	0.0
2003	22.1	12.6	9.5	2.7	--	6.9	6.5	0.4	6.3	0.0
2004	23.0	13.2	9.8	2.8	--	7.0	6.6	0.4	6.5	0.0
Projected										
2005	23.7	13.7	10.0	2.9	--	7.1	6.7	0.4	6.5	0.0
2006	24.9	14.4	10.6	3.1	--	7.4	7.0	0.4	6.8	0.0
2007	26.0	14.9	11.1	3.4	--	7.7	7.3	0.5	7.1	0.0
2008	27.3	15.4	11.8	3.6	--	8.2	7.7	0.5	7.6	0.0
2009	28.2	16.0	12.3	3.9	--	8.4	7.9	0.5	7.7	0.0
2010	29.5	16.5	13.1	4.1	--	9.0	8.5	0.5	8.3	0.0
2011	30.8	16.9	13.9	4.2	--	9.6	9.1	0.5	8.9	0.0
2012	32.1	17.4	14.8	4.4	--	10.4	9.8	0.5	9.7	0.0
2013	33.5	17.7	15.7	4.5	--	11.2	10.7	0.6	10.5	0.0
2014	34.8	18.1	16.7	4.6	--	12.1	11.5	0.6	11.3	0.0
2015	36.2	18.3	17.8	4.7	--	13.1	12.5	0.6	12.3	0.0
Historical Estimates				Per Capita Amount						
1999	$67	$43	$24	$9	--	$15	$14	$1	(5)	(5)
2000	67	42	25	9	--	16	15	1	(5)	(5)
2001	68	41	26	9	--	18	16	1	(5)	(5)
2002	71	41	29	9	--	20	19	1	(5)	(5)
2003	75	42	32	9	--	23	22	1	(5)	(5)
2004	77	44	33	9	--	23	22	1	(5)	(5)
Projected										
2005	79	45	33	10	--	24	22	1	(5)	(5)
2006	82	47	35	10	--	24	23	1	(5)	(5)
2007	85	48	36	11	--	25	24	1	(5)	(5)
2008	88	50	38	12	--	26	25	2	(5)	(5)
2009	90	51	39	12	--	27	25	2	(5)	(5)
2010	94	52	42	13	--	29	27	2	(5)	(5)
2011	97	53	44	13	--	30	29	2	(5)	(5)
2012	101	54	46	14	--	32	31	2	(5)	(5)
2013	104	55	49	14	--	35	33	2	(5)	(5)
2014	107	56	52	14	--	37	36	2	(5)	(5)
2015	111	56	54	14	--	40	38	2	(5)	(5)
Historical Estimates				Percent Distribution						
1999	100.0	63.7	36.3	13.3	--	23.1	21.3	1.8	20.8	0.0
2000	100.0	62.4	37.6	13.2	--	24.4	22.6	1.8	22.0	0.1
2001	100.0	60.9	39.1	12.9	--	26.1	24.3	1.8	23.7	0.1
2002	100.0	58.6	41.4	12.5	--	28.9	27.1	1.8	26.4	0.1
2003	100.0	56.9	43.1	12.0	--	31.1	29.4	1.7	28.7	0.1
2004	100.0	57.4	42.6	12.0	--	30.6	28.8	1.8	28.2	0.1
Projected										
2005	100.0	57.7	42.3	12.3	--	30.0	28.2	1.8	27.5	0.1
2006	100.0	57.6	42.4	12.6	--	29.8	28.0	1.8	27.4	0.1
2007	100.0	57.2	42.8	13.0	--	29.7	28.0	1.8	27.3	0.1
2008	100.0	56.6	43.4	13.4	--	30.1	28.3	1.8	27.7	0.1
2009	100.0	56.5	43.5	13.7	--	29.8	28.1	1.8	27.4	0.1
2010	100.0	55.7	44.3	13.7	--	30.5	28.8	1.7	28.2	0.1
2011	100.0	54.9	45.1	13.8	--	31.3	29.6	1.7	29.0	0.1
2012	100.0	54.1	45.9	13.6	--	32.3	30.6	1.7	30.0	0.1
2013	100.0	53.0	47.0	13.5	--	33.6	31.9	1.7	31.3	0.1
2014	100.0	51.9	48.1	13.3	--	34.8	33.2	1.7	32.6	0.0
2015	100.0	50.7	49.3	13.0	--	36.3	34.6	1.6	34.0	0.0
Historical Estimates				Annual Percent Change from Previous Year Shown						
1999	--	--	--	--	--	--	--	--	--	--
2000	1.8	-0.2	5.2	1.3	--	7.5	7.6	6.1	7.4	88.2
2001	1.6	-0.8	5.6	-0.5	--	8.9	9.5	1.3	9.5	-37.8
2002	5.7	1.6	12.0	2.1	--	16.8	17.7	5.5	17.8	29.9
2003	6.4	3.2	10.9	2.4	--	14.6	15.5	1.4	15.9	-11.9
2004	4.0	4.9	2.7	4.1	--	2.1	1.9	5.8	1.9	18.9
Projected										
2005	3.3	3.9	2.4	5.3	--	1.3	1.1	4.9	1.0	16.6
2006	5.1	4.9	5.4	7.8	--	4.4	4.4	3.9	4.5	0.0
2007	4.4	3.7	5.3	7.8	--	4.2	4.2	3.8	4.3	-1.0
2008	4.8	3.6	6.5	7.6	--	6.0	6.2	4.0	6.2	0.8
2009	3.6	3.4	3.8	6.2	--	2.7	2.6	3.9	2.6	1.0
2010	4.5	3.2	6.3	4.7	--	7.1	7.3	3.6	7.4	0.3
2011	4.3	2.8	6.3	4.6	--	7.0	7.2	3.3	7.4	-3.6
2012	4.3	2.7	6.4	3.3	--	7.7	8.0	3.2	8.1	0.2
2013	4.1	2.1	6.6	3.0	--	8.1	8.4	2.9	8.5	-0.3
2014	4.0	1.8	6.4	2.6	--	7.9	8.1	2.8	8.2	-0.2
2015	3.9	1.5	6.5	1.9	--	8.2	8.5	2.6	8.6	0.2

[1] The health spending projections were based on the 2004 version of the National Health Expenditures (NHE) released in January 2006.
[2] Includes Medicaid SCHIP Expansion and SCHIP.
[3] Subset of Federal funds.
[4] Subset of Federal and State and local funds. Includes Medicaid SCHIP Expansion.
[5] Calculation of per capita estimates is inappropriate.

NOTES: Per capita amounts based on July 1 Census resident based population estimates. 0.0 denotes less than $50 million for aggregate amounts, and 0 denotes less than $.50 for per capita amounts.
Numbers and percents may not add to totals because of rounding.
SOURCE: Centers for Medicare & Medicaid Services, Office of the Actuary.

Commercial insurance companies operate in the private sector and offer numerous health insurance benefits plans to serve the needs of employers, business, and government. However, the patient bears the ultimate responsibility for paying all medical bills and for filing all claims in compliance with his or her benefit plan's requirements. Some providers, particularly those who are in network, may choose to file for the patient to ensure a clean, timely claim. Beyond the deductible and coinsurance payment, most providers do not require the patient to be "insured." Therefore, the risk of an "aged claim" falls on the provider.

The term *commercial insurance* has historically been used to refer to traditional indemnity health plans that reimburse the fee for service, generally based on an 80/20 split, with the insurance company covering 80% of the allowable charge and the patient being responsible for the remaining 20% coinsurance. Most commercial insurance plans have predefined patient deductibles and coinsurance provisions. The physician's office staff is responsible for contacting the health plan payer to determine the patient's deductible and coinsurance status before rendering services.

Commercial Insurance "Nondisclosed" Payment Allowance

The traditional indemnity plan is based on predefined payment allowances that may vary by physician specialty and/or geographic location. Many indemnity insurers rely on at least one outside source of information, such as the St Anthony Relative Value for Physicians (RVP), to establish or evaluate their physician payment allowances.

It is important that billing for any service be the same for all carriers. Medicare does not allow billing for their services to be different from that of commercial payers. The allowed payments may differ, but the amount billed may not. Remember that all services rendered by physicians might not be covered by all insurance plans. Coverage for health services is defined in the patient's health insurance policy, which is based on a contract between the insurance company and the patient or employer. Each insurance company health plan offers different levels of medical and financial coverage.

Coordination of Benefits

Most commercial insurance health plans have coordination of benefits (COB) clauses that help to define primary and secondary payer status for a pending claim. Many plans also use the "gender rule" or the "birthday rule" to assign primary responsibility. Under the gender rule, coverage of the male in the household is primary, ie, billed first. Under the birthday rule, the plan of the parent whose birthday occurs first in a calendar year is the primary plan. If both parents have the same birthday, the plan that has covered a parent the longest is primary.

Relationship to Other Health Insurance Programs

The following list shows how government programs and automobile insurance generally relate to health insurance programs in terms of primary and secondary status. Benefits are paid from the primary carrier first. The secondary carrier payment, if any, then follows.

- *Medicare*. Commercial insurance is almost always primary to any public program, including Medicare. Therefore, beneficiaries age 65 or older who are covered by an employer health plan should use the commercial payer as the primary insurer.
- *Medicaid*. If a person is eligible for Medicaid as well as commercial insurance benefits, commercial insurance is always primary.
- *TRICARE*. When a beneficiary is covered under another medical insurance plan, TRICARE, which is the US Department of Defense military health system, is always secondary, except for Medicaid, the Indian Health Service, or any plan that is specifically designated as a TRICARE supplement.

- *Workers' compensation.* Expenses for medical care related to job-connected illness or injury are paid by the workers' compensation program. Only when benefits are exhausted under this program does commercial insurance assume responsibility for the balance.
- *Private automobile insurance.* In the case of an automobile accident, any amounts paid by commercial insurance when the claims are also payable under an automobile insurance policy may be subject to recovery under the Federal Claims Collections Act.

Claim Submission

It is the physician's responsibility to accurately report the level or type of service provided to a patient according to Current Procedural Terminology (CPT®) codes, guidelines, and conventions and the payer's reimbursement rules. Through accurate coding, the health plan's claim adjudication division will process the physician's claim and the physician will receive appropriate reimbursement.

Most commercial insurance companies are required to accept the CMS-1500 form for claims processing and have a "deadline" or a set time limit for which the claim is "processable." The period usually starts on the date of the physician service and may continue for three months, six months, or a year, depending on the policy. It is recommended that claims for patients with commercial insurance be filed within four to six days after the date of service. A claim filed on time but not settled expediently because of administrative delays should still be paid, even if the processing time extends beyond the filing date. Proof of filing, as well as evidence that the claim continues to be actively pursued, may be necessary. Failure to meet this objective may indicate serious billing problems.

Blue Cross Blue Shield Plans

Blue Cross Blue Shield plans are licensees under the Blue Cross Blue Shield Association that contract with physicians, hospitals, and various other health entities to provide services to their insured companies and individuals. Blue Cross Blue Shield refers to the persons they insure as subscribers, not policyholders, and they are issued a certificate, not a policy. The certificate defines the health care benefits and obligations of the medical plan. The word *plan* refers to each separately incorporated, locally administered corporation authorized to use the Blue Cross Blue Shield name and symbol.

Currently, 38 Blue Cross Blue Shield member plans exist in the United States, Puerto Rico, and the District of Columbia. Blue Cross primarily covers hospital services, outpatient care, some institutional services, and home care. By contrast, Blue Shield typically covers physician services and, in some cases, dental, outpatient, and vision care.

Collectively, Blue Cross Blue Shield member plans provide health care coverage for more than 94 million (or one in three) people in the 50 states, the District of Columbia, and Puerto Rico. In the United States, more than 80% of hospitals and nearly 90% of physicians contract directly with Blue Cross Blue Shield member plans. Collectively, Blue Cross Blue Shield member plans make up the nation's largest provider of managed care services. Blue Cross Blue Shield plans offer a variety of insurance products to all segments of the population including large employer groups, small businesses, and individuals.

The Blue Cross Blue Shield Association of America coordinates activities of Blue Cross Blue Shield plans nationally. The Blue Cross Blue Shield Web site can be accessed at www.bcbs.com. Local Blue Cross Blue Shield plans can be located by accessing them by zip code on the plan finder at www.bcbs.com/healthinsurance/planfinder.html. Blue Cross Blue Shield plans are organized locally and, in some states, both Blue Cross and Blue Shield share offices. In other states, they are entirely separate organizations. The national organization coordinates services and benefits among different Blue Cross Blue Shield plans for those with offices in multiple states and provides other related services.

Blue Cross Blue Shield plans differ from commercial carrier plans in that they can operate as nonprofit corporations and write contracts directly with providers. If nonprofit, the Blue Cross Blue Shield plan must obtain approval from its state insurance department before raising rates or changing coverage. Most Blue Cross Blue Shield plans offer health maintenance organization (HMO), preferred provider organization (PPO), and point-of-service (POS) plans.

Physician reimbursement under Blue Shield plans has historically been based on the usual, customary, and reasonable (UCR) payment method. Under this method, the allowable charge is the lower of either the physician's usual charge for a service the range of "customary" fees usually charged by physicians of similar training and experience for the same service within a geographic area at that point in time. Many plans use the resource-based relative value scale (RBRVS) to define payment schedules, while other plans use a fixed rate per patient, called capitation. Blue Shield plans, like other commercial insurance plans, will continue to shift their reimbursement methods away from UCR to RBRVS and capitated methods.

Most Blue Cross Blue Shield insurance can be classified into the following types of accounts:

- Local or regular business
- National
- Federal employee program
- Blue Card program
- National Account Service Company Operation (NASCO)

Local or Regular Business Account

Local accounts are those in which plan members are located within the plan's geographic territory. Blue Cross Blue Shield issues identification cards locally, and all identification contract numbers are preceded by the local plan's prefix. When a patient presents a local or regular business identification card, the following information is transmitted from the card to the claim form:

- Subscriber's name
- Subscriber's contract number, alpha prefix, and other suffixes
- Subscriber's group number
- Blue Cross Blue Shield plan code

This is just one example of information provided on the back of a Blue Cross card (see Figure 2-1) provided by Blue Cross Blue Shield of Kansas City. The back of each card should be reviewed. Note that instructions may differ among the various Blue Cross groups.

FIGURE 2-1

Blue Cross Blue Shield Identification Card

National Account
A national account plan is contracted with companies that have employees located in more than one geographic plan area. The employees are covered through a single national contract for coverage.

Federal Employee Program Account
The Blue Cross Blue Shield Association, on behalf of all Blue Cross Blue Shield plans, contracts with the US Office of Personnel Management (OPM) to provide government-wide service benefit plan coverage to millions of federal employees, dependents, and retirees through the Federal Employee Program (FEP). Each year the benefits and premiums are renegotiated with OPM. Benefits for 2006 for both standard and basic option plans are shown in Tables 2-2 and Table 2-3, respectively.

TABLE 2-2

BCBS 2006 Standard Option Benefits at a Glance: What You Pay

Services	Preventive Care Standard Option PPO Benefit	Standard Option Non-PPO Benefit*
Preventive screenings: Pap smears, mammograms, stool tests for blood, prostate specific antigen tests, cholesterol tests, sigmoidoscopies, and related office visit charge	$15 for each related office visit Nothing for preventive screening tests	Subject to $250 calendar year deductible 25% plan allowance for covered tests The preventive screening office visit is not covered
Routine physical exams, including a history and risk assessment, chest X-ray, EKG, urinalysis, CBC, and metabolic and general health panel tests annually	$15 for the office visit Nothing for related preventive screening tests	Not a benefit
Influenza & Pneumonia Immunizations—once every calendar year	$15 office visit copayment Nothing for immunizations	Subject to $250 calendar year deductible 25% plan allowance
Well Child Care upto age 22, including routine physical examinations, routine hearing tests, laboratory tests, immunizations, and related office visits	Nothing for covered charges	Nothing for covered charges
Dental Care for services listed in Section 5(h) of the *2006 Service Benefit Plan brochure* fee schedule	Your out-of-pocket costs are limited to a maximum allowable charge (MAC) Benefits paid according to the fee schedule in the *2006 Service Benefit Plan brochure*	Benefits paid according to the fee schedule in the *2006 Service Benefit Plan brochure* You are responsible for balance up to billed charges

Services	Physician's Care Standard Option PPO Benefit	Standard Option Non-PPO Benefit*
Inpatient services, including surgical and medical care	Subject to $250 calendar year deductible 10% PPA	Subject to $250 calendar year deductible 25% plan allowance
Outpatient surgery and related diagnostic tests such as X-rays, laboratory tests, and machine diagnostic tests**	Subject to $250 calendar year deductible 10% PPA	Subject to $250 calendar year deductible 25% plan allowance

TABLE 2-2

BCBS 2006 Standard Option Benefits at a Glance: What You Pay (*continued*)

Services	Standard Option PPO Benefit	Standard Option Non-PPO Benefit*
Home and office visits, second surgical opinions, outpatient consultations, and medical emergency care	$15 for the visit charge, with no deductible	Subject to $250 calendar year deductible 25% plan allowance
Outpatient physical, occupational, and speech therapy	$15 for each visit	Subject to $250 calendar year deductible
Physical, occupational and speech therapy—combined maximum of 75 visits per year		25% plan allowance

	Chiropractic Care	
Services	Standard Option PPO Benefit	Standard Option Non-PPO Benefit*
Spinal manipulations	$15 copayment for each visit Up to 10 spinal manipulations per year per person	Subject to $250 calendar year deductible 25% plan allowance Up to 10 spinal manipulations per year per person

	Maternity Care	
Services	Standard Option PPO Benefit	Standard Option Non-PPO Benefit*
Inpatient hospital care—Precertification is not required	Nothing for covered charges	$300 per admission copayment 30% plan allowance at Non-member hospitals
Physician care including delivery and pre-and post-natal care	Nothing for covered charges	Subject to $250 calendar year deductible 25% plan allowance

	Prescription Drugs	
Services	Standard Option PPO Benefit	Standard Option Non-PPO Benefit*
Prescription Drugs Mail Service Pharmacy	$10 copayment for generic drugs	$10 copayment for generic drugs
Up to a 90-day supply per prescription or refill	$35 copayment for brand name drugs	$35 copayment for brand name drugs
Prescription Drugs Retail Pharmacy Up to a 90-day supply per prescription or refill	25% PPA at the time of purchase	100% of billed charges at the time of purchase, file a claim, then receive 55% of average wholesale price (AWP) as reimbursement

TABLE 2-2

BCBS 2006 Standard Option Benefits at a Glance: What You Pay (*continued*)

Services	Hospital/Facility Care	
	Standard Option PPO Benefit	**Standard Option Non-PPO Benefit***
Hospital inpatient room and board and other inpatient hospital services—Precertification required	Unlimited days $100 per admission copayment	Unlimited days $300 per admission copayment 30% plan allowance at nonmember hospitals***
Hospital/Facility care—outpatient surgery	10% PPA	25% of plan allowance at member facilities and nonmember facilities
Hospital/Facility care—outpatient services including medical emergency care, diagnostic tests, renal dialysis, radiation therapy, and chemotherapy.	Subject to $250 calendar year deductible 10% PPA	Subject to $250 calendar year deductible 25% of plan allowance at member facilities and nonmember facilities
Outpatient physical, occupational and speech therapy—combined maximum of 75 visits per year	$15 for each visit	Subject to $250 calendar year deductible 25% of plan allowance at member facilities and nonmember facilities

Services	Accidental Injury	
	Standard Option PPO Benefit	**Standard Option Non-PPO Benefit***
Covered charges in connection with and within 72 hours after an accidental injury at a facility or in a physician's office. (See the definition of accidental injury in Section 10 of the *2006 Service Benefit Plan brochure*) Includes outpatient medical care, diagnostic tests, and ambulance transportation	Nothing for covered charges	Any difference between the plan allowance and the billed amount

Services	Mental Health and Substance Abuse	
	Standard Option PPO Benefit	**Standard Option Non-PPO Benefit***
Inpatient Hospital—precertification required	In full after $100 per admission copayment Unlimited days	$400 daily copayment at member hospitals and nonmember hospitals 100 days per calendar year for mental conditions 28 days per lifetime for substance abuse
Outpatient Facility Care	Subject to $250 calendar year deductible 10% PPA	Subject to the $250 calendar year deductible 25% plan allowance at member facilities and nonmember facilities Combined total of 25 visits per calendar year

TABLE 2-2

BCBS 2006 Standard Option Benefits at a Glance: What You Pay (*continued*)

Services	Standard Option PPO Benefit	Standard Option Non-PPO Benefit*
Inpatient Professional Care	Subject to $250 calendar year deductible 10% PPA	Subject to the $250 calendar year deductible 40% of plan allowance 100 days per calendar year for mental conditions 28 days per lifetime for substance abuse
Outpatient Professional Care—up to 2 hours per visit	$15 copayment per visit Treatment plan needed prior to 9th visit	Subject to the $250 calendar year deductible 40% of plan allowance Combined total for outpatient visits of 25 visits per calendar year per patient

	Other Services	
Services	Standard Option PPO Benefit	Standard Option Non-PPO Benefit*
Catastrophic Protection (Please refer to Section 4 in the *2006 Service Benefit Plan brochure* for charges applied to this benefit.)	100% payment level begins after you pay $4000 out-of-pocket in coinsurance, copayment and deductible expenses	100% payment level begins after you pay $6000 out-of-pocket in coinsurance, copayment and deductible expenses

PPA = Preferred Provider Allowance, the amount accepted as payment in full by most Preferred professionals and pharmacies.

Calendar Year Deductible = One $250 deductible per member per calendar year, $500 family limit each calendar year. Certain deductibles and coinsurance amounts do not apply to you if Medicare is your primary coverage for medical services (it pays first).

On limited occasions, such as for certain drugs requiring prior approval, you will need to file a claim for services received from Preferred providers.

*When you use Non-member facilities and Non-participating professionals, you are also responsible for the difference between the provider's charge and our payment. And when rendered by a Non-PPO provider, treatment of mental health and substance abuse is covered differently.

**Certain diagnostic cancer tests are paid differently.

***Emergency admissions to Non-member hospitals are paid at 100% of the Plan Allowance after the $300 per admission copayment.

Available at www.fepblue.org/benefits/benefits06/benftaagso-06.html. Accessed September 26, 2006.

TABLE 2-3

BCBS 2006 Basic Option Benefits at a Glance: What You Pay

	Preventive Care
Services	Basic Option Network Benefit*
Preventive screenings and related office visit charge, routine physical exams	$20 office visit copayment for primary care provider $30 office visit copayment for specialists Nothing for covered preventive screenings billed by your doctor
Well Child Care Up To Age 22, including routine physical examinations, routine hearing tests, laboratory tests, immunizations, and related office visits	Nothing for covered charges

TABLE 2-3

BCBS 2006 Basic Option Benefits at a Glance: What You Pay (*continued*)

Preventive Care	
Services	**Basic Option Network Benefit***
Routine Dental Care—See limitations in Section 5(h) of the *2006 Service Benefit Plan brochure*	$20 office visit charge 2 exams and cleanings per year Annual X-rays Sealants for children up to age 16

Physician's Care	
Services	**Basic Option PPO Benefit***
Surgical Care	$100 copayment per surgeon
Home and office visits, second surgical opinions, and consultations	$20 office visit charge for primary care provider $30 office visit copayment for specialists

Maternity Care	
Services	**Basic Option PPO Benefit***
Inpatient Hospital and Physician Care—Precertification is not required	Nothing for professional charges for pre-natal and post-natal care and delivery $100 copayment per admission for inpatient hospital care

Prescription Drugs	
Services	**Basic Option PPO Benefit***
Mail Service Pharmacy	Not a benefit
Retail Pharmacy	Up to an initial 34-day supply $10 copayment for generic drugs $30 copayment for formulary brand name drugs 50% coinsurance ($35 minimum) for nonformulary brand name drugs

Hospital/Facility Care	
Services	**Basic Option PPO Benefit***
Hospital Inpatient—Precertification required	$100 per day up to $500
Outpatient Facility Care, excluding laboratory and X-ray services	$40 per day per facility copayment
Outpatient Facility Care, laboratory and X-ray services	Nothing for covered charges
Outpatient Surgery	$40 copayment

TABLE 2-3

BCBS 2006 Basic Option Benefits at a Glance: What You Pay (*continued*)

Accidental Injury/Emergency Care	
Services	**Basic Option PPO Benefit***
Accidental Injury Care—emergency room	$50 copayment
Medical Emergency—emergency room	$50 copayment
Accidental Injury and Medical Emergency—Physician care	$50 copayment

Chiropractic Care	
Services	**Basic Option PPO Benefit***
Spinal Manipulations	Up to 20 spinal manipulations per year $20 copayment

Other Services	
Services	**Basic Option PPO Benefit***
Catastrophic Benefits	100% payment level begins after you pay $5000 out-of-pocket in coinsurance and copayment expenses

*Under Basic Option, benefits are not available for care that is performed by a Non-preferred provider, except in certain situations such as emergency care.

Available at www.fepblue.org/benefits/benefits06/benftaagbo-06.html. Accessed September 26, 2006.

The FEP identification card is a nationally recognized card with the words *Government-Wide Service Benefit Plan* across the top. All claims are processed through the local plan's office. Customers may use a toll-free customer service number when filing claims, requesting additional claim forms for patients, and requesting benefit information. Claim forms and other forms may be accessed online at www.fepblue.org/contactus/contactusforms.html. Table 2-4 provides a list of local and overseas contact numbers and address for the BlueCross Blue Shield Federal Employee Program.

Blue Card Account

The Blue Card Program is a national program that allows members to receive the same health care benefits and balance billing protection of their local Blue Plan when traveling or living outside of their Plan's area. Members also have access to the BlueCard Worldwide network of participating hospitals. The BlueCard Doctor and Hospital Finder can be accessed at www.bcbs.com/healthtravel/finder.html.

Plan program: A Blue Cross Blue Shield plan that participates in the Blue Card program.

Member: A person entitled to benefits under a subscription, certificate, or contract issued by a home plan.

Home plan: Blue Cross Blue Shield plan in which members receive care from a hospital or physician of a host plan.

Host plan: Blue Cross Blue Shield plan whose hospitals or physicians render care to a member of the home plan.

T A B L E 2-4

BCBS Overseas and Local Plans Customer Service Contact

	OVERSEAS	
Carefirst Blue Cross Blue Shield	P.O. Box 96242 Washington, DC 20090-6242	Toll-Free: 888-999-9862

	PUERTO RICO	
La Cruz Azul de Puerto Rico	Carr. 1 Km 17.3 P.O. Box 366068 San Juan, PR 00936-6068	888-272-9078

	ALABAMA	
Blue Cross and Blue Shield of Alabama	450 Riverchase Parkway East Birmingham, AL 35244	Toll-Free: 800-492-8872

	ALASKA	
Blue Cross and Blue Shield of Alaska	7001 220th Street SW Mountlake Terrace, WA 98043	Toll-Free: 800-562-1011

	ARIZONA	
Blue Cross and Blue Shield of Arizona	2444 West Las Palmaritas Drive Phoenix, AZ 85021	Toll-Free: 800-345-7562

	ARKANSAS	
Arkansas Blue Cross and Blue Shield	601 South Gaines Street Little Rock, AR 72201	Toll-Free: 800-482-6655 (AR only) Local: 501-378-2531

	CALIFORNIA	
Blue Cross of California	21555 Oxnard Street Woodland Hills, CA 91367	Toll-Free: 800-284-9093
Blue Shield of California	P.O. Box 7168 San Francisco, CA 94120-7168	Toll-Free: 800-824-8839

TABLE 2-4
BCBS Overseas and Local Plans Customer Service Contact (*continued*)

COLORADO		
Anthem Blue Cross and Blue Shield, Colorado	P.O. Box 36310 Louisville, KY 40233-6310	Toll-Free: 800-852-5957

CONNECTICUT		
Anthem Blue Cross and Blue Shield of Connecticut	P.O. Box 37790 Louisville, KY 40233-7790	Toll-Free: 800-438-5356

DELAWARE		
Blue Cross and Blue Shield of Delaware	One Brandywine Gateway Wilmington, DE 19899	Toll-Free: 800-721-8005

DISTRICT OF COLUMBIA		
CareFirst BlueCross BlueShield (Washington, DC)	P.O. Box 96242 Washington, DC 20090-6242	Toll-Free: 800-848-9766 (only in plan service area) Local: 202-484-1650

FLORIDA		
Blue Cross and Blue Shield of Florida	532 Riverside Avenue Jacksonville, FL 32231	Toll-Free: 800-333-2227

GEORGIA		
BlueCross BlueShield of Georgia	P.O. Box 7037 Columbus, GA 31908-7037	Toll-Free: 800-282-2473

HAWAII		
Hawaii Medical Service Association	818 Keeaumoku Street Honolulu, HI 96814	Toll-Free: 800-966-6198

IDAHO		
Blue Cross of Idaho Health Service	3000 East Pine Avenue Meridian, ID 83642	Toll-Free: 800-627-6656
Regence BlueShield of Idaho	1602 21st Avenue Lewiston, ID 83501	Toll-Free: 800-732-1209

TABLE 2-4

BCBS Overseas and Local Plans Customer Service Contact (*continued*)

	ILLINOIS	
Blue Cross and Blue Shield of Illinois	300 E. Randolph Chicago, IL 60601	Toll-Free: 800-972-8382

	INDIANA	
Anthem Blue Cross and Blue Shield, Indiana	1099 N. Meridian St. Suite 1100 Indianapolis, IN 46204	Toll-Free: 800-382-5520

	IOWA	
Wellmark Blue Cross and Blue Shield of Iowa	636 Grand Avenue Des Moines, IA 50309	Toll-Free: 800-532-1537

	KANSAS	
Blue Cross and Blue Shield of Kansas	1133 SW Topeka Blvd. Topeka, KS 66629	Toll-Free: 800-432-0379

	KENTUCKY	
Anthem Blue Cross and Blue Shield, Kentucky	10100 Linn Station Road Louisville, KY 40223	Toll-Free: 800-456-3967

	LOUISIANA	
Blue Cross and Blue Shield of Louisiana	5525 Reitz Avenue Baton Rouge, LA 70809	Toll-Free: 800-272-3029

	MAINE	
Anthem Blue Cross and Blue Shield of Maine	P.O. Box 37980 Louisville, KY 40233-7980	Toll-Free: 800-722-0203

	MARYLAND	
CareFirst BlueCross BlueShield (Maryland)	PO Box 801 Owings Mills, MD 21117	Toll-Free: 800-638-6756

	MASSACHUSETTS	
Blue Cross and Blue Shield of Massachusetts	401 Park Drive Landmark Center Boston, MA 02115	Toll-Free: 800-433-7766

TABLE 2-4

BCBS Overseas and Local Plans Customer Service Contact (*continued*)

MICHIGAN

Blue Cross and Blue Shield of Michigan	600 Lafayette East Detroit, MI 48226	Toll-Free: 800-482-3600

MINNESOTA

Blue Cross and Blue Shield of Minnesota	3535 Blue Cross Road St. Paul, MN 55122	Toll-Free: 800-859-2128

MISSISSIPPI

Blue Cross and Blue Shield of Mississippi	3545 Lakeland Drive Jackson, MS 39208	Toll-Free: 800-932-7724

MISSOURI

Blue Cross and Blue Shield of Kansas City	2301 Main Kansas City, MO 64108	Local: 816-395-2500
Blue Cross and Blue Shield of Missouri — Wellpoint	1831 Chestnut Street St. Louis, MO 63103	Toll-Free: 800-392-8043 Local: 314-923-4404

MONTANA

Blue Cross and Blue Shield of Montana	3360 10th Avenue South Great Falls, MT 59405	Toll-Free: 800-634-3569

NEBRASKA

Blue Cross and Blue Shield of Nebraska	7261 Mercy Road Omaha, NE 68180	Toll-Free: 800-223-5584

NEVADA

Anthem Blue Cross and Blue Shield Nevada	P.O. Box 36400 Louisville, KY 40233-6400	Toll-Free: 800-852-5957

NEW HAMPSHIRE

Anthem Blue Cross and Blue Shield — New Hampshire	P.O. Box 36500 Louisville, KY 40233-6500	Toll-Free: 800-852-3316

TABLE 2-4

BCBS Overseas and Local Plans Customer Service Contact (*continued*)

	NEW JERSEY	
Horizon Blue Cross Blue Shield of New Jersey	33 Washington Street Newark, NJ 07102	Toll-Free: 800-624-5078

	NEW MEXICO	
New Mexico Blue Cross and Blue Shield	12800 Indian School Road NE Albuquerque, NM 87112	Toll-Free: 800-245-1609

	NEW YORK	
Excellus Blue Cross and Blue Shield — Central New York, Syracuse	344 South Warren St. Syracuse, NY 13202	Toll-Free: 800-252-2209
Excellus Blue Cross and Blue Shield — Utica-Watertown	12 Rhoads Drive Utica, NY 13502	Toll-Free: 800-252-2209
Excellus Blue Cross and Blue Shield — Rochester	165 Court Street Rochester, NY 14647	Toll-Free: 800-584-6617
Blue Cross and Blue Shield of Western New York, Buffalo	1901 Main Street Buffalo, NY 14240	Toll-Free: 800-234-6008 Local: 716-884-5082
Blue Shield of Northeastern New York, Albany		Call the Buffalo, NY, Plan
Empire BlueCross BlueShield	P.O. Box 3876 Church Street, Station New York, NY 10008-3876	Toll-Free: 800-522-5566

	NORTH CAROLINA	
Blue Cross and Blue Shield of North Carolina	5901 Chapel Hill Road Durham, NC 27707	Toll-Free: 800-222-4739

	NORTH DAKOTA	
Blue Cross and Blue Shield of North Dakota	4510 13th Avenue SW Fargo, ND 58121	Toll-Free: 800-548-4026

TABLE 2-4
BCBS Overseas and Local Plans Customer Service Contact (*continued*)

OHIO		
Anthem Blue Cross and Blue Shield, Ohio	1351 William Howard Taft Road Cincinnati, OH 45206	Toll-Free: 800-451-7602

OKLAHOMA		
Blue Cross and Blue Shield of Oklahoma	1215 South Boulder Tulsa, OK 74102	Toll-Free: 800-722-3130 Local: 918-560-2004

OREGON		
Regence BlueCross BlueShield of Oregon	1148 Broadway Plaza Tacoma, WA 98402	Toll-Free: 800-962-2731

PENNSYLVANIA		
Blue Cross of Northeastern Pennsylvania	70 North Main Street Wilkes-Barre, PA 18711	Toll-Free: 800-618-3337
Capital Blue Cross	2500 Elmerton Avenue Harrisburg, PA 17110	Toll-Free: 800-344-5446
Highmark Blue Shield	1800 Center Street Camp Hill, PA 17089	Toll-Free: 800-779-6945 (Professional) Toll free: 800-556-1720 (Institutional)
Independence Blue Cross	1901 Market Street Philadelphia, PA 19103	Local: 215-241-4400

RHODE ISLAND		
Blue Cross and Blue Shield of Rhode Island	444 Westminster Street Providence, RI 02903	Toll-Free: 800-377-4418

SOUTH CAROLINA		
Blue Cross Blue Shield of South Carolina	4101 Percival Road Columbia, SC 29229	Toll-Free: 800-444-0025

TABLE 2-4

BCBS Overseas and Local Plans Customer Service Contact (*continued*)

	SOUTH DAKOTA	
Wellmark Blue Cross Blue Shield of South Dakota	1601 West Madison St. Sioux Falls, SD 57104	Toll-Free: 800-532-1537 (Hosp. Services) 888-800-1359 (Phys. Services)

	TENNESSEE	
Blue Cross and Blue Shield of Tennessee	801 Pine Street Chattanooga, TN 37402	Toll-Free: 800-572-1003 Local: 423-755-5707

	TEXAS	
Blue Cross and Blue Shield of Texas	4002 Loop 322 Abilene, TX 79602	Toll-Free: 800-442-4607

	UTAH	
Regence BlueCross BlueShield of Utah	2890 East Cottonwood Parkway Salt Lake City, UT 84121	Toll-Free: 800-421-4498

	VERMONT	
Blue Cross and Blue Shield of Vermont	445 Industrial Lane Montpelier, VT 05601	Toll-Free: 800-328-0365

	VIRGINIA	
Anthem Blue Cross and Blue Shield — Virginia	Federal Employee Program P.O. Box 27401 Mail drop VAH4A Richmond, VA 23279	Toll-Free: 800-552-6989

	WASHINGTON	
Premera Blue Cross	7001 220th Street SW Mountlake Terrace, WA 98043	Toll-Free: 800-562-1011
Regence BlueShield	1148 Broadway Plaza Tacoma, WA 98402	Toll-Free: 800-552-0733

TABLE 2-4
BCBS Overseas and Local Plans Customer Service Contact (*continued*)

WEST VIRGINIA		
Mountain State Blue Cross and Blue Shield	700 Market Square Parkersburg, WV 26102	Toll-Free: 800-535-5266

WISCONSIN		
Blue Cross and Blue Shield United of Wisconsin	401 West Michigan St. Milwaukee, WI 53203	Toll-Free: 800-242-9635

WYOMING		
Blue Cross and Blue Shield of Wyoming	4000 House Avenue Cheyenne, WY 82001	Local: 307-634-1393

Available at www.fepblue.org/contactus/contactuslocalplans.html. Accessed September 28, 2006.

National Account Service Company Operation Account

The National Account Service Company Operation (NASCO) is an automated claims processing system for any national account that contracts to be a part of the system. Contract benefits are processed and paid consistently nationwide. NASCO's owners are Wellpoint, Inc, Blue Cross Blue Shield of Michigan, Horizon Blue Cross Blue Shield of New Jersey, and the Blue Cross Blue Shield Association. NASCO has partnered for more than 15 years with the Blue Plans to develop innovative products and services that provide Blue Cross Blue Shield plans with progressive, cost-effective health care processing solutions. Information on NASCO can be accessed at www.nasco.com or by contacting info@nasco.com. NASCO can be contacted via phone at 678 441-0061 from 8:00 am to 4:30 pm (eastern time), Monday through Friday. The NASCO business office is located at 1200 Abernathy Road, Suite 1000, Atlanta, Georgia 30328.

Traditional Insurance Option

The traditional insurance option generally provides the same scope of benefits available to enrollees through their previous Blue Cross Blue Shield coverage. However, full benefits for inpatient hospital services are provided only following predetermination approval.

Members covered under the PPO option use the local plan's PPO network, while HMO members may have different plans depending on where they live.

MEDICARE

Medicare is the federal government's health insurance program created by Title XVIII of the Social Security Amendment of 1965 titled Health Insurance for the Aged and Disabled. The Medicare program is divided into four parts: Part A, Part B, Part C, and Part D.

When Medicare began on July 1, 1966, there were 19.1 million persons enrolled in the program. By the end of 1975, there were about 24 million enrollees; in 1985, almost 30 million enrollees; and in 2000, there were 40 million enrollees in Part B of the Medicare program.

To be enrolled in the Medicare program, persons must be 65 or older, retired on Social Security benefits, the spouse of a person paying into the Social Security system, or receiving Social Security disability benefits for a two-year period. Special eligibility provides coverage for those diagnosed with end-stage renal disease (ESRD), the medical expenses of kidney donors to persons with ESRD, the spouses and dependent children of workers who paid into Social Security, and retired federal employees of the Civil Service Retirement System and their spouses. Everyone eligible for Social Security benefits is automatically enrolled in Part A, which covers institutional care; Part B coverage must be elected and paid for with additional premiums. Beneficiaries are responsible for a deductible, copayments, and monthly premiums for Part B.

Part A

Part A of Medicare, also called Hospital Insurance (HI) for the Aged and Disabled, covers institutional providers of inpatient, hospice, and home health services.

Individuals who did not pay Medicare taxes while working and those individuals with less than 30 quarters of coverage must pay a premium to obtain Part A benefits. Currently, the premium for Part A is $393 per month. In addition, seniors with 30 to 39 quarters of coverage and certain disabled persons with 30 or more quarters of coverage will pay a premium of $216 in 2006.

A deductible is required for each spell of illness and is currently $952. In addition, if a participant is hospitalized for more than 60 days, a coinsurance applies as well. The daily coinsurance is $238 for the 61st through 90th days and $476 for the 91st through 150th days. The daily coinsurance for a skilled nursing facility for the 21st through 101st days is $119.

Voluntary enrollment in Part A is available for individuals not eligible for Social Security. However, applicants must be at least 65 years old and a US resident (ie, either a citizen or an alien lawfully admitted for permanent residence for not less than five years immediately prior to the application). Also, the individual must enroll in Part B.

Coverage Period

Entitlement to Part A Medicare benefits begins the first day of the month in which an individual eligible for retirement benefits as a Social Security retirement beneficiary, a qualified Railroad Retirement Account (RRA) beneficiary, or a survivor beneficiary under either program turns age 65. When Medicare entitlement to Social Security benefits for the first month of application for a spouse age 65 depends on entitlement of the primary beneficiary at age 62, the primary beneficiary will be considered to be entitled to benefits throughout the first month, thereby permitting the spouse also to be entitled to Medicare benefits for that month. Entitlement ends the last day of the month of death or the last day of the month before the month in which the beneficiary no longer meets the requirements for entitlement to Social Security monthly retirement or survivor benefits or is a qualified RRA beneficiary.

Disability Beneficiaries

Qualified railroad retirement disability beneficiaries and the following categories of Social Security beneficiaries are entitled to Part A coverage:

- Disabled workers
- Disabled widows and widowers between the ages of 50 and 65
- Certain men or women age 50 or older entitled to their mother's or father's insurance benefits
- Persons age 18 and older who receive Social Security benefits because they became disabled before reaching age 22

Medicare-qualified government employment is treated as Social Security qualifying employment for the purpose of providing Medicare disability benefits.

Disabled individuals may not receive Part A benefits until they have satisfied a 24-month "waiting period" during which they have been continuously disabled. An exception to this rule is made for individuals with amyotrophic lateral sclerosis (ALS); these individuals have no waiting period. Entitlement to benefits begins the first day of the 25th month of disability and continues until the end of the month following the month in which notice of termination of disability status is mailed to the beneficiary or, if earlier, the end of the month before the month in which age 65 is reached.

Medicare benefits and entitlement are extended for disability beneficiaries who attempt to return to work or who give up or lose their disability benefits for other reasons. Under one provision, Medicare coverage continues during a nine-month period of "trial work" and for up to 15 months thereafter. Other provisions allow beneficiaries who lose their disability eligibility, either because they return to work or for other reasons, to regain Medicare entitlement without being subject to the 24-month waiting period, again provided the second disability is the same as or directly related to the first disability. If the two disabilities are unrelated, the 24-month waiting period still can be avoided for (1) those workers who return to disability status within 60 months after the first disability and (2) widows, widowers, and adults disabled since childhood who return to disability status within 84 months.

Disability beneficiaries who are not yet 65 and continue to be disabled and who no longer are entitled to benefits solely because their earnings are in excess of the amount permitted may purchase Part A coverage after they have worked 48 months and have exhausted their extended period of Medicare eligibility. Enrollment can occur during special enrollment periods. It should be noted that Medicare would be the secondary payer for disability benefits in some cases.

Part B

Part B, also called Supplementary Medical Insurance (SMI) Benefits for the Aged and Disabled, provides benefits for services received from noninstitutional health care providers. Medicare Part B (Medical Insurance) primarily covers physician services in both hospital and nonhospital settings. Part B also covers other nonphysician services including laboratory tests, durable medical equipment, most supplies, diagnostic tests, ambulance services, flu vaccines, prescription drugs that cannot be self-administered, certain self-administered chemotherapy drugs, and blood. Expenditures for institutional services in hospital outpatient departments, ambulatory surgical centers, and home health agency services are covered.

The Medicare Part B premium was $78.20 per month in 2005 and $ 88.50 per month in 2006. Part B participants must also pay 20% coinsurance. The 2006 deductible for Part B participants is 124 per year. This amount may be higher if the beneficiary did not sign up for Part B when he or she first became eligible. The cost of Part B may go up 10% for each 12-month period that the beneficiary could have had Part B coverage but did not sign up for it. Part B premiums are usually deducted from the enrollee's monthly Social Security check.

Enrollees who do not receive Social Security benefits can pay monthly premiums to receive Part B Medicare. Table 2-5 contains examples of items not covered by Medicare, and Table 2-6 describes the condition for which Medicare covers the most common preventive services.

Who Is a Physician?

Medicare defines *physicians* to include doctors of medicine, psychiatrists, doctors of osteopathy, dentists, optometrists, and chiropractors. However, Medicare coverage is available only for those physicians licensed by the state in which they practice and only for services authorized by the state licensing agency and covered by Medicare. Physicians performing services in hospitals operated by the federal government within the scope of their federal employment are also covered, even if not licensed by the state. Intern and resident services that are part of an approved teaching program are covered under Part A,

TABLE 2-5

Examples of Items Not Covered Under Medicare Part B

Medicare generally does not cover preventive services, but here are the major exceptions for tests and a physician's interpretation of the results:

Welcome to Medicare Physical: The initial preventive physical will consist of a comprehensive examination that will allow the physician to diagnose problems early when treatment is more effective. In addition, the physician and office staff will provide education, counseling, and referral to other preventive services covered by Medicare.

Cardiovascular Screening Tests: Medicare coverage of cardiovascular screening blood tests, including tests for total cholesterol, high density lipoprotein, and triglycerides. Beneficiaries will be allowed to be screened every five years.

Diabetes Screening Tests: These tests to be covered include a fasting plasma glucose test and post-glucose challenges. Medicare allows for diabetes screening tests up to twice a year.

Mammography Screening: Women aged 35–39 are covered for one baseline mammogram. Women 40 and older are covered for one screening per year. Part B deductible is waived.

Pap Smears, Pelvic and Breast Exams: These tests are covered at three-year intervals, with annual exams covered for women at high risk of cervical or vaginal cancer or who are of childbearing age with an abnormality detected during the past three years.

Colorectal Screening Test: Anal fecal occult blood tests for those aged 50 and older, flexible sigmoidoscopy every four years for those aged 50 and older, colonoscopy every two years for high risk individuals, screening barium enemas every four years for those 50 and older not at risk and every two years for high risk patients.

Prostate Cancer Screening: Anal digital rectal exams and prostate specific antigen blood tests are covered for men of 50 years of age.

Glaucoma screening: Annual glaucoma screening for individuals at high risk for glaucoma, individuals with a family history of glaucoma, and individuals with diabetes.

Bone Marrow Measurement: These tests are covered for certain at-risk patients after a need for the test has been determined. These tests may be performed biannually or more often in certain cases.

Diabetes Self-Management: Education and training are covered if certified under a physician's comprehensive plan of care. Blood glucose monitors and testing strips are covered as durable medical equipment.

Vaccines: Medicare covers influenza, pneumococcal, and hepatitis B vaccinations, including payment for the vaccine plus payment for a physician's administration of the vaccine.

---

although teaching physicians may bill under Part B for direct patient care provided certain documentation is maintained.

Medicare is administered by the Centers for Medicare & Medicaid Services (CMS, formerly known as the Health Care Finance Administration [HCFA]), a federal agency within the Department of Health and Human Services. Large regional insurance companies, such as Blue Cross Blue Shield, that have been awarded Medicare contracts locally conduct the actual day-to-day operations of Medicare Part B. These companies are called Medicare carriers. Most physicians contact Medicare is through the local carrier's provider representative. All physicians and health care providers are required by law to bill Medicare for services rendered by completing the CMS-1500 claim form at no charge to the patient.

Medicare Part B reimburses for physician services according to the allowances defined in the Medicare fee schedule (MFS), which is based on RBRVS. Under RBRVS, physician payment allowances for the same service may vary from one locality to another based on the local geographic practice cost index (GPCI). However, all physicians in the same locality, regardless of their specialty, receive the same payment for the same service. Payment variations for a Medicare service within a region depend on (1) whether

TABLE 2-6

Medicare-Covered Preventive Services

Medicare generally does not cover preventive services, but here are the major exceptions for tests and a physician's interpretation of the results:

- **Screening Mammography.** Women aged 35 to 39 are covered for one screening, women 40 and older are covered for one screening per year. Part B deductible is waived and payment is $67.81.

- **Pap Smears, Pelvic and Breast Exams.** These tests are covered at 3-year intervals, with annual exams covered for women at high risk of cervical or vaginal cancer or who are of childbearing age with an abnormality detected during the past 3 years.

- **Colorectal Screening Test.** Anal fecal occult blood tests for those aged 50 and older, flexible sigmoidoscopy every 4 years for those aged 50 and older, colonoscopy every 2 years for high-risk individuals, screening barium enemas every 4 years for those 50 and older not at high-risk and every 2 years for high-risk patients.

- **Bone Marrow Measurement.** These tests are covered for certain at-risk patients after a need for the test has been determined. Tests may be performed biannually or more often in certain cases.

- **Prostate Cancer Screening.** Anal digital rectal exams and prostate-specific antigen blood tests are covered for men over 50.

- **Diabetes Self-management.** Education and training are covered if certified under a physician's comprehensive plan of care. Blood glucose monitors and testing strips are covered as durable medical equipment.

the physician participates with Medicare, (2) the facility where the service is performed, and (3) whether the claim is assigned.

Medicare Physician Fee Schedule

Physicians are paid by Medicare on a national fee schedule. This schedule applies to all physician services (refer to the earlier definition of *physicians*) and some services provided by other health care professionals, such as:

- Supplies and other services furnished incident to a physician's professional service provided they are integral in the patient's diagnosis or treatment
- Outpatient physical, occupational, and speech therapy
- Diagnostic X rays and other diagnostic tests, other than clinical lab procedures, that have their own fee schedule
- Radioactive therapies, including materials and technicians

Medicare Part B carriers generally pay 80% of the lower of the fee schedule amount or the actual physician's charge, with 20% being due from the patient. Fee schedule amounts are determined by multiplying the relative value by the geographic adjustment factor and the conversion factors. The *relative value,* set by CMS, is a relative ranking of the resources required for that procedure compared to all other procedures. The relative value reflects (1) the value of the physician's professional time, (2) the physician's practice expense, and (3) a factor for malpractice insurance costs. The geographic adjustment factor is a relative ranking of labor cost in each area (metropolitan statistical area [MSA], rural, etc) compared to all other areas; the conversion factor is a dollar amount set annually by CMS; and the conversion factor is $37.90 for 2006.

All participating physicians in a given area, regardless of specialty, are paid the same amount for the same service. Nonparticipating physicians are paid 5% less than participating physicians.

Adjustments to the Medicare Fee Schedule

In addition to the 5% discount for nonparticipating physicians, these other adjustments apply:

- *Anesthesiologists:* Medical direction is paid for at 50% when a single procedure is involved.
- *Assistants-at-surgery:* Payment under Part B is prohibited for physician assistants-at-surgery in hospitals with approved teaching programs. Otherwise, the lesser of 16% of the fee schedule or the actual charge is paid for these physician services, provided the services are required due to exceptional medical circumstances, complex medical procedures are performed that require more than one physician, and certain other conditions are met.
- *Physician assistants:* These professionals are paid 80% of whichever is less—the MFS or the actual charges. If performing as an assistant-at-surgery, the payment is the lesser of the actual charge or 85% of the amount payable if the service was provided by a physician serving in the same role.
- *Nurse practitioners and clinical nurse specialists:* These professionals are paid at 80% of the lesser of the actual charge or 85% of the fee schedule.
- *Clinical psychologists:* These professionals are paid at 100% of the fee schedule.

Understanding Medicare Participation

Each year, CMS invites all physicians to "participate" or "discontinue participation" by December 31 of that year. Medicare *participation* means that the physician agrees to accept assignment for all Medicare claims and to accept Medicare's allowable charge as payment in full for his or her services. Physicians who elect not to participate (referred to as "non-par" physicians) can still see Medicare patients and accept assignment on a claim-by-claim basis.

The number of physicians electing to participate in Medicare has steadily increased over the past 15 years. By participating, the physician agrees to:

- Accept assignment for all Medicare services provided (*Assignment* means the physician requests direct payment from Medicare and Medicare pays 80% of the fee schedule to the physician.)
- Accept Medicare's payment and the patient's deductible and coinsurance as payment in full for the services, regardless of the charge he or she makes
- Not to bill the patient for services determined by Medicare to be noncovered services or for certain elective procedures (However, the physician may bill the patient for other noncovered services provided notice of noncoverage was given before rendering services.)

Electing not to participate with Medicare means the physician has the choice, on a claim-by-claim basis, to accept assignment.

Payments to non-par physicians on assigned claims are 5% less than payments to participating physicians. For example, if the fee schedule amount for participating physicians is $100, the amount paid to a nonparticipating physician's assigned claim is $95.

For unassigned claims, the physician must adhere to Medicare-determined limiting charge limitations, also referred to as balance billing limits. The limiting charge is 115% of Medicare's allowable charge for participating physicians. Violation of the charge limitations is considered a violation of Medicare regulations, and overcharges must be referred to the patients within 30 days. Physicians can obtain the limiting charge amounts from their local Medicare carriers.

Advantages and Disadvantages of Participation

Effective September 1, 1990, regardless of the assignment status of a claim or the participation status of a physician, all physicians must submit bills to Medicare on behalf of their patients. As a result, what used to be an advantage for nonparticipating physicians, ie, not having to submit Medicare bills on behalf of their patients, has equalized, resulting in the same time constraints and costs to all practices.

On assigned claims, reimbursement is sent directly to the practice. This guarantees at least partial payment and can simplify bookkeeping for the staff. Additionally, the remittance advice received with the check provides important feedback to the practice regarding accuracy of coding, coverage information, and regulatory information, which is vital to improving reimbursements. This important information is lost when a nonparticipating practice does not accept assignment on the claim.

However, because payment can be collected "at time of service" on unassigned claims, the staff does not have to perform the extra step of updating the file when the payment is received. The file can be marked paid at the time of service and put away, thus saving time, increasing efficiency, and possibly avoiding mistakes.

Although nonparticipating physicians who do not accept assignment on a claim can collect the fee at the time of service, many do not. This means that the Medicare payment sent to the patient may be spent on something other than the physician's fee. This could become a burdensome and costly process if office staff does not have time to properly perform the collection function. Because the only amounts to be collected for assigned claims are the coinsurance and deductible, the practice is assured it will receive at least part of the reimbursement.

Collection from the patient poses less of a problem for participating physicians and those who accept assignment. In many circumstances, collection from the patient is avoided, because many Medicare enrollees carry supplemental insurance, which pays for some or all deductible and coinsurance balances. Most carriers have an arrangement whereby they send the necessary information to the appropriate supplemental insurer, thus eliminating this process for the office staff or the patient. (This advantage is usually only available to participating physicians.) Even though the practice must collect from two sources, it usually collects the total approved fee.

For a nonparticipating physician who does not accept assignment, the total limited fee can be collected at the time of service, which means no waiting, speedy cash flow, and no cost of collection. However, if the fee is not collected from the patient at the time of service, the practice runs the risk of collecting substantially less money or no money at all from the patient and must cover the cost and time of collection efforts. Also, as the result of subsequent medical necessity denials, the practice must refund any amounts previously collected to the patient. Nonparticipating physicians have additional requirements that participating physicians do not, such as completion of the elective surgery advance notice.

Carriers maintain and distribute a list of all participating physicians, groups, and clinics. This list, which is updated annually, is called the Medicare Participation Directory (MEDPARD). It contains the names, addresses, and phone numbers of all physicians, groups, and clinics that have elected participation for a calendar year. The vast distribution of MEDPARD could help increase the participating physician's patient base.

When referring a Medicare patient to a nonparticipating physician for outpatient care, hospitals are required to also provide, when practical, the name of a participating physician qualified to perform the same services. Medicare includes a statement reminding the patient about the participation program on all explanation of Medicare benefits statements for unassigned claims. Some carriers point out the amount of money the patient could have saved with a participating provider.

Although this consideration may not be paramount to all practices, it is important to think about how a physician's participation status affects the physician's Medicare patients. Many Medicare beneficiaries do not understand the participation program or assignment agreement, and an explanation does not always improve this understanding. Physician participation removes a burden from these patients, possibly helping them focus on "getting well" rather than worrying about how to pay for their medical care.

Medicare Outpatient Deductibles and Copayment

The 2005 Medicare Part B outpatient deductible was $110 per year; this amount can change every year. The beneficiary coinsurance responsibility in 2005 was 20% of the MFS payment allowance. The 2006 Medicare Part B outpatient deductible is 124 per year. However, payment rules vary based on physician participation status and whether the claim was taken under assignment.

If a participating physician charges $100 for a service and the participating allowance is $60, Medicare will reimburse 80% of $60, or $48, directly to the physician. The patient is responsible for 20% of $60, or $12, and the remaining $40 in excess of the allowance is written off as a Medicare participation contractual allowance.

Under the same scenario, except for a nonparticipating physician not accepting assignment, the MFS has a nonparticipating limiting charge allowance that is calculated at 115% of the participating allowance. This limiting charge value represents the charge amount the nonparticipating physician cannot exceed when billing Medicare beneficiaries without facing possible Medicare fines and penalties.

The limiting charges for the service with the $60 participating allowance are equal to 115% of $60, or $69. Consequently, the nonparticipating physician's charge cannot exceed $69. When billed to Medicare at $69, Medicare pays 95% of the 80%, or $52.44. The beneficiary is responsible for 20% of the allowance, or $13.80. Plus, the nonparticipating physician can collect the balance of the $69 charge ($69 − [$52.44 + $13.80], or $2.76) from the patient.

Coordination of Benefits: Medicare as Secondary Payer

Basically, the Medicare secondary payer (MSP) program's function is to coordinate the coverage of health benefits between the Medicare program and other health insurers, with particular emphasis on employer group health plans. Services payable under workers' compensation plans, the Federal Black Lung Program, and those authorized by Veterans Affairs have always been excluded from primary payment under Medicare but may coordinate secondary payer benefits. The following four types of insurance coverage circumstances make Medicare benefits (payments) secondary to other forms of insurance:

- Employer group health plan (EGHP) insurance for working-aged beneficiaries older than age 65 or the spouse of an employed individual of any age, with the beneficiary being covered under an EGHP

- Liability or "no-fault" insurance for automobile, homeowner's, or property claims that provides personal injury or medical expense coverage

- Disability insurance for beneficiaries younger than age 65 and disabled who are covered by a large group health plan (LGHP)

- Work-related illness or injury insurance such as workers' compensation, black lung, or Veterans Administration

Because the reporting of Medicare as secondary payer is mandated by CMS, physicians must actively identify MSP claims before billing Medicare as primary. This can be accomplished by having the patient fill out the MSP questionnaire, which asks a series of questions about the four categories of "other" insurers.

Both the MSP questionnaire and billing procedures for each of the four insurance categories are published in most Medicare carrier newsletters, making it easy and beneficial to review this information. Practices that fail to follow MSP requirements will experience Medicare denials, accumulated accounts receivable, irritated beneficiaries, and less than optimal reimbursement.

If a physician determines a beneficiary has EGHP insurance that makes Medicare the secondary payer, the physician must bill the private insurance first for all the services and supplies provided during the patient encounter. Because Medicare is not the patient's primary insurer, the physician is not obligated to bill using the physician's "Medicare rates" or limiting charges, nor is the physician obligated to abide by Medicare service and supply coverage limits, unless so defined by the primary insurer. The physician should bill at his or her standard or private insurance charges.

Practices unfamiliar with the MSP program assume that if the primary insurance payments exceed the Medicare allowable(s) for services rendered, the billing and collection process has been completed. This assumption not only prevents Medicare from tracking beneficiary COB, deductible, and coinsurance liabilities but also reduces legitimate payment optimization efforts.

The amount of the Medicare secondary payment (per service) is based on several factors. Medicare will pay the lowest of the following values:

- The billed charge minus the primary insurer's payment
- The amount Medicare would have paid as primary insurer (ie, 80% of the MFS allowable amount)
- The higher of (1) the fee schedule amount or (2) the other insurer's approved charge minus the amount the other insurer actually paid

Charges to the Patient

If the claim is assigned, the beneficiary's obligation remains 20% as a coinsurance payment plus any unmet deductible. The physician can charge the patient only if the primary insurer's payment is less than the patient's Medicare coinsurance and deductible.

The patient's coinsurance of $25 (ie, 20% times $125) cannot be collected from the patient because the primary payment ($120) satisfies this obligation. If the primary payment does not satisfy the beneficiary's obligation (eg, the primary payment was only $20), the physician can bill up to the deductible and coinsurance due, or $5.

Expenses that meet the beneficiary's Part B $124 deductible are credited to the deductible even if the primary insurer paid the entire bill and there is no Medicare benefit payable. The Part B deductible is credited on the basis of Medicare allowable charges, rather than the amount paid by the primary insurer.

Medicare Health Insurance Identification Card

The Medicare beneficiary health insurance identification card (see Figure 2-2) has four key areas to understand and use for efficient claim submission:

- *Beneficiary name.*
- *Medicare beneficiary health insurance claim number (HICN).* This is the beneficiary's unique identification number. It closely matches his or her nine-digit Social

FIGURE 2-2

Medicare Beneficiary Health Insurance Identification Card

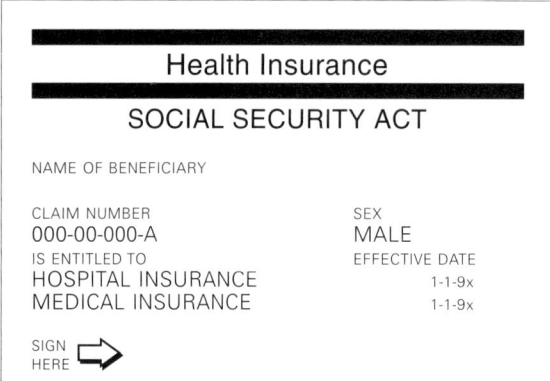

TABLE 2-7

Common Health Insurance Claim Number (HICN) Suffix Modifiers

A	Wage earner	B	Aged wife	B1	Husband
C1	Children	D	Aged widow	D4	Remarried widow
E	Mother (widow)	F1	Father	F2	Mother

TABLE 2-8

Most Common Prefixes for Railroad Retirement Beneficiaries

A	Retired railroad worker (annuitant)
MA	Spouse of an annuitant
WA	Widow or widower of an annuitant who is 60 years or older
WCA	Widow with a child in her care, or a child alone (of annuitant)
PA	Parent of a deceased annuitant
JA	Survivor "joint annuitant," an employee who is receiving a reduced annuity in order to guarantee payment to his widow
WD	Widow or widower of an employee who is 60 years or older
WCD	Widow with a child in her care, or child alone (of an employee)
PD	Parent of a deceased employee
H	Retired worker on a pension
MH	Spouse of a pensioner
WH	Widow or widower of a pensioner
WCH	Widow with a child in her care, or child alone (of a pensioner)
PH	Parent of a deceased pensioner

Security number and includes a one- or two-digit alphanumeric suffix modifier (see Table 2-7). The HICN represents a Railroad Retirement Board (RRB) beneficiary when prefix characters, instead of suffix modifiers, are added to the six- or nine-digit number (see Table 2-8).

- *Entitlement.* This defines what the beneficiary is entitled to. *Hospital insurance* indicates the beneficiary has Part A (hospital benefits). *Medical insurance* indicates the beneficiary has Part B (outpatient benefits).
- *Effective dates.* This defines the effective date for each benefit. Medicare will not pay for services before these dates.

Other Medicare Claim Submission Policies

Physicians must submit professional service claims using the CMS-1500 form on behalf of beneficiaries treated; electronic submission can also be used. Failure to bill on behalf of beneficiaries may subject a physician to a civil monetary penalty of up to $10,000 per violation. Physicians may not charge for preparing or filing Medicare claims. In addition, Medicare-assigned claims must be filed within one year from the date of service or the payment will be reduced by 10%. If the date of service was in October, November, or December, a practice has until the following December to submit the claim without the 10% payment reduction. The physician is responsible for accurately reporting the level or type of service provided to a patient according to the coding guidelines and reimbursement rules of the American Medical Association and CMS. The Medicare Part B Bulletin should be referred to for the latest coding changes and implementation dates.

How to File Primary Insurance if Not Medicare

When filing to a primary insurance carrier other than Medicare, all services, procedures, and supplies and the full charge amount (standard rates) are billed to the primary insurer. Medicare is identified as the secondary payer on the CMS-1500 form. The primary insurance information is entered for fields 11a through 11d on the CMS-1500 form, and information regarding Medicare as the secondary payer is entered for fields 9a through 9d. Before billing Medicare, the provider should wait to receive the primary EOB with payments and/or denials. In some instances electronic billing may benefit from tape-to-tape transfers.

How to File a Medicare Secondary Claim

Medicare should be billed after receiving the EGHP primary insurance EOB for partial payment, full payment, or denials for services rendered. If the primary insurer has not paid the bill in full, a claim for Medicare showing the full charge for the services should be prepared. (The full charge cannot exceed the limiting charge on a nonassigned claim to Medicare.) A copy of the primary insurance EOB or a copy of the check should be attached to the claim. Documentation should reflect primary allowed and payment amounts. The documentation should be marked or stamped in red with the following: "Medicare Secondary Payer." Electronic billers must file a paper claim when Medicare is the MSP. When completing the CMS-1500 form, the following items require special attention:

- Fields 11a through 11d: Beneficiary's information
- Fields 9a through 11d: Primary insurer information
- The amount paid by the primary insurer

Chapter 6 contains detailed instructions on completing a CMS-1500 form.

Relationship of Medicare to Other Health Insurance Programs

Following is a list of health insurance programs other than Medicare along with explanations of how the programs' payments relate to Medicare payments:

- *Commercial insurance.* Commercial insurance is always primary to any public program, including TRICARE and Medicare. Therefore, beneficiaries who are 65 or older and are covered by an employer health plan should use the commercial insurance as the primary insurer.
- *Medicaid.* As a rule of thumb, a federal program supersedes a state program. So, if a person is eligible for Medicaid as well as Medicare, Medicare is usually the primary payer. Furthermore, all claims must be submitted assigned.
- *Workers' compensation.* Expenses for medical care related to job-connected illness or injury are always paid by the workers' compensation program as primary.
- *Private automobile insurance.* Claims related to an automobile accident or other personal injury claims are always payable as primary under an automobile insurance policy and may be subject to recovery under the Federal Claims Collections Act.

When filing claims to Medicare as the primary payer, a number of different RBRVS-related payment policies may alter the traditional 80/20 payment split. An overview of special RBRVS payment policies is provided in the next section.

Medicare Advantage

The Medicare Advantage (MA) program allows Medicare beneficiaries to receive their Medicare benefits from private plans rather than from the traditional fee-for-service (FFS) program. There are five available plan types:

- **Health maintenance organizations (HMOs):** HMOs have comprehensive provider networks and members must use network providers in all nonemergency situations.
- **Local and regional PPOs:** Local PPOs have comprehensive networks, but members may use out-of-network providers if they pay higher cost sharing. The only difference between local and regional PPOs is the service area they choose to cover. Regional PPO plans were new in 2006. They must cover entire state-based regions. All plans that are not regional are considered local, meaning they define their own county-based local service areas. Regional PPOs must have PPO-like networks, which may sometimes be looser than the ones required of local PPOs.
- **Medicare Special Needs Plan:** Special needs plans are a special type of Medicare Advantage Plan that provides all Medicare Part A and Part B health care and services to people who can benefit the most from things like special care for chronic illnesses, care management of multiple diseases, and focused care management. These plans may limit membership to people in certain institutions (like a nursing home) eligible for both Medicare and Medicaid, or with certain chronic or disabling conditions.
- **Private fee-for-service (PFFS):** PFFS plans are not required to establish any networks, as long as they pay providers at least FFS Medicare rates. Because there are no network requirements, providers do not need to decide whether to participate in a plan until a plan member requests service from the provider.
- **Medicare Medical Savings Account (MSA) Plan:** MSAs are a type of Medicare Advantage Plan that has two parts. The first part is a high-deductible Medicare Advantage MSA Health Plan. This health plan won't begin to pay covered costs until you have met the annual deductible, which varies by plan. The second part is a Medical Savings Account into which Medicare deposits money that you may use to pay health care costs.

In practice, some of the distinctions between the plan types may be blurred. An HMO that has an out-of-network option may appear much like a PPO. As there is a great deal of variation in plan attributes within each type of plan and because the lines between plan types are not always clear, the statements about plan types should be seen as generalizations and may not apply to any individual plan. Some distinctions between the definitions of plan types are in law or regulation.

Local HMOs with an out-of-network option may be similar to local PPOs. The major difference is that HMOs are required to submit quality data for all services while PPOs must report some data only for services provided in-network. If a plan's sponsoring organization does not have an HMO license in the relevant state, CMS presumes the plan is a PPO and looser reporting requirements apply. A PFFS plan may not be a regional plan and is not required to have a provider network if it pays providers at least Medicare FFS rates.

In 2006, almost 100% of Medicare beneficiaries had MA plans available to them, an increase from 84% in 2005. Greater availability reflects growth in participation of coordinated care plans. In 2006, 80% of Medicare beneficiaries had a local HMO or PPO plan operating in their county or residence. PFFS plan availabilty also increased in 2006 to 80% of beneficiaries. See Table 2-9.

TABLE 2-9

Percentage of Medicare Beneficiaries With Access to MA Plans

	HMO or PPO	**PFFS**	**Any Local Plan**	**Regional PPO**	**Any MA Plan**
2006	80%	80%	99%	88%	100%
2005	67%	45%	84%	N/A	84%
2004	61%	31%	77%	N/A	77%

FIGURE 2-3

County Benchmarks for MA Plans, 2006

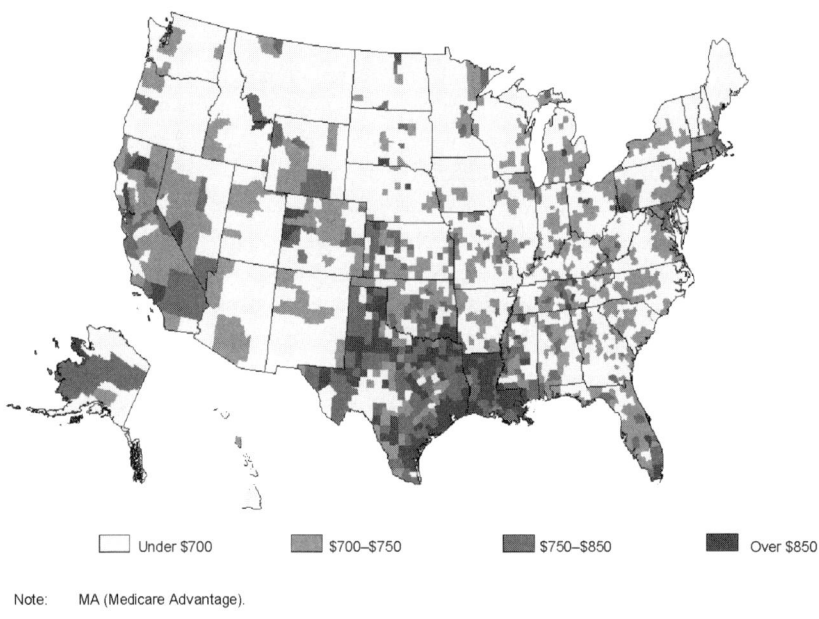

Note: MA (Medicare Advantage).
Source: CMS website, 2006.

Under MA, plans can charge a premium for additional benefits. This premium is in addition to the Part B premium. However, many plans do not charge any premium for the additional benefits. These plans are called zero-premium plans. Zero-premium MA plans are available to 84% of Medicare beneficiaries in 2006. HMOs are the most widely available zero-premium plans, with 54% of beneficiaries having access to one. Where there are no zero-premium plans, low-premium plans are often available. See Figure 2-3.

MA enrollees face cost-sharing requirements in addition to any plan premiums. FFS Medicare beneficiaries' average cost-sharing liability is higher than that of typical MA enrollees. An out-of-pocket (OOP) limit is one way to protect beneficiaries from high cost-sharing liability. MMA mandated that regional PPOs have an OOP limit on beneficiary cost-sharing liability for covered Medicare services provided in-network. Overall, 98% of beneficiaries have access to a plan that includes an annual OOP limit of $5000 or less, and 65% of beneficiaries have a plan available that includes an OOP limit of $2000 or less. While mandated by law all regional PPOs offer OOP limit, only 4% of Medicare beneficiaries live in regions where a regional plan with an OOP limit of $2000 or less is offered. Eighty seven percent of beneficiaries have access to a plan with expected cost-sharing of $500 or less for a six-day hospital stay. Availability of these plans is greater for HMOs and other local plans. Only 13% of beneficiaries have access to a regional PPO with this level of cost sharing. See Table 2-10.

Many beneficiaries will have numerous MA choices. More choices are available, not just because MA plans are entering new areas but also because more plans are entering already well-established MA areas. In 2006, almost half of all beneficiaries could choose from 16 or more MA plans on average and 5% could choose from more than 40 plans. Beneficiaries in Broward County, Florida, have the most choices available with 63 MA plans to choose from. These plan choices are in addition to the stand-alone prescription drug plan offerings. See Figure 2-4.

Several changes occurred in the MA program in 2006. Medicare payments to plans are determined differently. CMS no longer determines MA plan payments based solely on administratively set payment rates. Plans now submit formal bids, then CMS compares the bids with benchmarks (derived from old rates) to determine payment. The benchmark is a bidding target. CMS sets local plan benchmarks for every county administratively, as directed by law.

TABLE 2-10

Benefits Available in MA Plans

	HMO	PPO	PFFS	Regional PPO	Any MA Plan
Prescription drug plan	72%	63%	70%	88%	99%
Zero-premium prescription drug plans	48%	11%	25%	15%	68%
Out of pocket limit $5000 or less	53%	41%	75%	88%	98%
Out-of-pocket limit $2000 or less	28%	16%	37%	4%	65%
Cost sharing for 6-day hospital stay, $500 or less	63%	45%	43%	13%	87%

Source: CMS 2006 unpublished bid data.

MA = Medicare Advantage, HMO = health maintenance organization, PPO = preferred provider organization, PFFS = private fee-for-service

The 2006 benchmarks are the 2005 MA county payment rates, updated by the projected national growth rate in per capita Medicare spending. CMS determines the benchmarks for the MA regional PPOs by using a more complicated formula that incorporates the plan bids. The regions county benchmarks are aggregated to produce a component of the regional benchmark. This component is averaged with the regional PPO bids to produce the final regional benchmark. Every plan submits a separate set of bids to cover beneficiaries in each of its service areas. Each bid consists of up to three separate components:

- The bid for Medicare Part A and Part B
- The bid for supplemental benefits (if any) that the plan covers
- The bid for the Medicare Part D drug benefit (when offered)

FIGURE 2-4

Counties With MA Plans, 2006

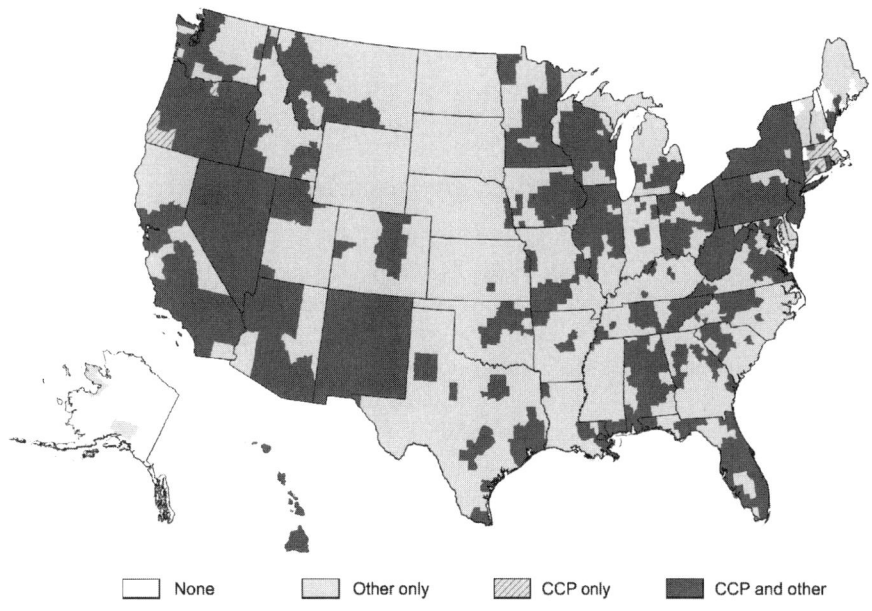

Note: MA (Medicare Advantage), CCP (coordinated care plan). Other includes private fee-for-service and regional preferred provider organizations.

Source: Medicare Health Plan Compare database, May 2006. Available at http://www.medicare.gov.

Another key change relates to the introduction of Medicare's Part D prescription drug benefit. Organizations that sponsor MA plans must include the Part D benefit, or an actuarially equivalent or enhanced drug benefit, in at least one of their plan offerings. Medicare now makes separate Part D payments to the MA plans that include the Part D benefits—Medicare Advantage Prescription Drug plans (MA-PDs)—as if they were stand alone prescription drug plans (PDPs).

Compliance Issues Concerning Medicare Billing

Because of the size and scope of the Medicare program, the government has several agencies and programs in place to identify and eliminate fraud, abuse, and program waste. Medicare, like the health care industry as a whole, uses compliance programs to police providers who, in turn, need to police themselves.

Laws and regulations that deal with fraud and abuse, such as the False Claims Act, have been in effect since before Medicare's inception. However, the Justice Department recently stated that health care fraud and abuse is its number two priority, second only to violent crime. As a result, the government has increased the number and severity of current laws that affect physicians and has added civil penalties of more than $10,000 per claim for billing errors.

Although the topic of compliance is a book unto itself, some issues that practices need to be aware of when billing Medicare include, but are not limited to, the following:

- Reassignment of payment
- Limiting charges (nonparticipating)
- Correct CPT code assignment and service utilization
- Diagnostic coding and medical necessity
- "Incident-to" billing for physician assistants, nurse practitioners (NPs), and other ancillary employees of the practice
- Evaluation and management (E/M) and CPT documentation guidelines
- Ancillary orders and supervision requirements
- Teaching physician and resident billing
- Routine waiver of copayments, deductibles, or professional courtesy discounts
- Stark I and II anti-referral and compensation regulations
- Credit balances
- Correct Coding Initiative edits

Medicare Supplemental Insurance: Medigap

Although Medicare Part A and Part B cover many health care costs, beneficiaries still have to pay Medicare's coinsurance and deductibles. There are also many medical services and items that Medicare does not cover.

Beneficiaries may purchase a Medicare supplemental insurance (Medigap) policy. Medigap is private insurance designed to help pay beneficiaries Medicare cost-sharing amounts. There are 12 standard Medigap policies (A-L), and each offers a different combination of benefits.

The best time to buy a policy is during a Medigap open enrollment period. For a period of six months from the date beneficiaries are first enrolled in Medicare Part B and are age 65 or older, ie, the beneficiary's open enrollment period, beneficiaries have a right to buy the Medigap policy of their choice. Beneficiaries cannot be turned down or charged higher premiums because of poor health if a policy is purchased during this period. When the Medigap open enrollment period ends, beneficiaries may not be able to buy the policy of their choice. They may have to accept whatever Medigap policy an insurance company is willing to sell.

Medicare SELECT

The state insurance counseling office can answer questions about Medicare and other health insurance information. They can also answer questions about Medicare SELECT, another type of Medicare supplemental health insurance that is sold by insurance companies and HMOs throughout most of the country.

Medicare SELECT is the same as standard Medigap insurance in nearly all respects. The only difference is that each insurer works with specific hospitals and, in some cases, specific physicians that beneficiaries must use, except in an emergency, to be eligible for full benefits. Medicare SELECT policies generally have lower premiums than other Medigap policies because of this requirement.

End-Stage Renal Disease Benefits

End-stage renal disease (ESRD) is defined by CMS as a "stage of kidney impairment that appears irreversible and permanent and requires a regular course of dialysis or kidney transplantation to maintain life." Benefits for qualified ESRD beneficiaries include all covered Part A and Part B items and services. Coverage is not limited to the items and services associated with renal disease. These beneficiaries are subject to all regular deductible, premium, and coinsurance provisions of both parts of Medicare. ESRD beneficiaries are not eligible to enroll in an HMO or a Medicare Advantage plan under Part C. However, if a beneficiary is already in a plan, he or she can stay in that plan or join another plan offered by the same company in the same state. If the beneficiary had a successful kidney transplant, he or she may be able to join a plan.

Medicare covers individuals who have not reached age 65 and who are suffering from ESRD. A covered individual is (1) a person who is currently insured by or entitled to Social Security or railroad retirement benefits or (2) the spouse or dependent child of such a person. Therefore, an individual receiving monthly Social Security benefits is entitled to Medicare coverage if he or she suffers from ESRD; however, that individual's dependents are not entitled to Medicare unless they suffer from renal disease.

Coverage Period

Medicare coverage begins the third month after the month in which a course of renal dialysis is initiated. The three-month waiting period does not apply in two instances. It does not apply when an individual participates in a self-care training program (in the expectation of completing the training and entering self-dialysis) before the beginning of the third month after the one during which the individual initiates a regular course of dialysis. In the case of a transplant candidate, coverage can begin as early as the month in which the patient is hospitalized for transplantation, provided the surgery takes place in that month or in the following two months.

When an individual receives a kidney transplant, coverage normally ends 36 months after the month of the transplant. If an individual does not receive a transplant, coverage normally ends 12 months after the month in which a regular course of dialysis is ended. If dialysis is resumed after one of these expiration dates, a new application must be submitted, but no waiting period is required.

Dialysis Coverage

Dialysis treatment is covered in various settings: an inpatient or outpatient hospital setting, an independent renal dialysis facility, and a patient's home. Varying levels of care apply to the different settings. A seriously ill patient may be treated as an inpatient at a hospital. After stabilization, maintenance dialysis treatments may be rendered in an outpatient setting at either a hospital or nonhospital facility. A patient may receive extensive attention and professionals may perform all services needed for dialysis at a renal dialysis facility. Or the patient may be placed in "self-care" where only minor assistance is given by facility technical personnel. In any of these settings, a patient can be taught to perform dialysis at home.

Maintenance dialysis treatment is covered on an outpatient basis. Even when maintenance peritoneal dialysis treatments extend over night, the treatments generally are considered outpatient services. If a patient is admitted as a hospital inpatient because inpatient services are required, the maintenance dialysis treatment is covered as an inpatient hospital service.

Medicare covers all supplies and equipment (including supportive equipment) needed to perform home dialysis, such as home hemodialysis, home intermittent peritoneal dialysis, and continuous ambulatory peritoneal dialysis. Medicare also covers the rental or purchase of kidney dialysis equipment for home use. This coverage includes delivery and installation service charges as well as equipment maintenance expenses. Medicare also covers home dialysis support services, which include periodic monitoring of the patient's home adaptation, visits by a qualified provider or facility personnel in accordance with a plan prepared and periodically reviewed by a professional team (including the individual's physician), installation and maintenance of dialysis equipment, and testing and treating water used in treatment.

Reimbursement for outpatient maintenance dialysis is based on a special prospective payment system (PPS) for nonhospital dialysis services. (Inpatient dialysis services are covered under hospital reimbursement rules.) The payment system is intended to reduce program costs by encouraging home dialysis. Under the dialysis payment system each facility receives a certain payment rate per treatment, called the composite rate. The current base rate for a freestanding facility is $128 and $132 for hospital-based facilities. In 2006, CMS calculated an update factor of 1.4% and a total add-on payment of 14.7% for hospital-based and free-standing facilities. Medicare pays 80% of the composite rate (reduced by any deductible or coinsurance obligations the beneficiary may have). This payment is considered Medicare's full compensation for all of the facility's per-treatment costs except for bad debts, the costs of physicians' direct patient care services, and certain "separately billable" laboratory services and drugs that are not included in the facility's composite rate (until lab services and drugs are included in the composite rate).

In addition to the composite rate, payments to the facilities for self-dialysis or home dialysis training sessions are supplemented as follows:

- A charge of $20 per training session for intermittent peritoneal dialysis, continuous cycling peritoneal dialysis, and hemodialysis training furnished up to three times per week
- A charge of $12 per training session for continuous ambulatory peritoneal dialysis (Only one training session per day is reimbursable, up to a maximum of 15 days.)

Under this payment system, an ESRD facility must furnish all necessary dialysis services, equipment, and supplies. If it fails to furnish (either directly or under arrangements) any part of the items and services covered under the composite rate, the facility cannot be paid any amount for the part of the items and services that it does furnish.

Suppliers

Suppliers who deal directly with ESRD patients instead of going through an approved facility are paid according to a single composite rate that is related to the amount that would have been payable to a hospital-based facility. These suppliers must have a written agreement with an approved provider or ESRD facility under which the supplier certifies that the provider or facility will provide the patient all self-care home dialysis support services and all other necessary dialysis services and supplies, including institutional dialysis services and supplies and emergency services.

The beneficiary has two payment choices: Method 1 and Method 2 (see Table 2-11). Under Method 1, the beneficiary chooses to receive necessary home dialysis equipment, supplies, and support services directly from the facility the beneficiary is associated with. Method 1 covers the equipment, supplies, and support services in the facility's composite rate. Under Method 2, the beneficiary chooses to make arrangements with an independent supplier. The beneficiary may either bill Medicare directly or have the facility or supplier bill Medicare under an assignment agreement. Medicare's payment under Method 2 is

TABLE 2-11

Method 1 and Method 2 Payment Chart for Home Dialysis Equipment, Supplies, and Support Services

Method	Home Dialysis Equipment	Home Dialysis Supplies	Home Dialysis Support Services
Method 1: Dealing with dialysis facility	Medicare pays 80% of the facility's composite rate.	Medicare pays 80% of the composite rate.	Medicare pays 80% of the composite rate.
Method 2: Dealing directly with a supplier	If equipment is bought or rented, Medicare Part B will pay 80% after the $124 annual deductible has been met.	Medicare Part B will pay 80% of approved charges for all covered supplies after the $124 annual deductible has been met.	Medicare Part B will pay the facility 80% of approved charges for all covered services after the $124 deductible has been met.

in accordance with the usual reasonable cost or reasonable charge rules, as appropriate. Specifically, payment will be denied if any of the following conditions are met:

- The supplier has not accepted assignment
- The supplies were furnished by a second supplier
- The monthly payment limit has been reached
- The claim is marked nonassigned and the evidence clearly shows that the supplier intends not to accept assignment

Clinical Diagnostic Laboratory Tests

Currently, fee schedules do not apply to clinical laboratory tests furnished by ESRD facilities, which are included in the ESRD composite rate. However, it is anticipated that lab test will be included in the composite rate in the near future. Fee schedules do apply to clinical laboratory tests performed for ESRD patients when the test is not covered under the ESRD composite rate.

Billing Procedures

It has been said that trying to understand Medicare regulations is like trying to photograph a fast-moving train; a clear image is hard to capture. Medicare rules and regulations change monthly, weekly, or even daily and, sometimes, retroactively. Despite the ever-changing and complex nature of Medicare, a fundamental understanding and knowledge of all Medicare rules and regulations to which health care providers must adhere is necessary. This is the only way compliance can be achieved. Compliance with all Medicare laws is mandatory. Basically, providers must submit claims to Medicare that are 100% correct. All eligibility, all benefits, all coverage requirements, all reimbursement issues, and all adjustment rules must be known. Billers cannot do as some have done in the past, ie, assume that if Medicare accepts and pays a claim the claim must be right or assume that the payer is responsible for determining if a claim is acceptable before reimbursing it. The federal government has ruled that it is the provider's responsibility (or anyone submitting claims on behalf of the provider) to submit only covered charges and to submit them correctly.

There is an established way by which participating providers are paid for services and supplies covered under the Medicare program and an established way by which benefits are provided to eligible Medicare beneficiaries. For the payment cycle to begin, a beneficiary must receive services from a participating provider. All providers must be participating in Part A to receive reimbursements. Services must meet a number of other requirements established through Medicare laws, regulations, and program instructions to be paid. The Medicare payment cycle exists in large part to ensure that all requirements are met before any Medicare payment is made. Medicare pays only for covered services rendered after the Medicare effective date of individual coverage. Every Medicare claim must indicate at least one diagnosis, and this diagnosis should support the medical necessity of the service billed. Also, any treatment provided must be reasonable and necessary. For inpatient services, the Quality Improvement Organization (QIO), formerly Peer Review Organization (PRO), makes this determination. For other services, the fiscal intermediary and/or carrier and other contractors who receive the claim for processing make the determination. Medicare is complex and has many players. Figure 2-5 illustrates the role that the federal government plays in Medicare.

Common Working File

Common working file (CWF) is a Medicare Part A and Part B benefit coordination and pre-payment claims validation system that uses localized databases maintained by designated contractors called *hosts*. Intermediaries and carriers are assigned to a host and are known as *satellites*. The satellites process claims using beneficiary data they have in their own files. The satellites receive this data from the CWF hosts via responses to claims processed for beneficiaries. Current claims are processed to the point of reimbursement computation. Just prior to payment, the satellite submits the claims to its CWF host site to verify entitlement and utilization on the claim. The CWF software also performs limited Part A/B crossover editing to ensure that the services are not paid twice on different types of claims. The hosts provide the satellites with responses to those claims. Satellites also submit special transactions such as Medicare Secondary Payment (MSP) data (primary insurer data when Medicare is secondary), ESRD (End-Stage Renal Disease) Method of Reimbursement Computation data (only intermediaries submit these transactions), and Certificate of Medical Necessity (CMN).

The common working file (CWF) contains eligibility and entitlement information for Medicare beneficiaries. The CWF is comprised of nine databases throughout the United States, which are referred to as hosts. The hosts maintain the CWF databases. Claims are processed using the CWF in the order they are received, regardless of the dates the services were incurred. This first-in–first-out method of processing requests facilitates prompt handling. Most claims are expedited quickly through the CWF; however, delays do occur. During such a delay, one of two responses may be received. The response "Not In Host's File" indicates that the beneficiary record for which the fiscal intermediary submitted a claim is not in the CWF region being accessed by the intermediary. Further research throughout the CWF hosts may be needed. The response "Beneficiary Not Found" may appear on the eligibility detail inquiry screen. This response indicates that the HICN entered cannot be found and that it may be necessary to check additional eligibility information, which is contained in CMS's national database.

FIGURE 2-5

Role of Federal Government in Medicare

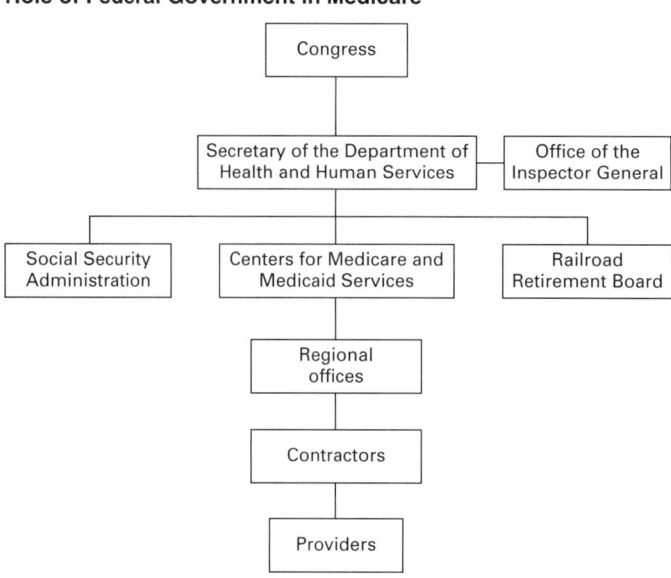

Inpatient Hospital Benefit Days

A patient with hospital insurance coverage is entitled to have payments made on his or her behalf for up to 90 days of covered inpatient hospital services in each spell of illness. Also, the patient has a lifetime reserve of 60 additional days. Payment should be made for the remaining days in the following order of priority:

1. The 60 full benefit days
2. The 30 regular coinsurance days
3. The 60 lifetime reserve coinsurance days

The number of days of care charged to a beneficiary for inpatient hospital services is always in units of full days. A day begins at midnight and ends 24 hours later. The midnight to midnight method is to be used to count days of care for Medicare reporting purposes, even if the hospital uses a different definition of *day* for statistical or other purposes. A part of a day, including the day of admission, counts as a full day. However, the day of discharge, death, or a day on which a patient begins a leave of absence is not counted as a day. (Charges for ancillary services on the day of discharge or death or the day on which a patient begins a leave of absence are covered.) If admission and discharge or death occur on the same day, the day is considered a day of admission and counts as one inpatient day. An example of coverage is provided in Figure 2-6.

FIGURE 2-6

Benefits Example for Billing Medicare Coinsurance and Lifetime Reserve Days

Patient Name: Smith, Jane   DOS: 1/1/06–7/1/06   Total charges: $525,000

The following is a breakdown on how to bill coinsurance days and lifetime reserved days, also UB's codes that should be billed when billing for coinsurance days and lifetime reserve days.

1/1/06–3/1/06 = 60 days

- All days are covered in full except for a $ $952 deductible.

3/02/06–3/31/06 = 30 days

- All days are coinsurance days. Medicare will pay for covered charges except $7140. (coinsurance days = $238 × 30 days)
- Value code 09 (Medicare coinsurance amount, first calendar year) is used. The screen should read **Value code 09 5820.00.** Value code 09 reports the Medicare coinsurance amounts charged in the year of admission. *This code does not apply to Part B claims.*
- Value code 11 (Medicare coinsurance amount, second calendar year) is used. Value code 11 reports to Medicare the coinsurance amount charged in the year of discharge for a bill that spans two calendar years. The amount reported reflects the number of coinsurance days used in the second calendar year of the billing period multiplied by the applicable coinsurance rate. *This code does not apply to Part B claims.*

4/01/06–6/01/06 = 60 days

- All days are lifetime reserve days. Medicare pays for all covered charges except $28,560. (lifetime reserve days = $476 × 60 days)
- Value code 8 (Medicare lifetime reserve amount, first calendar year) is used. The screen should read **Value code 08 23,280.00.**
- Value code 10 (Medicare lifetime reserve amount, second calendar year) is used. The amount reported reflects the number of lifetime reserve days used in the second calendar year of the billing period multiplied by the applicable lifetime reserve coinsurance rate.

6/02/06–7/01/06 = 30 days

- All days are noncovered. Medicare will determine the noncovered amount: $60,000 (ie, $2000 per day for 30 days).
- Other payment from Medicare would be determined by diagnosis-related group assignment and possibly cost outlier justification.

Lifetime Reserve Day Election
The last 60 days, known as lifetime reserve days, may be used once in an individual's lifetime. If a beneficiary is hospitalized for 150 days during the first covered spell of illness, all lifetime reserve days are expended. If a beneficiary is hospitalized for only 100 days during the first spell of illness, 50 lifetime reserve days remain for use during a subsequent spell of illness that requires hospitalization for more than 90 days. Payment is made for lifetime reserve days used unless the individual elects not to have payments made, thereby saving reserve days for a later time.

The beneficiary (or someone acting on his or her behalf) may elect not to use lifetime reserve days at the time of admission to a hospital or at any time thereafter, subject to the limitations on retroactive elections.

Hospitals are required to notify patients who have already used or will use 90 days of benefits in a spell of illness that they can elect not to use their reserve days for all or part of a stay. The hospital notice should be given when the beneficiary has five regular coinsurance days left and is expected to be hospitalized beyond that period. The hospital should immediately notify the patient of this option if it discovers the patient has fewer than five regular coinsurance days left. The hospital should annotate its records at the time that it informed the patient of this option. In addition, an appropriated election statement or form should be made available for inclusion in the patient's hospital record if he or she elects not to use reserve days. If a patient elects not to use reserve days, covered Part B services are billed on the CMS-1500 form. A Medicare beneficiary who is eligible for medical assistance under a state plan (Medicaid) should be advised that such assistance would not be available if he or she elects not to use the lifetime reserve days. However, this restriction on medical assistance payments does not apply to cases where the beneficiary has elected not to use lifetime reserve days.

Ordinarily, an election not to use reserve days will apply prospectively. If the election is filed at the time of admission to a hospital, it may be made effective beginning the first day of hospitalization or any day thereafter. If the election is filed later, it may be made effective beginning any day after the day it is file.

A beneficiary may retroactively elect not to use reserve days provided the beneficiary (or some other source) offers to pay the hospital for any of the services not payable under Part B and the hospital agrees to accept the retroactive election. In these cases, the hospital uses corrected-bill procedures. (The debit-credit procedure should be used by the intermediary if CMS has not rejected the prior bill. Otherwise, the intermediary should correct the original bill.) A beneficiary may file an election not to use the lifetime reserve days after the 90 days following discharge only if benefits are available from a third-party payer and the hospital agrees to the retroactive election. (The hospital manual should be consulted for further details.) All election formats (see Figure 2-7) should be documented and filed within the patient's medical record.

If a claim has not been filed for Part B ancillary services furnished on the hospital days in question, an election not to use reserve days may be revoked in whole or in part. An election may be revoked in part subject to the restriction on elections. The revocation must be submitted to the hospital in writing and be made part of the patient's hospital record. If a beneficiary is incapacitated, any individual permitted to sign the request for payment may file revocation on the beneficiary's behalf. However, an election not to use reserve days may not be revoked after the beneficiary dies. The revocation of an election not to use reserve days should specify the name of the hospital, the admission date of the stay to which it applies, and, if appropriate, the effective date of revocation. Figure 2-8 is a suggested format to use. Additional information is included in the Intermediary Manual, Part 3, Chapter 2, Coverage of Services (see www.cms.hhs.gov/manuals).

Blood Deductibles
Payment may not be made for the first three pints of whole blood or equivalent units of packed red cells received by a beneficiary in a benefit period. However, payment may be made for blood processing (ie, administration, storage) beginning with the first pint or unit in a benefit period. The Part A blood deductible applies only to the first three pints of blood furnished in a benefit period, even if more than one provider furnished blood.

FIGURE 2-7

Election Not to Use Lifetime Reserve Days

I do not wish to have Medicare benefits paid on my behalf under the lifetime reserve provisions of section 1812 (b) of the Social Security Act for services furnished me by [Name of Hospital] beginning _____.
                                                                                                                    Date

WHERE THE ELECTION MAY TERMINATE BEFORE THE END OF THE STAY IN ACCORDANCE WITH SECTION 3106.3 THE FOLLOWING MAY BE INCLUDED:

The last day to which this election applies is _____.
                                                                      Date

I understand that I will be responsible for all of the hospital's charges not reimbursed by Medicare because of this election, except those covered under Medicare Part B. Where Medicare Part B payments may be made for services furnished during the period covered by the election, I will be responsible for the deductible and 20% coinsurance amounts.

_____   _____
                               Signature   Date

_____
           HICN

FIGURE 2-8

Revocation of Election Not to Use Lifetime Reserve Days

I wish to revoke the election previously made by me or on my behalf not to use lifetime reserve days to pay for the inpatient hospital services furnished me by [Name of Hospital] during my stay there beginning [Admission Date]. [If appropriate, add: I wish to revoke my election not to use lifetime reserve days for the period from _____ to _____.] I understand that my lifetime reserve days will be used for these services (to the extent that I have such days available) but that I will still be responsible to pay the Medicare coinsurance amounts and any charges for services not covered under the Medicare program.

_____   _____
                               Signature   Date

_____
           HICN

The Part A and Part B blood deductibles are applied separately. Blood deductibles are in addition to any other applicable deductible and coinsurance amounts for which the patient is responsible. To be covered as a Part A service and count toward the blood deductible, the blood must be furnished on a day that counts as a day of inpatient hospital or extended care. Blood is not covered under Part A and does not count toward the Part A blood deductible when furnished to an inpatient after he or she has exhausted all benefit days in a benefit period or when the individual has elected not to use lifetime reserve days. However, if the patient is discharged on the first day of entitlement or on the provider's first day of participation, the provider is permitted to submit a bill with no accommodation charge but with ancillary charges including blood.

Blood furnished on an outpatient basis is subject to a Part B deductible applicable to the first three pints of whole blood or equivalent units of packed red cells received by a beneficiary in a calendar year. Payment for blood may be made to the hospital under Part B coverage only for blood furnished in an outpatient setting. The Part B blood deductible applies only to the first three pints of blood furnished in a calendar year, even if more than one provider furnished blood. The Part A and B blood deductibles are applied separately. The blood deductibles are in addition to any other applicable deductible and coinsurance amounts for which the patient is responsible.

The blood deductibles apply only to whole blood and packed red cells. The term *whole blood* means human blood or units of packed red cells, which are subject to either the Part A or Part B blood deductible, unless the individual, another person, or a blood bank replaces the blood or arranges to have it replaced. For replacement purposes, a pint of whole blood is considered equivalent to a unit of packed red cells. A deductible pint of whole blood or unit of packed red cells is considered replaced when a medically acceptable pint or unit is given or offered to the provider or, at the provider's request, to its blood supplier. Accordingly, where an individual or a blood bank offers blood as a replacement for a deductible pint or unit furnished a Medicare beneficiary, the provider may not charge the beneficiary for the blood, regardless of whether the provider or its blood supplier accepts the replacement offer. Thus a provider may not charge a beneficiary merely because it is the policy of the provider or its blood supplier not to accept blood from a particular source that has offered to replace blood on behalf of the beneficiary. However, a provider would not be barred from charging a beneficiary for deductible blood, if there is a reasonable basis for believing that replacement blood offered by or on behalf of the beneficiary would endanger the health of a recipient or that the prospective donor's health would be endangered by making a blood donation. Once a provider accepts a pint of replacement blood from a beneficiary or another individual acting on his or her behalf, the blood is deemed to have been replaced and the beneficiary may not be charged for the blood, even though the replacement blood is later found to be unfit and has to be discarded. When a provider accepts blood donated in advance, in anticipation of need by a specific beneficiary, whether the beneficiary's own blood, that is, an autologous donation, or blood furnished by another individual or blood assurance group, such donations are considered replacement for pints or units subsequently furnished the beneficiary.

Figure 2-9 provides tips for billing Medicare blood deductibles.

FIGURE 2-9

Billing Tips to Bill Medicare Blood Deductible

Patient: Smith, Jane
DOS: 1/02/06–01/20/06
No. Units Used: 15
Total Charge: $ 906

$906.00 ÷ 15 units = $60.40 per unit (or per pint)

Patient responsibility: 3 units x $60.40 = $181.20

Value Code 37 Pints of blood furnished	1500	
Value Code 38 Blood deductible pints	300	
Value Code 06 Medicare blood deductible (patient responsibility)		$181.20

These value codes should be used only with type of bill codes (FL 4) 11X, 13X, 18X, 21X, 71X, 72X, and 83X. The value code amount is the sum of the payment and contractual allowance.

TABLE 2-12

Sample Bill Types

111	Inpatient admit through discharge	131	Outpatient admit through discharge
112	Inpatient initial bill (includes admit date)	132	Outpatient initial billing
113	Inpatient interim bill (no admit/discharge date)	133	Outpatient interim bill
114	Inpatient final bill (includes discharge date)	134	Outpatient final bill
115	Inpatient late charge bill	135	Outpatient late charge

A UB-92 or UB-04 Editor can be consulted for additional type of bill (TOB).

Type of Bill

The type of bill (TOB) code provides specific information about the elements of the bill for Medicare (or other payer) billing purposes. The first digit of this three-digit number identifies the type of facility, the second digit classifies the type of care being billed (bill classification), and the third digit indicates the sequence of the bill for a specific episode of care (see Table 2-12). The TOB code and provider number (FL 51) must be consistent with the type of services rendered, especially for providers with multiple provider numbers. This field must be completed for Medicare billing and all other third-party payers. Blue Cross may stipulate which TOB codes are acceptable at the local level.

MEDICAID

Title XIX of the Social Security Act is a federal and state entitlement program that pays for medical assistance for certain individuals and families with low incomes and limited resources. This program, known as Medicaid, became law in 1965 as a cooperative venture jointly funded by federal and state governments (including the District of Columbia and the Territories) to assist states in furnishing medical assistance to eligible needy persons. Medicaid is the largest source of funding for medical and health-related services for America's poorest people.

Within broad national guidelines established by federal statutes, regulations, and policies, each state (1) establishes its own eligibility standards; (2) determines the type, amount, duration, and scope of services; (3) sets the rate of payment for services; and (4) administers its own program. Medicaid policies for eligibility, services, and payment are complex and vary considerably, even among states of similar size and geographic proximity. Thus, a person who is eligible for Medicaid in one state may not be eligible in another state, and the services provided by one state may differ considerably in amount, duration, and scope from services provided in a similar or neighboring state. In addition, Medicaid eligibility and services within a state can change during the year.

Medicaid was initially formulated as a medical care extension of federally funded programs that provide cash income assistance for the poor, with an emphasis on dependent children and their mothers, the disabled, and the elderly. Over the years, Medicaid eligibility has been expanded beyond its original ties with eligibility for cash programs. Legislation in the late 1980s ensured Medicaid coverage to an expanded number of low-income pregnant women, poor children, and some Medicare beneficiaries who are not eligible for any cash assistance program. Legislative changes also focused on increased access, better quality of care, specific benefits, enhanced outreach programs, and fewer limits on services.

Crossover Forms

Crossover forms are used for Medicare and Medicaid claims when the primary payer is Medicare and the secondary payer is Medicaid. When the claim is filed to Medicare, Medicaid is indicated as the secondary payer. After Medicare processes the claim, the electronic claims system automatically sends the claim to Medicaid. In the event that the claim does not automatically cross over, Medicaid uses the crossover form to file the claim as a hard copy. As a rule, whenever a crossover form is filed, the Medicare EOMB is attached and no other billing form is required.

Nonavailability Statement

A nonavailable statement is an official Department of Defense (DOD) document (DD form 1251) issued by the commander or a designee of a military treatment facility that certifies that a specific medical service or procedure was not available to the beneficiary at or through the military treatment facility.

Cost of Program

Medicaid data, as reported by the states, indicate that more than 42 million persons received health care services through the Medicaid program in 2003. The total expenditure for the nation's Medicaid program in 2004, excluding administrative costs, was $138.5 billion.

In most years since its inception, Medicaid has had rapid growth in expenditures, although the rate of increase has slowed somewhat in recent years. This rapid growth in Medicaid expenditures is due primarily to the:

- Increase in size of Medicaid-covered populations as a result of federal mandates, population growth, and economic recessions
- Expanded coverage and use of services
- Disproportionate share hospital (DSH) payment program, coupled with its inappropriate use to increase federal payments to states
- Increase in the number of very old and disabled persons requiring extensive acute and/or long-term health care and various related services
- Technological advances to keep more very low-birth-weight babies and other critically ill or severely injured persons alive and in need of continued extensive and costly care
- Increase in payment rates to providers of health care services, when compared to general inflation

The federal government pays a share of the medical assistance expenditures under each state's Medicaid program. That share, known as the Federal Medical Assistance Percentage (FMAP), is determined annually using a formula that compares the state's average per capita income level with the national income average. States with a higher per capita income level are reimbursed a smaller share of their costs. By law, the FMAP cannot be less than 50% or more than 83%. In 2006, the FMAPs varied from 50% in eight states to 76% in Mississippi and averaged 60% overall. See Table 2-13.

For the children added to Medicaid through the State Child Health Insurance Program (SCHIP), the FMAP average for all states is about 70%, compared to the general Medicaid average of 60%.

The federal government also reimburses states for 100% of the cost of services provided through facilities of the Indian Health Service, provides financial help to the 12 states that furnish the highest number of emergency services to undocumented aliens, and shares in each state's expenditures for the administration of the Medicaid program. Most administrative costs are matched at 50%, although higher percentages are paid for certain activities and functions, such as development of mechanized claims processing systems.

TABLE 2-13

Federal Medical Assistance Percentage by State

State	2006 FMAP	2007 FMAP
Alabama	69.51%	68.85%
Alaska	50.16%	51.07%
Arizona	66.98%	66.47%
Arkansas	73.77%	73.37%
California	50.00%	50.00%
Colorado	50.00%	50.00%
Connecticut	50.00%	50.00%
Delaware	50.09%	50.00%
District of Columbia	70.00%	70.00%
Florida	58.89%	58.76%
Georgia	60.60%	61.97%
Hawaii	58.81%	57.55%
Idaho	69.91%	70.36%
Illinois	50.00%	50.00%
Indiana	62.98%	62.61%
Iowa	63.61%	61.98%
Kansas	60.41%	60.25%
Kentucky	69.26%	69.58%
Louisiana	69.79%	69.69%
Maine	62.90%	63.27%
Maryland	50.00%	50.00%
Massachusetts	50.00%	50.00%
Michigan	56.69%	56.38%
Minnesota	50.00%	50.00%
Mississippi	76.00%	75.89%
Missouri	61.93%	61.60%
Montana	70.54%	69.11%
Nebraska	59.68%	57.93%
Nevada	54.76%	53.93%
New Hampshire	50.00%	50.00%
New Jersey	50.00%	50.00%
New Mexico	71.15%	71.93%
New York	50.00%	50.00%
North Carolina	63.49%	64.52%
North Dakota	65.85%	64.72%
Ohio	59.88%	59.66%
Oklahoma	67.91%	68.14%
Oregon	61.57%	61.07%
Pennsylvania	55.05%	54.39%
Rhode Island	54.45%	52.35%
South Carolina	69.32%	69.54%
South Dakota	65.07%	62.92%
Tennessee	63.99%	63.65%
Texas	60.66%	60.78%
Utah	70.76%	70.14%
Vermont	58.49%	58.93%
Virginia	50.00%	50.00%
Washington	50.00%	50.12%
West Virginia	72.99%	72.82%
Wisconsin	57.65%	57.47%
Wyoming	54.23%	52.91%

Except for SCHIP and the Qualifying Individuals (QI) Program (described in a later section), federal payments to states for medical assistance have no set limit (cap). Rather, the federal government matches (at FMAP rates) state expenditures for mandatory services, as well as for optional services that individual states decide to cover for eligible recipients, and matches (at the appropriate administrative rate) all necessary and proper administrative costs.

Eligibility for Medicaid

To be eligible for federal funds, states are required to provide Medicaid coverage for most individuals who receive federally assisted income-maintenance payments, as well as for related groups not receiving cash payments. Mandatory Medicaid eligibility groups include:

- Recipients of Aid to Families with Dependent Children (AFDC)
- Children younger than age 6 who meet the state's AFDC financial requirements or whose family income is at or less than 133% of the federal poverty level (FPL)
- Pregnant women whose family income is less than 133% of the FPL (services are limited to pregnancy, complications of pregnancy, delivery, and three months of postpartum care)
- Infants up to age 1 and pregnant women not covered under the mandatory rules whose family income is no more than 185% of the FPL (The percentage of FPL is set by each state.)
- Supplemental Security Income (SSI) recipients (or aged, blind, and disabled individuals in states that apply more restrictive eligibility requirements)
- Special protected groups (typically, individuals who lose their cash assistance from AFDC or SSI because of earnings from work or increased Social Security benefits, but who may keep Medicaid for a period of time)
- Recipients of adoption assistance and foster care who are under Title IV-E of the Social Security Act
- Certain Medicare beneficiaries (described later)
- All children born after September 30, 1983, in families with incomes at or below the FPL (These children must be given full Medicaid coverage until age 19. As of 2002, all children younger than 19 years of age who are from families meeting the FPL guidelines are covered.)

States also have the option to provide Medicaid coverage for other "categorically needy" groups. These optional groups share characteristics of the mandatory groups, but the eligibility criteria are more liberally defined. The broadest optional groups that states may cover (and for which they will receive federal matching funds) under the Medicaid program include:

- Children younger than age 21 who meet the AFDC income and resource requirements but who otherwise are not eligible for AFDC
- Recipients of state supplementary income payments
- Institutionalized individuals with income and resources below specified limits
- Certain aged, blind, or disabled adults whose income is greater than what is required for mandatory coverage but less than the FPL
- Persons receiving care under home- and community-based waivers
- Tuberculosis-infected persons who would be financially eligible for Medicaid at the SSI level (but only for tuberculosis-related ambulatory services and for tuberculosis drugs)
- Individuals belonging to federally sponsored Children's Health Insurance Programs
- "Medically needy" persons

The medically needy option allows states to extend Medicaid eligibility to additional persons. These persons would be eligible for Medicaid under one of the mandatory or optional groups, except that their income and/or resources are greater than the eligibility level set by their state. Persons may qualify immediately or may "spend down" by incurring medical expenses that reduce their income to be equal to or less than their state's medically needy income level.

Medicaid eligibility and benefit provisions for the medically needy do not have to be as extensive as for the categorically needy and may be quite restrictive. Federal matching funds are available for medically needy programs. However, if a state elects to have a medically needy program, federal requirements state that certain groups and certain services must be included, ie, children younger than age 19 and pregnant women who are medically needy must be covered and prenatal and delivery care for pregnant women as well as ambulatory care for children must be provided. A state may elect to provide medically needy eligibility to certain additional groups and may elect to provide certain additional services within its medically needy program. Currently, 38 states have a medically needy program and provide at least some medically needy services to at least some medically needy recipients. All remaining states use the "special income level" option to extend Medicaid to the "near poor" in medical institutional settings.

Personal Responsibility and Work Opportunity Reconciliation Act of 1996

Public Law 104-193, the Personal Responsibility and Work Opportunity Reconciliation Act of 1996, also known as the "welfare reform" bill, made restrictive changes regarding eligibility for SSI coverage that affected the Medicaid program. For example, legal resident aliens and other qualified aliens who entered the United States on or after August 22, 1996, are ineligible for Medicaid for five years. Medicaid coverage for most aliens entering before that date and coverage for those eligible after the five-year ban are state options; emergency services, however, are mandatory for both of these alien coverage groups. Medicaid can continue for aliens who lose SSI benefits because of the new restrictions regarding SSI coverage only if these persons can be covered for Medicaid under some other eligibility status (again with the exception of emergency services, which are mandatory). Public Law 104-193 also affected a number of disabled children who lost SSI as a result of the restrictive changes; however, their eligibility for Medicaid was reinstituted by Public Law 105-33, the BBA.

Temporary Assistance for Needy Families

Welfare reform also repealed the open-ended federal entitlement program, known as AFDC, and replaced it with Temporary Assistance for Needy Families (TANF), which provides states with grants to be spent on time-limited cash assistance. TANF generally limits a family's lifetime cash welfare benefits to a maximum of five years and permits states to impose a wide range of other requirements, in particular, those related to employment. However, the impact on Medicaid eligibility is not expected to be significant. Under welfare reform, persons who would have been eligible for AFDC under the AFDC requirements in effect on July 16, 1996, generally will still be eligible for Medicaid. Although most persons covered by TANF will receive Medicaid, the law does not require it.

Title XXI of the Social Security Act, known as the State Children's Health Insurance Program (SCHIP), is a new program initiated by the BBA. In addition to allowing states to craft or expand an existing state insurance program, SCHIP provides more federal funds for states to expand Medicaid eligibility to include a greater number of children who are currently uninsured. With certain exceptions, these children are from low-income families and would not qualify for Medicaid based on the plan that was in effect on April 15, 1997. Funds from SCHIP may be used to provide medical assistance to children during a presumptive eligibility period for Medicaid. This is one of several options from which states may select to provide health care coverage for children, as prescribed within the BBA's Title XXI program.

Medicaid coverage may begin as early as the third month prior to application, provided the person would have been eligible for Medicaid had he or she applied during that time. Medicaid coverage generally stops at the end of the month in which a person no longer meets the criteria of any Medicaid eligibility group. Under the BBA, states are allowed to provide 12 months of continuous Medicaid coverage (without reevaluation) for eligible children under the age of 19.

The medically needy Medicaid program does not have to be as extensive as the categorically needy program in a state, but there are certain requirements. A state with any medically needy program must provide certain services as a minimum (the state may also choose to include additional services). In addition, in any medically needy program, a state is required to provide coverage to certain persons (eg, certain children younger than age 18 and pregnant women who are medically needy). A state may elect to provide eligibility to other medically needy persons: aged, blind, and disabled persons; caretaker relatives of children deprived of parental support and care; and certain other financially eligible children up to age 21.

Medicaid does not provide medical assistance for all poor persons. Even under the broadest provisions of the federal statute, Medicaid does not provide health care services for very poor persons unless they are in one of the designated groups. Low income is only one test for Medicaid eligibility; assets and resources also are tested against established thresholds (as determined by each state, within federal guidelines).

Once eligibility for Medicaid is determined, coverage generally is retroactive to the third month prior to application. Medicaid coverage generally stops at the end of the month in which a person no longer meets the criteria of any Medicaid eligibility group. In addition to the Medicaid program, most states have additional "state-only" programs to provide medical assistance for specified poor persons who do not qualify for Medicaid. Federal matching funds are not provided for these state-only programs.

Scope of Medicaid Services

Title XIX of the Social Security Act requires a state to offer the following certain basic services to the categorically needy populations to receive federal matching funds:

- Inpatient hospital services
- Outpatient hospital services
- Prenatal care
- Physician services
- Nursing facility services for persons age 21 or older
- Home health care for persons eligible for skilled-nursing services
- Family planning services and supplies
- Rural health clinic services
- Laboratory and X-ray services
- Pediatric and family nurse practitioner services
- Nurse-midwife services
- Certain federally qualified ambulatory and health center services
- Early and periodic screening, diagnostic, and treatment services (for those younger than 21 years of age)

States may also receive federal assistance if they elect to provide other approved optional services. Optional services under the Medicaid program include clinic services, nursing facility services for the aged and disabled, intermediate care facilities for the mentally retarded, optometrist services and eyeglasses, prescribed drugs, prosthetic devices, dental services, and tuberculosis-related ambulatory services and drugs for qualifying persons.

Physician Application and Participation

As with Medicare, physicians must apply to Medicaid and receive a Medicaid physician identification number. Physicians who treat Medicaid patients must accept Medicaid's payment for services as payment in full. In most states, patients do not have a copayment and physicians are not allowed to balance-bill the patient.

Practices that provide services to Medicaid patients from more than one state, such as practices on state borders, must know about the coverage policies of the applicable states, because the policies can vary significantly.

Medicaid is a recipient program, meaning that benefit and coverage information varies month to month. Because most state Medicaid programs issue eligibility cards on a monthly basis to patients, the current status of every Medicaid patient should be reviewed before scheduling an appointment and providing services. Photocopying these cards at each visit helps verify the patient's status.

Medicaid Coordination of Benefits

Basically, Medicaid should be the payer of last resort in most situations. For a patient with both Medicare and Medicaid, Medicaid will often pay the Medicare Part B deductible, coinsurance, and monthly premium amounts.

Relationship to Other Health Insurance Programs

Medicaid is always secondary to Medicare. All Medicare claims filed with Medicaid must be assigned. Medicaid will only fill the Medigap such that the total amount does not exceed the Medicaid fee schedule. Therefore, Medicaid may pay nothing if the payment received from Medicare exceeds Medicaid's fee for the same service. Expenses for medical care related to job-connected illness or injuries are paid by the workers' compensation program as primary. Any amounts paid by commercial insurance arising from an automobile accident when the claims are also payable as primary under an automobile insurance policy may be subject to recovery under the Federal Claims Collections Act.

Medicaid Claim Submission

A significant development in Medicaid has been the growth in managed care as a service delivery mechanism, one that is different from the traditional FFS system. Under a managed care system, HMOs, prepaid health plans (PHPs), and comparable entities agree to provide a specific set of services to Medicaid enrollees, usually in return for a predetermined periodic payment per enrollee. Managed care programs seek to cost-effectively enhance access to quality care. Waivers may provide states with greater flexibility in designing and implementing their Medicaid managed care programs. Waiver authority under sections 1915(b) and 1115 of the Social Security Act is an important part of the Medicaid program. Section 1915(b) waivers allow states to develop innovative health care delivery or reimbursement systems. Section 1115 waivers allow statewide experimental demonstrations of health care reform to cover uninsured populations and to test new delivery systems without increasing costs. The BBA also provides states with a new option to use managed care. The number of Medicaid beneficiaries enrolled in some form of managed care program is growing rapidly, from 14% of enrollees in 1993 to 54% in 1998 to 59.11% in 2003.

Although each state Medicaid program has its own coverage and payment policies, the billing requirements for Medicaid are the same as those for Medicare. Most Medicaid programs accept the CMS-1500 form for physician services. However, because Medicaid coverage is limited, the need to correctly code CPT and *International Classification of Diseases, Ninth Edition, Clinical Modification* (ICD-9-CM) codes is very important. Some state programs offer electronic claim submission.

Providers must enroll in the Medicaid program before claims for services can be rendered. Once enrolled, the most recent Medicaid *Physician Billing Guide* must be obtained from the physician's state Medicaid office. It is important to carefully review the billing guidelines and special coding requirements relative to physician services being billed. Claims should be mailed within four to six days after the date of service. Some state programs deny payment if the claim is submitted 60 or 90 days after the date of service. Failure to meet this objective may indicate billing problems. It is best to define Medicaid recipients as a separate class in the billing software to make account follow-up with the physician's Medicaid office easier. Contact names for reimbursement assistance must be identified.

Medicaid Managed Care Programs

Many state Medicaid programs administer managed care programs for their Medicaid recipients. Table 2-14 lists states with comprehensive statewide health care reform demonstrations. Medicaid managed care trends from 1996 through 2005 and enrollment data are depicted in Table 2-15, Table 2-16, Figure 2-10, and Table 2-17.

Medicaid–Medicare Relationship

Medicare beneficiaries with low incomes and limited resources may also receive help from the Medicaid program. Medicare health care coverage is supplemented by services available under the state's Medicaid program, according to eligibility category. These additional services may include, for example, nursing facility care beyond the 100-day limit

TABLE 2-14

States With Comprehensive Health Care Reform Demonstrations as of December 31, 2005

State	Medicaid Enrollment	Expansion Enrollment	Managed Care Enrollment	% Enrolled in Managed Care
Arizona	995,208	142,838	888,801	89.31%
Delaware	143,237	14,587	108,795	75.95%
Hawaii	203,090	21,620	162,394	79.96%
Kentucky	708,203	0	644,713	91.04%
Maryland	717,040	0	486,691	67.88%
Massachusetts	1,026,904	97,180	622,780	60.65%
Minnesota	575,926	75,372	366,282	63.60%
Missouri	883,441	81,395	379,759	42.99%
New York	4,252,734	528,673	2,563,617	60.28%
Oklahoma	571,969	0	479,168	83.78%
Oregon	408,457	22,712	368,403	90.19%
Rhode Island	181,828	21,311	126,225	69.42%
Tennessee	1,221,978	51,814	1,221,978	100.00%
Texas	2,770,069	673,267	1,877,548	67.78%
Vermont	130,276	31,115	84,995	65.24%
Utah	206,716	17,956	188,079	90.98%
Wisconsin	820,948	91,256	380,109	46.30%
TOTALS	**15,818,024**	**1,871,096**	**10,950,337**	**69.23%**

Reprinted from Centers for Medicare and Medicaid Services. Available at: www.cms.hhs.gov/MedicaidDataSourcesGenInfo/Downloads/mmcee05.pdf. Accessed October 25, 2006.

The **unduplicated** managed care enrollment figures include enrollees receiving comprehensive benefits and limited benefits. This table also provides **unduplicated** Medicaid and expansion enrollment figures. The enrollment figures include individuals enrolled in state health care reform programs that expand eligibility beyond traditional Medicaid eligibility standards.

TABLE 2-15

Managed Care Trends, 1996–2005

Year	Total Medicaid Population	Managed Care Population	Other Population	% Managed Care Enrollment
2005	45,392,325	28,575,585	16,816,740	62.95%
2004	44,355,955	26,913,570	17,442,385	60.68%
2003	42,740,719	25,262,873	17,477,846	59.11%
2002	40,147,539	23,117,668	17,029,871	57.58%
2001	36,562,567	20,773,813	15,788,754	56.82%
2000	33,690,364	18,786,137	14,904,227	55.76%
1999	31,940,188	17,756,603	14,183,585	55.59%
1998	30,896,635	16,573,996	14,322,639	53.64%
1997	32,092,380	15,345,502	16,746,878	47.82%

The Total Medicaid population for 1997–2005 was collected by States at the same time the managed care enrollment numbers were collected instead of using 2082 data as in previous years. These figures represent point-in-time enrollment as of June 30th for each reporting year.

The **unduplicated** managed care enrollment figures include enrollees receiving comprehensive benefits and limited benefits. This table also provides **unduplicated** national figures for the Total Medicaid population and Other population. The statistics also include individuals enrolled in State health care reform programs that expand eligibility beyond traditional Medicaid eligibility standards.

Reprinted from Medicaid Managed Care Enrollment Report as of June 30, 2005, page 1.

TABLE 2-16

National Breakout of Managed Care Entities and Enrollment as of June 30, 2005

Managed Care Entity Type	# of Plans	# of Enrollees
Health Insuring Organization	5	500,780
Commercial Managed Care Organization	157	9,780,823
Medicaid-only Managed Care Organization	130	8,606,164
Primary Care Case Management	36	6,559,561
Prepaid Inpatient Health Plan	107	8,119,325
Prepaid Ambulatory Health Plan	43	4,986,161
Program of ALL-inclusive Care for the Elderly	33	11,824
Other	8	549,358
TOTAL	519	39,113,996

This table provides duplicated figures by plan type. The total number of enrollees include 10,538,411 individuals who were individuals who were enrolled in more than one managed care plan. It also includes individuals enrolled in State health care reform programs that expand eligibility beyond traditional Medicaid eligibility standards.

Reprinted from Medicaid Managed Care Enrollment Report as of June 30, 2005, page 1.

covered by Medicare, prescription drugs, eyeglasses, and hearing aids. For persons enrolled in both programs, services covered by Medicare are paid for by the Medicare program before any payments are made by the Medicaid program; Medicaid is always the "payer of last resort."

Certain other Medicare beneficiaries may receive help with Medicare premium and cost-sharing payments through their state Medicaid program. Qualified Medicare beneficiaries (QMBs) and specified low-income Medicare beneficiaries (SLMBs) are the best-known categories and the largest in numbers. QMBs are those Medicare beneficiaries

FIGURE 2-10

Total Annual Medicaid Population Distribution by Year: Managed Care v Other as of June 30, 2005

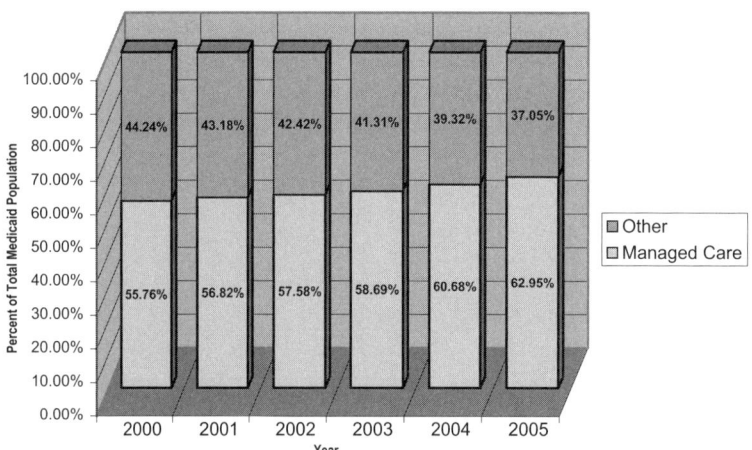

Reprinted from Medicaid Managed Care Enrollment Report as of June 30, 2005, page 2.

with resources at or less than twice the standard allowed under the supplemental security income (SSI) program and with incomes at or less than 100% of the federal poverty level (FPL). Medicaid pays the hospital insurance and supplementary medical insurance (SMI) premiums and the Medicare coinsurance and deductibles for QMBs, subject to limits that states may impose on payment rates. SLMBs are Medicare beneficiaries with resources similar to those of QMBs but with higher incomes, though still less than 120% of the FPL. The Medicaid program pays only the SMI premiums for SLMBs. A third category of Medicare beneficiaries that may receive help consists of disabled-and-working individuals. According to the Medicare law, disabled-and-working individuals who previously qualified for Medicare because of disability but who lost entitlement because of their return to work (despite the disability) are allowed to purchase Medicare hospital insurance and SMI coverage. If their income is less than 200% of the FPL but they do not meet any other Medicaid assistance category, these individuals may qualify to have Medicaid pay their hospital insurance premiums as qualified disabled-and-working individuals. According to CMS estimates, Medicaid currently provides some level of supplemental health coverage for 5 million Medicare beneficiaries within these three categories.

Medicare beneficiaries with incomes greater than 120% and less than 175% of the FPL are known as qualifying individuals (QIs). For these individuals, the BBA establishes a capped allocation to states for each of the 5 years beginning January 1998 for payment of all or some of the Medicare SMI premiums. Unlike QMBs and SLMBs who may be eligible for other Medicaid benefits in addition to their QMB/SLMB benefits, QIs cannot be otherwise eligible for medical assistance under a state plan. The payment of this QI benefit is 100% federally funded up to the state's allocation.

TRICARE AND CHAMPVA

TRICARE is the name of the Department of Defense's (DOD) managed health care program for active duty military, active duty service families, retirees and their families, some former spouses and survivors of deceased military members. TRICARE is the DOD's regional managed health care program for service families. It is a combination of Army, Navy, and Air Force resources under regional management. In the past, each service unit managed its resources independently under a central authority. This often resulted in duplication and misuse of resources. The program is now implemented on a regional basis throughout the country. TRICARE transitioned from 12 regions and

TABLE 2-17

Medicaid Managed Care Enrollment as of December 31, 2005

State	Medicaid Enrollment	Managed Care Enrollment	Percent in Managed Care
Alabama	819,256	472,884	57.72%
Alaska	98,557	0	0.00%
Arizona	995,208	888,801	89.31%
Arkansas	634,701	527,234	83.07%
California	6,508,414	3,282,341	50.43%
Colorado	389,115	371,077	95.36%
Connecticut	409,393	302,061	73.78%
Delaware	143,237	108,795	75.95%
Dist. of Columbia	142,224	91,732	64.50%
Florida	2,308,886	1,543,141	66.83%
Georgia	1,411,908	1,352,163	95.77%
Hawaii	203,090	162,394	79.96%
Idaho	171,451	141,571	82.57%
Illinois	1,900,600	148,900	7.83%
Indiana	834,244	597,899	71.67%
Iowa	327,308	279,855	85.50%
Kansas	282,597	159,511	56.44%
Kentucky	708,203	644,713	91.04%
Louisiana	991,931	735,339	74.13%
Maine	251,545	163,385	64.95%
Maryland	717,040	486,691	67.88%
Massachusetts	1,026,904	622,780	60.65%
Michigan	1,472,812	1,307,910	88.80%
Minnesota	575,926	366,282	63.60%
Mississippi	610,528	67,702	11.09%
Missouri	883,441	379,759	42.99%
Montana	83,241	55,023	66.10%
Nebraska	208,057	168,784	81.12%
Nevada	173,658	161,108	92.77%
New Hampshire	108,719	2,305	2.12%
New Jersey	831,122	564,729	67.95%
New Mexico	407,405	244,934	60.12%
New York	4,188,586	2,563,617	61.20%
North Carolina	1,250,507	814,068	65.10%
North Dakota	54,312	31,120	57.30%
Ohio	1,727,567	617,812	35.76%
Oklahoma	571,969	479,168	83.78%
Oregon	408,457	368,403	90.19%
Pennsylvania	1,731,139	1,557,560	89.97%
Puerto Rico	864,530	855,501	98.96%
Rhode Island	181,828	126,225	69.42%
South Carolina	832,727	118,893	14.28%
South Dakota	126,886	123,230	97.12%
Tennessee	1,221,978	1,221,978	100.00%
Texas	2,770,069	1,877,548	67.78%
Utah	206,716	188,079	90.98%
Vermont	130,276	84,995	65.24%
Virgin Islands	13,531	0	0.00%
Virginia	697,662	438,709	62.88%
Washington	*868,648	*868,648	*100%

(*continued*)

TABLE 2-17 (continued)

Medicaid Managed Care Enrollment as of December 31, 2005

State	Medicaid Enrollment	Managed Care Enrollment	Percent in Managed Care
West Virginia	293,797	132,749	45.18%
Wisconsin	820,948	380,109	46.30%
Wyoming	61,871	0	0.00%
TOTALS	**44,786,077**	**28,381,567**	**63.37%**

The unduplicated Medicaid enrollment figures include individuals in the State health care reform programs that expand eligibility beyond traditional Medicaid eligibility standards. The unduplicated managed care enrollment figures include enrollees receiving comprehensive and limited benefits.

* WA - the Total Medicaid and managed care enrollment numbers are estimations. WA was not able to submit the actual enrollment numbers for the December data collection due to system reconstruction.

7 contractors stateside to 3 regions and 3 contractors to better meet the health care needs of TRICARE beneficiaries. The new contracts were phased in from June through November 2004. Each of the three TRICARE regions (North, South, and West) in the United States has a regional contractor that helps coordinate medical services available through the military treatment facilities and through a network of civilian hospitals and providers. The regional contractors are responsible for a variety of functions, including establishing TRICARE provider networks, operating TRICARE service centers, providing customer service to beneficiaries, providing administrative support, such as enrollment, disenrollment, claims processing, and communicating and distributing educational information to beneficiaries and providers. The regional contractors work with the TRICARE regional offices (TROs) to manage TRICARE at a regional level. Both the regional contractors and the TROs receive overall guidance from TRICARE Management Activity (TMA).

TRICARE North Region

TRICARE's North region includes Connecticut, Delaware, the District of Columbia, Illinois, Indiana, Kentucky, Maine, Maryland, Massachusetts, Michigan, New Hampshire, New Jersey, New York, North Carolina, Ohio, Pennsylvania, Rhode Island, Vermont, Virginia, West Virginia, and Wisconsin (and some zip code areas in Iowa, Missouri, and Tennessee). Health Net Federal Services, Inc, is the new regional contractor providing health care services and network-provider support in the TRICARE North region. Contact information for the TRICARE North region is as follows:

Health Net toll-free telephone number
877 844-2273

Health Net Web site
www.healthnetfederalservices.com

Claims mailing address prime, prime remote, extra, and standard
(Claims processing information for TRICARE For Life, TRICARE Pharmacy and Dental programs is provided at www.tricare.osd.mil/claims/.)
North Region Claims
Palmetto GBA
PO Box 870140
Surfside Beach, SC 29587-9740

Toll-free telephone number for claims assistance
877 874-2273

TRICARE North Region Claims Web site
www.mytricare.com

TRICARE South Region

TRICARE's South region includes Alabama, Arkansas, Florida, Georgia, Louisiana, Mississippi, Oklahoma, South Carolina, Tennessee (excluding 35 Tennessee zip codes in the Fort Campbell, Kentucky, area), and Texas (excluding, only, the extreme southwestern El Paso area). Humana-Military is the regional contractor providing health care services and network provider support in the TRICARE South region. Contact information for the TRICARE South region is as follows:

Humana-Military toll-free telephone number
800 444-5445

Humana-Military Web site
www.humana-military.com

Claims mailing address prime, prime remote, extra, and standard
(Claims processing information for TRICARE For Life, TRICARE Pharmacy and Dental programs is provided at www.tricare.osd.mil/claims/.)
TRICARE South Region
Claims Department
PO Box 7031
Camden, SC 29020-7031

Toll-free telephone number for claims assistance
800 403-3950

TRICARE South region claims Web site
www.mytricare.com

TRICARE West Region

TRICARE's West region includes Alaska, Arizona, California, Colorado, Hawaii, Idaho, Iowa (except 82 Iowa zip codes that are in the Rock Island, Illinois, area), Kansas, Minnesota, Missouri (except the St Louis area), Montana, Nebraska, Nevada, New Mexico, North Dakota, Oregon, South Dakota, Texas (the southwestern corner, including El Paso, only), Utah, Washington, and Wyoming. Contact information for the TRICARE West region is as follows:

TriWest toll-free telephone number
888 874-9378

TriWest Web site
www.triwest.com

Claims mailing address prime, prime remote, extra, and standard
(Claims processing information for TRICARE For Life, TRICARE Pharmacy and Dental programs is provided at www.tricare.osd.mil/claims/.)
WPS/West Region Claims
PO Box 77028
Madison, WI 53707-7028

Toll-free telephone number for claims assistance
888 874-9378

TRICARE West region claims Web site
www.triwest.com

TRICARE offers families three choices: (1) TRICARE Prime, an HMO-type source of care with very low costs; (2) TRICARE Extra, an expanded network of providers that offers reduced cost-sharing, does not require enrollment, and can be used on a case-by-case basis; and (3) TRICARE Standard, which is the same as CHAMPUS, having the same benefits and cost-sharing structure.

Under TRICARE Prime, the provider files claims using the CMS-1500 form. Typically, the patient files his or her own claims under both TRICARE Standard and TRICARE Extra. Form DD2642-CHAMPUS (see Figure 2-11) is used by a beneficiary to file a claim. Claims must be filed within one year from the date of service or within one year from the date of discharge. Claims received after the filing date are denied. The following are some exceptions to the filing deadline:

- Retroactive eligibility (A copy of the determination must be submitted with the claim.)
- Administrative error
- Mental incompetence when no one else is legally responsible for the patient
- Late adjudication of the primary carrier's processing of the claim

TRICARE Prime

TRICARE Prime is a voluntary enrollment option that is much like a civilian HMO. Members living in an area where TRICARE Prime is offered enroll for a year at a time and normally receive care from within the Prime network of civilian and military providers.

Active-duty service members have automatic enrollment and must choose or are assigned to a primary care manager. Their families and all others who are eligible must take action to enroll. Enrollment of newborns and newly adopted children in TRICARE Prime is automatic if another family member is enrolled (unless the sponsor specifies otherwise). However, the children must be registered in the Defense Enrollment Eligibility Reporting System (DEERS) before their enrollment in TRICARE Prime becomes effective.

Active-duty families do not pay an annual enrollment fee. All others do pay an annual enrollment fee, but there are no annual deductibles and the patient's share of the costs for services under Prime is reduced. Members do not file claims when using TRICARE Prime network providers. Covered services are the same as those offered by TRICARE Standard (formerly called CHAMPUS) and include additional preventive and primary care services. For example, physical screenings are covered at no charge under TRICARE Prime but are not covered under TRICARE Extra and TRICARE Standard.

TRICARE Prime enrollees also have a POS option. This means that they can choose to receive nonemergency services without a referral from their primary care physician. However, if they receive care under the POS option, there is a $300 annual deductible for an individual or $600 for a family. After the deductible is satisfied, cost sharing for POS care is 50% of the TRICARE allowable charge. Members may also have to pay any additional charges by nonnetwork providers up to an amount 15% greater than the allowable charge. They also may have to pay the entire bill at the time service is provided and, after a claim is filed, wait for reimbursement of the government's share of the costs.

TRICARE Extra

Under TRICARE Extra, members do not enroll or pay an annual fee. They can seek care from any provider who is part of the TRICARE network, receive a discount on services, and pay reduced cost-shares (5% less than those of TRICARE Standard) in most cases. Members do not have to file any claims when network providers are used. Members must meet the normal annual outpatient deductible, just as they would under TRICARE Standard. (For active-duty pay grades E-4 and lower, the deductible is $50 for an individual or $100 for a family; for all other eligible persons, the deductible is $150 for an individual or $300 for a family.)

FIGURE 2-11
Form DD2642-CHAMPUS

- PATIENT'S COPY -

CHAMPUS CLAIM PATIENT'S REQUEST FOR MEDICAL PAYMENT	Form Approved OMB No. 0720-0006 Expires Mar 31, 2006

The public reporting burden for this collection of information is estimated to average 15 minutes per response, including the time for reviewing instructions, searching existing data sources, gathering and maintaining the data needed, and completing and reviewing the collection of information. Send comments regarding this burden estimate or any other aspect of this collection of information, including suggestions for reducing the burden, to Department of Defense, Washington Headquarters Services, Directorate for Information Operations and Reports (0720-0006), 1215 Jefferson Davis Highway, Suite 1204, Arlington, VA 22202-4302. Respondents should be aware that notwithstanding any other provision of law, no person shall be subject to any penalty for failing to comply with a collection of information if it does not display a currently valid OMB control number.

PLEASE DO NOT RETURN YOUR COMPLETED FORM TO THIS ADDRESS. RETURN COMPLETED FORM TO THE APPROPRIATE CHAMPUS CLAIMS PROCESSOR. IF YOU DO NOT KNOW WHO YOUR CLAIMS PROCESSOR IS, CONTACT A HEALTH BENEFITS ADVISOR OR TRICARE MANAGEMENT ACTIVITY (303) 676-3400.

PRIVACY ACT STATEMENT

AUTHORITY: 44 U.S.C. 3101; 10 U.S.C. 1079 and 1086; 38 U.S.C. 613; E.O. 9397.
PRINCIPAL PURPOSE(S): To evaluate eligibility for medical care provided by civilian sources and to issue payment upon establishment of eligibility and determination that the services/supplies received are authorized by law.
ROUTINE USE(S): Information from claims and related documents may be given to the Department of Health and Human Services and/or the Department of Transportation consistent with their statutory administrative responsibilities under CHAMPUS; to the Department of Justice for representation of the Secretary of Defense in civil actions; to the Internal Revenue Service and private collection agencies in connection with recoupment claims; and to Congressional offices in response to inquiries made at the request of the person to whom a record pertains. Appropriate disclosures may be made to other federal, state, local, foreign government agencies, private business entities, and individual providers of care, on matters relating to entitlement, claims adjudication, fraud, program abuse, utilization review, quality assurance, peer review, program integrity, third-party liability, coordination of benefits, and civil and criminal litigation related to the operation of CHAMPUS.
DISCLOSURE: Voluntary; however, failure to provide information will result in delay in payment or may result in denial of claim.

IMPORTANT - READ CAREFULLY

Federal Laws (18 U.S.C. 287 and 1001) provide for criminal penalties for knowingly submitting or making any false, fictitious or fraudulent statement or claim in any matter within the jurisdiction of any department or agency of the United States. Examples of fraud include situations in which ineligible persons knowingly use an unauthorized Identification Card in filing of a CHAMPUS claim; or where providers submit claims for treatment, supplies or equipment not rendered to, or used for CHAMPUS beneficiaries; or where a participating provider bills the beneficiary/patient (or sponsor) for amounts over the CHAMPUS-determined allowable charge; or where a beneficiary/patient (or sponsor) fails to disclose other medical benefits or health insurance coverage.

INCOMPLETE CLAIM FORMS WILL DELAY PAYMENT

NONAVAILABILITY STATEMENT REQUIREMENTS: If the patient resides within the catchment area of a Military Treatment Facility (MTF) or Uniformed Services Treatment Facility (USTF) (generally within a 40-mile radius of the MTF or USTF), the patient may need to obtain a Nonavailability Statement for some inpatient care that is not a bona fide emergency. *Contact your Health Benefits Advisor for more information. The claims processor will deny your claim if you need a nonavailability statement authorization and do not have one.*

* * * * * *

ITEMIZED BILL: Ask your provider to complete the HCFA Form 1500 for you. If the provider refuses, complete this form and attach an itemized bill which must be on the provider's billing letterhead. The bill must contain the following information:

1. Doctor's or provider's name/address (the one that actually provided your care). If there is more than one provider on the bill, circle his/her name;
2. Date of each service;
3. Place of each service;
4. Description of each surgical or medical service or supply furnished;
5. Charge for each service;
6. The diagnosis should be included on the bill. If not, make sure that you've completed block 8a on the form.

DRUGS: All prescriptions require the name of the patient; the name, strength, and quantity of each drug; NDC for each drug if available; the prescription number of each drug; the name and address of the pharmacy; and the name of the prescribing physician. Billing statements showing only total charges, or canceled checks, or cash register and similar type receipts are not acceptable as itemized statements, unless the receipt provides detailed information required above.

* * * * * *

TIMELY FILING REQUIREMENTS: All claims must be filed no later than one year after the services are provided; or for inpatient care, one year from the date of discharge. Contact a CHAMPUS Health Benefits Advisor or TRICARE Management Activity if you need the name and address of your claims processor. If a claim is returned for additional information, it must be resubmitted by the filing deadline, or within 90 days of the notice -- whichever date is later.

* * * * * *

WHERE TO OBTAIN ADDITIONAL FORMS: You may obtain additional claim forms from your claims processor, the Health Benefits Advisor at the nearest military treatment facility or TRICARE Management Activity, 16401 E. Centretech Pkwy., Aurora, CO 80011-9066.

* * * REMINDER * * *

Before submitting your claim to the claims processor be sure that you have:

1. **Completed all 12 blocks on the form.** *If not signed, the claim will be returned.*
2. Verified that the sponsor's SSN is correct.
3. Attached your provider's or supplier's bill which specifically identifies the doctor/supplier that provided your care.
4. Attached an Explanation of Benefits if there is other health insurance or Medicare supplemental insurance.
5. Obtained a Nonavailability Statement if required (see information above).
6. Attached DD Form 2527, "Statement of Personal Injury - Possible Third Party Liability CHAMPUS" if accident or work related. See instruction number 7 on reverse side.
7. Ensured that patient's name, sponsor's name and sponsor's SSN are on all attachments.
8. Made a copy of this claim and attachments for your records.

DD FORM 2642, APR 2003   PREVIOUS EDITION IS OBSOLETE.   COPY 1 - PATIENT'S COPY

FIGURE 2-11 (continued)

- PATIENT'S COPY -

1. PATIENT'S NAME (Last, First, Middle Initial)	2. PATIENT'S TELEPHONE NUMBER (Include Area Code) DAYTIME ( ) EVENING ( )
3. PATIENT'S ADDRESS (Street, Apt. No., City, State, and ZIP Code)	4. PATIENT'S RELATIONSHIP TO SPONSOR (X one) [ ] SELF [ ] STEPCHILD [ ] SPOUSE [ ] OTHER (Specify) [ ] NATURAL OR ADOPTED CHILD

5. PATIENT'S DATE OF BIRTH (YYYYMMDD)	6. PATIENT'S SEX (X one) [ ] MALE [ ] FEMALE	7. IS PATIENT'S CONDITION (X both if applicable) ACCIDENT RELATED? [ ] YES [ ] NO WORK RELATED? [ ] YES [ ] NO

8a. DESCRIBE CONDITION FOR WHICH THE PATIENT RECEIVED TREATMENT, SUPPLIES OR MEDICATION. IF AN INJURY, NOTE HOW IT HAPPENED. REFER TO INSTRUCTIONS BELOW.	8b. WAS PATIENT'S CARE (X one) [ ] INPATIENT? [ ] OUTPATIENT? [ ] DAY SURGERY?

9. SPONSOR'S NAME (Last, First, Middle Initial)	10. SPONSOR'S SOCIAL SECURITY NUMBER

11. OTHER HEALTH INSURANCE COVERAGE

a. Is patient covered by any other health insurance plan or program to include health coverage available through other family members? If yes, check the "Yes" block and complete blocks 11 and 12 (see instructions below). If no, you must check the "No" block and complete block 12. Do not provide CHAMPUS supplemental insurance information, but do report Medicare supplements. [ ] YES [ ] NO

b. TYPE OF COVERAGE (Check all that apply)
[ ] (1) EMPLOYMENT (Group)   [ ] (3) MEDICARE   [ ] (5) MEDICARE SUPPLEMENTAL INSURANCE
[ ] (2) PRIVATE (Non-Group)   [ ] (4) STUDENT PLAN   [ ] (6) OTHER (Specify)

	c. NAME AND ADDRESS OF OTHER HEALTH INSURANCE (Street, City, State, and ZIP Code)	d. INSURANCE IDENTIFICATION NUMBER	e. INSURANCE EFFECTIVE DATE (YYYYMMDD)
INSURANCE 1			
INSURANCE 2			

12. SIGNATURE OF PATIENT OR AUTHORIZED PERSON CERTIFIES CORRECTNESS OF CLAIM AND AUTHORIZES RELEASE OF MEDICAL OR OTHER INSURANCE INFORMATION.

a. SIGNATURE	b. DATE SIGNED (YYYYMMDD)	c. RELATIONSHIP TO PATIENT

HOW TO FILL OUT THE CHAMPUS FORM
You must attach an itemized bill (see front of form) from your doctor/supplier for CHAMPUS to process this claim.

1. Enter patient's last name, first name and middle initial as it appears on the military ID Card. Do not use nicknames.
2. Enter the patient's daytime telephone number and evening telephone number to include the area code.
3. Enter the complete address of the patient's place of residence at the time of service (street number, street name, apartment number, city, state, ZIP Code). Do not use a Post Office Box Number except for Rural Routes and numbers. Do not use an APO/FPO address unless the patient was actually residing overseas when care was provided.
4. Check the box to indicate patient's relationship to sponsor. If "Other" is checked, indicate how related to the sponsor; e.g., former spouse.
5. Enter patient's date of birth (YYYYMMDD).
6. Check the box for either male or female (patient).
7. Check box to indicate if patient's condition is accident related, work related or both. If accident or work related, the patient is required to complete DD Form 2527, "Statement of Personal Injury - Possible Third Party Liability CHAMPUS." The form may be obtained from the claims processor, Health Benefits Advisor or TRICARE Management Activity.
8a. Describe patient's condition for which treatment was provided, e.g., broken arm, appendicitis, eye infection. If patient's condition is the result of an injury, report how it happened, e.g., fell on stairs at work, car accident.
8b. Check the box to indicate where the care was given.
9. Enter the Sponsor's last name, first name and middle initial as it appears on the military ID Card. If the sponsor and patient are the same, enter "same."
10. Enter the Sponsor's Social Security Number (SSN).

11. By law, you must report if the patient is covered by any other health insurance to include health coverage available through other family members. If the patient has supplemental CHAMPUS insurance, do not report. You must, however, report Medicare supplemental coverage. Block 11 allows space to report two insurance coverages. If there are additional insurances, report the information as required by Block 11 on a separate sheet of paper and attach to the claim.
NOTE: All other health insurances except Medicaid and CHAMPUS supplemental plans must pay before CHAMPUS will pay. With the exception of Medicaid and CHAMPUS supplemental plans, you must first submit the claim to the other health insurer and after that insurance has determined their payment, attach the other insurance Explanation of Benefits (EOB) or work sheet to the CHAMPUS claim.
The CHAMPUS claims processor cannot process claims until you provide the other health insurance information.
12. The patient or other authorized person must sign the claim. If the patient is under 18 years old, either parent may sign unless the services are confidential and then the patient should sign the claim. If the patient is 18 years or older, but cannot sign the claim, the person who signs must be either the legal guardian, or in the absence of a legal guardian, a spouse or parent of the patient. If other than the patient, the signer should print or type his/her name in Block 12a. and sign the claim. Attach a statement to the claim giving the signer's full name and address, relationship to the patient and the reason the patient is unable to sign. Include documentation of the signer's appointment as legal guardian, or provide your statement that no legal guardian has been appointed. If a power of attorney has been issued, provide a copy.

DD FORM 2642 (BACK), APR 2003   COPY 1 - PATIENT'S COPY

FIGURE 2-11 (*continued*)

	CHAMPUS CLAIM **PATIENT'S REQUEST FOR MEDICAL PAYMENT**	*Form Approved* *OMB No. 0720-0006* *Expires Mar 31, 2006*

The public reporting burden for this collection of information is estimated to average 15 minutes per response, including the time for reviewing instructions, searching existing data sources, gathering and maintaining the data needed, and completing and reviewing the collection of information. Send comments regarding this burden estimate or any other aspect of this collection of information, including suggestions for reducing the burden, to Department of Defense, Washington Headquarters Services, Directorate for Information Operations and Reports (0720-0006), 1215 Jefferson Davis Highway, Suite 1204, Arlington, VA 22202-4302. Respondents should be aware that notwithstanding any other provision of law, no person shall be subject to any penalty for failing to comply with a collection of information if it does not display a currently valid OMB control number.

PLEASE DO NOT RETURN YOUR COMPLETED FORM TO THIS ADDRESS. RETURN COMPLETED FORM TO THE APPROPRIATE CHAMPUS CLAIMS PROCESSOR. IF YOU DO NOT KNOW WHO YOUR CLAIMS PROCESSOR IS, CONTACT A HEALTH BENEFITS ADVISOR OR TRICARE MANAGEMENT ACTIVITY (303) 676-3400.

PRIVACY ACT STATEMENT

AUTHORITY: 44 U.S.C. 3101; 10 U.S.C. 1079 and 1086; 38 U.S.C. 613; E.O. 9397.

PRINCIPAL PURPOSE(S): To evaluate eligibility for medical care provided by civilian sources and to issue payment upon establishment of eligibility and determination that the services/supplies received are authorized by law.

ROUTINE USE(S): Information from claims and related documents may be given to the Department of Health and Human Services and/or the Department of Transportation consistent with their statutory administrative responsibilities under CHAMPUS; to the Department of Justice for representation of the Secretary of Defense in civil actions; to the Internal Revenue Service and private collection agencies in connection with recoupment claims; and to Congressional offices in response to inquiries made at the request of the person to whom a record pertains. Appropriate disclosures may be made to other federal, state, local, foreign government agencies, private business entities, and individual providers of care, on matters relating to entitlement, claims adjudication, fraud, program abuse, utilization review, quality assurance, peer review, program integrity, third-party liability, coordination of benefits, and civil and criminal litigation related to the operation of CHAMPUS.

DISCLOSURE: Voluntary; however, failure to provide information will result in delay in payment or may result in denial of claim.

IMPORTANT - READ CAREFULLY

Federal Laws (18 U.S.C. 287 and 1001) provide for criminal penalties for knowingly submitting or making any false, fictitious or fraudulent statement or claim in any matter within the jurisdiction of any department or agency of the United States. Examples of fraud include situations in which ineligible persons knowingly use an unauthorized Identification Card in filing of a CHAMPUS claim; or where providers submit claims for treatment, supplies or equipment not rendered to, or used for CHAMPUS beneficiaries; or where a participating provider bills the beneficiary/patient (or sponsor) for amounts over the CHAMPUS-determined allowable charge; or where a beneficiary/patient (or sponsor) fails to disclose other medical benefits or health insurance coverage.

INCOMPLETE CLAIM FORMS WILL DELAY PAYMENT

NONAVAILABILITY STATEMENT REQUIREMENTS: If the patient resides within the catchment area of a Military Treatment Facility (MTF) or Uniformed Services Treatment Facility (USTF) (generally within a 40-mile radius of the MTF or USTF), the patient may need to obtain a Nonavailability Statement for some inpatient care that is not a bona fide emergency. Contact your Health Benefits Advisor for more information. The claims processor will deny your claim if you need a nonavailability statement authorization and do not have one.

* * * * * *

ITEMIZED BILL: Ask your provider to complete the HCFA Form 1500 for you. If the provider refuses, complete this form and attach an itemized bill which must be on the provider's billing letterhead. The bill must contain the following information:

1. Doctor's or provider's name/address (the one that actually provided your care). If there is more than one provider on the bill, circle his/her name;
2. Date of each service;
3. Place of each service;
4. Description of each surgical or medical service or supply furnished;
5. Charge for each service;
6. The diagnosis should be included on the bill. If not, make sure that you've completed block 8a on the form.

DRUGS: All prescriptions require the name of the patient; the name, strength, and quantity of each drug; NDC for each drug if available; the prescription number of each drug; the name and address of the pharmacy; and the name of the prescribing physician. Billing statements showing only total charges, or canceled checks, or cash register and similar type receipts are not acceptable as itemized statements, unless the receipt provides detailed information required above.

* * * * * *

TIMELY FILING REQUIREMENTS: All claims must be filed no later than one year after the services are provided; or for inpatient care, one year from the date of discharge. Contact a CHAMPUS Health Benefits Advisor or TRICARE Management Activity if you need the name and address of your claims processor. If a claim is returned for additional information, it must be resubmitted by the filing deadline, or within 90 days of the notice -- whichever date is later.

* * * * * *

WHERE TO OBTAIN ADDITIONAL FORMS: You may obtain additional claim forms from your claims processor, the Health Benefits Advisor at the nearest military treatment facility or TRICARE Management Activity, 16401 E. Centretech Pkwy., Aurora, CO 80011-9066.

* * * REMINDER * * *

1. **Completed all 12 blocks on the form.** *If not signed, the claim will be returned.*
2. Verified that the sponsor's SSN is correct.
3. Attached your provider's or supplier's bill which specifically identifies the doctor/supplier that provided your care.
4. Attached an Explanation of Benefits if there is other health insurance or Medicare supplemental insurance.
5. Obtained a Nonavailability Statement if required (see information above).
6. Attached DD Form 2527, "Statement of Personal Injury - Possible Third Party Liability CHAMPUS" if accident or work related. See instruction number 7 on reverse side.
7. Ensured that patient's name, sponsor's name and sponsor's SSN are on all attachments.
8. Made a copy of this claim and attachments for your records.

DD FORM 2642, APR 2003 PREVIOUS EDITION IS OBSOLETE. **COPY 2 - PROCESSOR'S COPY**

FIGURE 2-11 (continued)

1. PATIENT'S NAME (Last, First, Middle Initial)	2. PATIENT'S TELEPHONE NUMBER (Include Area Code) DAYTIME ( ) EVENING ( )
3. PATIENT'S ADDRESS (Street, Apt. No., City, State, and ZIP Code)	4. PATIENT'S RELATIONSHIP TO SPONSOR (X one) ☐ SELF ☐ STEPCHILD ☐ SPOUSE ☐ OTHER (Specify) ☐ NATURAL OR ADOPTED CHILD

5. PATIENT'S DATE OF BIRTH (YYYYMMDD)	6. PATIENT'S SEX (X one) ☐ MALE ☐ FEMALE	7. IS PATIENT'S CONDITION (X both if applicable) ACCIDENT RELATED? ☐ YES ☐ NO WORK RELATED? ☐ YES ☐ NO

8a. DESCRIBE CONDITION FOR WHICH THE PATIENT RECEIVED TREATMENT, SUPPLIES OR MEDICATION. IF AN INJURY, NOTE HOW IT HAPPENED. REFER TO INSTRUCTIONS BELOW.	8b. WAS PATIENT'S CARE (X one) ☐ INPATIENT? ☐ OUTPATIENT? ☐ DAY SURGERY?

9. SPONSOR'S NAME (Last, First, Middle Initial)	10. SPONSOR'S SOCIAL SECURITY NUMBER

11. OTHER HEALTH INSURANCE COVERAGE

a. Is patient covered by any other health insurance plan or program to include health coverage available through other family members? If yes, check the "Yes" block and complete blocks 11 and 12 (see instructions below). If no, you must check the "No" block and complete block 12. Do not provide CHAMPUS supplemental insurance information, but do report Medicare supplements. ☐ YES ☐ NO

b. TYPE OF COVERAGE (Check all that apply)
☐ (1) EMPLOYMENT (Group)   ☐ (3) MEDICARE   ☐ (5) MEDICARE SUPPLEMENTAL INSURANCE
☐ (2) PRIVATE (Non-Group)   ☐ (4) STUDENT PLAN   ☐ (6) OTHER (Specify)

	c. NAME AND ADDRESS OF OTHER HEALTH INSURANCE (Street, City, State, and ZIP Code)	d. INSURANCE IDENTIFICATION NUMBER	e. INSURANCE EFFECTIVE DATE (YYYYMMDD)
INSURANCE 1			
INSURANCE 2			

12. SIGNATURE OF PATIENT OR AUTHORIZED PERSON CERTIFIES CORRECTNESS OF CLAIM AND AUTHORIZES RELEASE OF MEDICAL OR OTHER INSURANCE INFORMATION.

a. SIGNATURE	b. DATE SIGNED (YYYYMMDD)	c. RELATIONSHIP TO PATIENT

HOW TO FILL OUT THE CHAMPUS FORM
You must attach an itemized bill (see front of form) from your doctor/supplier for CHAMPUS to process this claim.

1. Enter patient's last name, first name and middle initial as it appears on the military ID Card. Do not use nicknames.
2. Enter the patient's daytime telephone number and evening telephone number to include the area code.
3. Enter the complete address of the patient's place of residence at the time of service (street number, street name, apartment number, city, state, ZIP Code). Do not use a Post Office Box Number except for Rural Routes and numbers. Do not use an APO/FPO address unless the patient was actually residing overseas when care was provided.
4. Check the box to indicate patient's relationship to sponsor. If "Other" is checked, indicate how related to the sponsor; e.g., former spouse.
5. Enter patient's date of birth (YYYYMMDD).
6. Check the box for either male or female (patient).
7. Check box to indicate if patient's condition is accident related, work related or both. If accident or work related, the patient is required to complete DD Form 2527, "Statement of Personal Injury - Possible Third Party Liability CHAMPUS." The form may be obtained from the claims processor, Health Benefits Advisor or TRICARE Management Activity.
8a. Describe patient's condition for which treatment was provided, e.g., broken arm, appendicitis, eye infection. If patient's condition is the result of an injury, report how it happened, e.g., fell on stairs at work, car accident.
8b. Check the box to indicate where the care was given.
9. Enter the Sponsor's last name, first name and middle initial as it appears on the military ID Card. If the sponsor and patient are the same, enter "same."
10. Enter the Sponsor's Social Security Number (SSN).

11. By law, you must report if the patient is covered by any other health insurance to include health coverage available through other family members. If the patient has supplemental CHAMPUS insurance, do not report. You must, however, report Medicare supplemental coverage. Block 11 allows space to report two insurance coverages. If there are additional insurances, report the information as required by Block 11 on a separate sheet of paper and attach to the claim.
NOTE: All other health insurances except Medicaid and CHAMPUS supplemental plans must pay before CHAMPUS will pay. With the exception of Medicaid and CHAMPUS supplemental plans, you must first submit the claim to the other health insurer and after that insurance has determined their payment, attach the other insurance Explanation of Benefits (EOB) or work sheet to the CHAMPUS claim.
The CHAMPUS claims processor cannot process claims until you provide the other health insurance information.
12. The patient or other authorized person must sign the claim. If the patient is under 18 years old, either parent may sign unless the services are confidential and then the patient should sign the claim. If the patient is 18 years or older, but cannot sign the claim, the person who signs must be either the legal guardian, or in the absence of a legal guardian, a spouse or parent of the patient. If other than the patient, the signer should print or type his/her name in Block 12a. and sign the claim. Attach a statement to the claim giving the signer's full name and address, relationship to the patient and the reason the patient is unable to sign. Include documentation of the signer's appointment as legal guardian, or provide your statement that no legal guardian has been appointed. If a power of attorney has been issued, provide a copy.

DD FORM 2642 (BACK), APR 2003   COPY 2 - PROCESSOR'S COPY

Source: TRICARE. Available at: www.tricare.osd.mil/claims/Dd_2642.pdf.

TRICARE Standard

TRICARE Standard (formally known as CHAMPUS) pays a share of the cost of covered health services that members obtain from a non-network civilian health care provider. There is no enrollment in TRICARE Standard. The annual deductibles, cost-shares, and benefits are the same as for TRICARE Extra.

Members are free to choose their provider, but costs will be higher than with the other two TRICARE options. Members must file their own claims and perhaps pay more for care (up to 15% more than the allowable charge) if the provider seen does not participate in TRICARE Standard. Providers who do participate agree to accept the TRICARE Standard allowable charge as the full fee for the care received.

Eligibility

The categories of individuals eligible for TRICARE and CHAMPVA benefits include the following:

- Spouses of active-duty members of the uniformed services
- Unmarried children (including stepchildren) of active-duty members
- Members of the uniformed services receiving or entitled to receive retired, retainer, or equivalent pay based on duty in the service
- Spouses of retirees
- Unmarried children (including stepchildren) of retirees
- Widowers and widows of deceased active-duty members and deceased retirees who have not remarried
- Unmarried children of deceased active-duty members and deceased retirees
- Ex-spouses who have valid identification cards

For TRICARE standard cost-sharing purposes when preexisting medical conditions exist, family members of active-duty service members who died while on active duty and who were on active duty for at least 30 days before death continue to be treated as active-duty family members for one year after their active-duty sponsor dies.

To be eligible, children must be unmarried and younger than age 21 (age 18 for CHAMPVA). Financial dependence is not required, except for students and disabled children who have passed their 18th or 21st birthday. Dependent children are eligible if they are full-time students and have obtained a valid identification card.

The CHAMPVA sponsor (the active or retired military member) is not eligible for CHAMPVA benefits but is eligible for care from the VA.

When an individual reaches age 65 and becomes eligible for Medicare Part A, TRICARE benefits cease. If Social Security eligibility is not met, TRICARE benefits are extended indefinitely. Effective October 1, 1991, an individual younger than age 65 who becomes eligible for Medicare Part A as the result of a disability and who elects Medicare Part B coverage retains TRICARE as a secondary payer. Disabled spouses and dependent children of active-duty service members are entitled to Medicare Part A and TRICARE without the Medicare Part B requirement.

TRICARE Standard does not cover active-duty service members or dependent parents and parents-in-law.

TRICARE Reserve Select

TRICARE Reserve Select is a premium-based, three-tier TRICARE health plan available for purchase by qualified members of the Selected Reserve (SelRes), which carries the same covered benefits of TRICARE Standard and TRICARE Extra. Table 2-18 highlights tier eligibility.

Tier 1

Qualifying for TRS Tier 1 is a one-time opportunity for each period of qualifying active duty. If TRS is not purchased within the specified deadlines, the opportunity is forfeited. An IRR member who qualifies for TRS Tier 1 will have one year from the end of qualifying active duty or TAMP to find a position in the SelRe. The effective start date for TRS coverage is the date of accession into SelRes or the day following the end of TAMP, whichever is later.

Tiers 2 and 3

The Department of Defense determines what documentation is required to validate qualifications. Documentation for TRS Tier 2 is as follows:

- **Eligible Unemployment Compensation Recipients:** A statement of benefit, verification of receipt of unemployment compensation, or a letter of eligibility from the state office that administers the unemployment insurance program that identifies the member as eligible for unemployment insurance compensation and specifies the period of eligibility.
- **Nonavailability of Employer-Sponsored Health Care Plan:** A letter from the employer certifying the employer does not offer health care insurance to its employees or the company health insurance plan excludes these employees from participating in the company's health insurance plan and the reason why.
- **Self-Employed:** An IRS Form 1040 and Schedule SE filed for the most recent federal income tax return (If this is the first year of self-employment, documentation filed with federal, state, or local government officials to establish the business and the taxpayer identification number under which the business will operate)

Coverage under Tiers 2 and 3 is effective for one year at a time through December 31 of each year. (An applicant may be permitted to enter mid-year, for less than a year's coverage, with a qualifying life event.) If a member is a new accession into SelRes, he or she must complete Step 2 within 60 days of signing the service agreement. If Tier 2 or 3 coverage is purchased during the special 2006 one-time open season and the member's service agreement is effective through December 31, 2007, they will be automatically renewed for one year, calendar year 2007, at 2007 premium costs. Table 2-19 displays 2006 premiums.

Continued Health Care Benefit Program

The Continued Health Care Benefit Program (CHCBP) provides benefits similar to those provided by TRICARE Standard for a specific time period (1836 months) to eligible participants. Participants must enroll in CHCBP within 60 days after separation from active duty or loss of eligibility for military health care. Members who leave active duty voluntarily and those who accept the lump sum special separation benefit (SSB) or voluntary separation incentive (VSI) may also be entitled to CHCBP. Participants must pay monthly premiums.

Eligibility Verification

The DOD maintains a worldwide database on military family enrollment and eligibility through DEERS. Both active and retired military sponsors and all family members must be entered in the DEERS computer data banks. This includes newborns, who must be enrolled in DEERS before claims for their care as TRICARE-eligible patients can be processed. The sponsor must ensure that all participants are enrolled and keep the status of their family members current. If the sponsor fails to notify DEERS of a change in status and ineligible participants receive care, the amount paid by TRICARE for that care must be returned. Patients and providers can verify eligibility by calling the appropriate center:

- California only: 800 334-4162
- Alaska and Hawaii only: 800 527-5602
- All other states: 800 538-9552

TABLE 2-18

Tier Eligibility

Tier 1: Contingency Operations	Tier 2: Certified Qualifications	Tier 3: Other SelRes Members
■ Was called or ordered to AD for a period of more than 30 days in support of a contingency operation ■ Either — Served continuously on AD for 90 days or more or — Served less than 90 days due solely to an injury, illness, or disease incurred or aggravated while on AD ■ Executed a TRS Service Agreement (DD 2895) for continued service no later from AD for continued service in SelRes from the begin date of TRS coverage through the end date of coverage ■ Is a member of SelRes on the start date of TRS coverage (IRR members have one year after the last day of qualifying active duty, or the last day of TAMP coverage, to occupy a position in the SelRes or the opportunity to qualify for TRS Tier 1 is lost.)	■ Is one of the following: — An eligible unemployment compensation recipient as determined by state law — An employee whose employer does not offer a health plan to anyone working for the employer — In a category of employees not offered an employer-sponsored health benefits plan (not based on membership in the reserves) — Primarily self-employed as reported to the IRS (not including reported to the IRS (not including SelRes income) ■ Either — Qualified (Jul 1-Oct 31) or — Submitted documentation sufficient to verify a QLE (such as change in family composition, change in family employment, or change in family health plan coverage) or — Is a new accession into the SelRes ■ Executed a Service Agreement (DD 2895) for continued service from the begin date of TRS coverage to the end date of coverage ■ Is a member of SelRes on the start date of TRS coverage	■ Is a member of the SelRes ■ Does not qualify for Tier 1 or Tier 2 ■ Either — Qualified (Jul 1-Oct 31) or — Submitted documentation sufficient to verify a QLE (such as change in family composition, change in family employment, or change in family health plan coverage) or — Is a new accession into the SelRes ■ Executed a Service Agreement of (DD 2895) for continued service from the begin date of TRS coverage to the end date coverage ■ Is a member of SelRes on the start date of TRS coverage.

AD = active duty, QLE = qualifying life event, SelRes = selected reserve

TABLE 2-19

2006 Premiums

Member pays:	Tier 1: Contingency Operations	Tier 2: Certified Qualifications	Tier 3: Other Selected Reserve Members
TRS members only	$81.00	$145.29	$247.00
TRS members and family	$253.00	$451.52	$767.41

A valid uniformed services identification card is required to establish eligibility. Children younger than age 10 are not normally issued identification cards, except under unusual circumstances. Their eligibility is established on the basis of either parent's identification card. A "yes" in block 15b on the back of the card indicates eligibility. CHAMPVA beneficiaries are issued a CHAMPVA identification card (see Figure 2-12) after the VA determines eligibility.

TRICARE Participation

As with Medicare, physicians must apply and be approved by TRICARE for a patient to receive benefits for services. When the physician accepts assignment on a claim, he or she agrees to accept as payment the amount allowed by TRICARE, to write off the difference of the actual charge and the amount allowed by TRICARE, and to file the claim for the patient. The provider must collect any coinsurance amounts, noncovered items, or deductibles from the patient.

When the provider does not accept assignment, the practice may collect the full fee from the patient at the time service is rendered. In addition, the provider is not bound by UCR agreements and is not required to file claim forms.

TRICARE operates on a fiscal year instead of a calendar year. The fiscal year runs from October 1 to September 30. Consequently, beginning each October, the deductible amount of $150 per individual and $300 per family must be met before TRICARE will begin paying on claims.

Only participating providers may file appeals and have the right to information related to participating claims.

Nonparticipating Providers

Certain health care providers who see TRICARE patients but who do not "participate"—also known as "accepting assignment"—in the program are limited by federal law in how much they can charge TRICARE patients for the services they provide. Nonparticipating providers may charge no more than 15% above the TRICARE maximum allowable charge for their services.

Covered Benefits

TRICARE provides coverage for most medical and surgical conditions; contagious diseases; and nervous, mental, and chronic disorders, such as alcoholism and certain obesity surgeries. The program pays a coinsurance for drugs prescribed by physicians or dentists when obtained from a pharmacy by written prescription. Any service considered to be experimental in nature is not a covered benefit of the program. Some medication benefits programs that require copayments and not coinsurance are available. Some organ transplant operations are allowed, such as cornea, kidney, liver, and bone marrow, with some limitations imposed. Only active-duty dependents are eligible to receive one eye examination per year.

The provider should be aware that for a certain number of psychiatric visits (eg, 33 in Missouri, 22 in Illinois) an ongoing treatment report must be completed, regardless of the number of times he or she actually saw the patient. Otherwise, the patient will not receive further benefits or reimbursement from TRICARE. See Table 2-20 for an explanation of deductibles and coinsurance.

Claims should be submitted on form 501 or form CMS-1500. Because of the detailed information required for a TRICARE claim, form 501 should be used whenever possible.

Nonavailability Statement

Any CHAMPUS beneficiary who lives within the zip code catchment area of a uniformed services hospital must obtain a nonavailability statement (NAS) before CHAMPUS will share the cost of nonemergency inpatient care from a civilian source. The catchment area is defined by zip codes and is based on approximately a 40-mile radius surrounding the military medical facility.

The patient is responsible for obtaining the NAS waiver. Without the waiver, services could be denied for payment by CHAMPUS. All civilian hospital admissions require a nonavailability waiver from the military facility before admitting members who live within a catchment area surrounding a military medical facility.

TABLE 2-20

TRICARE Deductibles and Coinsurance

	Active Duty Family Members		
	TRICARE Prime	**TRICARE Extra**	**TRICARE Standard**
Annual Deductible	None	$150/individual or $300/family for E-5 & above; $50/$100 for E-4 & below	$150/individual or $300/family for E-5 & above; $50/100 E-4 below
Annual Enrollment Fee	None	None	None
Civilian Outpatient Visit	No cost	15% of negotiated fee	20% of allowable charges for covered service
Civilian Inpatient Admission	No cost	Greater of $25 or $14.35/day	Greater of $25 or $14.35/day
Civilian Inpatient Behavioral Health	No cost	Greater of $20 per day or $25 per admission	Greater of $20 per day or $25 per admission
Civilian Inpatient Skilled Nursing Facility Care	$0 per diem charge per admission No separate cost share for separately billed professional charges	$14.35/day ($25 minimum) Charge per admission	$14.35/day ($25 minimum) Charge per admission

	Retirees, Their Family Members, and Others		
	TRICARE Prime	**TRICARE Extra**	**TRICARE Standard**
Annual Deductible	NONE	$150/individual or $300/family	$150/individual or $300/family
Annual Enrollment Fee	$230/individual $460/family	None	None
Civilian Cost Shares	**N/A**	20% of negotiated fee	25% of allowable charges for covered service
Outpatient	$12	**N/A**	**N/A**
Emergency Care	$30		
Mental Health Visit	$25 $17 (group visit)		
Civilian Inpatient Cost Share	Greater of $11 per day or $25 per admission; no separate co-payment for separately billed professional charges	Lesser of $250/day or 25% of negotiated charges plus 20% of negotiated professional fees	Lesser of $535/day or 25% of billed charges plus 25% allowable professional fees
Civilian Inpatient Skilled Nursing Facility Care	$11/day ($25 minimum) charge per admission	$250 per diem cost share or 20% cost share of total charges, whichever is less, institutional services, plus 20% cost share of separately billed professional charges	25% cost share of allowable plus charges for institutional services, 25% cost share of allowable for separately billed professional charges.
Civilian Inpatient Behavioral Health	$40 per day; no charge for separately billed professional charges	20% of total charge. Plus, 20% of the allowable charge for separately billed professional services	High Volume Hospitals—25% per hospital specific per diem, plus 25% of the allowable charge for separately billed professional services; Low Volume Hospitals—$175 day or 25% of the billed charges, whichever is lower, plus 25% of the allowable charge for separately billed services

Available at: www.tricare.osd.mil/tricarecost.cfm. Accessed October 26, 2006.

Fourteen outpatient procedures require an NAS before civilian care can be rendered. These procedures include arthroscopy, breast mass or tumor excision, cataract removal, cystoscopy, dilation and curettage, gastrointestinal endoscopy, gynecologic laparoscopy, hernia repair, ligation or transection of fallopian tubes, myringotomy, neuroplasty, nose repair, strabismus repair, and tonsillectomy/adenoidectomy. The following situations also require an NAS:

- A patient has been receiving care from an outpatient civilian source and it is medically advisable that care continues from the civilian physician or source
- Space is not available at the military facility
- The military facility does not maintain the necessary medical equipment or personnel required for care or treatment
- The patient resides outside the catchment area
- The patient is covered by another insurance policy that is the primary payer

TRICARE for Life

The National Defense Authorization Act (NDAA) for Fiscal Year 2001 (Public Law 106–398) extended TRICARE health care and pharmacy benefits to:

- Medicare-entitled uniformed services retirees
- Medicare-entitled retired guard members and reservists
- Medicare-entitled family members and widows/widowers
- Medicare-entitled unremarried former spouses who meet TRICARE eligibility requirements

Pharmacy benefits began on April 1, 2001, and the TRICARE medical benefits began on October 1, 2001. The medical benefits are known as TRICARE for Life (TFL) and the pharmacy benefits are part of the TRICARE Pharmacy Program.

TFL is a permanent program funded through the Department of Defense Medicare-Eligible Retiree Health Care Fund and resourced with general revenues of the US Treasury and annual contributions from appropriations. TFL does not require annual authorization by Congress. *Dual-eligible* is the term used to describe a TRICARE beneficiary who is entitled to Medicare. TFL is for all TRICARE beneficiaries who are entitled to Medicare because of a disability, end-stage renal disease (ESRD), or age. Under federal law, a TRICARE beneficiary entitled to Medicare because of age, disability, or ESRD must enroll and pay the monthly Medicare Part B premium in order to remain TRICARE-eligible. If the member is an active duty family member entitled to Medicare, he or she is not required to purchase Part B until his or her active duty sponsor retires. A member will lose his or her TRICARE benefits if he or she disenrolls from Part B or stops paying the Part B premiums. TRICARE will not pay any claims for any period a member is entitled to Part A and not enrolled in Part B. If claims were paid, TRICARE may take action to recover payments made on the member's behalf.

If a member reaches age 65 and is not entitled to premium-free Medicare Part A under his or her own Social Security number (SSN), he or she needs to file for benefits under his or her spouse's (or divorced spouse's) SSN if he or she is 62 or older. If a member's spouse (or divorced spouse) is not yet 62, they must refile for benefits under his or her spouse's (or divorced spouse's SSN) when he or she turns 62. Such an individual's TRICARE benefits remain the same because he or she is entitled to premium-free Part A. The member will not transition to TRICARE for Life but may continue to enroll in TRICARE Prime if it is available in his or her area, or the member can use TRICARE Standard and TRICARE Extra.

Medicare and TRICARE are distinct programs governed by different federal laws and regulations. For either program to pay for health care services, the service must meet that program's requirements. Neither Medicare nor TRICARE can pay for services not considered medically necessary and appropriate for the particular patient's diagnosis, symptoms, or history.

While Medicare is the member's primary insurance, TRICARE acts as his or her secondary insurance, minimizing out-of-pocket expenses. TRICARE benefits include covering the coinsurance and deductible amounts incurred by Medicare. If a service is a benefit under both Medicare and TRICARE, there will be no out-of-pocket expense. After Medicare pays its portion of the claim, TRICARE pays the remaining amount (which would have been a member's responsibility). If a service is a benefit under both Medicare and TRICARE, but Medicare cannot pay because the member has used up his or her Medicare benefit, TRICARE will make payment as the primary payer. The member will be responsible for applicable TRICARE deductibles and cost shares. The network status of the provider determines the member's costs shares. Cost shares for services received from network providers will be TRICARE Extra cost shares. Services received from non-network providers will be TRICARE Standard cost shares. See Table 2-21 for cost distribution.

Services Covered by Medicare but not by TRICARE
If a service is a benefit under Medicare but not under TRICARE, TRICARE will make no payment for the service regardless of any action Medicare may take on the claim. The member is responsible for the Medicare deductible and cost shares.

Services Covered by TRICARE but not by Medicare
If a service is a benefit under TRICARE but not under Medicare, TRICARE will process the claim as the primary payer. The member is responsible for applicable TRICARE deductibles and cost shares. The network status of the member's provider determines the member's costs shares. Cost shares for services received from network providers will be TRICARE Extra cost shares. Services received from non-network providers will be TRICARE Standard cost shares.

Services not Covered by Medicare or TRICARE
Neither Medicare nor TRICARE will make payment on the claim. The member is responsible for the entire bill.

Coordination of Benefits (or Double Coverage)

Section 779 of Public Law 97-377, the FY83 Department of Defense Appropriations Act, changed the procedure for determining the primary payer in a double-coverage situation. According to this law, no TRICARE funds "shall be available for the payment for any service or supply for persons enrolled in any other insurance, medical service, or health plan to the extent that the service or supply is a benefit under the other plan."

In other words, TRICARE is the secondary payer to all other insurance, medical service, and health plans. The exception to this rule is Medicaid and the Indian Health Service. If the patient has Medicaid, TRICARE is the primary payer. With Indian Health Service claims, if the patient was treated at a facility other than an Indian Health Service facility, TRICARE is primary. This law went into effect on December 21, 1982. Active-duty families no longer have the option to file with TRICARE first. The exclusionary clause for policies in effect before 1966 no longer exists, and private plans are also included as double-coverage situations. This includes HMOs and PPOs.

Relationship to Other Government Medical Programs

TRICARE-eligible dependents of active-duty sponsors with Medicare Part A maintain TRICARE as the secondary payer. Non-active-duty dependents who are younger than age 65 and disabled maintain TRICARE as the secondary payer if they have Medicare Parts A and B. TRICARE always pays first for a person who is eligible for Medicaid as well as TRICARE benefits.

Expenses for medical care related to job-connected illness or injury that are paid by the workers' compensation program, or can be paid by such a program, are not covered by TRICARE. Responsibility for the balance is assumed by TRICARE only if benefits were

TABLE 2-21

TFL Costs for 2006 Health Care Coverage

Inpatient Services (Medicare Part A): Outside a Military Treatment Facility (MTF)			
	Medicare[1] Pays	**TRICARE[2] Pays**	**Member Pays**
Inpatient Hospitalization (Medical, Surgical, and Hospital-Based Psychiatric Care)	Days 1–60: 100% (after $952 deductible[4])	$952 deductible[4]	Nothing for services payable by Medicare and TRICARE
A new benefit period [6] must begin before Medicare will cover additional days.	Days 61–90: All but $238/day[4]	$238/day[4]	Nothing for services payable by Medicare and TRICARE
	Days 91–150[5]: All but $476/day[4]	$476/day[4]	Nothing for services payable by Medicare and TRICARE
	Days 151+: Not covered	The DRG-allowed[7] amount minus the patient's copayment/cost share	$250/day or 25% of institutional charges, whichever is less plus 20% of professional charges if care is delivered in a TRICARE network hospital[8]; $535/day[9] or 25% of billed charges for institutional services, whichever is less, plus 25% of allowable for professional charges if care is delivered in a non-network hospital
Inpatient Mental Health (Psychiatric Facility)[10]	Days 1–60: 100% (after $952 deductible[4]	$952 deductible[4]	Nothing for services payable by Medicare and TRICARE
Inpatient mental health care requires preauthorization. Care in excess of 30 days requires a waiver for secondary TRICARE coverage. If authorized, TRICARE pays cost share or deductible.	Days 61–90: All but $238/day[4]	$238/day[4]	Nothing for services payable by Medicare and TRICARE
	Days 91–150: All but $476/day[4]	$476/day[4]	Nothing for services payable by Medicare and TRICARE
A new benefit period[6] must begin before Medicare will cover additional days.	Days[11] 151+: Not covered	80% if network hospital[8]; 75% if non-network hospital	20% of institutional charges plus 20% of professional charges for services received in a network hospital[8]; For services received in a non-network hospital see TRICARE Reimbursement Manual Chap 2, Addendum A, page 10, for beneficiary payment information (see www.tricare.osd.mil/tricaremanuals/)

TABLE 2-21

TFL Costs for 2006 Health Care Coverage (*continued*)

Inpatient Services (Medicare Part A): Outside a Military Treatment Facility (MTF)			
	Medicare[1] Pays	**TRICARE[2] Pays**	**Member Pays**
Skilled Nursing Facility: *A beneficiary must be admitted to an inpatient hospital during a benefit period[6] for at least 3 days prior to receiving Medicare authorization to receive this benefit*	Days 1–20: 100%	Remaining beneficiary liability 5%	Nothing for services payable by Medicare and TRICARE
	Days 21–100: All but $119/day[4]	$119/day[4]	Nothing for services payable by Medicare and TRICARE
	Days 101+: Not covered	80% if network hospital[8]; 75% if non-network hospital	20% of TRICARE allowable charges if care delivered in a TRICARE network hospital; 25% of TRICARE allowable charges if care delivered in a non-network hospital
Hospice Care	95%	Remaining beneficiary liability 5%	Nothing for services payable by Medicare and TRICARE

Outpatient Services (Medicare Part B): Outside a Military Treatment Facility (MTF)			
	Medicare[1] Pays	**TRICARE[2] Pays**	**Member Pays**
Doctors Visits (Outside an MTF)	80%	20%	Nothing for services payable by Medicare and TRICARE
Emergency Room Visit	80%	20%	Nothing for services payable by Medicare and TRICARE
Mental Health Visit	50%	50%	Nothing for services payable by Medicare and TRICARE
Laboratory Services	100%	Remaining beneficiary liability (if any)	Nothing for services payable by Medicare and TRICARE
Radiology (X-rays)	80%	20%	Nothing for services payable by Medicare and TRICARE
Home Health Care	100% for approved services	Remaining beneficiary liability (if any)	Nothing for services payable by Medicare and TRICARE
Durable Medical Equipment	80%	20%	Nothing for services payable by Medicare and TRICARE
Outpatient Hospital Services	80%	20%	Nothing for services payable by Medicare and TRICARE

TABLE 2-21

TFL Costs for 2006 Health Care Coverage (*continued*)

Outpatient Services (Medicare Part B): Outside a Military Treatment Facility (MTF)			
	Medicare[1] Pays	**TRICARE[2] Pays**	**Member Pays**
Blood	Nothing for the first three pints; 80% for additional pints (beyond the first three)	100% of the cost of the three pints of blood; 20% first for additional pints (beyond the first three)	Nothing for services payable by Medicare and TRICARE
Chiropractic Services	80%	Not covered	20% Medicare cost-share

[1] All percentages paid by Medicare are for the Medicare approved amounts for services received from Medicare providers who accept Medicare assignment.

[2] TRICARE will pay the difference between Medicare's paid amount and Medicare's limiting charge (up to 115% of the allowable amount) for non-participating provider claims.

[3] TRICARE has a $3000 per fiscal year (October 1-September 30) catastrophic cap (a member's maximum out-of-pocket expense).

[4] Medicare amount that will change every calendar year.

[5] Lifetime Reserve days (91–150) are 60 additional days Medicare will pay for when a member is in a hospital for more than 90 consecutive days during a benefit period minus the $476/day coinsurance (in 2006). These 60 reserve days may only be used once.

[6] A benefit period begins when a beneficiary is admitted to a hospital or skilled nursing facility and continues until the beneficiary has been out the facility for at least 60 consecutive days.

[7] A reimbursement system using diagnosis-related groups (DRGs) that assigns payment levels to each DRG based on the average cost of treating all patients in a given DRG.

[8] A network hospital is one that has a contractual agreement with TRICARE.

[9] DRG per diem rate that will change every fiscal year.

[10] 190 days in a lifetime are available within a psychiatric facility.

[11] Medicare ceases to pay after day 150, unless a new benefit period begins. TRICARE will pay 75% or 80% and the beneficiary pays up to 25% depending on whether a network or non-network facility is used.

[12] The original Medicare plan does not cover health care when a member travels outside the United States and its territories, except for some emergency situations in Mexico and Canada.

exhausted under the workers' compensation program. Any amounts paid by TRICARE arising from an automobile accident when these same amounts are also payable, in whole or in part, under an automobile insurance policy may be subject to recovery under the Federal Claims Collections Act. Commercial insurance also supersedes TRICARE as primary, except under certain coverage conditions. Supplemental insurance policies that pay for coinsurance, deductibles, and cost shares are secondary; TRICARE remains the primary payer.

TRICARE as Secondary Payer

Beneficiaries may not waive benefits due from their primary insurance carrier. A claim must be filed first with the primary carrier. Failure to do so will result in denial of the claim by TRICARE. Limitations as a secondary payer include:

- Benefits will not be provided for services provided prior to coverage
- Benefits will not be paid at a higher rate by a secondary payer than would be paid in the absence of other coverage
- Benefits will not exceed patient liability
- Services must be covered

CHAMPVA

CHAMPVA, the Civilian Health and Medical Program of the Department of Veterans Affairs, was created in 1973 to provide a health benefits program for dependents of veterans with total, permanent, service-connected disabilities and for the surviving dependents of veterans who died as a result of service-connected conditions or who at the time of death were rated permanently and totally disabled from a service-connected condition. Members who receive TRICARE beneficiaries do not qualify for coverage under CHAMPVA. A CHAMPVA policy manual can be accessed at www.va.gov/hac/forbeneficiaries/champva/policymanual/cvapmchap1/1cltoc.asp.

A dependent's eligibility for benefits is determined by the VA. The prospective recipient must go to the nearest VA hospital or clinic to be reviewed for eligibility in the program. Persons eligible for CHAMPVA benefits are issued a CHAMPVA identification card by the VA. See Figure 2-12 for a sample identification card.

CHAMPVA eligibility is affected by a change in status such as marriage or divorce. Becoming eligible for Medicare or TRICARE also impacts coverage, as does age and scholastic status or marriage of children. Participants younger than age 65 who are eligible for Medicare must be enrolled in Part A and Part B to be eligible for CHAMPVA. Those older than 65 must meet the following conditions in order for benefits to be extended past age 65:

- If the beneficiary was 65 or older prior to June 5, 2001, and was otherwise eligible for CHAMPVA, and was entitled to Medicare Part A coverage, then the beneficiary will be eligible for CHAMPVA without having to have Medicare Part B coverage.
- If the beneficiary turned 65 on/or before June 5, 2001, and has Medicare Part A and Part B, the beneficiary must keep both Part A and Part B to be eligible.
- If the beneficiary turned 65 on or after June 5, 2001, the beneficiary must be enrolled in Medicare Parts A and Parts B to be eligible.
- The beneficiary is not required to enroll in Medicare Part D in order to become or remain CHAMPVA eligible.

The benefits under the CHAMPVA program are similar to the benefits received by dependents of retired or deceased military personnel in the TRICARE program. CHAMPVA has an outpatient deductible of $50 per person up to $100 per family per calendar year and a cost share of 25%. The cost share of 25% should be collected from the patient except when the patient has other health insurance.

CHAMPVA covers most health care services and supplies that are medically necessary. Some general exclusions to coverage include:

- Services determined to be medically unnecessary
- Services or supplies obtained as part of a grant, study, or research program

FIGURE 2-12
CHAMPVA Identification Card

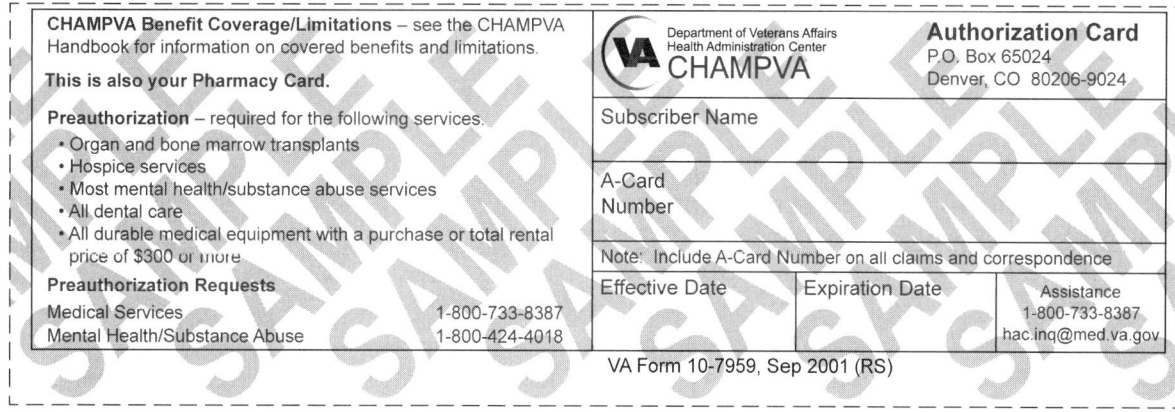

- Services or supplies related to experimental, investigational, or unproven procedures or treatment regimens or not provided in accordance with accepted professional medical standards
- Care for persons eligible for benefits under other government programs, except Medicaid and State Victims of Crime Compensation programs
- Care for which the beneficiary is not obligated to pay, such as services obtained at a health fair
- Care provided outside the scope of the provider's license or certification
- Service provided by a member of the immediate family of the beneficiary or person living in the household of the beneficiary
- Services rendered by providers suspended or sanctioned by any federal agency

Preauthorization is required for the following:

- Dental care
- Durable medical equipment with a purchase price or total rental price of $300 or more
- Hospice services
- Mental health or substance abuse services
- Transplants

CHAMPVA is always the secondary payer when other coverage is present, except when the other coverage is Medicaid, State Victims of Crime Compensation Programs, or supplemental CHAMPVA policies.

Beneficiaries must periodically complete a health insurance certification questionnaire. The participant is responsible for reporting changes in coverage status. Changes may be reported by phone; cancellation or termination of coverage must be in writing.

The CMS-1500 form should be used when submitting claims for CHAMPVA patients. A copy of any other EOB, if applicable, must be included with the submittal. The CHAMPVA claim form should not be used unless the provider is filing for the patient and payment is to go to the patient. Claims must be submitted within one year of the date of service. Reconsideration of claims and appeals must be submitted within one year from the date on the EOB.

CHAMPVA is administered through the VA's Health Administration Center. Although information may be available through other VA facilities, only the Health Administration Center is authorized to process CHAMPVA applications, determine eligibility, authorize benefits, and process claims. All inquires on CHAMPVA-related matters should be address to the center.

All new health care claims should be submitted to the following:

VA Health Administration Center
CHAMPVA Claims
PO Box 65024
Denver, CO 80206–9024

General information requests as well as requests for information on payment or reprocessing of a denied claim should be sent to the following:

VA Health Administration Center
CHAMPVA Claims
PO Box 65023
Denver CO 80206–9023
Phone: 800 733–8387 (Monday-Friday, 8:05 am-7:30 pm eastern time)
Fax: 303 331–7804
E-mail: hac.inq@va.gov

ALTERNATE HEALTH PLANS

In addition to traditional plans, several alternative systems or managed care plans have become prominent over the past few decades. These include HMOs, PPOs, independent practice associations (IPAs), physician/hospital organizations (PHOs), POSs, and self-funded plans. Most commercial and Blue Cross Blue Shield programs offer one or more of these alternatives.

Health Maintenance Organizations

HMOs provide comprehensive health care that ranges from physician services to hospitalization. Patients enrolled in an HMO pay a fixed amount per month or other payment period. Enrollment entitles patients to the full range of services offered by the HMO during the period of enrollment. An HMO can be viewed as a combination health insurer and health care delivery system. Many commercial and Blue Cross Blue Shield plans offer HMOs as an alternative to standard service contracts or indemnity plans.

Because HMOs are paid a fixed amount regardless of services provided, they generally attempt to reduce and control the costs of delivering health care through utilization review, ambulatory surgery vs inpatient surgery, second opinions, and preventive medicine.

Enrollees are instructed to use only "panel" or "participating" physicians, hospitals, ancillary centers, etc, that have contracted with the HMO. The patient may face financial responsibility for out-of-network charges. HMOs also save administrative costs by subcontracting key functions such as benefit communications management, physician enrollment and credentialing, claims processing, utilization review, and remittance management.

In an HMO program, the patient is usually responsible for a copayment, ranging from $10 to $50, for visits to a physician. The patient may seek care from a selected group of physicians. A patient who elects to see a physician who does not participate in the HMO network may forfeit all benefits for those services. If the patient is not admitted to an HMO hospital, the patient may not receive any benefits relating to the hospital bill and the physician will not receive payment even though he or she is an HMO provider of service. However, in an emergency situation, the patient will usually have 24 hours to transfer to an HMO facility unless his or her condition is life-threatening.

All four HMO types or models (described in the following paragraphs) share the common characteristic of operations, capitated reimbursement, and control over health care delivery and financing. The major differences between each model involve the relationship between the HMO and its participating physicians.

Staff Model
Staff model HMOs employ physicians who are typically paid a fixed salary to provide services to HMO beneficiaries. Staff models are considered "closed-panel" HMOs because physicians must be members of the HMO. Staff models have greater control over the practice patterns of physicians and may limit physician autonomy. As a result, staff model HMOs can more easily manage and control the use of health services.

Group Model
Group model HMOs primarily contract with larger, multispecialty physician groups; therefore, the physicians are employees of the group practice, not the HMO. Group models are also considered "closed panel" because physicians must be members of the group to gain access to HMO patients. Although the group model physician has more autonomy than a staff model physician, he or she must still adhere to internal utilization review and service cost goals that are set by the group practice to meet practicewide goals.

There are two categories of group model HMOs: captive and independent. They are differentiated by the amount of non-HMO work provided by a contracted multispecialty practice.

Captive Group Model In a captive group HMO, the physician group exists solely to provide services to the HMO. The group does not service non-HMO clients. In most cases, this HMO model was formed to service its members, recruit physicians, and provide administrative support services to the physicians. The most prominent example of a captive group model is the Kaiser Foundation Health Plan, in which the permanent medical groups provide all physician services to Kaiser's members.

Independent Group Model In an independent group HMO, the HMO contracts with an existing multispecialty group practice. In many cases, the group practice is the sponsor or owner of the HMO. An example of an independent group HMO is the Geisinger Health Plan of Danville, Pennsylvania, which is serviced by the Geisinger Clinics. As their name suggests, independent groups often service other contracts and patients in addition to the HMO members.

Individual Practice Association Model

Individual practice associations (IPAs) contract with independent physician groups for all specialties. The IPA is a separate legal entity that physicians are members of, but each practice retains its own office, staff, and physician identity. Each practice also assumes risks associated with patient care.

IPA HMOs recruit physicians from all specialties so they can offer a complete package of services while minimizing the need to refer patients to out-of-plan physicians. Although there may be more physician autonomy under an IPA, control of utilization and cost is much more difficult to manage. In addition, the IPA attempts to transfer financial risk back to the member practice, not the plan.

Physician compensation arrangements vary from IPA to IPA, yet the HMO usually pays a fixed amount per subscriber (a capitation fee) to the IPA. The IPA in turn pays its member physicians, usually on a FFS basis, as services are rendered to the HMO patients. Some plans may pay primary care physicians under a capitated arrangement and pay specialists on a discounted FFS arrangement, or vice versa. Under subcapitation, the specialist is paid on a capitated basis. Because specialists account for a majority of costs, some programs have reversed capitation, ie, the specialist is capitated and the primary care physician receives a fee for service. The incentive is for the primary care physician to do more. This arrangement illustrates how HMOs have become more aggressive and creative in their compensation arrangements so as to recruit and maintain a high quality of care and access to physicians of all specialties.

IPA physicians are paid from the pool of capitation funds. This provides them with an incentive to contain costs associated with providing care—if funds are exhausted, IPA physicians may not get paid for all the services they provide. On the other hand, if physicians provide services totaling less than the fund pool, IPA physicians may profit.

Network or Direct-Contract Model

Network or direct-contract HMOs contract with physicians at all levels and usually consist of each model type. The models contract directly with physicians to provide services to their members.

Physician reimbursement may vary between capitation and discounted fees for service, although capitation is more common. Direct-contract models retain more of the financial risk than IPA models do, as well as being more involved in managing utilization and cost controls.

According to a study by the Managed Care Information Center, Manasquan, New Jersey, HMOs are more likely to be organized as IPAs than any other model type. The study shows that 55.5% of HMOs are IPAs, 18.5% are mixed model HMOs, 12.3% are network model HMOs, 9.0% are group model HMOs, and 1.1% are staff model HMOs. The remaining HMOs are mixed models.

Physician Participation and General HMO Guidelines

A physician must apply and sign a contract to become a participating provider with any HMO group. The contract defines the patient group to be covered, the physician's scope of services, and the method of reimbursement (either discounted FFS or capitation). The provider must file insurance claim forms; collect any deductible, coinsurance, or copayment; and write off the difference of the actual billed charge and the allowed amount.

Figure 2-13 shows PPO and HMO enrollment from 1991 through 2005. The HMO plans offering fewer restrictions garner the highest market share as seen in Table 2-22, which shows the enrollment by type of HMO plan. Figure 2-14 shows the Medicare HMO enrollment growth rate data from 1996 through 2004.

Preferred Provider Organizations

A PPO is generally defined as a group of health care providers, including physicians, hospitals, and allied institutions, that agree to provide services to a specific pool of patients. PPOs are offered by insurance carriers, groups of physicians, and groups of hospitals.

Generally, there are financial incentives offered to plan holders to use physicians in the plan's PPO network. Participants who use in-network providers will benefit from lower deductibles, coinsurance, copayments, or other incentives. The physicians, in turn, benefit from access to new patients, increased patient utilization, and prompt FFS payment from the insurer. Under PPOs, the physician's reimbursement is based on a discounted fee schedule and payment is based on traditional FFS billing.

FIGURE 2-13

PPO and HMO Enrollment

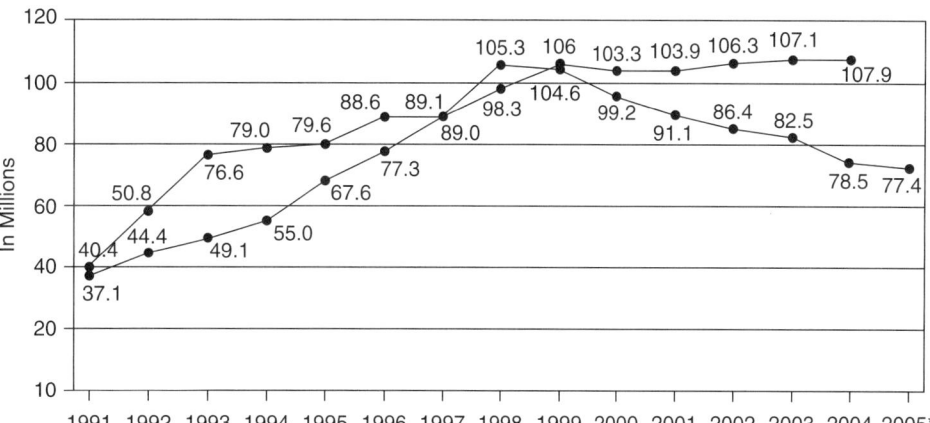

Data Source: Verispan LLC ©2006.

PPO enrollment numbers reflect eligible employees. HMO enrollment numbers represent actual members.

*PPO numbers for 2005 were unavailable at the time of publication.

TABLE 2-22

Enrollment by Type of HMO Plan

Plan Type	12/31/96	12/31/97	12/31/98	12/31/99	12/31/00	12/31/01	12/31/02	12/31/03	12/31/04	12/31/05
IPA	45,280,900	50,242,432	53,811,551	57,536,924	53,268	51,367	45,588	40,814	40,650	39,189
Network	8,361,900	15,233,840	21,539,232	23,753,198	24,027	19,949	21,044	22,180	21,113	21,038
Group	19,507,700	20,524,921	20,853,681	21,397,088	20,259	17,942	17,581	17,568	14,957	15,321
Staff	4,188,700	3,029,340	2,104,946	1,882,022	1,730	1,819	2,243	1,942	1,861	1,671

Data Source: Verispan LLC ©2006.

FIGURE 2-14

Medicare HMO Enrollment Growth Rate

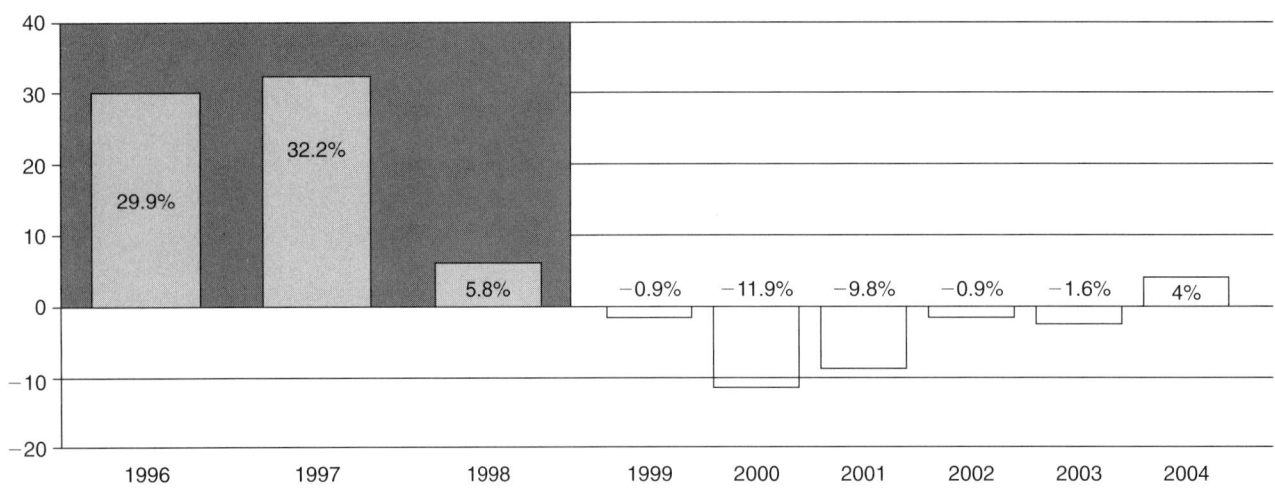

Data Source: Verispan LLC ©2006.

FIGURE 2-15

PPO Eligible Employees

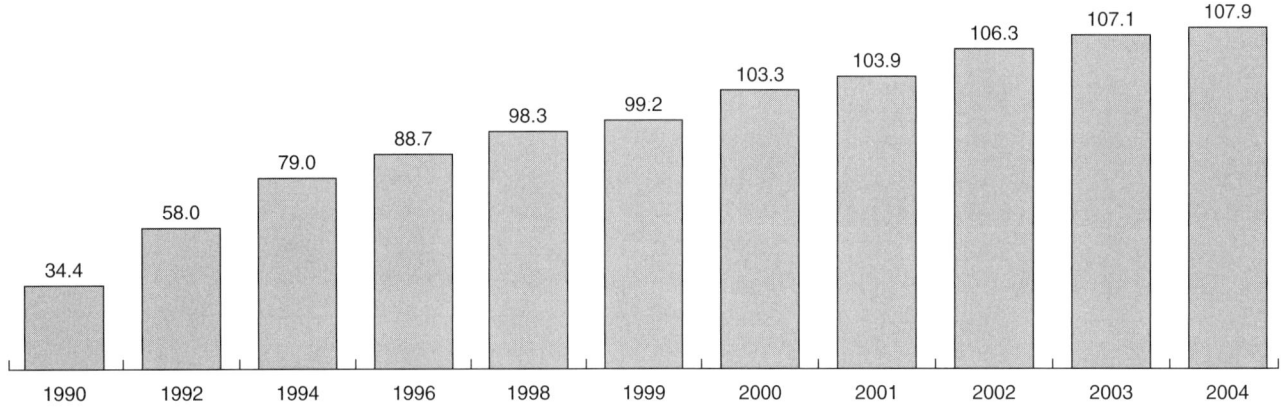

Data Source: Verispan LLC ©2006.
Verispan's Preferred Provider Organization Database—2006 Edition
Excludes employees eligible for worker's compensation and speciality plans.

PPOs derive many cost-saving benefits from strict payment policies and discounted fee schedules. They also use some of the same techniques that HMOs use to minimize utilization of services. Utilization review, second options, and ambulatory surgery are often used to reduce costs. Figure 2-15 depicts the significant increase in the PPO eligible employees from 1990 through 2005. Figure 2-16 shows the breakout of all PPOs by type as of 2005. Full service PPOs offer general medical/surgical, workers' compensation, and at least two specialty services.

PPO enrollment will continue to grow and hybrid PPO plans will continue to evolve in the coming years. Consequently, practices must review each contract presented to them and be aware of the plan's discounted fee schedule, contract requirements, leasing of discount payer lists, and potential risk incurred by the physician. Because each PPO plan varies in terms of coverage and benefit packages, office staff must be aware of all PPO plans the practice participates in and the policies and procedures that must be followed for successful claim submission. When managing PPO discounts, the provider must be wary

FIGURE 2-16

Breakout of All PPOs by Type, 1999 v 2006

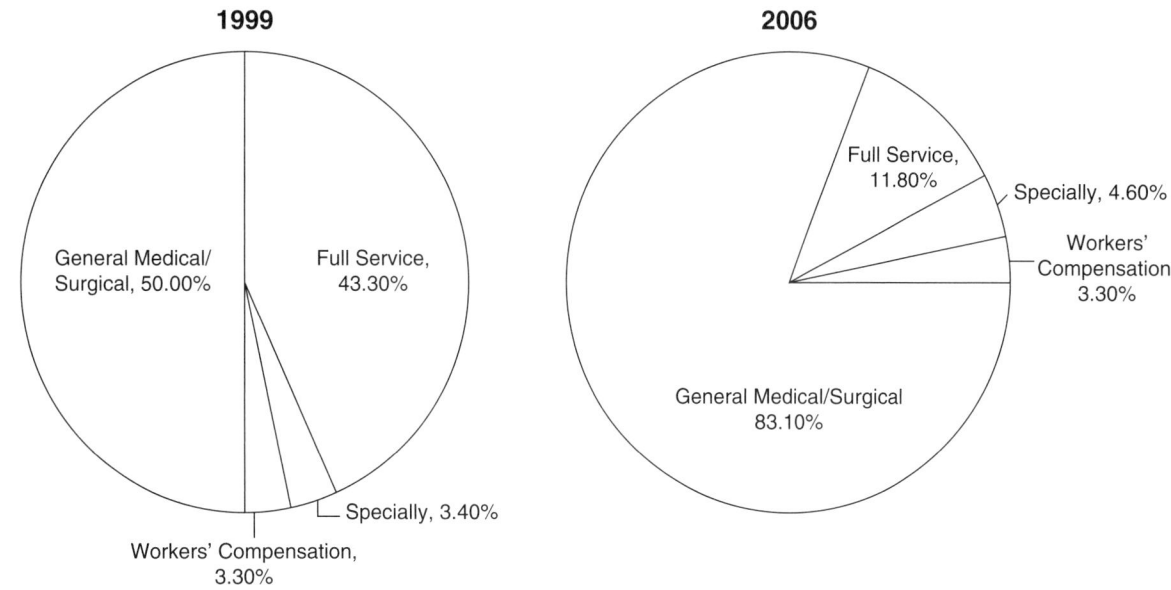

Data Source: Verispan LLC ©2006.

of the "silent PPO discount." This "discount" is a prevalent problem that can cost practices tens of thousands of dollars in due reimbursement that is improperly written-off. Some insurance plans with which the practice does not have a signed contract will indicate on their EOB that they are taking their "contractual PPO discount." Although the plan may be part of a PPO that the practice has a signed contact with, the plan is not a part of the PPO network. Apparently, traditional insurance plans buy fee schedules and physician listings of contracted providers from other insurance plans that have PPO contracts. The plans use the data to reduce their payments and convince practice staff that they must accept the "contractual PPO discount." Awareness of network health plans; PPO fee schedule amounts; and, if leasing discount, to whom is critical for eliminating this problem.

Point-of-Service Plans

Several commercial insurance plans have developed a new form of managed care that combines aspects of both PPOs and HMOs. It is called a point-of-service (POS) plan. Beneficiaries may select physicians and other health care providers who are members of the POS or they may select providers outside of the plan. Financial incentives, usually in the form of lower fees, are offered to subscribers to encourage them to use member providers.

Self-funded Plans: Employee Retirement Income Security Act of 1974

An increasing number of large corporations are dropping traditional health insurance from commercial carriers and insuring their employees through self-funded plans. To institute a self-funded plan, the corporation usually obtains an excess liability rider (re-insurance, stop loss coverage) and then establishes a reserve fund to pay employee medical bills.

A third-party administrator that establishes a PPO network or similar type of arrangement with physicians, hospitals, and other health care providers frequently manages self-funded plans. Incentives are provided to employees who seek care from providers who have contracted with the corporation through the third-party administrator to provide services at a discounted rate. These incentives may be in the form of first dollar coverage or bonuses to employees who do not use health care services unnecessarily. First dollar coverage refers to coverage that pays the entire amount covered without first applying a deductible.

Provider-Sponsored Organizations

A PSO is a MedicareAdvantage organization that is a public or private entity and is organized and operated by a health care provider or group of affiliated health care providers. Legislation in the Balanced Budget Act of 1997 legally defines a PSO as a public or private entity of affiliated providers who provide a substantial portion (60% for rural PSOs, 70% for urban PSOs) of the care. These providers take a substantial portion of the risk to do this on the budget (capitation) the government provides for Medicare patients. The reserve needed by a PSO is less than that required for an HMO. Any shortfall in reserves is usually covered by the state. PSOs can be formed by many types of entities, such as physician-hospital organizations (PHOs), which are an affiliate organization formed by physicians and hospitals that serve as collaborative providers.

WORKERS' COMPENSATION AND DISABILITY

Workers' compensation programs offer benefits to workers who are injured on the job or contract a job-related illness. Claimants are entitled to benefit payments as well as coverage of their medical cost for related services.

Workers' compensation is a state-required insurance plan in which employers make premium payments to a general fund. Each state may have different requirements that govern who is allowed to provide insurance. The level of benefits provided and types of injuries that are compensable also vary by state. Premiums depend on the type of work performed, the length of time the insurance has been in place, and the number of claims. The amount of insurance an employer must carry depends on the risk of employee job-related injuries. Laws regulating workers' compensation programs vary from state to state.

Not all employees are covered by state-regulated programs. The federal government administers the Federal Employees Compensation Act but has no role in the program. The Longshore and Harbor Workers' Compensation Act covers longshore, harbor, and other maritime workers. Railroad workers involved in interstate commerce as well as US Merchant Marines are covered by health insurance and disability benefits instead of workers' compensation. The Federal Black Lung Program covers coal miners receiving benefits for black lung disease. Other occupations carry their own workers' compensation programs.

An employee who is injured on the job either must go to a designated physician or select his or her own physician for an independent medical exam. The physician conducting the independent medical exam is paid a predefined amount. When treating a patient covered under a workers' compensation program, the provider should obtain a statement of injury form from the patient's employer. In addition, some programs require completion of special medical report forms for claims.

A commercial insurance carrier chosen by the employer may handle workers' compensation cases when allowed. PPO networks may charge commercial rates for workers' compensation cases. Publicly funded state programs run others. Before admission, the carrier should be notified and verification of coverage obtained. The patient should have a written authorization form (possibly in the form of an incident report) signed by a representative of the employer or the carrier should request documentation from the employer. The carrier must determine whether the employer recognizes responsibility for the injury. If so, a letter stating this obligation should be requested.

If the carrier denies a worker's compensation case, the patient has the right to appeal the denial to the state workers' compensation board and request a hearing. Provided the patient has an appeal pending, neither the hospital nor the physician can pursue payment from the patient, even though the claim may have been previously denied. Case status can be determined either through the carrier or through the state board of workers' compensation. Additional forms and filing requirements may vary from state to state.

The level of compensation and benefits provided will vary depending on the term of the employee's disability. Some injuries do not result in time lost from work that exceeds the waiting period for cash benefits. In these situations, the patient returns to work within a few days and only medical benefits are allowed.

In other cases, the patient's injury results in time lost from work on a temporary basis, ie, a temporary total disability. The employee is entitled to medical benefits as well as cash benefits for time lost from work. The employee will eventually return to work upon release by the physician. The employee may also return to work in a reduced capacity with the permission of the physician until full recovery is obtained.

An employee may be permanently disabled but not totally disabled. This is called permanent partial disability. An example is an injury that is severe enough to impair an employee's function and cause a permanent disability but does not totally disable the employee. Medical benefits are paid until the employee obtains maximum improvement, ie, to the point that further medical care is not beneficial. The employee may also receive a disability payment based on the percentage of disability that has occurred.

Permanent total disability occurs when an injury is so severe that the employee cannot return to work. In this case, the employee is entitled to medial coverage and cash benefits indefinitely.

SUMMARY

Chapter 2 covers types of insurance and third-party payers. A large quantity of important information is presented in this chapter. The following programs are discussed and reviewed in detail: Medicare, Medicaid, TRICARE, CHAMPVA, and Blue Cross Blue Shield. Additionally, commercial carriers and managed care plans are discussed. Current statistics and trends are provided on several aspects of these programs.

It is important for practice and other health care reimbursement staff to have a solid understanding of the information presented in this chapter. Additional information and guidance relating to Medicare secondary payer (MSP) can be found in Appendix D in the back of the book.

chapter 3

Electronic Claims Processing

OBJECTIVES

- Understand the basics of electronic data interchange (EDI).
- Know the advantages of using of EDI.
- Understand the shortcomings of EDI.
- Understand privacy concerns regarding electronic transmission of confidential medical information.
- Educate the claims staff on patient privacy issues.

Medicare is the industry leader in electronic claims processing. Medicare's processing rate for electronic media claims (EMCs), for May 2006 was approximately 99.4% for Part A and Part B claims for Fiscal Intermediaries and approximately 92.5% for Part B Medicare Carriers. In May 2006, Medicare processed a total of 16,509,594 Part A and Part B claims for Fiscal Intermediaries, of which 16,412,504 were processed electronically. Medicare processed 88,666,095 Part B claims for Medicare Carriers in May 2006, of which 80,132,527 were processed electronically. In 2005, Medicare received and processed 179,096,500 Part A and Part B claims for Fiscal Intermediaries, of which 177,062,821, or 98.9%, were processed electronically. It received and processed 983,967,962 Part B claims for Medicare Carriers, of which 89.1%, or 876,527,057, claims were processed electronically.

Historically, companies, including medical practices, have relied on paper as the medium for conducting their business. Records are maintained on paper and then mailed between companies to exchange information. Although the computer has become a staple in nearly all medical offices, the use of mail to transmit information on paper continues. Claims processors enter data into a form and mail the form to a third party; that third party then rekeys or scans the data into another business application. Inherent in this process are delays, excessive paperwork, and the potential for errors as information is transcribed or scanned. Beginning in the 1970s, certain industries such as banking moved to electronic data interchange (EDI). In the medical community, paper records are now giving way to electronic medical records, and the trend is expected to continue. The excerpt beginning on page 117 shows a survey from the America's Health Insurance Plans' Center for Policy and Research validating this trend toward electronic claims processing. Most claims are now submitted electronically. The survey displays data showing the dramatic increase in electronic claim processing over the past decade. It also shows the cost savings that can be realized by filing claims electronically rather than on paper.

Medical billing software helps providers manage financial information and reduces errors on claims submitted to Medicare and most other third-party payers. Medical billing software can be stand alone or integrated with other aspects of a medical practice such as patient medical records. It can be linked to the laboratory and other ancillary service areas and can interface with other software used to analyze claims for completeness, accuracy, and probability of being edited by Medicare.

Because EDI can simplify billing to all payers and can improve the cash-flow benefits to a practice, it is recommended that staff learn and submit EDI claims. This chapter will prepare a practice to do just that.

ADVANTAGES OF ELECTRONIC DATA INTERCHANGE

Switching to an EDI claims processing system has many advantages. EDI claims are processed much more quickly than paper claims. And EDI can be practically error free, which, in turn, increases claim acceptance rates. As an example, a private insurance carrier may require the use of procedure code 36415 when billing for venipuncture. Medicare requires G0001 for the same service. The software automatically selects the right code for each insurer. In addition, the costs for EDI are far less than for paper claims, with savings recognized both in labor costs and materials, including postage. Billing secondary payers is also faster, because a practice learns the amount that the primary payer will cover much more quickly. The top nine advantages of Medicare EDI, as noted by the Centers for Medicare & Medicaid Services (CMS), are listed in Table 3-1.

The following key questions should be addressed when exploring an EDI system:

- Is the system compliant with the Health Insurance Portability and Accountability Act (HIPAA) of 1996?
- Which fields can be changed and by whom?
- How quickly are Medicare and other payer requirements and changes reflected in the EDI system?
- Are credit balances resolved in compliance with Medicare requirements and state laws?
- What are the limitations of the EDI system, and is there a manual process to fill the gaps?
- Are EDI system reports routinely reviewed by management, with documentation of corrective actions?

The following document displays a survey prepared by the Center for Policy and Research of America's Health Insurance Plans. This survey shows that electronic claim submission has increased significantly over the past several years. The survey was based on aggregated data from nearly 25 million claims.

TABLE 3-1

Advantages of Using Medicare EDI

1. **Faster payment** on electronic claims. Electronic claims submitted in a standard format adopted for national use under HIPAA can be paid **after expiration of a 13-day waiting period, ie, as early as the 14th day after the date of receipt** while paper claims and electronic claims submitted in a non-HIPAA format can not be paid earlier than the 27th day after the date of receipt.
2. **Electronic** transactions are **cost effective**, and reduce the opportunity for error.
3. **Electronic claims** have lower administrative, postage, and handling costs than paper claims.
4. **On-line** acknowledgement of receipt of electronic claims.
5. **Standardized** formats reduce administrative costs since one format will meet billing requirements for all US health care payers under HIPAA, not only Medicare.
6. **Standardized** electronic claims submission and COB exchange and remittance receipt **reduce** system **costs**.
7. **Electronic** remittances are **sent** to a **provider-preferred** location.
8. **Claim** status and eligibility information in **24 hours** or less.
9. **Electronic funds transfer (EFT)** can have accounts receivable in provider's bank, drawing interest, in **two working days** after payment. Paper checks can take as long as **one week** to process.

Source: Reprinted from the Centers for Medicare & Medicaid Services. 2004 (September 16). Available at: *www.cms.hhs.gov/providers/edi/edi2.asp*. Accessed November 29, 2005.

An Updated Survey of Health Care Claims Receipt and Processing Times, May 2006

Electronic submission of health insurance claims more than tripled in the last decade, reducing administrative costs and allowing 98 percent of claims to be processed within 30 days of receipt.

Summary

Consumers, health care providers and insurers have a common interest in the prompt and accurate payment of medical claims. In the winter of 2005–2006, America's Health Insurance Plans (AHIP) conducted a survey of its members to examine the issue of claims processing and turnaround times for claim payments. The study is a follow-up to a survey done in 2002. A comparison of findings from the 2002 and 2006 studies shows that claims processing times have improved significantly in the past four years.

Here are some highlights of the latest survey:

- The percentage of claims received electronically was 75 percent in 2006, up from 44 percent in 2002.
- There is often a significant time lag before health insurance plans receive claims from health care providers. In 2006, 29 percent of claims were received from health care providers more than 30 days after the date of patient service, and 15 percent of claims were received from providers more than 60 days after the service was provided.
- According to the 2006 survey, health insurance plans processed 98 percent of "clean" claims within 30 days, up from 94 percent in 2002 (see Figure 1). Processing time is the number of days from when a claim is received until the claim is paid, denied, or "pended" for further information. ("Clean" claims are those for which no additional information is needed.) Fourteen percent of claims in the survey were "pended" or delayed, usually because of incomplete or incorrect information. On average, pended claims take an additional 9 days to process, while more information is being gathered from the provider.
- Approximately two-thirds (68 percent) of all claims are now adjudicated automatically; that is, processed without manual intervention. Among electronic claims, 71 percent were adjudicated automatically in 2006, up from 49 percent in 2002. Forty-four percent of paper claims were adjudicated automatically in 2006, up from 27 percent in 2002.

FIGURE 1

Average Time to Complete Processing After Receipt of "Clean" Claim

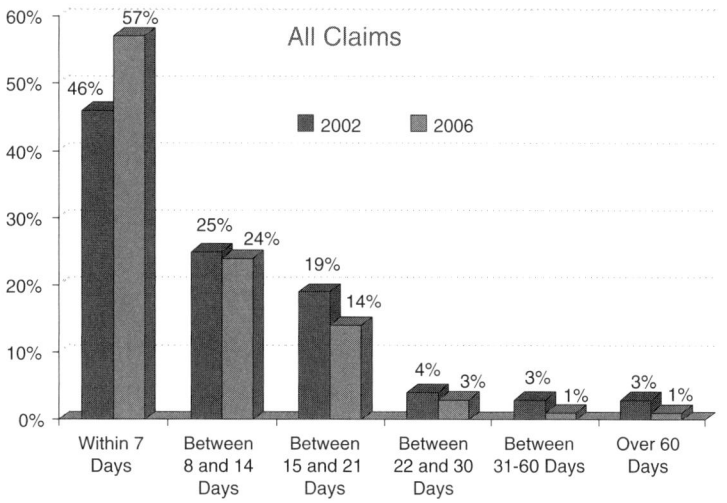

Reprinted with permission from America's Health Insurance Plans.

FIGURE 2
Types of Claims Submitted

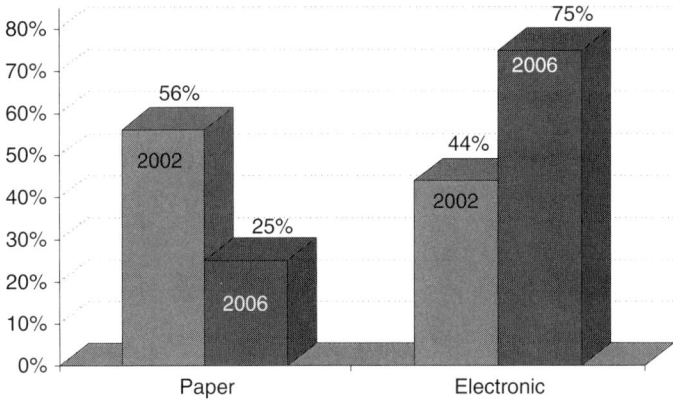

- Electronic claims are less costly to process than paper claims. The average cost of processing a clean electronic claim was 85 cents, nearly half the $1.58 cost of processing a clean paper claim. Pended claims requiring manual or other review cost $2.05 on average per claim to process.

The 2006 survey was based on aggregated data from nearly 25 million claims, processed by a total of 26 large and small health plans throughout the United States. The questionnaire and methodology were designed so that results would be comparable to prior surveys.[1]

Electronic vs. Paper Claims

Most claims are now submitted and processed electronically. From 2002 to 2006, the percent of claims filed electronically has risen substantially, from 44 percent to 75 percent (see Figure 2). At the same time, the percentage of claims submitted on paper dropped from 56 percent in 2002 to 25 percent in 2006. Surveys conducted in the 1990s found much lower percentages of claims filed electronically: 40 percent in 1999; 24 percent in 1995; and 2 percent in 1990.

Receiving and Paying Claims

With the rise of electronic claims systems, health care providers are submitting a greater share of claims within a week of the service date. In 2006, 30 percent of all claims were submitted within 7 days, compared to 19 percent in 2002 (see Figure 3).

FIGURE 3
Lag Time for Receiving Claims from Health Care Providers

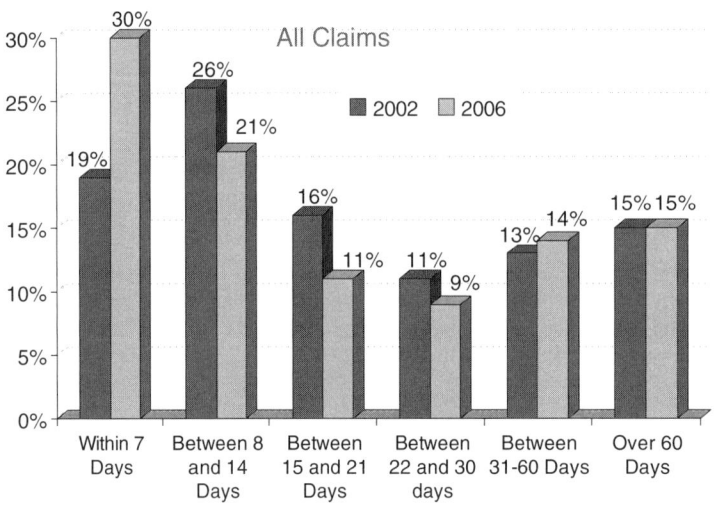

---

[1] For prior survey results, see "Results from an HIAA Survey on Claims Payment Processes," Health Insurance Association of America (March 2003). http://www.ahipresearch.org/PDFs/21_ClaimsPaymentProcessesSurveyChartbook.pdf>

Reprinted with permission from America's Health Insurance Plans.

However, a large number of claims continue to be received after long lag times. In 2006, 29 percent of claims were received more than a month after the date of patient service. This percentage remained largely unchanged from 2002 when 28 percent of claims were received after 30 days. Moreover, 15 percent of claims were received more than 60 days after the service date. Paper claims were slower to arrive than electronic claims, with 31 percent received more than 60 days after the date of service.

Ninety-seven percent of claims are paid directly to the health provider; the remaining three percent are reimbursed to the patient.

Average Claims Processing Time

Most claims are processed within 30 days of receipt. In 2006, 98 percent of all claims, paper or electronic, were processed within a month, up from almost 94 percent in 2002. Eighty-one percent of all claims were processed within two weeks of submission, compared with 71 percent in 2002. Fifty-seven percent of claims were processed within one week, an increase over the 46 percent rate in 2002.

In general, electronic claims are processed faster than paper claims. Sixty-nine percent of electronic claims are processed within 7 days; by contrast, only 29 percent of paper claims are processed within one week of receipt (see Figure 4). After two weeks, however, the disparity shrinks: about 85 percent of electronic claims are processed within 14 days, versus 69 percent of paper claims.

Automatically Adjudicated Claims

The percentage of claims that are automatically adjudicated—that is, processed without manual intervention—increased significantly for both paper and electronic claims from 2002 to 2006. Overall, 68 percent of claims were adjudicated automatically in 2006. Among electronic claims, 71 percent were adjudicated automatically in 2006, up from 49 percent in 2002. Forty-four percent of paper claims were adjudicated automatically in 2006, up from 27 percent in 2002 (see Figure 5).

Pended or Delayed Claims

If more information is needed to complete processing a claim, a claim may be "pended." For pended claims, the payment process is suspended until the information is received or verified, and the resulting "clean" claim is returned to the payment processing system. Overall, 14 percent

FIGURE 4

Average Time to Complete Processing After Claim Receipt

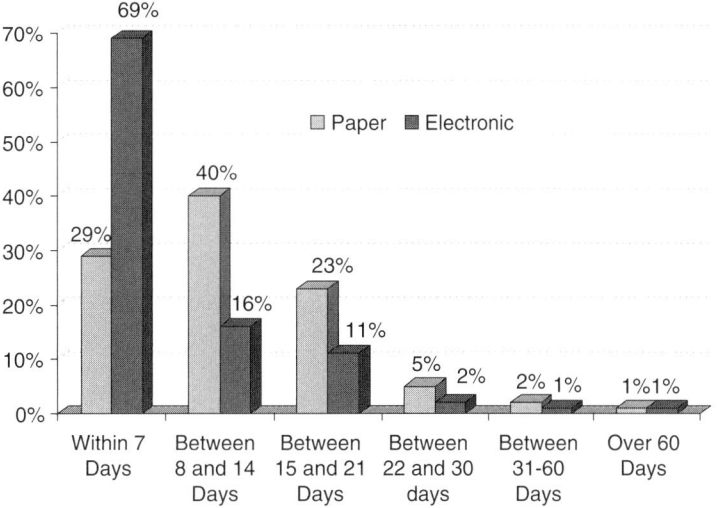

Reprinted with permission from America's Health Insurance Plans.

FIGURE 5

Percent of Claims Automatically Adjudicated, 2002 to 2006

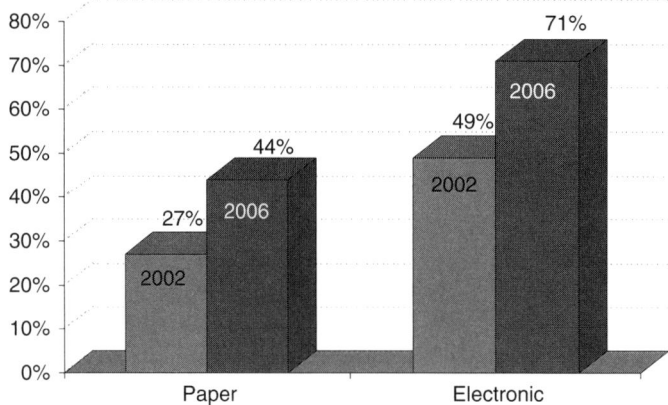

of total claims were pended in 2006. On average, pended claims require an additional 9 days to process, while more information is being sought.

Nearly half of all claims (48 percent) were pended due to the submission of duplicate claims (35 percent), lack of complete information or other information needed to justify the claim (12 percent), or invalid codes (1 percent). Twenty-four percent of pended claims were due to coverage issues, including no coverage based on date of service (8 percent), non-covered or non-network benefit or service (7 percent), coordination of benefits (5 percent), or coverage determination (4 percent). Other or miscellaneous reasons were the cause of the remaining 28 percent of pended claims.

The following breakdown shows the reasons for which claims were pended and the average number of days they were delayed in processing (see Table 1).

TABLE 1

Reasons for Pended/Delayed Claims

	Percent of Pending/Delayed Claims	**Average Number of Days Pended/Delayed**
Duplicate Claims Submitted	35%	9
Lack of Necessary Information	12%	11
No Coverage Based on Date of Service	8%	11
Non-covered/Non-network Benefit or Service	7%	5
Coordination of Benefits (COB)	5%	14
Coverage Determination	4%	8
Utilization Review	3%	10
Authorization	3%	20
Pre-existing Condition Review	1%	16
Invalid Codes Submitted	1%	25
Other*	21%	4
Total	100%	9

*Other reasons cited included: Medicare as primary payer, incorrect provider ID, no provider, ineligible provider, possible third-party liability (TPL), provider watch, member alert, multi-surgery manual pricing, and high dollar claims.

Reprinted with permission from America's Health Insurance Plans.

FIGURE 6
Average Cost to Process a Claim

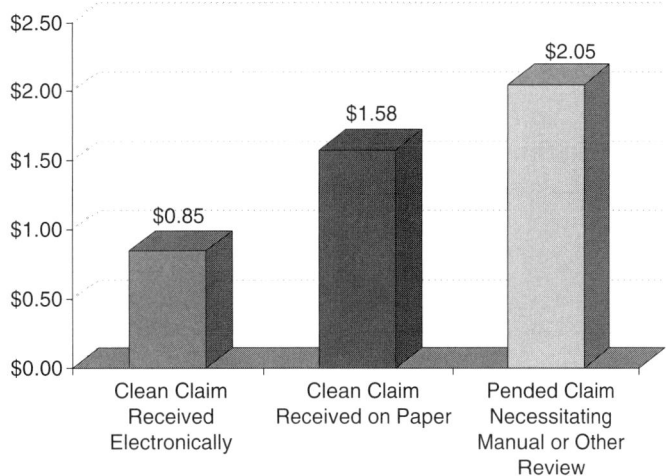

Cost of Processing Claims

Electronic claims are less costly to process than paper claims. Pended claims that necessitate manual or other review cost an average of $2.05 per claim (see Figure 6).

Acknowledgements

This census and report were compiled and written by Hannah Yoo and Karen Harner, Policy Analysts at AHIP's Center for Policy and Research. For further information, please contact Jeff Lemieux, Senior Vice President at AHIP's Center for Policy and Research, at 202.778.3200 or visit www.ahipresearch.org.

Reprinted with permission from America's Health Insurance Plans.

OPTIONS FOR PUTTING ELECTRONIC DATA INTERCHANGE INTO THE PRACTICE

A provider can incorporate an EDI system into the practice by using an EDI service bureau, a stand alone EDI system, or an integrated EDI system. Hiring an EDI service bureau is the least involved service option. Essentially, the practice hires another company to perform the EDI. A stand alone EDI system is a nonintegrated approach that can be implemented on a personal computer (PC). An integrated EDI system is a completely hands-off process that relies on computers to do all work. This approach integrates EDI with the practice's other business applications.

Many firms offer simple terminals or data entry devices specifically for submitting claims, and most practice management computer systems have capabilities for electronic claims submission. Computer vendors, Blue Cross Blue Shield, Medicare, and other organizations can provide information about setting up an EDI system.

MEDICAL BILLING SOFTWARE

Most EDI software contains claim-editing features that detect and report incomplete claims, invalid codes, and other problems that will cause a claim to be rejected. These basic edits flag or reject improper claims, eg, a prostatectomy for a female or a Pap smear for a male, and force the practice to file cleaner claims.

Software companies point out that electronic software can easily assimilate the ever-changing regulations and reimbursement policies affecting providers. Edits, essential for correct coding, are now handled by software, allowing for consistent, accurate bills. New software that works with voice recognition software to permit the computer to read a medical record and correctly code it is being developed. Human error decreases as the use of software and electronics increases.

Most practices have found that EDI is far less expensive than processing paper claims. Third-party payers also realize cost savings through the receipt of electronic claims. Payment posting and reconciliation of claims is far superior using EDI.

Basic Billing Software

Basic billing software relies heavily on user knowledge and data entry skills. It is widely distributed in the private sector. Users key most, if not all, claim information onto a claim facsimile. The software manipulates these entries to produce an electronic claim. Typical errors involve entry errors, incorrect or missing patient or provider information, incorrect or incomplete diagnosis codes, and/or invalid Current Procedural Terminology (CPT®) codes. Basic medical billing software, developed for mass markets, usually does not allow users to customize or override its programs. The greatest risk of claim error is in data entry.

Informational Software

Informational software augments basic software capabilities. It uses databases and linked files to recall patient, provider, diagnostic, and service information. Invalid code combinations, missing diagnoses, and other errors that might prevent processing of a claim can be brought to the user's attention before the claim is submitted for payment. Informational software does not appear to generate erroneous claims; it does provide tools to help providers code their claims accurately. Vulnerabilities are more likely to stem from improper software configuration and use. For example, limited procedure coding options for office visits may steer claims decisions to higher-valued procedure codes.

Interactive Software

Interactive software combines and enhances basic billing and informational software capabilities by giving the user options for correcting problems detected by the software. Interactive software is distinguished from other medical billing software by its ability to provide the user with information and the likely consequences (no pay, more pay, less pay) of their decisions.

Proprietary Software

Proprietary software may present the greatest risk of misuse. This type of software is developed for a specific user. Inner workings of proprietary software may be known only to a single person or a select few. Hidden programs may add or modify claim information, producing erroneous or fraudulent claims. Unlike commercially available software packages, which are manufactured for a broad market, proprietary software is created to meet the needs of a specific, single customer. Commercial software that produces inaccurate claims has a greater chance of detection and of being reported by honest medical providers. Proprietary software presents a vulnerability to Medicare because it is created for, and used by, a select few. Proprietary software, not commercial software, possesses the greatest risk of being intentionally designed to produce improper or inaccurate claims.

SHORTCOMINGS OF ELECTRONIC DATA INTERCHANGE

Although electronic claims are easier to submit, there are some risks in using EDI, eg, claims that require supplementary documentation must still be filed using the paper claim method. However, as EDI systems begin to accommodate the electronic transmission of reports, radiographs, and related information, in the future claims may be generated from an electronic medical record, which will enhance proper documentation.

Another risk of EDI is the potential for misuse of submitter numbers, a vulnerability currently being addressed by Medicare. Billing companies, their employees, and providers' employees have access to patient and provider information needed to access the Medicare system. Clearinghouses or their employees can misuse this information to generate false claims (without the medical provider's knowledge).

Each time information changes hands or is handled outside an automated system, the risk of error increases. Source documents pass through the hands of many people before information is entered into a software program. Practice employees or an outside billing agency may misinterpret source document information; inaccurately key information into the system; or add, delete, or modify information on source documents. Regardless if intentional or unintentional errors occur, the patient's medical record may not support the claim submitted to Medicare. This claim will be incorrect, resulting in overpayment or underpayment. Even the most automated practices, clearinghouses, and service bureaus still produce and mail a large number of paper claims. In most systems, a paper claim may be produced from the electronically stored data; however, it is important to note that payments are delayed by Medicare and most other carriers when submitted as paper claims. When claims are submitted electronically, payment is generally always made more quickly to the service provider.

The following risks of using EDI are of concern to all practices:

- An overreliance on computerized systems without comprehensive knowledge of their limitations can result in major billing problems.
- Failure to have well-organized, clear documentation of EDI system edits can leave the physician and practice open to increased compliance risks.
- If manual procedures are not implemented to fill the gap when the EDI system falls behind in changing edits as Medicare rules are changed, an increased risk of false claim allegations exists.
- By using less-experienced personnel (a cost savings touted by some EDI vendors), the physician's staff may not understand the underlying documentation requirements needed to support changing a diagnosis code when facing medical necessity denials.
- Simply having the capability to print extensive management, productivity, and compliance monitoring reports is no assurance that the reports are read in a timely manner or that problems will be acted on by responsible personnel. For example, multiple months of increasing frequency of claim denials could become a prosecutor's exhibit to support a False Claim Act allegation of reckless disregard.
- Anyone with access to a physician's electronic billing number and a telephone may be able to submit false claims for payment.
- Billing software that requires users to input extensive information increases the risk of claim error.

PRE-CLAIM SUBMISSION OPERATIONS

Before any claim can be generated and submitted for payment, the office staff must perform a number of pre-claim tasks critical to ensuring the validity and accuracy of the patient's billing data and submission of a "clean claim." The basic objectives of staff pre-claim operations include:

- Collecting complete and accurate patient and responsible party information.
- Determining the appropriate financial class or account type (eg, commercial insurance, Medicare, Medicaid) and correctly assigning primary and secondary insurance billing status when two insurance plans require coordination of benefits.
- Educating the patient as to their ultimate financial responsibility for services rendered and obtaining written waivers when necessary to support future collection efforts.

- Verifying all data collected before rendering services or submitting claims and obtaining updated profiles of insurance plan benefits using an insurance or employer verification form.
- Anticipating the need for collection through accounts receivable controls and quality data.

PRIVACY AND MEDICAL RECORDS

The trade and lay press are increasingly focusing on privacy issues regarding the electronic transmission of medical data and records. Fears of insecure private and confidential information are growing, fueled by well-publicized cases of inadvertent release of confidential information that was stored or transmitted electronically.

Present statutes include penalties for violating a patient's right to privacy. For violations of the privacy standards by the persons subject to them, these penalties include civil monetary penalties of up to $25,000 per person, per year, per standard. Substantial criminal penalties are applicable to certain statute violations that are done knowingly: up to $50,000 and one year in prison for obtaining or disclosing protected health information; up to $100,000 and up to five years in prison for obtaining protected health information under false pretenses; and up to $250,000 and up to 10 years in prison for obtaining protected health information with the intent to sell, transfer, or use it for commercial advantage, personal gain, or malicious harm. Some existing uses of information, such as reporting births and deaths and reporting abuse such as child abuse, would not be affected. After balancing privacy and other social values, the US Department of Health and Human Services (DHHS) permits disclosure of health information without individual authorization for the following national priority activities and for activities that allow the health care system to operate more smoothly:

- Public health
- Research
- Judicial and administrative proceedings
- Law enforcement
- Emergency circumstances
- Providing information to next of kin
- Identifying the body of a deceased person or the cause of death
- As authorized for governmental health data systems
- For activities related to national defense and security

HEALTH INSURANCE PORTABILITY AND ACCOUNTABILITY ACT AND ELECTRONIC DATA INTERCHANGE

HIPAA, signed by President Clinton on August 21, 1996, aims to improve the productivity of the American health care system. The law encourages development of information systems that are based on the exchange of standard management and financial data using EDI. The act also requires organizations that exchange health care transactions to follow national implementation guidelines for EDI. The DHHS Web site (www.aspe.hhs.gov/admnsimp/) and the CMS Web site (www.cms.hhs.gov/HIPAAGenInfo) have more information on EDI efforts under HIPAA. The Administrative Simplification Provisions under HIPAA are intended to reduce the costs and administrative burdens of health care by making possible the standardized, electronic transmission of many administrative and financial transactions that were previously performed manually on paper.

These provisions require the secretary of DHHS to adopt standards for electronic transactions and data elements for those transactions; unique health identifiers for individuals, employers, health plans, and health care providers; and security standards and safeguards for electronic information systems involved in those transactions. The secretary of DHHS is also responsible for standards to ensure the privacy of electronic transactions.

DHHS has developed and implemented a plan to meet the law's mandate. With the exception of privacy standards, CMS is charged with coordinating the plan and its implementation. These rules include standards for electronic transactions; national provider and employee identifiers; and security and privacy standards for electronic transmission of protected health information. (Chapter 11 of this book provides detailed information regarding HIPAA.)

The final rule, which was published in January 2004, establishes the standard for a unique health identifier to be used by the health care system and announces adoption of the national provider identifier (NPI) as that standard. Use of the NPI will improve the Medicare, Medicaid, and other federal and private health programs as well as the effectiveness and efficiency of the health care industry, in general, by simplifying the administration of the health care system and enabling the efficient electronic transmission of certain health information. The effective date for providers, clearinghouses, and large health plans was May 23, 2007, with small health plans having until May 23, 2008, to comply. Health care providers were able to apply for an NPI beginning May 23, 2005. (This document is available at www.aspe.hhs.gov/admnsimp/).

What Is Protected Under the Health Insurance Portability and Accountability Act Regulations?

Protected health information is individually identifiable information that is or was electronic and in the hands of a covered entity. Information becomes electronic when it is sent electronically or if it is maintained in a computer system. Information that is later printed as a *hard copy* is still considered *electronic* and thus is covered under the HIPAA regulations. Once information is electronic, it is forever covered under the regulations. HIPAA is clear that the information itself, rather than the record, is protected under the regulations.

Who Is Covered Under the Health Insurance Portability and Accountability Act Regulations?

The regulations limit the breath of the law to *covered entities*, which are defined as health plans, health care clearinghouses, and any health care provider who transmits health information in an electronic form in connection with what are called standard transactions. However, the law does not reach all individuals and companies that may receive, use, or disclose individually identified information, eg, an employer, workers' compensation company, or accountant who is provided the information for legitimate purposes is not regulated.

THE AMERICAN MEDICAL ASSOCIATION AND ELECTRONIC DATA INTERCHANGE

The following are EDI policies set by the American Medical Association (AMA). These policies can be accessed using the search function of the AMA Web site (www.ama-assn.org) and searching by policy number (eg, H-315.979).

H-315.979 Electronic Data Interchange Status Report
Our AMA will: (1) work to establish consensus on industry security guidelines for electronic storage and transmission of medical records as an important means of protecting patient privacy in a manner that avoids undue and non-productive burdens on physician practices; and (2) develop relevant educational tools or models in accordance with industry electronic security guidelines to assist physicians in compliance with state and federal regulations.
(CMS Report 7, I-98; Reaffirmation I-01; Reaffirmation A-02)

H-190.992 Electronic Claims Submission

It is the policy of the AMA to: (1) support, assist and encourage the use of electronic data interchange (EDI) and electronic media claims (EMC) by physicians; (2) support and continue its involvement in the development of uniform EMC format and technical requirements; (3) continue to support the elimination of the Medicare 14-day payment delay regulation following Medicare carrier receipt of a claim; and (4) oppose the establishment, at this time, of any time tables or plans for mandatory EMC or EDI use by physicians. (BOT Rep. W, A-90; Amended: CMS Rep. I-93-1; Modified: Sunset Report, I-00; Reaffirmation A-04)

H-190.983 Submission of Electronic Claims Through Electronic Data Interchange

The AMA: (1) will take a leadership role in representing the interests of the medical profession in all major efforts to develop and implement EDI technologies related to electronic claims submission, claims payment, and the development of EDI standards that will affect the clinical, business, scientific, and educational components of medicine; (2) supports aggressive time tables for implementation of EDI as long as the implementation is voluntary, and as long as all payers are required to receive standard electronic claims and provide electronic reconciliation prior to physicians being required to transmit electronic claims; (3) supports the acceptance of the ANSI 837 standard as a uniform, but not exclusive, standard for those physicians who wish to bill electronically; and (4) will continue to monitor the cost effectiveness of EDI participation with respect to rural physicians. (CMS Rep. I-93-1; Reaffirmation A-04)

H-190.980 Electronic Data Interchange and Telemedicine: Update

Our AMA will continue to help create a uniform data set for electronic claims transmission to public and private payers, through its leadership of the National Uniform Claim Committee, a committee chaired by the AMA that is comprised of key parties affected by health care electronic data interchange. (CMS Rep. 8, I-95; Reaffirmation I-01; Reaffirmation A-02)

H-190.978 National Clearinghouse for Health Care Claims

Our AMA: (1) adopts the following policy principles to encourage greater use of electronic data interchange (EDI) by physicians and improve the efficiency of electronic claims processing: (a) public and private payers who do not currently do so should cover the processing costs of physician electronic claims and remittance advice; (b) vendors, claims clearinghouses, and payers should offer physicians a full complement of EDI transactions (eg, claims submission; remittance advice; and eligibility, coverage and benefit inquiry); (c) vendors, clearinghouses, and payers should adopt American National Standards Institute (ANSI) Accredited Standard's Committee (ASC) Insurance Subcommittee (X12N) standards for electronic health care transactions and recommendations of the National Uniform Claim Committee (NUCC) on a uniform data set for a physician claim; (d) all clearinghouses should act as all-payer clearinghouses (ie, accept claims intended for all public and private payers); (e) practice management systems developers should incorporate EDI capabilities, including electronic claims submission; remittance advice; and eligibility, coverage and benefit inquiry into all of their physician office-based products; (f) states should be encouraged to adopt AMA model legislation concerning turnaround time for "clean" paper and electronic claims; and (g) federal legislation should call for the acceptance of the Medicare National Standard Format (NSF) and ANSI ASC X12N standards for electronic transactions and NUCC recommendations on a uniform data set for a physician claim. This legislation should also require that (i) any resulting conversions, including maintenance and technical updates, be fully clarified to physicians and their office staffs by vendors, billing agencies or health insurers through educational demonstrations and (ii) that all costs for such services based on the NSF and ANSI formats, including educational efforts be fully explained to physicians and/or their office staffs during negotiations for such contracted services; (2) continues to encourage physicians to develop electronic data interchange (EDI) capabilities and to contract with vendors and payers who accept American National Standards Institute (ANSI) standards and who provide electronic remittance advice as well as claims processing; (3) continues to explore EDI-related business opportunities; (4) continues to facilitate the rapid development of uniform, industry-wide, easy-to-use, low cost means for physicians to exchange electronically claims and eligibility information and remittance advice with payers and others in a manner that protects confidentiality of medical information and to assist physicians in the transition to electronic data interchange; (5) continues its leadership roles in the NUCC and WEDI; and (6) through its participation in the National Uniform Claim Committee, will work with third-party payers to determine the reasons for claims rejection and advocate methods to improve the efficiency of electronic claims approval. (BOT Rep. 9; A-96; Amended: CMS Rep. 11, I-96; Appended: Sub. Res. 702, A-00)

H-190.977 Electronic Data Interchange Status Report

(1) Principles for development of a uniform data set for a non-institutional electronic claim should: (a) build on, and seek needed improvements to, data elements in the existing CMS-1500 paper form and Medicare electronic claims National Standard Format and relate directly to and conform to American National Standards Institute, Accredited Standards Committee, Insurance Subcommittee standards; (b) be equivalent across products, contracts and government programs; (c) be as small as possible yet sufficient for use across the industry; (d) include data elements earmarked for one-time collection only, to avoid unnecessary duplication; (e) include data elements intended to serve as replacements for attachments; and (f) include standardization of optional or statutorily required elements. (2) The AMA will continue its dialogues with Community Health Information Networks and encourage sound, economic analyses of the costs and benefits to physicians of participating in these networks. (3) The AMA will continue to monitor and have input into the Medicare Transaction System (MTS), a unified Medicare claims processing system intended to consolidate and standardize operations. Public sector and proprietary review systems that may be used within MTS to detect fraud and abuse should adhere to AMA principles of medical review (eg, full disclosure of all payment and coding rules.) (4) The AMA will encourage private payers to use all available technology to provide medical practices with up-to-date information (on deductibles and other payment elements) that eliminates erroneous claims and reduces administrative costs. Expanded information on health insurance cards is one of the options available to accomplish this objective. (5) The AMA will encourage the National Uniform Claim Committee to develop and seek implementation by all payers (including Medicare and Medicaid) of proposals acceptable to physicians to standardize third-party paper and electronic payment reporting methods, including remittance advices, explanations of benefits, "reason codes," and other explanations of third-party payment adjustment and actions. (CMS Rep. 1, A-96)

H-190.976 Electronic Claims Submission

The AMA encourages insurance companies to adopt a standardized or open electronic claims submission protocol such as the National Standard Format (NSF) or American National Standards Institute (ANSI) such as utilized by Medicare, thus allowing physicians and other providers of health care to utilize Electronic Data Interchange (EDI) efficiently and economically without needing redundant and proprietary standards and software for electronic claims submission; and encourages insurance companies to provide sufficient toll free (800) telephone lines in order to transmit this information, realizing the overall economies available to them from the conversion of paper claims to EDI. (Res. 115, I-96)

H-190.975 Universality of CMS-1500 Form
The AMA will undertake the task of asking individual carriers and/or their representative organizations to maintain the universal contents and acceptance of specific data in the CMS-1500 Form so that it will remain as a truly universal form for the patient-doctor claim form. (Res. 107, I-96; Reaffirmed: Res. 139, A-99)

H-190.973 Uniform Physician and Physician Group Identifiers
The AMA strongly urges the Department of Health and Human Services that all payers, public and private, be required to accept the National Provider Identifier as the sole physician and physician group identifier on all claims. (Res. 818, A-97)

H-190.974 Status Report on the National Uniform Claim Committee and Electronic Data Interchange
The AMA advocates use of the National Uniform Claim Committee standard claims/encounters data set for implementation of the administrative simplification provisions of the Health Insurance Portability and Accountability Act of 1996 (HIPAA); and strongly advocates that the CPT coding system be designated as the coding system to be used to report physician services under the HIPAA. (CMS Rep. 2, A-97)

H-190.970 Status Report on the National Uniform Claim Committee and Electronic Data Interchange
The AMA advocates the following principles to improve the accuracy of claims and encounter-based measurement systems: (1) the development and implementation of uniform core data content standards (eg, National Uniform Claim Committee [NUCC] data set); (2) the use of standards that are continually modified and uniformly implemented; (3) the development of measures and techniques that are universal and applied to the entire health care system; (4) the use of standardized terminology and code sets (eg, CPT) for the collection of data for administrative, clinical, and research purposes; and (5) the development and integration of strategies for collecting and blending claims data with other data sources (e.g., measuring the performance of physicians on a variety of parameters in a way that permits comparison with a peer group). (CMS Rep. 2, I-97)

H-190.964 Electronic Claims
Our AMA policy is that ALL third party payers: (1) acknowledge receipt of each electronic claim received within 24 hours; and (2) accept or reject each electronic claim within 10 business days. (Res. 707, A-01; Reaffirmation 1-04)

H-390.864 Medicare Supplemental Insurers Shall Accept Electronic Transfer of Data
The AMA will work with other appropriate organizations to encourage CMS and/or Congress to require or otherwise ensure that non-Medigap Medicare supplemental insurers accept electronic claims data from Medicare carriers. (Sub. Res. 109, I-96)

H-330.954 Mandatory Transmission of Electronic Claims
Our AMA opposes: (1) mandation of the electronic submission of Medicare claims and supports the continued right of practitioners to have free choice, without penalty, to transmit claims data either by paper claim or electronically; and (2) the policy of local Medicare carriers of mandating that physicians choose between electronic remittance advice or standard paper remittance report until all secondary insurers accept the electronic remittance advice explanation of benefits in its present format. (Res. 815, A-93; Appended: Res. 107, I-00; Reaffirmation A-01)

H-190.986 Medical Insurance Overhead Costs

(1) The AMA, through participation with CMS on the National Uniform Claim Committee, will reexamine the paper Uniform Claim Form (CMS-1500) to address any documented shortcomings caused by recent changes in claims processing technology and inappropriate uses of the CMS-1500 by third-party payers. (2) The AMA urges the National Uniform Claim Committee to address problems resulting from the wide variations in electronic claims processing formats and to work toward greater uniformity of such formats. (3) The AMA will continue to participate actively in efforts such as those of the Workgroup on Electronic Data Interchange to help assure that proposals and recommendations are implemented in a way that will facilitate appropriate standardization in electronic data interchange while preserving the flexibility needed for special situations. (4) The AMA will seek, insofar as practical, to involve members who are in active practice in the discussions of the National Uniform Claim Committee, American National Standards Institute, and other groups directed toward improvement and standardization of claims processing methodology and formats. (CMS Rep. E, I-92; Reaffirmed and Modified: CMS Rep. 10, A-03)

H-190.981 Required Timely Reimbursements by all Health Insurers

Our AMA will prepare and/or seek sponsorship of legislation calling for all health insurance entities and third-party payers—inclusive of not-for-profit organizations and health maintenance organizations—to pay for "clean" claims when filed electronically within 14 days and paper claims within 30 days, with interest accruing thereafter. These time periods should be considered ceilings, not floors or fixed differentials between paper and electronic claims. (Sub. Res. 112, A-95; Modified: BOT Rep. 17, I-00; Reaffirmation A-02; Reaffirmed: Res. 815, I-02)

H-185.984 Toll-Free 24-Hour Insurance Information

(1) It is the policy of the AMA to initiate and support efforts to require that health insurance providers and third-party administrators maintain a toll-free 24-hour-a-day telephone line, or other confidential electronic means, to provide information about specific coverage and benefits available to any patient presenting for medical care. (2) Our AMA supports a requirement that health insurers provide physicians with toll-free telephone access to adequate personnel who can discuss and respond to questions regarding patient covered services within 24 hours. (3) Our AMA seeks legislation to require that, where a plan does not provide toll-free, 24-hour access to verify patient coverage eligibility, the patient's identification card from the plan will be deemed valid. (4) Our AMA continues its efforts to seek reinstatement by CMS of toll-free telephone lines for transmission of electronic claims. (5) The toll-free lines for questions and claims submission be available on a 24-hour basis. (6) The toll-free lines are not reinstated, our AMA seeks enactment of legislation requiring CMS provision of toll-free telephone lines. (Res. 76, A-91; Res. 707, A-97; Reaffirmed and Appended: Sub. Res. 114, I-98; Reaffirmed: Sub. Res. 828, A-99; Reaffirmation A-00)

PROVIDER ENROLLMENT CHAIN AND OWNERSHIP SYSTEM

CMS recognizes the need to evaluate its safeguards for electronic claims and developed a computer system called the Provider Enrollment Chain and Ownership System (PECOS). PECOS was developed to help ensure that only agencies authorized by a provider submit claims. PECOS has been used by Medicare's fiscal intermediaries since July 2002. It is now being used by all carriers. PECOS is a national system that will standardize the process used by carriers. It allows a one-time enrollment process for providers and health care suppliers, and makes updating existing information easier. It also eliminates the need to send duplicate information to both the local carrier and the Railroad Medicare Carrier (RMC). PECOS implementation was completed in 2004 when the National Supplier Clearinghouse was brought online.

The provider community should be educated concerning their liability for erroneous claims submitted to Medicare using their provider number(s). Remittance notices can be rerouted to a billing company or another address and providers may never see them. Providers should be made aware of their responsibility to review remittance notices.

CONCLUSION

The benefits of using EDI in your practice include speed, efficiency, improved cash flow, and fewer coding errors. As technology changes to address confidentiality and privacy concerns and more payers urge the use of EDI, the use of paper for claims processing will continue to decline. Programs written for commercial distribution to a large audience pose little risk of producing erroneous or false claims. Proprietary software, by its very nature, appears more likely to pose some risk of misuse or fraud. As with paper claims, humans (and not software) may be the greatest cause of claim error.

chapter 4

The Coding Systems

OBJECTIVES

- Understand how Current Procedural Terminology (CPT®) is organized.
- Recognize the format of CPT and CPT coding guidelines.
- Define Evaluation and Management (E/M) services as used in CPT.
- Understand the rules that apply to CPT coding for surgery.
- Understand how CPT modifiers are used.
- Understand the purpose of the National Correct Coding Initiative.
- Describe how the three levels of the Healthcare Common Procedure Coding System (HCPCS) differ.
- Recognize the HCPCS coding guidelines.
- Identify the three volumes of the *International Classification of Diseases, Ninth Revision, Clinical Modification* (ICD-9-CM) as they pertain to medical practices.
- Understand the general ICD-9-CM coding guidelines.
- Identify ICD-9-CM-specific coding symbols, abbreviations, and notations.
- Understand the purpose of ICD-9-CM fourth and fifth digits.
- Understand the difference between V and E codes and the difference between *Includes* and *Excludes* notes.
- Locate the Neoplasm and Hypertension tables in the ICD-9-CM index.
- Understand what the term *cross-reference* means.
- Recognize upcoming changes of the ninth and tenth revisions of ICD.

Practices use coding systems to communicate the procedures and services provided to patients and the reasons the procedures and services were provided. Physician practices benefit from learning how to properly use the coding systems in two ways.

First, appropriate use of codes helps ensure proper payment from third-party payers and patients. Payers may reject or delay payment on claims without codes or with codes that are used incorrectly. Payment may be denied or delayed because of the need for medical necessity, which is a leading cause of claims rejection or delay. Many third-party payers will not pay for a procedure or service if it is not medically necessary. Proper coding and an understanding of medical necessity can enhance a practice's relationship with patients. When claims are coded accurately and meet medical necessity, patients who file their own claims have fewer problems obtaining payment from their insurance company.

Second, appropriate use of codes reduces a practice's audit liability. If the reported codes do not accurately describe the procedures and services rendered, the physician may be accused of fraudulent billing, ie, billing for services and procedures other than those provided. One example of this is overcoding the Evaluation and Management (E/M) services level for a physician's office. Thus, learning how to code accurately and properly is in the practice's best interest.

The three coding systems most commonly used by physicians in the United States are *Current Procedural Terminology* (CPT®), the Healthcare Common Procedure Coding System (HCPCS) Level II codes, and the *International Classification of Diseases, Ninth Edition, Clinical Modification* (ICD-9-CM). Each system is unique and serves a specific purpose in communicating to third-party payers what the physician did and why.

Certain physicians use other coding systems, such as the *Diagnostic and Statistical Manual of Mental Disorders*, Fourth Edition (DSM-IV®), for psychiatric and mental health services; *Current Dental Terminology*, Third Edition (CDT-3), for dental services; and the American Society of Anesthesiologists (ASA) 2004 Crosswalk, a systematic listing of all AMA CPT codes, except pathology (80048-89356), with appropriate anesthesia CPT codes for reporting medical services and procedures that relate to the practice of the anesthesiologist. These codes are identical to the anesthesia codes listed separately in the ASA *Relative Value Guide* (RVG) in which base units, when appropriate, and time units are also included.

CPT PROCEDURE CODING

The codebook titled *Current Procedural Terminology (CPT)*, Fourth Edition, is updated and published annually by the American Medical Association (AMA). The CPT coding system consists of more than 8000 codes used to report the procedures and services carried out by providers. These codes make it possible to bill third-party payers. CPT codes are five-digit numbers accompanied by narrative descriptions. A two-digit numeric modifier may also be used for additional modification of the CPT code description. All third-party payers accept CPT codes.

A new edition of CPT is released each November, and the codes become effective on January 1 of the following year. Physicians should purchase the new CPT volume each year to ensure use of the most current codes. Submission of deleted or incorrect CPT codes may result in reimbursement delay or denial or audit liability. Copies of the CPT codebook are available from the AMA (www.amabookstore.com).

The *Coders Desk Reference* is a learning tool that helps the experienced coder as well as the novice. This book contains detailed descriptions and helps clarify the CPT codes; it also provides an anesthesia crosswalk. *Principles of CPT Coding* and *Coders Desk Reference* also give basic coding guidelines for ICD-9-CM and CPT coding. Another great resource is *CPT Assistant*, a monthly newsletter published by the AMA. This official coding newsletter helps rationalize the meaning behind the codes and provides practical coding advice, timely articles, clinical vignettes, and a question and answer section. *CPT Changes: An Insider's View*, another AMA publication, describes all annual changes for the current year as well as examples of the new codes.

CPT Organization

Codes in CPT are organized in six logical sections according to the types of services or procedures provided. Each section begins with guidelines that provide important coding rules and other information. It is important to be familiar with these six sections and the code number ranges in each section to better understand where to locate codes. The six CPT sections and their associated code ranges are:

- *Evaluation and Management Services (codes 99201-99499)*. Codes from this section are used to report office, hospital, consultative, nursing home, and other related "visit" services. CPT starts with this series of codes because they are the most frequently reported services by physicians.
- *Anesthesia (codes 00100-01999, 99100-99140)*. The codes in this section describe anesthesia services any physician can use.

- *Surgery (codes 10021-69990).* Surgery is the longest section in CPT. It includes codes that describe procedures ranging from simple wound repairs to organ transplants.
- *Radiology (codes 70010-79999).* Diagnostic radiology, diagnostic ultrasound, radiation oncology, and nuclear medicine are covered in this section.
- *Pathology and Laboratory (codes 80048-89356).* These codes describe laboratory tests and pathology services.
- *Medicine (codes 90281-99199, 99500-99602).* This section provides codes for a variety of medical services, ranging from immunizations to ECGs to psychotherapy to home health procedures and services.

The CPT codebook also provides information about the proper use and selection of codes, specifically:

- *Introduction.* This section contains explanations of and instructions for the use of the CPT code book.
- *Guidelines.* Guidelines, which precede each section, contain important information specific to the section and may include a discussion of applicable modifiers.
- *Category II Codes.* This section contains a set of supplemental tracking codes that can be used to measure performance. These codes are intended to facilitate data collection for quality of care by coding certain services and/or test results that support performance measures that have been agreed on as contributing to good patient care. Use of these codes is optional, and these codes may not be used as a substitute for Category I codes. Category II codes are published biannually: January 1 and July 1. The most current list can be accessed at www.ama-assn.org/go/cpt.
- *Category III Codes.* This section contains a set of temporary codes for emerging technology, services, and procedures. Use of these temporary codes allows data to be collected for a specific procedure or service. Unlisted codes do not make it possible for this specific data to be collected. If available, a Category III code must be used instead of a Category I unlisted code. Services and procedures described in this section utilize alpha-numeric characters. For example, 0019T denotes extracorporeal shock wave therapy involving the musculoskeletal system, not otherwise specified, low energy.
- *Appendices.* Nine appendices follow the Medicine section. Appendix A provides a complete list of the Level I two-digit numeric modifiers for CPT codes and their descriptions, as well as Level II modifiers (HCPCS). Appendix B summarizes code additions (●), deletions, and revisions (▲) that occurred for that year in the volume. Appendix B provides a quick reference for updating computer code databases used by some practices to generate claims. Appendix C contains clinical examples of the E/M services and their corresponding CPT codes. Appendix D contains a summary of CPT add-on codes that can be identified throughout the CPT codebook with a plus (✚) symbol. Appendix E contains a summary of CPT codes that are exempt from modifier 51 but have not been designated as CPT add-on codes. These codes are identified with a ⊘ symbol. Appendices F through I were added to *CPT 2005*. Appendix F is a listing of codes exempt from the use of modifier 63. Appendix G lists procedures that include conscious sedation as an inherent part of providing the procedure. Appendix H contains an alphabetic index of performance measures by clinical condition or topic. Appendix I includes genetic testing code modifiers that should be used in conjunction with CPT and HCPCS codes to provide diagnostic granularity of service to enable providers to submit complete and precise genetic testing information without altering test descriptors.
- *Index.* The index can be used to locate the correct CPT code for a procedure. A coder should *never* code directly from the index, because this can lead to coding errors. The index often lists a range of codes or multiple codes from which to choose. It is necessary to read the complete descriptions, notes or parenthetic phrases, and guidelines of each code to ensure proper selection.

CPT Format

The CPT coding system utilizes an indented format, like that shown in the following example. This format is used to save space. Reporting of indented codes requires caution because the indented portion refers back to a common portion of the code above that is not indented. The common portion is the portion printed before the semicolon (;). For example,

> Laryngoscopy, flexible fiberoptic;

is common to codes 31575 through 31578. Thus, code 31576 is used to report:

> Laryngoscopy, flexible fiberoptic; with biopsy

Following is an example of the indented format:

> 17106   Destruction of cutaneous vascular proliferative lesions (eg, laser technique); less than 10 sq cm
> 17107   10.0 to 50.0 sq cm
> 17108   over 50.0 sq cm
> 17110   Destruction (eg, laser surgery, electrosurgery, cryosurgery, chemosurgery, surgical curettement), of flat warts, molluscum contagiosum, or milia; up to 14 lesions

Another example is:

> 11200   Removal of skin tags, multiple fibrocutaneous tags, any area; up to and including 15 lesions
> +11201   each additional ten lesions (List separately in addition to code for primary procedure)

In addition to the indented format, the Surgery section uses a consistent "universal" format that helps a coder locate codes. Surgery codes are first arranged by body system, such as integumentary, musculoskeletal, respiratory, and so on. As appropriate, codes within a body system are then arranged from the top of the system to the bottom or from the outside of the body to the inside of the body. Codes are further organized into types of procedures, such as incision, excision, repair, etc.

CPT Symbols

The CPT codebook uses various symbols. These symbols and their meanings are described here:

- ● The solid circle (or bullet) appears to the left of codes that are new to the CPT codebook. *New* means the codes were not listed in the previous year's publication.
- ▲ A solid triangle (or delta) to the left of a code signifies that the code's narrative description has been revised since the previous year's edition of the codebook. Description changes may be significant or relatively minor. Appendix B shows the actual changes made to the code descriptors. In Appendix B, if the revisions include deleted language, a solid black line is marked through the description. If new text is added, the description is underlined.
- ►◄ The two triangles facing each other are used to indicate new and revised text other than the procedure descriptors.
- ⇨ The arrow is found within the professional edition of the CPT codebook and signifies that additional material regarding the application of the code can be found in *CPT Assistant* and *CPT Changes: An Insider's View*.
- ✚ The plus sign signifies add-on codes. Some procedures are carried out in addition to the primary procedure performed. All add-on codes are exempt from the multiple procedure concept.

⊘ This symbol indicates codes that are exempt from the use of modifier 51 but have not been designated as CPT add-on procedures or services.

⊙ This symbol identifies CPT codes that include conscious sedation as an inherent part of providing the procedure.

The solid circle and triangle symbols are useful when referring to a specific code, because they identify the changes in each new volume of the CPT codebook. Symbols are used for quick reference and to save the practice time from referencing Appendix B for each code it wishes to report.

CPT Notes

The CPT codebook contains several hundred notes and parenthetical remarks designed to assist with code selection. Notes precede groups of codes, follow a code(s) to which they apply, and, in at least one case, follow a section of codes. Parenthetical notes and remarks are typically provided to refer the coder to related procedures or, in the case of deleted codes, to refer to codes that replace the deleted ones.

To code properly, review all notes pertaining to the code being considered. Failure to read and understand notes can result in lower insurance reimbursements and audit liability.

CPT Index

The CPT index is an excellent starting point for locating codes. The page preceding the index gives instructions on how to use the index. Most codes can be located by looking under the:

- Name of the procedure or service (eg, incision, endoscopy)
- Organ system or body area (eg, lung, genitourinary)
- Patient's condition (eg, dislocation, pregnancy)
- Use of synonyms (eg, renal for kidney), eponyms (eg, Abbe-Estlander), or abbreviations (eg, ECG, CAT scan)

Subterms, which follow most main terms in the CPT codebook, should be reviewed carefully, because they may affect code assignments.

CMS Coding Guidelines

This section presents basic coding rules and special requirements for CMS that apply to frequently used sections of the CPT codebook.

National Correct Coding Initiative and CMS Directives

In August 1994, CMS (formerly HCFA) contracted with Adminastar Federal, Inc., for the development of the currently named National Correct Coding Initiative (NCCI) as part of CMS's effort to reduce coding errors and the inappropriate payments that result from those errors. Medicare has since incorporated the "edits," which are revised and updated quarterly, into their automated claims processing systems. Codes for services that are excluded by Medicare are not addressed by the NCCI.

The NCCI edits focus on multiple services billed to a patient on any particular day. Billing each service separately rather than globally is referred to as *unbundling* and may violate reimbursement regulations and leave a provider open to fraudulent billing charges. Most private insurance carriers have similar edits in place, with the same goal of identifying unbundled procedures. Understanding the NCCI and proper Medicare coding helps practices avoid these penalties and reduce delayed claim payments and unnecessary denials.

General Rules Bundling or fragmented billing errors occur in different ways, including:

- Fragmenting one service into separate component parts and billing each part separately
- Using several codes to describe a procedure when one comprehensive code will cover the entire procedure
- Separating the surgical approach from the surgical procedure when the approach is included in the procedure code

To prevent improper coding and billing, it is important to always use the most current edition of the NCCI. The most current version of the NCCI, which includes an overview of Medicare payment policies, can be downloaded from the CMS Web site (www.cms.hhs.gov/ physicians/ cciedits/default.asp). Hard copy, disk, or CD-ROM versions of the NCCI may be obtained from the National Technical Information Service (888 363-2068 or 703 605-6060 www.ntis.gov).

How to Use the NCCI Because the NCCI comes in different formats, the exact method for identifying code pairs may differ. However, the basic principles remain the same:

- A column 1 code is the principal code that describes a procedure.
- A procedure listed in column 2 is performed at the same time as a more complex primary procedure. The column 2 prcedure is often a component of the column 1 comprehensive code. However, there are many column 1/column 2 edits where there is no comprehensive or component relationship, but the codes should not be reported together for other reasons.
- Medicare considers all services necessary to accomplish a given procedure as included in the description of that procedure.
- Mutually exclusive procedures are two codes (procedures) that cannot reasonably be performed together based on the code definitions or anatomic considerations.

In Figure 4-1, code 17106 is the main procedure or comprehensive code. The codes in the second column are often considered components of the main procedure because they are necessary parts of the main procedure. The codes in column three are considered mutually exclusive to the main procedure because they cannot reasonably be performed at the same time on the same patient.

Medicare considers all services necessary to complete a given procedure to be included (bundled) in the description of that procedure. In some cases, procedures normally denied as bundled may be paid separately by using the appropriate modifier. In the hard copy of the NCCI, CCI modifier indicators are listed next to the codes to designate whether a modifier may be used with a particular code pair. In the electronic file, the modifier indicators are in a separate column. The indicators include the following:

0 No modifier is allowed. The procedures will not be paid separately under any circumstance.
1 Modifier is allowed. The procedures may be paid separately with the appropriate modifier.
9 Used for all code pairs whose deletion date is the same as their effective date.

Evaluation and Management Services (99201-99499)

Medical record documentation is required for each patient visit with a physician to record pertinent facts, findings, and observations about an individual's health history, including past and present illnesses, examinations, tests, treatments, and outcomes. The medical

FIGURE 4-1

Comprehensive, Component, and Mutually Exclusive Codes

Comprehensive Code	Component Codes	Mutually Exclusive Codes
17106	11100, 11900 11901	17107, 17108

Comprehensive Code

17106   Destruction of cutaneous vascular proliferative lesions (eg, laser technique); less than 10 sq cm

Component Codes

11100   Biopsy of skin, subcutaneous tissue and/or mucous membrane (including simple closure), unless otherwise listed single lesion

11900   Injection intralesional; up to and including seven lesions

11901   more than seven lesions

Mutually Exclusive Codes

17107   Destruction of cutaneous vascular proliferative lesions (eg, laser technique); 10.0–50.0 sq cm

17108   Destruction of cutaneous vascular proliferative lesions (eg, laser technique); over 50.0 sq cm

record chronologically documents the care of the patient and is an important element that contributes to high quality care. The medical record facilitates the following:

- The ability of the physician and other health care professionals to evaluate and plan the patient's immediate treatment and to monitor his or her health care over time
- Communication and continuity of care among physicians and other health care professionals involved in the patient's care

An appropriately documented medical record can reduce many of the "hassles" associated with claims processing and may serve as a legal document to verify the care provided, if necessary.

Because payers have a contractual obligation to enrollees, they may require reasonable documentation that services are consistent with the insurance coverage provided. They may request information to validate the site of service; the medical necessity and appropriateness of the diagnostic and/or therapeutic services provided; and/or that services provided have been accurately reported. To correctly document the services performed, specific requirements must be met to support the services rendered and to receive correct reimbursement for those services. When providing information to a payer, practice staff is encouraged to follow HIPAA's minimally necessary guideline (eg., do not forward entire charts).

General Principles of Medical Record Documentation

The principles of documentation that follow are applicable to all types of medical and surgical services in all settings. For E/M services, the nature and amount of physician work and documentation varies by type of service, place of service, and the patient's status. The general principles listed here may be modified to account for these variable circumstances in providing E/M services.

- The medical record should be complete and legible.
- The documentation of each patient encounter should include:
  - The chief complaint and/or reason for the encounter and relevant history, physical examination findings, and prior diagnostic test results,
  - Assessment, clinical impression, or diagnosis,
  - Plan for care, and
  - Date and a verifiable legible identity of the health care professional who provided the service.
- If not specifically documented, the rationale for ordering diagnostic and other ancillary services should be easy to infer.
- To the greatest extent possible, past and present diagnoses and conditions, including those in the prenatal and intrapartum period that affect the newborn, should be accessible to the treating and/or consulting physician.
- Appropriate health risk factors should be identified.
- The patient's progress, response to and changes in treatment, planned follow-up care instructions, and diagnosis should be documented.
- The CPT and ICD-9-CM codes reported on the health insurance claim form or billing statement should be supported by the documentation in the medical record.
- An addendum to a medical record should be dated the day the information is added to the medical record and not dated for the date the service was provided and validated by signature.
- Timeliness is essential, and a service should be documented during or as soon as practicable after it is provided to maintain an accurate medical record.
- The confidentiality of the medical record should be fully maintained consistent with the requirements of medical ethics and of law.

1995 and 1997 Evaluation and Management Guidelines

In 1995, CMS issued guidelines to help establish standards for medical record documentation for both the physician and the claims reviewer. These guidelines defined the documentation of the history, examination, and medical decision-making in the medical record to support the level of service billed by the health care provider. In 1997, CMS developed new guidelines that meet the 1995 documentation requirements but give the physician the choice of using the key elements or bullets from either a multisystem or body organ system. The 1995 guidelines are more generic and are not as specific as the 1997 guidelines.

At this time, a physician may use either the 1995 or 1997 guidelines; however, it is recommended that a physician use only one set of guidelines to avoid confusion. Within a facility of several physicians or specialists, one physician or specialist may choose to use the 1997 guidelines and another may use the 1995. The changes in the guidelines from 1995 to 1997 affected documentation of the history and the examination. The medical decision-making guidelines did not change. CMS also published proposed changes in June 2000, but these changes had not been put into affect at the time of this book's publication. Once the final 2000 guidelines are released, CMS will publish rules regarding use of the three sets of these guidelines.

History The 1995 and 1997 guidelines are very similar. A significant exception relates to the extended history of the presenting illness. Under the 1995 guidelines, the physician must document four elements of the history of the presenting illness to qualify for an extended history of the presenting illness. Under the 1997 guidelines, the physician may either document four elements or document the presence of three or more chronic or inactive conditions.

Examination The examination documentation requirements were greatly expanded under the 1997 guidelines. Although the categories for the different levels of examination remained the same, the requirements to meet those levels of care changed.

The 1995 guidelines include the use of descriptors such as "limited," "extended," or "complete." However, these 1995 guidelines provide no specifics on the number of elements or body areas that must be examined to meet each level of care. Because of this nonspecificity, it may be difficult for an auditor and coder to agree on the level of care provided.

The 1997 examination guidelines are more quantifiable. In these guidelines, a specific number of elements must be documented to qualify for a specific level of service, as demonstrated in the following examples:

> 1995 Expanded Problem-Focused Examination: A limited examination of the affected body area or organ system and other symptomatic or related organ system(s).
>
> 1997 Expanded Problem-Focused Examination: Examination should include performance and documentation of at least 6 elements identified by a bullet (•) in 1 or more organ system(s) or body area(s).

The guidelines for single organ exams may differ from those for the multisystem exam. The physician is not limited by specialty to use a specific type of exam. The nature of the presenting problem and medical necessity will determine the type of examination that is performed. (E/M guidelines for 1995 and 1997 can be accessed at www.cms.hhs.gov.)

The following criteria are presented in the proposed 2000 E/M coding guidelines.

Determining a Level of Care There are seven components to consider in determining the level of care: history, examination, medical decision-making, time, counseling, coordination of care, and nature of presenting problem. The first three components are the key components in determining a level of care. When time and counseling are major factors of the E/M visit, different guidelines apply.

History The history consists of four parts. Each part must be considered in determining a level of care. The four parts are chief complaint, history of present illness, review of systems (ROS), and past family and social history. A chief complaint is one sentence or phrase describing why the patient is seeing the provider at that instance. A chief complaint is indicated at all levels.

The history of present illness is a narrative describing the symptoms and events leading to the provider encounter. The symptom description has eight possible elements:

- *Location:* Where the symptom is located on the body (eg, chest, abdomen, arm)
- *Quality:* Distinguishing factor, grade (eg, piercing, throbbing, pulsitile)
- *Severity:* Degree of pain (eg, moderate, bad, slightly better)
- *Duration:* Frequency (eg, one day, a couple of hours, the past week)
- *Timing:* When the symptom occurs (eg, after dinner, all the time, upon sitting up)
- *Context:* The situation associated with the symptom (eg, since beginning an exercise program, after laying down)
- *Modifying factors:* What alleviates or worsens the symptom (eg, after taking ibuprofen, upon standing and walking, upon resting)
- *Associated signs and symptoms:* Other symptoms or signs that appear with the main symptom (eg, cough with dyspnea, fever, fatigue)

There are two levels of history of present illness: brief and extended. A level of *brief* requires one to three of the elements listed. A level of *extended* requires four or more elements or three or more chronic or inactive conditions. (The 1995 guidelines do not allow for the substitution of three or more conditions as an extended history of present illness.)

The ROS is the patient's response to specific questions about the different body systems. The recognized systems are as follows:

- Constitutional symptoms (fever, weight loss, etc)
- Eyes
- Ears, nose, mouth, throat
- Cardiovascular
- Respiratory
- Gastrointestinal
- Genitourinary
- Musculoskeletal
- Integumentary (skin and/or breast)
- Neurological
- Psychiatric
- Endocrine
- Hematologic/lymphatic
- Allergic/immunologic

There are three levels of the ROS. A level of *problem pertinent* requires documentation of the patient's positive responses and pertinent negative responses for the system related to the problem. A level of *extended* requires documentation of the patient's positive responses and pertinent negative responses for two to nine systems. A level of *complete* requires documentation of the patient's positive responses and pertinent negative responses to 10 or more systems.

When gathering information regarding past family and social history, three areas are considered: (1) the patient's past medical history, including past provider visits, hospitalizations, surgeries, current medications, allergies, and other pertinent past data; (2) the patient's family history as it relates to health and hereditary issues; (3) the patient's social history (eg, relationships, diet, occupation, smoker, drinker).

The two levels of past family and social history are pertinent and complete. A level of *pertinent* requires one specific item from any of the three areas. A level of *complete* requires a review of two or all three of the past family and social history areas, depending on the category of the E/M service. A review of all three history areas is required for services that by their nature include a comprehensive assessment or reassessment of the patient. A review of two of the three history areas is sufficient for other services. At least one specific item from two of the three history areas must be documented for a complete past family and social history for the following categories of E/M services: office or other outpatient services, established patient; emergency department; domiciliary care, established patient; and home care, established patient. At least one specific item from all of the three history areas must be documented for a complete past family and social history for the following categories of E/M services:

- Office or other outpatient services, new patient
- Hospital observation services
- Hospital inpatient services, initial care
- Consultations
- Comprehensive nursing facility assessments
- Domiciliary care, new patient
- Home care, new patient

Examination The second key component in determining the level of care is the examination. The requirements vary for the documentation of the exam depending on which guidelines are used. The 1997 guidelines are very specific and require documentation of a certain number of elements for each level of care. The 1995 guidelines state the different levels of exam, without giving specifics on what documentation must be present. Following are the four levels of exam:

- *Problem focused* requires the documentation of a limited examination of the affected body area or organ system.
- *Expanded problem focused* requires the documentation of a limited exam of the affected body area or organ system and additional symptomatic or related systems.
- *Detailed* requires the documentation of an extended examination of the affected area and other symptomatic or related organ systems.
- *Comprehensive* requires the documentation of a general multisystem exam or a complete exam of a single organ system.

Medical Decision-Making Medical decision-making refers to the complexity of establishing a diagnosis and/or selecting a management option. It is measured by the number of possible diagnoses and/or the number of management options that must be considered; the amount and/or complexity of medical records, diagnostic tests, and/or other information that must be obtained, reviewed, and analyzed; and the risk of significant complications, morbidity, and/or mortality, as well as comorbidities, associated with the patient's presenting problem(s), the diagnostic procedure(s), and/or the possible management options. The four types of medical decision-making are:

- *Straightforward.* The problems addressed are straightforward, having minimal decision-making complexity.
- *Low complexity.* Typically, the problem(s) addressed will (1) be of low severity, low urgency, and low risk of clinical deterioration and complications; (2) have a limited differential diagnosis and limited review of additional data; and (3) have straightforward diagnostic and/or therapeutic interventions, with a straightforward treatment plan. For the purpose of documentation, two of these three elements must either meet or exceed the requirement for low complexity.
- *Moderate complexity.* Typically, the problem(s) addressed will (1) be of moderate severity with a low to moderate risk of clinical deterioration; (2) require review of a detailed amount of additional information with an extended differential diagnosis; and (3) require complicated diagnostic and/or therapeutic intervention, with a complicated treatment plan. For the purpose of documentation, two of these three elements must either meet or exceed the requirement for moderate complexity.
- *Highly complex.* Typically, the problem(s) addressed will (1) be of high severity with a high risk of complications and clinical deterioration; (2) require review of an extensive amount of additional information with an extensive differential diagnosis; and (3) require highly complex multiple diagnostic and/or therapeutic interventions, with a highly complex treatment plan. For the purpose of documentation, two of these three elements must either meet or exceed the requirement for highly complex medical decision-making.

Table 4-1 shows the progression of the elements required for each level of medical decision-making. To qualify for a given type of decision-making, two of the three elements in

TABLE 4-1

Levels of Medical Decision-Making

Severity/ Urgency of Problem(s) and Risk of Complications and Deterioration	Differential Diagnoses and Amount/ Complexity of Data Reviewed	Treatment Plan Including Diagnostic and Therapeutic Tests, Procedures, and Interventions	Type of Decision-Making
Low	Limited	Straightforward	Low
Moderate	Detailed	Complicated	Moderate
High	Extensive	Highly complex	High

the table must either meet or exceed the requirements for that type of decision-making. The CMS guidelines (accessible at www.cms.hhs.gov) provide additional information and clarification regarding medical decision-making.

Time Time is calculated as either face-to-face or unit/floor. Face-to-face time is the time the physician spends face-to-face with the patient or family. Use face- to-face time for office visits and other outpatient visits.

Unit/floor time is for hospital and other inpatient visits. Intra-service time is calculated as the time spent both with the patient and the time spent on the floor.

When an excessive amount of time is spent with a patient, prolonged service codes may be required. Prolonged service codes are used when the time spent with the patient exceeds the regular time by more than 30 minutes.

Time is not counted for emergency department levels of service. The nature of emergency department work does not allow for accurate estimates of the time spent on the floor or with the patient.

Counseling and Coordination of Care When counseling and/or coordination of care dominates (more than 50%) the physician/patient and/or family encounter (face-to-face time in the office or other outpatient setting or floor/unit time in the hospital or nursing facility), time is considered the key or controlling factor to qualify for a particular level of E/M services. The total length of time of the encounter (face-to-face or floor time, as appropriate) and a full description or explanation of the counseling and/or activities performed to coordinate care must be documented in the medical record. The performance of a history and physical examination, although not required at each instance of counseling or coordination of care, should be referred to when appropriate. Medical decision-making associated with this service must be documented as part of counseling and coordination of care.

Nature of Presenting Problem The nature of the presenting problem determines the type of care the patient will receive. Severely ill or injured patients may be admitted to the hospital, critical care unit, or emergency department. Patients with less severe problems may be admitted for observation or referred to a physician office.

Determining the level of care documented first requires consideration of the three key components and then the four modifying factors. The procedure for new and established office visits in 2006 is described here. Other E/M service levels are determined in a similar manner. The most current CPT manual or carrier manual should be referenced for the most recent criteria.

New patient evaluations require all three of these key components: history, physical examination, and decision-making (see Table 4-2). All components must be met or exceeded for new patients for office visits, domiciliary care, home visits, office consultations, initial hospital care, initial inpatient consultations, hospital observation, emergency department services, and initial nursing facility assessments.

TABLE 4-2

New Patient Evaluations

Code	History	Physical	Decision-Making	Typical Time
99201	Problem focused	Problem focused	Straightforward	10 min
99202	Expanded problem focused	Expanded problem focused	Straightforward	20 min
99203	Detailed	Detailed	Low complexity	30 min
99204	Comprehensive	Comprehensive	Moderate complexity	45 min
99205	Comprehensive	Comprehensive	High complexity	60 min

Established patient evaluations require at least two of the three key components (Table 4-3), which must be met or exceeded for established patients in the office, home, domiciliary care, subsequent hospital care, nursing facility care.

When counseling or coordination of care exceeds 50% of the patient visit, time is the deciding factor in choosing a level of care. To use time, documentation in the chart must state the total length of time spent with the patient and the amount of time spent on counseling and coordination of care. Information on what was discussed with the patient should also be included. Table 4-4 shows a side-by-side comparison of E/M documentation guidelines.

TABLE 4-3
Established Patient Evaluations

Code	History	Physical	Decision-Making	Typical Time
99211	Minimal	Minimal	Minimal	5 min
99212	Problem focused	Problem focused	Straightforward	10 min
99213	Expanded problem focused	Expanded problem focused	Low complexity	15 min
99214	Detailed	Detailed	Moderate complexity	25 min
99215	Comprehensive	Comprehensive	High complexity	40 min

TABLE 4-4
Side-by-Side Comparison of E/M Documentation Guidelines

Code Component	1995 Requirements	1997 Requirements	Draft Guidelines (June 2000) The Good News—What's Different
Hx - History of Present Illness	• Specific requirements	• Specific requirements	• Clearer requirements • Explicit recognition of medication monitoring
Hx - Review of Systems	• Specific body area or organ system requirements	• Specific body area or organ system requirements	• Less required • Clearer • Examples are provided
Hx - Past, Family, Social History	• Brief information required	• Brief information required	• No difference
Physical Exam	• Specifically referenced general multi-system exam • Description of single system exams inadequate • 4 levels • Requirements not clear	• General multi-system exam and 10 single system exams • 4 levels • Very descriptive • Confusing shading & bullets format • Requirements often not relevant	• Physician *tailors* documentation to exam • Only 3 levels • Vignette examples • No bullets • No shading • Minimal counting • No irrelevant facts to record
Medical Decision Making	• 4 levels • Laundry list of examples not reflective of clinical assessments & plans	• 4 levels • Laundry list of examples not reflective of clinical assessments & plans	• Only 3 levels • Physician *tailors* documentation to assessment & plan of treatment • Vignette examples

* HX - History

Source: Centers for Medicare and Medicaid Services. Available at: www.cms.hhs.gov/medlearn.

Summary   Understanding the requirements for documenting each level of service is critical to coding. Because undercoding and overcoding of services are primary areas related to investigation of fraud and abuse, knowing how to properly code and document services is no longer an option but a necessity.

Selecting the CPT Procedure Code

The CPT coding process involves the following six basic steps that, when followed, increase the likelihood of accurate code selection:

1. Identify the procedures and services provided during the patient/physician encounter. This entails reviewing the patient's record, operative report, radiology, laboratory reports, and so on. Identification of routine services, such as an office visit, is fairly straightforward. Identification of multiple services or complex procedures (especially surgeries) requires a higher-level understanding of the CPT codebook and of billing rules.
2. Consult the index to locate the code numbers. Then determine the main terms for each procedure to be coded and identify those terms in the alphabetic index. Note any listed subterms below the main term and refer to cross-references provided in the index.
3. Locate the code(s) in the main body of the CPT codebook. Always refer to the code in the main body of the book; it may include notes or other important information that may affect code selection. Never code directly from the index.
4. Review the notes and parenthetical remarks associated with the codes, which contain special rules or information that may affect code selection. Also review the guidelines at the beginning of the section and subsection notes when included.
5. Code specific procedures and services after they have been identified. Select the name of the procedure or service that accurately identifies the service performed. Do not select a CPT code that merely approximates the service provided. If no such procedure or service exists, report the service using the appropriate unlisted procedure or service code.
6. Modify as necessary. Some situations require adding appropriate modifiers to codes. Modifiers are discussed later in this chapter.

Comparing the final code description with the procedure or service provided ensures that all components have been reported.

Selecting the E/M Services Code

Nearly one third of all services rendered by physicians nationwide are reported using codes from this section of the CPT codebook. Therefore, it is necessary to pay special attention to the rules related to coding E/M services. Rules for coding these services are in the E/M guidelines, beginning on page 1 of the CPT codebook.

E/M services are coded according to the *content* of the service provided. The extent of the history taken by the physician, the extent of the examination, and the complexity of medical decision-making involved are defined as *key components*. Four levels of history, four levels of examination, and four levels of decision-making are defined. In most cases, code selection depends on matching the levels of each key component provided with the levels specified in the codes.

For example, if the physician saw an established patient in the office, took an expanded problem-focused history, performed an expanded problem-focused examination, and determined that medical decision-making was of low complexity, code 99213 would be selected.

99213 *Office or other outpatient visit* for the evaluation and management of an established patient, which requires at least two of these three key components:

- an expanded problem focused history;
- an expanded problem focused examination;
- medical decision making of low complexity.

Counseling and coordination of care with other providers or agencies are provided consistent with the nature of the problem(s) and the patient's and/or family's needs.
Usually, the presenting problem(s) is of low to moderate severity. Physicians typically spend 15 minutes face-to-face with the patient and/or family.

When a new patient is evaluated, all three key components are necessary for establishing the numeric level of billing. All key components must meet or exceed the stated requirements to qualify for a particular level of E/M service. When an established patient is evaluated, only two of three key components are used for billing purposes. Two of the three components must meet or exceed the status requirements to qualify for a particular level of E/M services.

Code selection for E/M services can be affected by other factors, called *contributing factors*. These include the nature of the patient's presenting problem(s), the provision of counseling and/or coordination-of-care services, and the amount of time the physician spends with the patient. Although these factors are not key to choosing the E/M code, they can affect selection.

According to CPT E/M guidelines, time may become the controlling factor in selecting E/M codes only when more than 50% of the service rendered to the patient was related to counseling and/or coordination of care. Understanding how "time" is defined is important when time is used as the controlling factor in billing. For office E/M services, time is defined as time spent face-to-face with the patient and/or family; for hospital E/M services, time is defined as time spent on the patient's floor or unit and at the bedside rendering services for that patient.

All Medicare updates from local carriers should be read, because coding guidelines and documentation requirements change frequently.

E/M Documentation Guidelines

CMS's revised documentation guidelines for E/M services have been indefinitely delayed. Currently either the 1995 or 1997 guidelines may be used, whichever is most advantageous to the provider.

Surgery Coding

Special rules apply to the coding of surgical procedures. Two of the most important rules are discussed in the following paragraphs.

Surgical Package Rules

Beginning coders often ask what services are included with surgical procedures. To address this issue, the CPT system provides the "surgical package" (or global surgery) definition, which is given in the Surgery section guidelines. The definition specifies components included in the surgery code. The components include the operation itself; local infiltration; metacarpal/metatarsal/digital block or topical anesthesia; subsequent to the decision for surgery, one related E/M encounter on the date immediately prior to or on the date of the procedure (including history and physical); immediate postoperative care, including dictating operative notes and talking with the family and other physicians; writing orders; evaluating the patient in the postanesthesia recovery area; and typical postoperative follow-up care.

The Medicare definition of the surgical package delineates the number of preoperative and postoperative days included as well as the types of services included in the package. The Medicare global surgery package includes:

- A one-day preoperative period. This includes all preoperative visits by the surgeon in or out of the hospital beginning the day before surgery.
- Intraoperative services that are a part of the procedure.
- A standard 90-day postoperative period (or follow-up) that includes any services the surgeon provides during that time, unless service is provided for an unrelated condition. Minor surgical procedures include a 0- to 10-day postoperative period. There is no postoperative period for endoscopic diagnostic procedures performed through an existing body orifice.
- All medically necessary return trips to the operating room can be billed separately and will be paid at a reduced rate.

Several other payers have definitions of the surgical package that may differ from the ones listed here. Physicians and staff need to be aware of these differences and code accordingly. Local carriers should be contacted for clarification of their policies.

The global surgical package is very important in physician office claim submission. However, the surgical package is *not* applicable to hospital coding for the facility fee.

Separate Procedures

CPT codes were designed so that several procedures that are often performed together can be combined. The result is a minimum number of codes yet a complete picture of the services provided. In some cases, the CPT code system identifies certain procedures as *separate procedures*, which means the procedures can be coded separately when performed independently and not in conjunction with the major or primary procedure of which it is considered an integral component. For example, a transurethral resection of the prostate and a vasectomy are performed. Following the separate procedure guidelines, only code 52601 should be assigned, because it incorporates both the resection of the prostate and the vasectomy. Code 55250 is identified as a separate procedure and can be reported separately when only the vasectomy is performed:

52601   Transurethral electrosurgical resection of the prostate, including control of postoperative bleeding, complete (vasectomy, meatotomy, cystourethroscopy, urethral calibration and/or dilation, and internal urethrotomy are included)

55250   Vasectomy, unilateral or bilateral (separate procedure), including postoperative semen examination(s)

CPT Modifiers

The CPT code system contains two-digit numeric modifiers that are used to report situations in which the service or procedure was altered by some specific circumstance. In these situations, the circumstance does not affect the selection of the CPT code. For example, the physician performs a bilateral tympanostomy under general anesthesia. Because code 69436 is a unilateral procedure code, modifier 50 must be appended to identify this procedure as bilateral:

69436   with modifier 50 Tympanostomy (requiring insertion of ventilating tube), general anesthesia

The addition of modifier 50 indicates that the physician performed the procedure bilaterally.

All modifiers are listed in Appendix A of the CPT codebook. Certain modifiers have specific uses (ie, 21, 24, 25 with E/M services). Some modifiers are commonly used with certain types of codes (ie, surgery, medicine), so as not to preclude or restrict their use to only one specialty. The modifier that depicts the circumstance most accurately is the one to be used. Figure 4-2 is a list of the modifiers and their descriptors that are applicable to

(text continued on p. 151)

FIGURE 4-2

CPT Modifiers Found in the 2005 Codebook

Appendix A

Modifiers

This list includes all of the modifiers applicable to *CPT 2005* codes.

21 Prolonged Evaluation and Management Services: When the face-to-face or floor/unit service(s) provided is prolonged or otherwise greater than that usually required for the highest level of evaluation and management service within a given category, it may be identified by adding modifier 21 to the evaluation and management code number. A report may also be appropriate.

22 Unusual Procedural Services: When the service(s) provided is greater than that usually required for the listed procedure, it may be identified by adding modifier 22 to the usual procedure number. A report may also be appropriate.

23 Unusual Anesthesia: Occasionally, a procedure, which usually requires either no anesthesia or local anesthesia, because of unusual circumstances must be done under general anesthesia. This circumstance may be reported by adding modifier 23 to the procedure code of the basic service.

24 Unrelated Evaluation and Management Service by the Same Physician During a Postoperative Period: The physician may need to indicate that an evaluation and management service was performed during a postoperative period for a reason(s) unrelated to the original procedure. This circumstance may be reported by adding modifier 24 to the appropriate level of E/M service.

25 Significant, Separately Identifiable Evaluation and Management Service by the Same Physician on the Same Day of the Procedure or Other Service: The physician may need to indicate that on the day a procedure or service identified by a CPT code was performed, the patient's condition required a significant, separately identifiable E/M service above and beyond the other service provided or beyond the usual preoperative and postoperative care associated with the procedure that was performed. The E/M service may be prompted by the symptom or condition for which the procedure and/or service was provided. As such, different diagnoses are not required for reporting of the E/M services on the same date. This circumstance may be reported by adding modifier 25 to the appropriate level of E/M service. **Note:** This modifier is not used to report an E/M service that resulted in a decision to perform surgery. See modifier 57.

26 Professional Component: Certain procedures are a combination of a physician component and a technical component. When the physician component is reported separately, the service may be identified by adding modifier 26 to the usual procedure number.

32 Mandated Services: Services related to *mandated* consultation and/or related services (eg, PRO, third party payer, governmental, legislative or regulatory requirement) may be identified by adding modifier 32 to the basic procedure.

47 Anesthesia by Surgeon: Regional or general anesthesia provided by the surgeon may be reported by adding modifier 47 to the basic service. (This does not include local anesthesia.) **Note:** Modifier 47 would not be used as a modifier for the anesthesia procedures.

50 Bilateral Procedure: Unless otherwise identified in the listings, bilateral procedures that are performed at the same operative session, should be identified by adding modifier 50 to the appropriate five digit code.

51 Multiple Procedures: When multiple procedures, other than E/M services, are performed at the same session by the same provider, the primary procedure or service may be reported as listed. The additional procedure(s) or service(s) may be identified by appending modifier 51 to the additional procedure or service code(s). **Note:** This modifier should not be appended to designated "add-on" codes (see Appendix D).

52 Reduced Services: Under certain circumstances a service or procedure is partially reduced or eliminated at the physician's discretion. Under these circumstances the service provided can be identified by its usual procedure number and the addition of modifier 52, signifying that the service is reduced. This provides a means of reporting reduced services without disturbing the identification of the basic service. **Note:** For hospital outpatient reporting of a previously scheduled procedure/service that is partially reduced or cancelled as a result of extenuating circumstances or those that threaten the well-being of the patient prior to or after administration of anesthesia, see modifiers 73 and 74 (see modifiers approved for ASC hospital outpatient use).

53 Discontinued Procedure: Under certain circumstances, the physician may elect to terminate a surgical or diagnostic procedure. Due to extenuating circumstances or those that threaten the well being of the patient, it may be necessary to indicate that a surgical or diagnostic procedure was started but discontinued. This circumstance may be reported by adding modifier 53 to the code reported by the physician for the discontinued procedure. **Note:** This modifier is not used to report the elective cancellation of a procedure prior to the patient's anesthesia induction and/or surgical preparation in the operating suite. For outpatient hospital/ambulatory surgery center (ASC) reporting of a previously scheduled procedure/service that is partially reduced or cancelled as a result of extenuating circumstances or those that threaten the well being of the patient prior to or after administration of anesthesia, see modifiers 73 and 74 (see modifiers approved for ASC hospital outpatient use).

FIGURE 4-2 (*continued*)

54 **Surgical Care Only:** When one physician performs a surgical procedure and another provides preoperative and/or postoperative management, surgical services may be identified by adding modifier 54 to the usual procedure number.

55 **Postoperative Management Only:** When one physician performed the postoperative management and another physician performed the surgical procedure, the postoperative component may be identified by adding modifier 55 to the usual procedure number.

56 **Preoperative Management Only:** When one physician performed the preoperative care and evaluation and another physician performed the surgical procedure, the preoperative component may be identified by adding modifier 56 to the usual procedure number.

57 **Decision for Surgery:** An evaluation and management service that resulted in the initial decision to perform the surgery may be identified by adding modifier 57 to the appropriate level of E/M service.

58 **Staged or Related Procedure or Service by the Same Physician During the Postoperative Period:** The physician may need to indicate that the performance of a procedure or service during the postoperative period was: a) planned prospectively at the time of the original procedure (staged); b) more extensive than the original procedure; or c) for therapy following a diagnostic surgical procedure. This circumstance may be reported by adding modifier 58 to the staged or related procedure. **Note:** This modifier is not used to report the treatment of a problem that requires a return to the operating room. See modifier 78.

59 **Distinct Procedural Service:** Under certain circumstances, the physician may need to indicate that a procedure or service was distinct or independent from other services performed on the same day. Modifier 59 is used to identify procedures/services that are not normally reported together, but are appropriate under the circumstances. This may represent a different session or patient encounter, different procedure or surgery, different site or organ system, separate incision/excision, separate lesion, or separate injury (or area of injury in extensive injuries) not ordinarily encountered or performed on the same day by the same physician. However, when another already established modifier is appropriate it should be used rather than modifier 59. Only if no more descriptive modifier is available, and the use of modifier 59 best explains the circumstances, should modifier 59 be used.

62 **Two Surgeons:** When two surgeons work together as primary surgeons performing distinct part(s) of a procedure, each surgeon should report his/her distinct operative work by adding modifier 62 to the procedure code and any associated add-on code(s) for that procedure as long as both surgeons continue to work together as primary surgeons. Each surgeon should report the cosurgery once using the same procedure code. If additional procedure(s) (including add-on procedure(s)) are performed during the same surgical session, separate code(s) may also be reported with modifier 62 added. **Note:** If a co-surgeon acts as an assistant in the performance of additional procedure(s) during the same surgical session, those services may be reported using separate procedure code(s) with the modifier 80 or modifier 82 added, as appropriate.

63 **Procedure Performed on Infants less than 4 kg:** Procedures performed on neonates and infants up to a present body weight of 4 kg may involve significantly increased complexity and physician work commonly associated with these patients. This circumstance may be reported by adding modifier 63 to the procedure number. **Note:** Unless otherwise designated, this modifier may only be appended to procedures/services listed in the 20000-69999 code series. Modifier 63 should not be appended to any CPT codes listed in the **Evaluation and Management Services, Anesthesia, Radiology, Pathology/Laboratory, or Medicine** sections.

66 **Surgical Team:** Under some circumstances, highly complex procedures (requiring the concomitant services of several physicians, often of different specialties, plus other highly skilled, specially trained personnel, various types of complex equipment) are carried out under the "surgical team" concept. Such circumstances may be identified by each participating physician with the addition of modifier 66 to the basic procedure number used for reporting services.

76 **Repeat Procedure by Same Physician:** The physician may need to indicate that a procedure or service was repeated subsequent to the original procedure or service. This circumstance may be reported by adding modifier 76 to the repeated procedure/service.

77 **Repeat Procedure by Another Physician:** The physician may need to indicate that a basic procedure or service performed by another physician had to be repeated. This situation may be reported by adding modifier 77 to the repeated procedure/service.

78 **Return to the Operating Room for a Related Procedure During the Postoperative Period:** The physician may need to indicate that another procedure was performed during the postoperative period of the initial procedure. When this subsequent procedure is related to the first, and requires the use of the operating room, it may be reported by adding modifier 78 to the related procedure. (For repeat procedures on the same day, see modifier 76.)

79 **Unrelated Procedure or Service by the Same Physician During the Postoperative Period:** The physician may need to indicate that the performance of a procedure or service during the postoperative period was unrelated to the original procedure. This circumstance may be reported by using modifier 79. (For repeat procedures on the same day, see modifier 76.)

80 Assistant Surgeon: Surgical assistant services may be identified by adding modifier 80 to the usual procedure number(s).

81 Minimum Assistant Surgeon: Minimum surgical assistant services are identified by adding modifier 81 to the usual procedure number.

82 Assistant Surgeon (when qualified resident surgeon not available): The unavailability of a qualified resident surgeon is a prerequisite for use of modifier 82 appended to the usual procedure code number(s).

90 Reference (Outside) Laboratory: When laboratory procedures are performed by a party other than the treating or reporting physician, the procedure may be identified by adding modifier 90 to the usual procedure number.

91 Repeat Clinical Diagnostic Laboratory Test: In the course of treatment of the patient, it may be necessary to repeat the same laboratory test on the same day to obtain subsequent (multiple) test results. Under these circumstances, the laboratory test performed can be identified by its usual procedure number and the addition of modifier 91. **Note:** This modifier may not be used when tests are rerun to confirm initial results; due to testing problems with specimens or equipment; or for any other reason when a normal, one-time, reportable result is all that is required. This modifier may not be used when other code(s) describe a series of test results (eg, glucose tolerance tests, evocative/suppression testing). This modifier may only be used for laboratory test(s) performed more than once on the same day on the same patient.

99 Multiple Modifiers: Under certain circumstances two or more modifiers may be necessary to completely delineate a service. In such situations modifier 99 should be added to the basic procedure, and other applicable modifiers may be listed as part of the description of the service.

Anesthesia Physical Status Modifiers

The Physical Status modifiers are consistent with the American Society of Anesthesiologists ranking of patient physical status, and distinguishing various levels of complexity of the anesthesia service provided. All anesthesia services are reported by use of the anesthesia five-digit procedure code (00100-03108) with the appropriate physical status modifier appended.

Example: 00100-P1

Under certain circumstances, when another established modifier(s) is appropriate, it should be used in addition to the physical status modifier.

Example: 00100-P4-53

Physical Status Modifier P1: A normal healthy patient

Physical Status Modifier P2: A patient with mild systemic disease

Physical Status Modifier P3: A patient with severe systemic disease

Physical Status Modifier P4: A patient with severe systemic disease that is a constant threat to life

Physical Status Modifier P5: A moribund patient who is not expected to survive without the operation

Physical Status Modifier P6: A declared brain-dead patient whose organs are being removed for donor purposes

Modifiers Approved for Ambulatory Surgery Center (ASC) Hospital Outpatient Use

CPT Level I Modifiers

25 Significant, Separately Identifiable Evaluation and Management Service by the Same Physician on the Same Day of the Procedure or Other Service: The physician may need to indicate that on the day a procedure or service identified by a CPT code was performed, the patient's condition required a significant, separately identifiable E/M service above and beyond the other service provided or beyond the usual preoperative and postoperative care associated with the procedure that was performed. The E/M service may be prompted by the symptom or condition for which the procedure and/or service was provided. As such, different diagnoses are not required for reporting of the E/M services on the same date. This circumstance may be reported by adding modifier 25 to the appropriate level of E/M service. **Note:** This modifier is not used to report an E/M service that resulted in a decision to perform surgery. See modifier 57.

27 Multiple Outpatient Hospital E/M Encounters on the Same Date: For hospital outpatient reporting purposes, utilization of hospital resources related to separate and distinct E/M encounters performed in multiple outpatient hospital settings on the same date may be reported by adding modifier 27 to each appropriate level outpatient and/or emergency department E/M code(s). This modifier provides a means of reporting circumstances involving evaluation and management services provided by physician(s) in more than one (multiple) outpatient hospital setting(s) (eg, hospital emergency department, clinic). **Note:** This modifier is not to be used for physician reporting of multiple E/M services performed by the same physician on the same date. For physician reporting of all outpatient evaluation and management services provided by the same physician on the same date and performed in multiple outpatient setting(s) (eg, hospital emergency department, clinic), see **Evaluation and Management, Emergency Department, or Preventive Medicine Services** codes.

50 Bilateral Procedure: Unless otherwise identified in the listings, bilateral procedures that are performed at the same operative session should be identified by adding modifier 50 to the appropriate five digit code.

FIGURE 4-2 (*continued*)

52 Reduced Services: Under certain circumstances a service or procedure is partially reduced or eliminated at the physician's discretion. Under these circumstances the service provided can be identified by its usual procedure number and the addition of modifier 52, signifying that the service is reduced. This provides a means of reporting reduced services without disturbing the identification of the basic service. **Note:** For hospital outpatient reporting of a previously scheduled procedure/service that is partially reduced or cancelled as a result of extenuating circumstances or those that threaten the well-being of the patient prior to or after administration of anesthesia, see modifiers 73 and 74.

58 Staged or Related Procedure or Service by the Same Physician During the Postoperative Period: The physician may need to indicate that the performance of a procedure or service during the postoperative period was: a) planned prospectively at the time of the original procedure (staged); b) more extensive than the original procedure; or c) for therapy following a diagnostic surgical procedure. This circumstance may be reported by adding modifier 58 to the staged or related procedure. **Note:** This modifier is not used to report the treatment of a problem that requires a return to the operating room. See modifier 78.

59 Distinct Procedural Service: Under certain circumstances, the physician may need to indicate that a procedure or service was distinct or independent from other services performed on the same day. Modifier 59 is used to identify procedures/services that are not normally reported together, but are appropriate under the circumstances. This may represent a different session or patient encounter, different procedure or surgery, different site or organ system, separate incision/excision, separate lesion, or separate injury (or area of injury in extensive injuries) not ordinarily encountered or performed on the same day by the same physician. However, when another already established modifier is appropriate it should be used rather than modifier 59. Only if no more descriptive modifier is available, and the use of modifier 59 best explains the circumstances, should modifier 59 be used.

73 Discontinued Out-Patient Hospital/Ambulatory Surgery Center (ASC) Procedure Prior to the Administration of Anesthesia: Due to extenuating circumstances or those that threaten the well being of the patient, the physician may cancel a surgical or diagnostic procedure subsequent to the patient's surgical preparation (including sedation when provided, and being taken to the room where the procedure is to be performed), but prior to the administration of anesthesia (local, regional block(s) or general). Under these circumstances, the intended service that is prepared for but cancelled can be reported by its usual procedure number and the addition of modifier 73. **Note:** The elective cancellation of a service prior to the administration of anesthesia and/or surgical preparation of the patient should not be reported. For physician reporting of a discontinued procedure, see modifier 53.

74 Discontinued Out-Patient Hospital/Ambulatory Surgery Center (ASC) Procedure After Administration of Anesthesia: Due to extenuating circumstances or those that threaten the well being of the patient, the physician may terminate a surgical or diagnostic procedure after the administration of anesthesia (local, regional block(s), general) or after the procedure was started (incision made, intubation started, scope inserted, etc). Under these circumstances, the procedure started but terminated can be reported by its usual procedure number and the addition of modifier 74. **Note:** The elective cancellation of a service prior to the administration of anesthesia and/or surgical preparation of the patient should not be reported. For physician reporting of a discontinued procedure, see modifier 53.

76 Repeat Procedure by Same Physician: The physician may need to indicate that a procedure or service was repeated subsequent to the original procedure or service. This circumstance may be reported by adding modifier 76 to the repeated procedure/service.

77 Repeat Procedure by Another Physician: The physician may need to indicate that a basic procedure or service performed by another physician had to be repeated. This situation may be reported by adding modifier 77 to the repeated procedure/service.

78 Return to the Operating Room for a Related Procedure During the Postoperative Period: The physician may need to indicate that another procedure was performed during the postoperative period of the initial procedure. When this subsequent procedure is related to the first, and requires the use of the operating room, it may be reported by adding modifier 78 to the related procedure. (For repeat procedures on the same day, see 76.)

79 Unrelated Procedure or Service by the Same Physician During the Postoperative Period: The physician may need to indicate that the performance of a procedure or service during the postoperative period was unrelated to the original procedure. This circumstance may be reported by using modifier 79. (For repeat procedures on the same day, see 76.)

91 Repeat Clinical Diagnostic Laboratory Test: In the course of treatment of the patient, it may be necessary to repeat the same laboratory test on the same day to obtain subsequent (multiple) test results. Under these circumstances, the laboratory test performed can be identified by its usual procedure number and the addition of modifier 91. **Note:** This modifier may not be used when tests are rerun to confirm initial results; due to testing problems with specimens or equipment; or for any other reason when a normal, one-time, reportable result is all that is required. This modifier may not be used when other code(s) describe a series of test results (eg, glucose tolerance tests, evocative/suppression testing). This modifier may only be used for laboratory test(s) performed more than once on the same day on the same patient.

Source: Reprinted from American Medical Association. *CPT 2005.* Chicago, IL: American Medical Association; 2004: 401–405.

2005 CPT codes. (The latest edition of the CPT codebook should be consulted for the most up-to-date modifiers and codes.)

HCPCS PROCEDURE CODING

In the 1980s, when the use of electronic claims was increasing, CMS recognized the need for a nationwide standardized coding system. As a result, the Healthcare Common Procedure Coding System (HCPCS, pronounced "hick-picks") was created. Because Medicare and Medicaid pay for physicians' services as well as other medical services and supplies, CMS developed the following three levels of codes. Level I includes the five-digit CPT codes and two-digit modifiers. Level II includes alphanumeric codes that begin with a letter followed by four numbers. For example, G0103 indicates prostate cancer screening; prostate specific antigen test (PSA), total. Level II codes are usually used to report supplies and injections to Medicare and other payers. *CPT 2006* includes all Level I and Level II modifiers approved for physician and hospital outpatient use.

Level I: Current Procedural Terminology

The AMA developed and first published the five-digit CPT coding system in 1966. It is used to report procedures and services provided by physicians and other health care providers. In agreement with the AMA, CMS adopted the CPT coding system as the first level of HCPCS coding. The CPT codebook, which is copyrighted by the AMA, includes more than 8000 numeric codes and represents approximately 90% of HCPCS.

Level II: National HCPCS Codes

Level II codes (see Table 4-5) are for services and supplies not found in the CPT codebook, such as oral and injectable medications; durable medical equipment; prosthetics; orthotics; medical and surgical supplies; ambulance services; chiropractic, dental, certain vision services, and supplies; and temporary codes developed by CMS. Level II codes are five-digit alphanumeric codes, beginning with the letters A through V. As implied by the name, Level II national codes are used by all Medicare carriers (Part B) and intermediaries (Part A) and by Medicaid in all states.

Level III: Local HCPCS Codes

The Consolidated Appropriations Act of 2001, Public Law 106-554 (enacted December 21, 2000), instructed carriers to maintain and continue the use of Level III HCPCS codes (local codes) through December 31, 2003. Compliance with the Health Insurance Portability and Accountability Act of 1996 (HIPAA) requires deletion of any Level III codes as of that date. CMS developed Level II HCPCS codes (national codes) for providers to use in place of many of these local codes. These codes were discontinued as of December 31, 2003.

HCPCS Coding Guidelines

HCPCS Level II codes are reported on claims in the same manner as Level I (CPT) codes. Medicare requires physicians and hospitals to use certain Level II codes instead of less specific CPT codes in certain circumstances. For example, covered and injectable medications must be submitted with the specific Level II code that begins with "J," as well as the CPT code from the Medicine section. The Level II codes beginning with "A" must be used when billing covered supplies, such as surgical trays. Each Medicare carrier and intermediary can provide billing rules for Level II codes.

TABLE 4-5

HCPCS Level II (National) Modifiers for Hospital Outpatient Use

AH	Clinical psychologist
AJ	Clinical social worker
CC	Procedure code change (CC is used when the procedure code submitted was changed either for administrative reasons or because an incorrect code was filed.)
E1	Upper left, eyelid
E2	Lower left, eyelid
E3	Upper right, eyelid
E4	Lower right, eyelid
F1	Left hand, second digit
F2	Left hand, third digit
F3	Left hand, fourth digit
F4	Left hand, fifth digit
F5	Right hand, thumb
F6	Right hand, second digit
F7	Right hand, third digit
F8	Right hand, fourth digit
F9	Right hand, fifth digit
FA	Left hand, thumb
FP	Service provided as part of Medicaid Family Planning Program
G6	ESRD patient for whom less than six dialysis sessions have been provided in a month
GY	Item or service statutorily excluded or does not meet the definition of any Medicare benefit
GZ	Item or service expected to be denied as not reasonable and necessary
LC	Left circumflex, coronary artery (hospitals use with codes 92980-92984, 92995, 92996)
LD	Left anterior descending coronary artery (hospitals use with codes 92980-92984, 92995, 92996)
LL	Leasing/rental (The LL modifier is used when DME equipment rental is to be applied against the purchase price.)
LR	Laboratory round trip
LS	FDA-monitored intraocular lens implant
LT	Left side (used to identify procedures performed on the left side of the body)
MS	Six-month maintenance and servicing fee for reasonable and necessary parts and labor, which are not covered under any manufacturer or supplier warranty
PL	Progressive addition lenses
QM	Ambulance service provided under arrangement by a provider of services
QN	Ambulance service furnished directly by a provider of services
RC	Right coronary artery (hospitals use with codes 92980-92984, 92995, 92996)
RT	Right side (used to identify procedures performed on the right side of the body)
T1	Left foot, second digit
T2	Left foot, third digit
T3	Left foot, fourth digit
T4	Left foot, fifth digit
T5	Right foot, great toe
T6	Right foot, second digit
T7	Right foot, third digit
T8	Right foot, fourth digit
T9	Right foot, fifth digit
TA	Left foot, great toe
UE	Used durable medical equipment

ICD-9-CM CODING

The ICD-9-CM coding system reports patient illnesses, injuries, complaints, and/or symptoms, referred to as diagnoses. ICD-9-CM communicates to third-party payers the need or reason for medical services. Like CPT, the ICD-9-CM system consists of code numbers and narrative descriptions. Unlike CPT, ICD-9-CM codes may range from three to five digits, depending on the level of specificity defined. The physician or the coder should code to the highest level of specificity. All ICD-9-CM codes are numeric except for E and V codes.

ICD-9-CM was developed in 1978 by the US National Center for Health Statistics (NCHS) as a statistical classification system. It was created to replace the ICD-A system and to allow for better reporting of both inpatient and outpatient conditions. The ICD-A system and the ICD-9 system were developed by the World Health Organization (WHO) in Switzerland. The NCHS added the clinical modification (CM) so that the ICD-9 system could be used for insurance reimbursement in the United States. Virtually all third-party payers in the United States use ICD-9-CM coding system to describe patient conditions. It is updated annually in October. Physicians should use the most current ICD-9-CM coding books to ensure correct code assignment. There is not an expected release date for ICD-10-CM, tenth revision, according to the National Center for Health Statistics. In late 1991, the US Government Printing Office released the fourth edition of ICD-9-CM, which incorporates all changes made to ICD-9-CM since the 1980 printing of the third edition.

The purpose of ICD-9-CM coding is threefold: (1) to establish the medical necessity for a visit or service; (2) to provide statistics for morbidity and mortality rates; and (3) to take the written description of a disease or state and translate that information into numbers to produce a common language. The complete ICD-9-CM coding system consists of the following three volumes:

Volume 1: Diseases, Tabular List

Volume 2: Diseases, Alphabetic Index

Volume 3: Procedures, Tabular and Alphabetic Index

Physicians should only be concerned with Volumes 1 and 2. Volume 3, which contains codes and descriptions for procedures and an index to these codes, is used almost exclusively by hospitals. Volume 1 contains three-, four-, and five-digit codes and their associated descriptions. Volume 2 is the index to the codes in the tabular list of Volume 1. Following is a four-digit ICD-9-CM code taken from Volume 1:

685.0   Pilonidal cyst with abscess

Requirements

The Medicare Catastrophic Coverage Act, a law requiring all physicians to use ICD-9-CM codes when reporting patient diagnoses to Medicare, became effective on April 1, 1989. Lack of compliance on claims submitted to Medicare after June 1, 1989, results in serious penalties that range from nonpayment of assigned claims to fines of $2000 per occurrence on unassigned claims.

Although this law applies only to claims submitted to Medicare, the accurate use of ICD-9-CM codes for reporting diagnoses to all third-party payers is advisable for several reasons. First, payment may be denied or delayed if diagnosis codes are not used. Also, many third-party payers use software programs that compare the CPT codes to the ICD-9-CM codes. These programs, which test for logical relationships, would, for example, reveal a mismatch between a procedure listed as the removal of a cyst and the diagnosis of hypertension. Such a claim would probably be automatically denied for lack of medical necessity or reasonableness.

It is for these reasons that physicians should become familiar with the ICD-9-CM coding system and its rules. ICD-9-CM code ranges from 001.0 through V86.1 are used to report the reason for treatment. The following sections discuss the organization of the ICD-9-CM coding manual; the use of abbreviations, symbols, and notations; and general coding rules important to physician practices. The discussion is not intended to be exhaustive.

Organization

Volume 1, the tabular list, contains codes and descriptions for diseases, illnesses, injuries, complaints, symptoms, signs, findings, etc. It is organized into 17 chapters plus two supplementary sections. The supplementary sections are used when coding patients who are not being seen for a current illness (V codes) or when a patient's problem is due to an external cause related to injury or poisoning (E codes). Volume 2 is an alphabetic list of codes used as an index to the first volume.

Codes can contain either three digits (category), four digits (subcategory), or five digits (subclassification). The additional fourth and fifth digits typically provide additional information about the category that is pertinent to the body area or site or information about whether the patient did or did not present with complications. An example of each level of code follows:

345	Epilepsy and recurrent seizures
345.0	Generalized nonconvulsive epilepsy
345.01	Generalized nonconvulsive epilepsy with intractable epilepsy

In this example, 345 is the category. It is further defined by subcategory, in this case that the epilepsy is generalized as nonconvulsive. The subcategory is further defined by a fifth-digit subclassification, in this case that the patient has intractable epilepsy with generalized nonconvulsive epilepsy. Fifth-digit assignment is *not* optional. If such an assignment is available, it must always be coded to the greatest level of specificity. A claim submitted with ICD-9-CM code 345 would not be accepted because this code series demands five digits.

Symbols, Abbreviations, and Notations

Two symbols are used throughout Volume 1 of ICD-9-CM. The first symbol, the lozenge n, is used to show that the four-digit code is unique to the clinical modification system (ie, ICD-9-CM) rather than ICD-9. The second symbol, the section mark §, alerts the coder to the presence of fifth digits that need to be added to the code for more specificity. In many instances, definitions for the fifth digits are found on pages preceding the code. The section mark also indicates that there is a footnote at the bottom of the page that applies to all subdivisions in that code.

The abbreviations NEC and NOS are used in ICD-9-CM, and both have specific meanings and importance to coding and reimbursement. NEC, which means *not elsewhere classified*, is used when the coder lacks the information necessary to code the term to a more specific category. The ICD-9-CM index provides references to specific codes when such cases arise and uses the NEC abbreviation to guide the coder. In other cases, there may not be a code that completely describes the patient's condition. NEC is also used in these situations.

The abbreviation NOS, which means *not otherwise specified*, appears throughout the tabular list and is frequently associated with the unspecified codes. In fact, *not otherwise specified* means the same as *unspecified*. For example, a patient is seen by her physician for ringworm, but the type is unknown. This case would be coded as follows:

110.9	Dermatophytosis of unspecified site
	Ringworm NOS

When codes for unspecified conditions are reported to third-party payers, special attention may need to be given to the claim if reimbursement is expected. Many carriers suspend claims that list an unspecified diagnosis code for review. Therefore, a brief note attached to the claim explaining the patient's problem in more detail is prudent.

ICD-9-CM also uses notations to further assist the coder in selecting the appropriate code. Nonessential modifiers are one type of notation. In the index, main terms are shown in boldface type. The main term may be followed by a term or group of terms enclosed in parentheses. These terms are called nonessential modifiers, because they may or may not appear in the diagnostic statement in order for the code to be used. For example, under the main term "Encephalitis" in the index, seven nonessential modifiers are listed next to the main term:

Encephalitis (bacterial) (chronic) (hemorrhage) (idiopathic) (non-epidemic) (spurious) (sub-acute)

If the diagnostic statement contains one of these terms (eg, the patient has bacterial encephalitis), code 323.9 could be used. Conversely, if the diagnostic statement does not contain one of these terms, it could still be appropriate to use the code, depending on the circumstances. Nonessential modifiers give some examples of specific types of disorders that can be classified under this main term.

Essential modifiers, on the other hand, are indented line entries following the main term. They can represent differences in etiology, site, or other circumstances. For example, the main term "Burn" is followed by the subterm "arm(s)."

Another frequently used notation is the term *see also*. Found in the index and always printed in italics, this notation instructs the coder to refer to another category in addition to the one that the coder is referencing. For example, when coding toxic uninodular goiter, the coder might first look under "Toxic" in the index. Under "Toxic" the coder is instructed to "see also condition." The coder would look under the entry for the condition (in this case, goiter) to begin locating the proper code.

Notes

ICD-9-CM uses notes to convey information. There are two types of notes: those appearing with groups of codes and those appearing with specific codes. Each type has a specific meaning in ICD-9-CM. The first type, the Includes note, further define or give an example of the contents of a group of codes, as demonstrated in the following:

680   Carbuncle and furuncle
        Includes: Boil, furunculosis

The second type of notes, the Excludes note, means just the opposite of Includes notes. Because coders need to be aware of conditions that are excluded from groups of codes, it is critical to be aware of all Excludes notes. An example follows:

737   Curvature of spine
        Excludes: Congenital (754.2)

Thus, if a patient is suffering from congenital curvature of the spine, codes from the 737 group would not be reported.

In addition to Includes and Excludes notes, other notes may appear at the beginning of a section of codes and/or at the beginning of a chapter. These notes provide general coding guidance regarding the codes they precede. For example, five paragraphs of notes appear before the 369 group of codes for blindness and low vision, and Chapter 2, Neoplasms, provides extensive notes related to coding neoplasms. It is important to check for and read notes preceding codes because the notes may affect code selection.

Tables

There are three tables in the index that the coder should be aware of: the Hypertension Table, the Table of Neoplasms, and the Table of Drugs and Chemicals.

The Hypertension Table is found in the index of Volume 2 by looking up the term *hypertension*. It is further broken down by concurrent disease or state, such as pregnancy.

Each entry is followed by three columns that designate the hypertension state as malignant, benign, or unspecified.

The Table of Neoplasms is found in Volume 2 and has a special listing for neoplasms. It is broken down into four main categories:

- *Malignant*: A severe form of neoplasm possessing the property for destructive growth and metastasis.
- *Benign*: A nonmalignant neoplasm.
- *Uncertain behavior*: Pathology unable to determine type of neoplasm due to features that are present.
- *Unspecified*: There are insufficient data to be able to categorize the neoplasm.

The malignant designation may be further classified by whether the neoplasm is primary, secondary, or cancer in situ.

The Table of Drugs and Chemicals is found in Volume 2, Section 2. This table contains a classification of drugs and other chemical substances that is used to identify poisoning states and external causes of adverse effects.

Cross-Reference Terms

Cross-reference terms are found in the alphabetic index and instruct the coder to search elsewhere in the ICD-9-CM manual before assigning a code. The three types of terms are: see, see also, and see category. The *see* cross-reference directs the coder to an alternative term. The *see also* term directs the coder to look under another main term in the index, if all the information needed is not found under the first main term. The third type of cross-reference, *see category*, instructs the coder to a specific category in the tabular list. An important concept to remember is that for these cross-reference terms, one is directed to make a decision whether the referenced term applies or not. It does not necessarily mean to code that referenced term.

General ICD-9-CM Coding Guidelines

The process of coding with ICD-9-CM is much easier when the coder takes the following steps:

1. Review the entire medical record. Do not code from just the face sheet with a list of diagnoses and procedures. Query the physician if the information in the medical record is not consistent.
2. Review all subterms and look first in the alphabetic index for the main term. Then refer to any applicable notes for the term *nonessential modifiers*. Follow any cross-reference instructions.
3. Always verify the code numbers in the tabular list. Read and follow instructional terms and notes.
4. Code only three-digit codes for diseases if there are no fourth- or fifth-digit codes available.
5. Code only four-digit codes if there are no fifth-digit codes available.
6. Look for and be guided by the Includes and Excludes notes throughout the codebook. These may appear after a particular code or under category section titles.
7. When assigning multiple diagnoses, always sequence the principal diagnosis first.

ICD-9-CM Codes Validate Medical Necessity for Procedures

Current requirements for documenting medical necessity include the substitution of the final diagnosis code when a symptom leads to the performance of a procedure. For example, if a patient undergoes a chest X ray for "cough, sputum production, rales left lower lobe" and the study reveals "pneumonia," pneumonia should be reported as the diagnosis on the billing form (if it is available at the time of billing).

On the other hand, if a study demonstrates no pathology or a diagnosis that is not considered to validate medical necessity, the billing form should include a description of the indications or the clinical picture that led to the need for the study attended to it. For example, code *45378, Colonoscopy, flexible, proximal to splenic flexure; diagnostic, with or without collection of specimen(s) by brushing or washing, with or without colon decompression (separate procedure)*, may be denied for payment if the only positive findings are internal hemorrhoids. If the patient underwent the procedure because of a strong family history of colon cancer, code G0105 might be more appropriate if billing for a Medicare patient. Otherwise, an explanation describing the reason for performing the diagnostic procedure, such as "hematochezia not thought to be from rectal or perianal source," should be submitted along with the claim.

Fourth- and Fifth-Digit Codes

In many cases, there are fourth- and fifth-digit ICD-9-CM codes to select from. If there is a five-digit code, it must be used. If there is no five-digit code but there is a four-digit code, use the four-digit code. A three-digit code is used only if there are no four- or five-digit codes.

Fourth-digit codes are expanded completely below the category to which they apply. For example, in the 556 series of codes for ulcerative colitis, four-digit codes are provided, as shown in the following:

556.5   Left-sided ulcerative (chronic) colitis
556.6   Universal ulcerative (chronic) colitis
556.8   Other ulcerative colitis
556.9   Ulcerative colitis, unspecified

In some cases, as many as 10 (0 through 9) fourth-digit codes are provided; others may have only one or two. Also, fourth-digit codes do not always follow strict numerical order.

Fifth-digit codes are presented in two different ways in ICD-9-CM. First, all fifth-digit codes may be listed under the fourth-digit code. For example, code 054.1, Genital herpes, has five fifth-digit codes to choose from. The second method for presenting fifth-digit codes involves printing the fifth digits, along with their definitions, immediately above the four-digit codes to which they apply. For example:

The following fifth-digit subclassification is for use with category 531:
    0 without mention of obstruction
    1 with obstruction

These fifth digits are applied to the fourth-digit codes in the subcategory as appropriate. For example, if the patient has an acute gastric ulcer with perforation and obstruction, the correct code would be 531.11.

Many carriers have computer systems that can identify claims containing ICD-9-CM codes that require fourth or fifth digits. Claims that do not list fifth- or fourth-digit diagnosis codes when required may be denied.

Symptoms, Signs, and Ill-Defined Conditions

Some patients may present with symptoms or signs that defy immediate diagnosis. Nonetheless, a diagnosis must be listed if a claim is filed. Special codes can be used in such cases. Chapter 16 in ICD-9-CM provides codes to use in these situations. For example, a physician treats a patient who has burning and prickling sensations in his feet. Until a more definitive diagnosis is established, code *782.0, Disturbance of skin sensation*, can be listed.

In the absence of a definitive diagnosis, it is appropriate and preferable to list the symptom or other presenting problem. There can be legal consequences for those who list a code just to obtain payment or for those who list a diagnosis when the diagnosis is not attested to or documented by the physician. Instead, list the code for the symptom. For example, a patient presents with pain during urination, blood in the urine, slight fever, and back pain. The physician suspects bladder tumors but is unsure. Until the physician is sure of the diagnosis, the symptoms can be listed as the diagnosis, all of which support the need for services, such as an office visit.

Terrorism Codes

The US Federal Bureau of Investigation's definition of terrorism is "injuries resulting from the unlawful use of force or violence against persons or property to intimidate or coerce a Government, the civilian population, or any segment thereof, in furtherance of political or social objectives."

The two major classification systems used for mortality and morbidity statistics are the ICD-10-CM and ICD-9-CM. However, these two classification systems do not include categories of codes specific to terrorism. The NCHS developed a set of codes that allows the identification of death certificates through the National Vital Statistics System also for injuries and illnesses caused by terrorism reported on medical records used for statistics and reimbursement. The codes for terrorism are not substitute codes for operations of war, which are used during a declared state of war. Terrorism-related ICD-10 codes for mortality can be found in the new "U" chapter. Codes for morbidity are within the existing chapter for External Causes of Morbidity. Table 4-6 provides a list of terrorism diagnosis codes.

Coding for the Future

ICD-10-CM

The International Classification of Diseases (ICD), 10th revision and its Clinical Modification (CM) will replace the ICD-9-CM for statistics and billing in the United States. ICD-10 has certain applications today and is used in other countries around the world. The ICD-10 is copyrighted by the World Health Organization (WHO), which owns and publishes the classification. WHO is responsible for revising ICD, and a clinical modification (CM) was developed by the Department of Health and Human Services (DHHS) National Center for Health Statistics (NCHS), for use in the United States.

ICD-10-CM includes more then 23,000 codes and applies to more users then ICD-9-CM because it is designed to collect data on every type of health care encounter (eg, inpatient, outpatient, long term care, home health care, and hospice). The ICD structure developed by WHO and clinically modified for use in the United States is also expected to improve the quality of data input into clinical databases and there by, provide more information about patient healthcare encounters.

The WHO published ICD-10 in 1994 with a new name (International Statistical Classification of Diseases and Related Health Problems), and reorganized its three digit categories. While the title was amended to clarify content and purpose, and to reflect development of codes and descriptions beyond diseases and injuries, the familiar "ICD" was kept. ICD-10 contains clinical detail, expands information about previously classified diseases, and classifies diseases discovered since the last revision.

ICD-10 also incorporates organizational changes and new features, but its format and conventions remain unchanged. Chapter titles, organization, and Includes and Excludes notes are similar to ICD-9. The largest difference is that the new codes are alpha-numeric, and there is more detail in ICD-10-CM than in ICD-9-CM. All codes begin with a letter and are followed by up to five numbers. All letters of the alphabet are used, and valid codes can contain three, four, five or six characters.

TABLE 4-6

Diagnosis Codes for Terrorism

Classification for Morbidity (E Codes for ICD-9)

E979	Terrorism
E979.0	Terrorism involving explosion of marine weapons: depth charge; marine mine; mine NOS, at sea or in harbor; sea-based artillery shell, torpedo, underwater blast
E979.1	Terrorism involving destruction of aircraft: aircraft used as a weapon; aircraft burned, exploded, or shot down; crushed by falling aircraft
E979.2	Terrorism involving other explosions and fragments: antipersonnel bomb (fragments); blast NOS; explosions of artillery shell, breech-block, cannon block, mortar bomb, or munitions being used in terrorism; fragments from artillery shell, bomb, grenade, guided missile, land mine, rocket, shell, or shrapnel; mine NOS
E979.3	Terrorism involving fires, conflagration, and hot substances: conflagration NOS; fire NOS; petrol bomb; asphyxia; burns or other injury; collapse of, fall from, jump from, or hit by falling object in a burning building or structure; fire and melting of fittings and furniture in burning and smoldering building or structure
E979.4	Terrorism involving firearms: bullets from carbine, machine gun, pistol, rifle, or rubber (rifle); pellets from a shotgun
E979.5	Terrorism involving nuclear weapons: blast effects; exposure to ionizing radiation from nuclear weapons; fireball effect; heat from nuclear weapons and other direct and secondary effects of nuclear weapon
E979.6	Terrorism involving biological weapons: anthrax, cholera, or smallpox
E979.7	Terrorism involving chemical weapons: gases, fumes, and chemicals
E979.8	Terrorism involving other means: drowning and submersion; lasers; piercing or stabbing instruments
E979.9	Terrorism, secondary effects: excludes late effects of injury due to terrorism
E999	Late of effects of injury due to war operations and terrorism
E999.0	Late effect of injury due to war operations
E999.1	Late effect of injury due to terrorism

Classification for Mortality (U Codes for ICD-10)

*U01.0	Terrorism involving explosion of marine weapons: depth charge; marine mine; mine NOS, at sea or in harbor; sea-based artillery shell, torpedo, or underwater blast
*U01.1	Terrorism involving destruction of aircraft: aircraft used as a weapon; aircraft burned, exploded, or shot down; crushed by falling aircraft
*U01.2	Terrorism involving other explosions and fragments: antipersonnel bomb (fragments); blast NOS; explosion of NOS; artillery shell, breech-block, cannon block, mortar bomb, munitions being used in terrorism; own weapons; fragments from artillery shell, bomb, grenade, guided missile, land mine, rocket, shell, and shrapnel; mine NOS
*U01.3	Terrorism involving fires, conflagration, and hot substances: asphyxia; burns, other injuries (originating from fire caused directly by a fire-producing device or indirectly by any conventional weapon); petrol bomb; collapse of, fall from, hit by object, jump from burning building or structure; conflagration, fire, melting, or smoldering of fittings or furniture
*U01.4	Terrorism involving firearms: bullets from carbine, machine gun, pistol, rifle, or rubber (rifle); pellets (shotgun)
*U01.5	Terrorism involving nuclear weapons: blast effects; exposure to ionizing radiation from nuclear weapon; fireball effects; heat or other direct and secondary effects of nuclear weapons
*U01.6	Terrorism involving biological weapons: anthrax, cholera, or smallpox
*U01.7	Terrorism involving chemical weapons: gases, fumes, or chemicals
*U01.8	Terrorism, other specified: lasers; battle wounds; piercing or stabbing object injuries; drowned in terrorist operations NOS
*U01.9	Terrorism, unspecified
*U02	Sequelae of terrorism
*U03	Terrorism (suicide)
*U03.0	Terrorism involving explosions and fragments: aircraft used as a weapon; aircraft burned, exploded, or shot down; antipersonnel bomb (fragments); blast NOS; explosions of the following: NOS, artillery shell, breech-block, cannon block, mortar bomb, munitions being used in terrorism and own weapons; fragments from the following: artillery shells, bombs, grenades, guided missiles, land mines, rockets, shells, and shrapnel; mine NOS
*U03.9	Terrorism by other and unspecified means

ICD-10 Volumes

ICD-10-CM is published in three volumes.

- Volume 1 **Tabular List**
    - o Cause of death titles and codes
    - o Inclusion and exclusion terms for cause of death
- Volume 2 **Instruction Manual**: Description, guidelines, and coding rules
- Volume 3 **Alphabetical Index**: An alphabetical index to diseases and nature of injury, external causes of injury, and tables of drugs and chemicals

The ICD-10-CM coding system consists of 22 Chapters.

Chapter 1	A00-B99	Certain infection & parasitic diseases
Chapter 2	C00-D48	Neoplasms
Chapter 3	D50-D89	Disease of the blood and blood-forming organs & certain disorders involving the immune mechanism
Chapter 4	E00-E90	Endocrine, nutritional, & metabolic diseases
Chapter 5	F01-F99	Mental & behavioral disorders
Chapter 6	G00-G99	Disease of the nervous system
Chapter 7	H00-H59	Disease of the eye & adnexa
Chapter 8	H60-H95	Disease of the ear & mastoid process
Chapter 9	I00-I99	Disease of the circulatory system
Chapter 10	J00-J99	Disease of the respiratory system
Chapter 11	K00-K93	Disease of the digestive system
Chapter 12	L00-L99	Disease of the skin & subcutaneous tissue
Chapter 13	M00-M99	Disease of the musculoskeletal system and connective tissue
Chapter 14	N00-N99	Disease of genitourinary system
Chapter 15	O00-O99	Pregnancy, childbirth and the puerperium
Chapter 16	P00-P96	Certain conditions originating in the perinatal period
Chapter 17	Q00-Q99	Congenital malformations, deformations, and chromosomal abnormalities
Chapter 18	R00-R99	Symptoms, signs, and abnormal clinical and laboratory findings, not elsewhere classified
Chapter 19	S00-T98	Injury, poisoning and certain other consequences of external causes
Chapter 20	V01-Y98	External causes or morbidity
Chapter 21	Z00-Z99	Factors influencing health status and contact with health services
Chapter 22	U00-U99	Codes for special purposes

Supplemental classifications of the External causes of Morbidity (called external causes of injury or *E codes* in ICD-9-CM) and factors influencing Health Status (or *V codes*) are incorporated into the core of the ICD-10 classification system. This means that these codes and descriptions are located throughout the chapters of ICD-10, and they are no longer designated as *E codes* or *V codes*. ICD-10 E-codes classify the Endocrine System, not external causes. External causes, currently classified in ICD-9 as E codes will be *V codes* in ICD-10. The *V codes*, which are included in the ICD-9-CM Supplemental classification to report factors influencing health status, have been changed to U codes and Z codes in ICD-10.

Implementing ICD-10-CM

On May 29, 2002, the American Health Information Management Association (AHIMA) recommended to the National Committee on Vital and Health Statistics (NCVHS) that the current ICD-9-CM coding system be replaced as soon as possible. There are just as many positive reasons for adopting ICD-10-CM as negative ones. AHIMA tested more than 6000 medical encounters that used the ICD-10-CM in which the majority of participants were coding professionals from various health care fields. Most agreed that the ICD-10-CM system was an improvement over ICD-9-CM and felt that training would consist of a maximum of 16 hours face-to-face in a classroom setting or via Internet training. This revelation helps negate the criticism that the new system will be too complex for US coders to implement.

On July 24, 2003, Linda Kloss, CEO and executive vice president of AHIMA, wrote to the secretary of the US Department of Health and Human Services (DHHS) urging adoption of ICD-10-CM. A request to the President for his assistance in "pushing" the adoption was also made by Kloss. It is AHIMA's position that if ICD-10-CM is adopted soon and if the DHHS moves quickly, implementation of ICD-10-CM with upgrades could happen by late 2006. However, many feel this date is too presumptuous and will not be met.

Insurance companies oppose conversion to the ICD-10-CM system, because they feel it will be too costly. It has been estimated (or argued by some) that the price for implementing the new ICD-10-CM system, without proven benefits, could reach as high as $14 billion. Supporters of the ICD-10-CM conversion and the Rand Report, commissioned by the NCVHS, provide statistics to the contrary and state that the benefits of implementing this system will, in the long run, outweigh the cost of conversion.

Observation Services

Observation status was established in 1986 by CMS to allow an alternative method for physicians to oversee the care of patients in a hospital instead of the standard inpatient or outpatient settings. The intent was to allow a patient to remain in a hospital environment and be "observed" for any insidious complications that the patient may have but are not evident on initial examination by the emergency department and admitting physicians. This time period would allow certain clinical data and diagnostic exams to be performed and allow the physician to establish a more definitive diagnosis during this period of time.

Initially the length of time a patient could be in observation was not established nor were specific diagnoses presented to give the physician a better picture of which patients would be appropriate for this service. On July 1, 1996, CMS established a 48-hour maximum for use with Medicare claims and provided a better picture of what types of patients should be admitted into the observation service.

Definition
According to CMS guidelines:

> Observation services are defined as services that are furnished on hospital premises and include the use of a bed and monitoring by nursing and ancillary staff. These services are to be reasonable and necessary to evaluate an outpatient's condition or to determine the need for a possible inpatient admission.

A physician's order must be given in order for such services to be covered. Another individual authorized by State law and hospital bylaws to admit patients to the hospital or to order other outpatient tests can order observation services. Observation services are to be considered acute care services and handled accordingly.

These services typically do not exceed one day (24 hours); however, patients may require a second day (48 hours) for these services or sometimes on rare and exceptional cases more time can be given to the patient in Observation. Observation services should not be substituted for a patient who meets criteria for a medically necessary appropriate inpatient admission. Once the patient is admitted as an inpatient hospital admission, the patient should not be discharged to outpatient observation status.

General Guidelines for Outpatient Observation Services
Time begins for observation status when the patient is placed in an observation bed. No payment is made after 48 hours unless medical documentation clearly dictates the need for continued observation status in which the patient did not qualify for inpatient care.

Outpatient observation services should not be substituted when a patient is in the hospital for a one-day inpatient stay. The patient can be held liable for services beyond 48 hours. If this occurs, the patient must receive written notice of possible noncoverage of services that were provided.

One Day or Less Outpatient Observation Services
A patient is initially regarded as an outpatient if not formally admitted as an inpatient. Many observation patients, in particular those in a surgical setting, recover sufficiently to be released or discharged on the same day that observation services began. These patients would be classified as outpatients. Patients whose condition worsen or are determined after evaluation to require inpatient care are then formally admitted as inpatients on that particular day. This day is considered their first inpatient day.

Second Day Observation Services
Some patients require observation services overnight; they may be discharged or formally admitted on the following day. If not admitted or released on the following day, they are classified as outpatients. If formally admitted on the following day, that day is considered the patient's first inpatient day.

Services Denied on the Third Day of Observation Services
If a patient remains in observation status for a second night without a formal inpatient admission, further observation services are denied by Medicare. (Certain exceptional circumstances in a particular case may justify approval of an additional status.)

Types of Services Not Covered
Services that are not reasonable or necessary for the diagnosis or treatment but are provided for the convenience of the patient or physician are not covered. Services that are covered under Part A or as part of another Part B benefit, such as services covered under ambulatory surgical center payment rates, outpatient diagnostic testing charges, or routine preparation services prior to the testing, are not covered. In addition, the following services are not covered:

- Standing orders for observation following outpatient surgery
- Services ordered as inpatient services but billed as outpatient services
- Any substitution of an outpatient observation service for a medically appropriate inpatient admission
- Observation services provided for the convenience of the patient or the physician
- Observation services that exceed 48 hours, unless granted an exception by the fiscal intermediary

Billing Instructions
Although most physicians do not have direct exposure to the billing process, it is prudent that they have an understanding of what is involved in the process.

A CMS billing form 1450, also known as the UB-92, was used when billing for observation services (see Figure 4-3). Billing staff use the revenue code 762 for billing of observation services; once subject to the ambulatory surgery center (ASC) payment limitation, this is no longer the case.

Payment for Hospital Observation Services
Although the physician's business office handles information related to hospital observation services, it is prudent to understand this information and to understand how the billing process works. There are four CPT codes used to report E/M services. They include:

99217 Observation care discharge day management

This code is used for a patient on discharge from "observation status." This code cannot be used if the discharge is on the same day as the initial date of "observation status."

FIGURE 4-3
UB-92

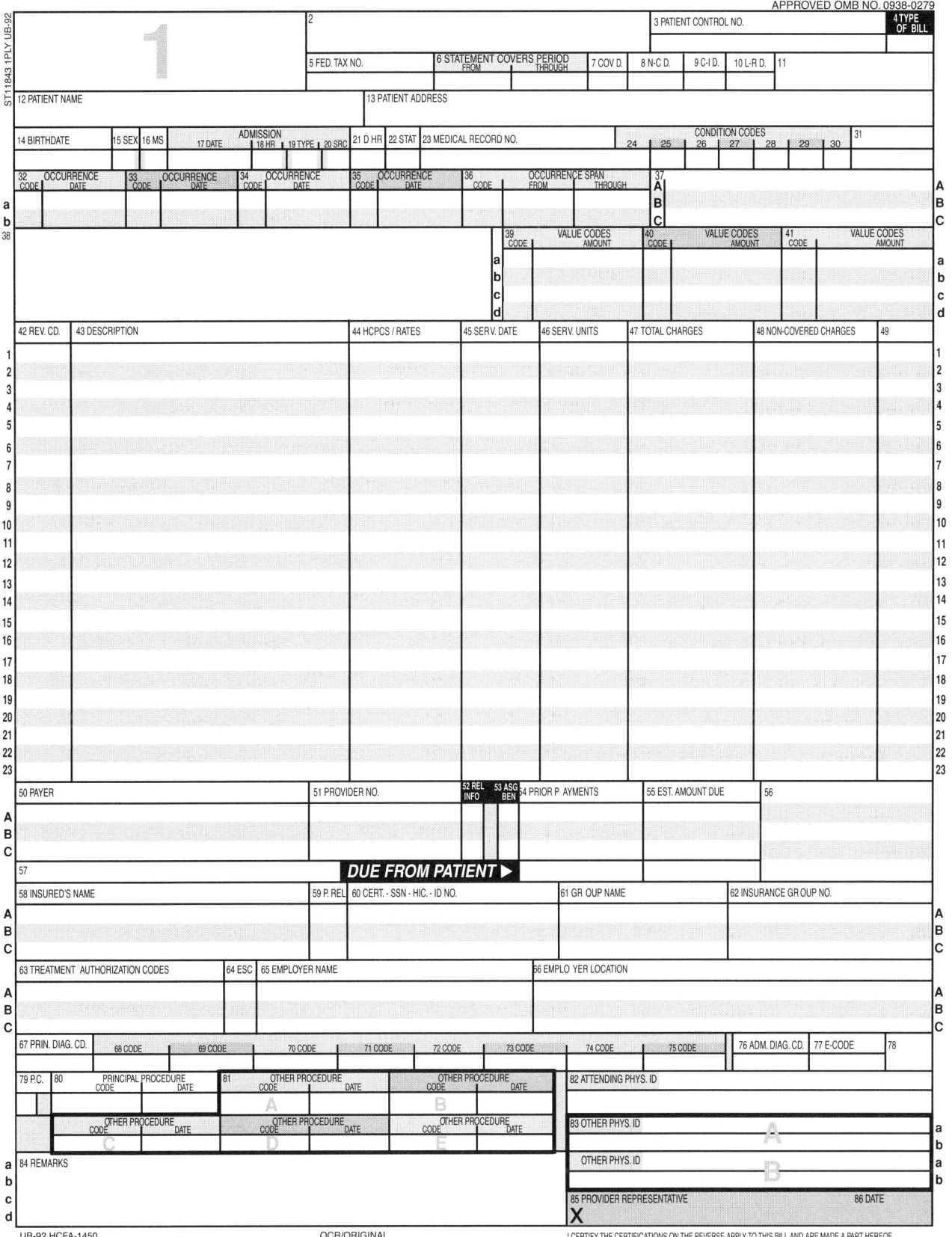

Source: Centers for Medicare and Medicaid Services. 2002 (September 27). Available at: www.hhs.gov/cmsforms/downloads/hcfa1450.pdf. Accessed July 1, 2006.

99218 Initial observation care

This code is used to denote that the problem for which the patient is admitted to "observation status" is of low severity.

99219 Initial observation care

This code is used to denote that the problem for which the patient is admitted to "observation status" is of moderate severity.

99220 Initial observation care

This code is used to denote that the problem for which the patient is admitted to "observation status" is of high severity.

Physician Billing for Observation Status After Admission to Observation

On the first day of admission to observation, the patient is billed with an initial observation care code. If discharged on this day, code 99217 cannot be used. Rather, codes 99234-99236 should be reported for observation or inpatient hospital care including the admission and discharge of the patient on the same date as appropriate. On the second calendar day, if the patient is expected to be discharged from observation status, the 99217 code should be used.

Admission to Inpatient Status From Observation

If the patient is admitted as an observation status case and then admitted as an inpatient on the same date, an initial hospital visit for E/M services should be billed. The observation discharge management code cannot be used in conjuction with a hospital admission.

Hospital Observation During Global Surgical Period

According to CMS guidelines,

> The global surgical fee includes payment for hospital observation services, which includes the codes 99217-99220, unless the criteria for use of CPT modifiers 24, 25, or 57 are met. These services are paid for in addition to the global surgical fee only if both of the following requirements are met:
>
>> Justification is seen in billing a hospital observation service with CPT modifiers 24, 25, or 57. The hospital observation service that is furnished by the surgeon meets all of the criteria.
>
> Example: Decision for Surgery During a Hospital Observation Period
>
> A patient is admitted to a hospital observation unit for observation by a neurosurgeon for a head injury. The surgeon makes the decision for surgery during this observation period, and modifier 57 is used to indicate that the decision was made for surgery. The surgeon would bill the appropriate level of hospital observation code along with modifier 57.
>
> Example: Hospital Observation Services During the Postoperative Period of a Surgery
>
> On the thirtieth day following a Billroth II procedure a patient is admitted to observation for abdominal pain by the surgeon who performed the surgery. The surgeon determines that the patient no longer requires surgery or observation and discharges the patient. The surgeon cannot bill for the observation services furnished during the global period because they were related to the previous surgery.
>
> Example: Billable Hospital Observation Service on the Same Day as the Procedure
>
> A patient presents to the emergency department with a scalp laceration. The laceration is repaired in the emergency department, and the patient is subsequently admitted to the observation unit for observation by the physician who repaired the scalp. The physician would bill the observation code with the CPT modifier 25 and the procedure code.
>
> Examples: Clarification of the Proper Use of Observation Status
>
> A patient comes to the hospital outpatient department to undergo a scheduled surgical procedure. The patient exhibits postoperative complications that extend past the usual recovery period. The patient is then seen by the physician who performed the surgery and placed in the observation unit. After a few hours, the patient no longer exhibits any

postsurgical complications. The physician is made aware of this and discharges the patient. Outpatient observation services begin when the patient is placed in the observation bed. The period of time that the patient is in the outpatient surgical suite and recovery room cannot be considered observation services.

A patient is scheduled to have a rhinoplasty performed on an outpatient basis. The patient expresses a preference to spend the night in the hospital following the procedure, despite the fact that the procedure does not require an overnight stay. This stay cannot be billed as an observation status case because it was not medically necessary. The patient must be notified of the noncoverage and the possibility of being billed for these extra services. If unforeseen circumstances do arise, the patient can be admitted.

Observation of Inpatient Care Services

According to AMA's *CPT 2006*, "The following codes are used to report observation or inpatient hospital care services provided to patients admitted and discharged on the same date of service":

99234   Observation or inpatient hospital care

This code is used to depict the problem that the patient was admitted to "observation status" or inpatient care for, namely a problem of low severity.

99235   Observation or inpatient hospital care

This code is used to depict the problem that the patient was admitted to "observation status" or inpatient care for, namely a problem of moderate severity.

99236   Observation or inpatient hospital care

This code is used to depict the problem that the patient was admitted to "observation status" or inpatient care for, namely a problem of high severity.

V Codes

V codes (V01-V86), which begin with the letter V, appear toward the end of Volume 1 under Supplementary Classification of Factors Influencing Health Status and Contact With Health Services. They are typically used when the patient is being seen for something other than a current illness or injury. A follow-up visit related to a history of major cardiovascular surgery that occurred four years ago would be an example. On occasion, V codes can be used for a principal diagnosis when the main reason for the visit is best described by the use of a V code (eg, encounter for radiation therapy). Table 4-7 is a reference to the V codes.

E Codes

E codes are supplementary and used to describe external causes of injuries, poisonings, or other adverse effects. E codes are never reported alone, nor are they ever reported as a principal diagnoses. They are an important component to the reimbursement of the claim. The E code can clarify why an accident happened, where it took place, and how it happened. This information is helpful when assigning liability to the appropriate insurance carrier for responsibility. The E codes are located in Volume 2 under Index to External Cause. The following excerpt from the ICD-9-CM Official Guidelines for Coding and Reporting (effective April 1, 2005, and available at www.cdc.gov/nchs/data/icd9/icdguide.pdf) explains the use of E codes:

Supplemental Classification of External Causes of Injury and Poisonings (E-codes, E800-E999)

. . . The use of E codes is supplemental to the application of ICD-9-CM diagnosis codes. E codes are never to be recorded as principal diagnoses (first-listed in non-inpatient setting) and are not required for reporting to the CMS.

TABLE 4-7

Sample Table of V Codes

V02.61	Hepatitis B carrier
V25.2	Encounter for sterilization
V42.0	Kidney replaced by transplant
V55.0	Attention to tracheostomy
V58.32	Encounter for removal of sutures
V58.61	Long-term (current) use of anticoagulants
V59.4	Kidney donor
V61.11	Counseling for victim of spousal or partner abuse
V67.2	Follow-up examination following chemotherapy
V72.0	Examination of eyes and vision

External causes of injury and poisoning codes (E codes) are intended to provide data for injury research and evaluation of injury prevention strategies. E codes capture how the injury or poisoning happened (cause), the intent (unintentional or accidental; or intentional, such as suicide or assault), and the place where the event occurred.

Some major categories of E codes include:

- Transport accidents
- Poisoning and adverse effects of drugs, medicinal substances and biologicals
- Accidental falls
- Accidents caused by fire and flames
- Accidents due to natural and environmental factors
- Late effects of accidents, assaults or self injury
- Assaults or purposely inflicted injury
- Suicide or self inflicted injury

These guidelines apply for the coding and collection of E code from records in hospitals, outpatient clinics, emergency departments, other ambulatory care settings and provider offices, and nonacute care settings, except when other specific guidelines apply.

a. **General E Code Coding Guidelines**

   1) **Used with any code in the range of 001-V86.1**

      An E code may be used with any code in the range of 001-V86.1, which indicates an injury, poisoning, or adverse effect due to an external cause.

   2) **Assign the appropriate E code for all initial treatments**

      Assign the appropriate E code for the initial encounter of an injury, poisoning, or adverse effect of drugs, not for subsequent treatment.

   3) **Use the full range of E codes**

      Use the full range of E codes to completely describe the cause, the intent and the place of occurrence, if applicable, for all injuries, poisonings, and adverse effects of drugs.

   4) **Assign as many E codes as necessary**

      Assign as many E codes as necessary to fully explain each cause. If only one E code can be recorded, assign the E code most related to the principal diagnosis.

   5) **The selection of the appropriate E code**

      The selection of the appropriate E code is guided by the Index to External Causes, which is located after the alphabetic index to diseases and by Inclusion and Exclusion notes in the Tabular List.

6) **E code can never be principal diagnosis**

   An E code can never be a principal (first listed) diagnosis.

7) **External cause code(s) with systemic inflammatory response syndrome (SIRS)**

   An external cause code(s) may be used with codes 995.93, Systemic inflammatory response syndrome due to noninfectious process without organ dysfunction, and 995.94, Systemic inflammatory response syndrome due to noninfectious process with organ dysfunction, if trauma was the initiating insult that precipitated the SIRS. The external cause(s) code should correspond to the most serious injury resulting from the trauma. The external cause code(s) should only be assigned if the trauma necessitated the admission in which the patient also developed SIRS. If a patient is admitted with SIRS but the trauma has been treated previously, the external cause codes should not be used.

b. **Place of Occurrence Guideline**

   Use an additional code from category E849 to indicate the Place of Occurrence for injuries and poisonings. The Place of Occurrence describes the place where the event occurred and not the patient's activity at the time of the event.

   Do not use E849.9 if the place of occurrence is not stated.

c. **Adverse Effects of Drugs, Medicinal and Biological Substances Guidelines**

   1) **Do not code directly from the Table of Drugs**

      Do not code directly from the Table of Drugs and Chemicals. Always refer back to the Tabular List.

   2) **Use as many codes as necessary to describe**

      Use as many codes as necessary to describe completely all drugs, medicinal or biological substances.

   3) **If the same E code would describe the causative agent**

      If the same E code would describe the causative agent for more than one adverse reaction, assign the code only once.

   4) **If two or more drugs, medicinal or biological substances**

      If two or more drugs, medicinal or biological substances are reported, code each individually unless the combination code is listed in the Table of Drugs and Chemicals. In that case, assign the E code for the combination.

   5) **When a reaction results from the interaction of a drug(s)**

      When a reaction results from the interaction of a drug(s) and alcohol, use poisoning codes and E codes for both.

   6) **If the reporting format limits the number of E codes**

      If the reporting format limits the number of E codes that can be used in reporting clinical data, code the one most related to the principal diagnosis. Include at least one from each category (cause, intent, place) if possible.

      If there are different fourth digit codes in the same three digit category, use the code for "Other specified" of that category. If there is no "Other specified" code in that category, use the appropriate "Unspecified" code in that category.

      If the codes are in different three digit categories, assign the appropriate E code for other multiple drugs and medicinal substances.

   7) **Codes from the E930-E949 series**

      Codes from the E930-E949 series must be used to identify the causative substance for an adverse effect of drug, medicinal and biological substances, correctly prescribed and properly administered. The effect, such as tachycardia, delirium, gastrointestinal hemorrhaging, vomiting, hypokalemia, hepatitis, renal failure, or respiratory failure, is coded and followed by the appropriate code from the E930-E949 series.

d. Multiple Cause E Code Coding Guidelines

If two or more events cause separate injuries, an E code should be assigned for each cause. The first listed E code is selected in the following order:

- E codes for child and adult abuse take priority over all other E codes.
- E codes for terrorism events take priority over all other E codes except child and adult abuse
- E codes for cataclysmic events take priority over all other E codes except child and adult abuse and terrorism
- E codes for transport accidents take priority over all other E codes except cataclysmic events and child and adult abuse and terrorism

The first-list E code should correspond to the cause of the most serious diagnosis due to an assault, accident, or self-harm, following the order of hierarchy listed above.

e. Child and Adult Abuse Guideline

1) Intentional injury

When the cause of an injury or neglect is intentional child or adult abuse, the first listed E code should be assigned from categories E960-E968, Homicide and injury purposely inflicted by other persons, (except category E967). An E code from category E967, Child and adult battering and other maltreatment, should be added as an additional code to identify the perpetrator, if known.

2) Accidental intent

In cases of neglect when the intent is determined to be accidental E code E904.0, Abandonment or neglect of infant and helpless person, should be the first listed E code.

f. Unknown or Suspected Intent Guideline

1) If the intent (accident, self-harm, assault) of the cause of an injury or poisoning is unknown

If the intent (accident, self-harm, assault) of the cause of an injury or poisoning is unknown or unspecified, code the intent as undetermined E980-E989.

2) If the intent (accident, self-harm, assault) of the cause of an injury or poisoning is questionable

If the intent (accident, self-harm, assault) of the cause of an injury or poisoning is questionable, probable or suspected, code the intent as undetermined E980E989.

g. Undetermined Cause

When the intent of an injury or poisoning is known, but the cause is unknown, use codes: E928.9, Unspecified accident, E958.9, Suicide and self-inflicted injury by unspecified means, and E968.9, Assault by unspecified means.

These E codes should rarely be used as the documentation in the medical record, in both the inpatient and outpatient settings, should normally provide sufficient detail to determine the cause of the injury.

h. Late Effects of External Cause Guidelines

1) Late effect E codes

Late effect E codes exist for injuries and poisonings but not for adverse effects of drugs, misadventures and surgical complications.

2) **A late effect E code (E929, E959, E969, E977, E989, or E999.1)**

A late effect E code (E929, E959, E969, E977, E989, or E999.1) should be used with any report of a late effect or sequela resulting from a previous injury or poisoning (905-909).

3) **Late effect E code with a related current injury**

A late effect E code should never be used with a related current nature of injury code.

4) **Use of late effect E codes for subsequent visits**

Use a late effect E code for subsequent visits when a late effect of the initial injury or poisoning is being treated. There is no late effect E code for adverse effects of drugs. Do not use a late effect E code for subsequent visits for follow-up care (eg, to assess healing, to receive rehabilitative therapy) of the injury or poisoning when no late effect of the injury has been documented.

i. **Misadventures and Complications of Care Guidelines**

1) **Code range E870-E876**

Assign a code in the range of E870-E876 if misadventures are stated by the provider.

2) **Code range E878-E879**

Assign a code in the range of E878-E879 if the provider attributes an abnormal reaction or later complication to a surgical or medical procedure, but does not mention misadventure at the time of the procedure as the cause of the reaction.

j. **Terrorism Guidelines**

1) **Cause of injury identified by the Federal Government (FBI) as terrorism**

When the cause of an injury is identified by the Federal Government (FBI) as terrorism, the first-listed E code should be a code from category E979, Terrorism. The definition of terrorism employed by the FBI is found at the inclusion note at E979. The terrorism E code is the only E code that should be assigned. Additional E codes from the assault categories should not be assigned.

2) **Cause of an injury is suspected to be the result of terrorism**

When the cause of an injury is suspected to be the result of terrorism a code from category E979 should not be assigned. Assign a code in the range of E codes based circumstances on the documentation of intent and mechanism.

3) **Code E979.9, Terrorism, secondary effects**

Assign code E979.9, Terrorism, secondary effects, for conditions occurring subsequent to the terrorist event. This code should not be assigned for conditions that are due to the initial terrorist act.

4) **Statistical tabulation of terrorism codes**

For statistical purposes these codes will be tabulated within the category for assault, expanding the current category from E960-E969 to include E979 and E999.1.

Coding Under Capitation

Coding under capitation is necessary because it drives cost management and cost centers. For example, all CPT codes or a list of all services included or excluded in the capitation rate must be in the managed care contract. Practices can also use CPT codes to determine provider productivity and compensation under capitation arrangements.

In a managed care setting, codes can be used to measure productivity for monetary rewards or continuation in the program. In many instances a relative value unit system is used.

TABLE 4-8

Anthrax-Related Diagnosis Codes

022.0-022.9	Anthrax	This series of diagnosis codes are to be used only when a patient is confirmed to have anthrax
795.31	Nonspecific positive findings for anthrax	This code is used when there is a positive nasal swab for anthrax
V01.81	Contact with or exposure to anthrax	This code is used to report exposure or reasonable suspicion of exposure to anthrax
V74.8	Special screening examination for other specified bacterial and spirochetal diseases	This code is used when there is a screening of an identified population but the patient is not symptomatic and has not been knowingly exposed to anthrax

Anthrax Coding

Anthrax is an infectious disease of warm-blooded animals (eg, cattle and sheep) caused by a spore-forming bacterium that is transmissible to humans, especially by handling infected products (as wool). The disease is characterized by external ulcerating nodules or by lesions in the lungs. The symptoms of anthrax are similar to those of flu or pneumonia. Human anthrax has three major clinical forms: coetaneous, inhalation, and gastrointestinal. If left untreated, anthrax in all forms can lead to septicemia and death. Testing can be performed if the patient thinks he or she has been exposed or has had contact to a communicable disease or biological agent. A patient may undergo this testing even without signs or symptoms. If the testing is performed and the bacterium is *not* present, the coder should use V01.81 (Other communicable diseases; anthrax). When a positive nasal swab comes back with *B*. Anthracis and the patient is treated with antibiotics, code 795.31 (Nonspecific positive findings for anthrax) is used. If a prophylactic antibiotic is prescribed, code V07.39 (Other prophylactic chemotherapy) is used. The only time a coder uses the anthrax codes 022.1-022.9 is when testing confirms that the patient has the anthrax bacillus bacteria.

SUMMARY

Accurate coding is necessary to determine reimbursement of health care services and for research and statistical data. Coding staff should code with the most precision and efficiency to accurately reflect the medical service and to reduce claim delays and denials. It is important to understand what documentation is necessary in the medical record per the AMA-CMS Documentation Guidelines to support the E/M level of service billed. Coders should be sure to choose the appropriate E/M code for the location and type of service provided to the patient. It also is necessary to know the importance of accurate ICD-9-CM coding and to understand how to code to the highest level of specificity. Understand that the diagnosis code is the only way to indicate to a payer the level of medical necessity to support the CPT code submitted. Coding and billing staff should be trained and should maintain careful knowledge of the most recent changes to codes and regulations

If the medical coding and billing is done incorrectly, the Office of the Inspector General may review medical coding of evaluation and management services, as well as other services provided. Physicians may be fined up to $10,000 for each item or service incorrectly billed. This is why physicians need to make sure that the staff or individual performing their medical billing, CPT-4, and ICD-9-CM coding knows how to do it accurately and effectively. Accurate coding and billing of services on a timely basis also will assist in receiving payment from carriers promptly, having a positive impact on operations and cash flow.

chapter 5

Billing for Ancillary Services

OBJECTIVES

- Know the history and basics of durable medical equipment, home health services, nursing homes (or skilled nursing facilities), ambulance services, and hospice care, and dietary or nutrition services.
- Understand covered services and how claims are filed for these specific ancillary service lines.
- Apply the rules specific to each service line.

This chapter introduces the following type of services: durable medical equipment (DME), home health services, nursing home care (or skilled nursing facilities [SNFs]), ambulance services, and hospice care. The history and basics of the services are introduced and specifics for each service, which include guidelines for reimbursement and specific conditions that must be met in order to receive reimbursement, are discussed.

DURABLE MEDICAL EQUIPMENT

In 1993, the Centers for Medicare and Medicaid Services (CMS) and the Department of Health and Human Services (DHHS) entered into contracts with carriers to perform all the duties associated with processing claims for DME, prosthetics, orthotics, and supplies (DMEPOS) under Part B of the Medicare program. The participating carriers (see Table 5-1) were designated as DME regional carriers (DMERCs).

DME furnished to a beneficiary for use in the patient's home is covered under Medicare Part B, whether furnished as a rented or purchased item. The equipment must meet the definition of *durable medical equipment*, ie, equipment that is reasonable and necessary for the diagnosis or treatment of an illness or injury or equipment that improves the functioning of a malformed body member. DME can withstand repeated use, is primarily and customarily used to serve a medical purpose, generally is not useful to a person in the absence of illness or injury, and is appropriate for use in the home. Table 5-2 lists covered and noncovered DME.

Payment for DME

Medicare Part B helps pay for medical equipment and supplies used in the home, such as wheelchairs, artificial limbs, braces, ostomy supplies, and hospital beds. DME is paid for using Medicare fee schedules. Payment is limited to the lower of the actual charge for the equipment or the fee schedule amount. Medicare pays the same amount regardless of whether the supplier "takes assignment." If the supplier takes assignment and if the beneficiary already has met the deductible for the year, Medicare pays 80% of the Medicare-approved charge and the beneficiary is responsible for the remaining 20%. The beneficiary may pay more if the supplier does not take assignment.

TABLE 5-1

Regional Carriers of Durable Medical Equipment

Carrier	Covered States/Territories	
Region A Health Now of New York, Inc 800 842-2052 TTY/TDD: 800 842-9519 www.umd.nycpic.com/dmerc.html	Connecticut Delaware Maine Massachusetts New Hampshire	New Jersey New York Pennsylvania Rhode Island Vermont
Region B AdminaStar Federal 800 270-2313 TTY/TDD: 317 841-4677 www.administar.com	Illinois Indiana Maryland Michigan Minnesota	Ohio Virginia Washington DC West Virginia Wisconsin
Region C Palmetto Government, Benefits Administration 866 270-4909 TTY/TDD: 800 788-5414 www.palmettogba.com	Alabama Arkansas Colorado Florida Georgia Kentucky Louisiana Mississippi	New Mexico North Carolina Oklahoma Puerto Rico South Carolina Tennessee Texas Virgin Islands
Region D Cigna Medicare 800 899-7095 TTY/TDD: 800 970-7494 www.cignamedicare.com	Alaska American Samoa Arizona California Guam Hawaii Idaho Iowa Kansas Missouri	Montana Nebraska Nevada North Dakota Marian Islands Oregon South Dakota Utah Washington Wyoming

TTY = Text telephone
TDD = Telecommunications device for the deaf

If a patient is not entitled to Part A benefits, payment may not be made under Part B for DME or oxygen provided in a facility. In addition, outpatients who use a facility's equipment or receive oxygen but do not take the equipment or oxygen system home are not covered by the fee schedule. In such a situation, an intermediary pays the facility based on reasonable cost.

DME is placed into one of six classes, which have separate regional fee schedules. The six classes include:

- Inexpensive or other routinely purchased DME
- Items requiring frequent and substantial servicing
- Customized items
- Prosthetic and orthotic devices
- Capped rental items
- Oxygen and oxygen equipment

TABLE 5-2

Covered and Noncovered Durable Medical Equipment

Items	Covered	Notes
Air cleaner	No	Environmental control equipment, not primarily medical in nature.
Air conditioner	No	Environmental control equipment, not primarily medical in nature.
Alternating pressure pad	Yes	If patient has, or is and highly susceptible to decubitus, mattresses and lambs wool pads, ulcers; and patient's physician has specified that he will be supervising its use in connection with his course of treatment.
Bathtub lift	No	Convenience item, not primarily medical in nature.
Bathtub seat	No	Comfort or convenience item, hygienic equipment, not primarily medical in nature.
Bed bath (home type)	No	Hygienic equipment, not primarily medical in nature.
Bed lifter (bed elevator)	No	Not primarily medical in nature.
Bedboards	No	Not primarily medical in nature.
Bed pans	Yes	If patient is bed confined.
Beds lounge (power or manual)	No	Not a hospital bed, comfort or convenience item, not primarily medical in nature.
Beds oscillating	No	Institutional equipment; inappropriate for home use.
Blood glucose analyzer	No	Unsuitable for home use.
Blood glucose monitor	Yes	If patient meets certain conditions.
Braille teaching text	No	Educational equipment; not primarily medical.
Cane	Yes	If patient's condition impairs ambulation.
Carafes	No	Convenience item; not primarily in nature.
Catheter	No	Nonreusable disposable supply.
Commode	Yes	If patient is confined to bed or room. Note: The term *room confined* means that the patient's condition is such that leaving the room is medically contraindicated. The accessibility of bathroom facilities generally would not be a factor in this determination. However, confinement of a patient to his or her home in a case where there are no toilet facilities in the home may be equated to room confinement. Moreover, payment may also be made if a patient's medical condition confines him/her to a floor of his/her home and there is no bathroom located on that floor.
Continuous passive motion (CPM) device	Yes	CPM devices are covered by the Medicare program as DME for patients who have received a total knee replacement. To qualify for such coverage, use of the device must commence within two days following surgery. In addition, coverage is limited to that portion of the three-week period following surgery during which the device is used in the patient's home.
Crutches	Yes	If patient's condition impairs ambulation.
Dehumidifiers (room or central heating system type)	No	Environmental control equipment; not primarily medical in nature.
Diathermy machines (standard pulse waves type)	No	Inappropriate for home use.
Disposable sheet and bag	No	Nonreusable disposable supplies, not rental-type items.
Elastic stockings	No	Nonreuseable supply; not rental type.
Electrical stimulation for wounds	No	Inappropriate for home use.
Elevators	No	Convenience item; not primarily medical in nature.
Emesis basins	No	Not primarily medical in nature.
Esophageal dilator	No	Physician instrument; inappropriate for use.

TABLE 5-2

Covered and Noncovered Durable Medical Equipment (*continued*)

Items	Covered	Notes
Exercise equipment	No	Not primarily medical in nature.
Fabric support	No	Nonreusable supplies, not rental-type items.
Face mask (oxygen)	Yes	If oxygen covered.
Face mask (surgical)	No	Nonreusable disposable item.
Grab bar	No	Self-help device, not primarily medical in nature.
Heat and massage foam cushion pad	No	Not primarily medical in nature; personal comfort item.
Heating and cooling plants	No	Environmental control equipment; not primarily medical in nature.
Heating pad	Yes	If the contractor's medical staff determines patient's medical condition is one for which the application of heat in the form of a heating pad is therapeutically effective and medical in nature.
Heat lamp	Yes	If the contractor's medical staff determines patients medical condition is one for which the application of heat in the form of a heat lamp is therapeutically effective.
Humidifier (room or central heating system types)	No	Environmental control equipment, not medical in nature.
Incontinent pads	No	Nonreusable supply; hygienic item.
Infusion pump	Yes	For external and implantable pumps, if the pump is used with an enteral or parenteral nutritional therapy system.
Injectors (hypodermic)	No	Noncovered self-administered drug supply.
Intermittent positive pressure breathing (IPPB) machine	Yes	If patient's ability to breathe is severely impaired.
Irrigating kit	No	Nonreuseable supply, hygienic equipment.
Lambs wool pad	Yes	Under the same conditions as alternating pressure pad and mattress.
Leotard	No	Personal comfort item.
Lymphedema pumps	Yes	Segmental and nonsegmental therapy types.
Massage devices	No	Personal comfort item; not primarily medical in nature.
Mattress	Yes	Only when hospital bed is medically necessary. Separate charge for replacement mattress should not be allowed when hospital bed with mattress is rented.
Medical oxygen regulator	Yes	If patient's ability to breathe is severely impaired.
Muscle stimulator	Yes	Under certain conditions.
Nebulizer	Yes	If patient's ability to breathe is severely impaired.
Overbed table	No	Convenience item.
Oxygen	Yes	If the oxygen has been prescribed for use in connection with medically necessary DME.
Oxygen humidifier	Yes	If a medical humidifier has been prescribed for use in connection with medically necessary durable equipment for purposes of moisturizing oxygen.
Parallel bar	No	Support exercise equipment, primarily for institutional use; in the home setting, other devices (eg, walker) satisfy the patient's needs.
Patient lift	Yes	If contractor's medical staff determines patient's condition is such that periodic movement is necessary to effect improvement or to arrest or retard deterioration in condition.
Percussor	Yes	For mobilizing respiratory tract secretions in patients with chronic obstructive lung disease, chronic bronchitis, or emphysema when patient or operator of powered percussors has received appropriate training by a physician of therapist and no one competent to administer manual therapy is available.

TABLE 5-2

Covered and Noncovered Durable Medical Equipment (*continued*)

Items	Covered	Notes
Portable oxygen system: Regulated (adjustable flow rate)	Yes	Under the conditions specified, refer all claims to medical staff for this determination.
Portable oxygen system: Preset (flow rate not adjustable)	No	Emergency, first-aid, or precautionary equipment, essentially not therapeutic in nature.
Portable paraffin bath unit	Yes	When the patient has undergone a successful trial period of paraffin therapy ordered by a physician and the patient's condition is expected to be relieved by long-term use of this modality.
Portable room heater	No	Not primarily medical in nature item.
Portable whirlpool pumps	No	Nor primarily medical in nature; personal comfort item.
Postural drainage boards	Yes	If patient has chronic pulmonary condition.
Preset portable oxygen unit	No	Emergency, first-aid, or precautionary equipment, essentially not therapeutic in nature.
Pulse tachometer	No	Not reasonable or necessary for monitoring pulse of homebound patient with or without a cardiac pacemaker.
Rolling chair	Yes	If the contractor's medical staff determines that the patient's condition is such that there is a medical need for this and it has been prescribed by the patient's physician in lieu of a wheelchair. Coverage is limited to rollabout chairs that have casters at least 5 inches in diameter and specifically designed to meet the needs of ill, injured, or otherwise impaired individuals. Coverage is denied for the wide range of chairs with smaller casters like those found in general use in homes, offices, and institutions for many purposes. This is not primarily medical in nature.
Sauna bath	No	Not primarily medical in nature; personal comfort item.
Seat lift	Yes	Under certain conditions, refer all claims to medical staff for this determination.
Self-contained pacemaker	Yes	When prescribed by a physician for a patient with a cardiac pacemaker.
Sitz bath	Yes	If the contractor's medical staff determines patient has infection or injury of the perineal area and the item has been prescribed by the patient's physician as part of planned regimen for treatment in the patient's home.
Spare tank of oxygen	No	Convenience or precautionary supply.
Speech teaching machine	No	Educational equipment; not primarily medical in nature.
Standing table	No	Convenience item; not primarily medical in nature.
Steams pack	Yes	These packs are covered under the same condition as heating pad.
Suction machine	Yes	If the contractor's medical staff determines that the machine specified on the claim is medically required and appropriate for home use without technical or professional supervision.
Surgical leggings	No	Nonreusable supply, not rental-type item.
Telephone alert system	No	These are emergency communications systems and do not serve a diagnostic or therapeutic purpose.
Telephone arms	No	Convenience item; not medical in nature.
Toilet seats	No	Not medical equipment.
Traction equipment	Yes	If patient has orthopedic impairment requiring traction equipment that prevents ambulation during the period of use. (Consider covering devices that can be used during ambulation, eg, cervical traction collar, under the brace provision.)
Trapeze bar	Yes	Covered if patient is to be confined and the patient needs a trapeze bar to sit up because of respiratory condition, to change body position for other medical reasons, or to get in and out of bed.
Treadmill exerciser	No	Exercise equipment; not primarily medical in nature.

TABLE 5-2

Covered and Noncovered Durable Medical Equipment (*continued*)

Items	Covered	Notes
Ultraviolet cabinet	Yes	For selected patients with generalized intractable psoriasis. Using appropriate consultation, the intermediaries should determine whether medical and other factors justify treatment at home rather than at alternative sites (eg, outpatient department of a hospital).
Urinal (autoclavable)	Yes	If patient is bed confined.
Urinal (autoclave hospital type)	Yes	If patient is bed confined.
Vaporizer	Yes	If patient has a respiratory illness.
Ventilator	Yes	For treatment of neuromuscular diseases, thoracic restrictive diseases, and chronic respiratory failure consequent to chronic obstructive pulmonary disease. Includes both positive and negative pressure types.
Walker	Yes	If patient's condition impairs ambulation.
Wheelchair	Yes	If patient's condition is such that without the use of a wheelchair he/she would otherwise be bed- or chair-confined. An individual may qualify for a wheelchair and still be considered bed confined.
Wheelchair (power operated) and wheelchair with other special features	Yes	If the patient's condition is such that a wheelchair is medically necessary and the patient is unable to operate the wheelchair manually. Any claim involving a power wheelchair or a wheelchair with other special features should be referred for medical consultation because payment for special features is limited to those that aremedically required because of the patient's condition. Note: A power-operated vehicle that may appropriately be used as a wheelchair can be covered.
Whirlpool bath equipment (standard)	Yes	If patient is homebound and has a condition for which the whirlpool bath can be expected to provide substantial therapeutic benefit justifying its cost. When patient is not homebound but has such a condition, payment is restricted to the cost of providing the services elsewhere (eg, an outpatient department of a participating hospital) if that alternative is less costly. In all cases, refer claim to medical staff for a determination.

Normally, payment for DME is made on a monthly rental basis. The payment amount is the lesser of the actual charge for the equipment or an amount determined according to a payment formula, as reduced by applicable Part B deductible and coinsurance requirements.

Under the DME payment formula, monthly rental payments are 10% of the "national limited payment amount" for the equipment.

Inexpensive Equipment

Payment for inexpensive DME is made on a rental basis or in a lump sum purchase amount that is based on the national limited payment amount, as updated by the Consumer Price Index. DME is considered inexpensive if it costs $150 or less or the secretary of DHHS determines it can be acquired by purchase at least 75% of the time. If rental rather than lump sum purchase is chosen, the total amount of rental payments may not exceed the allowed lump sum purchase amount.

Equipment Requiring Frequent and Substantial Servicing

DME that requires frequent and substantial servicing in order to avoid risk to the patient's health (ventilators, aspirators, intermittent positive pressure breathing [IPPB] machines, nebulizers) is paid for only on a monthly rental basis. The rented amount is based on the "average reasonable charge" in the area for such equipment, as updated by the Consumer Price Index.

Customized Items
DME that requires customization (unique construction or substantial modification to meet the specific needs of an individual patient) will be paid for in a lump sum amount. The carrier determines the payment amount by considering the equipment's maintenance and service needs. A wheelchair may not be considered a customized item unless it has been measured, fitted, or adapted to the patient's body size, disability, period of need, or intended use and has been so modified in accordance with instructions from the patient's physician. If the beneficiary requests an upgraded DME other than the standard allowable item, the beneficiary is responsible for the difference between the supplier's charge for the upgrade and the Medicare payment amount for the standard item.

Prosthetic Devices, Orthotics, and Prosthetics
Payment for prosthetic devices (other than parenteral and enteral nutrition, nutrients, supplies, and equipment), orthotics, and prosthetics (other than intraocular lenses) is made only on a lump sum basis. The allowed purchase price is based on a formula that weighs local and regional purchase prices.

Capped Rental Items
Rental payment can be made for only 13 months in most instances. After 13 months, payment can only be made for maintenance and servicing. Payment for rented equipment during the first three months of use is limited to 10% of the national limited purchase price; thereafter, payment is limited to 7.5% of the national limited purchase price. There are special rules for power-driven wheelchairs (which must be offered for purchase rather than rental from the beginning) and items used for 13 consecutive months. (As of November 2006, CMS implemented a rule in compliance with the Deficit Reduction Act (DRA) requiring suppliers to transfer title of capped rental items to the patient after 13 continuous months of rental payments.) In these cases, Medicare can pay for maintenance and servicing to the extent that the charges are reasonable and are not covered by the supplier's or manufacturer's warranty. Payment for equipment replacement may be made on either a rental or purchase basis if the useful life (generally five years) of the equipment has been reached.

Oxygen and Oxygen Equipment
A special formula based on a weighted average of local and regional Medicare past payment amounts is used to determine payment for oxygen and oxygen equipment. As of November 2006, CMS implemented a rule in compliance with the DRA requiring suppliers of oxygen and oxygen equipment to transfer title of oxygen equipment to the patient after 36 consecutive months of rental payments.

At the same time, CMS established separate payment classes and monthly payments for oxygen generating portable equipment (OGPE). OGPE are new, alternative oxygen equipment technologies that meet all of the patient's oxygen needs without delivery of oxygen contents. CMS also created separate classes for stationary and portable oxygen equipment, resulting in an increase in the monthly payment for delivery of oxygen contents for patient-owned portable tanks and cylinders.

Use in Patient's Home

DME must be used in the patient's home in order to be covered. For the purpose of rental or purchase of DME, "home" may be the patient's own dwelling, apartment, a relative's home, a home for the aged, or some other type of institution. Neither a hospital nor SNF may be considered a patient's home.

Certificate of Medical Necessity

Medicare requires a physician's prescription (supporting documentation) for DME. Called a *certificate of medical necessity* (CMN), this documentation must state the patient's diagnosis, prognosis, reason the equipment is required, and the doctor's estimated duration of need. Effective October 1, 2006, CMS has revised the CMN form physicians, providers, and suppliers use when billing to Medicare durable medical equipment regional carriers (DMERC). There was a transition period for claims with initial dates of service from October 1, 2006, through December 31, 2006, where claims for items requiring a CMN were accepted with either the old or new form. Beginning January 1, 2007, only the new revised form is accepted. The changes to the CMN forms have resulted in the following:

- Medicare Program Integrity Manual, Chapter 5, items and services having special DME review consideration has been revised.
- The new forms permit the use of signature and date stamps, which has resulted in the revision of Medicare Program Integrity Manual, Chapter 3 Section 3.4.1.1
- The new forms were approved by the Office and Management and Budget (OMB).
- For the CMS-484 form, the OMB # is 0938-0534.
- For the CMS forms 846, 847, 848, 849, 854, 10125, and 10126, the OMB # is 0938-0679.

Table 5-3 identifies the CMNs for claims with initial dates of service that were accepted during the transition period of October 1 through December 31, 2006. (Since January 1, 2007, the old forms have no longer been accepted.)

Table 5-4 identifies the newly revised CMNs that were accepted during the transition period for claims with initial dates of service of October 1 through December 31, 2006. As of January 1, 2007, these forms became effective for claims for items requiring a CMN.

Table 5-5 identifies the CMNs that were eliminated for claims with an initial date of service on or after October 1, 2006.

Medicare is developing a crosswalk to link legacy supplier numbers (national supplier clearinghouse [NSC]) to the new national provider identifiers (NPI) required under the Health Insurance Portability and Accountability Act (HIPAA). Until that crosswalk is completed, DMERCs will require continued submission of the legacy or NSC number. (Please note that Medicare DME suppliers are required to get an NPI for each location. The only exception to this is if the Medicare DME supplier is a sole proprietor. A sole

TABLE 5-3

Claims Accepted During Transition Period

DMERC Form	CMS Form	Items Addressed
484.2	484	Home oxygen therapy
01.01A	841	Hospital beds
01.02B	842	Support surfaces
04.03B	846	Lymphedema pumps
04.03C	847	Osteogenesis stimulators
06.02B	848	Transcutaneous electrical nerve stimulators (TENS)
07.02A	849	Seat lift mechanisms
09.02	851	External infusion pumps
10.02A	852	Parental nutrition
10.02B	853	Enteral nutrition
11.01	854	Section C continuation form

TABLE 5-4

Newly Revised CMNs Accepted During Transition Period

DME MAC Form	CMS Form	Items Addressed
484.03	484*	Oxygen
04.04B	846†	Pneumatic compression devices
04.04C	847	Osteogenesis stimulators
06.03B	848	Transcutaneous electrical nerve stimulators (TENS)
07.03A	849	Seat lift mechanisms
11.02	854	Section C continuation form

*The title on form CMS-484 has changed from Home Oxygen Therapy to Oxygen.
†The title of CMS-846 has changed from Lymphedema Pumps to Pneumatic Compression Devices.

TABLE 5-5

CMNs Eliminated

DME MAC Form	CMS Form	Items Addressed
01.02A	841	Hospital beds
01.02B	842	Support services

proprietor is eligible only for one NPI number.) Similarly, treating physicians and other providers (with the exception of small health plans, which were given an extra year) were required to begin using their NPI by May 2007. Medicare is also requiring those who submit bills on paper to obtain and use an NPI. CMS will issue further instructions when the crosswalk approaches operational status.

The official instructions issued to the DMERCs regarding this change can be found at www.cms.hhs.gov/Transmittals/downloads/R142Pl.pdf on the CMS Web site. These instruction include copies of the new forms. Physician assistants, nurse practitioners, and clinical nurse specialists may write and sign CMNs, provided they meet certain requirements. Suppliers may dispense DME based on a CMN signed and faxed by the physician, nurse practitioner, certified nurse specialists, or physician assistant. Corrections to a CMN need not be signed in full. If changes are made to section B of the CMN, the physician, nurse practitioner, certified nurse specialist, or physician assistant must line through the correction and initial and date the change.

Repairs, Maintenance, Replacement, and Delivery

Payment may be made for repair, maintenance, and replacement for medically required DME that the beneficiary owns or is purchasing, including equipment that had been used before the user enrolled in the program. Because renters usually recover the expense they incur with respect to maintaining the equipment they rent out, separately itemized charges for repair, maintenance, and replacement of rented equipment are not covered.

Repairs to equipment that the beneficiary has purchased or already owns are covered when necessary to make the equipment serviceable. Part of the repair charge may include the use of "loaner" equipment if required. The expense for repairs cannot exceed the estimated expense of purchasing or renting another item of equipment for the remaining period of medical need; no payment can be made for the excess.

Routine periodic servicing, such as testing, cleaning, regulating, and checking, is not covered. This type of routine maintenance is the beneficiary's responsibility. Purchasers of DME are given operating manuals that describe the type of servicing an owner may perform to maintain the equipment properly. Maintenance that is more extensive based on manufacturers' recommendations, if performed by authorized technicians, would be covered as repairs (eg, breaking down sealed components and performing tests that require specialized testing equipment not available to the beneficiary).

Reasonable costs or reasonable charges for delivery of DEM, whether rented or purchased, are covered if the provider or supplier customarily makes separate charges for delivery.

Supplies and Accessories

Reimbursement may be made for supplies (eg, oxygen) necessary for the effective use of DME. Such supplies include the drugs and biologicals that are put directly into the equipment to achieve the therapeutic benefit of the DME or to ensure proper functioning of the equipment (eg, tumor chemotherapy agents used with an infusion pump or heparin used with a home dialysis system). Coverage of such drugs or biologicals does not preclude the need for a determination that the drug or biological itself is reasonable and necessary for treatment of the illness or injury or to improve the functioning of a malformed body member. Reimbursement may be made for replacement accessories (such as hoses, tubes, mouthpieces, etc) for necessary DME, only if the beneficiary owns or purchases the equipment.

Home Oxygen Services

Medicare covers home oxygen services under the DME benefit. Claims for oxygen services provided in the beneficiary's home must include medical documentation provided by the patient's physician. The documentation must specify a diagnosis of the disease requiring home use of oxygen, the flow rate and oxygen concentration, and an estimate of the frequency and duration of use. The initial claim also must include the results of a blood gas study and a measurement of arterial oxygen saturation obtained by ear or pulse oximetry. A portable oxygen system is covered either as a necessary complement to a stationary system or by itself to provide an intermittent supply of oxygen for use during exercise by a patient who has a medical diagnosis or exercise-induced hypoxemia.

A new physician certification is required every 90 days for certain patients receiving home oxygen therapy. The recertification must be made if, at the time the home oxygen therapy is initiated, the patient has an initial arterial blood gas value at or greater than a partial pressure of 55 or arterial oxygen saturation at or greater than 89%. The recertification must be based on a follow-up test of these indications within the final 30 days of the 90-day period.

Change in Patient's Condition

A patient may sell or otherwise dispose of equipment purchased under the program and for which there is no further use (eg, recovery from the illness or injury that gave rise to the need for the equipment). The program is not authorized to repossess the equipment. If, after disposal, there is medical need for similar equipment, payment can be made for the rental or purchase of that equipment.

When payments stop because the patient's condition has changed and the equipment is no longer medically necessary, the patient is responsible for the remaining noncovered charges. Similarly, when payments stop because the patient dies, the patient's estate is responsible for the remaining noncovered charges.

NURSING HOME FACILITY

In 1965, Congress enacted the Medicare and Medicaid programs, making health care available to a large number of people who previously did not have health coverage. Prior to 1980, Medicaid and Medicare reimbursed nursing facilities on a retrospective reasonable cost basis. From 1980 to 1997, federal law directly linked Medicaid nursing home rates with minimum federal and state quality-of-care standards. As part of the

Omnibus Reconciliation Act of 1980, the Boren Amendment required that Medicaid nursing home rates be "reasonable and adequate to meet the costs which must be incurred by efficiently and economically operated facilities in order to provide care and services in conformity with applicable state and federal laws, regulations, and quality and safety standards." State Medicaid officials overwhelmingly came to oppose the amendment as impossible to implement operationally, believing that they were forced by the courts to spend too much on nursing homes at the expense of other services. In addition, the regulations required states to publish a public notice if the changes made to the state plan amendment were significant.

In 1997, the Balanced Budget Act repealed the Boren requirements and replaced them with a requirement that states implement a public process when changes in payment rates or methodologies are proposed. The new public process requirement applies to rates established on or after the October 1, 1997, effective date. CMS is in the process of developing regulations regarding implementation of this change.

The number of post-acute care providers is generally continuing to grow (see Table 5-6). From 1996 to 2005, the number of most types of post-acute care providers increased. From 1996 to 2005, inpatient rehabilitation facilities increased by 20%. The number of long-term care hospitals has doubled from 1996 to 2005. The number of home health agencies reached its peak in 1996 and then dropped in successive years. The numbers began to increase again in 2004, climbing 17% between 2002 and 2005.

Figure 5-1 reflects post-acute care spending, which has increased an average of 7% per year since 1999. Medicare spending for long-term care hospitals increased the most at 18% per year. CMS projected that total spending for post-acute care was $42 billion. Currently, post-acute care makes up about 13% of Medicare's total spending.

Long-term Care Terminology

Long-term care (LTC) refers to a comprehensive range of medical, personal, and social services coordinated to meet the physical, social, and emotional needs of people who are chronically ill or disabled. An *LTC facility* is defined as having three or more beds and providing LTC services throughout the facility or in a separately identifiable unit.

Skilled nursing care is received in a nursing facility that provides 24-hour nursing care for convalescent residents and those with LTC illnesses. This form of care is one step below hospital acute care, and regular medical supervision and rehabilitation therapy are usually available.

Personal care is customized to an individual's activities of daily living and self-administration of medications. Activities of daily living (ADLs) are everyday activities that include bathing, grooming, eating, toileting, and dressing. *Instrumental ADLs* include activities such as shopping, preparing meals, performing housework and heavy chores, laundering, managing finances, and performing yard work and maintenance. Medical and nursing care administered in an individual's home by a licensed provider is termed *home health care*.

TABLE 5-6

The Number of Post-Acute Care Providers

	1996	1998	2000	2002	2004	2005	Percent Change 1996–2005
Skilled nursing facilities*	14,548	16,079	16,275	15,089	15,784	15,625	7.4%
Home health agencies	9,808	9,284	7,317	6,888	7,148	8,082	−17.6
Inpatient rehabilitation facilities	1,031	1,078	1,102	1,181	1,206	1,235	19.8
Long-term care hospitals	183	209	240	286	307	375	105.0

Source: Online Survey, Certification, and Reporting system from CMS.

*Includes swing bed hospitals.

FIGURE 5-1

Spending for Post-Acute Care

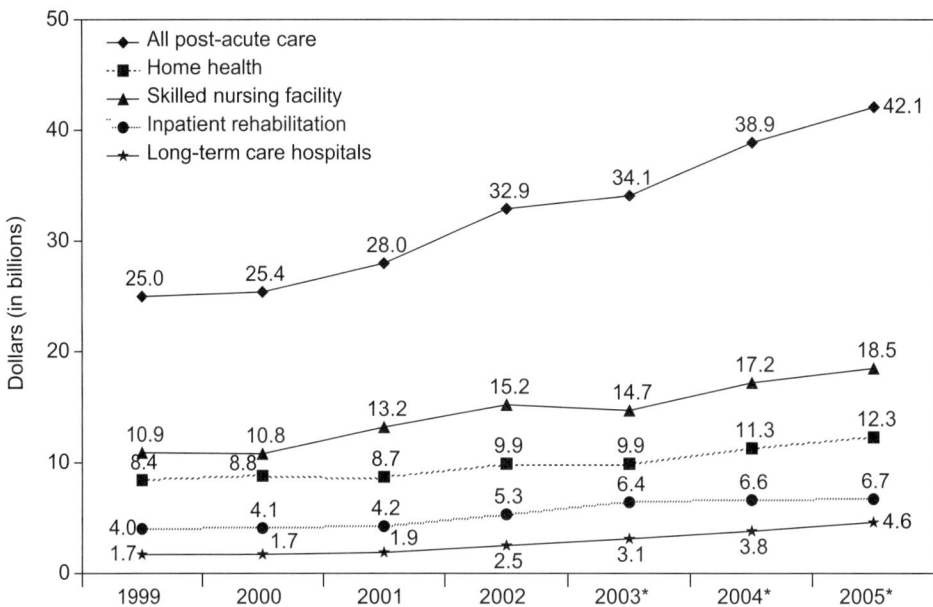

Source: Centers for Medicare & Medicaid Services, Office of the Actuary.

These numbers are program spending only and do not include beneficiary copayments.

*Estimated by CMS

Nursing Home Care and Services

Medicare program spending on skilled nursing facility (SNF) services grew an average of 21% per year from 1993 through 1998. During this period, Medicare paid SNFs based on theirs costs subject to some limits. Medicare program spending on SNF services fell from $13.1 billion to $10.1 billion in 1999 immediately following the implementation of the SNF prospective payment system (see Figure 5-2).

SNF spending grew at a slower rate between 2000 and 2005 after the implementation of the prospective payment system (PPS), however it still averaged 11% per year for the period. Contributing to the growth during this period were factors including the increases in the use of services and increases in the payment rates over the period.

Between 1999 and 2003, the number of Medicare admissions to SNFs grew at an average of 7%. Table 5-7 shows this increase. The increase in SNF use is exceeding the rate of growth in the Medicare population. During the same period, the average annual increase in Part A enrollees was 1.2%. SNF admissions increased 7% between 2002 and 2003. The number of SNF days increased 9% between 2002 and 2003.

Skilled nursing facility services may be provided in freestanding facilities or hospital-based facilities. In 2003, 90% of facilities were freestanding and 67% of the facilities were for profit (see Table 5-8).

Between 2000 and 2004, per-day costs for Medicare beneficiaries in free standing SNFs grew 3.7% annually on average. During the same period for-profit facilities had annual cost growth of 3.5%, lower than nonprofit at 4.4% average annual cost growth or government facilities at 4.5% average annual cost growth (see Figure 5-3). Table 5-9 shows freestanding skilled nursing facility Medicare margins by facility group for 2004.

Nursing homes provide basic and skilled care. Basic care includes services required to maintain a resident's ADL (ie, personal care, ambulation, supervision, and safety). Skilled care requires the services of a registered nurse for treatments and procedures on a regular basis. Skilled care also includes services provided by specially trained professionals such as physical, occupational, and respiratory therapists.

FIGURE 5-2
Medicare Spending for Skilled Nursing Facility Services

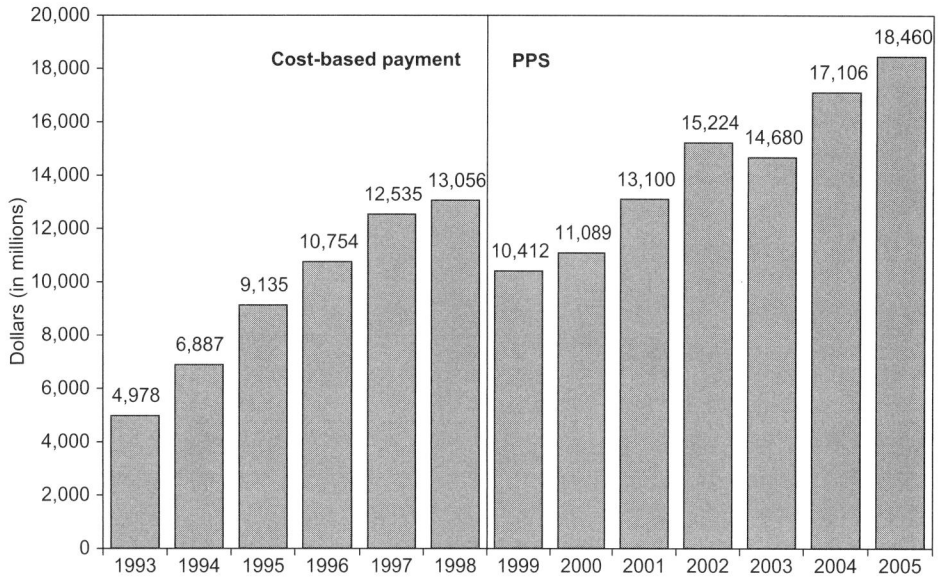

Source: CMS, Office of the Actuary, 2006.
PPS = prospective payment system
Spending is program spending for the calendar year.

TABLE 5-7
Medicare Skilled Nursing Facility Use

Year	Number of Admissions (Thousands)	Number of Days (Millions)	Days per Admission
1999	1,796	42.4	23.6
2000	1,824	43.8	24.0
2001	1,950	47.9	24.6
2002	2,223	54.7	24.6
2003	2,385	59.4	24.9
Average annual increase	7%	9%	1%

Source: Skilled nursing facility Medicare Provider Analysis and Review stay records from CMS, Office of Research, Development, and Information.

Data include facilities in Puerto Rico, Virgin Islands, and "unknown." Data do not include swing bed units.

The services nursing homes offer vary from facility to facility. Services often include:

- Room and board
- Monitoring of medication
- Personal care (including dressing, bathing, and toilet assistance)
- Twenty-four-hour emergency care
- Social and recreational activities

If a person leaves a LTC facility and returns to the community, a community interview is conducted to determine status. If he or she spends part of the reference period in the community and part in a LTC facility, a separate interview is conducted for each period.

TABLE 5-8

Characteristics of Skilled Nursing Facilities, 2003

Type of SNF	Facilities	Medicare Payments	Medicare-covered Stays
Freestanding	90%	90%	83%
Hospital-based	10	10	17
Urban	67	81	78
Rural	33	19	22
Large chain	15	20	17
Not large chain	85	80	83
For profit	67	71	64
Nonprofit	28	26	31
Government	5	3	4

Source: MedPAC analysis of the Provider of Services file and 2003 Medicare Provider Analysis and Review file.
SNF = skilled nursing facility

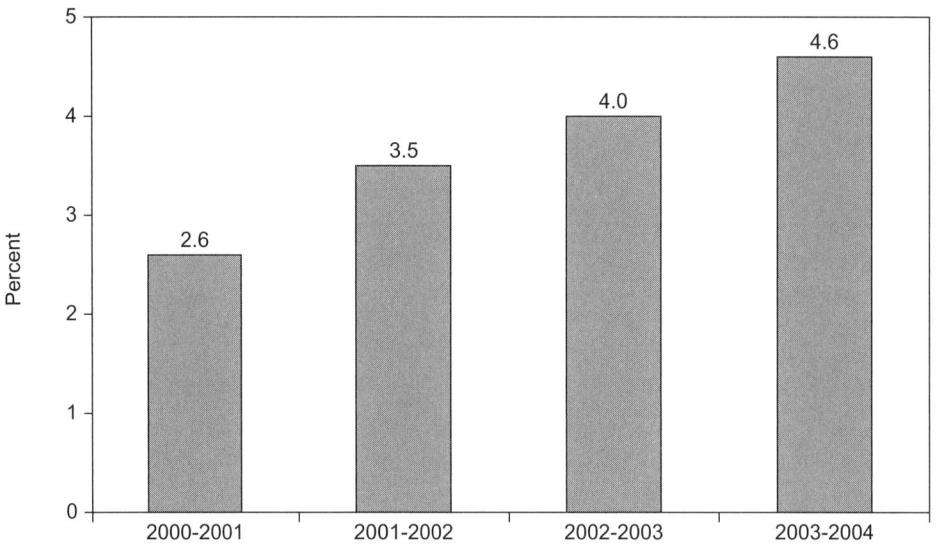

FIGURE 5-3

Medicare Costs per Day in Freestanding Skilled Nursing Facilities

Source: MedPAC analysis of Medicare cost report data from CMS.

Medicare per day cost growth was calculated from year to year among the cohort of freestanding skilled nursing facilities with cost report data in all five years. Cost per day is not adjusted for differences in case mix. Costs per day grew at an average annual rate of 3.7% between 2000 and 2004.

Hence, a beneficiary can be followed in and out of facilities and a continuous record is maintained regardless of where the person resides.

Covered Benefits

Medicare only pays for skilled care in a nursing facility that has a Medicare license. Insurance protection intended to cover major hospital care is provided without regard to income, but only restricted benefits are allowed for nursing home care. Medicare Part A pays for a semiprivate room, meals, skilled nursing and rehabilitative services, and other services and supplies (after a related three-day hospital stay). Most patients' health maintenance organization plans require them to have had a three-day hospital stay prior

TABLE 5-9

Freestanding Skilled Nursing Facility Medicare Margin, by Facility Group, 2004

Facility Type	Facilities Margin	Medicare
All facilities	11,049	13.5%
Urban	7,606	12.8
Rural	3,432	16.6
Large chain	2,043	18.2
Not large chain	9,006	12.0
For profit	8,374	16.1
Nonprofit	2,304	3.8
Government	371	−1.1

Source: MedPAC analysis of Medicare cost report and Provider of Service file from CMS.
Eleven facilities had missing urban or rural designations.

to admission in the SNF. There are exceptions, however, and the patient's insurance provider should be consulted to determine whether these restrictions apply.

The patient must meet specific criteria to receive treatment. These criteria include:

- The patient must be admitted into the SNF for treatment within 30 days of discharge from the hospital.
- The patient must enter the SNF for treatment of the same condition for which he or she was hospitalized.
- The patient must require daily skilled care for a condition that can be improved.
- The facility must be Medicare certified.
- The patient's physician must write a care plan that is carried out by the SNF.

Once the skilled needs are met, Medicare will no longer pay for services.

Prior Hospitalization Requirement

Services in an SNF are covered only after an individual has been transferred to the facility from a hospital in which he or she was a patient for not less than three consecutive calendar days before discharge in connection with the transfer. (In determining whether the required three-day period of hospitalization has been met, the date of admission, but not the day of discharge, is counted as a hospital inpatient day.) The hospital discharge that qualifies an individual for covered SNF services must have occurred on or after the first day of the month in which the individual reached age 65 or became entitled to Medicare due to disability or chronic renal disease. An individual is deemed to have been transferred from a hospital admitted to the SNF facility within 30 days after discharge from the hospital. (Here again, the day of discharge from the hospital is omitted in counting the 30 days.) No new qualifying period of hospitalization is required if the individual is readmitted to the same or another qualified facility within 30 days after discharge from the facility. This means that the period of extended care services may be interrupted briefly and then resume without a new period of hospitalization.

Despite this general 30-day transfer limitation, the law permits coverage admissions occurring more than 30 days after hospital discharge in the case of an individual whose condition is such that an active course of treatment in an SNF would not be medically appropriate within 30 days after hospital discharge. In such a case, the 30 day transfer period is increased to "such time as it would be medically appropriate to begin an active course of treatment."

To be covered, the extended care services must be for the treatment of a condition for which the beneficiary received inpatient hospital services or a condition that arose while the beneficiary was in the SNF for treatment of a condition that had required a prior medically necessary hospitalization. For purposes of determining whether an individual has met the three-day prior hospitalization requirement, it does not matter whether the hospital has a transfer agreement with the SNF; the hospital either must be a participating general or psychiatric hospital or an institution that meets the conditions of participating requirements.

Levels of Care

Services that qualify as either skilled nursing or rehabilitation services include the overall management and evaluation of a care plan; observation and assessment of the patient's changing condition; and patient education services.

Services that qualify as skilled nursing services include:

- Intravenous or intramuscular injections and intravenous feeding
- Enteral feeding that comprises at least 26% of daily calorie requirements and provides at least 501 ml of fluid per day
- Nasopharyngeal and tracheotomy aspiration
- Insertion and sterile irrigation and replacement of suprapubic catheters
- Application of dressings involving prescription medications and aseptic techniques
- Treatment of extensive decubitus ulcers or other widespread skin disorder
- Heat treatments that specifically have been ordered by a physician as part of active treatment and that require observation by a nurse to adequately evaluate the patient's progress
- Initial phases of a regimen involving administration of medical gases
- Rehabilitation nursing procedures, including the related teaching and adaptive aspects of nursing, that are part of active treatment (eg, the institution and supervision of bowel and bladder training programs)

Services that qualify as skilled rehabilitation services include:

- Ongoing assessment of rehabilitation needs and potential services concurrent with the management of a patient care plan, including tests and measurements of range of motion, strength, balance, coordination, endurance, functional ability, activities of daily living, perceptual deficits, speech, and language or hearing disorders
- Therapeutic exercises or activities that, because of the type of exercises employed or the condition of the patient, must be performed by or under the supervision of a qualified physical therapist or occupational therapist to ensure the safety of the patient and the effectiveness of the treatment
- Gait evaluation and training furnished to restore function in a patient whose ability to walk has been impaired by neurological, muscular, or skeletal abnormality
- Range of motion exercises that are part of the active treatment of a specific disease state that has resulted in loss of, or restriction of, mobility (as evidenced by the therapist's notes showing the degree of motion lost and the degree to be restored)
- Maintenance therapy, when the specialized knowledge and judgment of a qualified therapist is required to design and establish a maintenance program based on an initial evaluation and periodic reassessment of the patient's needs, and consistent with the patient's capacity and tolerance (eg, a Parkinson's patient not undergoing a rehabilitation regimen may require the services of a qualified therapist to determine what types of exercises will contribute the most to the maintenance of the patient's present level of functioning)
- Ultrasound, short-wave, and microwave therapy treatments by a qualified physical therapist
- Hot pack, hydro collator, infrared treatments, paraffin baths, and whirlpool in particular cases in which the patient's condition is complicated by circulatory deficiency,

areas of desensitization, open wounds, fractures, or other complications and the skills, knowledge, and judgment of a qualified physical therapist are required
- Services of a speech pathologist or audiologist when necessary for the restoration of function in speech or hearing

Personal care services that do not require the skills of qualified technical or professional personnel are not skilled services, except under circumstances specified (ie, when "special medical complications" are involved). Personal care services include, but are not limited to:

- Administration of routine oral medications, eye drops, and ointments
- General maintenance care of colostomy and ileostomy
- Routine services to maintain satisfactory functioning of indwelling bladder catheters
- Changes of dressings for noninfected postoperative or chronic condition
- Prophylactic and palliative skin care, including bathing and application of creams or treatment of minor skin problems
- Routine services to maintain satisfactory functioning of indwelling bladder catheters
- General maintenance care in connection with a plaster cast
- Routine care in connection with braces and similar devices
- Use of heat as a palliative and comfort measure, such as whirlpool and hydro collator
- Routine administration of medical gases after a regimen of therapy has been established
- Assistance in dressing, eating, and using the toilet
- Periodic turning and positioning in bed
- General supervision of exercises that have been taught to the patient, including the actual carrying out of maintenance programs (Helping a patient repeat exercises required to maintain bodily function do not require the skills of a therapist and would not constitute skilled rehabilitation services. Similarly, repetitious exercises to improve gait, maintain strength, or endurance; passive exercises to maintain range of motion in paralyzed extremities, which are not related to a specific loss of function; and assisted walking do not constitute skilled rehabilitation services.)

Hospital Providers of Extended Care Services (Swing-Bed Facilities)

Due to the shortage of rural SNF beds for Medicare patients, rural hospitals with fewer than 100 beds may be paid under Part A for furnishing covered nursing home services to Medicare beneficiaries. Such a hospital, known as a swing-bed facility, can "swing" its beds between hospital and SNF levels of care on an as-needed basis if it has obtained a swing-bed approval from CMS.

A hospital providing extended care services will be treated as an SNF for purposes of applying coverage rules. This means that services are subject to all of the Part A coverage: physician certification, deductible, and coinsurance provisions that are applicable to SNF extended care services. The following serve as examples of such provisions:

- SNF level of care days in a swing-bed facility are to be counted against total SNF benefit days available to Medicare Beneficiaries.
- Medicare beneficiaries receiving a SNF level of care in a swing-bed facility must first meet the three-day hospital stay requirement.
- Services needed and provided must be of the type and at the level to constitute extended care of SNF level services.

TABLE 5-10

SNF Care Paid for by Medicare

Days	Medicare Pays for Covered Services	Beneficiary Pays
1–20	Full cost	$0
21–100	All but $119 per day	Up to $119 per day
Beyond 100	$0	Full cost

The copayment is up to $119 per day for the year 2006. It can change each year. If the beneficiary has a Medigap policy with the Original Medicare Plan or is in a Medicare managed care plan or private fee-for-service plan, his or her costs may be different or he or she may have additional coverage.

Payment

The beneficiary is required to pay a coinsurance amount equal to one eighth of the inpatient hospital deductible for each day after the 20th and before the 101st day of SNF services furnished during a spell of illness. The coinsurance charge for 2006 is $119 per day. See Table 5-10.

Medicaid will pay only for nursing home care provided in a facility certified by the government to provide service to Medicaid recipients. SNFs and intermediate care facilities providing short-term care for a patient whose condition is stable or reversible are covered through Medicaid with a physician's authorization. Eligibility requirements and covered services vary widely from state to state. Medicaid reimbursement payments are generally made using one of three payment systems: cost base, per diem, and case mix. There is a greater use of prospective payment systems (per diem or case mix) than cost-based systems for nursing facility services. It is important to know that reimbursement may vary from state to state. It may also vary between providers and provider types.

A managed care plan will not help pay for care unless the nursing home has a contract with the plan.

Most Medicare supplemental insurance, often called Medigap plans, will help pay for skilled nursing care but only when Medicare covers that care. A Medigap policy may also pay for certain items or services not covered by Medicare. Medigap policies will pay supplemental benefits regardless of the providers used. Some people use employer group health plans or long-term care insurance to help cover nursing home costs.

LTC insurance is a private policy plan. The benefits and costs of these plans vary widely. LTC benefits are paid under the following circumstances:

- A policyholder suffers an impairment.
- A policyholder is unable to perform two ADLs.
- A policyholder has Alzheimer's or senile dementia.
- The policyholder's physician certifies that it is medically necessary.
- The waiting period is satisfied.

ALTERNATIVES TO NURSING HOME CARE

The Medicare program offers limited access to two unique programs for certain beneficiaries who need a comprehensive medical and social service delivery system. The two programs currently available are a Program of All-Inclusive Care for the Elderly (PACE) and a social managed care plan.

Program of All Inclusive Care for the Elderly

The Program of All Inclusive Care for the Elderly (PACE) is an optional benefit under both Medicare and Medicaid that focuses entirely on older people, those who are frail enough to meet their state's standards for nursing home care. PACE features comprehensive medical and social services that are provided at an adult health center, home, and/or inpatient facility. For most patients, the comprehensive service package permits them to continue living at home while receiving services, rather than be institutionalized. A team of doctors, nurses, and other health care professionals assess participants, develop care plans, and deliver all services that are integrated into a complete health care plan. PACE is available only in states that have chosen to offer PACE under Medicaid.

Eligible individuals who wish to participate must voluntarily enroll. PACE enrollees must be age 55 or older and meet the following requirements:

- Reside in a PACE service area
- Undergo screening by a team of physicians, nurses, and other health care professionals
- Sign and agree to the terms of the enrollment agreements

Services

PACE offers and manages all medical, social, and rehabilitative services that its enrollees need to preserve or restore their homes and communities and to maintain their quality of life. The PACE service package must include all Medicare and Medicaid services provided by the state. At a minimum, a PACE organization must provide an additional 16 services (eg, social work, drugs, nursing facility care). Minimum services that must be provided in the PACE center include primary care services, social services, restorative therapies, personal care and supportive services, nutritional counseling, recreational therapy, and meals. If an enrollee is receiving adult day care services, these services also include meals and transportation. Services are available 24 hours a day, seven days a week, 365 days a year. Generally, these services are provided in an adult day care setting but may also include in-home and other referral services that enrollees may need. This includes medical specialists, laboratory and other diagnostic services, and hospital and nursing home care.

An enrollee's need is determined by a PACE team of health care providers. A PACE team includes:

- Primary care physicians and nurses
- Physical, occupational, and recreational therapists
- Social workers
- Personal care attendants
- Dietitians
- Drivers

Payment

PACE receives a fixed monthly payment per enrollee from Medicare and Medicaid. The amounts are the same during the contract year, regardless of the services an enrollee may need. Persons enrolled in PACE also may have to pay a monthly premium, depending on their eligibility for Medicare and Medicaid.

Current Sites

Currently, 35 PACE sites exist; new sites are added each year. Sites are available in the following states:

California (4)	Massachusetts (6)	Ohio (2)	Tennessee (1)
Colorado (1)	Michigan (1)	Oregon (1)	Texas (2)
Florida (1)	Missouri (1)	Pennsylvania (4)	Washington (1)
Kansas (1)	New Mexico (1)	Rhode Island (1)	Wisconsin (1)
Maryland (1)	New York (4)	South Carolina (1)	

Social Managed Care Plan

A social managed care plan is an organization that provides the full range of Medicare benefits offered by standard managed care plans plus additional services that include care coordination, prescription drug benefits, chronic care benefits covering short-term nursing home care, a full range of home and community based services such as homemaker, personal care services, adult day care, respite care, and medical transportation. Other services that may be provided include eyeglasses, hearing aids, and dental benefits. These plans offer the full range of medical benefits that are offered by standard managed care plans plus chronic or extended care services. Membership offers other health benefits that are not provided through Medicare alone or most other senior health plans.

Current Social Managed Care Plan Sites

There are currently four social managed care plans participating in Medicare and each social managed care plan has eligibility criteria. These social managed care plans are located in Portland, Oregon; Long Beach, California; Brooklyn, New York; and Las Vegas, Nevada.

Kaiser Permanente, Portland, Oregon The enrollee must be 65 years of age or older, must have Medicare Part A and Part B, must continue to pay the Part B premium, and must live in Kaiser Permanente's social managed care plan service area. The enrollee cannot have end-stage renal disease (ESRD) or reside in an institutional setting. In order to receive the long-term care benefit, an expanded care resource coordinator will visit the enrollee at home to determine if he or she qualifies for nursing home certification based on criteria established by the State of Oregon Senior and Disabled Services. These criteria may include needing daily ongoing assistance from another person with one of the following activities of daily living: walking or transferring indoors, eating, managing medications, controlling difficult or dangerous behavior, controlling bowels or bladder, or requiring protection and supervision because of confusion or frailty.

SCAN, Long Beach, California The enrollee must be 65 years of age or older, must have Medicare Part A and Part B, must continue to pay the Part B premium, and must live in SCAN's service area. The enrollee cannot have ESRD. In addition, in order to receive extended home care services, members must have a nursing home certificate, which indicates that the members informal support system (such as a family member or care giver) is not sufficient to keep the member out of a nursing home.

Elderplan, Brooklyn, New York The enrollee must be 65 years of age or older, must have Medicare Part A and Part B, must continue to pay the Part B premium, and must live in Elderplan's service area. The enrollee cannot have ESRD. In order to receive chronic care benefits, the enrollee must meet state nursing home certifiable criteria.

Health Plan of Nevada, Las Vegas, Nevada The enrollee must be at least 65 years of age, or may under 65 if they are disabled. The enrollee must have Medicare Part A and Part B, must continue to pay the Part B premium and must live in Health Plan of Nevada's service area. The enrollee cannot have end-stage renal disease. For the long-term care benefit, the beneficiary must meet certain criteria based on established medical, psychological, functional, and social criteria as well as needing to be medically necessary.

HOME HEALTH CARE

Medicare spending for home health expenditures was $12.5 billion dollars in 2005 (see Figure 5-4). From 1992 to 1997, Medicare home health spending grew at an average annual rate of 20%. The payment system was cost based during this period. Spending began to fall in 1997 concurrent with the introduction of the interim payment system (IPS) based upon costs with limits, more restrictive eligibility, and increased scrutiny from the Office of Inspector General. The prospective payment system (PPS) replaced the IPS in 2000. Also eligibility for home health benefits was broadened slightly.

chapter 5 Billing for Ancillary Services

FIGURE 5-4

Spending for Home Health Care, 1992–2005

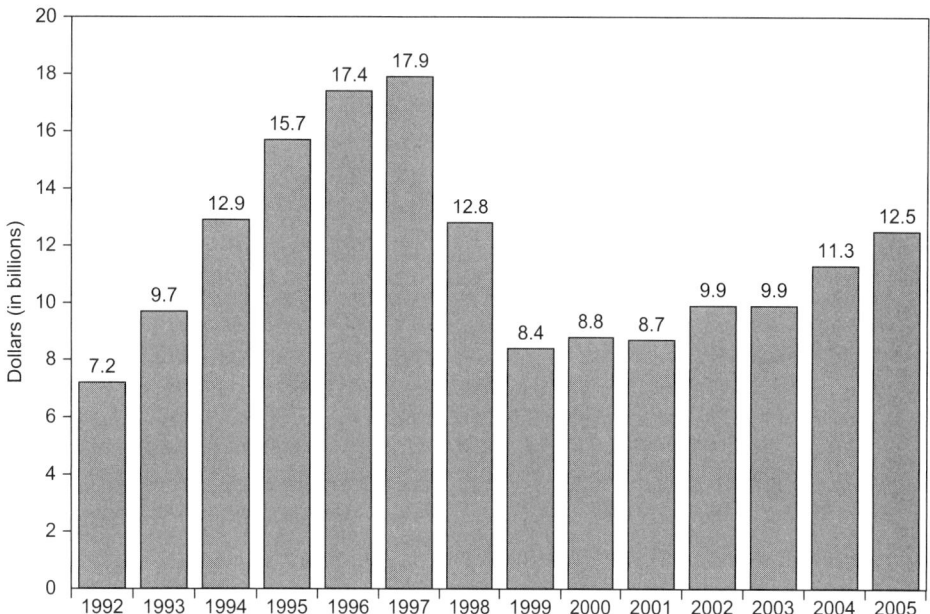

Source: CMS, Office of the Actuary, 2006.

In 2004, the payment system changed from fiscal year to calendar year.

TABLE 5-11

Medicare Home Health Care Use, 1992–2003

Year	People Served Number (Thousands)	Visits Number (Millions)	Visits Per Person Served
1992	2,506	132	53
1993	2,874	164	57
1994	3,179	209	66
1995	3,469	249	72
1996	3,600	265	74
1997	3,558	258	73
1998	3,062	155	51
1999	2,720	113	42
2000	2,461	91	37
2001	2,403	71	31
2002	2,544	73	31
2003	2,681	75	31

Source: CMS, Office of the Actuary, May 2005.

Continued enforcement of program standards remains. Chapter 10 discusses compliance and current compliance enforcement efforts.

Table 5-11 shows Medicare home health care utilization from 1992 through 2003. The total volume of home health care expanded rapidly as both the number of visits per user and number of users increased. The number of beneficiaries using home health care increased by more than one million between 1992 and 1996. The number of users fell by one million between 1997 and 2000.

TABLE 5-12

Aggregate Medicare Margins for All Freestanding Home Health Agencies, 2004

Agency Group	Number of Agencies	2004 Margin
All agencies	3,979	16.0%
Caseload		
Urban	2,546	15.9
Mixed	985	17.0
Rural	448	11.8
Type of Control		
Voluntary	686	12.4
Private	3,047	18.1
Government	246	8.1
Volume Group, Lowest to Highest		
First quintile	843	13.1
Second quintile	781	10.5
Third quintile	794	12.9
Fourth quintile	792	15.9
Fifth quintile	769	17.5

Source: MedPAC analysis of Medicare Cost Report file from CMS.

Some freestanding agencies were omitted because of data integrity concerns.

Table 5-12 shows Medicare margins for all freestanding home health agencies. Eighty percent of agencies had positive margins in 2004. The projected margin for 2006 is 14.7%.

Approximately 7.6 million patients received home health care in 2001. In addition to patients officially certified by a physician as "homebound," individuals eligible for home visits include those who would benefit from a home assessment because they have multiple problems, are on many medications, use the health care system excessively, are at risk for abuse or neglect, may need nursing home placement, or were recently discharged from a hospital because of acute illness, injury, surgery, or birth.

National health care expenditures on home health care totaled $41.3 billion in 2001. The vast majority of these expenditures were for services other than physician services. Most home care services are provided by facility-based home health agencies, which employ registered nurses, physical therapists, and home health aides.

Nurse practitioners, by nature of their license as a nurse and their legal authority to diagnose and treat, may perform either nursing visits or medical visits. In 1997, nurse practitioners gained the authority to bill Medicare for medically necessary home visits of the nature furnished by physicians.

The types and quantities of home health care services have changed since the implementation of the PPS (see Table 5-13). Before the PPS, the average number of visits per episode was 36. By 2002, the average number of visits per episode was 19. The mix of visits has shifted towards therapy and away from home health aide services. This includes physical, occupational, and speech therapy. Substantially higher payments for otherwise similar patients are generated by meeting the payment therapy threshold for a payment episode. For example, an episode for a patient with moderate clinical severity and moderate functional limitation would be paid at $2440 (base payment $\times$ case weight 1.08) if the episode did not meet the therapy threshold. It would be paid at $4440 (base payment $\times$ case weight 1.95) if the episode did meet the therapy threshold.

TABLE 5-13

Changes to the Home Health Product After the Prospective Payment System Started

	1997	2002
Average visits per episode	36	19
Average minutes per episode	1500	940
Percentage of therapy visits	9	26

Source: Pre-PPS CMS analysis of the National Claims History file; post-PPS MedPAC analysis of 5 percent Standard Analytic File.
The prospective payment system began in October 2000.

A homebound individual is normally unable to leave home, which takes considerable and taxing effort. A person may leave home for medical treatment or for nonmedical reasons that require brief absences from home (eg, religious services). The need for adult day care does not prohibit an individual from obtaining home health care for other medical conditions. Home health care patients receive skilled nursing care in their homes for the treatment of illness or injury. Skilled nursing care is a level of care that must be given or supervised by a licensed nurse and is under the general direction of a physician. Skilled nursing care services include:

- Giving intravenous injections
- Feeding patients through a tube
- Administering oxygen
- Changing sterile dressings on a wound

Any service that could be safely performed by a nonmedical person (or one's self) without the direct supervision of a licensed nurse is not covered. A home health agency (HHA) is an organization that provides this type of home care service, including skilled nursing care, physical therapy, occupational therapy, speech therapy, and care by home health aids.

A plan of care describes the kind of services and care that the beneficiary requires for his or her health problem. The physician works with a home health care nurse to decide what kind of services the beneficiary needs, what type of health care professional should give these services, and how often the services are needed.

All Medicare beneficiaries can receive home health care benefits if they meet the following four conditions:

- A physician has decided that the beneficiary needs medical care in the home and has made a plan for that home care.
- The beneficiary needs at least one of the following: intermittent skilled nursing care, physical therapy, speech pathology language services, or occupational therapy.
- The beneficiary is homebound.
- Medicare approves the HHA providing care for the patient.

Skilled Nursing Care

If a patient qualifies for home health services, Medicare covers either part-time or intermittent skilled nursing services. Skill nursing services are services that require the skills of a registered nurse or a licensed practical nurse (or licensed vocational nurse) under the supervision of a registered nurse; are reasonable and necessary to the treatment of the patient's illness or injury; and are needed on an intermittent basis. For purposes of receiving home health care, the phrase *part-time or intermittent care* means skilled nursing and home health aide services furnished up to 28 hours per week combined over any number of days per week provided they are furnished fewer than eight hours per day. Medicare may approve additional time up to 35 hours per week but fewer than eight hours per day on a case-by-case basis.

To meet the requirement for intermittent skilled nursing care, a patient must have a medically predictable, recurring need for skilled nursing services. In most instances, this definition is met if a patient requires a skilled nursing service at least once every 60 days. Because the need for intermittent skilled nursing care makes the patient eligible for other covered home health services, an intermediary should evaluate each claim involving skilled nursing services furnished less frequently than once every 60 days. In such cases, payment should be made only if documentation justifies a recurring need for reasonable, necessary, and medically predictable skilled nursing services.

Postinstitutional home health services are services furnished to a beneficiary in these instances: (1) after discharge from a hospital in which the beneficiary was an inpatient for not less than three consecutive days before being discharged and the services were initiated within 14 days of discharge or (2) after discharge from an SNF in which the beneficiary was provided posthospital extended care services and services were initiated within 14 days after discharge. If the first home stay requirement is not met, home health services are furnished under Part B.

Home health spell illness refers to a period of consecutive days beginning with the first day that an beneficiary is furnished postinstitutional home health services during a month in which the individual is entitled to benefits under Part A. It ends when the beneficiary has not received inpatient hospital, SNF, or home health services for 60 days.

An *episode of care* is a 60-day period starting on the day that the first billable services are provided to a beneficiary under a plan of care and ending 60 days later. On the 61st day that services are being provided, a new episode of care commences. A beneficiary can have an unlimited number of episodes of care and an episode can be shorter than 60 days. A beneficiary may have only one episode of care at a time. The 60-day episode of care is used to determine the amount of payment made on behalf of the beneficiary.

Medicare Coverage

Home health services are covered only if furnished by an HHA participating in the Medicare program and acting on a physician's certification. If the patient does not need therapy, skilled nursing care must be needed at least once every 60 days for the patient to qualify for home health benefits. There is no prior hospitalization requirement for a beneficiary to receive home health services.

Home health services are covered to varying degrees under Part A hospital and Part B supplementary medical insurance. Part C Medicare Advantage health plans also provide home health benefits but must do so only through Medicare-approved HHAs.

Prior to 1997 home health services always were covered under Part A when the patient was eligible under both Part A and Part B. Since January 1, 1998, for beneficiaries enrolled in Parts A and B, home health visits that are not part of the first 100 visits following a beneficiary's stay in a hospital or SNF are considered Part B home health services. If the beneficiary is enrolled only in Part A and qualifies for the home health benefit, all home health services fall under Part A.

For beneficiaries enrolled in Parts A and B, Part A pays only for postinstitutional home health services furnished during a home health spell of illness for up to 100 visits during such spell of illness for all beneficiaries. Since 1998, for beneficiaries enrolled in Part B, payment is transferred over a six-year period from Part A to Part B for postinstitutional home health services provided after the first 100 visits during a spell of illness requiring home health services following a beneficiary's stay in a hospital or SNF. Covered home health services that do not meet the definition of postinstitutional are covered under Part B.

The original Medicare plan covers the following home health care services:

- Part-time or intermittent skilled nursing care
- Part-time or intermittent home health aide services

- Physical and occupational therapy
- Speech language pathology services
- Medical supplies (not drugs or biologicals)
- DME

The original Medicare plan usually pays 80% of the approved amount for certain pieces of medical equipment.

Skilled Nursing Care on a Part-time or Intermittent Basis

Skilled nursing care includes services and care that can only be performed safely and correctly by a licensed nurse (either a registered nurse or licensed practical nurse).

Home Health Aid Services on a Part-time or Intermittent Basis

A home health aide does not have a nursing license. The aide provides services that support any services provided by a nurse. These services include help with personal care such as bathing, using the toilet, and dressing. Medicare does not cover home health aid services unless the patient is getting skilled care such as nursing care or other therapy.

Physical Therapy, Speech Language Pathology Services, and Occupational Therapy

Medicare covers the following types of therapy:

Physical therapy includes exercise to regain movement and strength to a body area and training on how to use special equipment or do daily activities, eg, getting in and out of a wheelchair or bathtub.

Speech language pathology services include exercise to regain and strengthen speech skills.

Occupational therapy helps the patient become able to do usual daily activities by himself or herself (eg, eating, getting dressed).

Beginning in January of 2006, a financial limitation ("therapy cap") was placed on outpatient rehabilitation services received by Medicare beneficiaries. These limits apply to outpatient Part B therapy services from all settings except outpatient hospitals and hospital emergency departments.

For physical therapy, including outpatient speech language pathology, there was a combined annual limit of $1,740 in 2006. For occupational therapy, the annual limit in 2006 was also $1,740. You must submit separate requests for exceptions from the combined physical therapy and speech language pathology cap and from the occupational therapy cap. In general, it is better to submit requests for exception from either therapy cap before the cap is exceeded.

However, CMS can grant exceptions to the caps at the request of the Medicare enrollee (or an agent acting for that person) if these services meet certain qualifications as medically necessary services; other types of exceptions are automatic. You must include a KX modifier on the claim identified as a therapy service with a GN, GO, or GP modifier when a therapy cap exception has been approved or if it meets all the guidelines for an automatic exception. This allows the bill for therapy services to be paid, even though they are above the therapy cap financial limits.

Medical Social Services, Supplies, and Equipment

Medical social services help a beneficiary with the social and emotional concerns related to an illness. Services include counseling and help in finding resources within a patient's community. Certain medical supplies, like bandages and gauze, are generally not covered. Medicare usually pays 80% of the approved amount for certain pieces of medical equipment, such as a wheelchair or walker. Medicare Part D covers some of the prescription drug costs of Medicare recipients.

Medical Supplies and DME

Covered medical supplies are items that, due to their therapeutic or diagnostic characteristics, are essential for an HHA to effectively implement the plan of care ordered by the physician for treating or diagnosing a patient's illness or injury. They include catheters and catheter supplies (eg, ostomy bags and ostomy care supplies); dressings and wound care supplies (eg, sterile gloves, gauze, and applicators); and intravenous supplies.

DME furnished by an HHA is reimbursed under Medicare Part B on a reasonable cost basis, with the beneficiary responsible for a 20% coinsurance. DME is not included in the home health prospective payment rate and has been eliminated from the consolidated billing requirement.

Exclusion of Drugs and Biologicals

Generally, drugs and biologicals as a home health benefit are excluded from coverage. In certain cases, they may be covered under Part B if administered by a physician as part of his or her professional services; the drugs cannot be self-administered. In addition, the administration of medication may be covered if the services of a licensed nurse are required to administer the medications safely and effectively for the reasonable and necessary treatment of the illness or injury.

Evaluation Visits

The cost of an initial evaluation visit by HHA personnel is considered an administrative expense of the HHA, because the patient has not been accepted for care. However, if, during the course of this initial evaluation, the patient is determined suitable for home health care by the HHA and is furnished the first skilled service as ordered under the physician's plan of treatment, the visit would become the first billable visit.

Outpatient Services

In certain instances, an outpatient service can be included as home health services. In most cases, a beneficiary would have to be homebound to be eligible for home health services. However, provision is made to cover services furnished under arrangements at a hospital, SNF, or rehabilitation center that require the use of equipment that cannot be made available at the beneficiary's home (eg, hydrotherapy) or are furnished while the beneficiary is at the facility to received services that require use of such equipment. The hospital or SNF must be a qualified provider of services. If special transportation arrangements must be made to bring the homebound patient to the institution providing these special services, the cost of transporting cannot be reimbursed as a home health service.

Medicaid Coverage

Medicaid pays for basic home health care and medical equipment including pay for homemaker, personal care, and other services that are not paid for by Medicare. There are Medicaid programs that pay some or all of Medicare's premiums and may also pay Medicare deductibles and coinsurance for certain individuals who are entitle to Medicare and have low income. Medicaid coverage differs from state to state.

Managed Care Plan Coverage

Medicare managed care plans are health care choices in some parts of the country. In most plans, beneficiary can only go to physicians, specialists, or hospitals on the plan's list. Medicare managed care plans must cover all Medicare Part A and Part B health care, including home health care. A beneficiary can only use a home health agency that works with the manage care plan.

AMBULANCE SERVICES

An origin-destination Healthcare Common Procedural Coding System (HCPCS) modifier (see Table 5-14) and the QM or QN modifier must be present for each base-rate ambulance trip and mileage revenue code line item. The modifier must indicate both origin and destination. The first position of the modifier is used to report the origin of service. The second position is used for the destination of service. For example, the first position is R if the origin is the patient's residence, and the second position is H if the destination is a hospital.

Ambulance Billing

An ambulance is a vehicle equipped for transporting the injured or the sick. An ambulance must be designed and equipped to respond to medical emergencies and, in nonemergency situations, be capable of transporting beneficiaries with acute medical conditions. The vehicle must comply with state or local laws governing the licensing and certification of an emergency medical transportation vehicle. At a minimum, the ambulance must contain a stretcher, linens, emergency medical supplies, oxygen equipment, and other lifesaving emergency medical equipment. It must also be equipped with emergency warning lights, sirens, and telecommunications equipment as required by state or local law. This equipment should include, at a minimum, one two-way voice radio or wireless telephone.

There are two types of ambulance services: ground (land or water) and air. The most common is ground ambulance service in which a patient is transported in a motor vehicle. Air ambulance service involves transporting a patient in a helicopter or airplane. There are six categories of service for ground ambulance and two categories for air ambulance, as follows:

- Ground Ambulance
    —*Basic life support:* Basic life support (BLS) is transportation by ground ambulance vehicle and the provision of medically necessary supplies and services, including BLS ambulance services as defined by the state. The ambulance must be staffed by an individual who is qualified in accordance with state and local laws as an emergency medical technician-basic (EMT-basic). These laws may vary from state to state or within a state. For example, in some jurisdictions an EMT-basic is permitted to operate limited equipment onboard the vehicle, assist more qualified personnel in performing assessments and interventions, and establish a peripheral intravenous (IV) line.
    —*BLS-emergency:* Emergency response is a BLS or advanced life support level 1 (ALS1) level of service that has been provided in immediate response to a 911 call or

TABLE 5-14
Origin and Destination Modifiers

D	Diagnostic or therapeutic site other than P or H
E	Residential, domiciliary, custodial facility (nursing home, not skilled nursing facility)
G	Hospital-based dialysis facility (hospital or hospital-related)
H	Hospital
I	Site of transfer (eg, airport or helicopter pad) between modes of ambulance transport
J	Nonhospital-based dialysis facility
N	Skilled nursing facility
P	Physician's office (includes health maintenance organization nonhospital facility, clinic, etc)
R	Residence
S	Scene of accident or acute event
X	Intermediate stop at physician's office en route to the hospital (includes health maintenance organization nonhospital facility, clinic, etc) NOTE: Only used as a destination code in the second position of a modifier.

the equivalent. An immediate response is one in which the ambulance provider or supplier begins as quickly as possible to take the steps necessary to respond to the call.

— *Advanced life support 1:* ALS1 is the transportation by ground ambulance vehicle and the provision of medically necessary supplies and services including the provision of an ALS assessment or at least one ALS intervention. ALS assessment is an assessment performed by an ALS crew as part of an emergency response that was necessary because the patient's reported condition at the time of dispatch was such that only an ALS crew was qualified to perform the assessment. An ALS assessment does not necessarily result in a determination that the patient requires an ALS level of service.

— *Advanced life support 2:* ALS2 is the transportation by ground ambulance vehicle and the provision of medically necessary supplies and services including (1) at least three separate administrations of one or more medications by intravenous push/bolus or by continuous infusion (excluding crystalloid fluids) or (2) ground ambulance transport and the provision of at least one of the following ALS2 procedures: manual defibrillation/ cardioversion, endotracheal intubation, central venous line, cardiac pacing, chest decompression, surgical airway, and intraosseous line.

— *Specialty care transport:* Specialty care transport (SCT) is hospital-to-hospital transportation of a critically injured or ill beneficiary by a ground ambulance vehicle, including the provision of medically necessary supplies and services, at a level of service beyond the scope of the EMT-paramedic. SCT is necessary when a beneficiary's condition requires ongoing care that must be furnished by one or more health professionals in an appropriate specialty area, eg, emergency or critical care nursing, emergency medicine, respiratory care, cardiovascular care, or a paramedic with additional training.

— *Paramedic intercept:* Paramedic intercept (PI) services are ALS services delivered by paramedics that operate separately from the agency that provides the ambulance transport. This type of service is most often provided for an emergency ambulance transport in which a local volunteer ambulance that can provide only BLS level service is dispatched to transport a patient. If the patient needs ALS services such as EKG monitoring, chest decompression, or intravenous therapy, another entity dispatches a paramedic to meet the BLS ambulance at the scene or once the ambulance is on the way to the hospital. The ALS paramedics then provide their services to the patient.

- Air Ambulance
  — *Fixed wing air ambulance:* Fixed wing (FW) air ambulance (airplane) is the transportation by a fixed wing aircraft that is certified by the Federal Aviation Administration (FAA) as a fixed wing air ambulance, including the provision of medically necessary services and supplies.
  — *Rotary wing air ambulance:* Rotary wing (RW) air ambulance (helicopter) is the transportation by helicopter that is certified by the FAA as a rotary wing ambulance, including the provision of medically necessary supplies and services.

Billing Requirements

Only one zip code is permitted per claim for ambulance service. More than one ambulance service may be reported on the same claim for a beneficiary if all points of pickup have the same zip code. Suppliers must prepare a separate claim for each trip if the points of pickup are located in different zip codes. For out-of-country claims, the provider indicates 00000 on the form. Claims will be rejected if the zip code information is missing or invalid or if multiple zip codes are reported on the same claim.

If more than one patient is transported at the same time, a separate claim form must be filed for each patient. Payment will be prorated based on the number of patients transported; ambulance fee schedule allowance; and level of medically appropriate service rendered. Cost for mileage requires two revenue code line items on the UB-92 form. Base rate and ambulance trip and mileage should be reported as separate revenue code line items.

Air ambulance transportation services may be covered only if the following conditions are met:

- The vehicle is specially designed and equipped for transporting the sick or injured. It must have customary patient care equipment including a stretcher, clean linens, first-aid supplies, and oxygen equipment and it must also have such other safety and life-saving equipment as required by state or local authorities.
- The ambulance crew consists of at least two members. One of these members must have adequate first-aid training.
- The beneficiary's medical condition requires immediate and rapid ambulance transportation that could not have been provided by land ambulance and either (1) the point of pick-up is inaccessible by land vehicle (this condition could be met in Hawaii, Alaska, and other remote or sparsely populated areas) or (2) great distances or other obstacles (eg, heavy traffic) are involved in getting the patient to the nearest hospital with appropriate facilities for treatment. The term *appropriate facility* refers to a hospital that is capable of providing the required level and type of care for the patient's illness and has available the type of physician or specialist needed to treat the beneficiary's condition.

Air ambulance transport is covered for the transfer of a patient from one hospital to another if the medical necessity criteria are met and the transferring hospital does not have adequate facilities to provide the medical services needed by the patient. The medical appropriateness is only established when the beneficiary's condition is such that the time needed to transport a beneficiary by land or the instability of transportation by land poses a threat to the beneficiary's survival or seriously endangers the beneficiary's health.

Following is a list of examples for which air ambulance transportation could be justified. The list is not all inclusive, nor is it intended to justify air transportation in all locales for the circumstances listed.

- Intracranial bleeding requiring neurosurgical intervention
- Cardiogenic shock
- Burns requiring immediate treatment in a burn center
- Conditions requiring treatment in a hyperbaric oxygen unit
- Multiple severe injuries
- Life-threatening trauma

The ambulance transport is covered only if the hospital to which the patient is transferred is the nearest one with appropriate facilities.

Documentation

All Medicare providers must remain abreast of Medicare rules, policies, and payment guidelines; make an independent determination if the service is medically necessary; and have supporting medical documentation available. The issue of medical necessity extends to the provider ordering the service as well as to the provider performing and/or billing the service. Medical necessity must be demonstrated at all levels of care.

Ambulance suppliers are required to retain documentation on file supporting ambulance services billed to Medicare. The purpose of documentation is to provide a permanent record of each patient's medical condition (at the time of transport) and the reason for transport. This information must meet ambulance transport medical necessity criteria.

The ambulance trip sheet for each leg of the trip should be maintained in the ambulance company's records and should include the following:

- Beneficiary name, address, phone number, and health insurance claim number
- Date and time of transport
- Indication of emergency or nonemergency situation

- Name of person who ordered the transport (if available)
- Patient's signature or representative's signature
- Patient's height and weight (reported only when an extra attendant is required)
- Reason for transport, patient's complaint, or current condition
- Patient assessment (by ambulance personnel), which should include the chronological narrative of care or service rendered by ambulance personnel
- "Indicate" the patient's past medical history
- Name and address of origin and destination
- Odometer reading at point of pick up and destination
- Number of loaded miles
- Itemization of specialized services and/or supplies
- Name of treating physician or receiving physician
- Names, titles, and signatures of ambulance personnel
- Name and address of the entity rendering ALS services, if not the transporting company
- Provider's vehicle number and license plate number
- Type of equipped vehicle used for transport (BLS or ALS)

Separate documentation of the following must be submitted with the claim for air ambulance services:

- The air ambulance was dispatched to pick up a Medicare beneficiary.
- The aircraft actually took off to make the pick up.
- The patient was pronounced dead before being loaded onto the ambulance for transport.
- An individual authorized by state law to make such pronouncements made the pronouncement of death.
- The dispatcher did not receive notice of death in sufficient time to abort the flight.

Noncovered services are (1) those in which the patient is pronounced dead after the ambulance has been called but before the ambulance arrives and in which a subsidy is received from a local municipality or (2) those in which the transport vehicle is owned and operated by a government or volunteer entity.

The two billing exceptions are if the patient refuses transport or if an ambulance arrives and it is determined that transport is not medically necessary based on assessment.

Ambulance Fee Schedule

On April 1, 2002, CMS implemented a new national fee schedule that applies to all ambulance services. Ambulance services covered under Medicare are paid based on the lower of the actual billed amount or the ambulance fee schedule. The fee schedule has been phased in over a five-year period. The fee schedule, now fully implemented, replaces the previous retrospective reasonable cost reimbursement system for providers and the reasonable charge system for ambulance suppliers. The ambulance fee schedule was subject to a five-year transition period, as follows:

	Reasonable Charge (%)	Fee Schedule (%)
Year 1 (4/1/02–12/31/02)	80	20
Year 2 (CY 2003)	60	40
Year 3 (CY 2004)	40	60
Year 4 (CY 2005)	20	80
Year 5 (CY 2006 and after)	0	100

TABLE 5-15

Ambulance Fee Schedule

Procedure Code	Locality	Base RVU	GPCI	Conversion Factor	Urban Base Rate	Rural Base Rate
A0425	99	1.00	0.917	1.00	6.05	6.11
A0426	99	1.20	0.917	190.82	217.84	219.99
A0427	99	1.90	0.917	190.82	344.91	348.32
A0428	99	1.00	0.917	190.82	181.53	183.33
A0429	99	1.60	0.917	190.82	290.45	293.32
A0430	99	2529.65	0.917	1.00	2424.67	3637.00
A0431	99	2941.08	0.917	1.00	2819.03	4228.54
A0432	99	1.75	0.917	190.82	317.68	320.82
A0433	99	2.75	0.917	190.82	499.21	504.15
A0434	99	3.25	0.917	190.82	589.97	595.82
A0435	99	1.00	0.917	1.00	7.18	10.77
A0436	99	1.00	0.917	1.00	19.14	28.17

The Medicare Prescription Drug, Improvement and Modernization Act of 2003 also established that for ambulance services furnished during the period July 1, 2004, through December 31, 2009, the ground ambulance base rate is subject to a floor amount. The floor amount is determined by establishing nine fee schedules based on each of the nine census divisions utilizing the same methodology as was used to establish the national fee schedule. If the regional fee schedule methodology for a given census division results in an amount applies for all providers and suppliers in the census division. If the regional fee schedule methodology for a given census division results in an amount greater than the national ground base rate, then the fee schedule portion of the base rate for that census division is equal to a blend of the national rate and the regional rate.

During the transition period prior to January 1, 2006, the AIF was applied to both the fee schedule portion of the blended payment amount (both national and regional, if it applied) and to the reasonable cost or charge portion of the blended payment amount separately, respectively, for each ambulance provider or supplier. These two amounts are added together to determine the total payment amount for each provider or supplier.

As of January 1, 2006, the total payment amount for air ambulance providers and suppliers is based on 100% of the national ambulance fee schedule. The total payment amount for ground providers and suppliers is based on either 100% of the national ambulance fee schedule or 60% of the national ambulance fee schedule and 40% of the regional ambulance fee schedule.

The AIF for calendar year 2006 is 2.5%. Part B coinsurance and deductible requirements apply. See Table 5-15.

HOSPICE CARE

Hospice care is provided by a public agency or private organization that is primarily engaged in providing pain relief, symptom management, and supportive services to care for terminally ill people who have a prognosis of a life expectancy of six months or less. The prognosis should be based on the physician's or medical director's clinical judgment regarding the normal course of the individual's illness. Hospice care is for all age groups, including children, adults, and the elderly, during their final stages of life. The goal of hospice is to care for patients and their families, not to cure the illness. A certification that the individual is terminally ill must be obtained in order to receive Medicare benefits. Under the program, an individual may elect to receive Medicare coverage for an unlimited number of election periods of hospice care, which consist of two 90-day periods and an unlimited number of 60-day periods. These benefits do not need to be used consecutively.

Hospice care includes the following covered services:

- Nursing care
- Nurse practitioner
- Medical social services
- Physicians' services
- Counseling services
- Short-term inpatient care
- Medical appliances and supplies, including drugs and biologicals
- Home health aide and homemaker services
- Physical therapy, occupational therapy, and speech-language pathology services
- Other items and services

Respite care is care given to a hospice patient by another caregiver so that the usual caregiver can rest. As a hospice patient, the beneficiary may have one person who takes care of the patient every day, eg, a family member. It may be necessary to someone to take care of the patient for a short time while the caregiver takes needed time away from his or her duties. During a period of respite care, the patient will be cared for in a Medicare-approved facility, such as a hospice facility, hospital, or nursing home. See Table 5-16.

Benefit Periods

Medicare coverage of hospice care is limited by time periods. A Medicare beneficiary may elect to receive hospice care for up to two periods of 90 days each and an unlimited number of subsequent periods up to 60 days each. A beneficiary electing to receive hospice care must choose to receive such care through a particular hospice program rather than other health care providers. Beneficiaries might elect to receive hospice benefits for two periods of 90 days each, a subsequent period of 30 days, and a subsequent extension period. At the start of each period of care, the physician must certify that the individual is terminally ill in order for the individual to continue receiving hospice care.

By choosing a particular hospice program, a beneficiary gives up the right during the elected period, except in exceptional and unusual circumstances, to receive hospice care from other hospice programs and to receive other Medicare services related to treatment of the terminal illness that are equivalent to or duplicative of hospice care. However, the beneficiary's chosen hospice program may arrange for services to be provided by another hospice program.

TABLE 5-16

Medicare Hospice Payment Categories and Rates, FY 2006

Category	Description	Base Payment Rate	Labor Rate	Share of Days
RHC	Home Care provided on a typical day	$126 per day	69%	93.0%
CHC	Home Care Provided during periods of crisis	$30.76 per hour	69%	4.1%
IRC	Inpatient provided for a short period to provide respite for primary caregiver	$131 per day	54	0.2%
GIC	Inpatient care to treat symptoms that can not be managed in another setting	$563 per day	64	2.7%

FY = fiscal year, RHC = routine home care, CHC = continuous home care, IRC = inpatient respite care, GIC = general inpatient care

Payment for CHC is an hourly rate for care delivered during periods of crisis if care is provided in the home for eight or more hours within a 24-hour period beginning at midnight. A nurse must deliver half of the hours of this care to qualify for CHC-level payment. The minimum daily payment rate at the CHC level is $246 per day (eight hours at $30.75 per hour); maximum daily payment at the CHC level is $738 per day (24 hours at $30.75 per hour).

The beneficiary's waiver of the right to receive Medicare services related to the treatment of his or her terminal illness and that are furnished during the elected period or are duplicative of hospice care does not apply to services furnished by the patient's attending physician. This applies provided the physician is not an employee of the hospice program and the services are not provided by or under arrangements made by the hospice program.

A beneficiary may revoke a hospice care election before the coverage period expires, thereby reinstating eligibility for other Medicare benefits. At any time after such a revocation, a new hospice care election may be made if the beneficiary is otherwise entitled to hospice care benefits within that period. A beneficiary also is entitled to change from one hospice program to another hospice program once per period. Such a change is not considered revocation of an election if the individual is otherwise entitled to hospice care benefits within that period.

An individual who has elected hospice care is liable for coinsurance payments for drugs and biologicals and for respite care. An individual is liable for a coinsurance payment for each palliative drug and biological prescription furnished by the hospice while the individual is not an inpatient. The amount of coinsurance for each prescription approximates 5% of the cost of the drug or biological to the hospice, up to $5, determined in accordance with the drug copayment schedule established by the hospice. The drug copayment schedule must be reviewed for reasonableness and be approved by the intermediary before it is used. The amount of coinsurance for each respite care day is equal to 5% of the payment made by CMS for each respite care day. For example, if Medicare pays $100 per day for inpatient respite care, the beneficiary will pay $5 per day. The beneficiary can stay in a Medicare-approved hospital or nursing home for up to five days each time the individual receives respite care. There is no limit to the number of times the individual can receive respite care. The amount paid for respite care can change yearly. The amount of the individual's coinsurance liability for respite care during a hospice coinsurance period may not exceed the inpatient hospital deductible applicable for the year in which the hospice coinsurance period begins.

The individual hospice coinsurance period begins on the first day an election is effect for the beneficiary and ends with the close of the first period of 14 consecutive days on each of which an election is not in effect for the beneficiary. The law states that no other copayment or deductibles may apply to hospice care services provided during a period, regardless of the setting in which the hospice services are furnished.

Hospice Reimbursement

Hospice providers are reimbursed based on a cost-related prospective payment method, subject to an annual cap amount that is determined and applied at the end of each hospice cap period. The intermediary calculates the cap amount at the end of the hospice cap period. The cap period runs from November 1 of each year through October 31 of the next year. Any payment in excess of the cap must be refunded by the hospice once the cap is determined. The hospice cap for October 1, 2005, through September 30, 2006, is $20,585.39 per beneficiary per year. The FY 2007 payment rates will be the FY 2006 payment rates, increased by 3.4% points, which is the total market basket percentage increase forecasted for FY 2007. The 2007 hospice payment rates are effective for care and services furnished on or after October 1, 2006, through September 30, 2007.

With the exception of payment for physician services, Medicare payment for hospice care is made at one of four predetermined rates for each day that a Medicare beneficiary is under the care of hospice. The four rates are prospective rates; there are no retroactive adjustments other than the application of the statutory "caps" on overall payments and on payments for inpatient care. The rate paid for any particular day varies depending on the level of care furnished to the beneficiary. The four levels of care into which each day of care is classified are shown in Table 5-17.

For each day that a Medicare beneficiary is under the care of a hospice, the hospice is reimbursed an amount applicable to the type and intensity of the services furnished to the

TABLE 5-17

Levels of Care

Revenue code	Description	Rate ($)	Wage Component Subject to Index ($)	Nonweighted Amount ($)
651	Routine home care	130.79	89.87	40.92
652	Continuous home care (Full rate = 24 hours of care $31.81 hourly rate)	763.36	524.50	238.86
655	Inpatient respite care	135.30	73.24	62.06
656	General inpatient care	581.82	372.42	209.40

TABLE 5-18

Codes Used to Determine Type of Service Location for Hospice Services

HCPCS Code	Definition
Q5001	Hospice care provided in patients home/residence
Q5002	Hospice care provided in assisted living facility
Q5003	Hospice care provided in nursing long-term care facility
Q5004	Hospice care provided in skilled nursing facility
Q5005	Hospice care provided in inpatient hospital
Q5006	Hospice care provided in inpatient hospice facility
Q5007	Hospice care provided in long-term care hospital
Q5008	Hospice care provided in inpatient psychiatric facility
Q5009	Hospice care provided in place not otherwise specified (NOS)

beneficiary for that day. Effective January 1, 2007, continuous home care will be based on the number of hours, *reported in increments of 15 minutes*, of continuous care furnished to the beneficiary on that day. **Rounding to the next whole hour is no longer applicable.** For the other categories a single rate is applicable for that category for each day.

When the patient is discharged from an inpatient unit, the appropriate home care rate is to be paid unless the patient dies as an inpatient. When the patient is discharged deceased, the inpatient rate (general or respite) is to be paid for the discharge date.

For services provided on or before December 31, 2006, HCPCS codes are required only to report procedures for attending physician services (revenue 657). Level of care revenue codes (651, 652, 655, or 656) do not require HCPCS coding.

For services provided on or after January 1, 2007, hospices must also report a HCPCS code along with each level of care revenue code to identify the type of service location where that level of care was provided. Table 5-18 provides the HCPCS codes that will be used to report the type of service location for hospice services.

Hospice Programs

Hospice programs can be found through a state's hospice organization or by calling 800 633–4227. The hospice must be Medicare-approved in order to get Medicare payment. More information about hospice care can be obtained from the following:

The National Hospice Organization
1700 Diagonal, Suite 625
Alexandria, VA 22314
800 658-8898
www.nho.org

The Hospice Association of America
228 7th Street, SE
Washington, DC 20003
202 546-4759
www.hospice-america.org

DIETARY AND NUTRITIONAL SERVICES

Dieticians are experts in food and nutrition. They help promote good health through proper eating. They also supervise the preparation and service of food, develop modified diets, participate in research, and educate individuals and groups on good nutritional habits. The goals of dieticians are to obtain, prepare, and serve flavorsome, attractive, and nutritious food to patients, family members, and health care providers. Nutrition professionals include registered dietician (RD) and dietetic technician, registered (DTR). Some RDs or DTRs call themselves *nutritionists*.

The majority of dieticians are clinical or therapeutic. Clinical dieticians provide individual and group educational programs for patients and family members about their nutrition and health. They assess patients' nutritional needs, develop and implement nutrition programs, and evaluate and report the results. They also confer with physicians and other health care professionals in order to coordinate medical and nutritional needs. Some clinical dietitians specialize in the management of overweight patients or the care of critically ill or renal (kidney) and diabetic patients. In addition, clinical dieticians in nursing care facilities, small hospitals, or correctional facilities may manage the food service department.

The medical nutrition therapy (MNT) benefit was created by the Medicare, Medicaid, and SCHIP Benefits Improvement and Protection Act (BIPA) of 2000. It was implemented on January 1, 2002. The MNT benefit authorizes dieticians and nutritionists who meet certain qualifications to be reimbursed directly by Medicare. Previously they were not considered Medicare suppliers, and nutrition counseling was only covered as part of other benefits, such as a hospital stay. Now MNT may be billed separately as a stand-alone benefit, and achieving provider status allows dieticians and nutritionists to bill for services under both the medical nutrition therapy and diabetes self-management training benefits.

The nutrition counseling benefit, while related, is separate from the diabetes outpatient self-management training (DSMT) benefit created by the Balanced Budget Act of 1997. DSMT is a comprehensive diabetes training program, of which general nutrition is only one component. The DSMT and medical nutrition benefits can be provided to the same beneficiary in the same year. However, they are different benefits and require separate referrals from physicians or qualified nonphysician practitioners. The medical evidence reviewed by CMS sugggests that the MNT benefit for diabetic patients is more effective if it is provided after completion of the initial DSMT benefit.

Medicare pays for medical nutrition therapy (MNT) for patients diagnosed with diabetes or a renal disease. For the purpose of disease management, covered services include:

- An initial nutrition and lifestyle assessment
- Nutrition counseling
- Information regarding managing lifestyle factors that affect diet
- Follow-up sessions to monitor progress

This covered benefit provides three hours of one-on-one counseling services for the first year and two hours of coverage for subsequent years. The dietician or nutritionist may choose how many units are provided per day. Based on medical necessity, additional hours may be covered if the treating physician orders additional hours of MNT based on a change in medical condition, diagnosis, or treatment regimen.

Coverage Information

Medicare provides coverage of MNT services based on a required physician referral; nonphysician practitioners cannot make referrals for this service. MNT services must be provided by a qualified dietician, licensed registered dietician, a licensed nutritionist that meets the registered dietician requirements, or a "grandfathered" nutritionist that was licensed as of December 12, 2000.

TABLE 5-19

HCPCS and CPT Codes for the Reporting of MNT Services

HCPCS/CPT	Code Descriptors	Instructions for Use
97802	Medical nutrition therapy; initial assessment and intervention, individual face-to-face with the patient, each 15 minutes (NOTE: This CPT code must only be used for the initial visit.)	This code is to be used once a year, for initial assessment of a new patient. All subsequent individual visits are to be coded as 97803. All subsequent Group visits are to be billed as 97804
97803	Re-assessment and intervention, individual, face-to-face with the patient, each 15 minutes	This code is to be billed for all individual reassessments and all interventions after the initial visit. This code should also be used when there is a change in the patient's medical condition that affects the nutritional status of the patient.
97804	Group (2 or more individual(s)), each 30 minutes	This code is to be billed for all group visits, initial and subsequent. This code can also be used when there is a change in a patients condition that affects the nutritional status of the patient and the patient is attending in a group setting.
G0270	Medical nutrition therapy, reassessment and subsequent intervention(s) following second referral in the same year for change in diagnosis, medical condition or treatment regimen (including additional hours needed for disease), individual, face to face with the patient, each 15 minutes	
G0271	Medical nutrition therapy, reassessment and subsequent intervention(s) following second referral in the same year for change in diagnosis, medical condition or treatment regimen (including additional hours needed for disease), group (2 or more individuals), each 30 minutes	

The above codes can only be paid if submitted by a registered dietician or nutrition professional who meets the specified requirements under Medicare. These services cannot be paid "incident to" physician services. The payments can be reassigned to the employer of a qualifying dietician or nutrition professional.

Coverage for diabetes-related MNT is provided as a Medicare part B benefit. The patient will pay 20% (as the coinsurance or copayment) of the Medicare-approved amount after meeting the yearly Medicare part B deductible.

A physician must prescribe these services and renew the referral yearly if continuing treatment is needed into another calendar year. See Table 5-19 for the HCPCS and CPT codes used to report MNT services.

Billing Requirements

When submitting claims to carriers, the appropriate HCPCS or CPT code and the corresponding diagnosis code must be reported on Form CMS-1500 (or the HIPAA 837 Professional electronic claim format).

When submitting claims to fiscal intermediaries (FIs), the appropriate HCPCS or CPT code, the appropriate revenue code, and the corresponding diagnosis code must be reported on Form CMS-1450 (or the HIPAA 837 Institutional electronic claim format).

As required by CMS, there are two specific bill types that are applicable for MNT. The applicable FI claim bill types and associated revenue codes for MNT are provided in

TABLE 5-20

Applicable FI Claim Bill Types and Associated Revenue Codes for MNT

Facility Type	Type of Bill	Revenue Code
Hospital outpatient	13X	0942
Critical access hospital	85X	0942

Table 5-20. Additional information on nutrition services can be found by accessing the Web site for the American Dietetic Association: www.eatright.org.

SUMMARY

This chapter introduces health care ancillary services and reviews specific guidelines for providing services as well as billing for reimbursement. The ancillary services reviewed in this chapter include DME, home health services, nursing homes or SNFs, ambulance services, and hospice care, and dietary services. It is important to understand the specific regulations and guidelines that apply, as well as the basics of these types of organizations and services when billing for these types of services. Internet resources and organizations supporting each of these ancillary service areas are listed in Appendix A.

chapter 6

Insurance Processing: Managing Insurance and Patient Accounts

OBJECTIVES

- Explain the pre-claim submission process.
- Recognize and describe the use of all forms used in insurance processing, including:
  — Patient information
  — Insurance coverage verification
  — Employer information
  — Assignment of benefits
  — Authorization to release medical-related information
  — Signature on file
  — Fact sheet
  — Medical cost estimate
  — Advance notice for elective surgery
  — Waivers of liability
- Recognize and describe the use of the different letters, such as:
  — Welcome
  — Filing supplemental claims
  — Deductible
- Understand the skills necessary for various front and back office positions.
- Understand the importance of and how to improve the collection process.

It is not enough to have knowledge of the different types of insurance and the ability to code services for reimbursement. A practice must be able to report to the insurance plan on the services it has provided so that the practice receives appropriate reimbursement.

Unfortunately, this is often easier said than done. Because there are so many different types of health plans and reimbursement methods continue to change, the health insurance industry does not follow a set of "universal policies" that standardize or simplify the claim submission process. Generally each insurance plan has its own set of policies and procedures for claim adjudication, and medical practices are expected to understand and adhere to all of them if they are to receive payment for services rendered.

"Pre-claim" insurance processes necessary to manage insurance claim processing, from collecting data to submitting a claim for appropriate payment, are discussed in this chapter. Forms that will help simplify data collection and report formats that will increase information management efficiency are also described and sample forms are provided.

An identifier is issued regardless of the practice configuration (ie, group, solo, partnership). This number remains constant as long as the physician has a Medicare affiliation.

For the purpose of issuing an NPI, a *physician* is defined as a doctor of medicine or osteopathy, dental medicine, dental surgery, podiatric medicine, optometry, or chiropractic medicine legally authorized to practice by the state in which he/she performs. A *health practitioner* includes, but is not limited to, physician assistant, certified nurse-midwife, qualified psychologist, nurse practitioner, clinical social worker, physical therapist, occupational therapist, respiratory therapist, certified registered nurse anesthetist, or any other practitioner as may be specified. A *group practice* is defined by Medicare as a group of two or more physicians and nonphysician practitioners legally organized in a partnership, professional corporation, foundation, not-for-profit corporation, faculty practice plan, or similar association.

A physician or supplier that bills Medicare for a service or item must include the name of the ordering/referring physician on the Centers for Medicare and Medicaid Services (CMS) CMS-1500 claim form.

If any procedure codes associated with consults, diagnostic radiology, diagnostic lab, or durable medical equipment, orthotics, and prosthetics are shown on the claim form, the name and NPI of the ordering physician must be entered in fields 17 and 17a of the CMS-1500 form. For electronic claims, the name and NPI go in record/field EAO-20.0 positions 80–94 in the electronic media claims format. The following guidelines apply:

- If the service is a diagnostic laboratory or radiology service, the assigned NPI of the ordering/referring physician must be entered in field 17a on form CMS-1500.
- If the performing physician is also the ordering physician, the physician must enter his/her name and NPI in fields 17 and 17a on form CMS-1500, confirming that the service is not the result of a referral from another physician.
- If the service is a consultative service, the name and NPI of the referring physician or other person meeting the statutory definition of a physician must be listed on form CMS-1500 in fields 17 and 17a.
- If the service was the result of a referral from a person not meeting the statutory definition of a physician or a limited licensed practitioner (pharmacist, midwife, psychologist), the billing physician must enter his/her name and NPI in fields 17 and 17a. In other words, the physician completes the form as if the patient initiated the service.
- If durable medical equipment, prosthetics, or orthotics are ordered, the name and NPI of the ordering physician must be entered on form CMS-1500 in fields 17 and 17a.

Claims that require the physician name and NPI but do not include them will be denied. Incorrect use of a surrogate NPI is a violation of Medicare billing requirements. Suppliers will be notified that they are in violation of the law and that continuation of this billing practice may result in referral to the Office of Inspector General (OIG).

NATIONAL PROVIDER IDENTIFICATION (NPI)

The Health Insurance Portability and Accountability Act (HIPAA) of 1996 mandated the adoption of a standard unique identifier for health care providers. On January 23, 2004, the final rule was published that adopted the National Provider Identifier (NPI) as this identifier. The final rule provides for a standard unique health identifier for health care providers. The NPI is a 10-digit number made up of a nine-digit number and a check digit. The objective of the NPI system is to assign a unique identifier number to each and every provider of health care services.

Implementation of the NPI eliminated the prior system, called Unique Physician Identification Numbers (UPIN), of multiple numbers for a single provider. NPI provides a single universally accepted unique national identification number for each health care provider. A provider's NPI number will not change once it is enumerated regardless of job or location changes. NPI numbers have replaced UPINs (Unique Physician Identification Numbers) and PINs (Physician Identification Numbers) for physicians and other practitioners. National Supplier Clearinghourse (NSC) numbers for suppliers and other Online Survey Certification and Reporting System (OSCAR) numbers for institutional providers will also be replaced by the NPI system. The National Plan and Provider Enumeration System (NPPES) will maintain all of the information previously found in the UPIN master file and the Provider of Services file. Information that will be available for NPIs is published in the National Provider Identifier (NPI) Dissemination notice.

All covered entities except small health plans must use NPIs to identify providers in standard transactions as of the compliance date, which was May 23, 2007. The compliance date for small health plans is May 23, 2008. Both the new UB-04 (CMS 1450) and revised CMS 1500 form have undergone adjustments in order to accommodate NPI numbers. Figure 6-1 displays a copy of the CMS NPI Timeline for Implementation.

The Final Rule requiring implementation of the NPI also requires health care providers that are organizations and that are covered entities under HIPAA to determine if they have "subparts" that should be assigned NPIs. The Final Rule also provides guidance to health care providers in making these determinations.

FIGURE 6-1

Reporting of NPIs on Claims Sent to Medicare

Professional Paper Claims sent to Carriers & DME Contractors

May 23, 2007 and thereafter

Revised CMS-1500 (08/05) forms received without an NPI to identify each provider for which data is reported on a claim, such as a rendering, referring or ordering physician, in addition to the billing provider, will be rejected by Medicare. Medicare legacy provider identifiers may no longer be reported on paper claims sent Medicare.

Institutional Paper Claims sent to Fiscal Intermediaries

May 23, 2007 and thereafter

UB-92 forms received will be rejected by Medicare whether or not they include an NPI. UB-04 forms received by Medicare will be rejected if an NPI is not used to identify each provider for which data is reported on the claim. UB-04 submitters may no longer send Medicare legacy provider identifiers on these paper claims.

Electronic Claims sent to Carriers, DME Contractors or Fiscal Intermediaries

May 23, 2007 and thereafter

X12 837 and NCPDP electronic claims submitted without an NPI will be rejected. Medicare legacy provider identifiers may no longer be reported on electronic claims sent to Medicare.

FIGURE 6-1 (continued)

An NPI must be used as the only identifier on X12 270 and 276 queries sent to Medicare and on X12 271 and 277 responses issued by Medicare. Medicare will begin to batch claims being paid according to the NPI submitted on the claims and to report only the NPI of the pay-to-provider on paper and electronic remittance advice transactions issued the provider for payment of those claims on the date when payment is being issued.

All COB claims issued will contain an NPI only for identification of each provider for which data is included in a claim. There will be an exception for small plans that request that Medicare continue to send Medicare legacy provider identifiers as well as NPIs through May 22, 2008. If a COB claim is sent to a small plan and the claim contains information about a provider that/who is not the billing, pay-to or rendering provider, such as a supervising or ordering physician, it may not be possible for Medicare to send a Medicare legacy provider identifier. Providers other than billing, pay-to and rendering providers are not required to be enrolled in Medicare as a condition for Medicare payment of another provider for the services, equipment or supplies furnished, ordered, supervised, etc. by a non-enrolled provider.

If a secondary provider is not enrolled in the Medicare program because that provider does not submit claims, is not paid by or does not render covered services to Medicare patients, there will not be a legacy provider identifier in the Medicare files for that provider. Prior to May 23, 2007, Medicare used surrogate UPINs to identify non-enrolled secondary providers, but surrogate UPINs will no longer be reported in any Medicare transactions after May 22, 2007. Surrogate UPINs were not unique to any provider but were used as a tool to bypass provider number editing for those providers. A surrogate UPIN would not be useful to any COB trading partner since the same surrogate UPINs were reported for many different non-enrolled providers.

Special Instructions for Paper Claims Submission

May 23, 2007 – Forward: CMS systems will only accept NPI numbers. Small health plans have an additional year to be NPI compliant.

Source: www.cms.hhs.com

EMPLOYEE JOB DESCRIPTION

One key to a successful practice is assignment of specific job responsibilities to office personnel. To clearly state each employee's responsibilities and to eliminate miscommunications, all employees should have written descriptions of their job duties. Job descriptions explain what is expected of employees and can be used to evaluate performance. Job descriptions can also be used to explain why employment decisions were made if an employee files personnel discrimination charges. The job descriptions provided in Tables 6-1 through 6-3 are examples that can be modified to fit the unique requirements of each practice.

PRE-CLAIM SUBMISSION OPERATIONS

Before any type of claim can be generated and submitted for payment, the office staff must perform numerous pre-claim tasks. These tasks are critical to ensuring the validity and accuracy of the patient's billing data and the submission of a "clean claim." The basic objectives of office staff pre-claim operations are to:

1. Collect the patient's and responsible parties' information completely and accurately.
2. Determine the appropriate financial class or account type (eg, commercial insurance, Medicare, Medicaid, etc) and correctly assign primary and secondary insurance billing status when two insurance plans require coordination of benefits.
3. Educate the patient as to his or her ultimate financial responsibility for services rendered and obtain written waivers when necessary to support future collection efforts.
4. Verify all data collected prior to rendering services or submitting claims and obtain updated profiles of insurance plan benefits using an insurance/employer verification form.
5. Anticipate the need for collection through accounts receivable controls and quality data.

APPOINTMENTS AND PREREGISTRATION

In most cases, new patients wishing to see a physician will call the physician group to make an appointment. This initial contact by the prospective patient is a perfect time to identify the reason for the visit, begin collecting patient demographic and insurance billing data, and schedule an appointment that is convenient for the physician and patient. It is also important to verify patient referral information and make arrangements to have necessary forms and authorizations completed, as applicable.

It is important to identify the reason for the visit, especially if your practice divides schedules, ie, lengthy new-patient visits and physicals during a certain period, medical procedures for another time slot, and basic follow-up visits throughout the day. If a practice is at capacity, it may take three or more days to obtain an appointment; this is time that can be spent verifying the patient information.

The patient's demographic and insurance information should be obtained during the initial telephone contact. A polite telephone interview can be performed and the information recorded using a patient information form.

It is helpful for both the patient and the practice to call the patient one or two days before the scheduled appointment. This will assist the patient who has forgotten and allow the practice to fill slots that may have gone unused. This is also a good time to gather information or remind the patient of the necessary information he or she will need to bring for the visit.

Patient Information Form

The patient information form is a vital document used to gather necessary demographic data about a patient, such as name, address, guardian or responsible party name, insurance company and health plan policy information, name of person or physician who referred the patient to the practice, etc. The form does not include any information related to medical conditions. The form is generally used only for insurance and payment-related information and/or for general marketing data. This form should be completed when a patient first visits the practice and at least once every year. Because approximately 20% of people move each year, the practice will use this form to keep records current.

Typically, the patient information form is designed to fit on standard size paper ($8\frac{1}{2} \times 11$) with plenty of space for patients to complete required information accurately (see Figure 6-2).

Not only is the patient information form valuable for gathering important insurance processing information but it is also a way of tracking and finding patients who become delinquent in their payments. Additional information such as secondary insurance coverage and special circumstances such as divorce can also be gathered.

The patient should be given information about the practice and the practice should collect as much patient information as possible about insurance coverage, including any toll-free numbers for eligibility verification and filing requirements. During the initial contact with the prospective patient, office staff may want to communicate the following policies to the patient:

- Basic services for the condition and physicians' fees
- The patient's financial responsibility for services provided during the initial visit
- An estimate of the costs associated with a new comprehensive history and physical
- Method of payment (health maintenance organization [HMO], preferred provider organization [PPO], or other third-party carrier: copayment, cash, check, or credit card)
- Payment policy for future visits.
- Financial counseling available prior to the visit

TABLE 6-1

Office Manager Job Responsibilities

- Recruit, orient, train, supervise, and evaluate all office personnel.
- Maintain personnel records, including resumes, employment history, salary or wage history, paid days off, and vacation time.
- Respond to calls from patients regarding billing, balance due, and secondary insurance.
- Assist with patient registration, billing, and collections.
- Prepare checks for the payment of accounts payable and present with supporting invoices to authorized check-signer.
- Prepare month-end financial statements and management reports.
- Ensure the billing system's daily receipts agree with deposit slips and the patient registration log.
- Make sure all tax reports are prepared and filed on a timely basis.
- Prepare and file physicians' correspondence.
- Maintain and reconcile the petty cash fund on a monthly basis.
- Reconcile all bank accounts each month.
- Maintain all office equipment.
- Maintain appropriate quantities of business supplies.
- Ensure that all office employees are cross-trained.
- Provide financial counseling to patients as needed regarding delinquent account balances.
- Perform routine internal control checks to identify potential problem areas.
- Manage billing and collection personnel to ensure compliance with office policies.

TABLE 6-2

Billing and Collection Staff Job Responsibilities

- Know current Medicare rules and regulations applicable to the practice.
- Keep the office manager and physicians informed of significant changes.
- Send out patient statements and insurance claims on a timely basis.
- Prepare and mail secondary insurance claim forms as soon as payments are received from primary insurance carriers.
- Respond to requests for medical records or other appropriate information by insurance carriers.
- Handle business and insurance carrier correspondence.
- Reply promptly to all requests for additional information regarding insurance issues.
- Post and reconcile explanations of benefits promptly upon receipt.
- File all explanations of benefits in billing business files.
- Age accounts receivable and follow up with timely telephone calls and collection letters.
- Prepare and mail collection letters to patients each month.
- List patients' accounts to send to the practice's outside collection agency for follow-up, subject to office manager approval.
- Promptly prepare appeal letters with supporting documentation to Medicare and insurance carriers for denials.
- Follow up weekly on insurance claims not paid within 30 days.
- Post payments to patients' accounts on a timely basis.
- Verify patients' insurance coverage in accordance with office policy.
- When applicable, obtain authorization numbers for insurance companies before service is provided.
- Prepare hospital inpatient summaries for use by the physicians when making rounds.

TABLE 6-3

Reception and Patient Registration Job Responsibilities

- Answer all telephone calls and switch to/from answering service.
- Schedule daily appointments and instruct patients as to information needed.
- Keep reception room organized, neat, and ready for patients. Greet patients and visitors, determine needs, and respond accordingly.
- Have first-time patients complete the new patient information sheet.
- Copy the patients' drivers licenses and insurance cards, front and back.
- Inform new patients of the office collection policy when they make their appointments.
- Ensure that established patients who arrive for appointments have the same insurance coverage, phone number, and address as at their last visit.
- Have established patients complete the new patient information sheet if they have not made appointments within the last 12 months.
- Maintain the appointment book and daysheet.
- Call patients to remind them of their appointments.
- Prepare charge tickets and retrieve and file charts for each day's patients.
- Check out patients; post charges; collect payments, copayments, or deductibles related to the visit; and post receipts.
- Collect overdue accounts receivable from patients when checking them out or before their appointments.
- Refer patients with overdue balances exceeding a designated amount to the office manager for financial counseling.
- Follow up on no-shows with letters or phone calls, as appropriate.
- Retrieve and distribute the office mail each day.
- Fulfill requests for copies of medical records from patients. Obtain the patients' signatures on requests for other physicians or payers.
- Assist in filing patients' charts.
- Make copies as requested by the physicians.
- Stamp and send outgoing mail.
- Substitute for other staff as needed.

FIGURE 6-2
New Patient Information Sheet

PATIENT INFORMATION

Name: (First) _____ (MI) _____ (Last) _____

Date of Birth _____ Age _____ Sex: ☐ M ☐ F   Marital Status: ☐ S ☐ M ☐ W ☐ D

Address: (Street) _____

(City, State, ZIP) _____

Phone #: _____ Social Security #: _____ Driver License #: _____

E-mail Address: _____

Work #: _____ Employer: _____

Employer's Address: _____

Referring Physician: _____ If Student, School Name: _____ Full/Part Time _____

RESPONSIBLE PARTY OR SPOUSE INFORMATION

Name: _____ Relationship to Patient: _____

Address: (Street) _____

(City, State, ZIP) _____

Phone #: _____ Social Security #: _____ Driver License #: _____

Work #: _____ Employer: _____

Employer's Address: _____

Friend or Relative Not Living with You: _____ Phone #: _____

Address: _____

INSURANCE INFORMATION

Medicare #: _____ Medicaid #: _____

Insurance Co: _____ Phone #: _____

Insurance Address: _____

Group #: _____ Certificate or I.D. #: _____

Insured's Name: _____ Relationship to Patient: ☐ Self ☐ Spouse ☐ Dependent

Insured's Employer: _____ Phone #: _____

Employer's Address: _____

Insured's Social Security #: _____ Date of Birth: _____ Sex: ☐ M ☐ F

E-mail Address: _____

If the patient it covered by another insurance policy, please complete the following information for coordination of benefits. This information will enable your insurance company to process your claim more quickly. Thank you!

INSURANCE INFORMATION

Insurance Co: _____ Phone #: _____

Insurance Address: _____

Group #: _____ Certificate or I.D. #: _____

Insured's Name: _____ Relationship to Patient: ☐ Self ☐ Spouse ☐ Dependent

Insured's Employer: _____ Phone #: _____

Employer's Address: _____

Insured's Social Security #: _____ Date of Birth: _____ Sex: ☐ M ☐ F

I hereby assign, transfer, and set over to [Name of Practice] all of my rights, title, and interest to my medical reimbursement benefits under my insurance policy. I authorize the release of any medical information needed to determine these benefits. This authorization shall remain valid until written notice is given by me revoking said authorization. I understand that I am financially responsible for all charges whether or not they are covered by insurance.

Patient's Signature _____ Date _____

A patient education brochure is an excellent way to communicate the practice's policies and procedures.

After identifying the reason for the visit, a tentative patient care plan is developed so all procedures and services planned for in the care plan (obstetrics, laboratory, surgery, injections, etc) can be verified for service coverage. This information is reviewed by the account manager or office manager to determine the prospective account's financial class, potential collectibility, creditworthiness, and need for patient-related financial counseling.

Registration/Demographic and Insurance Coverage Verification

Patient registration for capturing accurate information, including referring physician data and verification of all information provided by the patient, is often overlooked by staff due to time or perceived value. Demographic, financial, and referring physician information should be obtained.

Today, change is constant, making the need to obtain information for verification even more important. Insurance coverage or eligibility for public medical programs changes from one month to the next for thousands of Americans. Office staff must be alert for the use of forged health insurance identification cards and immediately report any suspected occurrences to the payer.

Practices must keep in mind that they are, in a broad sense, providers of "good-faith credit" for medical services rendered to patients. Too often, patients are extended "credit" without adequate review of their creditworthiness or a discussion of their ultimate financial responsibility.

The patient's registration information serves not only as the foundation for billing and collection but also as a tool for credit-granting decisions made by the practice. The collectibility of each patient account, whether by insurance or self-pay, is only as strong as the information obtained from the patient, its verification for accuracy, and the patient's understanding of his or her financial obligations.

In most practices, registration information provided by the patient on the demographic form is rarely verified for accuracy and completeness. All patient demographic and insurance information must be verified to:

- Confirm patient insurance coverage for the service to be rendered and to determine primary and secondary coordination of benefit coverage, which allows for accurate billing of covered services
- Serve as a quality assurance tool for correctly processing billing information (ultimately responsible for the success of collections)
- Assist in identifying patients who need financial counseling or assistance with obtaining medical assistance for services rendered
- Reduce unnecessary write-offs and negative adjustments for uncollectible charges due to denials, down-coding, or reduced payment because of nonverified coverage of services

INFORMATION VERIFICATION

To reach these objectives, all practices must implement a process of information verification by which all patients undergo a thorough verification of the demographic, financial, and insurance coverage information they submit. The verification coordinator must identify the primary carrier for proper coordination of benefits. Using the insurance coverage verification form, the primary insurance plan should be contacted first to confirm coverage of the patient's services. When verifying insurance coverage, each category of physician (medicine, surgery, primary care, etc) should ask about coverage and payment policies for services he or she performs relative to the patient's condition.

The office should verify all insurance information in each of the following situations, going online if necessary:

- The patient is to be admitted to the hospital or subject to an outpatient surgical procedure
- The patient will have many visits to the office over an extended period of time
- The patient will undergo a minor diagnostic or therapeutic procedure in the office
- The office believes the patient may have deductible responsibilities
- The office believes the patient's insurance may have changed or terminated
- For established patients, at least once a year, preferably between October and January

Employer Information and Insurance Verification Form

The employer information and insurance verification form is supplemented by the patient information form. This form provides specific information about the type and extent of insurance coverage the patient receives from his or her employer. The form is more discretionary, and some practices may find the additional information helpful while others may find that the information on the patient information form is adequate. Two different formats are shown in Figures 6-3 and 6-4.

How to Verify Insurance Coverage

The business support staff of a medical practice is responsible for verifying all patient demographics and insurance plan coverage for all services likely to be provided in the patient's care plan. This is done before the initiation of such services.

Before a patient is accepted as a new patient and before the initiation of services, registration staff obtains demographic and insurance information from the prospective patient using the patient demographic form. The patient demographic form can be filled out by: (1) interviewing the patient over the phone, (2) having the patient fill out the form and return it through the mail, or (3) having the patient complete the form in the office, upon his/her arrival. The staff also collects copies of hospital admission and patient information, if applicable, and makes copies of all insurance cards (front and back) and the guarantor's driver's license (front only). As the last step, staff gathers information regarding the patient's insurance plan coverage and the order of benefit coordination (ie, primary, secondary, or tertiary) for multiple policies.

Using this information, registration or billing staff verifies all patient demographic and insurance policy coverage information electronically or manually—making telephone contacts and cross-referencing information from different sources. Patient and guarantor addresses are cross-referenced with telephone directories, postal addresses, driver's licenses, employment confirmation, and other sources of current information. Each insurance plan identified by the patient is contacted to verify insurance coverage for patient services using one of the insurance coverage verification forms (ICVFs). Insurance plan coverage is verified one plan at a time, making sure to complete the insurance data section, benefits grid section, and the service coverage listing for all services pertinent to your practice.

Only confirmed and verified information is entered on the ICVF. Changes to the patient source document are made in red pen, initialed, and dated. If insurance plan coverage(s) cannot be verified, the reason must be indicated on the ICVF report. After all policy coverage(s) has been verified, the completed ICVF should be copied.
The original is placed in the patient's chart; the copy is stored in a three-ring binder labeled Insurance/Employer Health Plan Profiles. It is helpful to store the information alphabetically by insurance or employer name and to update the profiles for future reference.

FIGURE 6-3

Employer-Insurance Verification Information Form

Date: _____

Employer Name: _____

Employer Address: _____

Benefits Coordinator: _____ Phone: _____

Insurance Carrier: _____ Plan Name: _____

Policy #: _____ Plan #: _____ Group #: _____

Type of Plan: ☐ Traditional ☐ 80/20 ☐ HMO ☐ PPO ☐ Other: _____

Mail Insurance Forms to: ☐ Carrier   ☐ Employer

Billing Address: _____

Contact Person: _____ Phone Number: _____

Renewal Period – Medical Benefits and Limits Are Renewed on (M/D/Y): (Date): _____

E-mail Address: _____

Basic Coverage

Physician Payment Schedule: ☐ UCR ☐ RBRVS ☐ Other Data

Percentage of COB (ie, 80/20?): _____ % Insurance Coverage _____ % Patient Copayment

Annual Outpatient Deductible: _____ Amount of Deductible Remaining: _____

Maximum Benefit: _____

Noncovered Services: _____

Diagnostic Benefits

Percentage of COB (ie, 80/20?): _____ % Insurance Coverage _____ % Patient Copayment

Annual Outpatient Deductible: _____ Amount of Deductible Remaining: _____

Maximum Benefit: _____

Noncovered Services: _____

Major Medical Coverage

Annual Outpatient Deductible: _____

Amount of Deductible Remaining: _____

Maximum Benefit: _____

Noncovered Services: _____

Form Used: ☐ Company-Specific Form ☐ HCFA-1500 ☐ Other: _____

Notes: _____

_____

_____

FIGURE 6-4
Patient-Insurance Coverage Verification Form

Date: _____ Practice: _____ Verification By: _____
Patient Name: _____ Account #: _____
Date of Birth: _____ Social Security #: _____
Employer: _____ Phone/Contact: _____
E-mail Address: _____
Accident Date: _____ Accident Location: _____

Patient Care Plan
Dx: (1) _____ (2) _____
Dx: (3) _____ (4) _____
Patient Care Plans/Services: _____

Insurance Data
Insurance – 1
Billing Address: _____
Ins. Contact Name: _____ Phone: _____
Policy #: _____ Plan: _____ Group: _____
Coverage Effective Dates – (From) _____ (To) _____
Policyholder: _____ Relationship: _____

Insurance – 2
Billing Address: _____
Ins. Contact Name: _____ Phone: _____
Policy #: _____ Plan: _____ Group: _____
Coverage Effective Dates – (From) _____ (To) _____
Policyholder: _____ Relationship: _____

Basic Benefits	**Primary**	**Secondary**
1. Preexisting Wait Period		
2. Annual Deductible Amount	($)	
3. Deductible Paid to Date		
4. Out-of-Pocket Expenses:		
a. Coinsurance ($ or %)		
b. Copayment @ TOS?		
5. Calendar Year Maximum:	$ _____ / _____ days	$ _____ / _____ days
6. Lifetime Maximum:	$ _____ / _____ days	$ _____ / _____ days
7. Remaining Benefits:	$ _____ / _____ days	$ _____ / _____ days
8. Medical Records Required?	Y / N	Y / N
9. Coordinate Benefits (X-Over)?	Y / N	Y / N
10. 2nd Opinion Requirements?	Y / N	Y / N
11. Verified with (name):		
12. Phone # of Above:		
13. Date Verified:		

Procedures & Services	**Covered?**	**Coverage Details / Limits**
1. Office Services	Y / N	
2. Hospital	Y / N	
3. Consultations	Y / N	
4. ER Visits	Y / N	
5. Laboratory (Chem)	Y / N	
6. Procedures	Y / N	
7. Injections / Tx	Y / N	
8. Supplies	Y / N	
9. Drugs / Medications	Y / N	
10. Exclusions:		

Overview of the Patient Insurance Coverage Verification Forms

The Basic Patient Demographic Data Section, which is the first section of the ICVF, is used to track the start and completion of the entire ICVF report for each new patient. The fields for that section include:

- *Date:* Enter the date the verification process was initiated and completed.
- *Practice:* Enter the practice name (helpful for multispecialty practices).
- *Verification By:* Enter the name of the verification clerk.
- *Patient Name/Account Number:* Enter patient's name and add practice account number later.
- *Date of Birth:* Enter the patient's date of birth.
- *Social Security Number:* Enter the patient's Social Security number.
- *Employer:* Enter the name of the patient's employer.
- *Phone/Contact:* Enter the contact name and phone number for benefits management.
- *Accident Date:* If services are related to an accident (auto, workers' compensation, etc), enter the date of the accident.
- *Accident Location:* Define where the injury occurred.

The Patient Care Plan Section maintains the clinical data needed to begin inquiry as to coverage and benefits. The patient's reason for the appointment or previously confirmed diagnosis from another physician for which the patient will be seen (as in the case of a consultation) should be entered in this section. Possible services—both diagnostic and therapeutic—that may or will be performed should also be entered. The fields for this section include:

- *Dx: (1):* Enter the patient's primary diagnosis or complaint.
- *Dx: (2):* Enter the patient's secondary diagnosis or complaint.
- *Dx: (3):* Enter the patient's third diagnosis or complaint.
- *Dx: (4):* Enter the patient's fourth diagnosis or complaint.
- *Patient Care Plans/Services:* List the possible services that may be reasonably expected to be performed on this patient.

The Insurance Data Section is used to record and then verify insurance plan information provided by the patient for future billing and coordination of the patient's benefits. All insurance plans submitted by the patient should be verified individually. *Note:* It is extremely important to assign the proper order of multiple insurance plan coverages (ie, primary plan vs secondary plan). This section includes the following fields:

- *Insurance (1):* Enter the name of the carrier that has identified itself as the primary insurance plan.
- *Phone:* Enter the carrier's phone number(s).
- *Billing Address:* Enter the carrier's billing address.
- *Insurance Contact Name:* Enter the name of the insurance representative.
- *Phone:* Enter the insurance contact's direct line and extension.
- *Policy Number:* Enter the patient's verified policy number.
- *Plan:* Enter the patient's verified plan number.
- *Group:* Enter the patient's verified group number.
- *Coverage Effective Dates:* Enter insurance plan effective dates of coverage, identifying *From date* and *To date*.
- *Policyholder:* Enter verified policyholder's name.
- *Relationship:* Verify relationship of patient to policyholder.

After each insurance plan is verified separately, the section on benefits should be completed carefully. The Basic Benefits Section is presented as a grid to capture all insurance plan(s) information and for easy review of all plan benefits. The grid is divided into three columns: one for the insurance benefit question and one for each insurance plan: primary and secondary. Fields for this section include:

- *Preexisting Wait Period:* Some policies do not provide benefits for certain conditions for a predetermined period of time. *Example:* A 12-month waiting period for maternity (ie, no benefits until the plan is more than 12 months into effect). Enter Y or N. Some health plan policies do not provide benefits for certain conditions, diagnoses, or preexisting conditions regardless of the period of time. If this is the case, enter "non-covered" in the space provided.
- *Annual Deductible Amount:* Enter the annual deductible dollar amount, ie, the amount the patient must pay out-of-pocket before insurance will start to cover services.
- *Deductible Paid to Date:* Enter the deductible amount paid to date, ie, the amount the patient has paid toward the deductible to date (as of today). *Note:* The difference is collectible at time of service.
- *Out-of-Pocket Expenses:* Indicate whether the plan has a patient cost-sharing program, which may include copayment or coinsurance provisions.
    - Coinsurance equals the dollar amount or percentage of the patient's financial responsibility.
    - Copayment is the collection of a patient payment at time of service, usually $5 to $20 per visit (see insurance card).
- *Calendar Year Maximum:* Enter dollar amount and/or the number of days limited by the insurance policy as a total annual payable benefit, if applicable.
- *Lifetime Maximum:* Enter the maximum dollar amount and/or the number of days allowed by the insurance policy as a total payable benefit, if applicable.
- *Remaining Benefits:* Enter the dollar amount and/or the number of days available under the insurance policy for remaining payable benefits, if applicable.
- *Medical Records Required:* Indicate with a "Y" or "N" whether medical records or other supporting documents are required for claim processing and receiving payment for services rendered. If yes, make note on expanded insurance information sheet (page 2, 3, or 4 of the form).
- *Coordinate Benefits (Crossover):* Indicate with a "Y" or "N" whether the primary policy will coordinate or crossover the benefits with any secondary insurance.
- *Second Opinion Requirements:* Indicate with a "Y" or "N" whether the plan has second-opinion requirements for specific conditions before payment of service benefits.
- *Verified with (name):* Enter the name of the person from the insurance plan to whom the verification clerk has been speaking to identify policy coverage.
- *Phone Number of Above:* Enter the phone number of the person from the insurance plan to whom the verification clerk has been speaking to identify policy coverage.
- *Date Verified:* Enter date the above information was verified.

The Procedures and Services Section is designed to capture individual insurance policy coverage information for all services that may be provided by your physicians and practice. Because the services to be verified for coverage vary by specialty, determine the services your practice will need to verify most frequently.

Ask each insurance plan representative to provide coverage information on the anticipated services potential patients will likely receive. Here is a list of steps to take when interviewing each insurance representative:

- Ask the questions listed below for each service.
- Indicate on the report if the policy provides coverage (Y or N).
- Indicate if the policy has limitations or maximum coverage amounts.

- Ask what code is required for payment of the service. Compare this to the Current Procedural Terminology (CPT®) code and identify variations in coding requirements.
- Ask about any service limitations, coverage, or exclusions.
- Determine the maximum reimbursement amount for each procedure.

Inquire about special coding or payment policies that may affect reimbursement, particularly for surgical-related practices. Some additional questions to ask include:

- Do you use the current CPT book?
- When must the new CPT codes be used (ie, effective date)?
- How is payment allowance based? (Ask payer to send copy of allowance data.)
- How does your plan define "global surgical package" and "global surgical periods"?
- Are complications from surgery bundled in postoperative care or can treatment be reported separately with appropriate modifiers?
- Are there any reductions in payment if procedure is performed in an outpatient hospital setting?
- In what order are multiple surgical procedures reimbursed?
- What are your supply payment policies? Are Healthcare Common Procedure Coding System (HCPCS) codes required or is 99070 acceptable?
- How are injectable drugs reimbursed and how should they be reported (J codes)?

Remember to document as much pertinent information about the policy coverage as possible, because the verification document serves as the ultimate quality assurance tool for billing and collections.

Only after verifying the patient's insurance plan coverage, assigning any unquestioned financial classification or account type, and obtaining signed agreements with the patient concerning financial obligation should a patient be admitted to a practice. The billing supervisor or office manager should review all questionable information to determine the prospective patient's financial class, potential collectibility, creditworthiness, and the need for patient-related financial counseling and/or service deposit calculations.

Demographic information regarding the patient and guarantor can be cross-referenced and verified through multiple reference sources, including:

- Telephone directory or directory assistance
- Social Security office
- Post office
- Annual city directory (R. L. Polk directories cost approximately $120)
- Personal bank
- Employer
- Driver's license (Verification through the Department of Motor Vehicles requires a name, date of birth, Social Security number, and driver's license number.)
- County court offices: legal or auditor department (all public records)

Patient Confidentiality and Registration

Patient confidentiality must be paramount in all office procedures. A breach of confidentiality is a disclosure to a third party, without patient consent or court order, of private information that the physician has learned within the patient-physician relationship. Disclosure can be oral or written, by telephone or fax, or electronically, eg, via e-mail or health information networks. The medium is irrelevant, although special security requirements may apply to the electronic transfer of information.[1]

The registration process is an area of potential concern. Patients who arrive at your office are likely to fill out a registration log indicating their name, time of appointment, time of arrival, and other basic information, such as whether their insurance information has changed since their last visit. These registration logs become the basis of the office visit for that day and are important in updating and verifying pertinent information. However, a patient's privacy may be compromised when that information is seen by all subsequent patients. Some practices use logs that have information on only one patient per sheet of paper. As each patient is checked in, the paperwork on that patient is removed from the log. Others, concerned that multiple pieces of paper are more likely get lost, limit the information on the log to only the most basic, eg, name, time of appointment, and a query as to whether any information has changed. Patients who answer "yes" to the last question complete a form to update their information. Practice logs must not ask for information related to the reason for the visit, the diagnosis, or any other information that is private or confidential.

Most physician offices have a sign-in sheet at the reception window. A formal sign-in sheet provides the practice with a constant source of valuable information that will enhance practice operations. A sample sign-in sheet is shown in Figure 6-5. The sheet provides information about whether the patient is new or established; changes in address, employer, and insurance; and waiting time efficiency data based on appointment time and arrival data. As stated, it is important for privacy and security compliance that information on the sign-in sheet not be accessible to other patients or individuals who are not entitled to access.

After the patient signs in, the receptionist should greet the patient and review the data on the sign-in sheet. If the patient is new, he or she should be given the patient demographic information form on a clipboard and asked to complete it. Some practices also give the patient a medical history form to complete, which is incorporated into the patient's medical record. The receptionist or registration staff should ask to make photocopies of the patient's insurance card (front and back), special billing forms, and driver's license.

FIGURE 6-5

Sample Sign-in Sheet

Date _____

Patient's Name _____

Has your address, phone number, or insurance information changed since your last visit?
    yes ☐   no ☐

If **yes**, please complete the following:

Address _____
_____

Phone (home) _____
(work) _____
E-mail Address: _____

Is this a new workers' compensation claim?
    yes ☐   no ☐

Time of Arrival _____

Time of Appointment _____

Physician's Name _____

Please indicate reason for appointment:
    ☐ Office Visit
    ☐ Laboratory only
    ☐ Injection only
    ☐ Blood pressure check only

The patient must read, sign, and date the New Patient Information Sheet (shown in Figure 6-2). This form has a series of statements at the bottom. The statements read as follows:

> I hereby assign, transfer, and set over to [Name of Practice] all of my rights, title, and interest to my medical reimbursement benefits under my insurance policy. I authorize the release of any medical information needed to determine these benefits. This authorization shall remain valid until written notice is given by me revoking said authorization. I understand that I am financially responsible for all charges whether or not they are covered by insurance.

This statement informs the patient that he or she has "assigned" or transferred the right of direct reimbursement from any health plan, including those that involve nonparticipating physicians, to the practice in order for the reimbursement to be mailed directly to the practice. Second, the patient has given authorization to release any medical record information needed to coordinate benefits and reimbursement. Third, the authorization is enforced unless the patient is otherwise notified. Finally, the patient understands his or her financial responsibility for charges for services rendered.

Although the patient information form serves the practice's internal needs, the practice should obtain patient or guarantor signatures on the following forms for the following insurance types:

- Patients with commercial insurance:
    - Authorization to release medical-related information
    - Assignment of benefits and payment to provider
- Patients with Medicare:
    - Authorization to pay Medicare benefits (signature on file)
    - Authorization to release medical-related information
    - Assignment of benefits and payment to provider
- Patients with Blue Cross and Blue Shield or managed care plans:
    - Authorization to release medical-related information
    - Assignment of benefits and payment to provider

Assignment of Benefits and Payment to Provider Form

The assignment of benefits and payment to provider form is used as authorization to a patient's insurance plan to send payment directly to the provider. A sample is shown in Figure 6-6. This form is required when a provider renders services to a patient with an insurance plan that the provider does not participate in. If a provider does not participate in an insurer's plan, the checks are usually mailed to the patient or policyholder, making collection more difficult. The form is also used if the patient's policy prohibits direct payment to the provider. This form may be sent as a legal document to request direct payment.

The insurer will likely take one of three actions after receiving the authorization:

- Send payment to the practice in the name of the practice
- Send payment to the practice in the name of the patient
- Refuse to send payment to the practice and continue to send payment(s) to the patient

If the patient's insurance plan is one in which the provider(s) do not participate or when checks are mailed to the patient, the patient should fill out this form on his or her first visit to the practice. Once the form is completed, it is signed by the patient and a witness. A copy is made and sent with the claim. The original is retained in the patient's chart.

FIGURE 6-6

Assignment and Instruction for Direct Payment to Medical Providers

Private – Group Accident – Health Insurance Authorization of Benefits

Patient: _____

Policyholder: _____

Employer: _____ Group #: _____

Social Security #: _____ Policy #: _____

I hereby authorize and instruct that _____ Insurance Company pay authorized insurance benefits, on my behalf, by check made out and mailed to:

– or –

If my current policy prohibits direct payment to medical provider, then I hereby also instruct and direct you to make out the check to me and mail it as follows:

c/o _____

for professional or medical expense benefits allowable, and otherwise payable to me under my current insurance policy as payment toward the total charges for services rendered. *This is a direct assignment of my rights and benefits under this policy.* This payment will not exceed my indebtedness to the above-mentioned assignee, and I have agreed to pay, in a current manner, any balance of said professional service charges over and above this insurance payment amount. A photocopy of this Assignment shall be considered as effective and valid as the original.

I also authorize the release of information pertinent to my case to any insurance company, adjuster, or attorney involved in this case.

Signed and dated at the above named practice this _____ day of _____, 2,____.

_____
Signature of Policyholder

_____
Witness

_____
Signature of Claimant, if other than Policyholder

Authorization for Release of Medical-Related Information Form

Patient medical information is confidential and private. It cannot be released without the patient's consent. Because insurance companies sometimes need to refer to medical information before making a determination on a claim, patients need to sign an authorization to release medical information. A sample authorization for release of medical-related information form is shown in Figure 6-7.

Signature-on-File Form

Rather than having the patient sign each claim form being submitted, most practices have the patient sign a blanket statement called a signature-on-file form. By obtaining the patient's signature on this form, the practice can enter the words *signature on file* in the appropriate field of the claim form (on the CMS-1500, fields 12 and 13). This form can also be used to obtain blanket authorization for assignment of benefits. A sample form, acceptable for Medicare and other patients, is shown in Figure 6-8.

FIGURE 6-7

Authorization for Release of Medical-Related Information

1. I authorize Dr. _____ to disclose complete information to [name of insurance company] concerning his medical findings and treatment of the undersigned.

2. Further, I authorize him to testify without limitation, as to all medical findings and the treatment administered to the undersigned, in any legal action, suit, or proceedings to which I am, or may become, a party; and I waive on behalf of myself and any persons who may have an interest in the matter all provisions of law relating to the disclosure of confidential medical information.

   Signed,

   _____   _____
   Patient   Witness

   _____   _____
   Date   Place

FIGURE 6-8

Signature-on-File Form

I authorize any holder of medical or other information about me to release to [the Social Security Administration and Health Care Financing Administration or its intermediaries, carriers, and agents or name of insurance company], any information needed to determine the benefits for this or a related claim.

Also, I permit a copy of this authorization to be used in place of the original, and request payment of medical insurance benefits either to myself or to the party who accepts assignment. Regulations pertaining to Medicare assignment of benefits apply.

_____   _____
Signature   Date

PATIENT EDUCATION AND PREAUTHORIZATIONS

Each practice should have preestablished patient insurance policies and procedures for their office staff. Staff must consistently communicate, explain, and enforce the practice's payment policies to patients prior to the delivery of care.

By informing patients about the practice's insurance policies, patients are made aware of the following:

- In most cases, regardless of insurance status, patients are ultimately responsible for payment of all or some of their medical bills, and the amount due must be paid on demand as indicated by the practice.
- Unless the physician is under contract or has signed a participation agreement with a health insurance plan, the contract for the patient's health policy is between the patient and the health insurer. Although the patient is ultimately financially responsible, the practice will submit the primary insurance on behalf of the patient.
- Insurance does not usually cover or pay for all medical charges, and the patient will, in most cases, have some financial obligation for payment.
- Payment problems or the need for financial counseling to meet patient financial responsibilities must be brought to the attention of the billing staff before rendering service(s).

In addition, the billing staff should review the practice's basic policies to be able to answer the following questions:

- Does the practice automatically produce a claim form (standard CMS-1500 form) for all patients who have a primary insurance plan? Does automatic claim generation only apply to Medicare, Medicaid, managed care plans, etc?
- How is the coordination of benefits handled? Will the practice process primary payment and then automatically produce a claim form for patients who may have a supplemental insurance plan?
- At what point does the overdue insurance balance become the patient's responsibility? For example, when the office staff is having difficulty collecting payment from third-party payers, the staff should contact the patient to inform him or her of the problem and enlist his or her assistance. Some practices give the patient's insurance 60 days, then responsibility for the balance is transferred to the patient for immediate payment.

Patient Communications

Many practices find it helpful to provide their patients with explanatory letters or pamphlets regarding insurance processing policies. Various sample letters are described in the following sections as guides for your practice.

Welcome Letter
A practice may send a welcome letter that outlines the practice's insurance processing policies to new patients. The policies outlined in the sample letter shown in Figure 6-9 may not be appropriate for every practice. However, the letter provides a good example of how a practice can explain its policies to patients.

Insurance Fact Sheet
An insurance fact sheet is another way to explain insurance processing requirements to your patients. Considering the many different health insurance policies written today, it would be virtually impossible to create one insurance fact sheet to serve all patients. However, the practice can outline patient payment responsibilities and provide patients with useful names and phone numbers. A sample fact sheet is shown in Figure 6-10.

Medical Cost Estimate Form
Knowing what to plan for can lessen the burden for patients being treated for an illness or injury. Patients about to undergo medical treatment want to know what

FIGURE 6-9
Sample Welcome Letter

Family Medical Group   Lynn I. Hunt, MD
Seattle, Washington   Robert H. Squires, MD

Dear Patient:

We would like to welcome you to our practice. We want to ensure that you are pleased with the services we provide as well as our claim processing and payment procedures.

We are outlining our policies in the paragraphs that follow.

If you have health insurance other than those specifically mentioned below, we ask that you pay us and then collect reimbursement from your insurance company. At the time of your clinic visit, you will be provided with a form that contains all the information necessary for you to file your claim with your insurance company. You will also receive a statement of current charges and any balance due each month. An additional copy of this is provided, which you may also use to bill your insurance company for current charges. If there is a problem or if you have a question, please feel free to discuss it with us. We are here to help you with this process.

Blue Cross and Blue Shield: If you have King County Blue Shield, we will bill King County Blue Shield for the entire amount of your charges. Any charges or balances not covered by King County Blue Shield will be billed directly to you.

Medicaid recipients must present a current, valid card prior to treatment. Any appropriate copayments or deductibles as determined by your Medicaid eligibility are due at the time of service. Please ask to speak to the bookkeeper regarding questions and payment arrangements.

Medicare patients are asked to pay for services at the time of their visit, unless prior payment arrangements have been made. We will submit your claim to Medicare, and you will receive payment directly from Medicare. If you require help with your billings or have difficulty paying the difference between what is charged and what Medicare pays, please ask to speak with the bookkeeper. Arrangements can be made for those with special needs.

Thank you for coming to our practice. Please tell us if you have any difficulty with your insurance claims.

Sincerely,

Lynn Hunt, MD

Robert Squires, MD

the costs will be so they can prepare an appropriate budget. Also, by providing patients with the required financial information, the practice increases its odds of receiving prompt reimbursement. The form shown in Figure 6-11 can help your practice provide patients with this valuable information. It may be necessary to contact the offices of other physicians involved in your patient's care to obtain an estimate of their charges.

Required Medicare Forms

In addition to the signature-on-file form, Medicare requires nonparticipating physicians to have the patient sign two additional forms. The first pertains to elective surgery. When the nonparticipating physician plans to perform an elective surgery (one that can be scheduled in advance and for which a delay in performing the procedure does not cause serious damage to the patient), the physician does not accept assignment, and the fee is $500 or greater, the physician must notify the patient, in writing, of the anticipated cost and out-of-pocket expense. A notice for this purpose that is acceptable to Medicare is shown in Figure 6-12.

The second form (see Figure 6-13) pertains to services deemed by Medicare to be medically unnecessary or that are otherwise noncovered. When the physician knows that a procedure or service may not be paid for by Medicare because it has been determined to be medically unnecessary for treating a specified condition or when the physician has a legitimate reason to believe that Medicare will not cover the service, the physician must notify the patient, in writing, before providing the service. Consequently, the patient will be required to pay for the service. The patient must sign this form for it to be considered valid by Medicare, and a new form must be completed for each situation. A form is not to be used as a blanket statement. Both participating and nonparticipating physicians are required to provide this form in when applicable.

Insurance Advance Notice Service Waiver of Liability

A form similar to the Medicare advance notice (see Figure 6-14) can be used to notify patients with other insurance plans. This reinforces the patient's understanding of his or her financial responsibility for services to be rendered. The patient completes the form and it is stored in the patient's file.

Entry of Patient and Insurance Data

For practices with a computerized billing system, the patient demographic and insurance information is usually entered into the system before the initial date of service and before the information has been verified. Although there are many different software billing management programs, most have common data fields that are crucial for error-free insurance billing.

Because of the volume of data needed to a process claim, most computer systems separate the patient information section from the responsible party section and from the insurance assignment section with separate screens. The patient data for each of these three sections must be carefully reviewed and entered into the management system.

The most important section in insurance billing is the assignment of primary and secondary insurance plan status. This is vital to assuring proper coordination of benefits, clean claim processing, and appropriate reimbursement. Consequently, the data entry staff must understand all coordination of benefit rules when more than one insurance plan is involved in a patient's account and then input accurate data onto the insurance data entry screen.

Correct numbers and letters for policy numbers, plan numbers, group numbers, authorization or precertification numbers, and extra insurance information such as accident-related data must be placed in the respective fields. Your insurance plan utility file must be reviewed closely before any new insurance plans are added to a patient file. Multiple

FIGURE 6-10

Insurance Fact Sheet

At the time of your visit, you will be provided with a copy of our encounter form. The pink copy is to be attached to your insurance claim form and mailed to your insurance carrier.

You should follow these steps when completing your insurance claim form:

1. Be sure to fill out the top portion of the claim form.

2. It is not necessary for you to fill in the portions regarding diagnosis or procedures. That information is recorded on the encounter form by the physician's office.

3. The physician's name, address, and provider number are also on the encounter form. You do not need to add this to the claim form.

4. If you have not already paid for your services, we will anticipate your forwarding the insurance check directly to our office so that we may credit your account. It is not necessary for you to deposit the check. You may simply endorse the back of the check as follows:

    Pay to the order of James Smith, MD

    and send it to our office in the enclosed envelope.

5. If you have a supplemental policy, fill out the top portion of the claim form, attach the Explanation of Medical Benefits (detach from your check), a copy of the encounter form, and mail them. Do not bill your supplemental policy before receiving an Explanation of Medical Benefits from your primary policy.

Helpful phone numbers:

Blue Cross and Blue Shield: _____

Travelers: _____

Medicaid: _____

FIGURE 6-11
Medical Cost Estimate Form

Patient Name: _____ Date: _____

Explanation of Procedure: _____

_____

	Fee	*% Covered by Insurance*
Surgery:	_____	_____
Assistant Surgeon:	_____	_____
Consultation:	_____	_____
Hospital Visits:	_____	_____
Other Professional Services:	_____	_____
*Anesthesiologist:	_____	_____
*Pathologist:	_____	_____
Total	_____	_____
Approximate Out-of-Pocket Cost	_____	_____

While you are in the hospital, there may be charges for laboratory tests, medications, transfusions, or special care that we are unable to estimate. Be assured that we are sensitive to the rising cost of medical services and will make every effort to deliver quality medical care in the most cost-efficient manner possible, without compromising your good health.

You may wish to contact the hospital business office at _____ for further information about hospital charges. Remember your health insurance card on the day of admittance!

[*You may want to explain that these are required by the hospital for certain surgeries, when applicable.]

FIGURE 6-12

Advance Notice Form for Elective Surgery Greater Than $500

I do not plan to accept assignment for your surgery. The law requires that where assignment is not taken and the charge is $500 or more, the following information must be provided prior to surgery. These estimates assume that you have already met the $124 annual Medicare Part B deductible for 2006.

Type of Surgery : _____

_____

_____

_____

Estimated Charge for Surgery $ _____

Estimated Medicare Allowable Charge $ _____

Your Estimated Out-of-Pocket Expense $ _____

_____   _____
Patient Signature   Date

FIGURE 6-13
Medicare Advanced Notice Service Waiver

Physician's Notice

Medicare will only pay for services that it determines to be "reasonable and necessary" under Section 1862(a)(1) of the Medicare law. If Medicare determines that a particular service, although it would otherwise be covered, is "not reasonable and necessary" under Medicare program standards, Medicare will deny payment for that service. I believe that, in your case, Medicare is likely to deny payment for the following reasons:

_____

_____

Note: On the above line, a specific procedure code and description of procedure *must* be listed here before the beneficiary signs the form.

Medicare does not usually pay:

1. For this many treatments/shots/visits.
2. For this service/drug/vaccine.
3. Because the treatment has yet to be proven effective.
4. For this office visit unless it was emergency care.
5. For like services by more than one physician during the same time period.
6. For such an extensive procedure.
7. For this equipment or lab test.
8. Because the treatment is considered by Medicare to be "not reasonable or necessary."

Beneficiary Agreement

I, _____, have been informed on this date _____ by my physician (and/or staff) that he/she believes that Medicare is likely to deny payment for the service(s) identified above for the reasons stated. If Medicare denies payment, I agree to be personally and fully responsible for payment of the service(s) rendered.

Further, I will pay for these services on this date, understanding that the physician will bill my insurance(s) on my behalf. If the above physician is paid by my insurance, I will receive a refund for the portion of the bill covered by my insurance less any portion of the payment that is deemed my responsibility.

_____   _____
Beneficiary Signature   Staff/Witness Signature

FIGURE 6-14

Insurance Coverage Advanced Notice Service Waiver

Physician's Notice

Some health insurance plans will only pay for services that they determine to be "reasonable and necessary." If an insurance plan determines that a particular service, although it would otherwise be covered, is "not reasonable and necessary," the insurance plan may deny payment for that service.

I believe that, in your case, your health plan is likely to deny payment for _____

_____

Policyholder/Patient Agreement

I, _____, have been informed on this date _____ by my physician (and/or staff) that he/she believes that my health plan may deny payment for the service identified above for the reasons stated. If the health plan denies payment, I agree to be personally and fully responsible for payment of the service(s) rendered.

Further, I will pay for these services on this date, understanding that the physician will attempt to rebill my insurance(s) on my behalf. If the above physician is paid by my insurance, I will receive a refund for the portion of the bill covered by my insurance less any portion of the payment that is deemed my responsibility.

_____   _____
Policyholder/Patient Signature   Staff/Witness Signature

insurance entries for a single insurance plan can easily complicate account follow-up and management.

Another data field includes the patient's financial or account type, which defines the primary account type for management and reporting purposes. The patient's account type is sometimes classified as a primary payer type (ie, Medicare, Medicaid, Blue Cross Blue Shield, commercial, insurance only, self-pay, etc).

Capturing All Billable Services and Transaction Entry

The traditional way to receive appropriate reimbursement under a fee-for-service arrangement is for the physician to report all pertinent services provided to the patient in the medical record and capture all billable services for transaction entry into the billing system. Accurate coding and reporting for all services provided is crucial to successful pre-claim processing; the proper use of codes and a thorough knowledge of guidelines and conventions allow for the accurate reporting of physician services. Even under managed care plans, which reimburse primary care physicians on a capitated rate, complete medical documentation and coding of all services rendered is critical as is the review of resource allocation and costs associated with care. Documentation is also used to measure physician productivity, which determine profit sharing and continuity as a plan provider. Proper documentation and accurate coding are keys to successfully capturing all billable services.

Comprehensive Medical Record Documentation

Although the medical record is a clinical document, it is also the primary source of information for billing. Therefore, physicians must develop detailed and qualitative notes of patient evaluation and management (E/M) encounters, diagnostic and therapeutic treatments, supplies, orders, and so on.

In December 1994, the American Medical Association (AMA) and the Centers for Medicare & Medicaid Services (CMS) jointly distributed *New E/M Documentation Guidelines,* which thoroughly define all documentation components needed to meet and exceed level-of-service definition criteria. All practices should have received a copy of the guidelines from their Medicare carrier or should request a copy if not received. In 1997, new E/M guidelines were distributed; however, CMS allows either the 1994 or 1997 criteria to be used, whichever is more appropriate for the provider.

Transfer of Clinical and Treatment Information to Appropriate CPT and ICD-9-CM Codes

Physicians are responsible for making sure that all services rendered and all medications and supplies provided are identified and coded from the medical record. In addition, the patient's chief complaints, signs, symptoms, or qualified diagnosis(es) also need to be coded using valid *International Classification of Diseases, Ninth Edition, Clinical Modification* (ICD-9-CM) codes.

Because coding is the basis for appropriate reimbursement, the quality and accuracy of the practice's coding skills is extremely important. The coding staff should be encouraged to become certified procedural coders or become affiliated with associations that encourage certification and offer coding education programs. In-house code training systems are also helpful in fostering staff coding skills.

Key areas for coding skills include E/M level of service differentiation, CPT procedure and surgery coding, use of modifiers, supply and injectable drug billing, and the coding's potential impact on reimbursement. To properly coordinate insurance plan benefits between different physicians treating different diagnostic conditions, the most appropriate Level I and II HCPCS codes (services and supplies) and ICD-9-CM diagnostic codes must be supplied. Submittal of a clean claim is necessary to receive appropriate reimbursement.

To facilitate the charge capture process, most practices develop customized billing source documents, called encounter forms, to serve as internal charge forms.

Encounter Forms

Encounter forms, also referred to as charge tickets, are preprinted forms that list procedure codes and descriptions (and occasionally diagnostic codes) for services frequently rendered by the practice. The form usually contains basic practice and patient information and serves as an internal charge form and patient invoice. It is usually prenumbered for internal control.

Services and diagnoses are usually arranged by service classification: E/M services, injections, minor procedures, diagnostic tests, laboratory, and radiology services. Some forms are printed on two-ply carbonless paper (one copy for the practice, the other to serve as the patient's receipt). Others are printed with sequential numbers for tracking purposes. A sample encounter form is shown in Chapter 1, Figure 1-2.

Many practices use encounter forms because they are convenient. At the time of a visit, the physician or medical assistant simply checks off the services and patient diagnoses, the staff completes the charge information, and the charges are entered into the patient billing system. Unless required to file a claim, as in the case of Medicare, the patient is given a copy of the encounter form to file with his or her insurance claim. Encounter forms save time, can be used with many third-party payers, and simplify paperwork and bookkeeping.

However, encounter forms do have significant drawbacks. First, it is impossible to list the complete range of procedure and diagnosis codes likely to be used by your practice on the encounter form. This can lead to miscoding of services and diagnoses, because many practices inappropriately select the closest code rather than take the time to refer to the code manual to locate the correct code. Second, encounter forms cannot be submitted to Medicare, nor are they useful when submitting claims for nonroutine or unusual services. Plus, codes must be reviewed and updated annually. Finally, encounter forms are most often used with patients who pay at the time of the visit. Because the patient files his or her own claim, you may not know if the claim was denied or delayed due to improper coding. This lack of feedback can increase coding and other encounter form errors, which result in underpayments to patients and audit liability to physician practices.

Final assignment of the HCPCS and ICD-9-CM codes on the encounter form is often a shared responsibility between the physician, clinical support staff, and business office support staff. The physician knows what services and supplies were provided to a patient and what was documented. Although the clinical support team may assist in assigning HCPCS and ICD-9-CM codes, it is important to remember that the ultimate responsibility for improper coding on fraudulent claims lies with the provider whose signature is on the claim.

Service Verification and Transaction Entry of Services Rendered

After the services and diagnoses have been marked on the encounter form, the encounter form is brought to the cashiering/discharge area. This is where the clinical assistant and the in-office coding staff first review the encounter form as a quality assurance check. They are responsible for:

- Reviewing the encounter form for complete charge capture and code assignment (They review the patient's chart against the encounter form for all supplies, drugs, and services provided.)
- Assigning proper E/M type of service (ie, noting if the patient a new or established patient; noting if the encounter is an office visit or a consultation)
- Ensuring the compatibility of the ICD-9-CM diagnoses codes with each CPT procedure code or E/M level of service
- Assigning the ICD-9-CM diagnoses codes with fourth and fifth digits or to the highest specificity

When the coding staff is satisfied with the code assignment, the patient's account is pulled up on the transaction entry screen of the computer system. Again, most billing management systems have standardized data fields for transaction entry that correspond to the CMS-1500 claim form.

The key data fields to complete per charge line item include:

- Date of service (DOS): Sometimes defined as from and to dates
- Place of service code: Code 11 = office, code 21 = hospital inpatient, code 22 = hospital outpatient
- Transaction codes: Level I-CPT and Level II-HCPCS codes
- Coding modifiers
- Attending practice physician code: Defaults to provider ID number
- Standard charge amount or special insurance charge default
- Number of units
- Definition of (1-4) diagnoses using ICD-9-CM codes
- Assignment of diagnosis codes to individual line item (1-4) cross-references

On most billing systems, the last data field for transaction entry is for indicating that the line item is to be billed to insurance. Some systems ask "bill insurance?" with a yes/no field, other systems allow the operator to bill a specific insurance plan through the assignment of insurance codes. After all line items have been coded, the transaction charges are added to the patient's account and the account is flagged by the system to generate a claim.

Filing Claims and Effect on Accounts Receivable

To keep accounts receivable low, it is best to collect from patients with commercial insurance and then have them file insurance claims for office visits. This applies unless special circumstances require that arrangements be made with the patient. Special circumstances include situations in which patients are clearly incapable of filing claims, when the law requires the office to file the claim, or when patients forget to bring their checkbooks or credit cards or have no other way of making a payment. Remember, billed services become accounts receivable and it is always preferable to receive payment immediately.

To reemphasize the point, by collecting up front, you avoid filing commercial insurance claims and you maximize cash flow. An insurance claim that is filed for commercial insurance becomes an accounts receivable for the practice and thus is subject to all office policies and procedures necessary to obtain payment from the insurance company.

If the office does collect payment for the visit, there is no accounts receivable for that transaction. The more money the office can collect at the front desk, the better the practice's cash flow will be. The front desk should be able to collect some payment for at least 90% of all visits, even if a patient pays only $5. Some practices accept charge cards to enhance collections and then file claim for the patient. Although it may not be mandatory for the practice to file the insurance claim, timing and proper filing are enhanced when the practice completes this step.

INSURANCE CLAIMS PROCESSING AND SUBMISSION

If a patient does not pay at the time of service, the office must prepare and file an insurance claim form with the patient's insurance company to receive payment. The manner in which the insurance claim form is completed and submitted depends on the type of insurance. As discussed earlier, some insurance companies only process paper claims, while others accept electronically submitted claims. It is the insurance processing manager's responsibility to identify insurance claims that need to be generated on paper and those that can be sent electronically.

To receive appropriate payment from the insurance company, the office must prepare the insurance claim correctly, ie, prepare a "clean claim." This means that every relevant box on the claim form is completed. Any error in the claim completion may cause payment to be delayed or denied. Because many states' laws require it, the most common form used to file insurance claims is the type mandated for outpatient Medicare claims: the CMS-1500 form.

The CMS-1450 (UB-04 Form) is presently utilized to bill inpatient claims and some outpatient services. The National Uniform Billing Committee approved the UB-04 as the replacement for the UB-92 billing form. Effective May 23, 2007, all institutional billing must be on a UB-04 claim form. The UB-92 is no longer accepted.

In August 2006, the Office of Management and Budget approved the UB-04 billing form (CMS-1450) for use. The expiration date is August 31, 2009, and the new OMB number is 0938-0997. Additional information on the UB-04, along with the crosswalk from the UB-92 to the UB-04, can be viewed on the NUBC website at www.nubc.org.

The Uniform Bill Form

For more than a decade, the UB-92 form was used to bill inpatient and outpatient visits such as those to hospitals (inpatient/outpatient), skilled nursing facilities (SNF), comprehensive outpatient rehabilitation centers (CORF), etc. However, starting in May 2007, providers that used paper forms for claim submission had to switch to the UB-04 form (which carries the alternate designation CMS-1450 just like the old UB-92 form did). The change resulted from the HIPAA requirement that National Provider Identifiers (NPIs) appear on all claims; the UB-92 form did not have a field for reporting of NPIs.

Although mandated by CMS, the National Uniform Billing Committee (NUBC) maintains a complete list of allowable data elements and codes. The following describes the 86 form locaters on the UB-04:

Form Locater 1   Provider name, address, and telephone number
Form Locater 2   Not required; however, the State Uniform Billing Committees (SUBC) may assign this field and it is uniform within the state.

Form Locater 3 Patient's account/control number, assigned by the provider.

Form Locater 4 Type of bill has three characters. The first digit indicates the type of facility, the second digit classifies the type of care, and the third character (either a letter or digit) indicates the sequence of this bill in this particular episode of care.

First Digit: Type of Facility
1. Hospital
2. SNF
3. Home Health
4. Religious Nonmedical Hospital
5. Religious Nonmedical Extended Care
6. Intermediate Care
7. Clinic- or Hospital-Based Renal Dialysis Facility
8. Special Facility/Hospital Ambulatory Surgical Center (ASC) Surgery
9. Reserved for National Assignment

Second Digit: Classification
1. Inpatient (Medicare Part A)
2. Hospital-Based or Inpatient Medicare Part B
3. Outpatient
4. Other (Includes home health agency [HHA] medical and other health services not under a plan of treatment, SNF diagnostic clinical laboratory services to nonpatients, and referred diagnostic services)
5. Intermediate Care Level 1
6. Intermediate Care Level 2
7. Intermediate Care level 3
8. Swing Bed
9. Reserved for National Use

Second Digit: Classification (for clinics only)
1. Rural Health Clinic (RHC)
2. Hospital-Based or Independent Renal Dialysis Facility
3. Free-Standing Provider-Based Facility Federally Qualified Health Centers
4. Other Rehabilitation Facility (ORF)
5. Comprehensive Outpatient Rehabilitation Facility (CORF)
6. Community Mental Health Center

Second Digit: Classification (for special facilities only)
1. Hospice Nonhospital Based
2. Hospice Hospital Based
3. Ambulatory Surgical Center Services to Hospital Outpatients
4. Free-Standing Birthing Center
5. Critical Access Hospital
6. Residential Facility (Not used for Medicare)

Third Digit: Frequency
A. Admission/Election Notice (Hospice and Religious Nonmedical Health Care Facilities utilize this code for admission notice)
B. Hospice/Medicare Coordinated Care Demonstration/Religious Nonmedical Health Care Institution-Termination Revocation Notice
C. Hospice Change of Provider
D. Hospice/Medicare Coordinated Care Demonstration/Religious Nonmedical Health Care Institution Void/Cancel
E. Hospice Change of Ownership

F   Beneficiary-Initiated Adjustment Claim
G   Common Working File (CWF)-Initiated Adjustment Claim
H   CMS-Initiated Adjustment Claim
I   Initiated Adjustment Claim (other than provider)
J   Initiated Adjustment Claim-Other
K   OIG-Initiated Adjustment Claim
M   Medicare Secondary Payer (MSP)-Initiated Adjustment Claim
P   Professional Review Organization (PRO) Adjustment Claim
0   Nonpayment/Zero Claims
1   Admit Through Discharge
2   Interim-First Claim
3   Interim-Second Claim
4   Interim-Final Claim
5   Late Charge Only
7   Replacement of Prior Claim
8   Void/Cancel of a Prior Claim
9   Final Claim for a Home Health Prospective Payment System (PPS) Episode

Form Locater 5   Federal tax identification number.
Form Locater 6   Statement covers period (from and through dates). Do not overlap dates of a previous bill.
Form Locater 7   Covered days.
Form Locater 8   Noncovered days.
Form Locater 9   Coinsurance days.
Form Locater 10 Lifetime reserve days.
Form Locater 11 Not required; however, the SUBC may assign this field and it is uniform within the state.
Form Locater 12 Patient's last name, first name, middle initial as it appears on his/her insurance card.
Form Locater 13 Patient's complete mailing address.
Form Locater 14 Patient's birth date: MM-DD-YYYY.
Form Locater 15 Sex of the patient: M, F, or U.
Form Locater 16 Marital status: M, S, or W.
Form Locater 17 Admission date: MM-DD-YY.
Form Locater 18 Admission hour (given in military time).
Form Locater 19 Admission type:
  1   Emergency
  2   Urgent
  3   Elective
  4   Newborn
  5   Unknown

Form Locater 20 Source of Admission:
  1   Physician referral
  2   Clinic referral
  3   HMO referral
  4   Transfer from a hospital
  5   Transfer from an SNF
  6   Transfer from another health care facility
  7   Emergency room

8 Court/law enforcement
9 Info not available
A Transfer from a Rural Primary Care Hospital

Form Locater 21 Discharge hour (given in military time).

Form Locater 22 Patient status:

01 Discharged to home or self-care (routine discharge)
02 Discharged/transferred to another general hospital for inpatient care
03 Discharged/transferred to an SNF
04 Discharged/transferred to an intermediate care facility
05 Discharged/transferred to another type of institution
06 Discharged/transferred to home under care of organized home health service organization
07 Left against medical advice
08 Discharged/transferred to home under care of a home intravenous (IV) drug therapy provider
09 Admitted as an inpatient to this hospital
20 Expired
30 Still a patient
40 Expired at home (hospice claims only)
41 Expired in a medical facility
42 Expired—place unknown (hospice claims only)
50 Hospice—home
51 Hospice—medical facility
61 Discharged/transferred within this institution to a hospital-based Medicare-approved swing bed
71 Discharged/transferred/referred to another institution for outpatient services as specified by the discharge plan of care
72 Discharged/transferred/referred to this institution for outpatient services as specified by the discharge plan of care

Form Locater 23 Medical record number.

Form Locater 24–30 Condition codes: These codes are used by the provider to identify specific environmental conditions relating to the patient. The code may affect the way in which the insurance processes the claim.

Form Locater 31 Not required; however, the SUBC may assign this field and it is uniform within the state.

Form Locater 32-35 Occurrence codes and dates: These codes and dates define a significant event relating to the patient for this bill and may affect the way in which the insurance processes the claim.

Form Locater 36 Use if additional occurrence codes need to be added.

Form Locater 37 Internal control number (ICN), document control number (DCN).

Form Locater 38 Responsible parties' name and address. Hospice claims—Name, address and provider number of a transferring hospice is shown by the new hospice on this admission notice.

Form Locater 39–41 Value codes. Code and related dollar amounts identify data of a monetary nature that are necessary for the processing of this claim.

Form Locater 42 Revenue code: Describes a specific accommodation, ancillary service, or billing calculation.

Form Locater 43 Revenue description.
Form Locater 44 HCPCS/Rates (rates are shown for inpatient hospitals or SNF bills).
Form Locater 45 Service date.
Form Locater 46 Service units.
Form Locater 47 Total charges.
Form Locater 48 Noncovered charges.
Form Locater 49 Not required; however, the SUBC may assign this field and it is uniform within the state.
Form Locater 50 Payer identification.
Form Locater 51 Provider number.
Form Locater 52 Release of information.

- Y The provider has a signed permission to release information
- R Restricted
- N No release on file

Form Locater 53 Assignment of benefits.
Form Locater 54 Prior payments.
Form Locater 55 Estimated amount due.
Form Locater 56 Not required; however, the SUBC may assign this field and it is uniform within the state.
Form Locater 57 Not required; however, the SUBC may assign this field and it is uniform within the state.
Form Locater 58 Insured's name.
Form Locater 59 Relationship to the insured:

- 01 Patient is the insured
- 02 Spouse
- 03 Natural child/insured has financial responsibility
- 04 Natural child/insured does not have financial responsibility
- 05 Stepchild
- 06 Foster child
- 07 Ward of the court
- 08 Employee (patient is employed by the insured)
- 09 Unknown
- 10 Handicapped
- 11 Organ donor
- 12 Cadaver donor
- 13 Grandchild
- 14 Niece/nephew
- 15 Injured plaintiff
- 16 Sponsored dependant
- 17 Minor dependant of a minor dependant
- 18 Parent
- 19 Grandparent

Form Locater 60 Certificate, Social Security Number, insurance identification number assigned.
From Locater 61 Group name (name of group through which the insurance is provided to the insured).

Form Locater 62	Group number (number assigned by the insurance to identify the group).
Form Locater 63	Treatment authorization code.
Form Locater 64	Employment status code.
Form Locater 65	Employer name.
Form Locater 66	Employer location.
Form Locater 67	Principal diagnosis code.
Form Locater 68–75	Other diagnoses codes.
Form Locater 76	Admitting diagnosis.
Form Locater 77	E code (code for external cause of injury, poisoning, or adverse effects).
Form Locater 78	Not required.
Form Locater 79	Procedure coding method.
Form Locater 80	Principal procedure and date.
Form Locater 81	Other procedure codes and dates.
Form Locater 82	Attending/referring physician ID.
Form Locater 83	Other physician ID.
Form Locater 84	Remarks.
Form Locater 85	Provider representative signature.
Form Locater 86	Date claim signed and submitted to insurance.

CMS-1500 Universal Claim Form

The CMS-1500 form is often called the universal claim form because virtually all third-party payers accept it. In 1992, the CMS-1500 form was changed so that it could be scanned by payers using optical character recognition (OCR) equipment. As previously stated, Medicare requires that all physicians submit this form when providing services to Medicare patients.

In addition to using a special red ink for OCR purposes, the form was redesigned to allow for the reporting of additional information, such as the physician's NPI, which is required by Medicare. These forms may be obtained from a variety of vendors and are relatively inexpensive (see Chapter 1, Figure 1-1).

Instructions for Completing a CMS-1500 Form

Most insurance and managed care plans provide basic instructions for completing fields on the claim form in their physician manual. If there are no special requirements, all fields should be completed according to the requirements stated on the form. If the claim form is not computer-generated, it is best to type in all required information. If rehandwritten, staff should print all requirement information using all capital letters and black ink. The claim form is divided into two sections: patient information (fields 1–13) and physician information (fields 14–33). (See Figure 1-1 for a sample CMS-1500 form.)

Patient and Insured Information

Fields 1 through 13 ask for information about the patient and the insured and for a determination of whether the patient is a dependent. This information should be provided on the registration form at the patient's initial office visit or at the hospital. Practices that use computerized patient information-accounting systems can generate this information automatically by entering a single patient identification number assigned by the practice.

The following sections explain how to complete fields 1 through 13. Where applicable, special requirements for Medicare, Medicaid, TRICARE, CHAMPVA, and private plans are described.

Field 1: Type of Insurance   Indicate the type of insurance coverage applicable to a claim by checking the appropriate box. For example, if a Medicare claim is being submitted, check the Medicare box; for the Federal Employment Compensation Act (FECA)/Black Lung, check FECA. For private plans such as a Blue Shield, check OTHER.

Field 1a: Insured's ID Number   Enter the insured's primary identification number, including all letters. This number appears on the plan identification card. For Medicare, enter the health insurance claim number (HICN) from the Medicare card, including all the letters. For Medicaid, enter the Medicaid number from the current Medicaid card. It is sometimes called the billing number or recipient number. For TRICARE, enter the sponsor's Social Security number. Do not provide the patient's Social Security number unless the patient and sponsor are the same. If a sponsor is an active-duty security agent, enter "SECURITY." Additional information about sponsors is given in Chapter 9. For CHAMPVA, provide the sponsor's Social Security number. Add the number in field 5 on the CHAMPVA authorization card if there is no Social Security number. For private plans, enter the insured's subscriber, enrollee, or member number. This may be the certificate number; it is copied directly from the plan's identification number. Frequently, this number is the insured's Social Security number.

Field 2: Patient's Name   Enter the patient's last name, first name, and middle initial, if any, as shown on the identification card. The practice may know the patient by a nickname or the individual may want to be known by his or her middle name, but enter the name exactly as it appears on the card.

Field 3: Patient's Birth Date and Sex   Enter the patient's birth date and sex. Because many plans operated under different rules, providers should contact individual payers to determine how that payer handles date formats.

For Medicare, as of October 1, 1998, service providers are required to report eight-digit birth dates for fields 3, 9b, and 11a on form CMS-1500. This includes entering two-digit months (MM) and days (DD) and four-digit years (CCYY). The reporting requirement of eight-digit birth dates does require revision to form CMS-1500. Eight-digit birth dates must be reported with a space between month, day, and year (ie, MM DD CCYY). On form CMS-1500, the space between month, day, and year is delineated by a dotted, vertical line.

Field 4: Insured's Name   Enter the full name of the insured.

For Medicare, if there is a plan primary to Medicare through the patient's or spouse's employment or any other source, list the name of the insured on that policy. When the insured and the patient are the same, enter the word "SAME." If Medicare is primary, leave blank. For Medicaid, enter the full name of the insured. For private plans, enter the full name of the insured if it is different from that of the patient.

Field 5: Patient's Address   Enter the patient's mailing address on the first line, the city and state on the second line, and the zip code and telephone number on the third line.

For TRICARE, do not provide a post office box number. Enter the actual place of residence. If this is a rural address, the address must contain the route and box number. An army post office/fleet post office (APO/FPO) address should not be used for a patient's mailing address unless that person is actually residing overseas.

Field 6: Patient Relationship to Insured   After completing field 4, check the appropriate box for the patient's relationship to the insured.

For Medicare, enter the relationship of the individual whose coverage is the primary plan for the Medicare beneficiary.

For TRICARE, if the patient is the sponsor, check the "self" field. If "other" is checked, indicate how the patient is related to the sponsor, for example, former spouse, parent. Parents, parents-in-law, stepparents, and parents by adoption are not TRICARE/CHAMPVA eligible. These categories of dependents may have ID cards with privileges for the military treatment facility but not for TRICARE/CHAMPVA benefits. Grandchildren are not eligible unless they are legally adopted. Be certain that an ID card authorizes "CIVILIAN" medical benefits. Review the reverse side of the retiree's ID card (DD Form 2: Retired). An unnumbered field provides a date when civilian military care is no longer authorized. For example, the TRICARE beneficiary becomes eligible for Medicare. If the child is a stepchild, check the "child" box.

For private plans, if the patient is the insured, check "self."

Field 7: Insured's Address Enter the insured's address and telephone number. When this address is the same as the patient's address, enter the word "same." Complete this field only when fields 4 and 11 have been completed.

For TRICARE, enter the address for the active-duty sponsor's duty station or the retiree's mailing address. If the address is the same as the patient's address, enter "same." If the sponsor resides overseas, enter the APO/FPO address.

For private plans, enter "same" if the insured is the patient.

Field 8: Patient Status Check the appropriate box for the patient's marital status and indicate whether the patient is employed or is a full-time or part-time student.

Field 9: Other Insured's Policy or Group Number Enter the insured's last name and his/her first name for a plan that is secondary to the patient's primary insurance plan listed in field 2.

For Medicare, enter the last name, first name, and middle initial of the enrollee in a Medigap policy if it is different from that shown in field 2. Otherwise, enter "same" or enrollee's name. If no Medigap benefits are assigned, leave this space blank. Only participating physicians are to complete fields 9 and 9a–9d and only when the beneficiary wishes to assign benefits under a Medigap policy. Participating physicians and suppliers must enter the information required in field 9 and its divisions if the beneficiary requests this. A claim for which a beneficiary elects to assign benefits under a Medigap policy to a participating physician or supplier is called a mandated Medigap transfer or crossover.

Do not list other supplemental coverages that are not Medigap policies in field 9a–9d when a Medicare claim is submitted. If the private plan contracts with a Medicare carrier to send Medicare claim information electronically, other supplemental claims are forwarded automatically. If there is no such contract, the beneficiary must file his or her own supplemental claim.

Medigap is medical insurance offered by a private plan to individuals covered by Medicare. It is designed to supplement Medicare benefits by providing payment for charges that Medicare does not cover, such as deductibles, coinsurance, and other limitations imposed by Medicare. Medigap does not include limited benefit coverage available to Medicare beneficiaries for "specific diseases," such as cancer, or for "hospital indemnity" per day coverage. Medigap excludes policies offered by an employer to employees or former employees as well as policies offered by a labor union to members or former members.

For TRICARE, enter the name of the insured if it is different from that shown in field 2 (patient). For example, the patient may be covered under a plan held by a spouse, parent, or other person. (Fields 11a–11d should be used to report insurance plans covering the patient.) Field 11d should be completed before the office staff determines the need for completing fields 9a–9d. If field 11d is checked, fields 9a–9d must be completed.

For private plans, enter the name of the insured for insurance plans that are secondary to the patient's primary plan listed in field 2.

Field 9a: Other Insured's Policy or Group Number Enter the plan ID number, which is the policy or group number of the secondary insurance plan.

For Medicare, enter the policy and/or group number of the Medigap insured preceded by MEDIGAP, MG, or MGAP. Field 9d must be completed if you enter a policy and/or group number in field 9a. For TRICARE, enter the policy number of the other insured's plan. For private plans, list the policy number of the secondary plan.

Field 9b: Other Insured's Date of Birth For Medicare, enter the Medigap insured's eight-digit birth date (MM DD CCYY) and sex. Because so many plans operate under different rules, providers should contact individual payers to determine how that payer handles date formats.

Field 9c: Employer's Name or School Name Enter the employer's name or school name for the secondary insurance plan. For Medicare, leave this field blank if a Medigap PAYER ID is entered in field 9d. Enter the claims processing address for the Medigap insurer. Use an abbreviated street address, two-letter state postal code, and zip code copied from the Medigap enrollee's Medigap identification card. For example,

1257 Anywhere Street
Baltimore, MD 21204

should be reported as

1257 Anywhere St MD 21204

For TRICARE, enter the name of the employer or school.

Field 9d: Insurance Plan Name or Program Name Enter the name of the insurance program or plan that received the claim after the plan noted in field 1.

For Medicare, enter the nine-digit PAYERID number of the Medigap insurer. If no PAYERID number exists, enter the Medigap insurance program or plan name. If you are a participating provider and the beneficiary wants Medicare payment data forwarded to a Medigap insurer under a mandated Medigap transfer, all information in fields 9, 9a, 9b, and 9d must be complete and accurate. Otherwise, the Medicare carrier cannot forward the claim information to the Medigap insurer.

For TRICARE, enter the insurance plan name or the program name through which the individual has other health insurance benefits. On an attached sheet, provide a complete mailing address for all other insurance programs and enter the word "attachment."

Field 10: Indicate Whether Condition is Work-related or Accident-related If the services listed on the claim form are for a work-related or accident-related injury, check the "yes" box.

For Medicare, check "yes" or "no" to indicate whether employment, auto liability, or other accident involvement applies to one or more of the services described in field 24. Any fields checked "yes" indicate that there may be subrogation primary to Medicare. Identify primary insurance information in field 11.

For TRICARE, check "yes" or "no." However, if service was the result of an automobile accident, indicate the state where the accident occurred. The contractor will contact the patient for potential third-party liability information. If third-party liability is involved, the beneficiary is required to complete DD Form 2527, Statement of Personal Injury, Possible Third-party Liability.

For private plans, provide information concerning potential third-party liability.

Field 10d: Reserved for Local Use For Medicaid, if the patient is entitled to Medicaid, enter the patient's number preceded by the letters MCD. For TRICARE, use this field to indicate that there is other health insurance.

Field 11: Insured's Policy Group or FECA Number Enter the insured's policy group or FECA number. If the number is the same as in field 4, write "same."

For Medicare, this field must be completed by the physician who acknowledges having made a good faith effort to determine whether Medicare is the primary or secondary plan. If there is insurance primary to Medicare, enter the insured's plan ID number and complete fields 11a–11c. If there is no insurance primary to Medicare, enter the word "none."

Insurance Primary to Medicare Circumstances under which Medicare payment may be secondary to other insurance include:

- Group health plan coverage:

    — Working aged
    — Disability
    — End-stage renal disease

- No fault and/or other liability
- Work-related illness/injury:

    — Workers' compensation
    — Black lung
    — Veterans benefits

For a paper claim to be considered for Medicare secondary payer benefits, a copy of the primary payer explanation of benefits (EOB) must be forwarded along with the claim form. For TRICARE, if the patient has other insurance, enter the plan ID number and indicate whether Medicare covers the patient. (Fields 9a–9d should be used to report another primary insurance plan.)

Field 11a: Insured's Date of Birth Enter the insured's eight-digit (MM DD CCYY) birth date and sex if they are different from what is entered in field 3. For TRICARE, fill in the insured's eight-digit date of birth (MM DD CCYY) and sex (check box). Enter the date of birth and sex if they are different from that entered in field 3.

Field 11b: Employer's Name or School Name For Medicare, enter the employer's name, if applicable. If there is a change in the insured's insurance status, eg, retired, enter either a six-digit (MM DD YY) or eight-digit (MM DD CCYY) retirement date preceded by the word "retired." For TRICARE, enter the employer's or school's name, if applicable.

Field 11c: Insurance Plan Name or Program Name Enter the nine-digit PAYERID number of the primary insurer. If no PAYERID number exists, enter the complete primary insurance plan or program name, eg, Blue Shield of Illinois. If the primary payer's EOB does not contain the claims processing address, record the primary payer's claims processing address directly on the EOB.

For TRICARE, enter the insurance plan or program name. If the patient has supplemental TRICARE coverage, it is not necessary to report a claim with that insurance first unless the insurance can be considered a primary plan. For TRICARE purposes, supplemental policies are those policies that are specifically designed to supplement TRICARE benefits, eg, payment of the beneficiary's cost share or deductible liability. Remember, TRICARE is secondary to all other medical insurance, except Medicaid. When you submit the claim to the other insurer, attach a copy of the explanation of benefits (EOB) from the primary insurance plan to the TRICARE claim.

Field 11d: Indicate Whether There is Another Health Benefit Plan This information is not required by Medicare, so leave this field blank. For TRICARE, check yes or no to indicate whether there is another primary insurance plan. If secondary insurance, Medicare, or Medicaid covers the patient, enter that plan ID number. If Medicaid covers the patient, enter the word "Medicaid," followed by the Medicaid number.

For private plans, place an X in the yes box to indicate patient coverage by a third insurance plan. Enter the group number or group name if the patient is covered by an employer-paid medical insurance plan.

Field 12: Patient's or Authorized Person's Signature The patient or authorized representative must sign and enter either a six-digit date (MM DD YY), eight-digit date (MM DD CCYY), or an alphanumeric date (ie, January 1, 1998) unless the signature is on file. The patient or authorized representative must sign in this field unless the signature is on file in the practice or at the hospital. The signed authorization for the patient that is on file at the hospital should cover all inpatient and outpatient hospitalization services on the claim form. When the patient's representative signs, the relationship to the patient must be indicated. The patient's signature, which authorizes the release of medical information, is necessary to process the claim. The patient's signature also authorizes payment of benefits to the provider of services when the provider accepts assignment on the claim.

Medicare allows the provider to obtain a one-time lifetime authorization, which is kept on file. If the registration form required by Medicare (see Chapter 2, Figure 2-6) is used, a separate authorization is not necessary. If a signature is obtained, enter "Signature on File" in field 12.

When an illiterate or physically handicapped patient signs by the signature mark, the patient's name and address must be entered next to the mark.

For TRICARE, either parent should sign for a patient younger than 18 years of age, unless the services are confidential. If the patient is 18 or older but cannot sign the claim, the person who signs must be either the legal guardian or, in the absence of a legal guardian, the spouse or parent of the patient. The signer should write the patient's name in field 12, followed by the word "by" and his or her own signature. A statement must be attached to the claim giving the signer's full name and address, the signer's relationship to the patient, and the reason the patient is unable to sign. Also included, must be documentation of the signer's appointment as a legal guardian, an indication of whether a power of attorney has been issued, or a statement that a legal guardian has not been appointed if such is the case.

For private plans, it is important to maintain current signatures for patients and/or insureds. Use the words "signature on file" if a valid signature is available. Most insurance and managed care plans accept this, but they do have the right to request a copy of the actual signature.

Field 13: Insured's or Authorized Person's Signature The signature in this field authorizes payment of medical benefits to the physician or provider for services listed on the claim.

For Medicare, the signature in this field authorizes payment of mandated Medigap benefits to the participating physician or supplier if required Medigap information is included in field 9 and its subdivisions. The patient or his/her authorized representative must sign this field or the signature must be on file as a separate Medigap authorization. The Medigap assignment on file in the participating provider's office must be insurer specific. It may state that the authorization applies to all occasions of service until it is revoked.

If a private plan has offered the physician a contract for participation in its program and the physician has not signed the contract, even though the signature is in field 13, payment may not be sent to the practice.

Physician or Supplier Information

These fields describe diagnoses, procedures, and charges and give a history of the patient's condition. Most of this information is found on the patient's encounter form. **Note:** For date fields other than date of birth, all fields need to maintain a consistent format, either six-dight or eight-digit. Intermixing the two formats on the claim is not allowed.

Field 14: Date of Current Illness, Injury, Pregnancy Enter either a six-digit (MM DD YY) or eight-digit (MM DD CCYY) date of when the first symptoms began for the current illness, injury, or pregnancy (date of last menstrual period).

For Medicare for chiropractic services, enter either a six-digit (MM DD YY) or eight-digit (MM DD CCYY) date of the initiation of the course of treatment and then enter either a six-digit (MM DD YY) or eight-digit (MM DD CCYY) X-ray date in field 19. For private plans, this information is used to determine benefits or exclusions for preexisting conditions.

Field 15: Indicate Whether Patient Has Had Same or Similar Illness For Medicare, leave blank. For TRICARE, enter the date when the patient first consulted the physician for a similar condition. For private plans, enter the date when the patient first consulted the physician for a similar condition.

Field 16: Dates Patient Unable to Work in Current Occupation Enter the dates the patient has been employed and unable to work in his or her current occupation. Enter either six-digit (MM DD YY) or eight-digit (MM DD CCYY) dates when the patient is unable to work. This is important if the patient has employment-related insurance coverage or workers' compensation.

Field 17: Name of the Referring Physician or Other Source For Medicare, enter the name of the referring or ordering physician if the service or item was ordered or referred by a physician.

A *referring physician* is a physician who requests an item or service for the beneficiary for which payment may be made under the Medicare program. An *ordering physician* is a physician who orders nonphysician services for the patient, such as diagnostic laboratory tests, clinical laboratory tests, pharmaceutical services, and durable medical equipment.

The ordering/referring requirement became effective on January 1, 1992. All claims for Medicare-covered services and items that result from a physician's order or referral must include the ordering/referring physician's name and national provider identifier (NPI). An NPI is a unique number assigned to each physician or other practitioner who bills the Medicare program. This includes parenteral and enteral nutrition, immunosuppressive drug claims, diagnostic laboratory services, diagnostic radiology services, consultative services, and durable medical equipment.

Claims for other ordered/referred services that are not included in the preceding list must also show the ordering or referring physician's name and NPI. For example, a surgeon must complete fields 17 and 17a when a physician sends a patient for a consultation. When the ordering physician is also the performing physician (as is often the case with in-office clinical laboratory tests), the performing physician's name and assigned NPI must appear in fields 17 and 17a.

All physicians must obtain an NPI even though they may never bill Medicare directly. A physician who has not been assigned an NPI must contact the Medicare carrier.

When a patient is referred to a physician who also orders and performs a diagnostic service, a separate claim is required for the diagnostic service. Enter the original ordering or referring physician's name and NPI in fields 17 and 17a of the first claim form. Enter the ordering (performing) physician's name and NPI in fields 17 and 17a of the second claim form.

For TRICARE, provide the name and address of the physician, institutional provider, or other source who referred the patient to the provider of the services identified on the claim. This is required for all consultation services. If the patient was referred from a military treatment facility (MTF), enter the name of the MTF and attach part DD2161 of SF 513, Referral.

Field 17a: ID Number of Referring Physician For Medicare, enter the CMS-assigned NPI of the referring or ordering physician listed in field 17. Enter only the seven-digit base number and the one-digit check digit. When a claim involves multiple referring or ordering physicians, a separate CMS-1500 form must be used for each ordering or referring physician.

If the ordering or referring physician has not been assigned an NPI, one of the surrogate NPIs listed below must be used in field 17a. The surrogate NPI that is used depends on the circumstance and is used only until the physician is assigned an NPI. Enter the physician's name in field 17 and the surrogate NPI in field 17a. All surrogate NPIs, with the exception of retired physicians (RET000), are temporary and may be used only until an NPI is assigned.

Use the following surrogate NPIs for physicians who have not been assigned individual NPIs. Claims received with surrogate numbers will be tracked and may be audited.

- Residents who are issued an NPI in conjunction with activities outside their residency status must use that NPI. For interns and residents without NPIs, use the eight-character surrogate NPI RES00000.

- Retired physicians who were not issued an NPI may use the surrogate RET00000.

- Physicians serving in the Department of Veteran Affairs or the US armed services may use VAD00000.
- Physicians serving in the Public Health or Indian Health Services may use PHS00000.
- Medicare extends coverage and direct payment in certain areas to practitioners who are state licensed to order medical services including diagnostic tests or refer patients to Medicare providers without a supervising physician. Use the surrogate NPI NPP00000 on claims involving services ordered or referred by nurse practitioners, clinical nurse specialists, or any nonphysician practitioner who is state licensed to order clinical diagnostic tests.
- When the ordering or referring physician has not been assigned an NPI and does not qualify to use a surrogate NPI, use the surrogate NPI OTH00000 until an individual NPI is assigned.

Field 18: Hospitalization Dates Related to Current Services Enter either a six-digit (MM DD YY) or eight-digit (MM DD CCYY) date for when a medical service is furnished as a result of, or subsequent to, a related hospitalization.

Field 19: Reserved for Local Use For Medicare, enter either the six-digit (MM DD YY) or eight-digit (MM DD CCYY) date that the patient was last seen and the NPI of his or her attending physician when an independent physical or occupational therapist or physician providing routine foot care submits a claim. For physical and occupational therapists, entering this information certifies that the required physician certification (or recertification) is being kept on file.

Enter either a six-digit (MM DD YY) or eight-digit (MM DD CCYY) x-ray date for chiropractor services. By entering an X-ray date and the initiation date for course of chiropractic treatment in field 14, you are certifying that all relevant information requirements (including level of subluxation) are on file along with the appropriate x ray and that all are available for carrier review.

Enter drug name and dosage when submitting a claim for a drug that is not otherwise classified (NOC). Enter a concise description of an "unlisted procedure code" or an NOC code if one can be given within the confines of this field. Otherwise, submit an attachment with the claim.

Enter all applicable modifiers when modifier 99 (multiple modifiers) is entered in field 24d. If modifier 99 is entered on multiple lines of a single claim form, all applicable modifiers for each line item containing modifier 99 should be listed as follows: 1 = (mod), where the number 1 represents the line item and "mod" represents all modifiers applicable to the referenced line item.

Enter the statement "Homebound" when an independent laboratory renders an electrocardiogram tracing or obtains a specimen from a homebound or institutionalized patient.

Enter the statement "Patient refuses to assign benefits" when the beneficiary absolutely refuses to assign benefits to a participating provider. In this case, no payment may be made on the claim.

Enter the statement "Testing for hearing aid" when services that involve testing of a hearing aid(s) are billed to obtain intentional denials when other payers are involved.

When dental examinations are billed, enter the specific surgery for which the exam is being performed.

Enter the specific name and dosage when low-osmolar contrast material is billed, but only if HCPCS codes do not cover them.

Enter either a six-digit (MM DD YY) or eight-digit (MM DD CCYY) assumed and/or relinquished date for a global surgery claim when providers share postoperative care.

Enter the statement "Attending physician, not hospice employee" when a physician renders services to a hospice patient and the attending physician is not employed by the hospice providing the patient's care (in which the patient resides).

Enter demonstration ID number 30 for all national emphysema treatment trial claims.

Field 20: Outside Lab For Medicare, complete this field when billing for diagnostic tests subject to purchase price limitations. A "yes" indicates that the diagnostic test was performed outside the entity billing for the service. When a "yes" is annotated, field 32 must be completed. Enter the purchase price under charges (field 24f) if the yes field is marked. A "no" indicates that "no purchased tests are included on this claim." When billing for multiple purchased diagnostic tests, each test must be submitted on a separate claim form.

For private plans, leave blank unless instructions are given by a specific plan.

Field 21: Diagnosis or Nature of Illness or Injury Enter the patient's diagnosis and/or condition using ICD-9-CM code numbers. Enter up to four codes in priority order (primary condition, secondary condition, comorbid conditions, and complications). All narrative diagnoses for nonphysician specialties must be submitted on an attachment.

Field 22: Medicaid Resubmissions Leave this field blank. It is required by some Medicaid agencies if the agency is going to resubmit a claim. Show the resubmission code and the original claim reference number.

Field 23: Prior Authorization Number Enter the Professional Review Organization's (PRO's) prior authorization number for procedures that requiring PRO prior approval.

Enter the investigational device exemption (IDE) number when an investigational device is used in a Food and Drug Administration-approved clinical trial.

For physicians performing care plan oversight services, enter the six-digit Medicare provider number of the home health agency (HHA) or hospice when CPT code 99375 or 99376 or HCPCS code G0064, G0065, or G0066 is billed.

Enter the 10-digit Clinical Laboratory Improvement Act (CLIA) certification number for laboratory services billed by a physician office laboratory.

For TRICARE, attach a copy of the authorization, eg, mental health pre-authorization, heart–hung transplant authorization. For private plans, enter the preauthorization number if required.

Field 24a: Dates of Service Enter either the six-digit (MM DD YY) or eight-digit (MM DD CCYY) date for each procedure, service, or supply. When "from" and "to" are shown for a series of identical services, enter the number of days or units in column 24g.

Field 24b: Place of Service There are variations in the codes (see Table 6-4) used for place of service (POS). The previous CMS form (1–84) had specific codes printed on the reverse side for use in field 24b. CMS (12–90) has no such codes printed. Some insurance plans still require the old (1–84) POS codes, and many require the new (12–90) codes.

For Medicare, use the new POS codes. Identify the location, using a place of service code, for each item used or service performed. When a service is rendered to a hospital inpatient, use the "inpatient hospital" code. For TRICARE, use the new POS codes. For private plans, check the plan's billing instructions to determine which POS codes are required.

Field 24c: Type of Service The type of service code is listed here when required. For Medicare, providers are not required to complete this field. For private plans, some plans require the use of type of service codes. Otherwise, leave it blank.

Field 24d: Procedures, Services, Supplies Enter the five-digit CPT code or the HCPCS Level II or Level III number for the service. A maximum of three modifiers can be used in the space next to the code. The first modifier is added between the solid line and the dotted line on the form. If three modifiers are necessary, there should be two blank spaces between the second and third modifiers in the field to the right of the dotted line.

For Medicare, enter the procedures, services, or supplies, using the HCPCS codes. When applicable, show the HCPCS modifier with any procedure code. Enter the specific code without a narrative description. When reporting an "unlisted procedure" code

TABLE 6-4

Place of Service Codes

Code	Place of Service
01	Pharmacy
02	Unassigned
03	School
04	Homeless shelter
05	Indian Health Service free-standing facility
06	Indian Health Service provider-based facility
07	Tribal 638 free-standing facility
08	Tribal 638 provider-based facility
09	Prison-correctional facility
10	Unassigned
11	Office
12	Home
13	Assisted living facility
14	Group home
15	Mobile unit
16–19	Unassigned
20	Urgent care facility
21	Inpatient hospital
22	Outpatient hospital
23	Emergency room—Hospital
24	Ambulatory surgical center
25	Birthing center
26	Military treatment facility
27–30	Unassigned
31	Skilled nursing facility
32	Nursing facility
33	Custodial care facility
34	Hospice
35–40	Unassigned
41	Ambulance—land
42	Ambulance—air or water
43–48	Unassigned
49	Independent clinic
50	Federally qualified health center
51	Inpatient psychiatric facility
52	Psychiatric facility—partial hospitalization
53	Community mental health center
54	Intermediate care facility/mentally retarded
55	Residential substance abuse treatment facility
56	Psychiatric residential treatment center
57	Nonresidential substance abuse treatment facility
58–59	Unassigned
60	Mass immunization center
61	Comprehensive inpatient rehabilitation facility
62	Comprehensive outpatient rehabilitation facility
63–64	Unassigned
65	End-stage renal disease treatment facility

TABLE 6-4

Place of Service Codes (*continued*)

Code	Place of Service
66–70	Unassigned
71	Public health clinic
72	Rural health clinic
73–80	Unassigned
81	Independent laboratory
82–98	Unassigned
99	Other place of service

or an NOC code, include a narrative description in field 19, if a coherent description can be given within the confines of that box. Otherwise, submit an attachment with the claim.

For private plans, not all modifiers are accepted. It is best to check with the individual plan to see which modifiers it recognizes.

Field 24e: Diagnosis Code Enter the diagnosis code reference number as shown in field 21 to relate the date of service and the procedures performed to the appropriate diagnosis.

For Medicare, enter only one reference number per line item. When multiple services are performed, enter the primary reference number for each service—either a 1, a 2, a 3, or a 4. If two or more diagnoses are required for a procedure code (eg, Pap smears), reference only one of the diagnoses in field 21.

Field 24f: Dollar Charges Enter the charges for each listed service.

Field 24g: Days or Units Enter the number of days or units. This field is commonly used for multiple visits, units of supplies, anesthesia minutes, and oxygen volume. If only one service is performed, the numeral 1 must be entered.

Some services require that the actual number or quantity provided be clearly indicated on the claim form as units of service (eg, multiple ostomy or urinary supplies, medication dosages, or allergy testing procedures). When multiple services are provided, enter the actual number provided.

For anesthesia services, show the elapsed time in minutes in field 24g. Convert hours into minutes and enter the total minutes required for this procedure.

Field 24h: EPSDT Family Plan For Medicare, leave this field blank. This field is not required by Medicare. For Medicaid, use a checkmark or X if preventive services were provided under Medicaid.

Field 24i: EMG (Emergency) For Medicare, leave this field blank. This field is not required by Medicare. For TRICARE, it is best to mark this field to indicate that the service was provided in a hospital emergency department. For private plans, some plans may require that this field be marked to indicate the service was provided in a hospital emergency department.

Field 24j: Coordination of Benefits (COB) For Medicare, enter the NPI of the performing provider of services or supplies if he/she is a member of a group practice. Enter the first two digits of the NPI in field 24j. Enter the remaining six digits of the NPI in field 24k, including the two-digit location identifier.

When several different providers of services or suppliers within a group are billing on the same form CMS-1500, show the individual NPI in the corresponding line item.

For private plans, check this field if the patient is covered by one or more private plans. These plans are identified in fields 11 and 11a–11d.

Field 24k: Reserved for Local Use   For Medicare, enter the NPI of the performing provider of services or supplies if he/she is a member of a group practice. Enter the first two digits of the NPI in field 24j. Enter the remaining six digits of the NPI in field 24k, including the two-digit location identifier.

For TRICARE, enter the state license number of the provider. For private plans, this field is not required.

Field 25: Federal Tax ID Number   Enter the physician or supplier federal tax ID (employer identification number) or Social Security number. For Medicare, the participating physician's or supplier's federal tax ID number is required for a mandated Medigap transfer.

Field 26: Patient's Account Number   Enter the patient's account number that was assigned by the practice's accounting system. This is an optional way to enhance patient identification by the physician. Some private plans, Medicaid, and some Medicare carriers include this information on their EOBs. It is easier to identify patient and post payments if this number is entered. As a service, any account numbers entered here will be returned to you.

Field 27: Indicate Acceptance of Assignment   For Medicare, check the appropriate box to indicate whether the physician accepts assignment of benefits. If Medigap is indicated in field 9 and Medigap payment authorization is given in field 13, the physician must also be a Medicare participating physician and must accept assignment of Medicare benefits for all covered charges for all patients.

The following services can be paid for only on an assignment basis:

- Clinical diagnostic laboratory services
- Physician services provided to individuals entitled to both Medicare and Medicaid
- Participating physician or supplier services
- Services of physician assistants, nurse practitioners, clinical nurse specialists, nurse midwives, certified registered nurse anesthetists, clinical psychologists, and clinical social workers
- Ambulatory surgical center services for covered ASC procedures
- Home dialysis supplies and equipment paid under Method II

For TRICARE, check "yes" if the practice accepts assignment, check "no" if it does not. Failure to complete this field results in nonacceptance of assignment. "Accept assignment" means that the provider has agreed to be a participating TRICARE provider on the claim and will accept the allowable amount as the total amount payable. When a provider accepts assignment, payment will be made to the provider. If the provider does not accept assignment, payment will be made to the patient or sponsor.

For private plans, this field is not applicable to plans with which the physician has a contract.

Field 28: Total Charge   Enter total charges for the services reported on the claim (ie, the total of all charges in field 24f).

Field 29: Amount Paid   Enter the total amount the patient paid on covered services only.

For TRICARE, enter the amount received by the provider or supplier from the other plans or insurances. If the amount includes payment by any other insurance, the other insurance EOB, worksheet, or denial showing the amounts paid or denied must be attached to the TRICARE claim. Payment from the beneficiary should not be included.

Field 30: Balance Due   Enter the balance due (field 28 minus field 29). For Medicare, leave this field blank. This field is not required by Medicare.

Field 31: Signature of Physician or Supplier, Including Degrees or Credentials   Enter the signature of the physician and/or his or her representative and either the six-digit

(MM DD YY), eight-digit (MM DD CCYY), or alphanumeric date (eg, January 1, 1998) the form was signed.

For TRICARE, the signature of physician or supplier, including degree(s) or credentials and the date of the signature, is necessary unless other authorized signatures are on file with the contractor.

Field 32: Name and Address of Facility Where Services Were Rendered (If Other Than Home or Office) Enter the name and address of the facility if services were furnished in a hospital, clinic, laboratory, or facility other than the patient's home or the physician's office.

For Medicare, when the name and address of the facility where the services were furnished is the same as the biller's name and address shown in field 33, enter the word "SAME." Providers of a service (namely physicians) must identify the supplier's name, address, and NPI when billing for purchased diagnostic tests. When more than one supplier is used, a separate CMS-1500 form should be used to bill each supplier. This field is completed whether supplier personnel performed the work at the physician's office or at another location.

If modifier QB or QU is billed, indicating the service was rendered in a health professional shortage area (HPSA), the physical location where the service was rendered must be entered if other than the patient's home. However, if the address shown in field 33 is in an HPSA and is the same as where the services were rendered, enter the word "SAME."

If the supplier is a certified mammography-screening center, enter the six-digit FDA-approved certification number.

Complete this field for all laboratory work performed outside a physician's office. If an independent laboratory is billing, enter the place where the test was performed and the NPI, including the two-digit location identifier.

Field 33: Physician's, Supplier's Billing Name, Address, Zip Code, and Telephone Number Enter the physician and/or supplier's billing name, address, zip code, and telephone number.

For Medicare, enter the NPI, including the two-digit location identifier, for the performing physician who is not a member of a group practice. Enter the group NPI, including the two-digit location identifier, for the performing physician who is a member of a group practice. For TRICARE, enter the provider number. For private plans, enter the provider number for the plan.

Insurance Claim Processing Cycles

The number of insurance claims generated depends on your practice's volume of patients seen, type of services provided, and third-party payer mix. Based on the volume of claims, each practice must determine its individual "insurance claim billing cycle." Some practices generate claims at the end of each day, while others process claims only once a week. Keep in mind that the sooner a claim is generated and submitted, the faster the insurance plan is likely to process it.

Filing Primary Insurance Claims

Insurance claims must be filed for patients covered by Medicare, Medicaid, workers' compensation, and most managed care plans, as required by law or the plan's contract with the physician. A medical office generally files primary insurance claims for all services provided as a courtesy to the patient.

To generate a claim form for every patient account that is to be billed to insurance, the insurance processing manager bills by account number, insurance plan, or patient last name, using the "from" and "to" data fields to define the range of patients to be billed. The computer system then generates claims for patients meeting the selection criteria.

Once generated, the forms are separated and organized by insurance company name and address. The way in which the claims are selected impacts the amount of manual sorting needed by the office staff to mail out the claims.

Before mailing insurance claims, staff should make sure all forms from the patients required by insurance companies have been completed and mailed. For example, some insurance plans have their own authorization statement that must be signed by the patient and submitted to the insurance company before the physician can be paid. If another physician within an HMO or PPO referred a patient, make sure the appropriate referral forms have been completed and mailed, if applicable. Many managed care plans require the primary care physician to complete a physician referral form when a patient is referred to a specialist. To be paid, the specialist's offices must attach the form to their own insurance claim.

Filing Secondary Insurance Claims

Most medical practices also file secondary insurance claims for their patients. Secondary insurance policies generally cover the services or patient responsibilities not covered by primary insurance plans. In most cases, these types of policies act as a supplement to Medicare coverage. Medicare supplemental insurance, or a Medigap policy, is a health insurance plan designed specifically to fill in some of the gaps in Medicare coverage. All supplemental policies do not provide the same benefits. Some pay for the Medicare deductible and most pay the coinsurance amount. Some policies even cover a limited number of services not covered under the Medicare program.

An office must determine when a patient has a supplemental policy. If it does not, the office is likely to receive payment from Medicare and bill the patient for the coinsurance or deductible. Then, after waiting a period of time, the office finds out that the patient has not paid because he or she thought the office was filing the secondary insurance claim. This puts a strain on a practice's cash flow and creates older accounts receivable. The new patient information form must include a section that indicates if a secondary insurance policy is in force. In addition, front desk personnel should be trained to ask the patient if he or she has a supplemental policy, whether the patient is new or established.

The most important aspect of filing a patient's secondary insurance is timeliness. Because secondary insurance claims are for a relatively small amount of money, many practices do not file them in a timely manner. This delays the office's reimbursement and impedes its cash flow. It could also create inefficiencies because the collection personnel have to spend time collecting a large number of small-balance accounts.

Secondary insurance claims are submitted on the patient's behalf only after receiving notification from the primary insurance company as to the claim's disposition (ie, payment in full, partial payment, denials, etc). Usually within 30 days from claim receipt, the insurance carrier will send an EOB along with the payment to explain how the claim was processed.

An EOB accompanies the check from the insurance company and indicates all services submitted on the claim and how much of the charged amount for each service was:

- Approved for payment (ie, the allowance or allowable amount)
- Disallowed or contractually adjusted (ie, amount of allowance that is unrecoverable)
- Applied to the patient's annual deductible
- Applied to the patient's copayment responsibilities
- Reduced or denied with explanation of determination
- Applied to other sources, such as "withhold" fees in managed care plans

An EOB provides the practice with essential information about the patient's financial responsibilities and the coordination of benefits between multiple insurance plans. A sample EOB is shown in Figure 6-15. The actual EOB review process and payment posting is discussed later in this chapter; here we finalize how to process secondary insurance claims.

After the primary insurance EOB data have been posted in the transaction entry payment screen, the practice processes all patient accounts with secondary insurance plans

FIGURE 6-15
Explanation of Benefits

Participant Information:

Check #:	0123456789#
Participant:	Last, First
SS #:	987-65-4321
Group #:	00000

To assist us in serving you, please include participant information and patient's name when you direct inquiries to:

Claims Office
P.O. Box 00000
Anywhere, USA 00000
Telephone 999 888-9999

Explanation of Benefits

For services provided by: A.J. Johnson, MD

Patient/ Service	Service Date(s)	(A) Total − Charge	(B) Excluded − Amounts	(C) Not Payable − by Plan	(D) Co-insurance = Amount %	(E) Plan Paid Amount %
Last, F						
Office visit	02/17/06	56.00	11.00 EM	10.00 CA		35.00 100%
X-ray	02/17/06	268.00		250.00 DD	3.60 20%	14.40 80%
Lab	02/17/06	20.00		15.00 CA		5.00 100%
Totals		**344.00**	**11.00**	**275.00**	**3.60**	**54.40**

Payments made to:
03/05/05   A.J. Johnson, MD $54.40

Codes and Remarks

EM: This amount represents the discount that resulted from the patient using a preferred provider. The patient is not responsible for this amount.

CA: This is the patient's copayment amount for this charge. The patient is responsible for this amount.

DD: This amount was applied to the patient's deductible.

that continue to have an outstanding accounts receivable balance due. The billing system generates a claim that indicates the services provided and the amount paid by the other insurance plan. When submitting the secondary claim form, always attach a copy of the patient's EOB from the primary insurance company. The EOB assists the secondary payer in determining the coordination of benefits and ultimate patient responsibility.

Organizing Copies of Insurance Claim Forms

Depending on your billing system and whether your practice uses single-form or two-ply carbonless CMS-1500 forms, the practice may need to file copies of the claim forms generated. Most practices file copies of unpaid insurance claim forms in a centralized office location so that anyone can access the files and find unpaid insurance claims. Centralizing insurance claim forms allows for: (1) easy access when performing insurance follow-up procedures, (2) a quick review of the claim forms if such a review is required, and (3) easy tracing of unpaid claims to other source documents in the office.

For example, the hard copies of insurance claims should be traced to the computer-generated unpaid insurance report to ensure the report's accuracy. These hard copies can be used to trace to the patient's ledger accounts for internal control purposes. In this situation, insurance claim amounts must always agree with the patient's accounts receivable on the account ledger.

An easy way to centralize the unpaid forms is to keep the office copies in an alphabetical or numerical expandable folder until payment is received. For insurance claims that are filed electronically, the electronic claim submission edit report or a white paper printout of the actual insurance claim forms should be maintained in the centralized file.

As practical as this sounds, it may prove impractical for some medical offices. This is especially true for practices that file a large number of claim forms and for offices that file most of their claims electronically. Regardless of how an office files its claims, an important practice management goal is to make sure all unpaid insurance claim forms are maintained in one centralized location.

Medicare Supplemental Insurance Policy Letters

Supplemental policies are separate health plans provided by another insurer that serve as a secondary source of coverage. For example, Medigap plans are designed to supplement Medicare coinsurance, deductibles, and some noncovered or unpaid services from Medicare. Many Medicare patients have these policies.

Supplemental plans are to be billed after Medicare has made its determination on a claim. In many states, the Medicare carrier forwards a claim to the supplemental carrier on behalf of the patient if the physician is participating with Medicare. This is commonly referred to as crossover claims processing.

In other states, the patient is responsible for filing the claim with the carrier of the supplemental policy. In some cases, the practice submits the claim on behalf of the patient; in other cases, the patient submits the claim.

If your practice does not accept assignment on Medicare claims and a patient has a supplemental policy, the two sample letters shown in Figures 6-16 and 6-17 can be used to explain what the patient needs to do in each circumstance. Letters like these help to reduce the number of routine insurance calls to your office.

Deductible Letters

Often, patients are not sure whether they have met their annual deductible. Some patients can check online, or others may contact their plan to find out. However, for patients who are not sure, the sample letter shown in Figure 6-18 can be used to inform them about their deductible and the necessary payment they need to make to your practice.

FIGURE 6-16
Sample Letter for Billing a Supplemental Claim: Practice Will File

Dear Patient:

Supplemental policies are policies that pay for copayments, deductibles, and sometimes other services and procedures that are not paid by Medicare. They are billed for the part not paid for by your Medicare policy. This second billing may pay the majority, if not all, of the balance due our office after Medicare pays.

Should you have a supplemental insurance policy, we will be happy to submit a claim on your behalf once we receive your Explanation of Medicare Benefits and check. The Explanation of Medicare Benefits is the portion attached to your Medicare reimbursement check.

Any questions you have regarding payment of your claim should be directed to the Medicare office. Their toll-free number is 1-800-____-_____, or you may call our office and speak with the billing supervisor.

After the supplemental policy has made a determination on the claim, we will notify you if there is a remaining balance due.

Thank you.

Sincerely,

[Name of Office Manager or Physician]

FIGURE 6-17
Sample Letter for Billing a Supplemental Claim: Patient Will File

Dear Patient:

As required by law, we have submitted your Medicare insurance form for services we provided to you recently. In addition, you will find enclosed a completed insurance claim form for your supplemental policy. Upon receiving payment from Medicare, attach the Explanation of Medicare Benefits to the enclosed claim form before mailing it to your insurance carrier for processing.

Please do not send the form to the supplemental insurance company until you have been paid by Medicare and have attached the Explanation of Medicare Benefits to the form. Submitting the enclosed claim form without the Explanation of Medicare Benefits attached will result in a denied or delayed claim.

We are happy to provide our patients with this service. If you have any questions regarding this subject, please do not hesitate to call our office.

Sincerely,

[Name of Office Manager or Physician]

FIGURE 6-18
Sample Deductible Letter

Dear [Patient Name]:

Your insurance company has processed your claim in the amount of $_____ for services we provided to you on _____. A portion of the reimbursement was used to satisfy your annual deductible of $_____.

This means you are responsible for paying the first $_____ each year before your insurance begins making payments. You need to pay this amount to our office. This is shown on the enclosed Explanation of Medical [Medicare] Benefits stating the reimbursement paid by your insurance carrier to our office.

We appreciate your prompt attention to this bill. For your convenience, a return envelope is enclosed.

Sincerely,

[Name of Office Manager]

HANDLING BAD DEBTS

Most medical practices grant credit and subsequently collect on accounts receivable. Unfortunately, every business (or practice) has customers (or patients) who will not keep their promise to pay. Proper management of this bad debt enhances the provider's professional practice and relieves financial and personal stress.

Medical practices are vulnerable to bad debts. Medicine has been promoted to society as the caretaker and rescuer of the sick. Most physicians focus on the clinical side of the business and ignore or suppress their collection processes, thinking that will help ensure patient compliance and follow up, as their medical conditions require. Although physicians should not ignore or withhold necessary care from the underprivileged, they should be honest with themselves and their office staff as to how much they can give and yet remain financially viable. Likewise, patients who do have adequate financial resources should be held accountable for their agreed financial responsibility.

Some medical practices enter into financially unhealthy business arrangements with third-party payers that increase bad debt. Physicians often sign contracts without reading them thoroughly or asking for appropriate advice and help. Examples of onerous contract provisions agreed to by physicians are 90-day filing clauses, "hold harmless clauses" that absolve the patient of financial liability in the event of insurance company insolvency, and burdensome "hassle factor" procedures. These contractual requirements can increase bad debts that must be written off by the practice.

Continued, undisciplined provision of medical care to bad-debt patients has detrimental consequences to the physician, the practice, the patient, and the profession. The physician loses income necessary to maintain professional growth, emotional health, and a balanced lifestyle. The practice loses revenue necessary to maintain professional employees, purchase needed equipment, and meet office expenses. Patients who do not pay can also develop a sense of entitlement that transfers to and disrupts other parts of the patient-physician relationship. The profession suffers because it maintains charges that are higher than necessary to support this bad debt. These consequences can build fear, anger, and insecurity in the practice, inhibiting its operations and possibly leading to financial failure or ruin.

Patients may give the following reasons for not paying their medical bills:

- Medical care is too expensive.
- The care rendered is believed to be inappropriate or ineffective.
- A bill was never received due to inaccurate mailing address or insurance billing address.
- The patient misunderstands the level of reimbursement from the third parties.
- The patient is experiencing personal financial problems.
- The patient expects that medical care should be rendered for free.

Bad debts can be identified at any time. Accounts receivable that are more than 60 days old (or more than two billing cycles) should be considered bad unless a proper reason has been given or communication has occurred. Because the collectability of an account diminishes over time, past-due accounts should be addressed proactively.

The Collection Effort

The collection effort begins with the development of and adherence to the practice's collection policy (see Figure 6-19). This policy defines to the patient the rules the practice will follow in collecting accounts. Payment expectations must be clearly conveyed to the patient prior to his or her first visit. It must be written prospectively, agreed to by the providers, communicated to the staff, and implemented consistently for it to be effective.

The collection effort is most effective when it occurs while the patient is in the office. Many practices are afraid to ask their patients to pay their accounts. However, most patients will make some effort to pay their debt if the practice's staff asks politely but firmly.

Subsequent telephone calls and collection letters reminding patients of their debts and the practice's financial policy are important. Frequently, the patient will claim to have never received a bill or statement. Returned letters and notification of disconnected telephone service confirm the inaccuracy of billing information within the practice. Excuses or reasons for nonpayment must be considered. In a polite but firm voice, the caller should develop an agreement by which the patient will pay his or her account and then document the agreement in the billing record and in a confirmation letter to the patient. Consequences for noncompliance must be communicated to the patient at this time.

Collection efforts must follow all federal, state, and local laws. For instance, there are "blackout" times in most areas when telephone calls for collection efforts cannot be made. Collection letters (see Figure 6-20) should be professionally written and should not use abusive language. Failure to comply exposes the practice to lawsuit or ridicule.

The Collection Agency

If continued nonpayment occurs despite internal collection efforts, bad debts should be turned over to a collection agency. They should not be written off, particularly if payment is still anticipated. A special account or other subsidiary account of the accounts receivable should be used to control these collections.

Because use of collection agencies has financial and emotional consequences to the patient, each collection account and medical record must be prospectively reviewed by the affected provider. The practice may have a valid medicolegal reason for opting not to use a collection agency.

Collection agencies are available in most communities. Local medical societies often endorse agencies that meet professional standards. An agency should be chosen based on its professional service, pricing, and sensitivity to health care issues. Often, practices use more than one agency based on their specific needs.

FIGURE 6-19
Sample Collection Policy

Collection Agencies
The Hometown Clinic will use all reasonable means to collect owed funds. Defaults in payment of agreed amounts will be automatically referred to a collection agency for payment.

Responsibilities of the Patient
The patient is to contact the insurance company and/or other third parties for necessary precertifications needed for insurance or third-party payment prior to the office visit. The patient likewise must familiarize himself or herself with the precertification requirements of the third-party payer for services rendered out of the office. A telephone number on the back of the insurance card can usually be used to obtain this information.

At each office visit or patient encounter, the patient will provide a current mailing address and telephone number as well as current third-party information necessary for billing purposes. This information must be given primarily to a billing representative or receptionist. The doctor or nurse will need to know the identity of the insurance company to make proper referrals under the managed care contract; thus, proper identification is mandatory.

After each office visit or within one week of hospital discharge, the patient will speak with a receptionist or billing representative to make payment arrangements for the services rendered.

The patient is to contact his or her insurance company if payment is not made within 60 days.

The patient is to immediately make total payment when the debt is due.

The patient is to proactively prospectively discuss extenuating circumstances with the Clinic.

Responsibilities of the Clinic
The Clinic will provide an accurate statement of charges on the day of office service or within one week of hospital discharge.

The Clinic will make a best effort to obtain necessary precertifications for requested procedures required by contracted third parties to facilitate approval for payment thereof. Failure to obtain precertifications or approval from the insurance company does not necessarily mean that the requested procedure is not medically necessary; in this circumstance, the patient may be financially responsible for services ordered or rendered.

Upon receiving accurate third party information, the clinic will file an appropriate AMA-approved claim to the appropriate entity (eg, insurance company, employer, workers' compensation plan). The Clinic will make a good-faith effort in concert with the patient to follow up these claims to facilitate payment.

The Clinic will uniformly and fairly enforce this policy and procedure upon all patients.

I attest that I have read this financial policy and procedure and have been given an opportunity to ask questions. I accept this policy and procedure and will comply with it as part of my professional relationship with the Clinic.

_____   _____
Patient or Responsible Party   Date

_____   _____
Witness   Patient's Name

FIGURE 6-19 (*continued*)

Collection Agencies
The Hometown Clinic will use all reasonable means to collect owed funds. Defaults in payment of agreed amounts will be automatically referred to a collection agency for payment.

Responsibilities of the Patient
The patient is to contact the insurance company and/or other third parties for necessary precertifications needed for insurance or third-party payment prior to the office visit. The patient likewise must familiarize himself or herself with the precertification requirements of the third-party payer for services rendered out of the office. A telephone number on the back of the insurance card can usually be used to obtain this information.

At each office visit or patient encounter, the patient will provide a current mailing address and telephone number as well as current third-party information necessary for billing purposes. This information must be given primarily to a billing representative or receptionist. The doctor or nurse will need to know the identity of the insurance company to make proper referrals under the managed care contract; thus, proper identification is mandatory.

After each office visit or within one week of hospital discharge, the patient will speak with a receptionist or billing representative to make payment arrangements for the services rendered.

The patient is to contact his or her insurance company if payment is not made within 60 days.

The patient is to immediately make total payment when the debt is due.

The patient is to proactively prospectively discuss extenuating circumstances with the Clinic.

Responsibilities of the Clinic
The Clinic will provide an accurate statement of charges on the day of office service or within one week of hospital discharge.

The Clinic will make a best effort to obtain necessary precertifications for requested procedures required by contracted third parties to facilitate approval for payment thereof. Failure to obtain precertifications or approval from the insurance company does not necessarily mean that the requested procedure is not medically necessary; in this circumstance, the patient may be financially responsible for services ordered or rendered.

Upon receiving accurate third party information, the clinic will file an appropriate AMA-approved claim to the appropriate entity (eg, insurance company, employer, workers' compensation plan). The Clinic will make a good-faith effort in concert with the patient to follow up these claims to facilitate payment.

The Clinic will uniformly and fairly enforce this policy and procedure upon all patients.

I attest that I have read this financial policy and procedure and have been given an opportunity to ask questions. I accept this policy and procedure and will comply with it as part of my professional relationship with the Clinic.

_____   _____
Patient or Responsible Party   Date

_____   _____
Witness   Patient's Name

FIGURE 6-20

Sample Overdue Letter

HOMETOWN CLINIC
111 Main Street
HOMETOWN, STATE 00000

To: Mr. Joe Patient
     121 Main Street
     Hometown, State 00000

Account: 00000

Dear Mr. Patient:

Review of our records shows that you have a seriously overdue account with our clinic of

$ _____. Please remit this balance to us immediately.

If you do not believe this amount is correct, please contact our office by telephone immediately so that this account can be reconciled.

Our collection policy states that if this account is not reconciled within thirty (30) days, we will employ a collection agency to assist in its collection.

Thank you for your prompt attention to this very important matter.

Sincerely,

Suzie B. Manager

The Fair Credit Reporting Act

The Fair Credit Reporting Act (FCRA) is designed to protect the privacy of credit report information and to guarantee that information supplied by consumer reporting agencies (CRAs) is as accurate as possible. The FCRA requires that CRAs adopt reasonable procedures for meeting the needs of commerce for consumer credit, personnel, insurance, and other information in a manner that is fair and equitable to the consumer, with regard to the confidentiality, accuracy, relevancy, and proper utilization of such information. CRAs include many types of databases, eg, medical information services or credit bureaus, that collect information to help businesses evaluate consumers. If you report information about consumers to a CRA, you are considered a "furnisher" of information under the FCRA, and the CRA must send you a notice of your responsibilities.

The following extract is a summary of providers' responsibilities under FCRA. (The full publication, *Credit Reports: What Information Providers Need to Know,* can be accessed at www.ftc.gov/bcp/conline/pubs/buspubs/infopro.htm.) Items 2 and 5 of this extracted material apply only to furnishers who "regularly and in the ordinary course of their business" provide information to CRAs. All information providers must comply with the other responsibilities listed.

1. General Prohibition on Reporting Inaccurate Information—Section 623(a)(1)(A) and Section 623(a)(1)(C).

You may not furnish information that you know—or consciously avoid knowing—is inaccurate. If you "clearly and conspicuously" provide consumers with an address for dispute notices, you are exempt from this obligation but subject to the duties discussed in Item 3.

What does "clear and conspicuous" mean? Reasonably easy to read and understand. For example, a notice buried in a mailing is not clear or conspicuous.

2. Correcting and Updating Information—Section 623(a)(2).

If you discover that you've supplied one or more CRAs with incomplete or inaccurate information, you must correct it, resubmit to each CRA, and report only the correct information in the future.

3. Responsibilities After Notice of a Consumer Dispute From a Consumer—Sections 623(A)(1)(B) and 623(a)(3).

If a consumer writes to the address you specify for disputes to challenge the accuracy of any information you furnished and if the information is, in fact, inaccurate, you must report only the correct information to CRAs in the future. If you are a regular furnisher, you also will have to satisfy the duties in Item 2.

Once a consumer has given notice that he or she disputes information, you may not give that information to any CRA without also telling the CRA that the information is in dispute.

4. Responsibilities After Receiving Notice From a Consumer Reporting—Section 623(b).

If a CRA notifies you that a consumer disputes information you provided:

- You must investigate the dispute and review all relevant information provided by the CRA about the dispute.
- You must report your findings to the CRA.
- If your investigation shows the information to be incomplete or inaccurate, you must provide corrected information to all national CRAs that received the information.
- You should complete these steps within the time period that the FCRA sets out for the CRA to resolve the dispute—normally 30 days after receipt of a dispute notice from the consumer. If the consumer provides additional relevant information during the 30-day period, the CRA has 15 days more. The CRA must give you all relevant information that it gets within five business days of receipt and must promptly give you additional relevant information provided from the consumer. If you do not investigate and respond within the specified time periods, the CRA must delete the disputed information from its files.

5. Reporting Voluntary Account Closings—Section 623(a)(4).

You must notify CRAs when consumers voluntarily close credit accounts. This is important because some information users may interpret a closed account as an indicator of bad credit unless it is clearly disclosed that the consumer—not the creditor—closed the account.

6. Reporting Delinquencies—Section 623(a)(5).

If you report information about a delinquent account that is placed for collection, charged to profit or loss, or subject to any similar action, you must, within 90 days after you report the information, notify the CRA of the month and the year of the commencement of the delinquency that immediately preceded your action. This will ensure that CRAs use the correct date when computing how long derogatory information can be kept in a consumer's file.

How do you report accounts that you have charged off or placed for collection? For example:

- *A consumer becomes delinquent on March 15, 1998. The creditor places the account for collection on October 1, 1998.*

  In this case, the delinquency began on March 15, 1998. The date that the creditor places the account for collection has no significance for calculating how long the account can stay on the consumer's credit report. In this case, the date that must be reported to CRAs within 90 days after you first report the collection action is "March 1998."

- *A consumer falls behind on monthly payments in January 1998, brings the account current in June 1998, pays on time and in full every month through October 1998, and thereafter makes no payments. The creditor charges off the account in December 1999.*

  In this case, the most recent delinquency began when the consumer failed to make the payment due in November 1998. The earlier delinquency is irrelevant. The creditor must report the November 1998 date within 90 days of reporting the charge-off. For example, if the creditor charges off the account in December 1999, and reports this charge-off on December 31, 1999, the creditor must provide the month and year of the delinquency (ie, "November 1998") within 90 days of December 31, 1999.

- *A consumer's account becomes delinquent on December 15, 1997. The account is first placed for collection on April 1, 1998. Collection is not successful. The merchant places the account with a second collection agency on June 1, 2003.*

  The date of the delinquency for reporting purposes is "December 1997." Repeatedly placing an account for collection does not change the date that the delinquency began.

- *A consumer's credit account becomes delinquent on April 15, 1998. The consumer makes partial payments for the next five months but never brings the account current. The merchant places the account for collection in May 1999.*

  Since the account was never brought current during the period that partial payments were made, the delinquency that immediately preceded the collection commenced in April 1998 when the consumer first became delinquent.

Writing Off Bad Debt

Accounts that are more than 365 days old generally have a low chance of collection. Each provider and practice must decide what debt it should write off and whether it should continue to render professional service to patients with bad debt. This should follow local community professional standards.

SUMMARY

Effectively managing the claims processing function is essential for the success of every practice. It is particularly important to accurately collect patient data and related insurance information and to accurately complete insurance claim forms prior to the initial submission. A practice can save staff labor, time, and resources and improve on its receivables management by accurately collecting patient information and accurately filing claims the first time they are submitted for payment. A claim is less likely to be denied for missing information or inaccurate claim form information if a practice is able to do this. In addition, the majority of claims will be paid on the first submission it's the post-claim process will be much easier to manage. A practice can realize numerous efficiencies and will greatly reduce its volume of claims that goes to the collection processes. Additionally, practice cash flow will steady and receivables balances will remain more stable without dramatic increases in volume of accounts due to denials.

ENDNOTE

1. www.ama-assn.org/physlegl/legal/patient

chapter

7

After Submission of Claims

OBJECTIVES

- Understand third-party reimbursements.
- Interpret explanations of benefits (EOBs) and post payments.
- Improve management of accounts receivable.
- Understand how to handle difficult patient accounts.

The back office functions of insurance processing challenge even the most experienced physicians and their staffs. The success of most back office functions relies heavily on the success of the front office functions: ensuring the patient's understanding of his or her financial responsibilities and the practice's payment policies and procedures; collection of patient and insurance data; verification of information; and accurate coding and billing. It can be viewed that the account of a patient properly admitted is already half collected.

UNDERSTANDING THIRD-PARTY REIMBURSEMENTS

The amount a physician or patient is reimbursed for a service depends in part on the patient's insurance benefits. Traditional insurers often reimburse 80% of an agreed-upon fee schedule, with the patient paying 20% and possibly more to fully satisfy the physician's charge. Under managed care plans, patients typically pay fixed copayments of $5 to $50 (which vary, in part, depending upon whether the physician is in-network or out-of-network), with the remainder adjudicated by the insurance company. In most cases, patients are required to meet plan deductibles before the payer reimburses for the procedure or service.

The approved amount allowed for a service can vary from payer to payer, depending on the payer's reimbursement policy and/or fee schedule. (Physician practices are encouraged to obtain a copy of the insurer's fee schedule, preferably organized by CPT code.) Fees received from a patient covered by a health maintenance organization (HMO), preferred provider organization (PPO), or independent practice associations (IPA) may be based on a contract or on a capitation basis. Medicare has its own resource-based revenue value system fee schedule.

The following examples illustrate reimbursement of two payers: a commercial carrier and Medicare.

COMMERCIAL PAYER: EXAMPLE 1

Dr Smith charges $200 for a specific procedure. The patient's insurance company allows $187 and pays 80% of the allowable, or $149.60. Dr Smith does not have a negotiated contract with this insurance company. The patient has previously met her deductible and would thus be responsible for the difference (the copayment). Payment would be as follows:

Dr Smith's charge	$200.00	
Insurance payment	$149.60	
Patient coinsurance	$ 37.40	Amount due from patient $50.40
Remainder due	$ 13.00	

Dr Smith is obligated to collect the full amount of the $200 charge.

COMMERCIAL PAYER: EXAMPLE 2 (OUT-OF-NETWORK)

Using example 2, if the patient had previously met his deductible, payments would be as follows:

Dr Jones' charge	$50.00	
Insurance payment	$38.40	
Patient coinsurance	$ 9.60	Patient responsibility is $9.60
Contractual adjustment	$ 2.00	

In this example, the insurance company pays $38.40, the patient pays $9.60, and the physician writes off $2. The insurance company pays 80% of the allowed amount, or 80% of $48.

COMMERCIAL PAYER: EXAMPLE 3 (OUT-OF-NETWORK)

Dr Parsons provides a $100 service to a patient. Dr Parsons has a contract requiring he accept UCR minus 10% as his full fee. The patient's insurance states that $100 is UCR for this service and reimburses on the 80/20 basis. The patient has met her deductible. Payment would be as follows:

Dr Parsons' charge	$100.00
Approved charge	$ 90.00
Insurance payment	$ 72.00
Patient coinsurance	$ 18.00
Contractual adjustment	$ 10.00

In this example, the amount allowed by the insurance company is the same as the physician's charge. The insurance company pays $72, the patient pays $18, and the physician writes off $10.

COMMERCIAL PAYER: EXAMPLE 4 (IN-NETWORK)

Dr Black charges $300 for a specific procedure performed in her office. The fee schedule with the insurance company for this procedure is $120. The patient's copayments for office visits are $20. Payment would be as follows:

Dr Black's charge	$300.00
Insurance payment	$100.00
Patient payment	$ 20.00
Contractual adjustment	$180.00

Providers should beware of insurance companies that pay discounted amounts without a contractual agreement authorizing the reduced payments. These "silent PPOs" should be challenged and reported to the state insurance commissioner.

Because Medicare reimburses on the basis of the Medicare fee schedule (MFS), charges and limits on charges are fixed. Physicians who participate in the Medicare program always accept assignment and agree to accept the MFS amounts for participating physicians minus deductibles and copayments as payment in full. Physicians who elect non-participating physician status can accept or decline assignment for Medicare claims.

MFS-allowed amounts for nonparticipating physicians are set at an amount 5% lower than that provided to participating physicians. If the nonparticipating physician does not accept assignment on a claim, the total charge is limited to 115% of Medicare's participating allowed amount. A charge submitted in excess of the Medicare limiting charge is considered a violation of the charge limit. A provider found violating this limit is subject to fines of up to $10,000 per violation, plus triple the violative charges and possible exclusion from the Medicare program. Fee schedules for participating and nonparticipating physicians, including limiting charges, are published annually and available from the local carrier. A practice can obtain a fee schedule from Medicare by contacting its Medicare carrier.

Patients covered by Medicare must meet an annual outpatient deductible of $124 for 2006 ($110 for 2005) before Medicare will pay 80% of the allowed fee schedule amount, with the beneficiary responsible for the remaining 20%. Providers must contractually adjust or write off any amount greater than the approved charge. Balance billing above the approved charge is not permitted.

INTERPRETING EXPLANATION OF BENEFITS AND PAYMENT POSTING

Payments received in the office, either from insurance plans or from patients, must be posted to the patient's account. Insurance payments received through the mail or electronically are typically accompanied by an explanation of benefits (EOB). Payments from patients are received through the mail and at the time of the office visits. Payment is typically posted using a computerized billing system or on the individual patient account system is used. A tracking

MEDICARE: EXAMPLE 1

Dr Jones is *participating* with Medicare. She bills $125 for a service provided to a Medicare patient. The patient has previously met her deductible, and the MFS amount for the service is $100. Payment would be as follows:

Dr Jones' charge	$125.00
Medicare payment	$ 80.00
Patient coinsurance	$ 20.00
Amount of write-off	$ 25.00

Dr Jones can collect a maximum of $100 from the patient and Medicare combined, because $100 is the MFS amount. The difference, $25, would be written off of Dr Jones' receivables as a contractual adjustment. Participating physicians are allowed to charge more than the fee schedule amount even though they may only collect the amount specified by the fee schedule.

MEDICARE: EXAMPLE 2

Dr Smith does *not participate* with Medicare but is *accepting assignment* on this patient's claim. Although Dr Smith normally charges $325 to commercial carriers for the service provided to the patient, the MFS limiting charge amount that applies to nonparticipating physicians for the service is $267.65. Thus, Dr Smith can collect no more than $267.65 from the Medicare beneficiary. The patient has already met his Medicare deductible for the year. Payment would be as follows:

Dr Smith's charge	$267.65
Medicare's payment	$214.12
Patient coinsurance	$ 53.53
Remainder	$ 0.00

MEDICARE: EXAMPLE 3

Dr Parsons does *not participate* with Medicare and *does not accept assignment* on a patient's claim. The patient has met her annual deductible. Dr Parsons must restrict his charge for the service to the limiting charge amount provided on the MFS, $67.43. For the service provided, Medicare will allow an amount equal to that given a nonparticipating physician who accepts assignment, or $58.63. Payment would be as follows:

Dr Parsons' charge	$67.43
Medicare's payment	$46.91
Patient coinsurance	$20.52
Remainder	$ 0.00

Medicare will pay 80% of the allowed MFS amount. In this example, the patient is responsible for the difference between Dr Parsons' charge and the amount of the Medicare payment. Recall that Dr Parsons had to limit his charge to $67.43, the MFS amount that a nonparticipating physician is allowed to charge for the service when not accepting assignment.

system of accounts receivable (payments, contractual adjustments, write-offs) as well as carrier denials needs to be used to monitor reimbursement patterns and trends. A sample EOB is shown in Figure 7-1. Definitions of the terms used in the sample EOB can be accessed at www.tricare.osd.mil/eob/eob_statement.cfm.

Preposting Operations

Before posting an insurance payment to a patient's account, the practice should perform and document the following actions:

1. Compare the EOB with the original insurance claim and review each carefully. All services reported on the claim form should be represented on the EOB. (Some insurance EOBs list services by line item, while others provide a single line-item determination for all services.) Look for changes in CPT® coding by the insurance company (eg, determine if a service was downcoded or recoded). The goal is to identify charges that can be appealed or rebilled for payment.

2. Investigate all denied services, determine the reason for the denial, and appeal them, if appropriate. (Denials are usually indicated with zeros in the allowed amount or amount paid data field on the EOBs.)

3. Appeal all payment reductions based on the insurance company's UCR charge amount. Insurance companies use regional charge databases to inform a physician when the charge submitted exceeds the UCR norm. Unfortunately, the UCR data are often payer-specific, meaning that they are not the same for all insurers. Each insurance company may have its own UCR. The insurer will send a UCR letter explaining why the insurance company reduced the physician's fee and why the company believes the fee is too high for the practice area. However, unless the payer can provide appropriate documentation that the UCR is appropriate, the physician does not need to accept this amount. Also, do not bill at each insurance UCR. Uniform billing should be done for each service to all payers.

4. Address a payers request for additional information that appears on the EOB immediately. The goal is to get paid by the insurance company as quickly as possible. Each insurer also has a time limit on claim rectification.

Upon receipt, carefully post the information contained on the EOB to the computer or manual patient ledger card. An error in the posting process may cause the patient's account balance to be incorrect. Tracking EOBs by carrier helps to monitor similar payments for similar procedures and diagnoses.

Contractual Adjustments

After the EOB has been carefully reviewed, the insurance payment should be posted to the patient's account. On the patient's account balance record, the office must account for the difference between the charge submitted on the claim and the amount allowed contractually, always specifically identifying the type of adjustment made (eg, Medicaid, HMO or PPO, or a UCR reduction) in the patient record.

These types of adjustments generally are called *contractual adjustments*. A contractual adjustment is the difference between what a practice bills and what it is legally entitled to collect. For example, if a physician's normal fee is $1200 for a specific service and he or she has signed with a PPO that has a contractual reimbursement of only $1000 for the same service, the contractual adjustment is $200. It is important to ensure that contractual adjustments shown on the EOB are in accordance with the contract. It is not uncommon to see contractual discounts in error taken by payers for which the physician has approved no previous discount agreement.

Note: A practice should never lump all adjustments into an account called *credit adjustments*. Specifically identifying contractual adjustments and other write-offs is necessary to allow for analysis of trends and to more easily identify problems.

FIGURE 7-1
TRICARE Explanation of Benefits

PGBA or WPS
TRICARE Claims Administrator for Your Region

Prime Contractor

TRICARE EXPLANATION OF BENEFITS
This is a statement of the action taken on your TRICARE Claim.
Keep this notice for your records.

Date of Notice:	August 02, 2000
Sponsor SSN:	000-00-0000
Sponsor Name:	NAME OF SPONSOR
Beneficiary Name:	NAME OF BENEFICIARY

Benefits were payable to:

PATIENT, PARENT/GUARDIAN
ADDRESS
CITY STATE ZIP CODE

PROVIDER OF MEDICAL CARE
ADDRESS
CITY STATE ZIP CODE

Claim Number: 919533693-00-00

Services Provided By Date of Services		Services Provided		Amount Billed	TRICARE Approved	See Remarks
PROVIDER OF MEDICAL CARE						
07/08/2000	1	Office/outpatient visit, est	(99213)	$ 45.00	$ 38.92	1
07/08/2000	1	Comprehen metabolic panel	(88054)	20.00	19.33	1
07/08/2000	1	Automated hemogram	(85025)	12.00	12.00	1
Totals:				**$ 77.00**	**$ 70.25**	

Claim Summary		Beneficiary Liability Summary		Benefit Period Summary		
				Fiscal Year Beginning:		
Amount billed:	77.00	Deductible	0.00	October 01, 1999		
TRICARE Approved:	70.25	Copayment:	0.00		Individual	Family
Non-Covered:	6.75	Cost Share	17.56	Deductible:	150.00	150.00
Paid by Beneficiary:	0.00			Catastrophic Cap:		
Other Insurance:	0.00			**Enrollment Year Beginning:**		
Paid to Provider:	52.69			**December 01, 1999**		
Paid to Beneficiary:	0.00				Individual	Family
Check Number:				POS Deductible:	300.00	600.00
				Prime Cap:		856.32

Remarks

1 – CHARGES ARE MORE THAN ALLOWABLE AMOUNT

1-888-XXX-XXXX

THIS IS NOT A BILL
If you have questions regarding this notice, please call or write us at the telephone number/address listed above

Source: www.tricare.osd.mil/eob/eob_statement.cfm

Specific identification of contractual adjustments by payer alerts a practice to the insurance programs that are reducing charges the most. If a practice is writing off a large amount for a specific insurance plan, the appropriate staff member should investigate and determine whether it makes sense to continue with that insurance plan. At the same time, the practice should determine if such write-offs are reasonable and, if so, whether they can be reduced. Specifically identifying write-offs is also a smart way to account for withholding adjustments made by managed care plans.

Withhold Adjustments

A *withhold* is an amount withheld from a physician's reimbursement that may or may not be reimbursed, depending on the managed care plan's criteria for reimbursement. For example, if a physician's normal charge for a procedure is $1000 and he or she has signed a managed care contract that will only reimburse $800 for the same procedure, the managed care plan will approve $800 for payment and may subtract another 10% as a withhold adjustment. Therefore, the practice receives a check for $720 instead of $800. The $80 withheld should be accounted for separately in the office's computer system or other means of documentation if the practice uses a manual system.

At the end of the year, a practice should review how much was withheld by each managed care plan and then appeal for reimbursement of the withhold. If a plan does not reimburse the withhold, a plan representative should be asked to explain the plan's withhold policy. Written criteria that describe the withhold and indications for withhold should be provided at the beginning of the contractual period. It is necessary to reconfirm that there will be no changes at the anniversary of each contract period. For particular plans that do not reimburse the withhold, the practice must be aware that the true discounted amount is not actually the approved amount and that it is also reduced by the plan withhold. An office should never write off the withhold amounts or any claim that has been denied by an insurance company until the issue has been fully investigated by the office manager.

Fractional Payment of the Allowed Charge

After accounting for contractual adjustments and other reductions, an insurance plan usually pays only a fraction of the allowed charge. Medicare, for example, pays 80% of the allowed amount. Some indemnity plans pay 90%. The amount paid by the insurance plan should be posted to the patient's account in the computer or on a manual ledger account card. In particular in out-of-network situations, the balance of the account is the patient's responsibility. The patient portion should be identified in his or her contract. A patient must know his or her responsibility before care is rendered.

If the account balance is not paid, it should be billed in the next round of monthly statements. The office must pay close attention to the amount the patient is responsible for when posting insurance payments. This amount should be identified clearly when posting payment and contractual adjustments in the computer or on the patient's manual ledger account card. If errors are made during the posting process, the aging of accounts will be unreliable. Also, when patients' statements are mailed, they may contain incorrect balances due, which is likely to upset patients. In most cases, a patient's insurance plan will also send the patient their copies of the EOB.

Filing the EOBs

After EOBs are posted, they should be filed with the respective copies of insurance claim forms either in the patient's clinical file or in a separate business file set up for each patient. Some offices find it more efficient to maintain individual EOBs in notebooks referenced by the insurance company. Insurance claim forms and related EOBs must be kept together so that the practice can easily audit a patient's account history when the need arises. In addition, copies of all EOBs should be organized in a way that allows the office manager or billing supervisor to review them for consistency in payment on a periodic basis.

CONCLUSION

Understanding the processes that follow the submission of claims is critical in managing the reimbursement process. Staff members must understand third-party reimbursement, including how to interpret and handle the EOB to ensure proper amounts are being paid for the services rendered. Reviews should be conducted and internal controls put in place to ensure that payments and adjustments are properly posted to a patient's account and that the proper amounts have been paid by the appropriate source for services. If a practice adequately addresses these issues, its management of accounts will not only be more effective but also will be less time consuming and require fewer resources. The overall result of understanding and applying the information presented in this chapter is improved revenue collection and reduced compliance risks.

chapter

8

Managing Insurance Accounts Receivable

OBJECTIVES

- Understand what is needed to accurately prepare accounts receivable reports.
- Recognize the different types of accounts receivable follow-up letters and know when to include letters for claim inquiry on an assigned claim, for claim inquiry on an unassigned claim, and for inquiry to an insurance commissioner.

Coding and billing are important parts of the reimbursement process and tracking amounts due and payments received is critical to ensuring proper reimbursement. When insurance information is verified, it is also necessary to determine if the patient's deductible is met. Claims processing may be delayed if a practice must first determine if the charges of other providers (eg, hospital) apply to the deductible. The ability to determine and separate accounts receivable (A/R) responsibilities (ie, insurance and patient) improves a practice's ability to manage cash flow and more readily achieve an overall reduction in A/R.

The purpose of the A/R process is to collect the total amounts due from the insurance plan and the patient in the shortest time possible. To efficiently manage this process, practices must develop a systematic way to define all A/R collection activities. This is done using priority parameters to sort claims. In addition, protocols should be set for printing aging reports, and responsibilities assigned to appropriate staff members. Protocols for follow-up letters and collection agency referrals should also be established.

A/R REPORT PREPARATION

Most computer billing systems provide powerful A/R reporting capabilities that enable a practice to generate A/R reports based on different selection criteria, eg, account number, patient name, age of account (30, 60, 90 days, etc), account or insurance type, and balance due amount. Unfortunately, these reports are often underutilized, making the follow-up and collection processes even more difficult to manage. Most practices use either the patient account number or the patient last name to sort practice A/R reports. However, priority parameters that represent the different categories or data fields can serve as the primary A/R sort specification.

Instead of printing A/R reports by patient account number or name, practices should consider prioritizing accounts based on a combination of the following:

- Balance due (highest to lowest)
- Aging of account
- Account type, payer type, or insurance plan

- Financial responsibility (insurance vs patient)
- Date of claim submission or date of service

Prioritizing

Accounts are prioritized for a number of reasons. First, all practices have limited staff and practice management resources. By focusing on the accounts with the highest outstanding balances, any problems with these claims can be quickly identified and resolved by re-billing, thereby yielding a greater overall recovery. For example, some practices prioritize accounts in the following way:

1. Greater than $5000
2. $4000 to $4999
3. $3000 to $3999
4. $2000 to $2999
5. $1000 to $1999
6. $500 to $999
7. $100 to $499
8. $50 to $99
9. $1 to $49

Second, the longer an account remains in A/R, the probability of collecting the full amount falls dramatically.

By sorting A/R reports into account aging "buckets" (ie, 30, 60, 90, 120, etc), the practice can focus on the oldest accounts. Some practices print separate A/R reports by aging category (eg, accounts greater than 120 days) or from the oldest to youngest aging bucket.

Third, problems for different claims are frequently based on similar circumstances, which are related to the type of account. For example, if the practice billed a wrong CPT® code to Medicare for all patients, all beneficiary accounts affected may have A/R problems. Each account would need to be reviewed. When communicating with certain types of insurance companies to follow up on A/R problems, practice staff may want to organize the accounts into similar categories, account types, payer types, or specific insurance plans.

Fourth, identifying the reason for an A/R problem is difficult if the practice cannot separate patient responsibility from insurance responsibility. This often occurs because insurance was not verified before services were rendered. A/R systems that can track and separate out insurance and patient responsibility by A/R report are available and should be considered.

Time Value of Money

Most A/R report formats can be reprogrammed by either the office staff or software technical support group to facilitate the practice's desire to recover more A/R. Large A/R balances may result in the need to borrow money to cover a cash flow deficit. The *time value* of money (how much it actually costs the practice) can be calculated in the following way:

$$\text{amount owed} \times (\text{days owed} \div 365) \times \text{interest rate of a money market account}$$

For example, if $100 is owed for 120 days at an interest rate of 3% annually, the amount lost, if collected today, is:

$$\$100 \times (120 \div 365) \times 0.03 = \$0.99 \text{ or } 1\% \text{ of the total amount of the bill}$$

If a practice grosses $300,000 annually, it is losing about $3000 annually.

FOLLOW-UP OF UNPAID INSURANCE CLAIMS

The methods described in the following paragraphs can be used to collect on unpaid insurance claims. Tables 8-1 and 8-2 illustrate the system.

TABLE 8-1

Insurance Responses and Explanations to Unpaid Insurance Claims

- The claim is not on file. (This is the most common response.)
- Insurance is pending information.
  - Insurance carrier pended claim awaiting information from the insured.
  - Insurance carrier pended claim awaiting medical records from the provider.
  - Insurance carrier pended claim awaiting an outside audit.
  - Insurance carrier pended claim awaiting repricing from another company.
- Insurance carrier has processed the claim and the insured is responsible for the balance.
  - Balance was applied to patient's deductible or coinsurance.
  - Benefits have been exhausted or no coverage exists.
  - Claim was denied due to preexisting conditions.
  - Services rendered and items billed were not covered under the plan.
  - Policy was rescinded.
  - Insurance paid the insured.
- Insurance carrier denied claim.
  - Prior authorization was not obtained.
  - Claim denied for not filing timely.
  - Claim denied as a duplicate.
  - Due to injuries being work or auto related.
  - Insurance paid another provider.
- Insurance carrier pended claim awaiting an audit.
  - Ask what kind of audit is being done.
  - Ask when the claim was received.
  - Ask when the claim was sent to be audited.
  - Ask who is conducting the audit.
  - Ask how long the claim will remain in auditing.
- Insurance carrier pended claim for repricing.
  - Determine when the claim was received.
  - Determine when the claim was sent to be repriced.
  - Ask how long the claim will be in repricing.
  - Ask for the claim number assigned to the claim.
  - Verify name, address, and telephone number of repricing company (contact repricing company to expedite the process).
- Claim was applied to patient's deductible or coinsurance.
  - Determine when the claim was received.
  - Determine the amount that was applied to deductible or coinsurance.
- Benefits exhausted or no coverage.
  - Ask for date policy was terminated.
  - Ask if patient has any other policy under different group or under spouse.
  - Ask insurance to fax copy of denial.
  - Contact patient to obtain correct insurance information and then bill insurance with copy of denial letter from previous insurance.
- Policy rescinded.
  - Determine on what day policy was rescinded.
  - Determine why policy was rescinded (did patient either falsify or omit information on the application).

TABLE 8-1 (*continued*)

Insurance Responses and Explanations to Unpaid Insurance Claims

- Services and items not covered.
  — Find out the date claim was processed.
  — Find out the amount that was not covered.
  — Ask and determine if patient is responsible for noncovered charges.
- Insurance paid the insured.
  — Find out the date claim was processed.
  — Find out why assignment of benefits was not honored.
  — Try to get the insurance to reissue a check to the provider and have them recoup the payment from the insured.
  — Find out the amount, check number, and date of the payment.
  — If the insurance carrier refuses to reissue a check to the provider, bill the patient.
- Insurance denied claim for timely filing.
  — Find out the date claim was denied or claim number was assigned to claim.
  — Verify eligibility.
  — Find out the filing limit.
  — Ask if you can fax proof of filing, then fax proof of filing with a claim number.
- Insurance denied claim for no authorization.
  — Find out the date claim was denied or claim number was assigned to claim.
  — If authorization is on file, give to insurance representative.
  — Verify eligibility.
  — If authorization not on file:
    - Find out who was responsible for obtaining authorization (hospital, patient, physician).
    - Try to obtain original authorization from primary care physician.
    - If the primary care physician does not have authorization on file, ask if a retro-authorization can be done.
    - If a retro-authorization cannot be done, ask the insurer if an appeal can be made with medical records.
    - If an appeal with medical records is possible, obtain the appeals address, phone number, and name of the department or person handling the appeals.
- Claim denied as a duplicate.
  — Find out the date claim was denied or claim number was assigned to the claim.
  — Find out when original claim was processed and how it was processed.
- Insurance denied claim as work or auto related.
  — Find out the date of denial.
  — If work related, contact the patient's place of employment and obtain the date of injury, workers' compensation carrier name, claims address and phone number, and claim number assigned to the claim.
  — Send forms CMS-1500/CMS1450 (UB92) to workers' compensation insurance along with an itemized statement.
  — If auto related, contact the patient to obtain the date of the accident and auto insurance information.
  — If the auto insurance states that the claim is in litigation, ask if the insurer has a subrogation letter that can be sent to the insured.

Identifying Unpaid Claims

At least once a week, an office staff member should identify unpaid insurance claims that are at least 25 days old. By starting with claims that are 25 days old, the office has time to determine whether claim forms have been received by the insurance companies and entered into their computers. It is common to have insurance companies say they have no record of receiving claims when contacted.

TABLE 8-2

Follow-Up Procedures for Unpaid Claims

- Claim not on file:
    — Verify claims mailing address.
    — Verify eligibility, policy number, group number, and insured's name.
    — Ask what date the insurance carrier is currently processing claims for.
    — Ask if claim can be faxed.

- Insurance is pending information from the patient:
    — Find out what information is being requested (claim form, accident details, preexisting information, other insurance, or student verification).
    — Ask when information was requested.
    — Ask if information can be given by the provider. Review other accounts that patient may have to obtain information (eg, other insurance information).
    — Ask if information can be faxed. For example, if accident details are needed, the provider can fax the emergency department report.
    — If information can only be given by the patient, contact the patient.

- Insurance is pending information from the provider:
    — Find out which provider insurance carrier is contacting for requested information.
    — If medical records are needed, ask what specific records are needed (discharge summary, history and physical, etc).
    — Ask for the number assigned to the claim. Ensure that the claim number, patient name, policy number, and date of service are on the medical record.
    — Verify the address to which the requested records are to be sent.
    — If a preexisting review is being done and the provider needs records from other providers, send the names and numbers to the other physicians. Contact the other physicians and try to obtain the records.

Also, by starting with claims that are at least 25 days old, the office can refile claims early; the sooner a practice starts the follow-up process, the quicker claims will be paid on balance. A major goal of every medical practice is to consistently obtain payment within 30 to 45 days for all insurance claims filed. Also, many insurance contracts require that claims be filed within 90 days; thus, starting early prevents nonpayment for this reason.

This is where the revised A/R report discussed earlier in the chapter can be used to track payment type. Copies of claims, which should be centrally located usually using an alphabetized expandable file, can also be used when tracking unpaid claims. Some offices keep their office copies in the patients' charts. However, unless the office has a list of all unpaid claims, keeping copies in the charts will likely create inefficiencies because collection personnel will have to pull charts to follow up on accounts not knowing at any given time which claims are 25 days old.

Telephone Calls

For each claim that is at least 25 days old, the office should make an inquiry to each insurance company. Some insurance companies, including Medicare, have automated response units that facilitate the process. This inquiry must always be documented in the billing record. The name of the contact at the insurance company; the date and time of the contact; the reason the claim has not been paid; and the date payment can be expected should be documented. If made on paper, the documentation should be attached to each office copy of the unpaid claim until payment is received. If the office files a large number of claims electronically, the forms can be attached to the computer edit report that lists the electronically filed claims.

Not every practice calls every insurance company when bills are 25 days old. The decision to call depends on how many claims are filed each week, how large the balances are, and the capabilities of the office's collection personnel. However, every office should try to make these calls.

Tracer Claims

If calls cannot be made or if communications with the insurance companies fail, practices may want to use the tracer method. A tracer claim is a copy of the original claim form with the word *TRACER* stamped on it. The date of the tracer should be written on the original claim. The tracer claims are refiled with the respective insurance companies. This tracer designation indicates to most insurance companies that the office is inquiring about the status of an unpaid claim.

Refiling Claims: Rebilling

Depending on the outcome of the follow-up call, the office should refile claims according to the payer's instructions (via facsimile, if possible) or do whatever is necessary to get claims paid as quickly as possible. Practice staff members who make the calls must document with whom they spoke at the insurance companies in case a call-back to the insurance company is necessary. Duplicate billing is a concern of the Office of the Inspector General (OIG). When submitting an unpaid claim, be sure to write, "This is not a duplicate bill. We have not been paid on the original claim submitted."

Prompt Payment Laws and/or Regulations

Prompt payment laws and/or regulations have been implemented in 49 states and the District of Columbia. Employees responsible for follow-up on delinquent claims should be familiar with the prompt payment laws or regulations for their state. The different state laws and regulations as well as individual state contact information are included in Table 8-3.

TABLE 8-3

State Prompt Payment Laws, as of October 2003

State	Payment Timeframe	Penalty	Contact Information
Alabama	Paper: 45 calendar days Electronic: 30 calendar days	1.5% monthly	Alabama Department of Insurance Life and Health Division PO Box 303351 Montgomery, AL 36130-335 334 269-3550 www.aldoi.gov/
Alaska	All claim types: 30 calendar days	15% annually	Alaska Division of Insurance 9th Floor State Office Bldg 333 Willoughby Ave Juneau, AK 99801 907 465-2515 www.dced.state.ak.us/insurance/

State	Payment Timeframe	Penalty	Contact Information
Arizona	All claim types: 30 days or as specified in contract	Legal interest rate	Arizona Department of Insurance 2910 North 44th St Ste 210 Phoenix, AZ 85018 602 364-2499 www.id.state.az.us/index.html
Arkansas	Paper: 45 days Electronic: 30 days	12% annually	Arkansas Insurance Department 1200 West Third St Little Rock, AR 72201 501 371-2600 or 800 282-9134 www.state.ar.us/insurance/
California	Non-HMOs: 30 working days HMOs: 45 working days	15% annually $10 additional noninclusion of interest with payment	California Department of Insurance Consumer Communications Bureau 300 S Spring St South Tower Los Angeles, CA 90013 800 927-4357 or 213 897-8921 www.insurance.ca.gov/
Colorado	Paper: 45 calendar days Electronic: 30 calendar days	10% annually >90 days: 3% claim amount	Colorado Division of Insurance 1560 Broadway Suite 850 Denver, CO 80202 303 894-7499 (phone) 303 894-7490 (consumer information) 800 930-3745 (toll free) 303 894-7455 (fax) www.dora.state.co.us/insurance/
Connecticut	All claim types: 45 days or as stipulated by contract	15% annually	State of Connecticut Insurance Department PO Box 816 Hartford, CT 06142-0816 860 297-3800 www.ct.gov/cid/site/default.asp
Delaware	Paper: 45 days Electronic: 30 days	As agreed upon by contract, not in excess of 5% over the Federal Reserve discount rate. When there is no contract: a percentage rate 5% over the Federal Reserve discount rate.	Delaware Insurance Department 841 Silver Lake Blvd Dover, DE 19904 302 674-7300 www.state.de.us/inscom/
District of Columbia	All claim types: 30 days	1.5%: 31–60 days 2%: 61–120 days 2.5% thereafter	Department of Insurance and Securities Regulation 810 First St, NE Suite 701 Washington, DC 20002 Attention: Consumer Services Division 202 727-8000 www.disr.dc.gov

TABLE 8-3 (continued)

State	Payment Timeframe	Penalty	Contact Information
Florida	Paper: 40 days Electronic: 20 days	12% annually	Florida Department of Financial Services 200 East Gaines St Tallahassee, FL 32399-0300 850 413-3100 www.fldfs.com/
Georgia	All claim types: 15 working days	18% annually	Georgia Insurance Fire and Safety Commission 2 Martin Luther King, Jr Dr West Tower Suite 704 Atlanta, GA 30334 404 656-2070 or 800 656-2298 404 657-8542 (fax) www.inscomm.state.ga.us/
Hawaii	Paper: 30 days Electronic: 15 days	15% annually; fines may also be assessed	Hawaii Department of Commerce and Consumer Affairs PO Box 3614 Honolulu, HI 96811 808 586-2790 www.hawaii.gov/dcca/ins/
Idaho	Paper: 45 days Electronic: 30 days	Legal rate of interest as provided by law	Idaho Department of Insurance 700 West State St PO Box 83720 Boise, ID 83720-0043 208 334-4250 www.doi.state.id.us/
Illinois	All claim types: 30 days	9% annually	Illinois Department of Insurance Consumer Division 320 W Washington St Springfield, IL 62767 866 445-5364 www.ins.state.il.us/
Indiana	Paper: 45 days Electronic: 30 days	As provided by law	Indiana Department of Insurance 311 W Washington St Suite 300 Indianapolis, IN 46204-2787 317 232-2385 800 622-4461 (in-state WatsLine) www.state.in.us/idoi/
Iowa	Consistent with timeframes for claims decisions by group health plans established by US Department of Labor	10% annually	Iowa Insurance Division 330 Maple St Des Moines, IA 50319-0065. 515 281-5705 or 877 955-1212 www.iid.state.ia.us/

State	Payment Timeframe	Penalty	Contact Information
Kansas	All claim types: 30 days	1% monthly	Topeka office 420 SW 9th St Topeka, KS 66612-1678 785 296-3071 800 432-2484 (in state only) 785 296-2283 (fax) Wichita office 130 S Market St Suite 4030 Box 3850 Wichita, KS 67201-3850 316 337-6010 800 432-2484 (in state only) 316 337-6018 (fax) www.ksinsurance.org/
Kentucky	All claim types: 30 days (except organ transplants: 60 days)	12% annually: 31–60 days 18% annually: 61–90 days 21% annually: >91 days	Kentucky Department of Insurance 215 W Main St Frankfort, KY 40601 800 595-6053 800 462-2081 (TTY) www.doi.state.ky.us/kentucky/
Louisiana	Paper: submitted within 45 days, 45 days to pay Electronic: 25 days	12% annually	Louisiana Department of Insurance 1702 N 3rd St Baton Rouge, LA 70802-5143 225 342-5900 www.ldi.state.la.us/
Maine	All claim types: 30 days	18% annually (1.5% monthly)	Maine Bureau of Insurance 34 State House Station Augusta, ME 04333 800 300-5000 (in state) or 207 624-8475 207 624-8599 (fax) www.state.me.us/pfr/ins/ins_index.htm
Maryland	All claim types: 30 days	1.5% monthly: 31–60 days 2% monthly: 61–120 days 2.5% monthly: >121 days	Maryland Insurance Administration 525 Saint Paul Pl Baltimore, MD 21202 800 492-6116 or 410 468-2000 www.mdinsurance.state.md.us/
Massachusetts	All claim types: 45 days	1.5% monthly (not to exceed 18% annually)	Massachusetts Division of Insurance 1 South Station 5th Fl Boston, MA 02110-2208 617 521-7777 617 521-7575 (fax) www.state.ma.us/doi/
Michigan	All claim types: 45 days	12% annually	Office of Financial and Insurance Services 611 West Ottawa St 2nd Fl Lansing, MI 48933 517 373-1820 www.michigan.gov

T A B L E 8-3 (continued)

State	Payment Timeframe	Penalty	Contact Information
Minnesota	All claim types: 30 days	1.5% monthly	Minnesota Department of Commerce 85 7th Pl East Suite 500 St Paul, MN 55101 651 296-4026 651 296-2860 (TTY) 651 297-1959 (fax) www.state.mn.us/portal/mn/jsp/home.do?agency=Commerce
Mississippi	Paper: 35 days Electronic: 25 days	1.5% monthly	Mississippi Department of Insurance Attn: Consumer Services Division PO Box 79 Jackson, MS 39205-0079 601 359-3569 800 562-2957 601 359-1077 (fax) www.doi.state.ms.us/
Missouri	All claim types: within 10 days	12% annually	Missouri Department of Insurance 301 West High St PO Box 690 Jefferson City, MO 65102 573 751-4126 http://insurance.state.mo.us/
Montana	All claim types: 30 days	18% annually	Montana Department of Insurance 840 Helena Avenue Helena, MT 59601 800 332-6148 (in state) 406 444-2040 www.sao.state.mt.us
Nebraska	Paper: 45 days Electronic: 30 days	12% annually	Nebraska Department of Insurance Terminal Building 941 "O" St Ste 400 Lincoln, NE 68508-3639 402 471-2201 www.nol.org/home/ndoi/
Nevada	All claim types: 30 days	Prime rate at largest bank of Nevada, plus 6%	Carson City Office 788 Fairview Drive Ste 300 Carson City, NV 89701 775 687-4270 Las Vegas Office 2501 East Sahara Ave Ste 302 Las Vegas, NV 89104 702 486-4009 http://doi.state.nv.us/

State	Payment Timeframe	Penalty	Contact Information
New Hampshire	Paper: 30 calendar days Electronic: 15 calendar days	1.5% monthly	State of New Hampshire Insurance Department 56 Old Suncook Rd Concord, NH 03301-7317 800 852-3416 www.state.nh.us/insurance/
New Jersey	Paper: 40 calendar days Electronic: 30 calendar days or the time allowed under Medicare, whichever is shorter	10% annually	New Jersey Department of Banking and Insurance PO Box 325 Trenton, NJ 08625-0325 609 292-5360 www.state.nj.us/dobi/index.shtml
New Mexico	Paper: 45 days Electronic: 30 days	1.5% monthly	New Mexico Public Regulation Commission-Insurance Division PERA Building 1120 Paseo de Peralta PO Box 1269 Santa Fe, NM 87504-1269 505 827-4601 www.nmprc.state.nm.us/insurance/inshm.htm
New York	All claim types: 45 days	12% annually or the rate set by the commissioner of taxation and finance for corporate taxes	State of New York Insurance Department 25 Beaver St New York, NY 10004 800 342-3736 www.ins.state.ny.us/
North Carolina	All claim types: 30 days	18% annually	North Carolina Department of Insurance PO Box 26387 Raleigh, NC 27611 919 733-2032 www.ncdoi.com/
North Dakota	All claim types: 15 business days	None listed	North Dakota Department of Insurance 600 E Blvd Dept 401 Bismarck, ND 58505-0320 701 328-2440 701 328-4880 (fax)
Ohio	All claim types: 30 days	18% annually	The Ohio Department of Insurance 2100 Stella Ct Columbus, OH 43215-1067 614 644-2658 614 644-3743 (fax) www.ohioinsurance.gov/
Oklahoma	All claim types: 45 calendar days	10% annually	Oklahoma Insurance Department Box 53408 Oklahoma City, OK 73152-3408 405 521-2828 or 800 522-0071 www.oid.state.ok.us/

TABLE 8-3 (*continued*)

State	Payment Timeframe	Penalty	Contact Information
Oregon	All claims types: 30 days	12% annually	Oregon Department of Consumer and Business Services Insurance Division 350 Winter St NE Rm 440 Salem, OR 503 947-7980 503 378-4351 (fax) www.cbs.state.or.us/external/ins/
Pennsylvania	All claim types: 45 days	10% annually	Pennsylvania Insurance Department Room 1701 State Office Bldg 1400 Spring Garden St Philadelphia, PA 19130 215 560-2630 215 560-2648 www.ins.state.pa.us/ins/site/default.asp
Rhode Island	Paper: 40 days Electronic: 30 days	12% annually	Department of Business Regulation Insurance Division 233 Richmond St Suite 233 Providence, RI 02903-4233 401 222-2223 401 222-5475 (fax) www.dbr.state.ri.us/
South Carolina	Paper: 45 days Electronic: 30 days	6% annually	South Carolina Department of Insurance 300 Arbor Lake Dr Suite 1200 Columbia, SC 29223 803 737-6180 www.doi.state.sc.us/
South Dakota	Paper: 45 calendar days Electronic: 30 calendar days	None indicated	South Dakota Division of Insurance 118 W. Capitol Pierre, SD 57501 605 773-5369 (fax) www.state.sd.us/drr2/reg/insurance/
Tennessee	Paper: 30 days Electronic: 21 days	1% monthly	Tennessee Department of Commerce and Insurance 500 James Robertson Parkway 4th Fl Nashville, TN 37243 615 741-2218 www.state.tn.us/commerce/sfm/index.html
Texas	Paper: 45 days Electronic: 30 days	Upto $100,000 or, after 90 days, 18% annually	Texas Department of Insurance PO Box 149104 Austin, TX 78714-9104 512 463-6169 or 800 578-4677 www.tdi.state.tx.us/

State	Payment Timeframe	Penalty	Contact Information
Utah	All claim types: 30 days	As agreed upon by contract or 10% annually	Utah Insurance Department State Office Bldg Rm #3110 Salt Lake City, UT 84114-6901 800 439-3805 www.insurance.state.ut.us/
Vermont	All claim types: 45 days	12% annually	State of Vermont Insurance Division Insurance Division 89 Main St Drawer 20 Montpelier, VT 05620-3101 www.bishca.state.vt.us/InsurDiv/insur_index.htm
Virginia	All claim types: 40 days	As established by law	Virginia State Corporation Commission Bureau of Insurance 1300 East Main St Richmond, VA 23219 804 371-9967 www.scc.virginia.gov/
Washington	Clean claims 95% must be paid within 30 days Disputed claims: 95% must be paid or denied within 60 days	1% monthly	Washington State Office of the Insurance Commissioner The Central Bldg Ste 650/MS: TB-03 810 3rd Ave Seattle, WA 98104 800 562-6900 www.insurance.wa.gov/
West Virginia	Paper: 40 days Electronic: 30 days	10% annually	West Virginia Insurance Commission 1124 Smith St Charleston, WV 25301 304 558-3354 www.state.wv.us/insurance/WVICOnline/contact.htm
Wisconsin	All claim types: 30 days	12% annually	Office of the Commissioner of Insurance 125 South Webster St Madison, WI 53702 608 266-3585 http://oci.wi.gov/oci_home.htm
Wyoming	All claim types: 45 days	None listed	Wyoming Insurance Department Herschler Bldg 3rd Fl East 122 West 25th St Cheyenne, WY 82002 307 777-7401 http://insurance.state.wy.us/

As stated earlier, it is important for staff members to be familiar with the laws and regulations for their state relating to prompt payment laws and the appeal process. Table 8-4 contains charts provided by the Arizona Department of Insurance, showing its appeal process for health care.

Statistical data is shown in Table 8-5. The figures show that between 1999 and 2001, nearly 60% of Formal Appeals and more than 50% of Informal Reconsideration Appeals were overturned in favor of the health care consumer. The fiscal year 2004 and fiscal year 2005 data show that a significant percentage of claims referred to or decided by an independent medical review organization were overturned or partially overturned in favor of the consumer.

TABLE 8-4

Health Care Appeal Processes

The following flow charts graphically represent the two separate tracks available for health care appeals, as well as the time frames for review at each of the three levels.

Standard Health Care Appeal Process

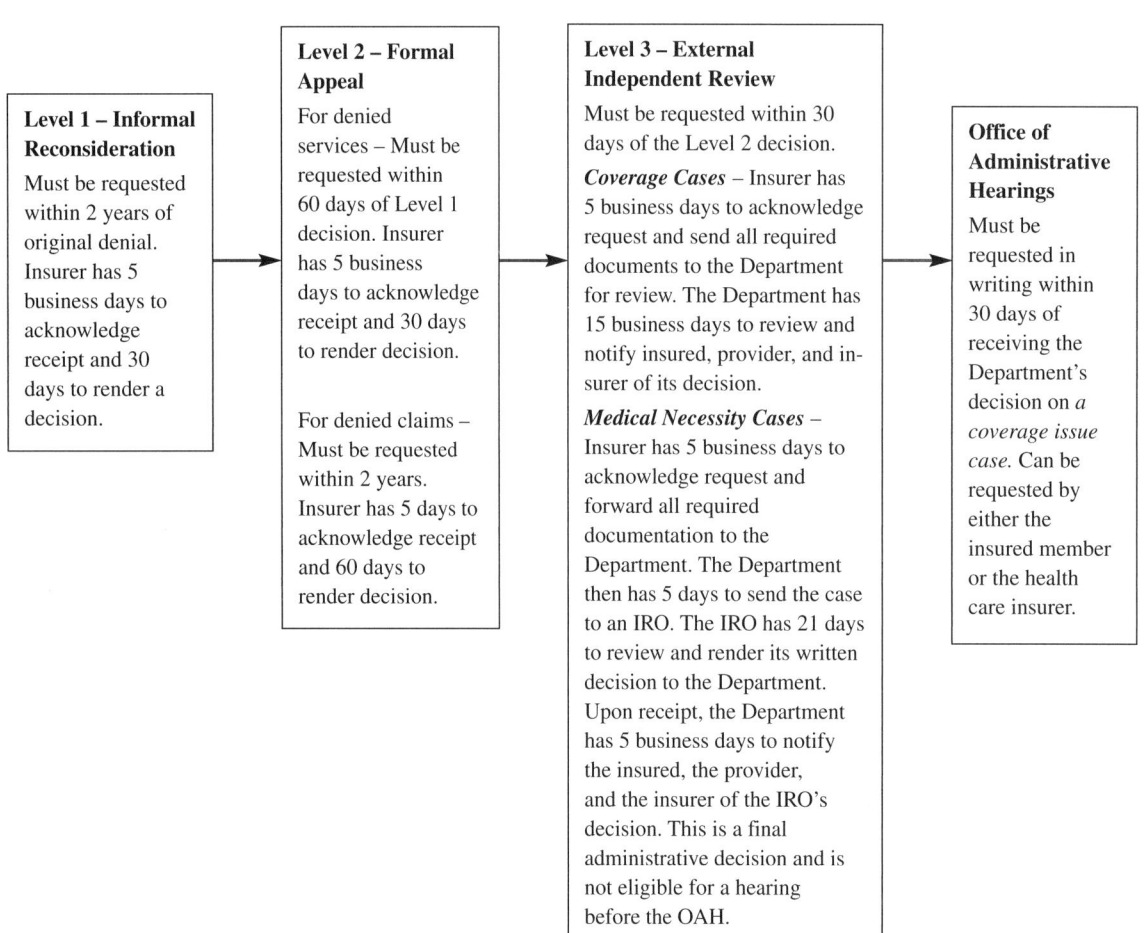

Level 1 – Informal Reconsideration
Must be requested within 2 years of original denial. Insurer has 5 business days to acknowledge receipt and 30 days to render a decision.

Level 2 – Formal Appeal
For denied services – Must be requested within 60 days of Level 1 decision. Insurer has 5 business days to acknowledge receipt and 30 days to render decision.

For denied claims – Must be requested within 2 years. Insurer has 5 days to acknowledge receipt and 60 days to render decision.

Level 3 – External Independent Review
Must be requested within 30 days of the Level 2 decision.
Coverage Cases – Insurer has 5 business days to acknowledge request and send all required documents to the Department for review. The Department has 15 business days to review and notify insured, provider, and insurer of its decision.
Medical Necessity Cases – Insurer has 5 business days to acknowledge request and forward all required documentation to the Department. The Department then has 5 days to send the case to an IRO. The IRO has 21 days to review and render its written decision to the Department. Upon receipt, the Department has 5 business days to notify the insured, the provider, and the insurer of the IRO's decision. This is a final administrative decision and is not eligible for a hearing before the OAH.

Office of Administrative Hearings
Must be requested in writing within 30 days of receiving the Department's decision on *a coverage issue case*. Can be requested by either the insured member or the health care insurer.

chapter 8 Managing Insurance Accounts Receivable

TABLE 8-4

Health Care Appeal Processes (*continued*)

Expedited Health Care Appeal Process

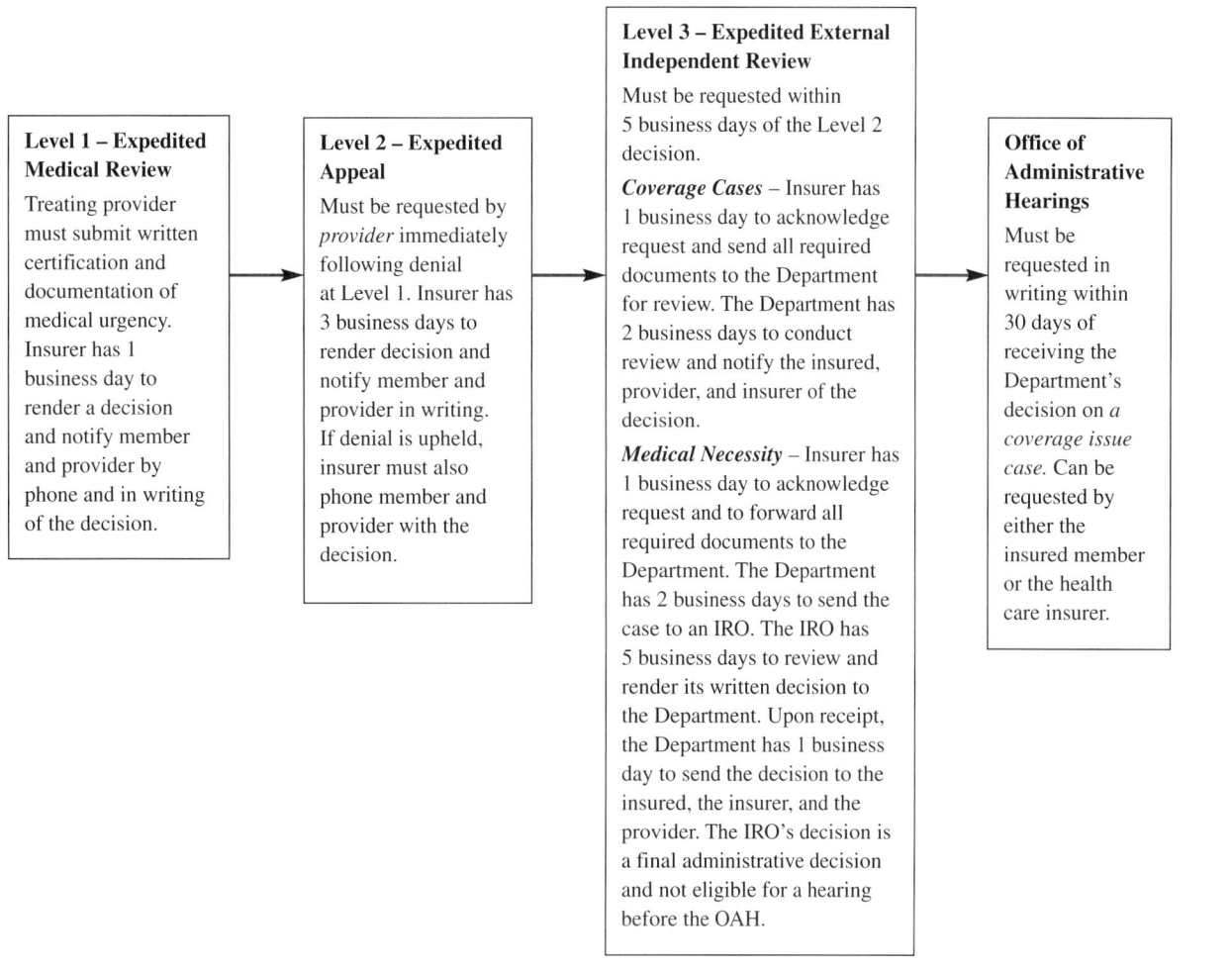

Level 1 – Expedited Medical Review

Treating provider must submit written certification and documentation of medical urgency. Insurer has 1 business day to render a decision and notify member and provider by phone and in writing of the decision.

Level 2 – Expedited Appeal

Must be requested by *provider* immediately following denial at Level 1. Insurer has 3 business days to render decision and notify member and provider in writing. If denial is upheld, insurer must also phone member and provider with the decision.

Level 3 – Expedited External Independent Review

Must be requested within 5 business days of the Level 2 decision.

Coverage Cases – Insurer has 1 business day to acknowledge request and send all required documents to the Department for review. The Department has 2 business days to conduct review and notify the insured, provider, and insurer of the decision.

Medical Necessity – Insurer has 1 business day to acknowledge request and to forward all required documents to the Department. The Department has 2 business days to send the case to an IRO. The IRO has 5 business days to review and render its written decision to the Department. Upon receipt, the Department has 1 business day to send the decision to the insured, the insurer, and the provider. The IRO's decision is a final administrative decision and not eligible for a hearing before the OAH.

Office of Administrative Hearings

Must be requested in writing within 30 days of receiving the Department's decision on *a coverage issue case*. Can be requested by either the insured member or the health care insurer.

Source: Arizona Department of Insurance Health Care Annual Appeals Report

TABLE 8-5

Health Care Appeals Statistics

Health Care Appeals Statistics For Fiscal Year 2004

Total number of health care appeals subject to External Review Process: 280

- *Number of cases decided by the Department as coverage issues:* **148**
    - 144 standard appeals
    - 4 expedited appeals
    - 133 upheld in favor of the health insurer
    - 1 overturned or partially overturned in favor of the consumer
    - 7 remain pending at year end
    - 7 were withdrawn
- *Number of cases decided by an independent medical review organization:* **85**
    - 79 standard appeals
    - 5 expedited appeals
    - 56 upheld in favor of the health insurer
    - 26 overturned or partially overturned in favor of the consumer
    - 3 remain pending at year end

TABLE 8-5

Health Care Appeal Statistics (*continued*)

- *Number of cases reviewed by the Department but referred to an independent medical review organization for medical decision:* **47**
    - 44 standard appeals
    - 3 expedited appeals
    - 28 upheld in favor of the health insurer
    - 18 overturned or partially overturned in favor of the consumer
    - 1 remaining pending at year end

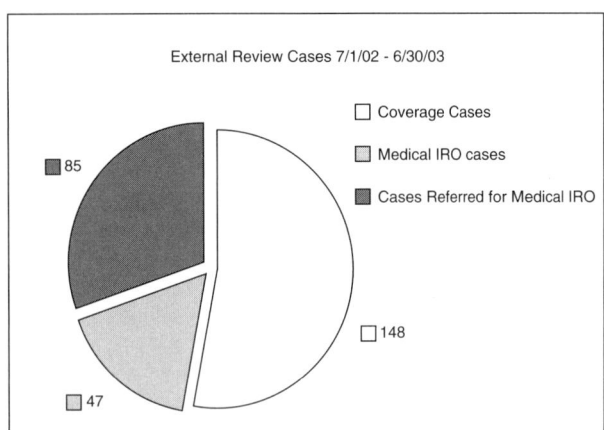

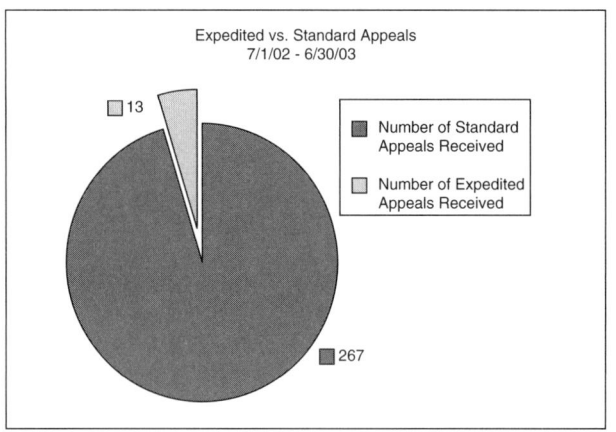

Health Care Appeals Statistics For Fiscal Year 2005

Total number of health care appeals subject to External Review Process: 288

- *Number of cases withdrawn as exempt from appeal process or settled by insurer:* **30**
- *Number of cases decided by the Department as coverage issues:* **145**
    - 133 standard appeals
    - 4 expedited appeals
    - 133 upheld in favor of the health insurer
    - 4 overturned or partially overturned in favor of the consumer
    - 8 remain pending at year end
- *Number of cases decided by an independent medical review organization:* **74**
    - 67 standard appeals
    - 4 expedited appeals
    - 47 upheld in favor of the health insurer
    - 21 overturned or partially overturned in favor of the consumer
    - 3 remain pending at year end
- *Number of cases reviewed by the Department but referred to an independent medical review organization for medical decision:* **39**
    - 35 standard appeals
    - 2 expedited appeals
    - 22 upheld in favor of the health insurer
    - 15 overturned or partially overturned in favor of the consumer
    - 2 remaining pending at year end

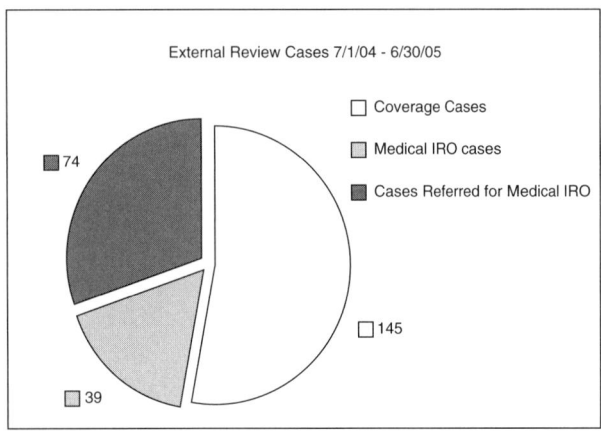

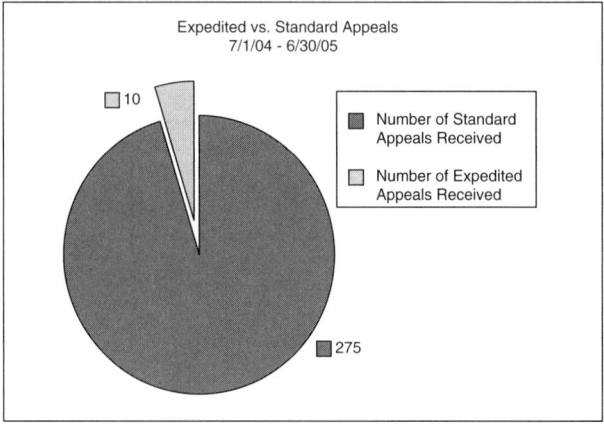

TABLE 8-5

Health Care Appeals Statistics (*continued*)

	Number of Expedited Medical Reviewers	Percentage of Expedited Medical Reviews Overturned	Number of Expedited Appeals	Percentage of Expedited Appeals Overturned	Number of Informal Reconsideration Appeals	Percentage of Informal Reconsideration Appeals Overturned	Number of Formal Appeals	Percentage of Formal Appeals Overturned
FY 2001	155	37%	38	37%	8,000	54%	2,724	59%
FY 2000	248	41%	N/A	N/A	8,025	59%	2,744	50%
FY 1999	459	21%	N/A	N/A	5,897	44%	1,936	49%

Source: Arizona Department of Insurance

INSURANCE A/R PROCESS OVERVIEW

As a summary of the insurance A/R process, the following steps may be taken to follow up on previously submitted claims:

1. Call the insurance company regarding claims submitted at least 25 days ago.
2. Send a tracer claim or claim inquiry letter to the insurance company (assigned or unassigned).
3. After 40 days, contact the patient to inform him or her of problems and enlist his or her assistance.
4. Make the second telephone contact by calling the insurance company regarding claims submitted at least 50 days ago.
5. At 60 days, bill the patient who is now financially responsible for charges. Inform the patient of what and with whom contact has been made with the insurer.
6. Request a review and insurance appeal with documentation.

Occasionally, insurance companies are slow to pay a claim. In these situations, you may want to consider inquiring about the status of the claim. For assigned claims, the practice may send a letter, similar to the one shown in Figure 8-1.

When an unassigned claim has been filed, the patient must make an inquiry to the insurance company. A letter from the patient (see Figure 8-2) to the slow-paying insurance company may help speed payment to the patient, which will in turn speed payment to your office. The practice can provide the letter to the patient to send to the insurance company.

When all reasonable efforts to collect from an insurance company have failed, a formal complaint may be filed with the state's Department of Insurance (see Figure 8-3).

Each state has its own laws and protocols to follow, thus inquiry should be made prior to the complaint. Some states require the patient to file the complaint and others allow the physician or both to file.

FIGURE 8-1

Sample Letter for Claim Inquiry on Assigned Claims

Physician or Group Name
Address
Phone
Applicable Identification Number(s)
Insurance Carrier
Claims Processing Department
Address

RE: Patient's Name
          Policyholder's Name
          Policy Number
          Patient's Identification Number

Dear Sir or Madam:

On [date], a claim was filed on behalf of the patient named above. To date, no payment has been received for this claim. We are requesting information regarding the following:

☐   Please verify amount of payment made to patient.

☐   Please review reimbursement due to under/overpayment of $_____.
       Other: _____

Insurance Company Reply:

☐   Payment was made to patient in the amount of $_____ on _____.
       Correct reimbursement should be $_____.

☐   Payment was made to your office on _____ for $_____.

☐   Other:

_____   _____   _____
Signature   Title   Date

FIGURE 8-2

Sample Letter for Claim Inquiry on Unassigned Claims

Patient's Name
Address
Phone Number

Insurance Company Name
Address

Attention: Supervisor of Claims Department

RE: Patient's Name
      Policyholder's Name
      Policy Number
      Patient's Identification Number

Dear Sir or Madam:

On [date] Dr [physician's name] of [include group or practice name, address, and applicable identification number], who is my physician, submitted an insurance claim for me in the amount of $_____ for my medical treatment. _____ weeks have passed and payment has not been received by me or my physician. Please check your records and contact me or Dr [physician's name] office immediately regarding this claim. I am anxious to settle this matter.

Yours truly,

Patient's Name

FIGURE 8-3

Sample Letter to Send to the Insurance Commissioner

Date

State Insurance Commissioner
Address
City, State, Zip Code

Dear Insurance Commissioner:

My physician filed the attached insurance claim form over thirty (30) days ago. Even after repeated attempts by my physician's office to contact the insurance company regarding the payment status of this claim, to this date my insurance company has not paid this claim and has provided no explanation to my physician for its nonpayment.

Please accept this letter as a formal written complaint against the insurance company. Your prompt attention to this matter would be greatly appreciated.

I am providing the insurance company and my physician with a copy of this notice.

Sincerely,

[Patient's Name]

cc: Practice Name
    Address

CONCLUSION

Good A/R management is critical to ensuring proper reimbursement and maintaining the practice's cash flow. Practice staff members should be knowledgeable of the steps involved in the A/R process and should be able to routinely perform these steps. Correct collection and entry of data is necessary for an accurate accounts receivable reporting system. A/R reports, which are used for follow-up purposes, may be printed using different formats. Practices should print reports using a format that maximizes efficiency in follow-up efforts.

Proper follow-up of unpaid insurance claims is also essential to managing the A/R process and maintaining proper cash flow for the practice. Specific actions to achieve this as well as sample letters are presented in this chapter. Practices often have difficulty getting an insurance carrier or other third-party payer to pay on a claim. The practice should aggressively follow the steps described here to collect a valid claim. This includes, but is not limited to, filing appeals and contacting various entities including state insurance commission offices or others able to assist in resolving claim payment issues.

Receivables are often written off and a practice does not receive the cash it has earned due to inadequate follow-up or the difficulties encountered during the collection process. A practice should make every effort to collect all monies it has earned and is due for providing valid reimbursable services to its patients.

In summary, the A/R management process is vital to a practice's operation and proper management and follow-through is critical to ensuring proper cash flow.

chapter

9

Requests for Appeals and Review

OBJECTIVES

- Understand why appeals are made to insurance companies.
- Know how to process a request for a Medicare review.
- Recognize the use of a letter to request a review.

For years, providers have ignored the fact that they are granted the right to appeal a denied claim. As a result, they have forfeited what would otherwise be a valid insurance claim.

An appeal of a denied claim to both private insurance carriers and government health care programs must be handled correctly; otherwise, the right to appeal may be permanently lost. Unfortunately, the appeals process can and does vary among insurance companies as well as governmental payers. The steps for appealing denied claims to private insurance companies are outlined in the participating provider agreement or in the provider handbook (also known as the provider policies and procedures manual). State Medicaid programs usually publish the appeals process in the state Medicaid manual. A short explanation of the Medicare appeals process can be accessed at www.cms.hhs.gov/medlearn/appeals_broch.pdf; providers will also find an explanation of the appeals process on their Medicare carrier's Web site.

Chapters 1 and 8 discussed and displayed appeal statistics from the State of Arizona Department of Insurance Health Care Appeals Annual Report for fiscal year ending June 30, 2001, through fiscal year ending June 30, 2005. It was noted that for the fiscal year ending June 30, 2005, of the 74 cases decided by an independent medical review organization, 21% to 28.4% were overturned or partially overturned in favor of the consumer. Of the 39 cases reviewed by the Department of Insurance but referred to an independent medical review organization for medical decision, 15% to 38.5% were overturned or partially overturned in favor of the consumer. Although the number of claims in these specific categories was relatively low, the rate at which the claims were overturned is significant. It definitely was advantageous for the consumer or provider of services to file appeals in the above cases. In addition, the above information does not include statistics or data for claims that were overturned by the insurance carrier, which is generally the first step during the appeals process. Both Chapter 1 and Chapter 8 discuss and provide contact information that providers can utilize to file appeals with their local states in the event appeals are unsuccessful at the insurance carrier level.

Regardless of which appeals process is used, the provider must carefully document each step in the process and make copies of all correspondence with the insurance carrier, which is to be kept on file. This file should include all cover letter(s), medical records, and correspondence with other providers. In addition, all correspondence should be sent to the carrier using a method that allows for tracking to ensure the carrier receives documents on time. Finally, if the provider corresponds with the carrier via facsimile or e-mail, a hard copy of the fax or e-mail along with the cover page and report page should be retained.

FIGURE 9-1
Sample Letter for Requesting a Review

Insurance Company Name
Review Appeals Department
Address

RE: Patient's Name
 Policyholder's Name
 Contract or Policy Number
 Claim Number
 Submission Date

Dear Madam or Sir:

We are requesting a review of the above-identified claim on behalf of your beneficiary. A signed authorization for release of information is enclosed, allowing you to correspond directly with our office regarding this claim.

In reviewing this claim, please consider the following facts and circumstances:

1.

2.

3.

4.

5.

(Etc)

The enclosed [consultation, laboratory, operative, etc] report(s) support our position. We appreciate your prompt attention to this review.

Sincerely,

[Name of Physician]
[Identification Number(s)]

The first step in appealing a denied claim is to draft an appeal letter. Providers can download template appeal letters from a number of Web sites. However, because the reasons for claim denial vary, the appeal letter must be reviewed and modified to fit the specific circumstances of the case. At a minimum, the appeal letter (see Figure 9-1) should state clearly why the charge should be allowed and the medical necessity, if applicable. In addition, necessary documents (such as hospital progress notes) should be attached to help support the claim that the denial was inappropriate.

A periodic sampling of past appeal letters will enable the practice to see how often and/or how quickly the practice was paid after an appeal was filed. This "appeal audit" could reveal a pattern of unusual denial affirmations, which may be due, in part, to a poorly drafted appeal letter or, possibly, failure to include supporting documents. An appeal letter that simply asks for a review of the denied or reduced charge should never be sent. The letter must explain to the insurance company why the amount should be paid. Otherwise, the insurance company will assume it was correct in initially denying or reducing the charge. A letter asking only for a review of a claim is a waste of time; it will not result in a paid claim.

REQUESTS FOR REVIEW

Requesting a review is a simple process that often results in a more favorable determination on a claim. First, the provider should send a letter to the carrier or insurance payer requesting a review. The letter should identify the claim to be reviewed (by claim number, patient name, patient identification number) and clearly state the reasons why the determination should be changed. Any appropriate supporting documents, including information or explanations that were not provided with the claim when it was initially submitted, should be included to help the reviewer see why the determination should be changed.

MEDICARE PART B APPEAL RIGHTS

As with most insurance carriers, Medicare has a formal administrative appeals process by which physicians and patients may challenge the determination of a claim. If the provider is dissatisfied with the Medicare carrier's initial determination and the determination is subject to appeal, a review may be requested.

The Medicare appeals process has recently undergone significant changes. First, Congress enacted the Benefits Improvement and Protection Act (BIPA) of 2000 (Public Law 106-554), which modified the Medicare appeals process in an effort to streamline the process of appealing a Medicare claim. The appeals process was further modified with enactment of the Medicare Prescription Drug, Improvement and Modernization Act of 2003 (Medicare Reform), Public Law 108-173. The purpose of this act is to lessen the complexity of the appeals process.

Currently, there are five levels to the Medicare appeals process prior to a judicial review of the claim. The five levels are:

- Level 1: Review
- Level 2: Hearing officer hearing
- Level 3: Review by administrative law judge
- Level 4: Review by departmental appeals board
- Level 5: Judicial review in US District Court

Figure 9-2 is a diagram of the new Medicare appeals process.

The first level of appeal, the review, is an examination of a claim by carrier personnel who are independent of those originally involved; the review request can be submitted either in writing or by calling the carrier. (It is recommended that providers submit review requests in writing.) To assist providers, the Centers for Medicare and

FIGURE 9-2

Comparison of Former and Current 1869 Fee-for-Service Appeals

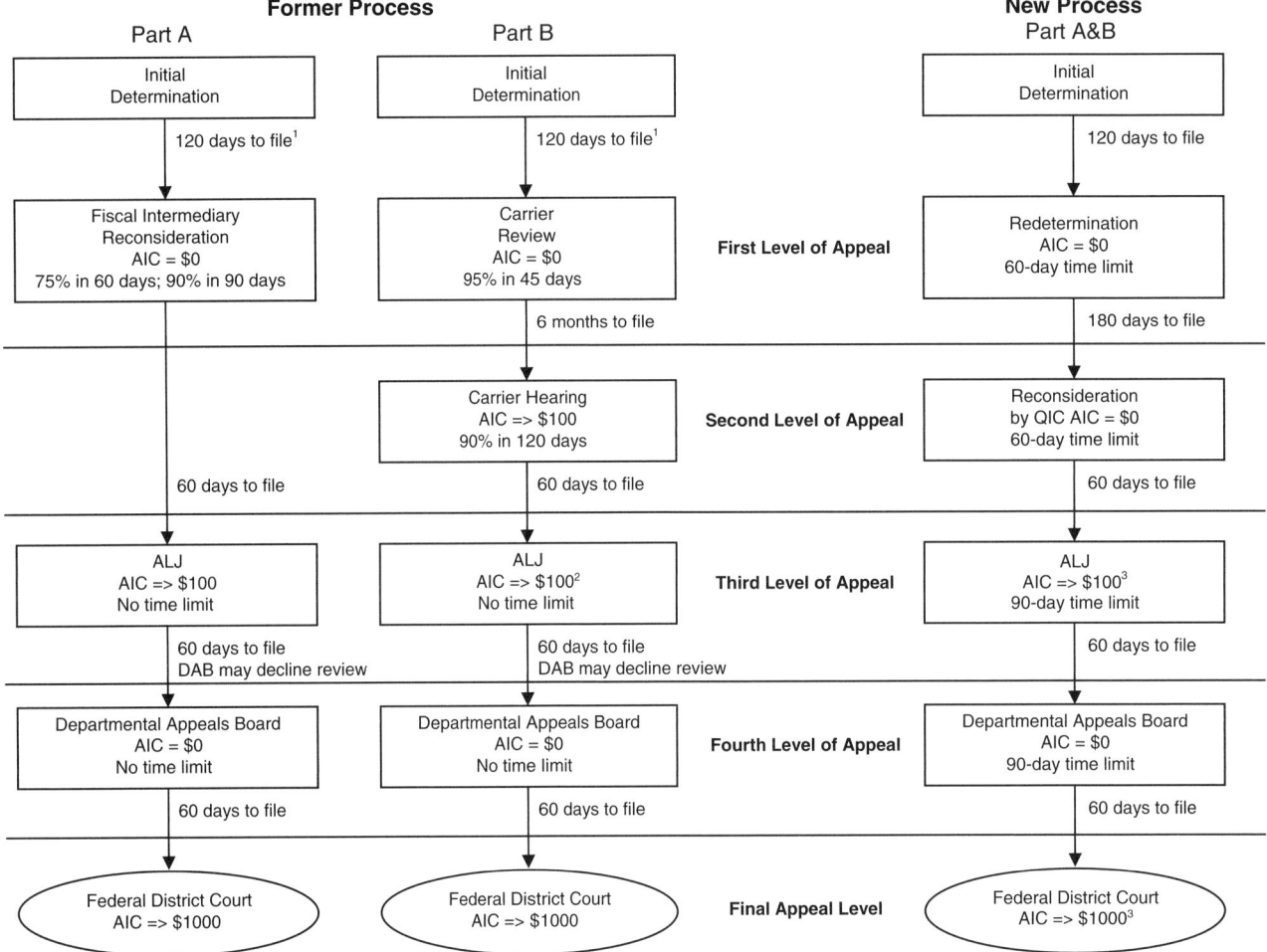

[1] For initial determinations prior to 10/1/02, the time frame to file was 6 months for a review and 60 days for a reconsideration.

[2] For initial determinations prior to 10/1/02, the AIC required for an ALJ hearing was $500 for all services other than home health.

[3] Starting in 2005, the AIC requirement for an ALJ hearing and Federal District Court will be adjusted in accordance with the medical care component of the consumer price index.

Source: Federal Register, Vol. 70, No. 44, March 8, 2005, p. 11426. Available at: www.sdfmc.org/ClassLibrary/Page/Information/DataInstances/220/Files/1277/Federal_Register_March_8_2005_Responses_to_Questions.pdf. Accessed January 3, 2006.

Medicaid Services (CMS) developed a downloadable review request form: Form CMS-1964 (see Figure 9-3) (http://cms.hhs.gov/forms). However, this form is not required for submission.

The request for a review must be made within 120 days of the initial determination indicated on the explanation of Medicare benefits (EOMB). However, the provider may receive a 120-day extension to the filing requirement if good cause is shown. Examples of good cause include:

- Circumstances beyond the patient's control, including mental or physical impairment or communication difficulty
- Death of a patient or advanced age (Advanced age is met automatically if the individual is 75 prior to the date services under dispute began.)
- Incorrect or incomplete information about the subject claim furnished by official source(s) (the CMS, intermediary, or social security office) to the individual

FIGURE 9-3
Form CMS-1964

DEPARTMENT OF HEALTH AND HUMAN SERVICES
CENTERS FOR MEDICARE & MEDICAID SERVICES

FORM APPROVED
OMB NO. 0938-0033

REQUEST FOR REVIEW OF PART B MEDICARE CLAIM
Medical Insurance Benefits – Social Security Act

NOTICE – Anyone who misrepresents or falsifies essential information requested by this form may upon conviction be subject to fine and imprisonment under Federal Law.

1. Carrier's Name and Address	2. Name of Patient
	3. Health Insurance Claim Number

4. I do not agree with the determination you made on my claim as described on my Explanation of Medicare Benefits dated:

5. MY REASONS ARE: (Attach a copy of the Explanation of Medicare Benefits, or describe the service, date of service, and physician's name. NOTE: If the date on the Explanation of Medicare Benefits mentioned in Item 4 is more than 120 days ago, include your reason for not making this request earlier.)

6. Describe illness or injury:

7. ☐ I have additional evidence to submit. (Attach such evidence to this form.)
   ☐ I do not have additional evidence.

COMPLETE ALL OF THE INFORMATION REQUESTED. SIGN AND RETURN THE FIRST COPY AND ANY ATTACHMENTS TO THE CARRIER NAMED ABOVE. IF YOU NEED HELP, TAKE THIS AND YOUR NOTICE FROM THE CARRIER TO A SOCIAL SECURITY OFFICE, OR TO THE CARRIER. KEEP THE DUPLICATE COPY OF THIS FORM FOR YOUR RECORDS.

8. SIGNATURE OF *EITHER* THE CLAIMANT *OR* HIS REPRESENTATIVE

Claimant	Representative	
Address	Address	
City, State and ZIP Code	City, State and ZIP Code	
Telephone Number	Date	Telephone Number	Date

Form CMS-1964 (09/91)

F I G U R E 9-3 (*continued*)

PRIVACY ACT ADVISORY STATEMENT

COLLECTION AND USE OF MEDICARE INFORMATION

We are authorized by the CENTERS FOR MEDICARE & MEDICAID SERVICES to ask you for information needed in the administration of the Medicare program. Social Security's authority to collect information is in section 205(a), 1872 and 1875 of the Social Security Act, as amended.

The information we obtain to complete your Medicare claim is used to identify you and to determine your eligibility. It is also used to decide if the services and supplies you received are covered by Medicare and to insure that proper payment is made.

The information may also be given to other providers of services, carriers, intermediaries, medical review boards, and other organizations as necessary to administer the Medicare program. For example, it may be necessary to disclose information about the Medicare benefits you have used to a hospital or doctor.

Additional disclosures are made through routine uses for information contained in systems of records. Disclosures of this information via routine uses may be made to: a congressional office from the record of an individual in response to an inquiry from the congressional office made at the request of that individual; the Department of Justice, to a court or other tribunal, or to another party before such tribunal, when HHS is a party to litigation or has an interest in such litigation; or a contractor for the purpose of collating, analyzing, aggregating or otherwise refining or processing records in this system for developing, modifying and/or manipulating ADP Software. See the notice for system No. 09-70-0512, titled "Review and Fair Hearing Case Files," as last published in the *Federal Register*, Privacy Act Issuances 1989 Comp., Vol. 1, page 413.

You should be aware that P.L. 100-503, the "Computer Matching and Privacy Protection Act of 1988," permits the government to verify information by way of computer matches.

With one exception, which is discussed below, there are no penalties under social security law for refusing to supply information. However, failure to furnish information regarding the medical services rendered or the amount charged would prevent payment of the claim. Failure to furnish any other information, such as name or claim number, would delay payment of the claim.

It is mandatory that you tell us if you are being treated for a work related injury so we can determine whether worker's compensation will pay for the treatment. Section 1877(a)(3) of the Social Security Act provides criminal penalties for withholding this information.

According to the Paperwork Reduction Act of 1995, no persons are required to respond to a collection of information unless it displays a valid OMB control number. The valid OMB control number for this information collection is 0938-0033. The time required to complete this information collection is estimated to average 15 minutes per response, including the time to review instructions, search existing data resources, gather the data needed, and complete and review the information collection. If you have any comments concerning the accuracy of the time estimate(s) or suggestions for improving this form, please write to: CMS, Attn: PRA Reports Clearance Officer, 7500 Security Boulevard, Baltimore, Maryland 21244-1850.

- Delay resulting from efforts to secure supporting evidence, when the individual did not realize that the evidence could be submitted after filing a request
- Unusual or unavoidable circumstances that demonstrate that the individual could not reasonably be expected to have been aware of the need to file in a timely manner
- Destruction or other damage of the individual's records that was responsible for the delay in filing

A provider of services to Medicare beneficiaries may appeal (request a review of) an initial claim determination if at least one of the following conditions is true:

- The provider accepted assignment on the claim.
- The provider did not accept assignment on the claim, the claim was denied as not reasonable and necessary, and no waiver of liability was obtained from the beneficiary, thus requiring the provider to return any money collected for that service to the beneficiary.
- The provider is a nonparticipating physician, practitioner, or supplier taking assignment for a specific service.
- The provider is acting as the duly authorized representative of the beneficiary.

Before requesting a review, the EOMB should be checked to determine if (1) the allowed amount shown for that procedure is the proper allowance for that service and (2) rebundling and/or global surgery edits have been correctly applied. The appeals process *cannot* resolve complaints regarding the Medicare fee schedule or national policy decisions. Appeals should be filed only on those claims in which an error has been made or extenuating circumstances were overlooked.

Once the review is requested and additional supporting documentation submitted to the carrier, the carrier must render a decision on the review within 60 days, per BIPA.

The second level of appeal, a hearing, takes place if the provider is dissatisfied with the review determination. The provider must file a request for a hearing within 180 days of the review determination; this time limit may be extended by the hearing officer if circumstances warrant. One important distinction between a review and a hearing is that a hearing is only permitted if the Medicare-allowed amount (less any outstanding deductible) is $100 or greater (combined); a review has no dollar minimum. Another distinction involves the individual conducting the hearing; these individuals, known as hearing officers or qualified independent contractors (QICs), are not carrier employees; they are outside individuals contracted by CMS to conduct hearings. The purpose of the hearing is to give the provider another opportunity to present the reason(s) for the provider's dissatisfaction and receive a new determination based on the information presented at the hearing level. The individual requesting a hearing has the right to be represented by a qualified individual of choice, including a coding expert, health care consultant, or attorney.

There are three types of hearings: on the record, by telephone, and in person. On the record (OTR) hearings are hearings in which the hearing officer reviews documentation submitted by both the carrier and the provider and makes a determination based on his or her conclusions drawn from the documents. The documentation can include the original claim, EOMB, medical record, progress notes from outside sources (eg, a hospital record), and statements from the physician. Generally, an OTR hearing is faster than the other two types of hearings, because the hearing officer usually has all needed documents prior to the date of the hearing.

During a telephone hearing, the provider or his or her agent contacts the hearing officer by telephone and presents his or her case. The telephone conversation is recorded and transcribed and gives the provider an opportunity to speak directly with the hearing officer as opposed to relying on documentation to state his or her case.

An in-person hearing is the traditional type of hearing in which the provider or agent is offered the opportunity to present both oral testimony and written evidence to support his or her position. The in-person hearing also allows the provider the chance to dispute the information used by the carrier or reviewer to deny the claim.

The hearing officer must handle a request for a hearing in one of the following ways:

- Dismiss the request
- Remand the claim for payment
- Accept a withdrawal of the complaint by the claimant or representative
- Transfer the request for the hearing if out-of-area jurisdiction applies
- Transfer to the case appropriate party if the issues are outside of the hearing officer's responsibility

If the hearing officer does not respond within 60 days following the date of the hearing, the provider may automatically appeal the decision to the next level. If a minimum of $100 remains in controversy following the hearing officer's decision, the provider may request an appeal of the hearing officer's determination before an administrative law judge (ALJ). The request must be filed in writing and submitted to the ALJ within 60 days of the hearing officer's decision. The ALJ appeal is before the ALJ and on the record and the parties are likely represented by either a coding expert or legal counsel. Following this proceeding, the ALJ must make his or her determination within 90 days.

Under BIPA, ALJs are employed by the Social Security Administration (SSA) and consequently often hear cases unrelated to Medicare claim denials. However, the Medicare Reform Act of 2003 called for the transfer of responsibility for Medicare ALJ appeals from SSA to the Department of Health and Human Services (DHHS) no earlier than July 1, 2005, but not later than October 1, 2005. As part of the transfer, the secretary of DHHS must ensure the independence of ALJs from CMS and its contractors and must place ALJs in an office that is organizationally and functionally separate from CMS. The office of ALJ will be under the supervision of the secretary and shall not report to any other officer of DHHS. The secretary must also provide for an appropriate geographic distribution of ALJs to ensure timely access to hearings throughout the United States.

If the provider is dissatisfied with the ALJ's decision, he or she may request a review by the Departmental Appeals Board (DAB) within 60 days of the ALJ's decision. The DAB has more than 70 staff members, including the chair; four other members of the DAB (the board); eight ALJs (including the chief ALJ); four administrative appeals judges (AAJs) (Medicare Appeals Council); and the attorneys, paralegals, program analysts, and clerical staff who support the judges and provide ADR services. The DAB renders the final decisions of DHHS and must do so within 90 days of the proceeding. More information about the DAB may be found at the DAB Web site (www.hhs.gov/dab/).

The final step in the appeals process is judicial review; providers may appeal the DAB's determination by filing with the federal district court. The filing must occur no more than 60 days following the DAB's determination and the amount in controversy must exceed $1000. At this point, the case is moved into the judicial system and all judicial rules apply (rules of evidence, federal court protocols, etc). It is therefore highly recommended that the provider seek legal counsel for representation before the federal court.

As mentioned, the Medicare Reform Act modified the Medicare appeals process in several areas. These areas include:

- Effective October 1, 2004, providers and suppliers who bring appeals of Medicare claims may not introduce new evidence at the ALJ level of review unless they show good cause as to why the evidence was not introduced at an earlier level of review.
- The Medicare Reform Act expands written notice requirements of initial determinations and redeterminations by carriers, reconsiderations by QICs, and ALJ decisions.

Specifically, the notice that denies a claim must include the reasons for the determination, the procedures for obtaining additional information, and notification of the right to seek a redetermination and instructions on how to initiate an appeal.

- The number of QICs is reduced from 12 to 4 and the requirements that must be satisfied in order for an entity to contract with CMS as a QIC have been modified.
- Providers or suppliers are allowed to appeal a denial on behalf of an individual who subsequently dies if there is no one else available to pursue the appeal. The provision is effective immediately for items and services furnished on or after December 8, 2003.
- Starting in 2005, the jurisdictional amount for ALJ hearing requests and for requests for judicial review are increased for all beneficiaries each year by the percentage increase in the medical care component of the Consumer Price Index for urban customers, rounded to the nearest multiple of $10.
- CMS has been given the authority to create a process that allows providers and suppliers to correct minor errors or omissions in claims without having to file an appeal. The process was to take effect not later than December 8, 2004.
- Effective May 1, 2005, appeals of redeterminations by the fiscal intermediaries (generally Part A claims, including hospital, skilled nursing facility, home health, outpatient hospital services, and hospice claims) will go through the QIC reconsideration.
- Appeals of Part B redeterminations (generally Part B claims, including claims for physician's services and durable medical equipment) will continue to go to a fair hearing for the remainder of 2005. Reconsiderations of Part B determinations on or after January 2006 will be conducted by the QIC.
- On March 5, 2005, CMS issued an Interim Final Rule establishing new regulations for implementing the new appeals process for claim denials required by Section 521 of BIPA of 2000 and the Medicare Modernization Act (MMA) of 2000.

More often than not, it is to the provider's advantage to challenge denials not prohibited from appeal. Denials are typically the result of computer edits, in which a computer program automatically denied a claim based on the CPT® code combinations on the claim. However, computer edits often do not consider outside factors such as modifiers or different diagnoses for different procedures, thus causing claims to be denied in error. Additionally, claims processors may lack experience or make errors in keystrokes during data entry causing a denial.

The following list provides documentation sources that have proven useful as support for providers during the appeals process:

- X-ray reports
- Test results
- Medical history
- Documentation of severity or acute onset
- Consultation reports
- Billing forms
- Referrals
- Plan of treatment
- Nurses' notes
- Physicians' notes
- Ambulance trip sheets
- Operative reports
- Hospital progress notes
- Copies of communications between the physician and/or beneficiary, hospital, carrier, laboratory, etc

CONCLUSION

Knowledge of the appeals and review process as well as the ability to request a review or file an appeal of a claim is an important component of practice management. Many providers ignore the fact that they have a right to appeal a denied claim. This can result in the loss of payment from a valid insurance claim. Proper documentation is a key component of the review and appeal process. It is critical that a practice clearly document each step it performs during the review and appeal process. It is also imperative that detailed and accurate patient medical record and billing file documentation be in place.

A practice should have a process in place to review all denied claims to ensure the denial is correct. If the claim should not have been denied, the practice should request a review or file an appeal as appropriate and should be prepared to file more than one appeal to ensure that the matter is ultimately satisfactorily resolved. Guidelines for filing reviews and appeals can generally be located in the participating provider agreement or provider handbook. The Medicare appeals process can be accessed at www.cms.hhs.gov/medlearn/appeals_broch.pdf.

chapter 10

Compliance Programs and the Office of the Inspector General

OBJECTIVES

- Understand the history of compliance programs in the United States.
- Understand why compliance programs are important for health care providers.
- Understand the seven core elements of an effective compliance program.

This chapter focuses on compliance programs, a concept virtually unheard of before the passage of the Health Insurance Portability and Accountability Act (HIPAA) of 1996, Public Law 104-191, on August 21, 1996. HIPAA launched a new effort by the federal government, joined in part by the individual states, to eliminate fraud, abuse, and waste in the US health care system.

The Department of Health and Human Services (DHHS), through the Centers for Medicare and Medicaid Services (CMS), routinely reports its findings on fraud and abuse to Congress. Table 10-1 shows the estimated improper payments by type of error for Medicare. In a news release on November 10, 2005, the CMS Administrator, Mark B. McClellan, MD, PhD, announced that due to aggressive oversight and new improvement efforts, the number of improper fee-for-service Medicare claims have been reduced by one-half in one year from 10.1% in 2004 to 5.2% in 2005, a $9.5 billion reduction in improper payments. In 1996, the first year the Medicare improper payment rate was reported, the error rate was 14.2%. CMS has been able to achieve an unprecedented reduction in the error rate in spite of a growing volume of claims and increased complexities in payment processing. Table 10-2 and Figure 10-1 show estimated improper payments and that physician documentation controls the two largest causes: lack of medical necessity and unsupported charges. To address this growing problem, DHHS developed and issued "guidance documents" in the form of model compliance plans designed to assist providers in creating their own internal mechanisms to reduce improper payments. (The model plans can be downloaded at www.oig.hhs.gov/fraud/complianceguidance.html.) Since the inception of compliance programs, their direct value to health care providers has been the subject of a myriad of trade journal articles, seminars, and speeches. Numerous model compliance plans have been issued by the Office of the Inspector General (OIG) covering providers from large hospital systems to small physician groups, making it impossible for health care providers to be unaware of the government's encouragement to establish compliance programs.

This chapter reviews the history and reasoning behind the concept of compliance programs, the seven core elements that must be included for a program to be effective and thus worthwhile to the provider, the role of the compliance officer, and the risks to the provider for failure to implement a compliance program. Table 10-3 provides a summary of industry statistics showing compliance enforcement activity. *Qui tam* is a legal term, an

TABLE 10-1

National Error Rates by Year

Year	Total Dollars Paid	Overpayments		Underpayments		Overpayments + Underpayments	
		Payment	Rate	Payment	Rate	Improper Payments	Rate
1996	$168.1 B	$23.5 B	14.0%	$0.3 B	0.2%	$23.8 B	14.2%
1997	$177.9 B	$20.6 B	11.6%	$0.3 B	0.2%	$20.9 B	11.8%
1998	$177.0 B	$13.8 B	7.8%	$1.2 B	0.6%	$14.9 B	8.4%
1999	$168.9 B	$14.0 B	8.3%	$0.5 B	0.3%	$14.5 B	8.6%
2000	$174.6 B	$14.1 B	8.1%	$2.3 B	1.3%	$16.4 B	9.4%
2001	$191.3 B	$14.4 B	7.5%	$2.4 B	1.3%	$16.8 B	8.8%
2002	$212.8 B	$15.2 B	7.1%	$1.9 B	0.9%	$17.1 B	8.0%
2003	$199.1 B	$20.5 B	10.3%	$0.9 B	0.5%	$12.7 B	6.4%
2004	$213.5 B	$20.8 B	9.7%	$0.9 B	0.4%	$21.7 B	10.1%
2005	$234.1 B	$11.2 B	4.8%	$0.9 B	0.4%	$12.1 B	5.2%

TABLE 10-2

Summary of Error Rates by Category

Type of Error	1996 Net	1997 Net	1998 Net	1999 Net	2000 Net	2001 Net	2002 Net	2003 Net	2004 Net	2005 Net
No Documentation Errors	1.9%	2.1%	0.4%	0.6%	1.2%	0.8%	0.5%	5.4%	3.1%	0.7%
Insufficient Documentation Errors	4.5%	2.9%	0.8%	2.6%	1.3%	1.9%	1.3%	2.5%	4.1%	1.1%
Medically Unnecessary Errors	5.1%	4.2%	3.9%	2.6%	2.9%	2.7%	3.6%	1.1%	1.6%	1.6%
Incorrect Coding Errors	1.2%	1.7%	1.3%	1.3%	1.0%	1.1%	0.9%	0.7%	1.2%	1.5%
Other Errors	1.1%	0.5%	0.7%	0.9%	0.4%	−0.2%	0.0%	0.1%	0.2%	0.2%
IMPROPER PAYMENTS	13.8%	11.4%	7.1%	8.0%	6.8%	6.3%	6.3%	9.8%	10.1%	5.2%
CORRECT PAYMENTS	86.2%	88.6%	92.9%	92.0%	93.2%	93.7%	93.7%	90.2%	89.9%	94.8%

abbreviation of "qui tam pro domino rege quam pro sic ipso in hoc parte sequitur," which means "who as well for the King as for himself sues in this matter." Private citizens are able to file a lawsuit in the name of the US Government charging fraud by those who receive or use government funds and share in monies received. According to the US Department of Justice, qui tam lawsuits have returned more than $8.4 billion to the government since Congress amended the False Claims Act in 1986. US Department of Justice False Claims Act statistics from 1987 through 2004 are shown in Table 10-3.

THE QUALITY OF CARE STANDARD

One of the most difficult compliance issues facing physicians and other health care providers involves the quality of patient care. Failure to provide adequate diagnoses and treatments can result in charges of substandard care. And providing tests or services not generally accepted by certain health care standards may result in charges that the physician is providing medically unnecessary services. With fee-based payers alleging medically unnecessary services and capitated payers alleging substandard care, the range of

FIGURE 10-1

National Error Rates by Category, 2004 vs 2005

reasonableness is being squeezed. Only those physicians who provide not too much and not too little will be found to be promoting just the right amount of service (see Figure 10-2).

With the intense focus on government regulation and the ever-increasing scrutiny of health care providers, development and implementation of a compliance program has become important, if not vital, for all health care providers. Although the OIG has not made the development and implementation of

TABLE 10-3
Qui Tam Explosion Since 1987

FRAUD STATISTICS - OVERVIEW
October 1, 1986 - September 31, 2005
Civil Division, U.S. Department of Justice

FY	NEW MATTERS[1]		SETTLEMENTS AND JUDGMENTS[2]					RELATOR SHARE AWARDS[3]		
	NON QUI TAM	QUI TAM	NON QUI TAM[2] TOTAL	QUI TAM WHERE U.S. INTERVENED OR OTHERWISE PURSUED	QUI TAM WHERE U.S. DECLINED	QUI TAM TOTAL	TOTAL QUI TAM AND NON QUI TAM	WHERE U.S. INTERVENED OR OTHERWISE PURSUED	WHERE U.S. DECLINED	TOTAL
1987	361	66	86,479,949	0	0	0	86,479,949	0	0	0
1988	246	60	172,843,696	355,000	35,431	390,431	173,234,127	88,750	8,638	97,388
1989	236	95	197,202,180	15,111,719	0	15,111,719	212,313,899	1,446,770	0	1,446,770
1990	256	82	193,239,367	40,483,367	75,000	40,558,367	233,797,734	6,590,936	20,670	6,611,606
1991	243	90	270,945,467	69,705,771	69,500	69,775,271	340,720,738	10,667,537	18,750	10,686,287
1992	357	119	136,862,236	134,099,447	994,456	135,093,903	271,956,139	24,196,648	259,784	24,456,432
1993	329	132	187,234,076	171,438,383	5,978,000	177,416,383	364,650,459	25,636,134	1,756,902	27,393,036
1994	291	222	706,187,897	379,646,074	1,822,323	381,468,397	1,087,656,294	70,112,579	538,897	70,651,476
1995	236	277	279,522,866	245,463,627	1,813,200	247,276,827	526,799,693	46,475,379	517,238	46,992,617
1996	187	363	247,357,271	124,565,203	14,033,433	138,598,636	385,955,907	22,193,539	3,896,058	26,089,597
1997	185	533	468,549,359	622,666,381	7,136,144	629,802,525	1,098,351,884	65,938,921	1,981,346	67,920,267
1998	119	470	151,585,794	432,813,410	29,225,385	462,038,795	613,624,589	69,660,944	8,527,750	78,188,694
1999	141	481	196,613,009	454,268,984	62,509,047	516,778,031	713,391,040	49,414,054	17,593,462	67,007,516
2000	96	367	367,887,197	1,202,552,907	1,814,847	1,204,367,754	1,572,254,951	183,600,387	391,733	183,992,120
2001	88	309	494,496,974	1,175,104,715	125,726,963	1,300,831,678	1,795,328,652	187,475,850	30,294,843	217,770,693
2002	63	320	113,692,470	1,066,606,748	29,866,186	1,096,472,934	1,210,165,404	159,198,889	5,593,086	164,791,975
2003	93	334	703,003,368	1,429,086,502	87,140,070	1,516,226,572	2,219,229,940	308,280,386	19,322,900	327,603,286
2004	113	415	115,656,023	556,072,685	9,474,879	565,547,564	681,203,587	109,627,498	2,433,638	112,061,136
2005	100	394	276,794,983	1,119,347,507	22,396,229	1,141,743,736	1,418,538,719	160,199,544	6,175,933	166,375,477
TOTAL	3,740	5,129	5,366,154,182	9,239,388,430	400,111,093	9,639,499,523	15,005,653,705	1,500,804,745	99,331,628	1,600,136,373

FIGURE 10-2

The Quality of Care Standard

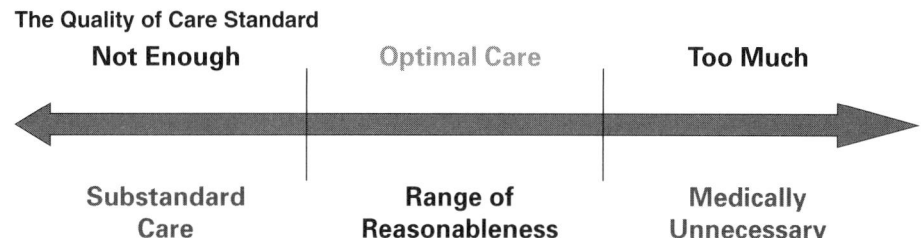

a compliance program mandatory, failure to develop an effective compliance program leaves physicians and other providers at risk for significant fines and penalties, including, but not limited to, exclusion from the federal Medicare and Medicaid programs as well as possible imprisonment. Penalties and fines are not illusory, and the number of cases investigated by the government is increasing. The value of a compliance program is recognized once it is implemented; a compliance program developed and implemented before any government investigation will be considered as a mitigating factor in an investigation of a provider. The government typically writes its own style of a compliance program (usually referred to as Corporate Integrity Agreements) for providers after an investigation, with little input from the provider. Having a "voluntary" complianced program definitely is preferred.

The OIG Model Compliance Program Guidance for Individual and Small Group Physician Practices (see Appendix B) was issued in its final form in September 2000 (and released on October 5, 2000). The final guidance addresses many of the concerns and comments raised by physicians who have long believed that compliance programs were too expensive and complex for their practices. The OIG's model compliance program for physicians identifies the following four basic compliance risks for physician practices:

- Accurate coding and billing
- Reasonable and necessary services
- Adequate clinical and CMS-1500 documentation
- Avoidance of improper inducements, kickbacks, and self-referrals

Thirteen additional risk areas are specified in the OIG guidance document, including gain sharing arrangements, professional courtesy discounts, unlawful advertising, and third-party billing services. Physicians are reminded that they remain responsible for billing errors and false claims submitted by third-party billing services, even if the physician had no knowledge of the impropriety (as noted in the OIG model).

Model plans already released by the OIG include those for nursing facilities; Medicare+Choice programs; hospices; the durable medical equipment, prosthetics, and orthotics supply industry; home health agencies; clinical laboratories; and hospitals. The OIG released program guidance for ambulance suppliers on March 24, 2003, and pharmaceutical manufacturers on May 5, 2003. Supplemental compliance program guidance for hospitals was issued on January 27, 2005. Original compliance program guidance for hospitals was issued on February 23, 1998. By issuing these draft programs for different types of providers, the OIG is encouraging the development of compliance programs tailored to each organization's needs, recognizing that the expense and complexity of a compliance program for a hospital need not be replicated by a small physician office. However, the basics of the compliance program remain similar for all providers, and the goals of the OIG remain the same. Former DHHS Inspector General June Gibbs Brown has said, "Adopting a voluntary compliance program is a lot like practicing preventive medicine; it helps identify and treat small problems before they become big problems."

Simply put, a compliance program is a combination of education, guidance, and audit procedures that allows the health care provider to maintain and monitor its efforts toward correct billing and coding. A well-developed and effective compliance program should reduce the number of claims rejected due to improper coding and billing. The risk of allegations of fraud, abuse, and waste should be decreased by the creation of an audit trail that documents the provider's efforts and commitment to follow all applicable rules and guidelines.

An effective compliance program will establish and implement a process and procedures that include checks and edits to ensure correct billing and coding. Compliance programs also give providers and their staffs a structure for keeping up with the complex and changing rules of Medicare, Medicaid, TRICARE (formerly the Civilian Health and Medical Program of the Uniformed Services [CHAMPUS]), and the other federal- and state-funded health programs. Employees are trained on issues that relate to billing and coding and on procedures to report problems, with anonymity a goal if not a guarantee. Importantly, a compliance program also should include a process to correct any identified problems.

SEVEN BASIC ELEMENTS OF AN EFFECTIVE COMPLIANCE PROGRAM

The OIG, in an effort to help create guidelines that allow for individual provider needs and differences while still clearly identifying the essentials of a compliance program, identified the following seven basic steps to developing a compliance program:

1. Establishing compliance standards through the development of a code of conduct and written policies and procedures.
2. Assigning compliance monitoring efforts to a designated compliance officer and other appropriate bodies.
3. Conducting comprehensive training and education on practice ethics and policies and procedures, including proper billing and coding procedures and specifically on any problem areas identified from monitoring and auditing.
4. Develop open, accessible lines of communication that encourage reporting of suspected violations, such as an anonymous drop box or hotline.
5. Enforcing disciplinary standards through well-publicized guidelines to ensure employees are aware that compliance is treated seriously and that violations will be dealt with consistently and uniformly.
6. Start an ongoing program of monitoring and auditing to monitor compliance with internal personnel or external sources.
7. Responding appropriately to detected violations through the investigation of allegations and the disclosure of incidents to appropriate government entities using the compliance officer, legal counsel, or outside assistance if needed.

Written Standards of Conduct and Policies

The development and distribution of written standards of conduct as well as written policies and procedures that promote the provider's commitment to compliance are vital for an effective compliance program. An initial step is to develop a code of conduct. This code should reflect the provider's philosophy as to coding, billing, patient care, and documentation. Additionally, the provider should develop a policies and procedures manual that includes all internal policies including, but not limited to, those on office procedures, billing, coding, documentation, collections and adjustments, patient quality of care, marketing, patient outreach, and employee hiring and firing. For each procedure there should be a description that include the individual (by job title) responsible for the procedure, what training is required, the method for completing the procedure, the documentation and process for reporting misconduct, and the steps for correcting misconduct. The policies and procedures manual may be developed using information available from other groups; however, it should be customized to reflect the unique characteristics of the practice. Additionally, providers should review and include publications from the government and other sources that apply to their practice. The policies and procedures manual must be updated as changes occur in law or policy. A manual that sits on a shelf with no changes, modifications, or revisions will not meet the spirit and intent of the OIG and will not protect the provider as it should.

The policies and procedures manual must be readily available to all employees. If individual copies are not provided to each employee, employees must know where the information is located. As noted in the following section on training, all new employees should be trained on the information contained in the manual.

If the provider's resources are limited, the OIG recommends focusing on those areas that put the practice at highest risk. A review of the policies and procedures currently in place, analysis of frequent rejections of claims, and an evaluation of employee and patient complaints are good starting points to identify these high-risk areas.

The Compliance Officer

The provider must designate a chief compliance officer and other appropriate individuals who will operate and monitor the compliance program. The compliance officer's duties include:

- Overseeing and enforcing the compliance program
- Ensuring that all reports of possible misconduct are promptly investigated
- Monitoring the compliance program to ensure its effectiveness
- Maintaining records of all reports made to or by the compliance officer including the resolution of the problem and the response to the reporting party
- Maintaining documentation of all compliance training and orientation of employees
- Creating and distributing a periodic and regular report of all activities, problems, and responses relating to the program as well as the general effectiveness of the program
- Developing a method to revise and improve the compliance program and providing training as needed

The compliance officer is key to the success of the compliance program. Optimally, the compliance officer should have a background and experience in billing and coding, effective communication skills, and an eye for detail. If this function is performed internally, the compliance officer should be a high-ranking officer or employee. The compliance officer should report directly to the board of directors or trustees and the chief executive officer.

An alternative to an internal compliance officer, especially for smaller physician practices and other health care providers, may be to select an outsourced consultant, billing company, or other entity to act as the compliance officer. Another alternative is to divide the responsibilities of the compliance officer among staff members who may be designated as *compliance contacts*.

Education and Training Program

The compliance program must include mandatory training of all employees, including the providers and all staff. Each employee must be made aware of his or her individual obligations to uphold the standards outlined in the code of conduct and the adverse consequences, including legal sanctions that may be imposed if the standards are not met. Periodic meetings should be held to inform staff of any regulatory and policy changes including, but not limited to, changes in Medicare and Medicaid.

The level of training may vary depending on the individual's job function. For example, coders and billers must have a greater level of understanding regarding correct coding rules, regulations, and procedures than a receptionist who may need to understand only the importance of compliance with all laws. All employees should be tested periodically to determine the understanding of their particular training.

Documentation of all training is imperative. Details and records including the schedule and content of all training must be kept, and sign-in sheets for attendees must maintained in the training records. A description of all materials distributed, including policies and procedures manuals, checklists, and any other compliance-related information along with the periodic tests and their results, should be included in the compliance officer's documentation. In addition, each personnel file should detail information of all conferences, in-services, and other training.

Educational and reference material should be available to employees at all times. The compliance library should include current information from Medicare and Medicaid publications and bulletins; current editions of the *International Classification of Diseases, Ninth Edition, Clinical Modification* (ICD-9-CM), Current Procedural Terminology (CPT®) codebook, Healthcare Common Procedure Coding System (HCPCS), and Correct Coding Initiative; and all other materials that the compliance officer determines necessary for the provider's particular practice. Smaller practices can use an office bulletin board to post and update compliance information.

Internet-based education has emerged as a viable, effective way to meet the training component of the OIG's "elements of an effective compliance program." The Internet has several important, genuine advantages for delivering information that include:

- Internet-based training and education is available 24 hours a day, 7 days a week, making it available for use by all shifts. Plus, it can be accessed anywhere there is an Internet connection.
- Internet-based training and education is well suited to the health care industry because the same program can be used across all geographic locations operated by the provider.
- The Internet affords features and functionality well suited to effective training, such as interactive quizzing, case studies, and benchmark testing. With reporting and tracking capabilities, compliance staff has instant records of who has been trained and who requires further training.
- Content can be added to the Internet platform as soon as it is created, allowing providers access to a constantly expanding curriculum that is responsive to new trends and developments

Figure 10-3 shows a compliance training tool that takes full advantage of the benefits of the Internet platform, with lessons on functional compliance integrated with legal and regulatory requirements. An online demonstration can be found at www.complianceedge.com where the viewer will be able to access some of the various menu items shown in Figure 10-3.

Process for Reporting Complaints

A compliance program cannot be effective without a clearly delineated procedure for reporting possible problems or violations. Each employee must be aware of his or her individual responsibility to immediately report any possible problems. The overall process must be user friendly and allow for prompt resolution of reported problems. Hotlines or e-mail that allow for anonymous communication may be advisable. For providers with a small number of employees, a suggestion box, "open door policy," or outside hotline service to report problems may be considered. Whatever approach is taken, a log to record the reported problem and actions taken will be strong evidence of the provider's commitment to compliance.

All employees must understand that reporting fraud or abuse is required; failure to report fraudulent or abusive activity is a violation of policy and procedure; and no retribution will

FIGURE 10-3

Sample Compliance Training and Education Tool

Internet-based tool featuring self-paced lessons, grouped in suggested courses representing major functional areas within provider settings. Lesson takes approximately 60 minutes to complete. Each lesson includes:

- Pretest
- Purpose of lesson
- Lesson objectives
- Setting the stage
- Laws/regulations
- Case studies/examples
- Pop-up windows
- Job-specific applications
- Summary
- Posttest
- Reporting features

EXAMPLES OF SPECIFIC LESSONS MAY INCLUDE

Advance notification of Medicare Non-Coverage

Medical necessity certification

Physician compliance: The Stark Law

Physician False Claims and Anti-Kickback Law

Patient Rights: Privacy, Confidentiality, & Care Participation

Compliance with outpatient technical modifiers

Physician recruitment: Anti-Kickback and Stark Law

Physician billing at teaching hospitals (PATH)

Physician recruitment and tax-exempt status

Related party transactions

Courtesy: Ernst & Young LLP, and Intellinex.

follow when filing a good-faith report of fraudulent or abusive activity. A periodic report to employees that includes information about problems discovered through the compliance efforts (without violation of confidentiality) and their resolution will encourage employees in their vigilance.

Disciplinary Procedures and Guidelines

The compliance program must include a system for responding to allegations of improper and illegal activities and for enforcing appropriate disciplinary action against employees who have violated internal compliance policies, applicable statutes, regulations, or federal health care program requirements. The compliance officer must respond quickly to any violations or problems. A thorough investigation and immediate and appropriate corrective and disciplinary actions are critical. Discipline must be consistent for infractions and violations. Ignoring problems, including failure to properly discipline the employee, may expose the provider to criminal and civil prosecution. Quick, decisive action sends a message that the provider will not tolerate inappropriate behavior.

Compliance Monitoring and Audits

Periodic monitoring and audits are effective ways to ensure that proper billing and coding procedures are in place and being followed. If time allows, qualified employees may perform this function or the provider may contract with an experienced consultant for these services. Whether conducted by an employee or contractor, a baseline must be established to determine the level of accuracy for the coding and billing process. The number of errors found in the baseline audit will also determine how often repeat audits should be performed (ie, monthly, quarterly, or yearly).

Retrospective audits are often used to illustrate how the organization manages the coding and billing processes. However, before performing a retrospective audit, a procedure for refunding overpayments if errors are found in the claims process should be established. It may also be advisable to consult counsel on the refund process. Statistically valid random samples for retrospective audits should not be selected without careful consideration, because carriers or other payers can easily use the results of such audits and may extrapolate the results to all prior claims. Audits may reveal services that were not previously billed and undercoded claims, the correction of which offsets overcoded claims.

For the most comprehensive coverage, an independent compliance risk assessment or audit may be performed by or under the supervision of legal counsel or other outside expert. This audit should include a review of all contracts and cover compliance with federal and state laws and regulations and all operating procedures. Although a smaller organization may be reluctant to expend the funds for this audit, it can be an excellent tool for discovering compliance risks that can be corrected before they become major problems.

Example reports from an outsourced monitoring service show results for evaluation and management (E/M) and CPT procedure coding by an ear-nose-throat (ENT) physician are shown in Figures 10-4 and 10-5. These figures show that the physician's use of Levels 4 and 5 codes for established patient visits was significantly less than his peers and that septoplasty and nasal endoscopy procedures were significantly higher in volume than for most other ENT physicians. Comparisons like these can identify practice profiles that may be targeted for investigation by carriers or other payers.

Most practice billing systems provide reports that compare the current month's volume by HCPCS/CPT code to prior months, quarters, or years. These comparisons can be used to identify unexplained variations that could be the result of improper coding or billing practices. This compliance monitoring process can be performed manually or it may be computerized. Typically, the manual process is limited to specific claims that may be targeted based on prior experience, professional judgement, or random selection. Computerized compliance monitoring systems offer the advantages of monitoring 100% of claims, automating the process, and maintaining continuous coverage (regardless of vacations, illness, etc). The most advanced computerized compliance monitoring systems include:

- The ability to easily interface with virtually any billing system
- All Medicare Correct Coding Initiatives, both National Coverage Determinations (NCDs) and Local Coverage Determinations (LCDs), and Medicaid edits

FIGURE 10-4

Physician Benchmarking: Evaluation and Management Distribution

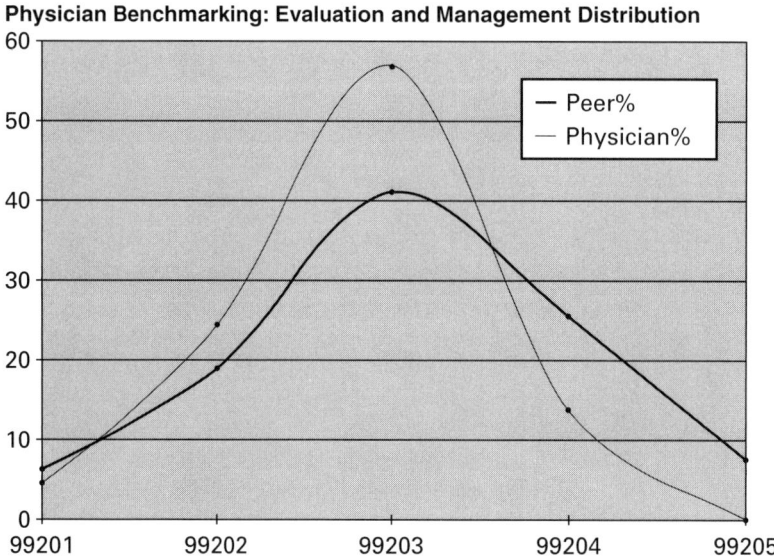

FIGURE 10-5

Physician Benchmarking: Variances From National Peers

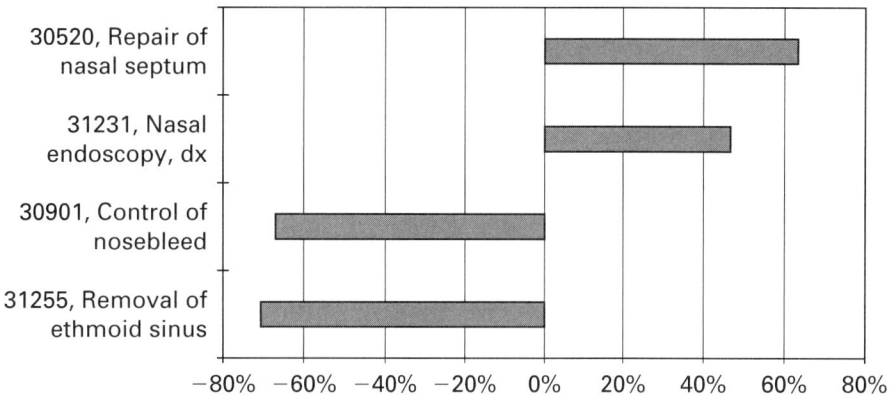

- Edits for all CPT and ICD-9-CM coding rules
- The ability to sort all edit results and other reports by date of service, account, payer, ICD-9-CM or HCPCS/CPT codes, age, sex, case length, etc
- Peer comparisons to Medicare and other payer normal distributions
- Summary graphs and detailed, drill-down reports
- The ability to monitor productivity, revenue, patterns of care, and significant variations from other peer norms and/or prior trends

Investigation and Remediation of Systemic Problems and Nonemployment or Retention of Sanctioned Individuals

Systemic, rather than isolated, coding and billing problems are of most concern to the OIG. Because of this, the OIG stresses the importance of the compliance officer who looks for trends and patterns of abuse. The compliance officer must initiate prompt steps to investigate all reports or indications of suspected noncompliance to determine whether a material violation of applicable law or compliance program requirements has occurred. If a material problem is found, the compliance officer must immediately take all steps necessary to correct the problem. This may include an immediate refund of overpayments, termination of the responsible employee, and/or a report to the government. However, it is advisable to consult with legal counsel or other outside experts prior to reporting to the government.

The OIG also encourages the compliance officer to determine whether the presence of individuals under investigation may hinder the process. If so, such individuals may be relocated until the investigation is completed. At the same time, the compliance officer should take all necessary steps to prevent the destruction of records or other evidence that may be pertinent to the investigation. All such information and evidence should be placed in a safe location by the compliance officer.

The OIG also requires providers to verify that all employees and contractors have been checked to ensure that they are not under sanctions. The OIG's List of Excluded Individuals/Entities (LEIE) is available on the Internet at http://oig.hhs.gov/fraud/exclusions.html. LEIE provides information regarding individuals and entities currently excluded from participation in Medicare, Medicaid, and all Federal health care programs. Individuals and entities who have been reinstated are removed from the LEIE. LEIE has both an online searchable database as well as two different types of downloadable databases on the site. The data is updated regularly to reflect the status of health care providers who have been excluded from participation in the Federal health care programs, including the Medicare and Medicaid programs. The General Services Administration also maintains an up-to-date Internet listing of debarred contractors on its Excluded Parties List System (EPLS) at http://epls.arnet.gov/.

Potential Medicare issues to be investigated by the OIG can be accessed via the Annual OIG Work Plan (http://oig.hhs.gov/publications/workplan.html). The work plan also provides a complete listing of the projects the OIG plans to conduct. Tables 10-4 and 10-5 summarize selected OIG Work Plan projects for 2006 that involved physician services.

COMPLIANCE AND INTERNAL CONTROLS

It is management's responsibility to establish effective internal controls. These are checks and balances to reduce the risks of transactions being recorded improperly or not being recorded at all. Effective internal controls also reduce the risk of embezzlement. Table 10-6 is an example of an internal control checklist.

Management should review its practice's internal controls using this checklist to identify major deficiencies in internal control. Deficiencies should then be addressed by reassigning tasks to improve the separation of duties by using an external accountant or consultant to provide additional independent control.

THE VALUE A COMPLIANCE PROGRAM BRINGS TO THE PROVIDER

An effective compliance program establishes an atmosphere in which commitment to proper coding, billing, and adherence to all rules and regulations is clearly articulated. The use of such a plan allows for promotion of policies and procedures used to locate and identify problems and the ability to report them when they are found; setting rules for the consistent and even-handed discipline of wrongdoers; and self-reporting to the government if overpayments or other material errors have been made. The provider who meets the standards of an effective compliance program may minimize the potential cost and disruption of a full-scale government audit and investigation, be permitted to negotiate a fair monetary settlement, and avoid an OIG exclusion preventing the entity from doing business with federal health care programs.

TABLE 10-4

OIG Projects for Medicare Physicians and Other Health Professionals

- Billing Service Companies
- Medicare Payments to VA Physicians
- Care Plan Oversight
- Ordering Physicians Excluded From Medicare
- Physician Pathology Services
- Cardiography and Echocardiography Services
- Physical and Occupational Therapy Services
- Payment to Providers of Care for Initial Preventive Physical Examination
- Part B Mental Health Services
- Wound Care Services
- "Long Distance" Physician Claims
- Potential Duplicate Physicial Therapy Claims

TABLE 10-5

Other OIG Medicare Projects

Hospitals

- Adjustments for Graduate Medical Education Payments
- Payments for Observation Services versus Inpatient Admissions for Dialysis Services
- Medical Education Payments for Dental and Podiatry Residents
- Nursing and Allied Health Education Payments
- Inpatient Prospective Payment System Wage Indices
- Inpatient Rehabilitation Facilities Payments
- Inpatient Hospital Payment for New Technologies
- Inpatient Psychiatric Hospitals
- Inpatient Rehabilitation Payments – Late Assessments
- Long Term Care Hospital Payments
- Critical Access Hospitals
- Organ Acquisition Costs
- Rebates Paid to Hospitals
- Coronary Artery Stents
- Outpatient Outlier and Other Charge-Related Issues
- Outpatient Department Payments
- Unbundling of Hospital Outpatient Services
- "Inpatient Only" Services Performed in an Outpatient Setting
- Diagnosis-Related Group Coding
- Hospital Reporting of Restraint-Related Deaths

Home Health

- Home Health Outlier Payments
- Enhanced Payments for Home Health Therapy
- Medicare Home Health Agency Survey and Certification Deficiencies
- Accuracy of Data on the Home Health Compare Web Site

Nursing Homes

- Skilled Nursing Facility Rehabilitation and Infusion Therapy Services
- Use of Additional Funds Provided to Skilled Nursing Facilities
- Skilled Nursing Facilities' Involvement in Consecutive Inpatient Stays
- Skilled Nursing Facility Payments for Day of Discharge
- Skilled Nursing Facility Consolidated Billing
- Nursing Home Deficiency Trends
- Nursing Home Residents Minimum Data Set Assessments and Care Planning
- Enforcement Actions Against Noncompliant Nursing Homes
- Imaging and Laboratory Services in Nursing Homes
- State Compliance with Compliant Investigation Guidelines
- Prescription Drug Plan Formularies and Dually Eligible Nursing Home Residents

Hospice

- Oversight of Hospice Providers
- Hospice Payments to Nursing Facilties

Medical Equipment and Supplies

- Durable Medical Equipment Payments for Beneficiaries Receiving Home Health Services
- Medicare Payments for Therapeutic Footware
- Medical Necessity of Durable Medical Equipment
- Medicare Pricing of Equipment and Supplies
- Home Blood Glucose Testing Supplies

TABLE 10-5

Other OIG Medicare Projects (*continued*)

Drug Reimbursement
- Computation of Average Sales Price
- Collecting and Maintaining Average Sales Price Data
- Effectiveness of Average Sales Price Cost Controls
- Medicare Payments for Oral Antiemetic Medications
- Monitoring of Market Prices for Part B Drugs
- Duplicate Payments for Part B Drugs Under the Competitive Acquisition Program
- Medicare Reimbursement for End State Renal Disease Drugs
- Adequacy of Reimbursement Rate for Drugs Under the Average Sales Price

Part D Administration
- CMS Program Integrity Safeguards for Medicare Drug Plan Applicants
- Beneficiary Awareness of the Medicare Part D Low-Income Subsidy
- Tracking Beneficiaries Ture Out-of-Pocket Costs for Part D Prescription Drug Coverage
- Prescription Drug Plan and Marketing Materials for Prescription Drug Benefits
- Auto-Enrollment of Dual Eligibles into Medicare Part D Plans
- Medicare Prescription Drug Benefit Pharmacy Access in Rural Areas
- Monitoring Fluctuation in Drug Prices Under Prescription Drug Plans and Medicare Advantage Prescription Drug Plans
- Coordination and Oversight of Medicare Part B and D to Avoid Duplicate Payments
- Enrollee Access to Negotiated Prices for Covered Part D Drugs
- Prescription Drug Plans' Use of Formularies
- Coordination Between State Pharmaceutical Assistance Programs and Medicare Part D
- Prescription Drug Plans' and Medicare Advantage Drug Plans' Implementation of Required Programs to Deter Fraud, Waste, and Abuse
- Prescription Drug Cards
- Employer Subsidies for Drug Coverage
- Medicare Part D Drug Benefit Payments
- State Contributions to Drug Benefit Costs Assumed by Medicare
- Medicare Part D Risk-Sharing Payments and Recoveries
- Prescription Drug Benefit

Other Medicare Services
- Laboratory Services Rendered During an Inpatient Stay
- Independent Diagnostic Testing Facilities
- Therapy Services Provided by Comprehensive Outpatient Rehabilitation Facilities
- Followup on Medicare Part B Payments for Ambulance Services
- Followup on Medicare Part B Payments for Radiology Services
- Emergency Health Services for Undocumented Aliens
- Separately Billable Laboratory Services under the End Stage Renal Disease Program
- Ground Ambulance Services
- Laboratory Profiency Testing
- Medicare Pricing of Laboratory Services
- Quality of Care in Dialysis Facilities
- Preventive Care Services

Managed Care
- Regional Plan Stabilization Fund
- Adjusted Community Rate Proposals
- Followup on Adjusted Community Rate Proposals

TABLE 10-5

Other OIG Medicare Projects (*continued*)

- Administrative Costs
- Managed Care Encounter Data
- Enhanced Managed Care Payments
- Duplicate Medicare Fee-For-Service Payments
- Marketing Practices of Managed Care Organizations
- Medicare Capitation Payments to Managed Care Plans After a Beneficiary's Death
- Medicare Advantage Regional Plans: Availability, Physician Participation, and Beneficiary Enrollment in Rural Areas
- Dissemination of Beneficiary Information Materials by Medicare Advantage Prescription Drug Plans

Contractor Operations

- Pre-award Reviews of Contract Proposals
- Contractors' Administrative Costs
- Pension Segmentation
- Pension Costs Claimed
- Unfunded Pension Costs
- Pension Segment Closing
- Postretirement Benefits and Supplemental Employee Retirement Plan Costs
- CMS Oversight of Contractor Performance
- Program Safeguard Contractor Performance
- Accuracy of the Provider Enrollment, Chain, and Ownership System
- Duplicate Medicare Part B Payments
- Handling of Beneficiary Inquiries
- Provider Education and Training
- Medicare Appeals Process

TABLE 10-6

Internal Control Checklist

- The person preparing and making deposits is not authorized to sign checks.
- A person other than the check signer can review bank statements, canceled checks, and endorsements of canceled checks for any irregularities.
- Bank accounts are reconciled monthly and reviewed by a person other than a check signer.
- Patient encounter forms are prenumbered and accounted for on a daily basis.
- The person posting payments to patient accounts does not open the mail or prepare deposits.
- Patients on the sign-in sheet are reconciled to the daily report of charges.
- Daily reports of payments received are reviewed for unposted patient charges.
- The contractual adjustments for the month and year-to-date appear reasonable based upon the practice's payer mix and payer contracts.
- A sample of patient charges is traced from the explanation of benefits to each individual patient account, and payments are traced to deposit slips.
- Write-offs of patient accounts are reviewed monthly for appropriateness.
- Individual passwords are required for access to the computer system and are not shared.
- All practice employees are bonded and undergo reference checks, which include the comparison of their names to Medicare exclusion lists.

CONCLUSION

The OIG is committed to its stated goal of combating fraud, abuse, and waste in the US health care system. An active compliance program is strong evidence of a provider's equal commitment to this goal. Developing and implementing a compliance program can appear to be a daunting task. The resources and time needed to complete the project are substantial; however, the rewards are even greater. Increased revenue, streamlined procedures, and well-educated staff are all benefits of a good compliance program. Many resources are available to help develop a compliance program. Whether a provider chooses to create his or her own program or enlist the services of an outside firm, an effective compliance program is the best way to protect the provider both financially and legally.

chapter

11

Health Insurance Portability and Accountability Act: Administrative Simplification

Health care is the largest billing system in the United States, with expenditures in 2006 topping $1.7 trillion and projected expenditures of $3.4 trillion in 2012.[1] With so many payers, providers, clearinghouses, billing services, and practice management vendors each claiming a proprietary piece of the trillion-dollar pie, health care costs were cutting deeper into the economy than expected.

Health care leaders had tried to move the industry into an efficient technology infrastructure, but with so many peripheral influences, the consensus was that health care needed a series of regulations to move it forward. Other industries such as manufacturing, retail online sales, banking, and transportation had made the transition. Now it was health care's turn.

Government and private industries collaborating in the early 1990s examined the effect electronic technology would have in minimizing administrative costs of health care transactions. It became clear that the savings generated from such a transition would be substantial. These findings provided some of the impetus behind the Administrative Simplification provisions in the Health Insurance Portability and Accountability Act of 1996 (HIPAA).

Because it promises to make health care business transactions smoother and reimbursement times quicker, Administrative Simplification is highly important to medical practices. But electronic transmission containing protected health information (PHI) comes with administrative, technical, and physical safeguards, explained in this chapter.

ADMINISTRATIVE SIMPLIFICATION OBJECTIVES

To address such chronic, systemic issues as the costs associated with paper-based transaction systems; multiple nonstandard health care data formats; and the misuse, errors relating to, and loss of health care records, HIPAA's Administrative Simplification has three overall objectives. The first objective is to improve efficiency and effectiveness of the health care system through electronic exchange of administrative and financial information. The second objective is to protect security and privacy of transmitted and stored administrative and financial information. Objective three is to identify sources of fraud and abuse, estimated at $16 billion a year.

When articulated as three straightforward objectives, Administrative Simplification seems manageable. However, the details of the Transactions, Privacy, and Security Rules are extensive. Despite their depth and complexity, many of the provisions call for appropriate and reasonable actions on your part, which are based on the size and intricacy of your business. This is known as *scalability*. Additionally, the majority of specifications are "technologically neutral"—meaning you have a choice of inputs (hardware and software systems) as long as the measures reflected in the standards are met.

Key Terms

A **covered entity** refers to any health plan, health care clearinghouse, or health care provider that chooses to transmit health information electronically. Health care providers, such as physicians, hospitals, dentists, or long-term care facilities that electronically transmit any of four types of medical information—claims or encounter information, eligibility requests, referrals and authorizations, and claim-status inquiries—must transmit the information using HIPAA standards. A different standard applies to health plans and health care clearinghouses: they must be able to receive those four transaction types, as well as conduct four others electronically: premium payment, claim payment and remittance advice, enrollment and disenrollment, and coordination of benefits. Any covered entity must comply with HIPAA's requirements.

A **covered transaction** is information exchanged electronically between two covered entities using the HIPAA-defined electronic data interchange (EDI) transaction standards for the exchange. For example, the transmission of an electronic claim by a physician to a health plan and the electronic transmission of a referral from one physician to another or to a lab or hospital are considered covered transactions. However, a patient sending an e-mail message to a physician that includes patient-identifiable information would not be a covered transaction because the patient is not a covered entity.

Electronic data interchange (EDI) refers to the computer-to-computer exchange of routine business information using publicly available standards. These standards, now being applied to health care, have been used in the retail, banking, and financial industries for years. The actual exchange of this information is called a *transaction*.[2]

HIPAA STANDARDS

There are four sets of standards within HIPAA. A *standard* is a requirement, and a *rule* is a document that includes the standards. Each rule begins with a Notice of Proposed Rule-Making (NPRM). HHS presents the NPRM for public comment and revisions and then publishes the final rule in the Federal Register. The rule's effective date may be 30 to 60 days after it is published, which allows time for public comment or for the agency to amend errors. With few exceptions, the deadline for compliance or implementation is 24 months after the rule's effective date. Each of the four sets of standards includes various sets of activities that your practice has either completed or is in the process of completing and revising (see Table 11-1).

Enforcement

Because enforcing HIPAA is such an overwhelming task, HHS has split the assignment of monitoring and enforcement between the Centers for Medicare & Medicaid Services (CMS) and the Office for Civil Rights (OCR). While OCR has enforcement authority for the privacy rule, CMS has enforcement authority for the remaining three HIPAA Administrative Simplification standards, which include transactions, code sets, identifiers, and security.

On February 16, 2006, HHS published a final rule that details the foundations and procedures for imposing civil money penalties on covered entities that violate any of the HIPAA Administrative Simplification Rules.[3] This final rule, which amends the interim rule published on April 17, 2003, applies to all of the Administrative Simplification Rules, rather than just to the privacy standards. In addition, it amends the previously existing rules "relating to the process for imposition of civil money penalties. Among other matters, the final Rule clarifies the investigation process. It also establishes the basis for liability, determination of the penalty amount, grounds for waiver, conduct of the hearing, and the appeal process."[4] The final Rule became effective on March 16, 2006.

TABLE 11-1

HIPAA Timeline

Standards Name	Date of Final Rule Publication	Deadline for Implementation	Comments
Transactions and Code Sets	August 17, 2000	October 16, 2002 October 16, 2003 April 16, 2003	TCS is now in effect.
Privacy Rule	Published December 28, 2000, but effective April 14, 2001. Modifications finalized August 14, 2002.	April 14, 2003	In effect. Office for Civil Rights at HHS is enforcement agency for this Rule.
Security Rule	Notice of Proposed Rule Making published on August 12, 1998. Final rule published February 20, 2003.	Effective date, April 21, 2003. Compliance date, April 21, 2005.	In effect. Centers for Medicare and Medicaid Services (CMS) is the enforcement agency.
National Identifier Standards	National Provider Identifier Rule issued January 23, 2004.	Effective date, May 23, 2005. Compliance date, May 23, 2007.	NPI must be used by covered entities to identify providers on all HIPAA-covered transactions that call for health care provider identifiers.

Are you a covered entity?

The Administrative Simplification standards adopted by HHS under HIPAA apply to any entity that is:

- a health care provider that conducts certain transactions in electronic form (referred to as a *covered entity*)
- a health care clearinghouse
- a health plan.[5]

Therefore, any health care provider that submits health information electronically in a designated HIPAA transaction is a covered entity. The electronic submission of a claim for reimbursement is one type of HIPAA transaction. The electronic claim contains information that can identify a patient, including, but not limited to, name, address, zip code, phone number, Social Security number, e-mail address, or driver's license number.[6]

HIPAA PRIVACY RULE

The *Standards for Privacy of Individually Identifiable Health Information* ("Privacy Rule") establishes a set of national standards to protect certain health information. The Privacy Rule applies to all covered entities and establishes conditions under which protected health information (PHI) can be used or disclosed in a health care environment. It also sets forth specific rights to patients so that they can have greater control over how health information about them is used and disclosed.[7]

By now, most practices have implemented the Privacy Rule and have found a relative comfort zone in understanding the Privacy Rule, but some aspects of the application of those privacy standards may still be unclear. So, allow the following to serve as a refresher on the Privacy Rule.

Use and Disclosure of Protected Health Information

There are several types of permitted disclosures—meaning you can send protected health information (PHI) externally without written permission or authorization from the patient.

Contact your privacy official for any questions about permitted disclosures in your state. HIPAA defers to state laws if a relevant state law is more stringent.

In most cases, public laws allow you freedom to conduct your own business, unless there is a stipulation against it. HIPAA is just the opposite. The Privacy Rule gives physicians specific guidelines for when to disclose PHI. The basic principle is that a health care provider and its employees, as a covered entity, cannot use or disclose PHI, except as permitted or required by the Rule.

To determine if information about a patient is PHI, begin by asking three questions.

1) Is the information created or received by a health care provider, health plan, employer, or health care clearinghouse? *(Did you create the information?)*
2) AND, does the information relate to the past, present, or future diagnosis or treatment of a physical or mental condition? *(Does the information relate to the patient's diagnosis or treatment?)*
3) OR, does it relate to a payment claimed or paid for a past, present, or future diagnosis or treatment of a physical or mental condition? *(Will the information be used to file a claim or to secure payment for services?)*

Next, ask yourself if the information is individually identifiable? Individually identifiable information is specific information about the patient, such as name, zip codes, Social Security number, date of birth, e-mail address, telephone number, photos, medical record numbers, etc. To use or disclose this information, determine whether you need permission to disclose it.

To "use" PHI means that you or a member of your staff uses a patient's protected health information internally. To "disclose" PHI means that you send a patient's protected health information outside the office. You are allowed to use and disclose patient information, but you must have a reason for each use or disclosure.

The basic premise of the Privacy Rule is that you must identify a permission (or a reason), even those that come with special requirements, to use or disclose patient information.[8] Within the Privacy Rule, there are 11 permissions that pertain to how you can use and disclose PHI. In general, the Privacy Rule permits you to use and disclose health information within parameters of these 11 permissions without written permission from the patient. However, nine remaining areas require specific policies and procedures on how you will manage PHI (see Table 11-2).

In order to ensure that your organization is compliant with the HIPAA Privacy Rule, you must:

- Appoint a privacy official, and seek initial HIPAA awareness training.
- Develop a privacy team.

TABLE 11-2

Permissions & Special Requirements for Disclosing PHI

Permissions	Special Requirements
Required disclosures, such as to public health agencies	Verification
Disclosures to the patient	Minimum necessary
Your own treatment, payment, operations	Business associates
Others' treatment, payment, operations	Personal representatives
Legally assigned personal representatives (friends, family)	Marketing
Disaster relief organizations	Psychotherapy notes
Incidental disclosures	Use or disclosure consistent with Notice of Privacy Practices
Public purpose	Use or disclosure consistent with other documents
Authorization	State laws (consent or other law)
De-Identification	
Limited data set	

- Determine how your office will respond to patient requests.
- Develop forms for patients to complete for each request, including an authorization form.
■ Decide how you will manage documentation requirements for use and disclosure.
■ Find out what privacy and security gaps might exist by conducting a "gap analysis."
■ Map out how PHI flows through your office.
■ Develop a Notice of Privacy Practices (NPP), and distribute it to all patients upon their first visit. Log patient signatures acknowledging receipt of the NPP.[9]

The Privacy Rule gives patients rights with regard to their health information and sets rules and limits on who can look at and receive their health information. In order to ensure that this information is protected but does not interfere with health care, PHI can be used and shared in several ways:

■ For a patient's treatment and care coordination
■ To pay doctors and hospitals for health care and help run their businesses
■ With family, relatives, friends or others the patient identifies who are involved with their health care or their health care bills, unless the patient objects
■ To make sure doctors give good care and nursing homes are clean and safe
■ To protect the public's health, such as by reporting when the flu is in a particular area
■ To make required reports to the police, such as reporting gunshot wounds[10]

Unless this law allows electronic exchange of health information under "treatment, payment, and health care operations," a patient's health information cannot be used or shared without his or her written permission. For example, if written authorization has not been given by the patient, a provider cannot use identifiable health information for marketing purposes, give information to the patient's employer, or share private notes about mental health counseling sections. Covered entities that are required to follow the Privacy Rule must comply with patients' right to:

■ See and obtain a copy of their health records
■ Request corrections be added to their health information
■ Receive a notice that tells them how their health information may be used and shared
■ Decide if they want to give their permission before their health information can be used or shared for certain purposes, such as for marketing
■ Get a report on when and why their health information was shared for certain purposes.[11]

If a patient feels that a covered entity violated his or her (or another patient's) health information privacy rights or committed any other violation of the Privacy Rule, the patient may file a complaint with the Office for Civil Rights (OCR). OCR has been designated by the Secretary of HHS as responsible for enforcing the Privacy Rule. Enforcement is based on complaints, and HHS is obligated to follow up on every complaint.

If your organization does fall under investigation or a representative from HHS visits your office, you will be responsible for producing significant records that document your privacy efforts. Investigations such as these are costly to you and to taxpayers, so your best defense is good communication. If you are aware that a patient has a problem, discuss it with the patient before he or she files a complaint.

However, if a patient does file a health information privacy complaint with OCR, the complaint must:

■ Be filed in writing, either on paper or electronically (mail, fax, or e-mail)
■ Name the entity that is the subject of the complaint
■ Describe the acts or omissions believed to be in violation of the applicable requirements of the Privacy Rule
■ Be filed within 180 days of when the patient knew that the act or omission occurred (extended by OCR only if the patient shows "good cause")[12]

Protecting patient confidentiality is of the utmost importance. Because patients expect to experience an atmosphere of confidentiality with their physician, they often reveal bits of information about their personal, spiritual, and professional lives. However, once the detailed medical record leaves the examining room, it goes through the hands of many people in the office, most of whom need access to only certain pieces of the information.

Need to Know, or Minimum Necessary

The notion of "need to know" may not be new to many industries, but it is to health care. In HIPAA, "need to know" is referred to as *minimum necessary*.

In order to ensure that all aspects of the HIPAA Privacy Rule are being met, it is crucial to assign a privacy official. Your privacy official is the person responsible for developing and implementing the policies, procedures, and privacy compliance program. The privacy official becomes the office's primary HIPAA expert. There are several components to choosing your organization's privacy official (see Table 11-3).

Your practice's privacy official also leads the privacy team. The privacy team will help ensure that minimum necessary standards are met by, for instance, making a list of persons who have access to specific portions of patient files. In addition, the practice will be required to designate passwords that control user access to patient files.

Notice of Privacy Practices

If yours is a new practice, the privacy official will need legal assistance building a Notice of Privacy Practices (NPP), also referred to as a Notice of Information Practices. Existing practices should already have an NPP in place.

The NPP serves three main purposes. The first is to spell out how your practice will use and disclose PHI, with or without a patient's consent, for treatment, payment, and health care operations; how medical information about payment may be used and disclosed; and how the patient can gain access to his or her medical information. The second purpose is to detail what actions the staff will take to protect the patient's privacy. The third purpose of the NPP is to spell out the patient's rights under HIPAA's Privacy Rule.[13]

Not many providers can afford to hire a lawyer to develop their own NPP. Therefore, it is a good idea to evaluate several NPPs, and create one that works best for you. Several helpful web sites are the North Carolina Health Care Information and Communications Alliance (www.nchica.org), the American Medical Association (www.ama-assn.org), HIPAA Collaborative of Wisconsin (www.hipaacow.org), and Pacific Retirement Services (www.retirement.org/hipaa).

While examining the web sites, it is important to remember that these are only sample documents. It can be risky to rely on someone else's NPP, unless you fully understand what it means and how the plan will affect your practice. If you are called to defend your privacy practices in a civil or criminal case, a lawyer will likely use your NPP as "Exhibit A."

TABLE 11-3

How to Designate a Privacy Official

- Create a job description
- Establish qualifications
- Establish a reporting structure
- Discuss salary or bonuses for taking on the additional responsibilities
- Document the level of independent decision-making authority given to the privacy official
- Consult with an attorney on documentation
- Encourage the privacy official to obtain a privacy designation offered through the American Accreditation Health Care Commission (www.urac.org) or the American Health Information Management Association (www.ahima.org)

Once your NPP has been developed, it is important to know how and when to distribute it. Anyone who enters your practice, whether a patient or not, may request to see the NPP. The Privacy Rule permits all persons to shop around and review NPPs from any covered entity prior to becoming a patient.

The NPP should be distributed to each patient on his or her first day of service and also posted where it can easily be seen in a common area of the practice. Present the NPP when the patient first arrives, and ask the individual to read and sign the acknowledgment form at the end of the NPP. By signing, the person is not agreeing to the NPP's contents, he or she is only acknowledging receipt. If an individual refuses to sign, keep a log of the response. However, you cannot deny care to a patient who refuses to acknowledge receipt.[14]

If at some point you want to change some portion of your NPP, you can do so. Because it is a legal document, you must carefully reconstruct the language you want to alter and it is certainly recommended that you seek the advice of an attorney. Be certain when developing your NPP that it includes a statement claiming that your practice reserves the right to make a revision and that it describes how the practice will provide recipients with the revised version. If a material change regarding use and disclosure of PHI is made, your practice must follow a legal process that your attorney should describe to you, including resending the NPP to all patients who have already acknowledged receipt. After making the change, post the revised version in a common area, and continue offering the document to all new patients.

Administrative, Physical, and Technical Safeguards

The Privacy Rule imparts mandates for administrative, physical, and technical safeguards pertaining to oral, paper, and electronic protected health information (ePHI). Often referred to as "the mini Security Rule within the Privacy Rule," these safeguards correspond with those you'll find in both the Privacy and Security Rules.

"Safeguards" refers to the measures you take to protect confidential patient information. HIPAA obligates you to protect the confidentiality of health information in your practice.

Administrative Safeguard

Administrative safeguards, included in both the Privacy and the Security Rules, are "administrative actions, and policies and procedures, to manage the selection, development, implementation, and maintenance of security measures to protect electronic protected health information and to manage the conduct of the covered entity's workforce in relation to the protection of that information."[15] The Privacy Rule requires covered entities to perform 10 administrative tasks to protect the privacy of health information, and the practice's management team must take action to meet the requirements. Table 11-4 details the required administrative tasks.[16]

Technical Safeguards

Due to technology advancements in the health care industry, technical safeguards are becoming more and more important. New security challenges emerge as technology improves, and health care organizations are faced with the task of protecting electronic protected health information (EPHI) from a variety of internal and external risks. Implementation of the Technical Safeguards standards signifies good business practices for technology policies and procedures within a covered entity.[17]

Table 11-5 illustrates some of the technical safeguard issues that may arise with employees.

To the average worker, technical safeguards may sound complicated, but they are much easier to comprehend when put into simple language. Table 11-6 defines many of the terms associated with the Technical Safeguards and computer security.

Physical Safeguards

An essential step in protecting ePHI is to implement reasonable and appropriate physical safeguards for information systems and related equipment and facilities. Physical safeguards represent smart business practices, and most of them are built on common sense.

TABLE 11-4

HIPAA Privacy Administrative Tasks and How to Do Them

What to Do	How to Do It
Appoint a privacy official.	The privacy official may also be the office manager. The privacy official is responsible for developing and implementing the privacy policies and procedures. Delegate a privacy team to help the privacy official, although the privacy official is accountable for privacy. The privacy official also may be the designation security official, as required by the Security Rule.
	Appoint a contact person to receive complaints.
	Send the Privacy Official to training. Expect a six- to eight-month learning curve.
	Keep the privacy official in contact with health-law attorney for legal advice.
Develop HIPAA policies and procedures	Develop your own or adopt and revise a set of policies and procedures from a vendor. Your policies and procedures can be scaled—if you're a small practice, you don't need 200 pages of policies and procedures.
	You must follow your policies and procedures. If you amend them, keep the old policies for six years, and retrain your entire staff in the new policy or procedure.
Develop and implement safeguards.	It's one thing to write a policy that tells staff to lock the doors at night or to keep voices down so that other patients can't hear, and another thing to practice privacy all the time.
	Safeguards prevent unintended uses and disclosures. Safeguards include the administrative, technical, and physical processes in this section.
Develop a documentation process.	Develop new documentation habits that put into writing how you use and disclose patient information, patient activities and requests, and document policies and procedures.
	Keep documentation for six years from the date the record was created or six years from when it was last used, whichever is later.
Train your staff.	HIPAA requires that you train your staff on your policies and procedures. Set aside one to two hours to train employees in appropriate groups: ■ Persons with direct patient contact, ■ Persons with little or no direct contact, and ■ Persons with management responsibilities.
	Keep a record of who attended training, and test them for understanding.
	Retrain if there are unintentional breaches.
	Train staff members when they accept new responsibilities.
	Train new staff when they come on board.
	Ask staff members to sign confidentiality agreements or an acknowledgment at the completion of training. These agreements should state that PHI cannot be disclosed even after the employee leaves the practice.
Develop a process for complaints.	Include a process for making complaints in your NPP so that patients will complain to you rather than the Secretary of HHS.
	Identify this process in your policies and procedures.
	Determine who receives the complaint and who follows up on the complaint.
	Designate a process to complete if the complaint is significant.
	Develop a plan to mitigate serious complaints.
Develop sanctions.	Develop a policy and procedure that sanctions employees and volunteers for intentional breaches and unintentional incidents. NOTE: Be certain you can live with your sanctions. Don't say you'll suspend an employee after three privacy breaches unless you intend to do so.
Mitigate breaches.	Develop a policy and procedures for mitigating any harmful effect that comes from a privacy violation. This includes breaches caused by business associates. Your privacy official is most likely the person to follow this policy.

TABLE 11-4 (*continued*)

HIPAA Privacy Administrative Tasks and How to Do Them

What to Do	How to Do It
Do not allow intimidation or retaliation.	Develop a policy that states you will not intimidate, harass, or retaliate against any patient for exercising any right under the HIPAA Privacy Rule, including the right to file a complaint.
Do not ask patients to waive rights.	Develop a policy that states you will not ask patients to waive their rights before you will treat them.

TABLE 11-5

Technical Safeguard Issues

Technical Safeguard Issue	Description
Sharing passwords	Even the sharing of passwords between physicians and office manager is no longer allowed.
Internet shopping	Computers left open to the Internet can leave medical records exposed to outsiders.
Friends and family e-mail lists	Do you send and receive personal e-mails at the office? Each time you receive an e-mail from a nonsecure site such as AOL or Earthlink, you are exposing your computer to viruses.
Computer games	Are you aware of what is on each employee's desktop? Are there games that can crash your network? Games may contain viruses that damage network data.
Remote access	Do the physicians in your practice download medical records from home via nonsecure Internet providers, update the records, and e-mail them back to the office?
"Minimum necessary"	Who has access to the medical records? Employees' passwords should give them only the level of information they need to do their job.

TABLE 11-6

Technical Safeguard Terms[18]

Technical Safeguard Term	What It Means
Access control	Access control includes policies and procedures to allow staff access using one password only and to guarantee that each person's password is not shared by others.
Emergency access procedure	Establish, and implement as needed, procedures for obtaining necessary ePHI during an emergency.
Encryption and decryption	Implement a mechanism to code and decode ePHI.
Audit controls	A person or software program that checks to make sure the right people have access to the right information.
Authentication	A process to make sure the person logging on really is that person.
Transmission security	Put in place technical security measures to guard against unauthorized access to PHI that is being electronically transmitted.
Contingency planning	The plan you follow if something happens to your electronic data.
Encryption	Similar to a locked door, but instead of using a key to enter, the program uses random bits of information with different lengths.
Passwords	The unique set of numbers and/or letters that identifies you as the user. Make sure that you and your staff do not share passwords with anyone.
Media controls	Receiving and removing information from hardware and software in and out of a facility. For example, when you donate used computers to the local college, you must eliminate the "media" or data on your computer before it goes to someone else.
Security incident	A breach. Someone may hack into the system, but, more likely, an employee has shared information that should not have been shared.

- Do you lock the doors?
- Is the building protected from environmental hazards and unauthorized intrusion?
- Keep medical records away from public view. Can any computer screens be seen by the public when you or a staff member steps away?
- Laptops and handheld computers: Are they put into a safe or locked up when you're away?
- Patient files: Are they protected from access by non-authorized persons?
- Building maintenance: Do maintenance workers have access to medical records? Have your personnel been trained about HIPAA and signed confidentiality agreements?

Walk around the inside and outside of your building, even if you've implemented the Privacy Rule. It simply makes good sense to run through a privacy checklist from time to time.

Why bother with the Privacy Rule?

- It's the law.
- It will protect your office assets.
- As you and your colleagues move into an electronic environment, patients will have greater confidence in you and your staff if they know you take privacy seriously.

HIPAA SECURITY RULE

Privacy is about controlling what information is permitted to be used and disclosed and to whom. Security is about controlling access to PHI. Privacy and Security go hand in hand. You can't ensure confidentiality of electronic health files without a plan to manage security of those records.

In 2003, Hurricane Isabel damaged many businesses along the Eastern seaboard. Depending on their level of preparedness, some medical and dental facilities were up and running within 24 hours. Others had to wait 30 days. Practices with electronic health records stored off site made a phone call to their storage vendor and requested an upload of patient records that had been backed up before the hurricane hit. With the flip of a switch, doctors had access to their patients' records and were back to work while their counterparts who used paper records were sending drenched files to an industrial freezer in hopes their records could be restored.

A disaster recovery plan, one of the Security Rule requirements, is good business. What would you do if a fire raged through your office? Do you know where your practice's insurance policy is kept? Could you set up temporary offices in a nearby school or with a fellow practitioner?

And what about background checks? Do you think doctors should bother with them when there are only three or four employees total? Ask a doctor who has been the subject of theft whether a background check might have uncovered a guilty staff member's malicious history.

The Administrative Simplification provisions of HIPAA required the HHS to establish national standards for the security of electronic health care information. The final rule adopting HIPAA standards for security was published in the Federal Register on February 20, 2003. Unlike the Privacy Rule, which applies to protected health information (PHI) in electronic, oral, and paper media, the final Security Rule applies only to *electronic* protected health information (ePHI). Both rules cover PHI "at rest" (storage) and "during transmission." The Privacy Rule defines authorized and required uses and disclosures of such information as well as the rights patients have with respect to it. The Security Rule defines protections for such information.

Three key definitions of properties comprise the foundation for security of ePHI: *integrity*, *confidentiality*, and *availability*.

- *Integrity* is the property that such information has "not been altered or destroyed in an unauthorized manner."
- *Confidentiality* is the property that such information is "not made available or disclosed to unauthorized persons or processors."

- *Availability* is the property that such information is "accessible and useable upon demand by an authorized person."

These properties, as well as other security attributes, are embodied in the three types of security standards previously discussed: *administrative safeguards*, *physical safeguards*, and *technical safeguards*. Within administrative, physical, and technical safeguard categories are *standards* and *implementation specifications*. Covered entities are required to comply with the standards and to follow the implementation specifications, which define what needs to be done to achieve compliance with the Security Rule. Implementation specifications are categorized by either *required* or *addressable*, which will be discussed in the next section.

It is important to note several characteristics of the Security Rule.

1. "In general, the security standards will supersede any contrary provision of State law."[19]
2. The security standards establish "a minimum level of security that covered entities must meet."

Accordingly, compliance with the Security Rule is designed to provide "a floor of protection of all electronic protected health information," but take into consideration that covered entities are of different sizes and complexities, and, thus, likely to require different means to achieve protection of electronic protected health information. As a result, the Security Rule is considered "technologically neutral."[20]

The foundation of the Security Rule is that security protections must be "reasonable and appropriate," as assessed in a required risk analysis and study of risk management measures. The Security Rule is designed to be "scalable and flexible." A small physician practice will have a different array of security protections than a large practice, clinic, or hospital, with the selection of security protections determined by the risk analysis.

Many of the protections you build will be reflected and documented in written (paper or electronic form) policies and procedures that must be kept current, with such documentation retained for six years from date of creation or date last in effect. Similar documentation must be created and maintained that memorializes "actions, activities, and assessments" pertaining to the Security Rule.

Both types of documentation must be made available to members of the practice workforce who are responsible for or affected by the Security Rule. Figure 11-1 exemplifies a sample risk analysis. And therein is the key to implementing the Security Rule. Your policies and procedures will depend on the outcome of your risk analysis.

FIGURE 11-1

Sample Risk Analysis

Below is an example of a portion of a risk analysis that you might conduct in your practice. As you will see, you will have to protect passwords to computer software that gives access to databases containing ePHI.

1. Your objective is to ensure that passwords are protected.
2. Survey the workforce to determine how each person protects his or her password.
3. Ask each person if he or she has disclosed his or her password to another member of the workforce.
4. Observe computer stations to note if there are any posted password reminders.
5. Based on the findings of the survey and observations, assess the practice's vulnerability.
6. Determine if there have been any database intrusion security incidents as a result of a breakdown in password protection.
7. Prepare policies and procedures for protecting passwords, based on mitigating past, existing, or potential vulnerabilities.
8. Make password protection policies and procedures a key element of the practice's training and make sure the workforce understands how vulnerable the practice could be if passwords were compromised.
9. Assess and update this portion of the practice's overall risk analysis, both on a periodic basis and after any related security incident that involves a breakdown of password protection.

FIGURE 11-2
Structure of the Security Rule

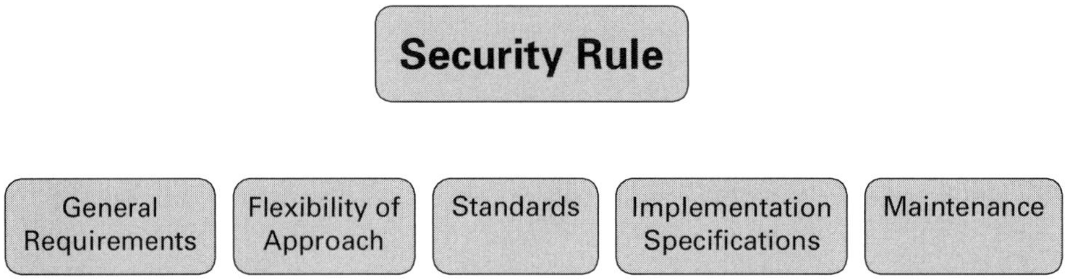

[Security Rule]

[General Requirements] [Flexibility of Approach] [Standards] [Implementation Specifications] [Maintenance]

General Rules

There are five general rules in HIPAA's Security Rule. Refer to Figure 11-2 for an overview of the structure.

General Requirements

There are four general requirements in the general rules:

1. Ensure the confidentiality, integrity, and availability of all ePHI the covered entity creates, receives, maintains, or transmits.
2. Protect against any reasonably anticipated threats or hazards to the security or integrity of such information.
3. Protect against any reasonably anticipated uses or disclosures of such information that are not permitted or required under Privacy of Individually Identifiable Health Information.
4. Ensure compliance with the Security Rule by its workforce.[21]

These requirements provide the foundation for the administrative, physical, and technical safeguards.

Flexibility of Approach

The general rule provides for flexibility of approach in complying with the Security Rule. Because of its importance in providing a foundation for the scalability of administrative, physical, and technical safeguards, the two parts of this rule are reproduced here:

1. Covered entities may use any security measures that allow the covered entity to reasonably and appropriately implement the standards and implementation specifications as specified in Security Standards for the Protection of Electronic Protected Health Information.
2. In deciding which security measures to use, a covered entity must take into account the following factors:
    a. The size, complexity, and capabilities of the covered entity.
    b. The covered entity's technical infrastructure, hardware, and software security capabilities.
    c. The costs of security measures.
    d. The probability and criticality of potential risks to electronic protected health information.[22]

Implementation Specifications

There are two types of implementation specifications: required and addressable. If an implementation specification is designated "required," a covered entity must implement the specification. The term *addressable* is more complicated and provides the covered entity with options. These options are outcomes of the risk analysis that the practice conducts. When analyzing a particular addressable implementation specification for a standard, the practice must determine "whether each implementation specification is a *reasonable and appropriate* safeguard in its environment, when analyzed with reference to the likely contribution to protecting the entity's electronic protected health information."[23]

In this and other addressable implementation specifications, the covered entity must balance the safeguard specification with the degree of risk mitigation the specification affords, taking into consideration its analysis of risk, strategy for risk mitigation, security protections already in place, and cost of implementation. If the covered entity determines that the implementation specification is a reasonable and appropriate safeguard, it must implement the specification.

If your practice determines that the implementation specification is not reasonable and appropriate, you have two options, for each of which you must document why the implementation specification is not reasonable and appropriate.

First, if the specification is required, you must document why it is not reasonable and appropriate and implement one or more alternative equivalent measures, or a combination of such measures, *if reasonable and appropriate*. Second, if you can otherwise document that the standard can be met, the covered entity may choose to implement neither the implementation specification nor alternative equivalent measure(s). In either circumstance, written documentation of the decision is critical.

To address an implementation specification, you have three choices.

Do it	Comply with the standard. Document how you will comply.
Don't do it	Document why this standard doesn't apply to you.
Alternate measure	You have an alternate approach. Document your decision, document your rationale, and document what you plan to do instead.

Maintenance

This part of the general rule requires that covered entities review their security measures periodically and make modifications as necessary to ensure that they continue to provide "reasonable and appropriate protection of electronic protected health information."

Privacy and Security Overlap

Not as many people understand the Security Rule because it appears to contain technology jargon. At the hospital level or large physician network level, it will be imperative to create a more sophisticated secure environment. In larger health environments, a computer systems engineer will offer strategies to protect information from malicious, intentional or unintentional acts. The engineer will also audit persons who have access to systems and block access to those who shouldn't be looking at PHI. But you won't have to be a "techie" to understand what's important about HIPAA Security.

As you get to know the ins and outs of the Security Rule, you'll see that it's more about people and business management than it is about technology. Begin by leveraging what you learned about privacy, because the Privacy and Security Rules overlap. One major difference is that they use different terms to describe similar concepts (see Table 11-7).

Get to Know the Security Safeguards

Most likely the administrative, physical, and technical safeguards look familiar to you because you've already implemented 60 percent of the Security Rule when implementing the Privacy Rule.

Here we'll present the safeguards, then present a checklist of actionable items for you to manage your Security implementation (see Tables 11-8 through 11-10).

TABLE 11-7

Leverage Privacy to Meet Security

Privacy	Security
Minimum Necessary	Access Control
	Information Access Management
Verification	Person or Identity Authentication
Sanctions	Sanctions
Training	Training
Business Associate contracts	Business Associate contracts
Policies and Procedures	Policies and Procedures
Uses and disclosures (NPP)	Information System Activity Review
Complaints to Covered Entity	Incident Procedures
Notice of Privacy Practices	Evaluation
Technical Safeguards	Facility Access Control
	Workstation Security
	Device and Media Controls

TABLE 11-8

Administrative Safeguards

Standards	Sections	Implementation Specifications	(R)=Required, (A)=Addressable
Security Management Process	164.308(a)(1)	Risk Analysis	(R)
		Risk Management	(R)
		Sanction Policy	(R)
		Information System Activity Review	(R)
Assigned Security Responsibility	164.308(a)(2)		(R)
Workforce Security	164.308(a)(3)	Authorization and/or Supervision	(A)
		Workforce Clearance Procedure	(A)
		Termination Procedures	(A)
Information Access Management	164.308(a)(4)	Isolating Health Care Clearinghouse Function	(R)
		Access Authorization	(A)
		Access Establishment and Modification	(A)
Security Awareness and Training	164.308(a)(5)	Security Reminders	(A)
		Protection from Malicious Software	(A)
		Log-in Monitoring	(A)
		Password Management	(A)
Security Incident Procedures	164.308(a)(6)	Response and Reporting	(R)
Contingency Plan	164.308(a)(7)	Data Backup Plan	(R)
		Disaster Recovery Plan	(R)
		Emergency Mode Operation Plan	(R)
		Testing and Revision Procedure	(A)
		Applications and Data Criticality Analysis	(A)
Evaluation	164.308(a)(8)		(R)
Business Associate Contracts and Other Arrangement	164.308(b)(1)	Written Contract or Other Arrangement	(R)

TABLE 11-9

Physical Safeguards

Standards	Sections	Implementation Specifications	(R)=Required, (A)=Addressable
Facility Access Controls	164.310(a)(1)	Contingency Operations	(A)
		Facility Security Plan	(A)
		Access Control and Validation Procedures	(A)
		Maintenance Records	(A)
Workstation Use	164.310(b)		(R)
Workstation Security	164.310(c)		(R)
Device and Media Controls	164.310(d)(1)	Disposal	(R)
		Media Re-use	(R)
		Accountability	(A)
		Data Backup and Storage	(A)

TABLE 11-10

Technical Safeguards

Standards	Sections	Implementation Specifications	(R)=Required, (A)=Addressable
Access Control	164.312(a)(1)	Unique User Identification	(R)
		Emergency Access Procedure	(R)
		Automatic Logoff	(A)
		Encryption and Decryption	(A)
Audit Controls	164.312(b)		(R)
Integrity	164.312(c)(1)	Mechanism to Authenticate Electronic Protected Health Information	(A)
Person or Entity Authentication	164.312(d)		(R)
Transmission Security	164.312(e)(1)	Integrity Controls	(A)
		Encryption	(A)

TRANSACTIONS AND CODE SETS

Overview of Transactions

In its simplest form, codes are published sets of numbers that people and computers use to identify a patient's diagnosis; the physician's recommended procedures to relieve pain and, if possible, heal the patient; and purchase of medical equipment and pharmaceuticals. Codes evolved from years of vague and inconsistent communications to established standards that tracked common illness and treatment. As electronic transactions began to take hold in the health care industry, vendors developed claim forms, vendor-specific and payer-specific codes, referral forms, prior authorizations, and explanations of benefits/explanations of payment (EOB/EOP). HIPAA finally standardized these administrative functions on August 17, 2000 when final transaction and code set standards were published by the federal government.

HIPAA transaction standards are the rules that standardize the electronic exchange of administrative information. Health care providers must comply with six sets of rules, including four of the eight covered-transaction standards:

- General provisions
- Code Sets
- Four transaction standards
  - Health care claims or equivalent encounter information
  - Eligibility for a health plan
  - Referral certification and authorization
  - Health care claim status

General Provisions

The value of using the transaction standards is that all covered entities engaged in a health care transaction communicate in a common language, whether they be a physician and payer handling a claim or a physician inquiring of a health plan about a plan beneficiary's eligibility. Not surprisingly, then, covered entities are prohibited from changing data definitions or other data specifications in conducting the transaction.

It is imperative that you verify that your vendor's transactions are based on HIPAA standards because, as the covered entity, you are ultimately responsible for HIPAA compliance. Your system vendor is a business associate under HIPAA and must provide you with assurance that working on your behalf it is using HIPAA-compliant specifications. But compliance is based solely on implementation of standards covered by entities. The term is not directly relevant to vendors and applies only indirectly to business associates, through you as the covered entity.

Code Sets

Code sets define much of the medical information or data content used in the transactions. A *code set* is defined as "any set of codes used to encode data elements, such as tables of terms, medical concepts, medical diagnostic codes, or medical procedure codes. A code set includes the codes and descriptors of the codes."[24]

The code sets fall into four categories:

- Codes for diseases, impairments, or other health-related problems.
- Codes for the causes of the injuries, diseases, impairments, or other health-related problems.
- Actions taken to prevent, diagnose, treat, or manage diseases, injuries, and impairments.
- Any substances, equipment, supplies, or other items used to perform these actions.

There are six defined code sets that underlie the transaction standards. They are:

- International Classification of Diseases, 9th Edition, Clinical Modification (ICD-9-CM), Volumes 1 and 2, as updated and distributed by HHS[25], for the following conditions:
  - Diseases
  - Injuries
  - Impairments
  - Other health-related problems and their manifestations
  - Causes of injury, disease, impairment, or other health-related problems.
- International Classification of Diseases, 9th Edition, Clinical Modification, (ICD-9-CM) Volume 3 Procedures, as updated and distributed by HHS[26], for procedures or

actions taken for diseases, injuries, and impairments on hospital inpatients reported by hospitals:
- Prevention
- Diagnosis
- Treatment
- Management

- National Drug Codes (NDC), as maintained and distributed by HHS[27], for reporting by retail pharmacies[28]:
  - Drugs
  - Biologics
- Code on Dental Procedures and Nomenclature, as maintained and distributed by the American Dental Association[29], for dental services.
- The combination of Health Care Financing Administration Common Procedure Coding System (HCPCS), as maintained and distributed by HHS[30], and Current Procedural Terminology, Fourth Edition (CPT-4), as maintained and distributed by the American Medical Association, for physician and other health care services, including, but not limited to:
  - Physician services
  - Physical and occupational therapy services
  - Radiologic procedures
  - Clinical laboratory tests
  - Other medical diagnostic procedures
  - Transportation services, including ambulance
- The Healthcare Common Procedure Coding System (HCPCS), as maintained and distributed by HHS[31], for all other substances, equipment, supplies, or other items used in health care services, with the exception of drugs and biologics, including, but not limited to:
  - Medical supplies
  - Orthodontic and prosthetic devices
  - Durable medical equipment

Although code set rules will have greater meaning to your vendor, you must be aware of the rules and the code values that are relevant to your practice. What is important is that when physicians in Denver or Kansas City or Miami treat a patient for a cold, they all use the same diagnostic and treatment codes to submit a claim for reimbursement, regardless of what health-benefit plans their patients carry.

Transaction Standards

When a patient visits your practice, you will conduct several administrative tasks, including compiling patient identifiable information with health-related information to create PHI. A HIPAA transaction contains patient-identifiable information and health-related information using information from the code sets. This also means that the transaction contains details about the patient and the patient's health that can be used to identify that person. If the transaction is sent electronically to fulfill an administrative function, it must be transmitted using the standard.

For health care providers such as physician practices, there are four standards of the eight in the HIPAA Transactions Rule that apply to administrative processes. The practice may choose to use all, some, or none. These standards are:

- Health claims or equivalent encounter information
- Eligibility for a health plan
- Health claim status
- Referral certification and authorization.

Before further discussion of the above four standards, it is important to note that there are four other Transaction Rule standard transactions that generally will *not* apply to or be used by a physician's practice: enrollment and disenrollment in a health plan, health care payment and remittance advice, health plan premium payments, and coordination of benefits. However, the practice should know two things about these four standards: They complete the reimbursement process that was initiated using the standard transactions on the provider side. Not only do payers have to be able to receive your standard transactions, if you so choose to send them, but they also must be able to respond using their four standard transactions. This process, when fully implemented, should lead to measurable improvement in the speed of transactions and in their resolution.

Health Claims or Equivalent Encounter Information

According to the final rule,[32] the health care claims or equivalent encounter information transaction is defined by the transmission of either of the following:

- A request from a health care provider to a health plan to obtain payment for health care. The request includes necessary accompanying information, known as the *data content*.
- If there is no direct claim for payment, because the health care provider rendered services under a health plan benefits contract other than charges or reimbursement rates for specific services, such as an HMO contract, the transaction is the transmission of encounter information for the purpose of reporting health care.

Associated with each standard transaction is an Implementation Guide. These are available via the Internet from Washington Publishing Company (www.wpi-edi.org). These Implementation Guides are important documents and give instructions on the implementation specifications for the transaction standards. These Implementation guides are lengthy and technical and best left to your systems and software vendors.

Talk to your information management or coding staff, and they'll tell you the claim/encounter transaction is the most frequent HIPAA transaction. This transaction allows the practice to be reimbursed. To keep it simple, the HIPAA professional claim encounter, the most widely used claim, requires four levels of information—the person or entity doing the billing, the person or entity to be paid, information about the claim, and information about the service. HIPAA allows up to 50 service lines where your office inserts procedure codes. Note that all this information is gathered by people like you in the office before getting to the coder or billing company.

After successfully filing a claim, your office receives a remittance advice transaction that describes the payer's reimbursement. When using this HIPAA transaction, the office becomes more efficient due to easier billing, fewer resubmitted claims, and no paper coordination of benefits.

Eligibility for a Health Plan, Inquiry, and Response

The eligibility for a health plan transaction is defined as the transmission of either of the following:

- An inquiry from a health care provider to a health plan, or from one health plan to another, to obtain any of the following information about a benefit plan for an enrollee:
    - Eligibility to receive health care under the health plan
    - Coverage of health care under the health plan
    - Benefits associated with the benefit plan.
- A response from a health plan to a health care provider's (or another health plan's) inquiry.

HIPAA allows the provider to ask for information about patients in a batch (all at once) or individually.

Ideally, the financial staff conducts eligibility inquiries the day before the patient arrives to determine financial risk. An eligibility inquiry allows you to ask and receive information about the patient's coverage so that the physician and patient team can determine the best clinical and financial solution.

To conduct a HIPAA Eligibility Inquiry and Response transaction, you first need four categories of information:

- Payer: A group or organization that holds the eligibility information
- Provider: A group or person making the inquiry
- Subscriber/patient: The information about the person who requests treatment
- Benefits of the subscriber/patient: The service provided

Armed with information from these four categories, the office can create three levels of inquiries:

- Level One: Is this patient a member of your plan?
- Level Two: Is this type of service covered?
- Level Three: Is this specific procedure code/diagnosis covered?

Your practice management system vendor should provide technical support, as well as answer the following questions, for you.

1. How will the claim status inquiry and response streamline my claim status process?
2. Does my system allow me to submit and receive claim status transactions?
3. Does my system have all of the necessary codes in the four information categories?
4. Does my system process the response and update the status of the claim in my accounts receivable?
5. How quickly should I get a response if I use the HIPAA eligibility inquiry?
6. Can I set up the system to "age" submitted claims? For example, if claims are older than 20 days, can I submit a claims status inquiry?

As with all inquiries with your vendors (business associates), be sure to get responses in writing.

Health Care Claim Status, Inquiry, and Response

A health care claim-status transaction is defined as either the transmission of either an inquiry to determine the status of a health care claim or a response about the status of a health care claim. This transaction may be the most important electronic transaction that any provider can implement. Once you file the claim, your interest is in receiving timely reimbursement. In the paper-transaction world, it is not unusual to have missing or incorrect information on a claim submission. Thankfully, many of the front-end tools that clearinghouses and billing services use today for electronic claims will identify and mitigate the time-consuming chores of fixing those errors.

But many times you do not know the status of a claim. You should be aware that payers who respond to claims status inquiries find claim status responses as costly as you do in terms of time expended that could have been more productive elsewhere. Perhaps the claim status inquiry and response using the electronic standard will prove of significant benefit to both payers and providers in eliminating time spent on the telephone, which is labor intensive and costly for both parties. Computer-to-computer request and response transactions concerning claim status save time and dollar resources for your staff and the payer.

Referral Certification and Authorization

According to the final rule,[33] the referral certification and authorization transaction is defined as any of the following transmissions:

- A request for the review of health care to obtain an authorization for the health care

- A request to obtain authorization for referring an individual to another health care provider
- A response to a request described herein.

The "referrals and prior authorizations" is the best transaction for getting the staff back to delivering patient care. This transaction facilitates exchange of information with other physicians such as specialists concerning a patient's treatment and also opens electronic communications with health plans concerning treatment or medication that goes beyond that originally approved. This type of communication is more efficient and labor saving than having to do such communication on paper or by telephone.

National Identifier Standards

The National Provider Identifier (NPI) Rule is the fourth Rule included in the administrative simplification provisions and is also discussed in Chapter 6. All covered entities must be in compliance with the NPI provisions by May 23, 2007. Although small plans have until May 23, 2008 to come into compliance, all other covered entities were required to be in compliance with the NPI provisions by May 23, 2007. After the deadline, covered entities, including health plans, may not conduct noncompliant transactions.[34] The NPI will assist in establishing simpler electronic transmission of HIPAA standard transactions, as well as provide more efficient coordination of benefits transactions.

The NPI is a 10-digit, intelligence free (does not carry information about health care providers, such as the state in which they practice or their specialization) number that will be used to identify you to your health care partners, including all payers, in all HIPAA standard transactions. The NPI will replace the identifiers currently being used in HIPAA standard transactions with Medicare and other health plans. It is mandatory that you have an NPI prior to enrolling with Medicare.[35]

In terms of NPIs, there are two types of health care providers:

- Type 1: Health care providers who are individuals, including physicians, dentists, and all sole proprietors. An individual is eligible for only one NPI.
- Type 2: Health care providers who are organizations, including physician groups, hospitals, nursing homes, and the corporation formed when an individual incorporates him/herself. Organizations must determine if they have "subparts" that need to be uniquely identified with their own NPIs in HIPAA standard transactions. A subpart is a component of an health care organization provider that provides health care and is not itself a separate legal entity.[36]

Once you obtain your NPI and share it with your health care partners—including payers, clearinghouses, vendors, and other health care organizations—your partners must integrate the NPI into their systems and processes.

Staff training is critical, and all employees should have an understanding of the NPI. Certain staff members need to know the requirements of its use and where it appears in transactions.

Training should include:[37]

- Identifying all responsibilities or processes that transpire as a result of the NPI. This includes how and when to distribute a provider's NPI, how to protect it, and when it should be collected from other providers for use in standard transactions.
- Developing a plan for who will be responsible for ensuring that NPIs are kept current.
- Informing staff of what to do if another provider's NPI is needed in a HIPAA standard transaction and is unknown.
- Educating your staff on how NPIs from other organizations will be collected and validated for use in HIPAA standard referral transactions.
- Creating a process for sharing your NPI with your business partners for billing purposes.

Besides affecting the HIPAA standard transactions, implementation of the NPI may have affected business processes and systems that you rely on every day. Those that should be reviewed include:[38]

- Computer systems and software, such as the Practice Management System, Electronic Medical Records, and ePrescribing
- Document imaging or archival systems
- Workflow processes for routing or indexing. Internal and external reports could be affected.
- *All* HIPAA standard transactions are impacted by the NPI, not just electronic ones. Make sure that the needs of the payment and remittance advice, claims status inquiry and response, and eligibility inquiry and response are all reviewed.

The Secretary has delegated to the Administrator of the Centers for Medicare and Medicaid Services (CMS) authority to enforce the identifier provisions. CMS will focus on obtaining voluntary compliance and use a complaint-driven approach for enforcement. CMS's approach will utilize the flexibility granted by the Social Security Act to consider good faith efforts to comply when assessing individual complaints.

CMS recognizes that transactions often require the participation of two covered entities, each of whom is required to comply with HIPAA and that noncompliance by one covered entity may put the second covered entity in a difficult position. CMS also understands that if one of the covered entities is a small health plan, which has a later compliance date, compliance by the covered trading partner may be especially challenging. Therefore, during the 12 month period immediately following the May 23, 2007 compliance date for all covered entities except small health plans, CMS intends to look at both covered entities' good faith efforts to come into compliance with the NPI standards. It will then be determined on a case-by-case basis whether reasonable cause for the noncompliance exists and, if so, the extent to which the time for resolving the noncompliance should be extended. Also for the 12-month period immediately following the May 23, 2007 compliance date, CMS will not impose penalties on covered entities that arrange contingency plans if they have made reasonable and diligent efforts to become compliant.[39]

CONCLUSION

Implementing the provisions of HIPAA Administration Simplification is a continuing effort. Going forward, it is important to note that there are certain things you can do to increase the value of your efforts tactically and strategically. Ensure that you have put into action the following steps:

- Assign a privacy official
- Assign a security official
- Develop policies and procedures for both
- Regularly train staff on security procedures
- Develop and follow internal processes to mitigate problems

REFERENCES

1. Heffler S., et al, "Health spending projections for 2002–2012: spending on hospital services and prescription drugs continues to drive health care's share of the economy upward," *Web Exclusives: A Supplement to Health Affairs*, January–June 2003: W3-55.
2. Hartley, Carolyn, and Edward J. Jones, *HIPAA Plain & Simple: A Compliance Guide for Health Care Professionals* (Chicago: AMA, 2004).
3. From http://www.cms.hhs.gov/Enforcement/04_GeneralEnforcementInformation .asp#TopOfPage.

4. Department of Health and Human Services, Office of the Secretary, "45 CFR Parts 160 and 16: HIPAA Administrative Simplification: Enforcement; Final Rule." *Federal Register*, v. 71, n. 32, February 16, 2006, p. 8390. This document is available electronically at www.cms.hhs.gov/Enforcement.
5. Content from www.hhs.gov/HIPAAGenInfo "Are You a Covered Entity?"
6. Hartley, Carolyn P., and Edward J. Jones, *HIPAA Plain & Simple: A Compliance Guide for Health Care Professionals* (Chicago: AMA, 2004).
7. Department of Health and Human Services, OCR Privacy Brief, p. 1, "Summary of the HIPAA Privacy Rule." This document is available electronically at http://www.hhs.gov/ocr/privacysummary.pdf.
8. Hartley, Carolyn P., and Edward J. Jones, *HIPAA Plain & Simple: A Compliance Guide for Health Care Professionals* (Chicago: AMA, 2004), 58.
9. Hartley, Carolyn P., and Edward J. Jones, *HIPAA Plain & Simple: A Compliance Guide for Health Care Professionals* (Chicago: AMA, 2004), 58.
10. From http://www.hhs.gov//ocr/hipaa/consumer_summary.pdf.
11. "Privacy and Your Health Information," available online at http://www.hhs.gov/ocr/hipaa/consumer_summary.pdf.
12. Office for Civil Rights Fact Sheet. "How to File a Health Information Privacy Complaint with the Office for Civil Rights." This document is available electronically at http://www.hhs.gov/ocr/privacyhowtofile.htm.
13. Hartley, Carolyn P., and Edward J. Jones, *HIPAA Plain & Simple: A Compliance Guide for Health Care Professionals* (Chicago: AMA, 2004), 69.
14. Hartley, Carolyn P., and Edward J. Jones, *HIPAA Plain & Simple: A Compliance Guide for Health Care Professionals* (Chicago: AMA, 2004), 71–72.
15. Department of Health and Human Services HIPAA Security Series 2. "Security Standards: Administrative Safeguards. Volume 2, Paper 2, pp. 2–3. This document can be found electronically at http://www.cms.hhs.gov/EducationMaterials/Downloads/SecurityStandardsAdministrativeSafeguards.pdf.
16. Hartley, Carolyn P., and Edward J. Jones, *HIPAA Plain & Simple: A Compliance Guide for Health Care Professionals* (Chicago: AMA, 2004), 102–104.
17. Department of Health and Human Services HIPAA Security Series 4. "Security Standards: Technical Safeguards. Volume 2, Paper 4, pp. 1–2. This document can be found electronically at http://www.cms.hhs.gov/EducationMaterials/Downloads/SecurityStandardsTechnicalSafeguards.pdf.
18. Definitions for these terms have been simplified. For a full review of legal terms and definitions, consult the Security Rule at www.cms.gov.
19. 68 *Federal Register* 8355.
20. "The standards do not allow organizations to make their own rules, only their own technology choices." 68 *Federal Register* 8343.
21. 68 *Federal Register* 8376.
22. 68 *Federal Register* 8376-8377.
23. 68 *Federal Register* 8377.
24. 65 *Federal Register* 50367
25. Information on computer files of the ICD-9-CM is available via the Internet at the U.S. Department of Commerce's National Technical Information Service (NTIS). Go to www.ntis.gov, and go to Product Families: Health.
26. Ibid.
27. Information on the National Drug Code is available via the Internet at the U.S. Food and Drug Administration's Center for Drug Evaluation and Research (CDER) at www.fda.gov/cder/ndc/.
28. Retail pharmacies are required to use the NDC codes. The final rule of August 17, 2000, was modified on February 20, 2003, to eliminate the NDC standard for "reporting drugs and biologics in all non-retail pharmacy transactions."
29. The American Dental Association in Chicago, IL can be reached via the Internet at www.ada.org.
30. Information on computer files of the Health Care Financing Administration Common Procedure Coding System (HCPCS) is available via the Internet at the U.S. Department of Commerce's National Technical Information Service (NTIS). Go to www.ntis.gov, and go to Product Families: Health.

31. Ibid.
32. 65 *Federal Register* 50370.
33. 65 *Federal Register* 50371.
34. "Guidance on Compliance with the HIPAA National Provider Identifier (NPI) Rule." This document can be found electronically at http://www.cms.hhs.gov/NationalProvidentStand/Downloads/NPI_Contingency.pdf.
35. Centers for Medicare and Medicaid Services, "The Who, What, When, Why & How of NPI: Information for Health Care Providers." August 2006. This document can be found electronically at http://www.cms.hhs.gov/MedicareProviderSupEnroll/downloads/EnrollmentSheet_WWWWH.pdf.
36. Ibid.
37. Department of Health and Human Services, "NPI Tip Sheet: Tips for Health Care Professionals – Preparing Your Office Staff for NPI." April 2006, pp. 1–2.
38. Ibid.
39. "Guidance on Compliance with the HIPAA National Provider Identifier (NPI) Rule." This document can be found electronically at http://www.cms.hhs.gov/NationalProvIdentStand/Downloads/NPI_Contingency.pdf.

appendix

Internet Resources

Coding and Billing Resources		
American Medical Association (AMA)	www.ama-assn.org/	AMA is a voluntary membership organization of physicians that is the patient's advocate and the physician's voice. It sets standards for the profession of medicine. The AMA is also the developer of the CPT®.
American Academy of Professional Coders (AAPC)	www.aapc.com	AAPC is the largest professional network of CPT, ICD-9-CM, and HCPCS coders in the nation who share a common interest in procedural and diagnostic coding issues.
CMS 1500 Claim Form	www.nucc.org/	This site features the 1500 claim form from The National Uniform Claim Committee.
Central Office on ICD-9-CM and Level I HCPCS (CPT-4 codes) for hospital providers and certain Level II HCPCS codes	www.icd-9-cm.org/	Created through a written memorandum of understanding between the AHA, World Health Organization, and National Center for Health Statistics in 1963, the Central Office on ICD-9-CM serves as a clearinghouse for issues related to the use of ICD-9-CM, maintains the integrity of the classification system, recommends revisions to the system as needed, and develops educational material and programs on ICD-9-CM. The public-private partnership now also includes CMS and AHIMA.
Departmental Appeals Board (DHHS)	www.hhs.gov/dab/	*The Departmental Appeals Board* provides prompt, fair, and impartial dispute resolution services to parties in many different kinds of disputes involving components of the Department of Health and Human Services. The DAB encourages the use of mediation and other forms of alternative dispute resolution. The Board Chair is also the dispute resolution specialist for the Department of Health and Human Services.
Evaluation and Management Audit Tools	www.donself.com/documentsframe.html	This site offers a variety of auditing forms and score sheets that can be used to assign the appropriate Evaluation and Management codes.
Evaluation and Management Coding Guidelines	www.cms.hhs.gov/MLNEdWebGuide/25_EMDOC.asp	This site contains the 1995 and 1997 Official Evaluation and Management Coding Guidelines from CMS.
Healthcare Common Procedure Coding System (HCPCS)	www.cms.hhs.gov/medhcpcsgeninfo/	Information on Level II of the HCPCS coding system that is used primarily to identify products, supplies, and services not included in the CPT-4 codes can be found on this CMS site.

345

Medicare Ambulance Fee-For-Service Schedule	www.cms.hhs.gov/center/ambulance.asp?	Site provides information on ambulance services including coding, billing, payment, and fee schedule information.
Medicare Regulations and Guidance	www.cms.hhs.gov/home/regsguidance.asp	Site provides information on regulations and guidance for Medicare and Medicaid programs.
Medicare Online Training	www.cms.hhs.gov/medlearn	This site specializes in self-paced Medicare training provided by CMS.
National Correct Coding Initiative (CCI) Reference Tools	www.ntis.gov/product/-correct-coding.htm	NTIS, in cooperation with CMS, offers a series of look-up references that show which codes cannot be used together in Part B reimbursement claims.
Outpatient Code Editor	www.ntis.gov/product/hcfa-outpatient-code-editor.htm	Hospitals and other facilities with outpatient billing will find this software an important tool. It combines CCI edits with the ambulatory payment classifications (APC) assignment program designed to meet mandated Medicare outpatient prospective payment system (OPPS) implementation.
TRICARE	www.tricare.osd.mil/	This site provides detailed comprehensive information on the TRICARE program.
UB-92 Claim Form, UB-04 Claim Form	www.nubc.org/	This site features the UB-92 claim form and the UB-04 claim form from The National Uniform Billing Committee. (UB-04 will be effective March 1, 2007).
World Health Organization (WHO)	www.who.int/en/	The World Health Organization is the United Nations' specialized agency for health.

Compliance Resources

EMTALA	www.emtala.com/	A resource for current information about the Federal Emergency Medical Treatment and Active Labor Act, also known as COBRA or the Patient Anti-Dumping Law.
Federal Trade Commission Telemarketing Fraud	www.ftc.gov/bcp/conline/edcams/telemarketing/index.html	This Web site provides information for consumers about more telemarketing fraud as well as resource materials for educators, providers, and community organizations.
Health Care Compliance Association (HCCA)	www.hcca-info.org/	HCCA is an organization solely dedicated to improving the quality of health care compliance. It provides resources for ethics and compliance professionals.
Health Hippo	hippo.findlaw.com/	Health Hippo is a collection of policy and regulatory materials related to health care.
Healthfinder	www.healthfinder.gov/	Healthfinder® is a free gateway to reliable consumer health and human services information developed by the US Department of Health and Human Services.

Health Insurance Portability and Accountability Act (HIPAA)	www.cms.hhs.gov/hipaageninfo/	This CMS site gives detailed information on the Health Insurance Portability and Accountability Act (HIPAA).
National Healthcare Anti-Fraud Association (NHCAA)	www.nhcaa.org/	Founded in 1985 by several private health insurers and federal and state law enforcement officials, NHCAA is a unique, issue-based organization comprising private- and public-sector organizations and individuals responsible for the detection, investigation, prosecution, and prevention of health care fraud.

Government Resources and Agencies

Agency for Healthcare Research and Quality	www.ahrq.gov	This Web site provides practical health care information, research findings, and data to help consumers, health providers, health insurers, researchers, and policymakers make informed decisions about health care issues.
Centers for Medicare and Medicaid Services	www.cms.gov/	The federal agency that administers Medicare, Medicaid, and SCHIP.
CMS Contact Information Directory	www.cms.hhs.gov/contacts	This site provides state telephone contact information regarding issues relating to the Medicare, Medicaid, and SCHIP Programs.
Department of Health and Human Services (DHHS)	www.hhs.gov	Top-level site with information on DHHS agencies on the Internet, news and public affairs, what's new, research data, and policy; contains a topic index.
Government Printing Office (GPO) Access on the Web	www.gpoaccess.gov/	This site provides access to the *Federal Register*, congressional bills, congressional record, public laws, and US code.
Medicare Part B EDI Helpline		The EDI Helpline is a regional number Medicare customers can call to access information and material regarding electronic data interchange. Telephone numbers are listed by state.
Medicare Payment Advisory Commission (MedPAC)	www.medpac.gov/	MedPAC is an independent federal body that advises the US Congress on issues affecting the Medicare program.
National Practitioner Data Bank (NPDB) and the Healthcare Integrity and Protection Data Bank (HIPDB)	www.npdb-hipdb.com/	NPDB and HIPDB are part of the government's efforts to improve health care quality and alleviate the financial burden that health care fraud and abuse impose on the nation.
Occupational Safety and Health Administration (OSHA) Bloodborne Pathogen Directive	www.osha.gov/SLTC/bloodbornepathogens/index.html	OSHA expects health care providers to minimize serious health risks faced by workers exposed to blood and other potentially infectious materials, such HIV, Hepatitis B, and Hepatitis C.

Office of Inspector General	http://oig.hhs.gov/ http://oig.hhs.gov/fraud/exclusions.html	This site provides guidance and information relating to fraud prevention and detection. The OIG's List of Excluded Individuals/Entities (LEIE) provides a listing of individuals and/or entities excluded from participation in all Federal health care programs, including Medicare and Medicaid.
The Public Health Data Standards Consortium	www.cdc.gov/nchs/otheract/phdsc/phdsc.htm	The consortium expands public health involvement in existing health data standards and content organizations and facilitates development of new public health data standards.
White House Federal Briefing Room: Health Statistics	www.whitehouse.gov/fsbr/health.html	This site contains statistical health information updated on a monthly basis. Topics include vital statistics, use of health services, prevention and risk, health status, reportable diseases, and health care expenditures.

Medical Ethics Resources

American Society of Law, Medicine and Ethics (ASLME)	www.aslme.org	The mission of ASLME is to provide high-quality scholarship, debate, and critical thought to the community of professionals at the intersection of law, medicine, and ethics.
American Psychological Association (APA) Ethics Information	www.apa.org/ethics/ethics.html	APA provides links to ethical principles, statements, and guidelines for psychologists, online services, and guidelines for the care of animals.
Bioethical Services of Virginia	www.bsvinc.com	This site offers an array of medical ethics programming functions for community hospitals, state facilities for individuals with mental retardation, mental health institutes, and community services boards.
Bioethics	www.medweb.emory.edu/	This site contains a fairly complete list of bioethics resources from MedWeb.
Bioethics Online Service	www.mcw.edu/bioethics/	This site contains a list of bioethics resources from the Medical College of Wisconsin.
Dental Ethics	www.cpmcnet.columbia.edu/health.sci/dental.toc/Dental_Educational_Software/Dental-Ethics/ethics-welcome.html	This site contains ethical questions and answers in dentistry from the Columbia-Presbyterian Medical Center.
Genetics and Ethics	www.ethics.ubc.ca/brynw/	Links on this Web site include the Human Genome Project, journals, public action groups, genetics and the law, and general philosophy resources.
Human Subjects and Research Ethics	www.psych.bangor.ac.uk/deptpsych/Ethics/HumanResearch.html	A pointer to information about the ethical aspects of research involving human subjects as participants.
MacLean Center for Clinical Ethics	www.ccmemac4-.bsd.uchicago.edu/CCME.html	This site consists of interdisciplinary-based resources on practical ethical concerns confronting patients and health professionals.

Medical Ethics Exhibit	www.learner.org/exhibits/medicalethics/	Is assisted suicide legal? What are the potential benefits and dangers of human cloning research? Should patients be entitled to any medical treatment they want? These and other questions are explored through the Annenberg/CPB Project, Medical Ethics.
National Reference Center for Bioethics Literature (NRCBL)	www.adminweb.georgetown.edu/nrcbl/	NRCBL is a specialized collection of books, journals, newspaper articles, legal materials, regulations, codes, government publications, and other relevant documents concerned with issues in biomedical and professional ethics.

Professional Associations and Other Resources

American Academy of Physician Assistants (AAPA)	www.aapa.org/	AAPA is the only national organization that represents physician assistants in all specialties and all employment settings.
American Ambulance Association (AAA)	www.the-aaa.org/	The American Ambulance Association (AAA) is an association representing ambulance services across the United States.
American Association of Retired Persons (AARP)	www.aarp.org/	AARP is the nation's leading organization for people age 50 and older.
American College of Emergency Physicians	www.acep.org/	The American College of Emergency Physicians is a medical specialty society that was formed in 1969 to improve emergency care by setting high standards for emergency medical education and practice.
American College of Healthcare Executives (ACHE)	www.ache.org/	ACHE is an international professional society of nearly 30,000 health care executives.
American College of Nurse Practitioners (ACNP)	www.acnpweb.org	Founded in 1993, ACNP is a national nonprofit membership organization focused on keeping nurse practitioners current on legislative, regulatory, and clinical practice issues.
American College of Physician Executives (ACPE)	www.acpe.org/	Founded in 1975 as the American Academy of Medical Directors, the ACPE, represents physician members with management or administrative responsibilities in hospitals, group practices, managed care, government, universities, the military, and industry.
American Dietetic Association (ADA)	www.eatright.org/	The American Dietetic Association is the nation's largest organization of food and nutrition professionals with nearly 65,000 members.
American Health Information Management Association (AHIMA)	www.ahima.org/	AHIMA is the professional association that represents more than 50,000 health information management professionals.

American Health Lawyers Association (AHLA)	www.healthlawyers.org/	The American Health Lawyers Association (Health Lawyers) is the nation's largest, nonpartisan, 501(c)(3) educational organization devoted to legal issues in the health care field.
American Hospital Association (AHA)	www.aha.org	AHA is the national organization that represents and serves all types of hospitals, health care networks, and their patients and communities.
America's Health Insurance Plans (AHIP)	www.ahip.org	AHIP is a trade association representing nearly 1,300 member plans providing benefits to more than 200 million Americans.
Association of American Medical Colleges (AAMC)	www.aamc.org/	AAMC is a nonprofit association comprising the 125 accredited US medical schools; the 17 accredited Canadian medical schools; nearly 400 major teaching hospitals and health systems, including 68 Department of Veterans Affairs medical centers; nearly 96 academic and professional societies representing 109,000 faculty members; and the nation's 67,000 medical students and 104,000 residents.
Catholic Health Association of the United States (CHA)	www.chausa.org/	Founded in 1915, CHA serves the nation's Catholic health care organizations.
Doctors Guide to the Internet—Medical Conferences & Meetings	www.docguide.com/crc.nsf	The Congress Resource Centre (CRC) is a one-stop site of organized links and information designed to facilitate planning and scheduling for a featured congress.
Healthcare Billing and Management Association (HBMA)	www.hbma.com/	Founded in 1993, HBMA is the only trade association representing third-party medical billers.
Healthcare Conventions	www.healthopps.com/health11.html	This site provides a searchable database of health care-related conventions and job fairs.
Healthcare Financial Management Association (HFMA)	www.hfma.org/	HFMA is the nation's leading personal membership organization for more than 34,000 financial management professionals employed by hospitals, integrated delivery systems, long-term and ambulatory care facilities, managed care organizations, medical group practices, public accounting and consulting firms, insurance companies, government agencies, and other health care organizations.
healthgrades.com Physician Report Cards	www.healthgrades.com/prc/index.cfm?ct1	A searchable database that provides a list of physicians in the specialty and geographic area specified.
Medical Group Management Association (MGMA)	www.mgma.com/	Founded in 1926, MGMA is the leading organization representing medical group practice nationwide.
Modern Physician Magazine	www.modernphysician.com/	*Modern Physician* is a monthly business news magazine written for physician executives who are key players in the effort to reshape America's major medical institutions.

National Association for Healthcare Quality (NAHQ)	www.nahq.org	The NAHQ is the nation's leading organization for health care quality professionals providing education and development opportunities for professionals at all management levels and within all health care settings.
National Association for Home Care and Hospice (NAHC)	www.nahc.org	The NAHC is the nation's largest trade association representing the interests of home care agencies, hospices, home care aide organizations, and medical equipment suppliers.
National Association of Insurance Commissioners (NAIC)	www.naic.org/	NAIC is the organization of insurance regulators from the 50 states, the District of Columbia, and the four US territories. The site includes access to information on committee activities, insurance regulators, upcoming events, state regulations, and more.
National Association of Psychiatric Health Systems	www.naphs.org/	Created in 1933, the National Association of Psychiatric Health Systems today represents delivery systems working to coordinate a full spectrum of treatment services, including inpatient, residential, partial hospitalization, and outpatient programs as well as prevention and management services.
National Association of Public Hospitals and Health Systems	www.naph.org/	The National Association of Public Hospitals and Health Systems has represented the nation's urban safety net health systems and the people they serve since 1981.
National Association of State Medicaid Directors (NASMD)	www.medicaid.aphsa.org/NASMD.htm	The NASMD is a bipartisan, professional, nonprofit organization of representatives of state Medicaid agencies.
National Center for Health Statistics (NCHS)	www.cdc.gov/nchs/	The NCHS is the nation's principal health statistics agency. It provides comprehensive statistical information on a wide and diverse range of data and topics.
National Committee for Quality Assurance (NCQA)	www.ncqa.org/	NCQA is a private, not-for-profit organization that assesses and reports on the quality of the nation's managed care plans.
National IPA Coalition (NIPAC)	www.nipac.org/	NIPAC is the leading resource for physician organizations that manage risk contracts. Their mission is "to enhance physician-directed managed healthcare."
National Uniform Billing Committee (NUBC)	www.nubc.org/	The NUBC was brought together by the American Health Association (AHA) in 1975 to develop a single billing form and standard data set that could be used nationwide by institutional providers and payers for handling health care claims. It includes the participation of all major national provider and payer organizations.
New England Journal of Medicine	www.nejm.org/	The New England Journal of Medicine on-line offers subscribers access to full text plus several additional features.

Professional Association of Healthcare Office Managers (PAHCOM)	www.pahcom.com/	PAHCOM is a nationwide organization dedicated to providing a strong professional network for physician practice managers.
WebDoctor	www.gretmar.com/webdoctor/journals.html	WebDoctor is an index to on-line medical journals.

State Medical Boards

Alaska	www.dced.state.ak.us/occ/pmed.htm	
Alabama	www.bmedixon.home.mindspring.com/	
Arizona	www.docboard.org/bomex/index.htm	
California	www.medbd.ca.gov	
Colorado	www.dora.state.co.us/medical	
Connecticut	www.state.ct.us/dph	
District of Columbia	www.dchealth.com/lra/news.stm	
Florida	www.doh.state.fl.us/mqa	
Georgia	www.sos.state.ga.us/ebd-medical/	
Iowa	www.docboard.org/ia/ia_home.htm	
Idaho	www.idacare.org	
Illinois	www.state.il.us/dpr	
Indiana	www.ai.org/serv/hpb_lookup_ia	
Kansas	www.ink.org/public/boha/	
Kentucky	www.state.ky.us/agencies/kbml	
Massachusetts	www.massmedboard.org/	
Maryland	www.docboard.org/md/default.htm	

Maine	www.docboard.org/me/me_home.htm	
Michigan	www.commerce.state.mi.us/bhser/home.htm	
Minnesota	www.bmp.state.mn.us/	
Missouri	www.ecodev.state.mo.us/pr/healarts/	
Mississippi	www.msbml.state.ms.us	
Montana	www.com.state.mt.us/license/pol/pol_boards/med_board/board_page.htm	
North Carolina	www.docboard.org/nc	
Nebraska	www.hhs.state.ne.us/	
New Hampshire	www.state.nh.us/medicine	
New Jersey	www.state.nj.us/lps/ca/medical.htm	
Nevada	www.state.nv.us./medical/	
New York	www.health.state.ny.us/nysdoh/opmc/main.htm	
Ohio	www.state.oh.us/med/	
Oklahoma	www.osbmls.state.ok.us/	
Oregon	www.bme.state.or.us/	
Pennsylvania	www.dos.state.pa.us/bpoa/medbd.htm	
Rhode Island	www.docboard.org/ri/main.htm	
South Carolina	www.llr.state.sc.us./me.htm	
South Dakota	www.state.sd.us/dcr/medical/med-hom.htm	
Tennessee	www.state.tn.us/health	
Texas	www.tsbme.state.tx.us/	

Utah	www.commerce.state.ut.us/dopl/disc.htm	
Virginia	Licensing at www.dhp.state.va.us	Board at www.dhp.state.va.us/levelone/med.htm
Vermont	www.docboard.org/vt/vermont.htm	
Washington	Press releases at www.doh.wa.gov/publicat/Publications.htm	MQAC at www.doh.wa.gov/hsqa/hpqad/MQAC
Wisconsin	www.badger.state.wi.us/agencies/drl/	
West Virginia	www.wvdhhr.org/wvbom/	

appendix

B

Office of the Inspector General Compliance Program for Individual and Small Group Physician Practices

The following article titled "OIG Compliance Program for Individual and Small Group Physician Practices" comes from the Office of the Inspector General (OIG) and serves as a reference tool for practice managers, staff, and physicians. Implementation of a quality compliance program can improve practice operations and increase efficiency as well as reduce compliance risks. Billing and other types of errors can be minimized, thereby accelerating insurance claim processing by payers and reducing the time it takes to otherwise receive payment when information needs to be corrected.

Once a compliance program has been implemented, it should be routinely monitored and reviewed to be effective. Changes to the compliance program should be implemented as the need arises. The program should automatically be reviewed if systems, processes, or structural changes are made within the practice. The guidance that follows will give the practice a solid foundation on which to build and maintain its compliance program.

Appendix B provides a reprint of the article—which originally appeared in the October 5, 2000, *Federal Register*—in its entirety. The article is also accessible on the Web site of the Office of the Inspector General (http://oig.hhs.gov/authorities/docs/physician.pdf).

DEPARTMENT OF HEALTH AND HUMAN SERVICES

Office of Inspector General

OIG Compliance Program for Individual and Small Group Physician Practices

AGENCY: Office of Inspector General (OIG), HHS.

ACTION: Notice.

SUMMARY: This **Federal Register** notice sets forth the recently issued Compliance Program Guidance for Individual and Small Group Physician Practices developed by the Office of Inspector General (OIG). The OIG has previously developed and published voluntary compliance program guidance focused on several other areas and aspects of the health care industry. We believe that the development and issuance of this voluntary compliance program guidance for individual and small group physician practices will serve as a positive step towards assisting providers in preventing the submission of erroneous claims or engaging in unlawful conduct involving the Federal health care programs.

FOR FURTHER INFORMATION CONTACT: Kimberly Brandt, Office of Counsel to the Inspector General, (202) 619–2078.

SUPPLEMENTARY INFORMATION:

Background

The creation of compliance program guidances is a major initiative of the OIG in its effort to engage the private health care community in preventing the submission of erroneous claims and in combating fraudulent conduct. In the past several years, the OIG has developed and issued compliance program guidances directed at a variety of segments in the health care industry. The development of these types of compliance program guidances is based on our belief that a health care provider can use internal controls to more efficiently monitor adherence to applicable statutes, regulations and program requirements.

Copies of these compliance program guidances can be found on the OIG web site at http://www.hhs.gov/oig.

Developing the Compliance Program Guidance for Individual and Small Group Physician Practices

On September 8, 1999, the OIG published a solicitation notice seeking information and recommendations for developing formal guidance for individual and small group physician practices (64 FR 48846). In response to that solicitation notice, the OIG received 83 comments from various outside sources. We carefully considered those comments, as well as previous OIG publications, such as other compliance program guidance and Special Fraud Alerts, in developing a guidance for individual and small group physician practices. In addition, we have consulted with the Health Care Financing Administration and the Department of Justice. In an effort to ensure that all parties had a reasonable opportunity to provide input into a final product, draft guidance for individual and small group physician practices was published in the **Federal Register** on June 12, 2000 (65 FR 36818) for further comments and recommendations.

Components of an Effective Compliance Program

This compliance program guidance for individual and small group physician practices contains seven components that provide a solid basis upon which a physician practice can create a voluntary compliance program:
• Conducting internal monitoring and auditing;
• Implementing compliance and practice standards;
• Designating a compliance officer or contact;
• Conducting appropriate training and education;
• Responding appropriately to detected offenses and developing corrective action;
• Developing open lines of communication; and
• Enforcing disciplinary standards through well-publicized guidelines.

Similar components have been contained in previous guidances issued by the OIG. However, unlike other guidances issued by OIG, this guidance for physicians does not suggest that physician practices implement all seven components of a full scale compliance program. Instead, the guidance emphasizes a step by step approach to follow in developing and implementing a voluntary compliance program. This change is in recognition of the financial and staffing resource constraints faced by physician practices. The guidance should not be viewed as mandatory or as an all-inclusive discussion of the advisable components of a compliance program. Rather, the document is intended to present guidance to assist physician practices that voluntarily choose to develop a compliance program.

Office of Inspector General's Compliance Program Guidance for Individual and Small Group Physician Practices

I. Introduction

This compliance program guidance is intended to assist individual and small group physician practices ("physician practices")[1] in developing a voluntary compliance program that promotes adherence to statutes and regulations applicable to the Federal health care programs ("Federal health care program requirements"). The goal of voluntary compliance programs is to provide a tool to strengthen the efforts of health care providers to prevent and reduce improper conduct. These programs can also benefit physician practices[2] by helping to streamline business operations.

Many physicians have expressed an interest in better protecting their practices from the potential for erroneous or fraudulent conduct through the implementation of voluntary compliance programs. The Office of Inspector General (OIG) believes that the great majority of physicians are honest and share our goal of protecting the integrity of Medicare and other Federal health care programs. To that end, all health care providers have a duty to ensure that the claims submitted to Federal health care programs are true and accurate. The development of voluntary compliance programs and the active application of compliance principles in physician practices will go a long way toward achieving this goal.

Through this document, the OIG provides its views on the fundamental components of physician practice compliance programs, as well as the principles that a physician practice might consider when developing and implementing a voluntary compliance program. While this document presents basic procedural and structural guidance for designing a voluntary compliance program, it is not in and of itself a compliance program. Indeed, as recognized by the OIG and the health care industry, there is no "one size fits all" compliance program, especially for physician practices. Rather, it is a set of guidelines that physician practices can consider if they choose to develop and implement a compliance program.

As with the OIG's previous guidance,[3] these guidelines are not mandatory. Nor do they represent an all-inclusive document containing all components of a compliance program. Other OIG outreach efforts, as well as other Federal agency efforts to promote compliance,[4] can also be used in developing a compliance program. However, as explained later, if a physician practice adopts a voluntary and active compliance program, it may well lead to benefits for the physician practice.

A. Scope of the Voluntary Compliance Program Guidance

This guidance focuses on voluntary compliance measures related to claims submitted to the Federal health care programs. Issues related to private payor claims may also be covered by a compliance plan if the physician practice so desires.

The guidance is also limited in scope by focusing on the development of voluntary compliance programs for individual and small group physician practices. The difference between a small practice and a large practice cannot be determined by stating a particular number of physicians. Instead, our intent in narrowing the guidance to the small practices subset was to provide guidance to those physician practices whose financial or staffing resources would not allow them to implement a full scale, institutionally structured compliance program as set forth in the Third Party Medical Billing Guidance or other previously released OIG guidance. A compliance program can be an important tool for physician practices of all sizes and does not have to be costly, resource-intensive or time-intensive.

B. Benefits of a Voluntary Compliance Program

The OIG acknowledges that patient care is, and should be, the first priority of a physician practice. However, a practice's focus on patient care can be enhanced by the adoption of a voluntary compliance program. For example, the increased accuracy of documentation that may result from a compliance program will actually assist in enhancing patient care. The OIG believes that physician practices can realize numerous other benefits by implementing a compliance program. A well-designed compliance program can:

- Speed and optimize proper payment of claims;
- Minimize billing mistakes;
- Reduce the chances that an audit will be conducted by HCFA or the OIG; and
- Avoid conflicts with the self-referral and anti-kickback statutes.

The incorporation of compliance measures into a physician practice should not be at the expense of patient care, but instead should augment the ability of the physician practice to provide quality patient care.

Voluntary compliance programs also provide benefits by not only helping to prevent erroneous or fraudulent claims, but also by showing that the physician practice is making additional good faith efforts to submit claims appropriately. Physicians should view compliance programs as analogous to practicing preventive medicine for their practice. Practices that embrace the active application of compliance principles in their practice culture and put efforts towards compliance on a continued basis can help to prevent problems from occurring in the future.

A compliance program also sends an important message to a physician practice's employees that while the practice recognizes that mistakes will occur, employees have an affirmative, ethical duty to come forward and report erroneous or fraudulent conduct, so that it may be corrected.

---

[1] For the purpose of this guidance, the term "physician" is defined as: (1) a doctor of medicine or osteopathy; (2) a doctor of dental surgery or of dental medicine; (3) a podiatrist; (4) an optometrist; or (5) a chiropractor, all of whom must be appropriately licensed by the State. 42 U.S.C. 1395x(r).

[2] Much of this guidance can also apply to other independent practitioners, such as psychologists, physical therapists, speech language pathologists, and occupational therapists.

[3] Currently, the OIG has issued compliance program guidance for the following eight industry sectors: hospitals, clinical laboratories, home health agencies, durable medical equipment suppliers, third-party medical billing companies, hospices, Medicare+Choice organizations offering coordinated care plans, and nursing facilities. The guidance listed here and referenced in this document is available on the OIG web site at http://www.hhs.gov/oig in the Electronic Reading Room or by calling the OIG Public Affairs office at (202) 619-1343.

[4] The OIG has issued Advisory Opinions responding to specific inquiries concerning the application of the OIG's authorities, in particular, the anti-kickback statute, and Special Fraud Alerts setting forth activities that raise legal and enforcement issues. These documents, as well as reports from the OIG's Office of Audit Services and Office of Evaluation and Inspections can be obtained via the Internet address or phone number provided in Footnote 3. Physician practices can also review the Health Care Financing Administration (HCFA) web site on the Internet at http://www.hcfa.gov, for up-to-date regulations, manuals, and program memoranda related to the Medicare and Medicaid programs.

C. Application of Voluntary Compliance Program Guidance

The applicability of these recommendations will depend on the circumstances and resources of the particular physician practice.

Each physician practice can undertake reasonable steps to implement compliance measures, depending on the size and resources of that practice. Physician practices can rely, at least in part, upon standard protocols and current practice procedures to develop an appropriate compliance program for that practice. In fact, many physician practices already have established the framework of a compliance program without referring to it as such.

D. The Difference Between "Erroneous" and "Fraudulent" Claims To Federal Health Programs

There appear to be significant misunderstandings within the physician community regarding the critical differences between what the Government views as innocent "erroneous" claims on the one hand and "fraudulent" (intentionally or recklessly false) health care claims on the other. Some physicians feel that Federal law enforcement agencies have maligned medical professionals, in part, by a perceived focus on innocent billing errors. These physicians are under the impression that innocent billing errors can subject them to civil penalties, or even jail. These impressions are mistaken.

To address these concerns, the OIG would like to emphasize the following points. First, the OIG does not disparage physicians, other medical professionals or medical enterprises. In our view, the great majority of physicians are working ethically to render high quality medical care and to submit proper claims.

Second, under the law, physicians are not subject to criminal, civil or administrative penalties for innocent errors, or even negligence. The Government's primary enforcement tool, the civil False Claims Act, covers only offenses that are committed with actual knowledge of the falsity of the claim, reckless disregard, or deliberate ignorance of the falsity of the claim.[5] The False Claims Act does not encompass mistakes, errors, or negligence. The Civil Monetary Penalties Law, an administrative remedy, similar in scope and effect to the False Claims Act, has exactly the same standard of proof.[6] The OIG is very mindful of the difference between innocent errors ("erroneous claims") on one hand, and reckless or intentional conduct ("fraudulent claims") on the other. For criminal penalties, the standard is even higher—criminal intent to defraud must be proved beyond a reasonable doubt.

Third, even ethical physicians (and their staffs) make billing mistakes and errors through inadvertence or negligence. When physicians discover that their billing errors, honest mistakes, or negligence result in erroneous claims, the physician practice should return the funds erroneously claimed, but without penalties. In other words, absent a violation of a civil, criminal or administrative law, erroneous claims result only in the return of funds claimed in error.

Fourth, innocent billing errors are a significant drain on the Federal health care programs. All parties (physicians, providers, carriers, fiscal intermediaries, Government agencies, and beneficiaries) need to work cooperatively to reduce the overall error rate.

Finally, it is reasonable for physicians (and other providers) to ask: what duty do they owe the Federal health care programs? The answer is that all health care providers have a duty to reasonably ensure that the claims submitted to Medicare and other Federal health care programs are true and accurate. The OIG continues to engage the provider community in an extensive, good faith effort to work cooperatively on voluntary compliance to minimize errors and to prevent potential penalties for improper billings before they occur. We encourage all physicians and other providers to join in this effort.

II. Developing a Voluntary Compliance Program

A. The Seven Basic Components of a Voluntary Compliance Program

The OIG believes that a basic framework for any voluntary compliance program begins with a review of the seven basic components of an effective compliance program. A review of these components provides physician practices with an overview of the scope of a fully developed and implemented compliance program. The following list of components, as set forth in previous OIG compliance program guidances, can form the basis of a voluntary compliance program for a physician practice:

• Conducting internal monitoring and auditing through the performance of periodic audits;

• Implementing compliance and practice standards through the development of written standards and procedures;

• Designating a compliance officer or contact(s) to monitor compliance efforts and enforce practice standards;

• Conducting appropriate training and education on practice standards and procedures;

• Responding appropriately to detected violations through the investigation of allegations and the disclosure of incidents to appropriate Government entities;

• Developing open lines of communication, such as (1) discussions at staff meetings regarding how to avoid erroneous or fraudulent conduct and (2) community bulletin boards, to keep practice employees updated regarding compliance activities; and

• Enforcing disciplinary standards through well-publicized guidelines.

These seven components provide a solid basis upon which a physician practice can create a compliance program. The OIG acknowledges that full implementation of all components may not be feasible for all physician practices. Some physician practices may never fully implement all of the components. However, as a first step, physician practices can begin by adopting only those components which, based on a practice's specific history with billing problems and other compliance issues, are most likely to provide an identifiable benefit.

The extent of implementation will depend on the size and resources of the practice. Smaller physician practices may incorporate each of the components in a manner that best suits the practice. By contrast, larger physician practices often have the means to incorporate the components in a more systematic manner. For example, larger physician practices can use both this guidance and the Third-Party Medical Billing Compliance Program Guidance, which provides a more detailed compliance program structure, to create a compliance program unique to the practice.

The OIG recognizes that physician practices need to find the best way to achieve compliance for their given circumstances. Specifically, the OIG encourages physician practices to participate in other provider's compliance programs, such as the compliance programs of the hospitals or other settings in which the physicians practice. Physician Practice Management companies also may serve as a source of compliance program guidance. A physician practice's participation in such compliance programs could be a way, at least partly,

---
[5] 31 U.S.C. 3729.
[6] 42 U.S.C. 1320a–7a.

to augment the practice's own compliance efforts.

The opportunities for collaborative compliance efforts could include participating in training and education programs or using another entity's policies and procedures as a template from which the physician practice creates its own version. The OIG encourages this type of collaborative effort, where the content is appropriate to the setting involved (i.e., the training is relevant to physician practices as well as the sponsoring provider), because it provides a means to promote the desired objective without imposing excessive burdens on the practice or requiring physicians to undertake duplicative action. However, to prevent possible anti-kickback or self-referral issues, the OIG recommends that physicians consider limiting their participation in a sponsoring provider's compliance program to the areas of training and education or policies and procedures.

The key to avoiding possible conflicts is to ensure that the entity providing compliance services to a physician practice (its referral source) is not perceived as nor is it operating the practice compliance program at no charge. For example, if the sponsoring entity conducted claims review for the physician practice as part of a compliance program or provided compliance oversight without charging the practice fair market value for those services, the anti-kickback and Stark self-referral laws would be implicated. The payment of fair market value by referral sources for compliance services will generally address these concerns.

B. Steps for Implementing a Voluntary Compliance Program

As previously discussed, implementing a voluntary compliance program can be a multi-tiered process. Initial development of the compliance program can be focused on practice risk areas that have been problematic for the practice such as coding and billing. Within this area, the practice should examine its claims denial history or claims that have resulted in repeated overpayments, and identify and correct the most frequent sources of those denials or overpayments. A review of claim denials will help the practice scrutinize a significant risk area and improve its cash flow by submitting correct claims that will be paid the first time they are submitted. As this example illustrates, a compliance program for a physician practice often makes sound business sense.

The following is a suggested order of the steps a practice could take to begin the development of a compliance program. The steps outlined below articulate all seven components of a compliance program and there are numerous suggestions for implementation within each component. Physician practices should keep in mind, as stated earlier, that it is up to the practice to determine the manner in which and the extent to which the practice chooses to implement these voluntary measures.

Step One: Auditing and Monitoring

An ongoing evaluation process is important to a successful compliance program. This ongoing evaluation includes not only whether the physician practice's standards and procedures are in fact current and accurate, but also whether the compliance program is working, *i.e.*, whether individuals are properly carrying out their responsibilities and claims are submitted appropriately. Therefore, an audit is an excellent way for a physician practice to ascertain what, if any, problem areas exist and focus on the risk areas that are associated with those problems. There are two types of reviews that can be performed as part of this evaluation: (1) A standards and procedures review; and (2) a claims submission audit.

1. Standards and Procedures

It is recommended that an individual(s) in the physician practice be charged with the responsibility of periodically reviewing the practice's standards and procedures to determine if they are current and complete. If the standards and procedures are found to be ineffective or outdated, they should be updated to reflect changes in Government regulations or compendiums generally relied upon by physicians and insurers (*i.e.*, changes in Current Procedural Terminology (CPT) and ICD–9–CM codes).

2. Claims Submission Audit

In addition to the standards and procedures themselves, it is advisable that bills and medical records be reviewed for compliance with applicable coding, billing and documentation requirements. The individuals from the physician practice involved in these self-audits would ideally include the person in charge of billing (if the practice has such a person) and a medically trained person (*e.g.*, registered nurse or preferably a physician (physicians can rotate in this position)). Each physician practice needs to decide for itself whether to review claims retrospectively or concurrently with the claims submission. In the Third-Party Medical Billing Compliance Program Guidance, the OIG recommended that a baseline, or "snapshot," be used to enable a practice to judge over time its progress in reducing or eliminating potential areas of vulnerability. This practice, known as "benchmarking," allows a practice to chart its compliance efforts by showing a reduction or increase in the number of claims paid and denied.

The practice's self-audits can be used to determine whether:

• Bills are accurately coded and accurately reflect the services provided (as documented in the medical records);

• Documentation is being completed correctly;

• Services or items provided are reasonable and necessary; and

• Any incentives for unnecessary services exist.

A baseline audit examines the claim development and submission process, from patient intake through claim submission and payment, and identifies elements within this process that may contribute to non-compliance or that may need to be the focus for improving execution.[7] This audit will establish a consistent methodology for selecting and examining records, and this methodology will then serve as a basis for future audits.

There are many ways to conduct a baseline audit. The OIG recommends that claims/services that were submitted and paid during the initial three months after implementation of the education and training program be examined, so as to give the physician practice a benchmark against which to measure future compliance effectiveness.

Following the baseline audit, a general recommendation is that periodic audits be conducted at least once each year to ensure that the compliance program is being followed. Optimally, a randomly selected number of medical records could be reviewed to ensure that the coding was performed accurately. Although there is no set formula to how many medical records should be reviewed, a basic guide is five or more medical records per Federal payor (*i.e.*, Medicare, Medicaid), or five to ten medical records per physician. The OIG realizes that physician practices receive reimbursement from a number of different payors, and we would encourage a physician practice's auditing/monitoring process to consist of a review of claims from all Federal payors from which the practice receives reimbursement. Of course, the larger the sample size, the larger the comfort level

---

[7] *See* Appendix D.II. referencing the Provider Self-Disclosure Protocol for information on how to conduct a baseline audit.

the physician practice will have about the results. However, the OIG is aware that this may be burdensome for some physician practices, so, at a minimum, we would encourage the physician practice to conduct a review of claims that have been reimbursed by Federal health care programs.

If problems are identified, the physician practice will need to determine whether a focused review should be conducted on a more frequent basis. When audit results reveal areas needing additional information or education of employees and physicians, the physician practice will need to analyze whether these areas should be incorporated into the training and educational system.

There are many ways to identify the claims/services from which to draw the random sample of claims to be audited. One methodology is to choose a random sample of claims/services from either all of the claims/services a physician has received reimbursement for or all claims/services from a particular payor. Another method is to identify risk areas or potential billing vulnerabilities. The codes associated with these risk areas may become the universe of claims/services from which to select the sample. The OIG recommends that the physician practice evaluate claims/services selected to determine if the codes billed and reimbursed were accurately ordered, performed, and reasonable and necessary for the treatment of the patient.

One of the most important components of a successful compliance audit protocol is an appropriate response when the physician practice identifies a problem. This action should be taken as soon as possible after the date the problem is identified. The specific action a physician practice takes should depend on the circumstances of the situation. In some cases, the response can be as straight forward as generating a repayment with appropriate explanation to Medicare or the appropriate payor from which the overpayment was received. In others, the physician practice may want to consult with a coding/billing expert to determine the next best course of action. There is no boilerplate solution to how to handle problems that are identified.

It is a good business practice to create a system to address how physician practices will respond to and report potential problems. In addition, preserving information relating to identification of the problem is as important as preserving information that tracks the physician practice's reaction to, and solution for, the issue.

Step 2: Establish Practice Standards and Procedures

After the internal audit identifies the practice's risk areas, the next step is to develop a method for dealing with those risk areas through the practice's standards and procedures. Written standards and procedures are a central component of any compliance program. Those standards and procedures help to reduce the prospect of erroneous claims and fraudulent activity by identifying risk areas for the practice and establishing tighter internal controls to counter those risks, while also helping to identify any aberrant billing practices. Many physician practices already have something similar to this called "practice standards" that include practice policy statements regarding patient care, personnel matters and practice standards and procedures on complying with Federal and State law.

The OIG believes that written standards and procedures can be helpful to all physician practices, regardless of size and capability. If a lack of resources to develop such standards and procedures is genuinely an issue, the OIG recommends that a physician practice focus first on those risk areas most likely to arise in its particular practice.[8] Additionally, if the physician practice works with a physician practice management company (PPMC), independent practice association (IPA), physician-hospital organization, management services organization (MSO) or third-party billing company, the practice can incorporate the compliance standards and procedures of those entities, if appropriate, into its own standards and procedures. Many physician practices have found that the adoption of a third party's compliance standards and procedures, as appropriate, has many benefits and the result is a consistent set of standards and procedures for a community of physicians as well as having just one entity that can then monitor and refine the process as needed. This sharing of compliance responsibilities assists physician practices in rural areas that do not have the staff to perform these functions, but do belong to a group that does have the resources. Physician practices using another entity's compliance materials will need to tailor those materials to the physician practice where they will be applied.

Physician practices that do not have standards or procedures in place can develop them by: (1) Developing a written standards and procedures manual; and (2) updating clinical forms periodically to make sure they facilitate and encourage clear and complete documentation of patient care. A practice's standards could also identify the clinical protocol(s), pathway(s), and other treatment guidelines followed by the practice.

Creating a resource manual from publicly available information may be a cost-effective approach for developing additional standards and procedures. For example, the practice can develop a "binder" that contains the practice's written standards and procedures, relevant HCFA directives and carrier bulletins, and summaries of informative OIG documents (*e.g.,* Special Fraud Alerts, Advisory Opinions, inspection and audit reports).[9] If the practice chooses to adopt this idea, the binder should be updated as appropriate and located in a readily accessible location.

If updates to the standards and procedures are necessary, those updates should be communicated to employees to keep them informed regarding the practice's operations. New employees can be made aware of the standards and procedures when hired and can be trained on their contents as part of their orientation to the practice. The OIG recommends that the communication of updates and training of new employees occur as soon as possible after either the issuance of a new update or the hiring of a new employee.

1. Specific Risk Areas

The OIG recognizes that many physician practices may not have in place standards and procedures to prevent erroneous or fraudulent conduct in their practices. In order to develop standards and procedures, the physician practice may consider what types of fraud and abuse related topics need to be addressed based on its specific needs. One of the most important things in making that determination is a listing of risk areas where the practice may be vulnerable.

To assist physician practices in performing this initial assessment, the OIG has developed a list of four potential risk areas affecting physician practices. These risk areas include: (a) Coding and billing; (b) reasonable and necessary services; (c) documentation;

---

[8] Physician practices with laboratories or arrangements with third-party billing companies can also check the risk areas included in the OIG compliance program guidance for those industries.

[9] The OIG and HCFA are working to compile a list of basic documents issued by both entities that could be included in such a binder. We expect to complete this list later this fall, and will post it on the OIG and HCFA web sites, as well as publicize this list to physician organizations and representatives (information on how to contact the OIG is contained in Footnote 3; HCFA information can be obtained at www.hcfa.gov/medlearn or by calling 1-800-MEDICARE).

and (d) improper inducements, kickbacks and self-referrals. This list of risk areas is not exhaustive, or all-encompassing. Rather, it should be viewed as a starting point for an internal review of potential vulnerabilities within the physician practice.[10] The objective of such an assessment is to ensure that key personnel in the physician practice are aware of these major risk areas and that steps are taken to minimize, to the extent possible, the types of problems identified. While there are many ways to accomplish this objective, clear written standards and procedures that are communicated to all employees are important to ensure the effectiveness of a compliance program. Specifically, the following are discussions of risk areas for physician practices:[11]

a. Coding and Billing. A major part of any physician practice's compliance program is the identification of risk areas associated with coding and billing. The following risk areas associated with billing have been among the most frequent subjects of investigations and audits by the OIG:

• Billing for items or services not rendered or not provided as claimed;[12]

• Submitting claims for equipment, medical supplies and services that are not reasonable and necessary;[13]

• Double billing resulting in duplicate payment;[14]

• Billing for non-covered services as if covered;[15]

• Knowing misuse of provider identification numbers, which results in improper billing;[16]

• Unbundling (billing for each component of the service instead of billing or using an all-inclusive code);[17]

• Failure to properly use coding modifiers;[18]

• Clustering;[19] and

• Upcoding the level of service provided.[20]

The physician practice written standards and procedures concerning proper coding reflect the current reimbursement principles set forth in applicable statutes, regulations[21] and Federal, State or private payor health care program requirements and should be developed in tandem with coding and billing standards used in the physician practice. Furthermore, written standards and procedures should ensure that coding and billing are based on medical record documentation. Particular attention should be paid to issues of appropriate diagnosis codes and individual Medicare Part B claims (including documentation guidelines for evaluation and management services).[22] A physician practice can also institute a policy that the coder and/or physician review all rejected claims pertaining to diagnosis and procedure codes. This step can facilitate a reduction in similar errors.

b. Reasonable and Necessary Services. A practice's compliance program may provide guidance that claims are to be submitted only for services that the physician practice finds to be reasonable and necessary in the particular case. The OIG recognizes that physicians should be able to order any tests, including screening tests, they believe are appropriate for the treatment of their patients. However, a physician practice should be aware that Medicare will only pay for services that meet the Medicare definition of reasonable and necessary.[23]

Medicare (and many insurance plans) may deny payment for a service that is not reasonable and necessary according to the Medicare reimbursement rules. Thus, when a physician provides services to a Medicare beneficiary, he or she should only bill those services that meet the Medicare standard of being reasonable and necessary for the diagnosis and treatment of a patient. A physician practice can bill in order to receive a denial for services, but only if the denial is needed for reimbursement from the secondary payor. Upon request, the physician practice should be able to provide documentation, such as a patient's medical records and

---

[10] Physician practices seeking additional guidance on potential risk areas can review the OIG's Work Plan to identify vulnerabilities and risk areas on which the OIG will focus in the future. In addition, physician practices can also review the OIG's semiannual reports, which identify program vulnerabilities and risk areas that the OIG has targeted during the preceding six months. All of these documents are available on the OIG's webpage at http://www.hhs.gov/oig.

[11] Appendix A of this document lists additional risk areas that a physician practice may want to review and incorporate into their practice standards and procedures.

[12] For example, Dr. X, an ophthalmologist, billed for laser surgery he did not perform. As one element of proof, he did not even have laser equipment or access to such equipment at the place of service designated on the claim form where he performed the surgery.

[13] Billing for services, supplies and equipment that are not reasonable and necessary involves seeking reimbursement for a service that is not warranted by a patient's documented medical condition. See 42 U.S.C. 1395i(a)(1)(A) ("no payment may be made under part A or part B [of Medicare] for any expenses incurred for items or services which * * * are not reasonable and necessary for the diagnosis or treatment of illness or injury or to improve the functioning of the malformed body member"). See also Appendix A for further discussion on this topic.

[14] Double billing occurs when a physician bills for the same item or service more than once or another party billed the Federal health care program for an item or service also billed by the physician. Although duplicate billing can occur due to simple error, the knowing submission of duplicate claims—which is sometimes evidenced by systematic or repeated double billing—can create liability under criminal, civil, and/or administrative law.

[15] For example, Dr. Y bills Medicare using a covered office visit code when the actual service was a non-covered annual physical. Physician practices should remember that "necessary" does not always constitute "covered" and that this example is a misrepresentation of services to the Federal health care programs.

[16] An example of this is when the practice bills for a service performed by Dr. B, who has not yet been issued a Medicare provider number, using Dr. A's Medicare provider number. Physician practices need to bill using the correct Medicare provider number, even if that means delaying billing until the physician receives his/her provider number.

[17] Unbundling is the practice of a physician billing for multiple components of a service that must be included in a single fee. For example, if dressings and instruments are included in a fee for a minor procedure, the provider may not also bill separately for the dressings and instruments.

[18] A modifier, as defined by the CPT–4 manual, provides the means by which a physician practice can indicate a service or procedure that has been performed has been altered by some specific circumstance, but not changed in its definition or code. Assuming the modifier is used correctly and appropriately, this specificity provides the justification for payment for those services. For correct use of modifiers, the physician practice should reference the appropriate sections of the *Medicare Provider Manual. See Medicare Carrier Manual* Section 4630. For general information on the correct use of modifiers, a physician practice can consult the National Correct Coding Initiative (NCCI). *See* Appendix F for information on how to download the NCCI edits. The NCCI coding edits are updated on a quarterly basis and are used to process claims and determine payments to physicians.

[19] This is the practice of coding/charging one or two middle levels of service codes exclusively, under the philosophy that some will be higher, some lower, and the charges will average out over an extended period (in reality, this overcharges some patients while undercharging others).

[20] Upcoding is billing for a more expensive service than the one actually performed. For example, Dr. X intentionally bills at a higher evaluation and management (E&M) code than what he actually renders to the patient.

[21] The official coding guidelines are promulgated by HCFA, the National Center for Health Statistics, the American Hospital Association, the American Medical Association and the American Health Information Management Association. *See* International Classification of Diseases, 9th Revision, Clinical Modification (ICD–9 CM)(and its successors); 1998 Health Care Financing Administration Common Procedure Coding System (HCPCS) (and its successors); and Physicians' CPT. In addition, there are specialized coding systems for specific segments of the health care industry. Among these are ADA (for dental procedures), DSM IV (psychiatric health benefits) and DMERCs (for durable medical equipment, prosthetics, orthotics and supplies).

[22] The failure of a physician practice to: (i) document items and services rendered; and (ii) properly submit the corresponding claims for reimbursement is a major area of potential erroneous or fraudulent conduct involving Federal health care programs. The OIG has undertaken numerous audits, investigations, inspections and national enforcement initiatives in these areas.

[23] "* * * for the diagnosis or treatment of illness or injury or to improve the functioning of a malformed body member." 42 U.S.C. 1395y(a)(1)(A).

physician's orders, to support the appropriateness of a service that the physician has provided.

c. *Documentation.* Timely, accurate and complete documentation is important to clinical patient care. This same documentation serves as a second function when a bill is submitted for payment, namely, as verification that the bill is accurate as submitted. Therefore, one of the most important physician practice compliance issues is the appropriate documentation of diagnosis and treatment. Physician documentation is necessary to determine the appropriate medical treatment for the patient and is the basis for coding and billing determinations. Thorough and accurate documentation also helps to ensure accurate recording and timely transmission of information.

i. Medical Record Documentation. In addition to facilitating high quality patient care, a properly documented medical record verifies and documents precisely what services were actually provided. The medical record may be used to validate: (a) The site of the service; (b) the appropriateness of the services provided; (c) the accuracy of the billing; and (d) the identity of the care giver (service provider). Examples of internal documentation guidelines a practice might use to ensure accurate medical record documentation include the following: [24]

• The medical record is complete and legible;

• The documentation of each patient encounter includes the reason for the encounter; any relevant history; physical examination findings; prior diagnostic test results; assessment, clinical impression, or diagnosis; plan of care; and date and legible identity of the observer;

• If not documented, the rationale for ordering diagnostic and other ancillary services can be easily inferred by an independent reviewer or third party who has appropriate medical training;

• CPT and ICD–9–CM codes used for claims submission are supported by documentation and the medical record; and

• Appropriate health risk factors are identified. The patient's progress, his or her response to, and any changes in, treatment, and any revision in diagnosis is documented.

The CPT and ICD–9–CM codes reported on the health insurance claims form should be supported by documentation in the medical record and the medical chart should contain all necessary information. Additionally, HCFA and the local carriers should be able to determine the person who provided the services. These issues can be the root of investigations of inappropriate or erroneous conduct, and have been identified by HCFA and the OIG as a leading cause of improper payments.

One method for improving quality in documentation is for a physician practice to compare the practice's claim denial rate to the rates of other practices in the same specialty to the extent that the practice can obtain that information from the carrier. Physician coding and diagnosis distribution can be compared for each physician within the same specialty to identify variances.

ii. HCFA 1500 Form. Another documentation area for physician practices to monitor closely is the proper completion of the HCFA 1500 form. The following practices will help ensure that the form has been properly completed:

• Link the diagnosis code with the reason for the visit or service;

• Use modifiers appropriately;

• Provide Medicare with all information about a beneficiary's other insurance coverage under the Medicare Secondary Payor (MSP) policy, if the practice is aware of a beneficiary's additional coverage.

d. *Improper Inducements, Kickbacks and Self-Referrals.* A physician practice would be well advised to have standards and procedures that encourage compliance with the anti-kickback statute [25] and the physician self-referral law.[26] Remuneration for referrals is illegal because it can distort medical decision-making, cause overutilization of services or supplies, increase costs to Federal health care programs, and result in unfair competition by shutting out competitors who are unwilling to pay for referrals. Remuneration for referrals can also affect the quality of patient care by encouraging physicians to order services or supplies based on profit rather than the patients' best medical interests.[27]

In particular, arrangements with hospitals, hospices, nursing facilities, home health agencies, durable medical equipment suppliers, pharmaceutical manufacturers and vendors are areas of potential concern. In general the anti-kickback statute prohibits knowingly and willfully giving or receiving anything of value to induce referrals of Federal health care program business. It is generally recommended that all business arrangements wherein physician practices refer business to, or order services or items from, an outside entity should be on a fair market value basis.[28] Whenever a physician practice intends to enter into a business arrangement that involves making referrals, the arrangement should be reviewed by legal counsel familiar with the anti-kickback statute and physician self-referral statute.

In addition to developing standards and procedures to address arrangements with other health care providers and suppliers, physician practices should also consider implementing measures to avoid offering inappropriate inducements to patients.[29] Examples of such inducements include routinely waiving coinsurance or deductible amounts without a good faith determination that the patient is in financial need or failing to make reasonable efforts to collect the cost-sharing amount.[30]

Possible risk factors relating to this risk area that could be addressed in the practice's standards and procedures include:

• Financial arrangements with outside entities to whom the practice

---

[24] For additional information on proper documentation, physician practices should also reference the *Documentation Guidelines for Evaluation and Management Services,* published by HCFA. Currently, physicians may document based on the 1995 or 1997 E&M Guidelines, whichever is most advantageous to the physician. A new set of draft guidelines were announced in June 2000, and are undergoing pilot testing and revision, but are not in current use.

[25] The anti-kickback statute provides criminal penalties for individuals and entities that knowingly offer, pay, solicit, or receive bribes or kickbacks or other remuneration in order to induce business reimbursable by Federal health care programs. *See* 42 U.S.C. 1320a–7b(b). Civil penalties, exclusion from participation in the Federal health care programs, and civil False Claims Act liability may also result from a violation of the prohibition. *See* 42 U.S.C. 1320a–7a(a)(5), 42 U.S.C. 1320a–7(b)(7), and 31 U.S.C. 3729–3733.

[26] The physician self-referral law, 42 U.S.C. 1395nn (also known as the "Stark law"), prohibits a physician from making a referral to an entity with which the physician or any member of the physician's immediate family has a financial relationship if the referral is for the furnishing of designated health services, unless the financial relationship fits into an exception set forth in the statute or implementing regulations.

[27] *See* Appendix B for additional information on the anti-kickback statute.

[28] The OIG's definition of "fair market value" excludes any value attributable to referrals of Federal program business or the ability to influence the flow of such business. *See* 42 U.S.C. 1395nn(h)(3). Adhering to the rule of keeping business arrangements at fair market value is not a guarantee of legality, but is a highly useful general rule.

[29] *See* 42 U.S.C. 1320a–7a(a)(5).

[30] In the OIG Special Fraud Alert "Routine Waiver of Part B Co-payments/Deductibles" (May 1991), the OIG describes several reasons why routine waivers of these cost-sharing amounts pose concerns. The Alert sets forth the circumstances under which it may be appropriate to waive these amounts. *See* also 42 U.S.C. 1320a–7a(a)(5).

may refer Federal health care program business;[31]
- Joint ventures with entities supplying goods or services to the physician practice or its patients;[32]
- Consulting contracts or medical directorships;
- Office and equipment leases with entities to which the physician refers; and
- Soliciting, accepting or offering any gift or gratuity of more than nominal value to or from those who may benefit from a physician practice's referral of Federal health care program business.[33]

In order to keep current with this area of the law, a physician practice may obtain copies, available on the OIG web site or in hard copy from the OIG, of all relevant OIG Special Fraud Alerts and Advisory Opinions that address the application of the anti-kickback and physician self-referral laws to ensure that the standards and procedures reflect current positions and opinions.

2. Retention of Records

In light of the documentation requirements faced by physician practices, it would be to the practice's benefit if its standards and procedures contained a section on the retention of compliance, business and medical records. These records primarily include documents relating to patient care and the practice's business activities. A physician practice's designated compliance contact could keep an updated binder or record of these documents, including information relating to compliance activities. The primary compliance documents that a practice would want to retain are those that relate to educational activities, internal investigations and internal audit results. We suggest that particular attention should be paid to documenting investigations of potential violations uncovered by the compliance program and the resulting remedial action. Although there is no requirement that the practice retain its compliance records, having all the relevant documentation relating to the practice's compliance efforts or handling of a particular problem can benefit the practice should it ever be questioned regarding those activities.

Physician practices that implement a compliance program might also want to provide for the development and implementation of a records retention system. This system would establish standards and procedures regarding the creation, distribution, retention, and destruction of documents. If the practice decides to design a record system, privacy concerns and Federal or State regulatory requirements should be taken into consideration.[34]

While conducting its compliance activities, as well as its daily operations, a physician practice would be well advised, to the extent it is possible, to document its efforts to comply with applicable Federal health care program requirements. For example, if a physician practice requests advice from a Government agency (including a Medicare carrier) charged with administering a Federal health care program, it is to the benefit of the practice to document and retain a record of the request and any written or oral response (or nonresponse). This step is extremely important if the practice intends to rely on that response to guide it in future decisions, actions, or claim reimbursement requests or appeals.

In short, it is in the best interest of all physician practices, regardless of size, to have procedures to create and retain appropriate documentation. The following record retention guidelines are suggested:

- The length of time that a practice's records are to be retained can be specified in the physician practice's standards and procedures (Federal and State statutes should be consulted for specific time frames, if applicable);
- Medical records (if in the possession of the physician practice) need to be secured against loss, destruction, unauthorized access, unauthorized reproduction, corruption, or damage; and
- Standards and procedures can stipulate the disposition of medical records in the event the practice is sold or closed.

Step Three: Designation of a Compliance Officer/Contact(s)

After the audits have been completed and the risk areas identified, ideally one member of the physician practice staff needs to accept the responsibility of developing a corrective action plan, if necessary, and oversee the practice's adherence to that plan. This person can either be in charge of all compliance activities for the practice or play a limited role merely to resolve the current issue. In a formalized institutional compliance program there is a compliance officer who is responsible for overseeing the implementation and day-to-day operations of the compliance program. However, the resource constraints of physician practices make it so that it is often impossible to designate one person to be in charge of compliance functions.

It is acceptable for a physician practice to designate more than one employee with compliance monitoring responsibility. In lieu of having a designated compliance officer, the physician practice could instead describe in its standards and procedures the compliance functions for which designated employees, known as "compliance contacts," would be responsible. For example, one employee could be responsible for preparing written standards and procedures, while another could be responsible for conducting or arranging for periodic audits and ensuring that billing questions are answered. Therefore, the compliance-related responsibilities of the designated person or persons may be only a portion of his or her duties.

Another possibility is that one individual could serve as compliance officer for more than one entity. In situations where staffing limitations mandate that the practice cannot afford to designate a person(s) to oversee compliance activities, the practice could outsource all or part of the functions of a compliance officer to a third party, such as a consultant, PPMC, MSO, IPA or third-party billing company. However, if this role is outsourced, it is beneficial for the compliance officer to have sufficient interaction with the physician practice to be able to effectively understand the inner workings of the practice. For example, consultants that are not in close geographic proximity to a practice may not be effective compliance officers for the practice.

---

[31] All physician contracts and agreements with parties in a position to influence Federal health care program business or to whom the doctor is in such a position to influence should be reviewed to avoid violation of the anti-kickback, self-referral, and other relevant Federal and State laws. The OIG has published safe harbors that define practices not subject to the anti-kickback statute, because such arrangements would be unlikely to result in fraud or abuse. Failure to comply with a safe harbor provision does not make an arrangement per se illegal. Rather, the safe harbors set forth specific conditions that, if fully met, would assure the entities involved of not being prosecuted or sanctioned for the arrangement qualifying for the safe harbor. One such safe harbor applies to personal services contracts. *See* 42 CFR 1001.952(d).

[32] *See* OIG Special Fraud Alert "Joint Venture Arrangements" (August 1989) available on the OIG web site at http://www.hhs.gov/oig. *See also* OIG Advisory Opinion 97–5.

[33] Physician practices should establish clear standards and procedures governing gift-giving because such exchanges may be viewed as inducements to influence business decisions.

[34] There are various Federal regulations governing the privacy of patient records and the retention of certain types of patient records. Many states also have record retention statutes. Practices should check with their state medical society and/or affiliated professional association for assistance in ascertaining these requirements for their particular specialty and location.

One suggestion for how to maintain continual interaction is for the practice to designate someone to serve as a liaison with the outsourced compliance officer. This would help ensure a strong tie between the compliance officer and the practice's daily operations. Outsourced compliance officers, who spend most of their time offsite, have certain limitations that a physician practice should consider before making such a critical decision. These limitations can include lack of understanding as to the inner workings of the practice, accessibility and possible conflicts of interest when one compliance officer is serving several practices.

If the physician practice decides to designate a particular person(s) to oversee all compliance activities, not just those in conjunction with the audit-related issue, the following is a list of suggested duties that the practice may want to assign to that person(s):

• Overseeing and monitoring the implementation of the compliance program;

• Establishing methods, such as periodic audits, to improve the practice's efficiency and quality of services, and to reduce the practice's vulnerability to fraud and abuse;

• Periodically revising the compliance program in light of changes in the needs of the practice or changes in the law and in the standards and procedures of Government and private payor health plans;

• Developing, coordinating and participating in a training program that focuses on the components of the compliance program, and seeks to ensure that training materials are appropriate;

• Ensuring that the HHS–OIG's List of Excluded Individuals and Entities, and the General Services Administration's (GSA's) List of Parties Debarred from Federal Programs have been checked with respect to all employees, medical staff and independent contractors;[35] and

• Investigating any report or allegation concerning possible unethical or improper business practices, and monitoring subsequent corrective action and/or compliance.

Each physician practice needs to assess its own practice situation and determine what best suits that practice in terms of compliance oversight.

Step Four: Conducting Appropriate Training and Education

Education is an important part of any compliance program and is the logical next step after problems have been identified and the practice has designated a person to oversee educational training. Ideally, education programs will be tailored to the physician practice's needs, specialty and size and will include both compliance and specific training.

There are three basic steps for setting up educational objectives:

• Determining who needs training (both in coding and billing and in compliance);

• Determining the type of training that best suits the practice's needs (*e.g.*, seminars, in-service training, self-study or other programs); and

• Determining when and how often education is needed and how much each person should receive.

Training may be accomplished through a variety of means, including in-person training sessions (*i.e.*, either on site or at outside seminars), distribution of newsletters,[36] or even a readily accessible office bulletin board. Regardless of the training modality used, a physician practice should ensure that the necessary education is communicated effectively and that the practice's employees come away from the training with a better understanding of the issues covered.

1. Compliance Training

Under the direction of the designated compliance officer/contact, both initial and recurrent training in compliance is advisable, both with respect to the compliance program itself and applicable statutes and regulations. Suggestions for items to include in compliance training are: The operation and importance of the compliance program; the consequences of violating the standards and procedures set forth in the program; and the role of each employee in the operation of the compliance program.

There are two goals a practice should strive for when conducting compliance training: (1) All employees will receive training on how to perform their jobs in compliance with the standards of the practice and any applicable regulations; and (2) each employee will understand that compliance is a condition of continued employment. Compliance training focuses on explaining why the practice is developing and establishing a compliance program. The training should emphasize that following the standards and procedures will not get a practice employee in trouble, but violating the standards and procedures may subject the employee to disciplinary measures. It is advisable that new employees be trained on the compliance program as soon as possible after their start date and employees should receive refresher training on an annual basis or as appropriate.

2. Coding and Billing Training

Coding and billing training on the Federal health care program requirements may be necessary for certain members of the physician practice staff depending on their respective responsibilities. The OIG understands that most physician practices do not employ a professional coder and that the physician is often primarily responsible for all coding and billing. However, it is in the practice's best interest to ensure that individuals who are directly involved with billing, coding or other aspects of the Federal health care programs receive extensive education specific to that individual's responsibilities. Some examples of items that could be covered in coding and billing training include:

• Coding requirements;

• Claim development and submission processes;

• Signing a form for a physician without the physician's authorization;

• Proper documentation of services rendered;

• Proper billing standards and procedures and submission of accurate bills for services or items rendered to Federal health care program beneficiaries; and

• The legal sanctions for submitting deliberately false or reckless billings.

3. Format of the Training Program

Training may be conducted either in-house or by an outside source.[37]

---

[35] The HHS–OIG "List of Excluded Individuals/Entities" provides information to health care providers, patients, and others regarding individuals and entities that are excluded from participation in Federal health care programs. This report, in both an on-line searchable and downloadable database, can be located on the Internet at http://www.hhs.gov/oig. The OIG sanction information is readily available to users in two formats on over 15,000 individuals and entities currently excluded from program participation through action taken by the OIG. The on-line searchable database allows users to obtain information regarding excluded individuals and entities sorted by: (1) The legal bases for exclusions; (2) the types of individuals and entities excluded by the OIG; and (3) the States where excluded individuals reside or entities do business. In addition, the General Services Administration maintains a monthly listing of debarred contractors, "List of Parties Debarred from Federal Programs," at http://www.arnet.gov/epls.

[36] HCFA also offers free online training for general fraud and abuse issues at *http://www.hcfa.gov/medlearn*. See Appendix F for additional information.

[37] As noted earlier in this guidance, another way for physician practices to receive training is for the physicians and/or the employees of the practice to attend training programs offered by outside entities, such as a hospital, a local medical society or a

Training at outside seminars, instead of internal programs and in-service sessions, may be an effective way to achieve the practice's training goals. In fact, many community colleges offer certificate or associate degree programs in billing and coding, and professional associations provide various kinds of continuing education and certification programs. Many carriers also offer billing training.

The physician practice may work with its third-party billing company, if one is used, to ensure that documentation is of a level that is adequate for the billing company to submit accurate claims on behalf of the physician practice. If it is not, these problem areas should also be covered in the training. In addition to the billing training, it is advisable for physician practices to maintain updated ICD–9, HCPCS and CPT manuals (in addition to the carrier bulletins construing those sources) and make them available to all employees involved in the billing process. Physician practices can also provide a source of continuous updates on current billing standards and procedures by making publications or Government documents that describe current billing policies available to its employees.[38]

Physician practices do not have to provide separate education and training programs for the compliance and coding and billing training. All in-service training and continuing education can integrate compliance issues, as well as other core values adopted by the practice, such as quality improvement and improved patient service, into their curriculum.

4. Continuing Education on Compliance Issues

There is no set formula for determining how often training sessions should occur. The OIG recommends that there be at least an annual training program for all individuals involved in the coding and billing aspects of the practice.[39] Ideally, new billing and coding employees will be trained as soon as possible after assuming their duties and will work under an experienced employee until their training has been completed.

Step Five: Responding To Detected Offenses and Developing Corrective Action Initiatives

When a practice determines it has detected a possible violation, the next step is to develop a corrective action plan and determine how to respond to the problem. Violations of a physician practice's compliance program, significant failures to comply with applicable Federal or State law, and other types of misconduct threaten a practice's status as a reliable, honest, and trustworthy provider of health care. Consequently, upon receipt of reports or reasonable indications of suspected noncompliance, it is important that the compliance contact or other practice employee look into the allegations to determine whether a significant violation of applicable law or the requirements of the compliance program has indeed occurred, and, if so, take decisive steps to correct the problem.[40] As appropriate, such steps may involve a corrective action plan,[41] the return of any overpayments, a report to the Government,[42] and/or a referral to law enforcement authorities.

One suggestion is that the practice, in developing its compliance program, develop its own set of monitors and warning indicators. These might include: Significant changes in the number and/or types of claim rejections and/or reductions; correspondence from the carriers and insurers challenging the medical necessity or validity of claims; illogical patterns or unusual changes in the pattern of CPT–4, HCPCS or ICD–9 code utilization; and high volumes of unusual charge or payment adjustment transactions. If any of these warning indicators become apparent, then it is recommended that the practice follow up on the issues. Subsequently, as appropriate, the compliance procedures of the practice may need to be changed to prevent the problem from recurring.

For potential criminal violations, a physician practice would be well advised in its compliance program procedures to include steps for prompt referral or disclosure to an appropriate Government authority or law enforcement agency. In regard to overpayment issues, it is advised that the physician practice take appropriate corrective action, including prompt identification and repayment of any overpayment to the affected payor.

It is also recommended that the compliance program provide for a full internal assessment of all reports of detected violations. If the physician practice ignores reports of possible fraudulent activity, it is undermining the very purpose it hoped to achieve by implementing a compliance program.

It is advised that the compliance program standards and procedures include provisions to ensure that a violation is not compounded once discovered. In instances involving individual misconduct, the standards and procedures might also advise as to whether the individuals involved in the violation either be retrained, disciplined, or, if appropriate, terminated. The physician practice may also prevent the compounding of the violation by conducting a review of all confirmed violations, and, if appropriate, self-reporting the violations to the applicable authority.

The physician practice may consider the fact that if a violation occurred and was not detected, its compliance program may require modification. Physician practices that detect violations could analyze the situation to determine whether a flaw in their compliance program failed to anticipate the detected problem, or whether the compliance program's procedures failed to prevent the violation. In any event, it is prudent, even absent the detection of any violations, for physician practices to periodically review and modify their compliance programs.

Step Six: Developing Open Lines of Communication

In order to prevent problems from occurring and to have a frank discussion

---

carrier. This sort of collaborative effort is an excellent way for the practice to meet the desired training objective without having to expend the resources to develop and implement in-house training.

[38] Some publications, such as OIG's Special Fraud Alerts, audit and inspection reports, and Advisory Opinions are readily available from the OIG and can provide a basis for educational courses and programs for physician practice employees. *See* Appendix F for a partial listing of these documents. *See* Footnote 3 for information on how to obtain copies of these documents.

[39] Currently, the OIG is monitoring a significant number of corporate integrity agreements that require many of these training elements. The OIG usually requires a minimum of one hour annually for basic training in compliance areas. Additional training may be necessary for specialty fields such as claims development and billing.

[40] Instances of noncompliance must be determined on a case-by-case basis. The existence or amount of a monetary loss to a health care program is not solely determinative of whether the conduct should be investigated and reported to governmental authorities. In fact, there may be instances where there is no readily identifiable monetary loss to a health care provider, but corrective actions are still necessary to protect the integrity of the applicable program and its beneficiaries, *e.g.*, where services required by a plan of care are not provided.

[41] The physician practice may seek advice from its legal counsel to determine the extent of the practice's liability and to plan the appropriate course of action.

[42] The OIG has established a Provider Self-Disclosure Protocol that encourages providers to voluntarily report suspected fraud. The concept of voluntary self-disclosure is premised on a recognition that the Government alone cannot protect the integrity of the Medicare and other Federal health care programs. Health care providers must be willing to police themselves, correct underlying problems, and work with the Government to resolve these matters. The Provider Self-Disclosure Protocol can be located on the OIG's web site at: www.hhs.gov/oig. *See* Appendix D for further information on the Provider Self-Disclosure Protocol.

of why the problem happened in the first place, physician practices need to have open lines of communication. Especially in a smaller practice, an open line of communication is an integral part of implementing a compliance program. Guidance previously issued by the OIG has encouraged the use of several forms of communication between the compliance officer/committee and provider personnel, many of which focus on formal processes and are more costly to implement (e.g., hotlines and e-mail). However, the OIG recognizes that the nature of some physician practices is not as conducive to implementing these types of measures. The nature of a small physician practice dictates that such communication and information exchanges need to be conducted through a less formalized process than that which has been envisioned by prior OIG guidance.

In the small physician practice setting, the communication element may be met by implementing a clear "open door" policy between the physicians and compliance personnel and practice employees. This policy can be implemented in conjunction with less formal communication techniques, such as conspicuous notices posted in common areas and/or the development and placement of a compliance bulletin board where everyone in the practice can receive up-to-date compliance information.[43]

A compliance program's system for meaningful and open communication can include the following:

• The requirement that employees report conduct that a reasonable person would, in good faith, believe to be erroneous or fraudulent;

• The creation of a user-friendly process (such as an anonymous drop box for larger practices) for effectively reporting erroneous or fraudulent conduct;

• Provisions in the standards and procedures that state that a failure to report erroneous or fraudulent conduct is a violation of the compliance program;

• The development of a simple and readily accessible procedure to process reports of erroneous or fraudulent conduct;

• If a billing company is used, communication to and from the billing company's compliance officer/contact and other responsible staff to coordinate billing and compliance activities of the practice and the billing company, respectively. Communication can include, as appropriate, lists of reported or identified concerns, initiation and the results of internal assessments, training needs, regulatory changes, and other operational and compliance matters;

• The utilization of a process that maintains the anonymity of the persons involved in the reported possible erroneous or fraudulent conduct and the person reporting the concern; and

• Provisions in the standards and procedures that there will be no retribution for reporting conduct that a reasonable person acting in good faith would have believed to be erroneous or fraudulent.

The OIG recognizes that protecting anonymity may not be feasible for small physician practices. However, the OIG believes all practice employees, when seeking answers to questions or reporting potential instances of erroneous or fraudulent conduct, should know to whom to turn for assistance in these matters and should be able to do so without fear of retribution. While the physician practice may strive to maintain the anonymity of an employee's identity, it also needs to make clear that there may be a point at which the individual's identity may become known or may have to be revealed in certain instances.

Step Seven: Enforcing Disciplinary Standards Through Well-Publicized Guidelines

Finally, the last step that a physician practice may wish to take is to incorporate measures into its practice to ensure that practice employees understand the consequences if they behave in a non-compliant manner. An effective physician practice compliance program includes procedures for enforcing and disciplining individuals who violate the practice's compliance or other practice standards. Enforcement and disciplinary provisions are necessary to add credibility and integrity to a compliance program.

The OIG recommends that a physician practice's enforcement and disciplinary mechanisms ensure that violations of the practice's compliance policies will result in consistent and appropriate sanctions, including the possibility of termination, against the offending individual. At the same time, it is advisable that the practice's enforcement and disciplinary procedures be flexible enough to account for mitigating or aggravating circumstances. The procedures might also stipulate that individuals who fail to detect or report violations of the compliance program may also be subject to discipline. Disciplinary actions could include: Warnings (oral); reprimands (written); probation; demotion; temporary suspension; termination; restitution of damages; and referral for criminal prosecution. Inclusion of disciplinary guidelines in in-house training and procedure manuals is sufficient to meet the "well publicized" standard of this element.

It is suggested that any communication resulting in the finding of non-compliant conduct be documented in the compliance files by including the date of incident, name of the reporting party, name of the person responsible for taking action, and the follow-up action taken. Another suggestion is for physician practices to conduct checks to make sure all current and potential practice employees are not listed on the OIG or GSA lists of individuals excluded from participation in Federal health care or Government procurement programs.[44]

C. Assessing A Voluntary Compliance Program

A practice's commitment to compliance can best be assessed by the active application of compliance principles in the day-to-day operations of the practice. Compliance programs are not just written standards and procedures that sit on a shelf in the main office of a practice, but are an everyday part of the practice operations. It is by integrating the compliance program into the practice culture that the practice can best achieve maximum benefit from its compliance program.

III. Conclusion

Just as immunizations are given to patients to prevent them from becoming ill, physician practices may view the implementation of a voluntary compliance program as comparable to a form of preventive medicine for the practice. This voluntary compliance program guidance is intended to assist physician practices in developing and implementing internal controls and procedures that promote adherence to Federal health care program requirements.

As stated earlier, physician compliance programs do not need to be time or resource intensive and can be developed in a manner that best reflects the nature of each individual practice. Many of the recommendations set forth in this document are ones that many physician practices already have in place and are simply good business practices that can be adhered to with a

---

[43] In addition to whatever other method of communication is being utilized, the OIG recommends that physician practices post the HHS–OIG Hotline telephone number (1–800–HHS–TIPS) in a prominent area.

[44] *See* Footnote 35 for information on how to access these lists.

reasonable amount of effort. By implementing an effective compliance program, appropriate for its size and resources, and making compliance principles an active part of the practice culture, a physician practice can help prevent and reduce erroneous or fraudulent conduct in its practice. These efforts can also streamline and improve the business operations within the practice and therefore innoculate itself against future problems.

Dated: September 27, 2000.

June Gibbs Brown,

Inspector General.

Appendix A: Additional Risk Areas

Appendix A describes additional risk areas that a physician practice may wish to address during the development of its compliance program. If any of the following risk areas are applicable to the practice, the practice may want to consider addressing the risk areas by incorporating them into the practice's written standards and procedures manual and addressing them in its training program.

I. Reasonable and Necessary Services

A. Local Medical Review Policy

An area of concern for physicians relating to determinations of reasonable and necessary services is the variation in local medical review policies (LMRPs) among carriers. Physicians are supposed to bill the Federal health care programs only for items and services that are reasonable and necessary. However, in order to determine whether an item or service is reasonable and necessary under Medicare guidelines, the physician must apply the appropriate LMRP.[1]

With the exception of claims that are properly coded and submitted to Medicare solely for the purpose of obtaining a written denial, physician practices are to bill the Federal health programs only for items and services that are covered. In order to determine if an item or service is covered for Medicare, a physician practice must be knowledgeable of the LMRPs applicable to its practice's jurisdiction. The practice may contact its carrier to request a copy of the pertinent LMRPs, and once the practice receives the copies, they can be incorporated into the practice's written standards and procedures manual. When the LMRP indicates that an item or service may not be covered by Medicare, the physician practice is responsible to convey this information to the patient so that the patient can make an informed decision concerning the health care services he/she may want to receive. Physician practices convey this information through Advance Beneficiary Notices (ABNs).

B. Advance Beneficiary Notices

Physicians are required to provide ABNs before they provide services that they know or believe Medicare does not consider reasonable and necessary. (The one exception to this requirement is for services that are performed pursuant to EMTALA requirements as described in section II.A). A properly executed ABN acknowledges that coverage is uncertain or yet to be determined, and stipulates that the patient promises to pay the bill if Medicare does not. Patients who are not notified before they receive such services are not responsible for payment. The ABN must be sufficient to put the patient on notice of the reasons why the physician believes that the payment may be denied. The objective is to give the patient sufficient information to allow an informed choice as to whether to pay for the service.

Accordingly, each ABN should:

I. Be in writing;
II. Identify the specific service that may be denied (procedure name and CPT/HCPC code is recommended);
III. State the specific reason why the physician believes that service may be denied; and
IV. Be signed by the patient acknowledging that the required information was provided and that the patient assumes responsibility to pay for the service.

The Medicare Carrier's Manual[2] provides that an ABN will not be acceptable if: (1) The patient is asked to sign a blank ABN form; or (2) the ABN is used routinely without regard to a particularized need. The routine use of ABNs is generally prohibited because the ABN must state the specific reason the physician anticipates that the specific service will not be covered.

A common risk area associated with ABNs is in regard to diagnostic tests or services. There are three steps that a physician practice can take to help ensure it is in compliance with the regulations concerning ABNs for diagnostic tests or services:

1. Determine which tests are not covered under national coverage rules;
2. Determine which tests are not covered under local coverage rules such as LMRPs (contact the practice's carrier to see if a listing has been assembled); and
3. Determine which tests are only covered for certain diagnoses.

The OIG is aware that the use of ABNs is an area where physician practices experience numerous difficulties. Practices can help to reduce problems in this area by educating their physicians and office staff on the correct use of ABNs, obtaining guidance from the carrier regarding their interpretation of whether an ABN is necessary where the service is not covered, developing a standard form for all diagnostic tests (most carriers have a developed model), and developing a process for handling patients who refuse to sign ABNs.

C. Physician Liability for Certifications in the Provision of Medical Equipment and Supplies and Home Health Services

In January 1999, the OIG issued a Special Fraud Alert on this topic, which is available on the OIG web site at *www.hhs.gov/oig/frdalrt/index.htm*. The following is a summary of the Special Fraud Alert.

The OIG issued the Special Fraud Alert to reiterate to physicians the legal and programmatic significance of physician certifications made in connection with the ordering of certain items and services for Medicare patients. In light of information obtained through OIG provider audits, the OIG deemed it necessary to remind physicians that they may be subject to criminal, civil and administrative penalties for signing a certification when they know that the information is false or for signing a certification with reckless disregard as to the truth of the information. (*See Appendix B* and *Appendix C* for more detailed information on the applicable statutes).

Medicare has conditioned payment for many items and services on a certification signed by a physician attesting that the physician has reviewed the patient's condition and has determined that an item or service is reasonable and necessary. Because Medicare primarily relies on the professional judgment of the treating physician to determine the reasonable and necessary nature of a given service or supply, it is important that physicians provide complete and accurate information on any certifications they sign. Physician certification is obtained through a variety of forms, including prescriptions, orders, and Certificates of Medical Necessity (CMNs). Two areas where physician certification as to whether an item or service is reasonable and necessary is essential and which are vulnerable to abuse are: (1) Home health services; and (2) durable medical equipment.

By signing a CMN, the physician represents that:

1. He or she is the patient's treating physician and that the information regarding the physician's address and unique physician identification number (UPIN) is correct;
2. the entire CMN, including the sections filled out by the supplier, was completed *prior* to the physician's signature; and
3. the information in section B relating to whether the item or service is reasonable and necessary is true, accurate, and complete to the best of the physician's knowledge.

Activities such as signing blank CMNs, signing a CMN without seeing the patient to verify the item or service is reasonable and necessary, and signing a CMN for a service that the physician knows is not reasonable and necessary are activities that can lead to criminal, civil and administrative penalties. Ultimately, it is advised that physicians carefully review any form of certification (order, prescription or CMN) before signing it to verify that the information contained in the certification is both complete and accurate.

---

[1] HCFA has recently developed a web site which, when completed by the end of the year 2000, will contain the LMRPs for each of the contractors across the country. The web site can be accessed at http://www.lmrp.net.

[2] The relevant manual provisions are located at MCM, Part III, §§ 7300 and 7320. This section of the manual also includes the carrier's recommended form of an ABN.

D. Billing for Non-covered Services as if Covered

In some instances, we are aware that physician practices submit claims for services in order to receive a denial from the carrier, thereby enabling the patient to submit the denied claim for payment to a secondary payer.

A common question relating to this risk area is: If the medical services provided are not covered under Medicare, but the secondary or supplemental insurer requires a Medicare rejection in order to cover the services, then would the original submission of the claim to Medicare be considered fraudulent? Under the applicable regulations, the OIG would not consider such submissions to be fraudulent. For example, the denial may be necessary to establish patient liability protections as stated in section 1879 of the Social Security Act (the Act) (codified at 42 U.S.C. 1395pp). As stated, Medicare denials may also be required so that the patient can seek payment from a secondary insurer. In instances where a claim is being submitted to Medicare for this purpose, the physician should indicate on the claim submission that the claim is being submitted for the purpose of receiving a denial, in order to bill a secondary insurance carrier. This step should assist carriers and prevent inadvertent payments to which the physician is not entitled.

In some instances, however, the carrier pays the claim even though the service is non-covered, and even though the physician did not intend for payment to be made. When this occurs, the physician has a responsibility to refund the amount paid and indicate that the service is not covered.

II. Physician Relationships with Hospitals

A. The Physician Role in EMTALA

The Emergency Medical Treatment and Active Labor Act (EMTALA), 42 U.S.C. 1395dd, is an area that has been receiving increasing scrutiny. The statute is intended to ensure that all patients who come to the emergency department of a hospital receive care, regardless of their insurance or ability to pay. Both hospitals and physicians need to work together to ensure compliance with the provisions of this law.

The statute imposes three fundamental requirements upon hospitals that participate in the Medicare program with regard to patients requesting emergency care. First, the hospital must conduct an appropriate medical screening examination to determine if an emergency medical condition exists.[3] Second, if the hospital determines that an emergency medical condition exists, it must either provide the treatment necessary to stabilize the emergency medical condition or comply with the statute's requirements to effect a proper transfer of a patient whose condition has not been stabilized.[4] A hospital is considered to have met this second requirement if an individual refuses the hospital's offer of additional examination or treatment, or refuses to consent to a transfer, after having been informed of the risks and benefits.[5]

If an individual's emergency medical condition has not been stabilized, the statute's third requirement is activated. A hospital may not transfer an individual with an unstable emergency medical condition unless: (1) The individual or his or her representative makes a written request for transfer to another medical facility after being informed of the risk of transfer and the transferring hospital's obligation under the statute to provide additional examination or treatment; (2) a physician has signed a certification summarizing the medical risks and benefits of a transfer and certifying that, based upon the information available at the time of transfer, the medical benefits reasonably expected from the transfer outweigh the increased risks; or (3) if a physician is not physically present when the transfer decision is made, a qualified medical person signs the certification after the physician, in consultation with the qualified medical person, has made the determination that the benefits of transfer outweigh the increased risks. The physician must later countersign the certification.[6]

Physician and/or hospital misconduct may result in violations of the statute.[7] One area of particular concern is physician on-call responsibilities. Physician practices whose members serve as on-call emergency room physicians with hospitals are advised to familiarize themselves with the hospital's policies regarding on-call physicians. This can be done by reviewing the medical staff bylaws or policies and procedures of the hospital that must define the responsibility of on-call physicians to respond to, examine, and treat patients with emergency medical conditions. Physicians should also be aware of the requirement that, when medically indicated, on-call physicians must generally come to the hospital to examine the patient. The exception to this requirement is that a patient may be sent to see the on-call physician at a hospital-owned contiguous or on-campus facility to conduct or complete the medical screening examination as long as:

1. All persons with the same medical condition are moved to this location;
2. there is a bona fide medical reason to move the patient; and
3. qualified medical personnel accompany the patient.

B. Teaching Physicians

Special regulations apply to teaching physicians' billings. Regulations provide that services provided by teaching physicians in teaching settings are generally payable under the physician fee schedule only if the services are personally furnished by a physician who is not a resident or the services are furnished by a resident in the presence of a teaching physician.[8]

Unless a service falls under a specified exception, such as the Primary Care Exception,[9] the teaching physician must be present during the key portion of any service or procedure for which payment is sought.[10] Physicians should ensure the following with respect to services provided in the teaching physician setting[11]

- Only services actually provided are billed;
- Every physician who provides or supervises the provision of services to a patient is responsible for the correct documentation of the services that were rendered;
- Every physician is responsible for assuring that in cases where the physician provides evaluation and management (E&M) services, a patient's medical record includes appropriate documentation of the applicable key components of the E&M services provided or supervised by the physician (e.g., patient history, physician examination, and medical decision making), as well as documentation to adequately reflect the procedure or portion of the services provided by the physician; and
- Unless specifically excepted by regulation, every physician must document his or her presence during the key portion of any service or procedure for which payment is sought.

C. Gainsharing Arrangements and Civil Monetary Penalties for Hospital Payments to Physicians to Reduce or Limit Services to Beneficiaries

In July 1999, the OIG issued a Special Fraud Alert on this topic, which is available on the OIG web site at *www.hhs.gov/oig/frdalrt/index.htm*. The following is a summary of the Special Fraud Alert.

The term "gainsharing" typically refers to an arrangement in which a hospital gives a physician a percentage share of any reduction in the hospital's costs for patient care attributable in part to the physician's efforts. The civil monetary penalty (CMP) that applies to gainsharing arrangements is set forth in 42 U.S.C. 1320a–7a(b)(1). This section prohibits any hospital or critical access hospital from knowingly making a payment directly or indirectly to a physician as an inducement to reduce or limit services to Medicare or Medicaid beneficiaries under a physician's care.

It is the OIG's position that the Civil Monetary Penalties Law clearly prohibits any gainsharing arrangements that involve payments by, or on behalf of, a hospital to physicians with clinical care responsibilities to induce a reduction or limitation of services to Medicare or Medicaid beneficiaries. However, hospitals and physicians are not prohibited from working together to reduce unnecessary hospital costs through other

---

[3] See 42 U.S.C. 1395dd(a).
[4] See 42 U.S.C. 1395dd(b)(1).
[5] See 42 U.S.C. 1395dd(b)(2) and (3).
[6] See 42 U.S.C. 1395dd(c)(1)(A).
[7] Hospitals and physicians, including on-call physicians, who violate the statute may face penalties that include civil fines of up to $50,000 (or not more than $25,000 in the case of a hospital with less than 100 beds) per violation, and physicians may be excluded from participation in the Federal health care programs.
[8] 42 CFR 415.150 through 415.190.
[9] 42 CFR 415.174.
[10] Id.
[11] This section is not intended to be and is not a complete reference for teaching physicians. It is strongly recommended that those physicians who practice in a teaching setting consult their respective hospitals for more guidance.

arrangements. For example, hospitals and physicians may enter into personal services contracts where hospitals pay physicians based on a fixed fee at fair market value for services rendered to reduce costs rather than a fee based on a share of cost savings.

D. Physician Incentive Arrangements

The OIG has identified potentially illegal practices involving the offering of incentives by entities in an effort to recruit and retain physicians. The OIG is concerned that the intent behind offering incentives to physicians may not be to recruit physicians, but instead the offer is intended as a kickback to obtain and increase patient referrals from physicians. These recruitment incentive arrangements are implicated by the Anti-Kickback Statute because they can constitute remuneration offered to induce, or in return for, the referral of business paid for by Medicare or Medicaid.

Some examples of questionable incentive arrangements are:

• Provision of free or significantly discounted billing, nursing, or other staff services.

• Payment of the cost of a physician's travel and expenses for conferences.

• Payment for a physician's services that require few, if any, substantive duties by the physician.

• Guarantees that if the physician's income fails to reach a predetermined level, the entity will supplement the remainder up to a certain amount.

III. Physician Billing Practices

A. Third-Party Billing Services

Physicians should remember that they remain responsible to the Medicare program for bills sent in the physician's name or containing the physician's signature, even if the physician had no actual knowledge of a billing impropriety. The attestation on the HCFA 1500 form, *i.e.*, the physician's signature line, states that the physician's services were billed properly. In other words, it is no defense for the physician if the physician's billing service improperly bills Medicare.

One of the most common risk areas involving billing services deals with physician practices contracting with billing services on a percentage basis. Although percentage based billing arrangements are not illegal *per se*, the Office of Inspector General has a longstanding concern that such arrangements may increase the risk of intentional upcoding and similar abusive billing practices.[12]

A physician may contract with a billing service on a percentage basis. However, the billing service cannot directly receive the payment of Medicare funds into a bank account that it solely controls. Under 42 U.S.C. 1395u(b)(6), Medicare payments can only be made to either the beneficiary or a party (such as a physician) that furnished the services and accepted assignment of the beneficiary's claim. A billing service that contracts on a percentage basis does not qualify as a party that furnished services to a beneficiary, thus a billing service cannot directly receive payment of Medicare funds. According to the *Medicare Carriers Manual* Section 3060(A), a payment is considered to be made directly to the billing service if the service can convert the payment to its own use and control without the payment first passing through the control of the physician. For example, the billing service should not bill the claims under its own name or tax identification number. The billing service should bill claims under the physician's name and tax identification number. Nor should a billing service receive the payment of Medicare funds directly into a bank account over which the billing service maintains sole control. The Medicare payments should instead be deposited into a bank account over which the provider has signature control.

Physician practices should review the third-party medical billing guidance for additional information on third-party billing companies and the compliance risk areas associated with billing companies.

B. Billing Practices by Non-Participating Physicians

Even though nonparticipating physicians do not accept payment directly from the Medicare program, there are a number of laws that apply to the billing of Medicare beneficiaries by non-participating physicians.

Limiting Charges

42 U.S.C. 1395w–4(g) prohibits a nonparticipating physician from knowingly and willfully billing or collecting on a repeated basis an actual charge for a service that is in excess of the Medicare limiting charge. For example, a nonparticipating physician may not bill a Medicare beneficiary $50 for an office visit when the Medicare limiting charge for the visit is $25. Additionally, there are numerous provisions that prohibit nonparticipating physicians from knowingly and willfully charging patients in excess of the statutory charge limitations for certain specified procedures, such as cataract surgery, mammography screening and coronary artery bypass surgery. Failure to comply with these sections can result in a fine of up to $10,000 per violation or exclusion from participation in Federal health care programs for up to 5 years.

Refund of Excess Charges

42 U.S.C. 1395w–4(g) mandates that if a nonparticipating physician collects an actual charge for a service that is in excess of the limiting charge, the physician must refund the amount collected above the limiting charge to the individual within 30 days notice of the violation. For example, if a physician collected $50 from a Medicare beneficiary for an office visit, but the limiting charge for the visit was $25, the physician must refund $25 to the beneficiary, which is the difference between the amount collected ($50) and the limiting charge ($25). Failure to comply with this requirement may result in a fine of up to $10,000 per violation or exclusion from participation in Federal health care programs for up to 5 years.

Specifically, 42 U.S.C. 1395u(l)(A)(iii) mandates that a nonparticipating physician must refund payments received from a Medicare beneficiary if it is later determined by a Peer Review Organization or a Medicare carrier that the services were not reasonable and necessary. Failure to comply with this requirement may result in a fine of up to $10,000 per violation or exclusion from participation in Federal health care programs for up to 5 years.

C. Professional Courtesy

The term "professional courtesy" is used to describe a number of analytically different practices. The traditional definition is the practice by a physician of waiving all or a part of the fee for services provided to the physician's office staff, other physicians, and/or their families. In recent times, "professional courtesy" has also come to mean the waiver of coinsurance obligations or other out-of-pocket expenses for physicians or their families (*i.e.*, "insurance only" billing), and similar payment arrangements by hospitals or other institutions for services provided to their medical staffs or employees. While only the first of these practices is truly "professional courtesy," in the interests of clarity and completeness, we will address all three.

In general, whether a professional courtesy arrangement runs afoul of the fraud and abuse laws is determined by two factors: (i) How the recipients of the professional courtesy are selected; and (ii) how the professional courtesy is extended. If recipients are selected in a manner that directly or indirectly takes into account their ability to affect past or future referrals, the anti-kickback statute—which prohibits giving anything of value to generate Federal health care program business—may be implicated. If the professional courtesy is extended through a waiver of copayment obligations (*i.e.*, "insurance only" billing), other statutes may be implicated, including the prohibition of inducements to beneficiaries, section 1128A(a)(5) of the Act (codified at 42 U.S.C. 1320a–7a(a)(5)). Claims submitted as a result of either practice may also implicate the civil False Claims Act.

The following are general observations about professional courtesy arrangements for physician practices to consider:

• A physician's regular and consistent practice of extending professional courtesy by waiving the entire fee for services rendered to a group of persons (including employees, physicians, and/or their family members) may not implicate any of the OIG's fraud and abuse authorities so long as membership in the group receiving the courtesy is determined in a manner that does not take into account directly or indirectly any group member's ability to refer to, or otherwise generate Federal health care program business for, the physician.

• A physician's regular and consistent practice of extending professional courtesy by waiving otherwise applicable copayments for services rendered to a group of persons (including employees, physicians, and/or their family members), would not implicate the anti-kickback statute so long as membership in the group is determined in a

---

[12] This concern is noted in Advisory Opinion No. 98–4 and also the Office of Inspector General Compliance Program Guidance for Third-Party Medical Billing Companies. Both are available on the OIG web site at http://www.hhs.gov/oig.

manner that does not take into account directly or indirectly any group member's ability to refer to, or otherwise generate Federal health care program business for, the physician.

• Any waiver of copayment practice, including that described in the preceding bullet, does implicate section 1128A(a)(5) of the Act if the patient for whom the copayment is waived is a Federal health care program beneficiary who is not financially needy.

The legality of particular professional courtesy arrangements will turn on the specific facts presented, and, with respect to the anti-kickback statute, on the specific intent of the parties. A physician practice may wish to consult with an attorney if it is uncertain about its professional courtesy arrangements.

IV. Other Risk Areas

A. Rental of Space in Physician Offices by Persons or Entities to Which Physicians Refer

In February 2000, the OIG issued a Special Fraud Alert on this topic, which is available on the OIG web site at *www.hhs.gov/oig/frdalrt/index.htm*. The following is a summary of the Special Fraud Alert.

Among various relationships between physicians and labs, hospitals, home health agencies, etc., the OIG has identified potentially illegal practices involving the rental of space in a physician's office by suppliers that provide items or services to patients who are referred or sent to the supplier by the physician-landlord. An example of a suspect arrangement is the rental of physician office space by a durable medical equipment (DME) supplier in a position to benefit from referrals of the physician's patients. The OIG is concerned that in such arrangements the rental payments may be disguised kickbacks to the physician-landlord to induce referrals.

Space Rental Safe Harbor to the Anti-Kickback Statute

To avoid potentially violating the anti-kickback statute, the OIG recommends that rental agreements comply with all of the following criteria for the space rental safe harbor:

• The agreement is set out in writing and signed by the parties.

• The agreement covers all of the space rented by the parties for the term of the agreement and specifies the space covered by the agreement.

• If the agreement is intended to provide the lessee with access to the space for periodic intervals of time rather than on a full-time basis for the term of the rental agreement, the rental agreement specifies exactly the schedule of such intervals, the precise length of each interval, and the exact rent for each interval.

• The term of the rental agreement is for not less than one year.

• The aggregate rental charge is set in advance, is consistent with fair market value, and is not determined in a manner that takes into account the volume or value of any referrals or business otherwise generated between the parties for which payment may be made in whole or in part under Medicare or a State health care program.

• The aggregate space rented does not exceed that which is reasonably necessary to accomplish the commercially reasonable business purpose of the rental.

B. Unlawful Advertising

42 U.S.C. 1320b–10 makes it unlawful for any person to advertise using the names, abbreviations, symbols, or emblems of the Social Security Administration, Health Care Financing Administration, Department of Health and Human Services, Medicare, Medicaid or any combination or variation of such words, abbreviations, symbols or emblems in a manner that such person knows or should know would convey the false impression that the advertised item is endorsed by the named entities. For instance, a physician may not place an ad in the newspaper that reads "Dr. X is a cardiologist approved by both the Medicare and Medicaid programs." A violation of this section may result in a penalty of up to $5,000 ($25,000 in the case of a broadcast or telecast) for each violation.

Appendix B: Criminal Statutes

This Appendix contains a description of criminal statutes related to fraud and abuse in the context of health care. The Appendix is not intended to be a compilation of all Federal statutes related to health care fraud and abuse. It is merely a summary of some of the more frequently cited Federal statutes.

I. Health Care Fraud (18 U.S.C. 1347)

Description of Unlawful Conduct

It is a crime to knowingly and willfully execute (or attempt to execute) a scheme to defraud any health care benefit program, or to obtain money or property from a health care benefit program through false representations. Note that this law applies not only to Federal health care programs, but to most other types of health care benefit programs as well.

Penalty for Unlawful Conduct

The penalty may include the imposition of fines, imprisonment of up to 10 years, or both. If the violation results in serious bodily injury, the prison term may be increased to a maximum of 20 years. If the violation results in death, the prison term may be expanded to include any number of years, or life imprisonment.

Examples

1. Dr. X, a chiropractor, intentionally billed Medicare for physical therapy and chiropractic treatments that he never actually rendered for the purpose of fraudulently obtaining Medicare payments.

2. Dr. X, a psychiatrist, billed Medicare, Medicaid, TRICARE, and private insurers for psychiatric services that were provided by his nurses rather than himself.

II. Theft or Embezzlement in Connection with Health Care (18 U.S.C. 669)

Description of Unlawful Conduct

It is a crime to knowingly and willfully embezzle, steal or intentionally misapply any of the assets of a health care benefit program. Note that this law applies not only to Federal health care programs, but to most other types of health care benefit programs as well.

Penalty for Unlawful Conduct

The penalty may include the imposition of a fine, imprisonment of up to 10 years, or both. If the value of the asset is $100 or less, the penalty is a fine, imprisonment of up to a year, or both.

Example

An office manager for Dr. X knowingly embezzles money from the bank account for Dr. X's practice. The bank account includes reimbursement received from the Medicare program; thus, intentional embezzlement of funds from this account is a violation of the law.

III. False Statements Relating to Health Care Matters (18 U.S.C. 1035)

Description of Unlawful Conduct

It is a crime to knowingly and willfully falsify or conceal a material fact, or make any materially false statement or use any materially false writing or document in connection with the delivery of or payment for health care benefits, items or services. Note that this law applies not only to Federal health care programs, but to most other types of health care benefit programs as well.

Penalty for Unlawful Conduct

The penalty may include the imposition of a fine, imprisonment of up to 5 years, or both.

Example

Dr. X certified on a claim form that he performed laser surgery on a Medicare beneficiary when he knew that the surgery was not actually performed on the patient.

IV. Obstruction of Criminal Investigations of Health Care Offenses (18 U.S.C. 1518)

Description of Unlawful Conduct

It is a crime to willfully prevent, obstruct, mislead, delay or attempt to prevent, obstruct, mislead, or delay the communication of records relating to a Federal health care offense to a criminal investigator. Note that this law applies not only to Federal health care programs, but to most other types of health care benefit programs as well.

Penalty for Unlawful Conduct

The penalty may include the imposition of a fine, imprisonment of up to 5 years, or both.

Examples

1. Dr. X instructs his employees to tell OIG investigators that Dr. X personally performs all treatments when, in fact, medical technicians do the majority of the treatment and Dr. X is rarely present in the office.

2. Dr. X was under investigation by the FBI for reported fraudulent billings. Dr. X altered patient records in an attempt to cover up the improprieties.

V. Mail and Wire Fraud (18 U.S.C. 1341 and 1343)

Description of Unlawful Conduct

It is a crime to use the mail, private courier, or wire service to conduct a scheme to defraud another of money or property. The term "wire services" includes the use of a telephone, fax machine or computer. Each use of a mail or wire service to further fraudulent activities is considered a separate crime. For instance, each fraudulent claim that is submitted electronically to a carrier would be considered a separate violation of the law.

Penalty for Unlawful Conduct

The penalty may include the imposition of a fine, imprisonment of up to 5 years, or both.

Examples

1. Dr. X knowingly and repeatedly submits electronic claims to the Medicare carrier for office visits that he did not actually provide to Medicare beneficiaries with the intent to obtain payments from Medicare for services he never performed.

2. Dr. X, a neurologist, knowingly submitted claims for tests that were not reasonable and necessary and intentionally upcoded office visits and electromyograms to Medicare.

VI. Criminal Penalties for Acts Involving Federal Health Care Programs (42 U.S.C. 1320a–7b)

Description of Unlawful Conduct

False Statement and Representations

It is a crime to knowingly and willfully:

(1) make, or cause to be made, false statements or representations in applying for benefits or payments under all Federal health care programs;

(2) make, or cause to be made, any false statement or representation for use in determining rights to such benefit or payment;

(3) conceal any event affecting an individual's initial or continued right to receive a benefit or payment with the intent to fraudulently receive the benefit or payment either in an amount or quantity greater than that which is due or authorized;

(4) convert a benefit or payment to a use other than for the use and benefit of the person for whom it was intended;

(5) present, or cause to be presented, a claim for a physician's service when the service was not furnished by a licensed physician;

(6) for a fee, counsel an individual to dispose of assets in order to become eligible for medical assistance under a State health program, if disposing of the assets results in the imposition of an ineligibility period for the individual.

Anti-Kickback Statute

It is a crime to knowingly and willfully solicit, receive, offer, or pay remuneration of any kind (*e.g.*, money, goods, services):

• for the referral of an individual to another for the purpose of supplying items or services that are covered by a Federal health care program; or

• for purchasing, leasing, ordering, or arranging for any good, facility, service, or item that is covered by a Federal health care program.

There are a number of limited exceptions to the law, also known as "safe harbors," which provide immunity from criminal prosecution and which are described in greater detail in the statute and related regulations (found at 42 CFR 1001.952 and www.hhs.gov/oig/ak). Current safe harbors include:

• investment interests;
• space rental;
• equipment rental;
• personal services and management contracts;
• sale of practice;
• referral services;
• warranties;
• discounts;
• employment relationships;
• waiver of Part A co-insurance and deductible amounts;
• group purchasing organizations;
• increased coverage or reduced cost sharing under a risk-basis or prepaid plan; and
• charge reduction agreements with health plans.

Penalty for Unlawful Conduct

The penalty may include the imposition of a fine of up to $25,000, imprisonment of up to 5 years, or both. In addition, the provider can be excluded from participation in Federal health care programs. The regulations defining the aggravating and mitigating circumstances that must be reviewed by the OIG in making an exclusion determination are set forth in 42 CFR part 1001.

Examples

1. Dr. X accepted payments to sign Certificates of Medical Necessity for durable medical equipment for patients she never examined.

2. Home Health Agency disguises referral fees as salaries by paying referring physician Dr. X for services Dr. X never rendered to the Medicare beneficiaries or by paying Dr. X a sum in excess of fair market value for the services he rendered to the Medicare beneficiaries.

Appendix C: Civil and Administrative Statutes

This Appendix contains a description of civil and administrative statutes related to fraud and abuse in the context of health care. The Appendix is not intended to be a compilation of all federal statutes related to health care fraud and abuse. It is merely a summary of some of the more frequently cited Federal statutes.

I. The False Claims Act (31 U.S.C. 3729–3733)

Description of Unlawful Conduct

This is the law most often used to bring a case against a health care provider for the submission of false claims to a Federal health care program. The False Claims Act prohibits knowingly presenting (or causing to be presented) to the Federal Government a false or fraudulent claim for payment or approval. Additionally, it prohibits knowingly making or using (or causing to be made or used) a false record or statement to get a false or fraudulent claim paid or approved by the Federal Government or its agents, like a carrier, other claims processor, or State Medicaid program.

Definitions

False Claim—A "false claim" is a claim for payment for services or supplies that were not provided specifically as presented or for which the provider is otherwise not entitled to payment. Examples of false claims for services or supplies that were not provided specifically as presented include, but are not limited to:

• a claim for a service or supply that was never provided.

• a claim indicating the service was provided for some diagnosis code other than the true diagnosis code in order to obtain reimbursement for the service (which would not be covered if the true diagnosis code were submitted).

• a claim indicating a higher level of service than was actually provided.

• a claim for a service that the provider knows is not reasonable and necessary.

• a claim for services provided by an unlicensed individual.

Knowingly—To "knowingly" present a false or fraudulent claim means that the provider: (1) Has actual knowledge that the information on the claim is false; (2) acts in deliberate ignorance of the truth or falsity of the information on the claim; or (3) acts in reckless disregard of the truth or falsity of the information on the claim. It is important to note the provider does not have to deliberately intend to defraud the Federal Government in order to be found liable under this Act. The provider need only "knowingly" present a false or fraudulent claim in the manner described above.

Deliberate Ignorance—To act in "deliberate ignorance" means that the provider has deliberately chosen to ignore the truth or falsity of the information on a claim submitted for payment, even though the provider knows, or has notice, that information may be false. An example of a provider who submits a false claim with deliberate ignorance would be a physician who ignores provider update bulletins and thus does not inform his/her staff of changes in the Medicare billing guidelines or update his/her billing system in accordance with changes to the Medicare billing practices. When claims for non-reimbursable services are submitted as a result, the False Claims Act has been violated.

Reckless Disregard—To act in "reckless disregard" means that the provider pays no regard to whether the information on a claim submitted for payment is true or false. An example of a provider who submits a false claim with reckless disregard would be a physician who assigns the billing function to an untrained office person without inquiring whether the employee has the requisite knowledge and training to accurately file such claims.

Penalty for Unlawful Conduct

The penalty for violating the False Claims Act is a minimum of $5,500 up to a maximum of $11,000 for *each* false claim submitted. In addition to the penalty, a provider could be found liable for damages of up to three times the amount unlawfully claimed.

Examples

• A physician submitted claims to Medicare and Medicaid representing that he had personally performed certain services when, in reality, the services were performed by a nonphysician and they were not reimbursable under the Federal health care programs.

• Dr. X intentionally upcoded office visits and angioplasty consultations that were submitted for payment to Medicare.

• Dr. X, a podiatrist, knowingly submitted claims to the Medicare and Medicaid programs for non-routine surgical procedures when he actually performed routine, non-covered services such as the cutting and trimming of toenails and the removal of corns and calluses.

II. Civil Monetary Penalties Law (42 U.S.C. 1320a–7a)

Description of Unlawful Conduct

The Civil Monetary Penalties Law (CMPL) is a comprehensive statute that covers an array of fraudulent and abusive activities and is very similar to the False Claims Act. For instance, the CMPL prohibits a health care provider from presenting, or causing to be presented, claims for services that the provider "knows or should know" were:

• not provided as indicated by the coding on the claim;
• not medically necessary;
• furnished by a person who is not licensed as a physician (or who was not properly supervised by a licensed physician);
• furnished by a licensed physician who obtained his or her license through misrepresentation of a material fact (such as cheating on a licensing exam);
• furnished by a physician who was not certified in the medical specialty that he or she claimed to be certified in; or
• furnished by a physician who was excluded from participation in the Federal health care program to which the claim was submitted.

Additionally, the CMPL contains various other prohibitions, including:

• offering remuneration to a Medicare or Medicaid beneficiary that the person knows or should know is likely to influence the beneficiary to obtain items or services billed to Medicare or Medicaid from a particular provider;
• employing or contracting with an individual or entity that the person knows or should know is excluded from participation in a Federal health care program.

The term "should know" means that a provider: (1) Acted in deliberate ignorance of the truth or falsity of the information; or (2) acted in reckless disregard of the truth or falsity of the information. The Federal Government does not have to show that a provider specifically intended to defraud a Federal health care program in order to prove a provider violated the statute.

Penalty for Unlawful Conduct

Violation of the CMPL may result in a penalty of up to $10,000 per item or service and up to three times the amount unlawfully claimed. In addition, the provider may be excluded from participation in Federal health care programs. The regulations defining the aggravating and mitigating circumstances that must be reviewed by the OIG in making an exclusion determination are set forth in 42 CFR part 1001.

Examples

1. Dr. X paid Medicare and Medicaid beneficiaries $20 each time they visited him to receive services and have tests performed that were not preventive care services and tests.

2. Dr. X hired Physician Assistant P to provide services to Medicare and Medicaid beneficiaries without conducting a background check on P. Had Dr. X performed a background check by reviewing the HHS–OIG List of Excluded Individuals/Entities, Dr. X would have discovered that he should not hire P because P is excluded from participation in Federal health care programs for a period of 5 years.

3. Dr. X and his oximetry company billed Medicare for pulse oximetry that they knew they did not perform and services that had been intentionally upcoded.

III. Limitations on Certain Physician Referrals ("Stark Laws") (42 U.S.C. 1395nn)

Description of Unlawful Conduct

Physicians (and immediate family members) who have an ownership, investment or compensation relationship with an entity providing "designated health services" are prohibited from referring patients for these services where payment may be made by a Federal health care program unless a statutory or regulatory exception applies. An entity providing a designated health service is prohibited from billing for the provision of a service that was provided based on a prohibited referral. Designated health services include: clinical laboratory services; physical therapy services; occupational therapy services; radiology services, including magnetic resonance imaging, axial tomography scans, and ultrasound services; radiation therapy services and supplies; durable medical equipment and supplies; parenteral and enteral nutrients, equipment and supplies; prosthetics, orthotics, prosthetic devices and supplies; home health services; outpatient prescription drugs; and inpatient and outpatient hospital services.

New regulations clarifying the exceptions to the Stark Laws are expected to be issued by HCFA shortly. Current exceptions articulated within the Stark Laws include the following, provided all conditions of each exception as set forth in the statute and regulations are satisfied.

Exceptions for Ownership or Compensation Arrangements

• physician's services;
• in-office ancillary services; and
• prepaid plans.

Exceptions for Ownership or Investment in Publicly Traded Securities and Mutual Funds

• ownership of investment securities which may be purchased on terms generally available to the public;
• ownership of shares in a regulated investment company as defined by Federal law, if such company had, at the end of the company's most recent fiscal year, or on average, during the previous 3 fiscal years, total assets exceeding $75,000,000;
• hospital in Puerto Rico;
• rural provider; and
• hospital ownership (whole hospital exception).

Exceptions Relating to Other Compensation Arrangements

• rental of office space and rental of equipment;
• bona fide employment relationship;
• personal service arrangement;
• remuneration unrelated to the provision of designated health services;
• physician recruitment;
• isolated transactions;
• certain group practice arrangements with a hospital (pre-1989); and
• payments by a physician for items and services.

Penalty for Unlawful Conduct

Violations of the statute subject the billing entity to denial of payment for the designated health services, refund of amounts collected from improperly submitted claims, and a civil monetary penalty of up to $15,000 for each improper claim submitted. Physicians who violate the statute may also be subject to additional fines per prohibited referral. In addition, providers that enter into an arrangement that they know or should know circumvents the referral restriction law may be subject to a civil monetary penalty of up to $100,000 per arrangement.

Examples

1. Dr. A worked in a medical clinic located in a major city. She also owned a free standing laboratory located in a major city. Dr. A referred all orders for laboratory tests on her patients to the laboratory she owned.

2. Dr. X agreed to serve as the Medical Director of Home Health Agency, HHA, for which he was paid a sum substantially above the fair market value for his services. In return, Dr. X routinely referred his Medicare and Medicaid patients to HHA for home health services.

3. Dr. Y received a monthly stipend of $500 from a local hospital to assist him in meeting practice expenses. Dr. Y performed no specific service for the stipend and had no obligation to repay the hospital. Dr. Y referred patients to the hospital for in-patient surgery.

IV. Exclusion of Certain Individuals and Entities From Participation in Medicare and other Federal Health Care Programs (42 U.S.C. 1320a–7)

Mandatory Exclusion

Individuals or entities convicted of the following conduct must be excluded from participation in Medicare and Medicaid for a minimum of 5 years:

(1) a criminal offense related to the delivery of an item or service under Medicare or Medicaid;

(2) a conviction under Federal or State law of a criminal offense relating to the neglect or abuse of a patient;

(3) a conviction under Federal or State law of a felony relating to fraud, theft, embezzlement, breach of fiduciary responsibility or other financial misconduct against a health care program financed by any Federal, State, or local government agency;

(4) a conviction under Federal or State law of a felony relating to the unlawful manufacture, distribution, prescription, or dispensing of a controlled substance.

If there is one prior conviction, the exclusion will be for 10 years. If there are two prior convictions, the exclusion will be permanent.

Permissive Exclusion

Individuals or entities convicted of the following offenses, may be excluded from participation in Federal health care programs for a minimum of 3 years:

(1) a criminal offense related to the delivery of an item or service under Medicare or Medicaid;

(2) a misdemeanor related to fraud, theft, embezzlement, breach of fiduciary responsibility or other financial misconduct against a health care program financed by any Federal, State, or local government agency;

(3) interference with, or obstruction of, any investigation into certain criminal offenses;

(4) a misdemeanor related to the unlawful manufacture, distribution, prescription or dispensing of a controlled substance;

(5) exclusion or suspension under a Federal or State health care program;

(6) submission of claims for excessive charges, unnecessary services or services that were of a quality that fails to meet professionally recognized standards of health care;

(7) violating the Civil Monetary Penalties Law or the statute entitled "Criminal Penalties for Acts Involving Federal Health Care Programs;"

(8) ownership or control of an entity by a sanctioned individual or immediate family member (spouse, natural or adoptive parent, child, sibling, stepparent, stepchild, stepbrother or stepsister, in-laws, grandparent and grandchild);

(9) failure to disclose information required by law;

(10) failure to supply claims payment information; and

(11) defaulting on health education loan or scholarship obligations.

The above list of offenses is not all inclusive. Additional grounds for permissive exclusion are detailed in the statute.

Examples

1. Nurse R was excluded based on a conviction involving obtaining dangerous drugs by forgery. She also altered prescriptions that were given for her own health problems before she presented them to the pharmacist to be filled.

2. Practice T was excluded due to its affiliation with its excluded owner. The practice owner, excluded from participation in the Federal health care programs for soliciting and receiving illegal kickbacks, was still participating in the day-to-day operations of the practice after his exclusion was effective.

Appendix D: OIG–HHS Contact Information

I. OIG Hotline Number

One method for providers to report potential fraud, waste, and abuse problems is to contact the OIG Hotline number. All HHS and contractor employees have a responsibility to assist in combating fraud, waste and abuse in all departmental programs. As such, providers are encouraged to report matters involving fraud, waste and mismanagement in any departmental program to the OIG. The OIG maintains a hotline that offers a confidential means for reporting these matters.

Contacting the OIG Hotline

By Phone: 1–800–HHS–TIPS (1–800–447–8477)
By E-Mail: *HTips@os.dhhs.gov*
By Mail: Office of Inspector General, Department of Health and Human Services, Attn: HOTLINE, 330 Independence Ave., SW., Washington, DC 20201

When contacting the Hotline, please provide the following information to the best of your ability:

• Type of Complaint:

Medicare Part A
Medicare Part B
Indian Health Service
TRICARE
Other (please specify)

• HHS Department or program being affected by your allegation of fraud, waste, abuse/mismanagement:

Health Care Financing Administration (HCFA)
Indian Health Service
Other (please specify)

Please provide the following information. (However, if you would like your referral to be submitted anonymously, please indicate such in your correspondence or phone call.)

Your Name
Your Street Address
Your City/County
Your State
Your Zip Code
Your email Address

• Subject/Person/Business/Department that allegation is against.

Name of Subject
Title of Subject
Subject's Street Address
Subject's City/County
Subject's State
Subject's Zip Code

Please provide a brief summary of your allegation and the relevant facts.

II. Provider Self-Disclosure Protocol

The recommended method for a provider to contact the OIG regarding potential fraud or abuse issues that may exist in the provider's own organization is through the use of the Provider Self-Disclosure Protocol. This program encourages providers to voluntarily disclose irregularities in their dealings with Federal health care programs. While voluntary disclosure under the protocol does not guarantee a provider protection from civil, criminal, or administrative actions, the fact that a provider voluntarily disclosed possible wrongdoing is a mitigating factor in OIG's recommendations to prosecuting agencies. Although other agencies may not have formal policies offering immunity or mitigation for self-disclosure, they typically view self-disclosure favorably for the self-disclosing entity. Self-reporting offers providers the opportunity to minimize the potential cost and disruption of a full-scale audit and investigation, to negotiate a fair monetary settlement, and to avoid an OIG permissive exclusion preventing the provider from doing business with Federal health care programs. In addition, if the provider is obligated to enter into an Integrity Agreement (IA) as part of the resolution of a voluntary disclosure, there are three benefits the provider might receive as a result of self-reporting:

• If the provider has an effective compliance program and agrees to maintain its compliance program as part of the False Claims Act settlement, the OIG may not even require an IA;

• In cases where the provider's own audits detected the disclosed problem, the OIG may consider alternatives to the IA's auditing provisions. The provider may be able to perform some or all of its billing audits through internal auditing methods rather than be required to retain an independent review organization to perform the billing review; and

• Self-disclosing can help to demonstrate a provider's trustworthiness to the OIG and may result in the OIG determining that it can sufficiently safeguard the Federal health care programs through an IA without the exclusion remedy for a material breach, which is typically included in an IA.

Specific instructions on how a physician practice can submit a voluntary disclosure under the Provider Self-Disclosure Protocol can be found on the OIG's internet site at www.hhs.gov/oig or in the **Federal Register** at 63 FR 58399 (1998). A physician practice may, however, wish to consult with an attorney prior to submitting a disclosure to the OIG.

The Provider Self-Disclosure Protocol can also be a useful tool for baseline audits. The protocol details the OIG's views on the appropriate elements of an effective investigative and audit plan for providers. Physician practices can use the self-disclosure protocol as a model for conducting audits and self-assessments.

In relying on the protocol for audit design and sample selection, a physician practice should pay close attention to the sections on self-assessment and sample selection. These two sections provide valuable guidance regarding how these two functions should be performed.

The self-assessment section of the protocol contains information that can be applied to audit design. Self-assessment is an internal financial assessment to determine the monetary impact of the matter. The approach of a review can include reviewing either all claims affected or a statistically valid sample of the claims.

Sample selection must include several elements. These elements are drawn from the Government sampling program known as RAT–STATS.[1] All of these elements are set forth in more detail in the Provider Self-Disclosure Protocol, but the elements are (1) Sampling unit, (2) sampling frame, (3) probe, (4) sample size, (5) random numbers, (6) sample design and (7) missing sample items. All of these sampling items should be clearly documented by the physician practice and compiled in the format set forth in the Provider Self-Disclosure Protocol. Use of the format set forth in the Provider Self-Disclosure Protocol will help physician practices to ensure that the elements of their internal audits are in conformance with OIG standards.

Appendix E: Carrier Contact Information

Medicare

A complete list of contact information (address, phone number, email address) for Medicare Part A Fiscal Intermediaries, Medicare Part B Carriers, Regional Home Health Intermediaries, and Durable Medical Equipment Regional Carriers can be found on the HCFA web site at *www.hcfa.gov/ medicare/incardir.htm*.

Medicaid

Contact information (address, phone number, email address) for each State Medicaid carrier can be found on the HCFA web site at *www.hcfa.gov/medicaid/ mcontact.htm*. In addition to a list of Medicaid carriers, the web site includes contact information for each State survey agency and the HCFA Regional Offices.

Contact information for each State Medicaid Fraud Control Unit can be found on the OIG web site at *www.hhs.gov/oig/oi/ mfcu/index.htm*.

Appendix F: Internet Resources

Office of Inspector General—U.S. Department of Health and Human Services

www.hhs.gov/oig

This web site includes a variety of information relating to Federal health care programs, including the following:
Advisory Opinions
Anti-kickback Information
Compliance Program Guidance
Corporate Integrity Agreements
Fraud Alerts
  Links to web pages for the:
Office of Audit Services (OAS)
Office of Evaluation and Inspections (OEI)
Office of Investigations (OI)
OIG List of Excluded Individuals/Entities
OIG News
OIG Regulations
OIG Semi-Annual Report
OIG Workplan

Health Care Financing Administration

www.hcfa.gov

This web site includes information on a wide array of topics, including the following:

Medicare

National Correct Coding Initiative
Intermediary-Carrier Directory
Payment
Program Manuals
Program Transmittals & Memorandum
Provider Billing/HCFA Forms
Statistics and Data

Medicaid

HCFA Regional Offices
Letters to State Medicaid Directors
Medicaid Hotline Numbers
Policy & Program Information
State Medicaid Contacts
State Medicaid Manual
State Survey Agencies
Statistics and Data

HCFA Medicare Training

www.hcfa.gov/medlearn

This site provides computer-based training on the following topics:
HCFA 1500 Form
Fraud & Abuse
ICD–9–CM Diagnosis Coding
Adult Immunization
Medicare Secondary Payer (MSP)
Women's Health
Front Office Management
Introduction to the World of Medicare
Home Health Agency
HCFA 1450 (UB92)

Government Printing Office

www.access.gpo.gov

This site provides access to Federal statutes and regulations pertaining to Federal health care programs.

The U.S. House of Representatives Internet Library

uscode.house.gov/usc.htm

This site provides access to the United States Code, which contains laws pertaining to Federal health care programs.

[FR Doc. 00–25500 Filed 10–4–00; 8:45 am]

BILLING CODE 4152-01-P

---

[1] Available through the OIG web site at http://www.hhs.gov/oas/ratstat.html.

appendix C

Medicare Modernization Act

On December 8, 2003, President George W. Bush signed into law the Medicare Prescription Drug, Improvement and Modernization Act (MMA) of 2003. This landmark legislation provides seniors and people living with disabilities with a prescription drug benefit, more choices and better benefits under Medicare, the most significant improvement to the senior health care in nearly 40 years.

The below information is presented describing current benefits and enrollment information for the Medicare Prescription Drug Program. Following this, information is presented describing the Medicare Prescription Drug Discount Card and the Transitional Assistance Program. Additional information and updates can be accessed at www.cms.hhs.gov/medicarereform/. This site is frequently updated with news and information on the program.

OVERVIEW

Medicare Prescription Drug Program

As of January 1, 2006, new Medicare prescription drug plans were available to people with Medicare. Insurance and other private companies will work with Medicare to offer these drug plans and make prescription drug coverage available to all 42 million Medicare beneficiaries, including the approximately 6.5 million low-income beneficiaries who are also enrolled in Medicaid. This means that as of January 1, 2006, Medicaid no longer paid for most of the prescription drugs for people with both Medicare and Medicaid.

2005: New Preventive Benefits are covered, including:

- A one-time initial wellness physical exam within 6 months of the day you first enroll in Medicare Part-B.
- A one-time initial wellness physical exam within 6 months of the day you first enroll in Medicare Part-B.
- A one-time initial wellness physical exam within 6 months of the day you first enroll in Medicare Part-B.

These benefits add to the preventive services that Medicare already covers, such as cancer screenings, bone mass measurements and vaccinations.

2006: Prescription Drug Benefits were available as of January 2006 to all people with Medicare, and they were able to enroll in plans that cover prescription drugs. Plans might vary, but in general, this is how they work:

- The Medical recipient will choose a prescription drug plan and pay a premium of about $35 a month.

Reprinted from www.cms.hhs.gov/medicarereform/.

- The recipient will pay the first $250 (called a "deductible").
- Medicare then will pay 75% of costs between $250 and $2,250 in drug spending. The Medicare recipient will pay only 25% of these costs.
- The recipient will pay 100% of the drug costs above $2,250 until you reach $3,600 in out-of-pocket spending.
- Medicare will pay about 95% of the costs after the recipient has spent $3,600.
- Some prescription drug plans may have additional options to help you pay the out-of-pocket costs.

Extra help will be available for people with low incomes and limited assets. Most significantly, people with Medicare in the greatest need, who have incomes below a certain limit won't have to pay the premiums or deductible for prescription drugs. If the Medicare recipient qualifies, they will only pay a small co-payment for each prescription they need.

Other people with low incomes and limited assets will get help paying the premiums and deductible. The amount they pay for each prescription will be limited.

Medicare Advantage plan choices will be expanded to include regional preferred provider organization plans (PPOs). Regional PPOs will help more people with Medicare have multiple choices for Medicare health coverage, no matter where they live. PPOs can help you save money by choosing from doctors and providers on a plan's "preferred" list, but usually don't require you to get a referral. PPOs are among the most common and popular plans right now for working Americans.

All of these options are voluntary. You can choose to remain in the traditional Medicare plan you have today.

For the latest information about Medicare, visit www.medicare.gov, or call 1-800-MEDICARE (1-800-633-4227). TTY users should call 1-877-486-2048. The Medicare Prescription Drug benefit is designed to allow broad access to medications and also to provide extra help with drug plan costs for people with limited income and resources.

Access to Medications

The Centers for Medicare and Medicaid Services (CMS) requires Medicare prescription drug plans to include at least two medications within each class of drugs. However, as a safeguard for certain vulnerable populations, CMS designates six classes of drugs "of special interest." Medicare prescription drug plans are required to offer virtually all available medications in those drug categories. Three of these categories include medications used frequently by people with mental illnesses: antidepressants (used to treat depression), antipsychotics (used to treat psychosis and delusions), and anticonvulsants (used as mood stabilizers).

If a medication is not covered by a plan, and the recipients doctor believes it is medically necessary for them to take it, the recipient or the doctor can ask the plan for an exception to pay for the drug needed. Generally, CMS requires a plan to give you an answer within 72 hours, but the time frame may "expedited" to 24 hours in case of an emergency. Authorized representatives may file an exception on the recipient's behalf. If the request for exception is denied, the recipient still has the option of using the plan's appeal process.

Enrollment into the program began November 15, 2005 and continued through May 15, 2006. If the recipient joined by December 31, 2005, their Medicare prescription drug plan coverage, began on January 1, 2006. If they joined after that, their coverage will be effective the first day of the month after the month they joined. In general, you can join or change plans once each year between November 15 and December 31. However, if a plan was not joined by May 15, 2006, and the recipient does not have a drug plan that covers as much or more than a Medicare prescription drug plan, and they are eligible by that date, they will have to pay more (on a monthly basis) to join at a later date.

Medicare Prescription Drug Discount Card and Transitional Assistance Program

The Medicare Prescription Drug Discount Card and Transitional Assistance Program was enacted into law on December 8, 2003 as part of the Medicare Prescription Drug, Improvement, and Modernization Act of 2003. The Administration worked with Congress to provide this voluntary program to give immediate relief to seniors and disabled people covered under Medicare to help reduce their costs for prescription drugs now, before the new Medicare drug benefit is implemented on January 1, 2006. Today, Medicare beneficiaries without outpatient drug coverage pay among the highest prices for prescription drugs, as much as 20 percent higher than people who have drug coverage. Under the Medicare Prescription Drug Discount Card Program, we expect beneficiaries to save an estimated 10 to 15 percent on their total drug spending, with discounts of up to 25 percent or more on individual prescription drugs.

Starting in May, Medicare beneficiaries, except for those who have Medicaid drug coverage, will have the opportunity to enroll in a Medicare-approved prescription drug discount card, which will help to lower their prescription drug costs. Beginning in June, 2004, the discount cards will provide discounts off the regular cash price of prescription drugs. The cards are primarily intended for individuals without outpatient prescription drug insurance. The discount card program is not intended to be a prescription drug benefit, but rather a discount card program to help people until the Medicare drug benefit takes effect on January 1, 2006.

In addition, beginning in June 2004, Medicare will provide $600 in 2004 and up to an additional $600 in 2005 to Medicare beneficiaries whose incomes are not more than 135 percent of the poverty line ($12,123 for single individuals or $16,362 for married individuals in 2003 - these income levels will vary slightly for subsequent years) if they do not have certain other drug coverage. These funds will be provided through the Medicare-approved drug discount card in which the beneficiary enrolls. When applying the $600 toward prescription drug purchases, beneficiaries at or below 100 percent of poverty will pay 5 percent coinsurance and beneficiaries above 100 percent of poverty will pay a 10 percent coinsurance. Since, on average, Medicare beneficiaries without prescription drug insurance would otherwise pay about $1,400 in 2004, the discounts and $600 in assistance, which many of them will be eligible for, will be of substantial help.

Private sector discount card programs that meet standards set by Medicare can qualify for a Medicare approval/endorsement to provide discounts. Medicare will make sure that beneficiaries have at least two choices of approved cards in each State.

CMS will provide information about the prescription drug prices offered by the approved discount card programs and other information about the Medicare-approved cards and other pharmacy assistance opportunities, through www.medicare.gov and 1-800-MEDICARE. We plan to make this information available so that beneficiaries can make informed decisions about the options that best meet their prescription drug needs.

Medicare-approved discount card programs can charge a beneficiary an enrollment fee up to $30 per year. Medicare will pay the enrollment fee for beneficiaries who qualify for the $600. More information about this program can be found at www.cms.hhs.gov/discountdrugs/.

Eligibility for the Medicare-Approved Prescription Drug Discount Card & $600

Drug Discount Card Eligibility: Medicare beneficiaries are eligible for the drug discount card program if they are enrolled under Part A or B, so long as the beneficiary is not receiving outpatient drug benefits through Medicaid, including 1115 waivers.

$600 Eligibility: Beneficiaries are eligible for up to $600 a year toward prescription drugs if their income is not more than 135% of the poverty line ($12,123 for single individuals or $16,362 for married individuals in 2003). Also, to qualify for these funds, beneficiaries must not be receiving outpatient drug coverage from other sources, including Medicaid, TRICARE, group health insurance or health insurance coverage, or FEHBP. Generally, once a person qualifies for the $600, they are qualified until the new Medicare drug benefit begins.

Enrollment Process

CMS has established a simple and convenient enrollment process.

- To enroll, the beneficiary will first select the discount card program that best meets his or her needs. The beneficiary will then submit basic information on an enrollment form

to the selected approved discount card program about his or her Medicare and Medicaid status. If the beneficiary wants the $600, he or she also must submit income and other information about retirement and other health benefits, and attest to its truthfulness.
- CMS will verify this information and notify the approved discount card program of the beneficiary's eligibility and enrollment outcome.
- Beneficiaries who are eligible are enrolled and may start obtaining discounts and, if receiving the $600, using these funds to purchase prescription drugs, as early as the first day of the following month.
- Individuals found to be ineligible for either the discount card or the $600 may request a reconsideration if they continue to believe they qualify.

Changing Approved Discount Card Programs

An eligible beneficiary can enroll in an approved discount card program at any time. After the initial election, the beneficiary will have the option, for 2005, of choosing a different card program during the annual coordinated election period, between November 15 and December 31, 2004.

- In addition a beneficiary may change cards during a special election period under certain circumstances, such as if the beneficiary has a change in residential status to a long-term care facility, a move outside of the area served by the beneficiary's approved program, or elects or disenrolls from a Medicare managed care plan.

Qualifications Sponsor Must Meet for Medicare-Approval

A non-governmental organization that meets all of the qualifications can receive a Medicare endorsement. Multiple organizations may combine capabilities to meet the various requirements. The types of qualifications sponsors must meet include:

- Having relevant organizational experience, including experience in adjudicating and processing pharmacy claims at the point of sale and negotiating with prescription drug manufacturers and others for low prices on prescription drugs
- Being financially stable and reputable
- Meeting service area and pharmacy network access standards
- Administering transitional assistance
- Providing negotiated prices on prescription drugs
- Managing the eligibility and enrollment process
- Providing customer service
- Providing a grievance process
- Complying with HIPAA privacy provisions
- Agreeing to provide data to CMS

Service Area and Pharmacy Network Access

A State is the smallest service area permitted under this program. If the service area includes additional states, then the entire additional state must be included.

Medicare-approved drug discount cards must provide convenient access to retail pharmacies. The minimum requirements are that:

- in urban areas, 90% of Medicare beneficiaries live within 2 miles of a participating pharmacy;
- in suburban areas, 90% of Medicare beneficiaries live within 5 miles; and
- in rural areas, 70% of beneficiaries live within 15 miles.

Medicare-approved programs may offer a mail order option in addition to their contracted retail pharmacy network., but and they are prohibited from providing a mail-order only program, and they may not require enrollees to use mail-order pharmacies.

Prescription Drug Offering

Covered Drugs and Formulary: Nearly all prescription drugs that can be purchased at retail pharmacies are eligible for discounts and use of the $600. Syringes and medical supplies associated with the injection of insulin - needles, alcohol, and gauze - are also included. We anticipate that many approved programs will use formularies to obtain deeper discounts on prescription drugs. A formulary is a specific list of drugs for which discounts are offered. However, even if a drug is not on the sponsor's formulary, the $600 can still be used to purchase the prescription drug.

If an approved discount card program uses a formulary, at a minimum, each program must offer a discount on the types of drugs commonly needed by Medicare beneficiaries (both seniors and individuals with disabilities) in more than 200 classes of drugs.

Rebates, Discounts, & Pass Through: Medicare-approved discount card programs must obtain rebates from drug manufacturers and other discounts to help lower the costs of prescription drugs purchased by their enrollees. We expect that a substantial share of these rebates and discounts will be passed through to card enrollees at the point of sale. Because approved programs will be competing for Medicare beneficiaries, the programs will have an incentive to offer the lowest possible prices.

Over-the-Counter (Non-Prescription) Drugs: Approved discount card programs, if they choose, may offer discounts on over-the-counter drugs. However, the $600 cannot be used to purchase these drugs.

Preventing "Bait and Switch:" Approved discount card programs can update their prices and list of drugs offered for a discount on a weekly basis. However, CMS will monitor drug price changes, and will identify if programs deviate from expected changes, such as those in average wholesale price.

$600 Proration and Rollover

To encourage Medicare beneficiaries to enroll in the program earlier rather than later, but to provide sufficient time for beneficiaries to learn about the drug card program and their option to join, in 2004 eligible beneficiaries will receive the full $600. In 2005, however, the $600 will be prorated depending on when a beneficiary first applies for the funds. The $600 will be reduced for late enrollees every quarter by $150 starting in April 2005. In most cases, funds made available but not spent in one calendar year may carry over into the following year and will remain available through early 2006.

Customer Service and Information & Outreach

Approved discount card sponsors will be required to provide program information, such as enrollment fees and prescription drug prices, to eligible Medicare beneficiaries. They also have to provide a process to reduce medication errors, such as drug interactions and other safety features, like allergy alerts.

Medicare approved drug discount card programs will each maintain a toll-free customer call center that is open during usual business hours.

Privacy

Approved discount card sponsors must comply with the HIPAA privacy provisions protecting beneficiaries' health information. A beneficiary's protected health information (PHI) can only be used for the health care operations and marketing of products and services that come under the scope of the Medicare endorsement. The statute provides additional restrictions beyond the HIPAA privacy provisions that prevent a sponsor from seeking authorization from a beneficiary to use PHI for any activity outside the scope of the Medicare endorsement, including marketing.

CMS Oversight and Reporting

General oversight: The Medicare program will operate a grievance and complaint tracking system, including intake from 1-800-MEDICARE. Complaints and reported information will be analyzed to identify trends that indicate poor card sponsor performance, including those related to:

- Savings garnered and shared by manufacturer and pharmacy;
- Appropriate management of the $600 funds;
- Enrollment and disenrollment;
- Marketing;
- Pharmacy network access;
- Customer service; and
- Confidentiality of enrollee records.

Intermediate Sanctions and Termination: CMS and OIG may impose intermediate sanctions, civil monetary penalties (CMPs), or terminate a contract based on a sponsor's failure to meet the requirements or standards set by Medicare for this program.

CMS Educational and Outreach Efforts

Medicare will provide general information about how the program operates, and who can qualify and how to join, as well as some comparative information on card sponsors at least 30 days prior to the initial enrollment date through www.medicare.gov and 1-800 MEDICARE. Other information sources will include a dedicated brochure for beneficiaries, a section in the *2005 Medicare & You* handbook, a national multi-media campaign, and State Health Insurance Programs and community organizations, among others.

- **Price comparison website** will provide a mechanism for Medicare beneficiaries to compare negotiated prices, fees, and other card program features. The negotiated prices displayed will be a drug's maximum price for an approved sponsor's service area. Actual prices may vary, but will not be more than the posted prices.

- **1-800-MEDICARE** will be used to answer questions about the program, walk-through price comparison website, log calls, and refer to appropriate sponsor or other resources (such as, make appropriate referrals for eligibility determination or to their State Pharmacy Assistance Program).

Medicare Managed Care Plans Offering "Exclusive Card Programs"

Medicare managed care plans (ie, Part C organizations providing coordinated care plans, and Medicare cost reimbursement contractors) may offer "exclusive card programs" that limit enrollment to their own Medicare managed care plan members. In wrapping the discount card around the plan's drug benefit (if any), the plan can apply the $600 toward drug benefit copayments and deductibles, as well as apply the balance of the $600 to additional drugs that either are not covered under the plan's benefit or for drugs when the plan's benefit cap is reached.

Options for States

States can coordinate with a Medicare-approved program, or encourage their own privately run program to apply for endorsement - such programs must meet the qualifications for endorsement. States may also choose to pay the enrollment fees for non-low income beneficiaries and coinsurance for low-income beneficiaries receiving the $600. However, no federal matching payments are available for these state expenditures.

General Solicitation & Application Review Process

Organizations will need to complete a detailed application concerning their qualifications and all facets of their proposed drug discount card program. There will be no specific limit to the total number of Medicare-approved drug discount card programs. All qualified applicants can enter into a contract with CMS.

- There will be a separate application for Medicare managed care exclusive card sponsors.

Competition for "Special Endorsement"

In addition to the general endorsement to offer a Medicare-approved drug discount card program, organizations will have the opportunity to apply for "special endorsement" to provide transitional assistance to:

- residents of long term care (LTC) facilities, to include nursing facilities and skilled nursing facilities, through long term care pharmacies, and to
- American Indians/Alaska Natives (AI/ANs) who use Indian Health Service, Indian Tribe and Tribal Organization, and Urban Indian Organization (I/T/U) pharmacies.

A special endorsement to provide discounts only (not transitional assistance) may also be granted to sponsors who serve residents of the U.S. territories, which include American Samoa, Commonwealth of the Northern Mariana Islands, Guam, Commonwealth of Puerto Rico, and the Virgin Islands, through retail pharmacies in these regions and mail order.

Special endorsement for providing access to each type of pharmacy—long term care pharmacies, I/T/U/ pharmacies, and pharmacies serving territories—will be competitively awarded to the card sponsors with the best plans.

Transitional Assistance in the Territories

Transitional assistance in the territories is a separate and distinct program from the Medicare-approved prescription drug discount cards. Territories will be asked to submit plans for using a one-time prescription drug assistance grant (totaling $35 million across the territories) to provide transitional assistance for covered drugs to some or all low-income Medicare beneficiaries with incomes below 135 percent of the poverty line, including beneficiaries with Medicaid.

Impact Analysis Results

Estimated Uptake	2004	2005
Discount only	2.6M	2.7M
Prescription drug assistance	4.7M	4.7M
Total	7.3M	7.4M
Discount Savings	$1.4-$1.8B	$2.0-$2.7B
Estimated Savings from TA	$2.4B	$2.6B

Enrollment uptake is based on an estimated 15.4 million beneficiaries who are eligible for (and can benefit from) either the card only, or for the card and $600.

Sponsor Costs: A $30 annual enrollment fee covers all (or nearly all) of a sponsors' costs of operations, assuming these fees are collected in 2004 and 2005 (fee not allowed in 2006 transition period), which would allow a sponsor to pass through a substantial share of the rebates, discounts, and other price concessions they negotiate with manufacturers and pharmacies.

appendix

D

Medicare Secondary Payer Guide

Medicare Secondary Payer (MSP) refers to situations where the Medicare program does not have primary responsibility for paying a beneficiary's medical expenses. The Medicare beneficiary may be entitled to other coverage, which should pay before Medicare. From the time the Medicare program began in 1966, providers of health care grew accustomed to billing Medicare first for services to Medicare beneficiaries. Legislative provisions during the years of 1980–1993 have changed this method of paying for health care costs and have resulted in more situations in which Medicare is no longer the primary payer. Because of these laws, the MSP program was initiated by the CMS (formerly the Health Care Financing Administration). There are eight (8) basic groups of individuals to whom MSP applies. One or more laws made Medicare a secondary payer for each group.

PRE-1980 LEGISLATIVE PROVISIONS

Until 1980, the Medicare program was the primary payer in all cases except those involving workers compensation (including black lung) benefits. Medicare was also precluded from making payment for services paid for by the Department of Veterans Affairs or other governmental entities.

Workers Compensation: Effective July 1, 1966

Medicare is secondary payer for items or services covered under a workers compensation law or plan of the United States or a state. The workers compensation carrier should be billed first for work-related illnesses or injuries.

If a claim is contested, the workers compensation board should notify you. Pending the workers compensation board decision, you may bill Medicare. Include with your bill a copy of the notice from the workers compensation board. Conditional primary payments may be made if the compensation carrier will not pay promptly. Follow up action will be taken to recover conditional payments.

Medicare reverts to primary status for all future medical expenses not reimbursed, once the beneficiary has exhausted all appeals under workers compensation.

Veterans Administration Benefits (VA): Effective July 1, 1966

The VA may authorize private physicians and other suppliers to render services, at Federal expense, to certain veterans with service connected disabilities and, in certain circumstances, with non-service connected disabilities. It is generally advantageous for Medicare beneficiaries who are veterans to have items and services paid for by the VA where possible. The VA has no deductible or co-insurance requirements. An authorization issued by the VA binds the VA to pay in full for the items and services provided.

When a physician accepts veterans as patients and bills the VA, the physician must accept the VA's "usual and customary" charge determination as payment in full. Therefore, neither the patient nor any other party can be charged an additional amount. Medicare

Reprinted with permission from the Upstate Medicare Division–Part B. Available at: www.umd.nycpic.com/Guide-MSP.html. Accessed June 12, 2006.

may supplement VA payments when the VA claim is for Part B services and is filed by the veteran rather than by a physician or supplier. When a Medicare claim is submitted, it must indicate which services were billed to the VA and whether the beneficiary submitted a claim to the VA for payment.

Federal Black Lung Program: Effective July 1, 1973

If the Medicare beneficiary is entitled to Black Lung medical benefits under the Federal Coal Mine Act, Medicare is secondary payer to the Federal Black Lung Program. Claims should sent to the Department of Labor first at the following address:

Federal Black Lung Program
P.O. Item 828
Lanham-Seabrook, MD 20703-0828

If all services were not covered by the Federal Black Lung Program, Medicare can then be billed for those services. A copy of the denial notice from the Department of Labor must be included with the claim. If the services rendered to a black lung beneficiary were solely for a non-black lung condition, Medicare should be billed as primary.

POST-1980 LEGISLATIVE PROVISIONS

Since 1980, a series of changes in the Medicare law have also resulted in Medicare being the secondary payer for individuals:

- Who are age 65 or older and working with coverage by an employer-sponsored or employee organization group health plan.
- Who are age 65 or older and who are covered by a working spouse's employer group health plan (EGHP). The working spouse can be any age.
- With coverage under automobile, no-fault, or liability insurance.
- With kidney failure, for up to the first 30 months of Medicare entitlement if they have coverage under their own employer-sponsored or employee organization group health plan, or if coverage is provided them because they are the spouse or dependent of an individual with EGHP coverage.
- Who are disabled and have coverage under their own large group health plan (LGHP) because of their current employment, or who are disabled and have coverage under the LGHP of a family member who is currently employed. An LGHP is a plan provided by an employer who employs 100 or more persons or a plan belonging to a multi-employer plan where at least one employer has 100 or more full or part-time employees.

Automobile Medical or No-Fault Insurance: Omnibus Reconciliation Act of 1980, effective December 5, 1980.

Medicare is the secondary payer of claims for medical items and services to the extent that payment has been made, or can reasonably be expected to be made, for items or services under automobile liability insurance, uninsured motorist insurance, or underinsured motorist insurance. The other insurance must be billed first.

In the case where the automobile liability carrier will not pay promptly, where a proper claim has been filed, conditional payments may be made. These conditional payments are subject to recovery if the individual later receives payment from an automobile liability insurer.

An individual's refusal to file a proper claim with the appropriate primary insurer or no-fault carrier is not a basis for making a conditional Medicare payment.

Other Liability Insurance: Omnibus Reconciliation Act of 1980, effective December 5, 1980.

Medicare is the secondary payer of claims for medical items and services to the extent that payment has been made or can reasonably be expected to be made for items or services under homeowner's liability insurance, malpractice insurance, product liability insurance, and general casualty insurance. This insurance is sometimes called "medical payment coverage," "personal injury coverage," or "medical expense coverage," and must be billed first.

In the case where the liability insurance carrier will not pay promptly, where a proper claim has been filed, conditional payments may be made. These conditional payments are subject to recovery if the individual later receives payment from a liability carrier.

An individual's refusal to file a proper claim with the appropriate primary insurer or no-fault carrier, is not a basis for making a conditional Medicare payment.

End Stage Renal Disease (ESRD): Omnibus Reconciliation Act 1981, Omnibus Budget Reconciliation Act (OBRA) of 1987, Omnibus Budget Reconciliation Act (OBRA) of 1990, Omnibus Budget Reconciliation Act (OBRA) of 1993, and the Balanced Budget Act (BBA) of 1997.

The Omnibus Reconciliation Act of 1981 provided for Medicare to be the secondary payer after benefits payable under an EGHP. Medicare is secondary for a period of up to 12 months for individuals entitled to Medicare solely on the basis of ESRD. These provisions applied to items and services furnished on or after October 1, 1981, for beneficiaries whose 12 month entitlement period began on or after October 1, 1981.

Medicare entitlement usually begins with the third month after the month in which the beneficiary starts a regular course of dialysis. Medicare will be the secondary payer after the EGHP for the first nine months of the individual's entitlement. Individuals who have undertaken a course in self-dialysis training or have received a kidney transplant during the three month waiting period are exempt from the waiting period. Medicare entitlement is immediate and will be secondary payer after the EGHP for the first 12 months of the individual's entitlement.

OBRA of 1990 amended these rules to state that Medicare is the secondary payer for benefits payable under an EGHP starting with the Medicare Part A entitlement date. This change applies to all 12-month periods that were in effect November 5, 1990. Also under OBRA 1990, Medicare is the secondary payer under an EGHP for a period of 18-months starting with the Medicare Part A entitlement date, or eligibility to Medicare, on or after February 1, 1990.

Under the provisions of the Omnibus Reconciliation Act of 1981 and the OBRA of 1990, the following rules apply:

- Persons must be younger than age 65 and Medicare eligible solely as a result of ESRD. Also, if the beneficiary turns 65 during the coordination period or dually entitled to disability benefits, Medicare becomes the primary payer at that point.
- An EGHP is any health plan that is of or contributed to by an employer or employee pay-all plan, providing coverage to employees and dependents without regard to the enrollee's employment status (i.e., full-time, part-time, or retired). These provisions are applicable regardless of the size of the employer.
- Medicare may not make conditional primary payments on behalf of an ESRD beneficiary who is covered by an EGHP if the plan could reasonably be expected to pay for the services.
- If an EGHP pays benefits as a primary payer, but pays less than the amount which Medicare would have paid in the absence of EGHP coverage, secondary Medicare benefits may be paid.
- If an EGHP denies payment for particular services because they are not covered by the plan, primary Medicare benefits may be paid for those services. However, an employer plan can not refuse to cover renal services. This is a violation of MSP provisions of law.

OBRA of 1993 provided that Medicare will remain the secondary payer throughout the entire 18-month coordination period, even if the beneficiary becomes entitled to Medicare based on disability or age before the coordination period ends. Additionally, a coordination period will start for aged or disabled beneficiaries if the ESRD provisions begin to apply and Medicare had already been secondary payer due to the working aged or disabled provisions. Upon completion of the 18-month coordination period, Medicare will revert to primary status and will remain primary as long as Medicare dual entitlement exists. If the beneficiary loses ESRD eligibility or entitlement after the coordination period has ended, then the working aged or disability MSP provisions begin to apply. This change is effective August 10, 1993.

Note: If ESRD-based eligibility or entitlement ceases, Medicare is the primary payer unless plan coverage is in effect by virtue of current employment status.

The BBA of 1997 permanently extends the ESRD coordination period to 30 months for individuals whose coordination period began on or after March 1, 1996. Therefore, individuals who have not completed an 18-month coordination period by July 31, 1997, will have a 30-month coordination period under the new law.

Working Aged: Tax Equity Fiscal Responsibility Act (TEFRA) of 1982, Deficit Reduction Act (DEFRA) of 1984, and Consolidated Omnibus Budget Reconciliation Act (COBRA) of 1985.

The working aged provisions apply to beneficiaries age 65 and over who have health insurance through their own current employment or the employment of a spouse (of any age). Employers with 20 or more employees must offer employees age 65 and over health coverage equivalent to that of their younger employees. Medicare is secondary payer when the employee accepts this EGHP coverage. If the beneficiary does not accept their own or their spouse's employer plan, Medicare is the primary payer. However, if this choice is made, the EGHP cannot pay supplemental benefits for Medicare covered services. Medicare can pay primary benefits for Medicare covered items and services which are not covered under the EGHP.

The "20 or more employee" threshold is met when an employer has 20 or more full and/or part-time employees for each working day in each of 20 or more calendar weeks in the current calendar year or the preceding calendar year. The 20 calendar weeks do not have to be consecutive. The requirements of the MSP law are based on the number of employees, not the number of people covered under the plan. EGHPs assure correct application of the "20 or more employees" rule by taking the following steps:

- At the beginning of a calendar year, employers should examine their records to determine whether they had 20 or more employees for each working day in each of 20 or more calendar weeks during the preceding calendar. If so, the threshold has been met, and Medicare is secondary payer for working aged people covered by the EGHP for the entire calendar year that has just begun. Once employers have met the requirement in a particular year, they must provide primary coverage for the remainder of the year and throughout the following year.

- If employers have not satisfied the threshold during the previous calendar year, it is still possible that they will meet it at some point during the new calendar year. Once employers reach the threshold, Medicare becomes secondary payer from that point on through the remainder of that year and throughout the next year. Medicare does not become secondary payer retroactively for the part of the year before the threshold is reached.

The MSP requirements for the working aged apply to both multiple employer plans and to multi-employer plans. A multiple employer plan is a plan sponsored by more than one employer. A multi-employer plan is a plan jointly sponsored by employers and unions under the Taft-Hartley Law. Under multi-employer plans, an employer typically pays a premium based on the hours that a union employee worked. The premium dollars go into a special health and welfare fund which administers benefits.

For EGHPs with more than one sponsor or contributor, there are three possible scenarios that come into play in determining whether the plan is primary:

- Where all of the employers have less than 20 employees, Medicare is primary payer for all working aged people enrolled in the plan because the plan is not subject to the MSP provisions.

- Where all of the employers have 20 or more employees, Medicare is secondary payer for all working aged people enrolled in the plan.

- Where at least one of the employers has 20 or more employees, even if some have less than 20, Medicare is secondary payer for all working aged people enrolled in the plan.

There is one exception: An EGHP may exempt those working aged people enrolled through an employer with fewer than 20 employees. In that case, Medicare would become primary payer for specifically identified working aged people enrolled through an employer with fewer than 20 employees. The EGHP must be able to document its decision to exempt such people. The plan may then offer those people coverage that supplements Medicare.

Employers must follow the Internal Revenue System aggregation rules to determine whether the "20 or more employee" threshold is met. (See 26 U.S.C. Sections 52(a), 52(b), 414(m), and 414(n)(2) of the Internal Revenue Code.)

Disability: The Omnibus Budget Reconciliation Act (OBRA) of 1986, Omnibus Budget Reconciliation Act (OBRA) of 1990, Omnibus Budget Reconciliation Act (OBRA) of 1993, and the Balanced Budget Act (BBA) of 1997.

Medicare is the secondary payer for people under age 65 who have Medicare because of disability and who are covered under a LGHP. Coverage under the LGHP must be due to the beneficiary's employment or the employment of a family member. Medicare eligibility due to disability occurs when an individual has received 24 consecutive months of Social Security disability payments. ESRD beneficiaries are excluded from the disability provisions. The disability provisions are effective for services rendered on or after January 1, 1987. The Balanced Budget Act (BBA) of 1997 made the disability provisions of MSP law permanent.

A disabled individual who receives sick pay or disability benefits, on which FICA tax is paid, is considered to be an employee by the status of "active individual" with the employer. Prior to August 10, 1993, "active individual" status was determined by sending a certification form to the beneficiary's employer. The "active individual" status was abolished effective August 10, 1993, with the enactment of OBRA of 1993. OBRA of 1993 states that the individual or the spouse of the individual must be actually working for the disability provisions to apply.

An LGHP is a plan sponsored or contributed to by an employer or employee organization, such as a union. The term LGHP includes plans in which employees pay all the costs. The plan:

- Provides health care to employees, former employees, the employer, business associates of the employer or their families, and
- Covers employees of at least one employer with 100 or more employees.

A group health plan that covers employees of a least one employer that had 100 or more employees on 50 percent or more of its business days during the preceding calendar year, meets the definition of an LGHP. An LGHP which is a multiple or multi-employer plan may not exempt people enrolled through an employer with less than 100 employees from the MSP disability provision.

Employers must follow the Internal Revenue System aggregation rules to determine whether the 100 or more employee threshold is met. (See 26 U.S.C. Sections 52(a), 52(b), 414(m), and 414(n)(2) of the Internal Revenue Code.)

INFORMATION REQUIRED ON CLAIM FORMS FOR MSP INVOLVED SERVICE

1. The beneficiary's name, address, and Health Insurance Claim Number.
2. Other insurance information (Item 10 and 11 on the 1500 claim form or Item 5 on the 1490S claim form).
   Instructions for Item 10:
   a. If condition is work related, check appropriate Item.
   b. If auto accident related, check the appropriate Item and annotate the date of accident.

c. Check "other liability" only if you have information that the payment liability lies with another insurer (personal injury cases, etc.) and annotate date of accident in this Item. Do not use "other" Item to signify "none of the above."

Instructions for Item 11:
Providers are required to complete Item 11 of the 1500 claim form when billing Medicare for services rendered to indicate that a good faith effort has been made to determine whether other insurance, primary to Medicare, exists for the beneficiary. The provider must indicate whether there is no primary insurance by stating "NONE" or that there is insurance primary to Medicare by indicating the policy or group number in Item 11. This information is mandatory after March 1, 1996.

Whenever Item 11 indicates that there is other insurance primary to Medicare, the provider must also complete the following items on the 1500 claim form giving specific information about that coverage:

Item 11a - indicate the insured's date of birth and sex.
Item 11b - indicate the employer's name or a retirement date for the insured.
Item 11c - indicate the insurance plan or program name.
Item 4 - indicate the name of the insured.
Item 6 - indicate the appropriate patient relationship to the insured.
Item 7 - indicate the insured's address and phone number.

3. For a paper claim to be considered for Medicare secondary benefits, a copy of the primary payer's explanation of benefits notice must be forwarded along with the claim form. The copy of the primary payer's explanation of benefits notice must identify the insurer who made the primary payment. Electronic claim submission formats contain specific records associated with the other payer information.

Effective April 1, 1996, assigned claims submitted to the Medicare carrier which are not in compliance with the above billing requirements will be rejected. No appeals rights will be available for these claim denials.

Note: Under the requirements for mandatory claim submission by physicians, the physician should submit the claim to Medicare on a 1500 claim form whenever the physician has sufficient information to do so. Where the physician does not have sufficient information to submit a proper claim, beneficiary submitted claims will be accepted.

SECONDARY BENEFITS CALCULATION

Medicare may pay secondary benefits when a physician, supplier or beneficiary bills a third party payer for primary benefits and that payer does not pay the entire charge for the items or services. This general rule applies when the physician or supplier does not accept, and is not obligated to accept, the third party payment as full payment. The method of calculating the Medicare secondary amount is the same whether the claim is assigned or unassigned.

Medicare secondary benefits are not payable when:

1. The third party payer pays the physician's or supplier's charges in full; or
2. The physician or supplier is either obligated to accept, or voluntarily accepts, a third party payment as full payment.

Note: In general, workers compensation medical benefits constitute a service benefit, ie, the payment constitutes full discharge of the patient's liability for services. In such cases, physicians and suppliers are obligated to accept the workers compensation payment as payment in full, and no secondary Medicare benefits are payable. However, if workers compensation pays for Medicare covered services and under the workers compensation plan the physician or supplier is not obligated to accept the payment as payment in full, Medicare secondary benefits may be payable.

I. Calculating Medicare Secondary Payments

A. General: When a proper claim has been filed (i.e., a claim that is filed in a timely manner and meets all other filing requirements of the third party payer), the amount of secondary benefits payable is the lowest of:

1. the actual charge by the physician or supplier (or the amount he or she is obligated to accept as payment in full, if that is less than the charges) minus the amount paid by the third party payer;
2. the amount Medicare would pay if services were not covered by a third party payer;
3. the higher of the Medicare fee schedule or other amount which would be payable under Medicare (without regard to any Medicare deductible and/or coinsurance amounts) or the third party payer's allowable charge (without regard to any deductible or coinsurance amounts imposed by the policy or plan) minus the amount actually paid by the third party payer.

To calculate the amount of Medicare secondary benefits payable on a given claim, it is generally necessary to have the following information not otherwise required in processing Medicare claims:

1. The amount paid by the third party payer; and
2. The third party payer's allowable charge.

This information can generally be derived from the third party payer's explanation of benefits (EOB). In the event that we cannot readily determine the third party payer's allowable charge from the EOB, we will assume, in the absence of evidence to the contrary, that the actual charge is the third party payer's allowable charge.

Example:

Example 1: An individual received treatment from a physician who charged $175. The individual's Part B deductible had been met. As a primary payer, an employer plan allowed $150 of the charge and paid 80 percent of this amount, or $120. The fee schedule amount for this treatment is $125. The Medicare secondary payment is calculated as follows:

1. Actual charge by the physician minus the third party payment:

    $$\$175 - \$120 = \$55.$$

2. Medicare payment determination in the usual manner:

    $$.80 \times \$125 = \$100.$$

3. Employer plan allowable charge of $150 minus employer plan payment of $120 = $30. (Employer plan allowable charge of $150 is higher than the Medicare fee schedule amount of $125.)
4. Pay $30 (lowest of amounts in steps 1, 2, or 3).

Example 2: An individual received treatment from a physician who charged $250. The individual had previously met $50 of the $100 Part B deductible for that year. As primary payer, an automobile insurer allowed the $250 charge in full. The insurer deducted $100 from the $250 physician charge to meet its own deductible and paid 80 percent of the remaining $150, or $120. The Medicare fee schedule amount for this treatment is $200. The Medicare secondary payment is calculated as follows:

1. Actual charge by the physician minus the third party payment:

    $$\$250 - \$120 = \$130.$$

2. Medicare payment determination in the usual manner:

    $$\$200 - \$50 = \$150 \times .80 = \$120.$$

> 3. Third party payer's allowable charge of $250 minus its payment of $120 = $130. (The third party payer's allowable charge of $250 is higher than Medicare's fee schedule amount of $200).
> 4. Pay $120 (lowest of amounts in steps 1, 2, or 3).
>
> The beneficiary's Medicare deductible is credited with $50, the amount that would have been credited to the deductible based on the fee schedule amount of $200 payable if Medicare had been primary payer. The beneficiary's Medicare deductible has now been met in full since $50 of the $100 deductible was met previously.
>
> The beneficiary cannot be billed by the physician because the sum total of the primary payment ($120) and the Medicare payment ($120) exceeds the fee schedule amount ($200).

B. When a third party payer pays for certain services rendered to an individual but does not pay for other services, or the benefits available under the policy or plan have been exhausted, Medicare may pay for the services for which the third party payer did not pay, provided they are otherwise covered.

> **Example:**
>
> A physician charges $600 for his/her services related to an on the job injury. He/she also charges $400 for the services of an independent physical therapist in his/her office, which were for treatment of a preexisting condition unrelated to the job injury. The fee schedule amount for the physician's services is $400, and the fee schedule amount for the therapist's services is $300. The beneficiary previously met the Medicare Part B deductible. Workers compensation paid a fee schedule amount of $375 for the work related injury, which the physician was required to accept as payment in full for his/her services, but workers compensation did not pay for physical therapy related to the preexisting condition. Since the workers compensation payment is payment in full for the physician's services, no secondary Medicare benefits are payable for these services. However, Medicare may pay for the covered physical therapy services (provided by an independent physical therapist) not covered by workers compensation. Medicare pays primary benefits of $240 (80 percent of the fee schedule amount of $300) for the independent therapist's services.

C. Third Party Payment Includes Both Medicare Covered and Non-Covered Services. To determine the amount of third party payment for covered services when a bill includes both Medicare covered and non-covered services, and it cannot be determined from the third party payer's EOB how much of its payment is for Medicare covered services, we will allocate the third party payment proportionately to the Medicare covered and non-covered services. To do this, we determine the ratio of the charges for covered services to the total charges and multiply the third party allowable charge and payment by that ratio. The results are, respectively, the third party allowable charge and the amount of the third party payment considered to be for Medicare covered services.

D. Effect of Failure to File Proper Claim. The term "proper claim" means one that is filed in a timely manner and meets all other filing requirements specified by the third party payer (e.g., mandatory second opinion, prior notification before seeking treatment).

When a physician, supplier, or beneficiary who is not physically or mentally incapacitated receives a reduced third party payment because of failure to file a proper claim, the Medicare secondary payment is the amount that Medicare would have paid if the third party payer had paid on the basis of a proper claim.

The physician, supplier, or beneficiary must inform CMS that a reduced payment was made, and the amount that the third party would have paid if a proper claim had been filed. If a greater secondary payment was made because the physician, supplier, or beneficiary fails to provide such notice, and we later discover that the third party payment was a reduced amount because of failure to file a proper claim, the difference between the Medicare payment and the amount that Medicare should have paid, on the basis of a proper claim for third party payment, is an overpayment. This amount will be recouped plus any applicable interest.

However, when failure to file a proper claim was attributable to the physical or mental incapacity of the beneficiary, consider the primary claim to have been properly filed, and pay secondary benefits without regard to any third party benefit reduction attributable to failure to file a proper claim.

Example:

A beneficiary receives services for which the physician's charges are $1000. The primary payer's allowed charge is also $1000, of which it would pay 80 percent or $800. However, the primary payer requires that the beneficiary submit a second opinion regarding the medical need for this service as a condition for filing a proper claim. Since the beneficiary failed to do so, the primary payer rejected the claim and refused to reimburse the beneficiary for the service. Medicare determines its secondary payment, in this case, as if the primary payer had paid on the basis of a proper claim. The Medicare fee schedule amount for this service is $800. The secondary payment is calculated as follows:

1. Actual charge by the physician minus what the third party payer would have paid on the basis of a proper claim:

   $$\$1000 - \$800 = \$200.$$

2. Medicare payment determination in the usual manner:

   $$.80 \times \$800 = \$640.$$

3. The primary payer's allowable charge of $1000 (which is higher than Medicare's fee schedule amount of $800) minus what the primary payer would have paid on the basis of a proper claim ($800) equals $200.

4. Pay $200 (lowest of amounts in steps 1, 2, or 3).

The beneficiary can be billed $800 by the physician (the amount of the third party payer reduction).

II. Effect of Primary Payments on Deductibles and Coinsurance

A. General: Expenses that would be credited to a beneficiary's cash or deductibles if Medicare were primary payer are credited to the deductibles if the expenses are reimbursed by a third party payer. This is true even if the third party payer paid the entire bill and there are no expenses in whole or in part, the Part B deductible is credited on the basis of Medicare fee schedule amount rather than the amount paid by the third party payer.

After deductibles are credited, a third party payer's payments are applied to satisfy a beneficiary's obligation to pay a Part B coinsurance amount.

Example:

An individual who had previously met $20 of the $100 Part B deductible, incurred $80 in charges, which were paid in full by the third party payer. The Medicare fee schedule amount was $50. No Medicare benefits are payable. The individual is credited with an additional $50 toward the Part B cash deductible and now has satisfied a total of $70.

The beneficiary cannot be billed by the physician because the sum total of the primary payment ($80) and the Medicare payment ($0) exceeds the fee schedule amount ($50).

B. Crediting the Deductible for Non-Inpatient Therapeutic Psychiatric Services: The Part B deductible for non-inpatient psychiatric services is credited on the basis of 62.5% of the Medicare fee schedule amount. This is because incurred expenses for non-inpatient therapeutic psychiatric services are limited to 62.5% of the Medicare fee schedule amount. Accordingly, Medicare pays no more than 50% of the Medicare fee schedule amount for non-inpatient therapeutic psychiatric services, i.e., 80% of 62.5% of the fee schedule amount. (Unmet Part B deductible reduces the percentage of the fee schedule amount payable by Medicare.)

Example:

An individual received non-inpatient psychiatric services from a physician for which the physician charged $500. None of the individual's $100 Part B deductible had been met. A third party payer allowed charges in full and paid $400 (80% of the $500). The Medicare fee schedule amount for the services was also $500. The $100 Part B deductible is credited in full by the first $160 of the fee schedule amount ($62.5\% \times \$160 = \$100$).

The beneficiary cannot be billed by the physician because the sum total of the primary payment ($400) and the Medicare secondary payment ($100) equals the physician's charges.

III. Right of Physician or Supplier to Charge Beneficiary

A. When a beneficiary has been paid by a third party payer, the amounts a physician or supplier who accepts assignment may collect for a Medicare covered services from the beneficiary are limited to the following:

1. The amount paid or payable by the third party payer to the beneficiary. If this amount exceeds the amount which would be payable by Medicare as primary payer (without regard to deductible or coinsurance), the physician or supplier may retain the third party payment in full without violating the conditions of assignment.
2. If the third party payment is less than the applicable Medicare deductible and coinsurance amounts, the difference between the fee schedule amount (or the amount the physician is obligated to accept as payment in full, if less) and the sum of the third party primary payment and the Medicare secondary payment.

Example:

A physician charges $262 for a service. The plan allows $262 but pays a primary payment of only $112 because of a $150 plan deductible. The Medicare fee schedule amount is $200. The amount that Medicare pays as secondary payer is $80 since the Medicare secondary payment amount cannot exceed the amount Medicare would pay as primary payer ($200 fee schedule amount minus the $100 Part B deductible, $100 \times 80\% = \$80$). The combined primary plan payment and Medicare secondary payment is $192 ($112 + $80).

The physician may charge the beneficiary $8, the difference between the Medicare fee schedule amount ($200) and the sum of the primary payment ($112) plus the Medicare secondary payment ($80). The $8 charge to the beneficiary represents the portion of the Part B deductible and coinsurance amounts in excess of the plan payment (the $100 Part B deductible is credited in full). The remaining $12 of the plan payment is applied to the beneficiary's Part B coinsurance obligation of $20, leaving him/her responsible for the remaining coinsurance obligation of $8.

B. Right to Charge the Beneficiary Where a Physician or Supplier Has Failed to File Proper Claim. If a physician or supplier receives, from a payer that is primary to Medicare, a payment that is reduced because the physician or supplier failed to file a proper claim, he/she may charge the beneficiary an amount equal to any third party payment reduction attributable to failure to file a proper claim. However, the physician or supplier may charge the beneficiary this amount only if the physician or supplier can show that he/she or the beneficiary failed to file a proper claim for a reason other than the mental or physical incapacity of the beneficiary.

C. Duplicate Payments. In any case in which a physician or supplier has received a primary payment from Medicare and a duplicate primary payment from a third party payer, the physician or supplier is instructed to refund to the beneficiary any Medicare deductible and coinsurance amounts that were paid by the beneficiary that were duplicated by the third party payment. If the third party payment <u>exceeds</u> the deductible and coinsurance amounts, then the excess constitutes a Medicare overpayment because it duplicates all or part of the amount Medicare has paid and should therefore be collected from the physician or supplier. Medicare must be reimbursed within 60 days of the receipt of the duplicate payment. A copy of the letter to the physician or supplier is sent to the beneficiary.

IRS/SSA/CMS DATA MATCH

In 1989, Congress passed a law that will help Medicare get back money that it paid for services where it was not primary. This law will enable Medicare to get accurate information about a beneficiary's health insurance.

The law requiring the Data Match was enacted with the Omnibus Budget Reconciliation Act (OBRA) of 1989 and was extended through 1998 by the Omnibus Budget Reconciliation Act (OBRA) of 1993. OBRA of 1989 authorizes CMS (Centers for Medicare & Medicaid Services), the Internal Revenue Service (IRS), and the Social Security Administration (SSA) to share information about where Medicare beneficiaries or their spouses are working and whether they have employment-related health insurance.

The process for sharing information from the other agencies is called Data Match. The Data Match will help Medicare find cases in which another insurer should have paid first. A designated Medicare contractor has contacted employers to confirm health insurance coverage information. The Data Match contractor maintains all of this information.

The Data Match contractor creates MSP records, which are loaded to a central processing file called the "Common Working File" (CWF). The MSP records created are also sent to CMS for matching against Medicare payment records. CMS then forwards any matches between the MSP record and the payment records to the contractor who originally made the payment so that recovery can be initiated. These recoveries are sought directly from the insurer responsible for payment on a primary basis.

Although the Data Match process has been extremely beneficial in identifying situations in which another insurer should have paid before Medicare, there have been situations in which beneficiaries have been inappropriately identified, by their employers or previous employers, as having insurance primary to Medicare. This causes Medicare claim denials. To correct claim denials due to a Data Match record, the Upstate Medicare Division (a CMS-contracted Medicare Part B carrier that processes claims for 45 counties in upstate New York), for example, utilizes the IRS/SSA/CMS Data Match Correction/Referral process to correct the record. Under this process, the Data Match contractor is responsible for coordinating the development of cases in which beneficiary and employer information do not agree. The Data Match contractor will contact the employer or health and welfare fund to obtain corrected information because that entity provided the original information in the Data Match. The Data Match contractor tracks those cases to ensure that multiple contacts (by contractors) to an employer regarding a particular beneficiary are not made, corrects any records with incorrect data (if applicable), and responds to all entities involved in the discrepancy once a final determination has been made.

The Upstate Medicare Division will forward cases to the Data Match contractor where discrepancies exist between information supplied by the beneficiary and the employer. Wherever possible, we try to facilitate the correction process by forwarding any readily available data from an employer to the Data Match contractor. The Upstate Medicare Division can act on its own to correct a Data Match record only in the following situations:

- The beneficiary or employer gives a retirement date that falls within 6 months before or after the date the record was established by the Data Match contractor and the MSP record currently shows no retirement date. Retirement dates not meeting this criteria or existing retirement dates which require a change must be corrected in CWF by the Data Match contractor.
- A letter from the beneficiary's or family member's employer is received stating corrected information which is complete, on company letterhead and supported by the signature of the employer's authorized representative. In this situation, the Upstate Medicare Division may not necessarily change the record but may intercede and issue claim payments until the Data Match contractor ultimately corrects the record.

The Data Match contractor will respond to referrals made by Medicare contractors within a reasonable time frame as obligated by their contract to perform this function. Upon notice of corrections made by the Data Match contractor, the Upstate Medicare Division automatically reprocesses any claims affected by the change in the record.

THE MSP DEPARTMENT FUNCTION

The MSP Department consists of specially-trained individuals who deal solely with cases where another carrier has responsibility to pay before Medicare. The purpose of this unit is to save Trust Fund dollars. The MSP Department is subdivided into two units. The MSP Claims Unit deals with prepayment detection of inappropriate billings for primary benefits. The MSP Correspondence and Recovery Unit deals with post-payment recovery and adjustment of previously processed claims.

MSP Claims Unit - The MSP Claims Unit performs the following functions:

1. Data entry for all claims received claiming secondary benefits. These claims are submitted by the beneficiary or physician with an explanation of benefits (EOB) showing how the services were paid or if the services were denied by the primary insurer. A coordination of benefits is performed to determine the correct secondary payment.
2. Claim suspensions are researched for other insurer involvement. Such claims would contain indication of other insurer involvement in Item 10 a-c or 11 a-c, 4, 6, and 7 of the 1500 claim form or Item 5 of the 1490S claim form.
3. Development questionnaires are generated and evaluated. MSP records are established based on decisions resulting from the questionnaire evaluation process. The records are, from that point on, used as flags in future claim processing. The flags result in system actions such as to suspend claims for review or automatic claim denial.

MSP Correspondence and Recovery Unit - The MSP Correspondence and Recovery Unit performs the following functions:

1. Review and adjustment of all correspondence inquiries related to MSP.
2. Initiate recovery of inappropriate primary payments made on previously processed claims. These recovery activities can go back as far as the beginning of the other insurance coverage period. Leads to follow for recovery activities are obtained from various sources to include the MSP claims unit, beneficiary, provider, and insurer correspondence, and the IRS/SSA/CMS Data Match Project.

SUMMARY

By being more informed in the MSP guidelines, you can assist us in assuring that claims are processed in an efficient and timely manner. This will avoid unnecessary delays when claims have to be suspended during external development. It will save time and money for everyone involved when claims are paid right the first time. It will avoid the expense and time associated with overpayment recovery actions and possible litigation.

If you have any questions concerning Medicare as secondary payer, please call us at 877 567-7173. Also, please address all MSP correspondence to Upstate Medicare Division, P.O. Box 5211, Binghamton, N.Y. 13902-5211.

appendix

E

MSP Recoveries/Debt-Related Issues

Q1: How does a Medicare Secondary Payer (MSP) debt arise?

A1: An MSP debt arises when Medicare learns that it made primary payment for services provided to a Medicare beneficiary that should have been the primary payment responsibility of another third party payer. The law requires Medicare to recover the payment from a party the law or regulations identify as responsible to repay Medicare.

Q2: Why didn't Medicare pay right in the first place?

A2: Medicare contractors make every effort to avoid mistaken primary payments. There are other cases where Medicare may not learn that the group health plan coverage existed until after some claims have been paid.

If a workers' compensation, no-fault or liability insurance does not pay a beneficiary's claim promptly, the law requires Medicare to make a "conditional" primary payment. Medicare recovers its "conditional" primary payments from the insurance proceeds once the beneficiary's claim is resolved.

Q3: What process does Medicare use to recover MSP debts?

A3: The recovery process begins with a "recovery demand letter" to an entity responsible for resolving the debt. The letter explains how the debt arose; provides detail about Medicare's recovery claim; and explains what must be done to resolve the matter. The matter may be resolved either through payment or presentation of a documented valid defense.

If the responsible entity does not resolve the matter timely, Medicare sends a second "recovery demand letter". A copy of the original "recovery demand letter" is provided. This second letter explains that, if the matter is not resolved within 60 days, Medicare will refer the debt to the Department of Treasury for further collection action. This letter is often referred to as a "Notice of Intent to Refer" letter.

If the matter is still not resolved 60 days after the date of the "Notice of Intent to Refer" letter, Medicare refers the debt to the Department of Treasury for further collection actions. Treasury may collect the debt in a variety of ways, including offset of Federal payments to the responsible entity. Treasury may also ask the Department of Justice to take legal action to collect the debt.

Q4: Who is responsible for resolving group health plan-related MSP debts?

A4: The law makes all entities "responsible for payment under a group health plan" jointly and severally responsible for resolving these debts. These entities include the employer sponsoring or contributing to the plan; other plan sponsors

---

Reprinted with permission from the American Benefits Council. Available at: www.americanbenefitscouncil.org/documents/msp_recoveries_faq.pdf. Accessed June 12, 2006.

(eg, a union or other employee organization); the insurer or third party administrator (TPA) (TPAs administer plans for employers that self-insure); and the plan itself if it is a separate legal entity.

Q5: **How do group health plan-related MSP debts occur?**

A5: A provider bills Medicare for primary payment for services provided to a Medicare beneficiary for whom a group health plan should have been the primary payer and Medicare mistakenly pays.

Group health plans are primary payers for aged beneficiaries covered as a result of their own or a spouse's current employment status; disabled beneficiaries covered as a result of their own or a family member's current employment status; beneficiaries with end-stage renal disease for a 30-month coordination period) covered on any basis (including retirement).

Q6: **How does Medicare pick whom to pursue for this type of MSP debt?**

A6: Medicare law allows for the pursuit of recoupment of a Medicare mistaken payment to all entities who are individually or jointly liable for repayment. In 1997, Medicare began sending the recovery demand letters to the employer (if known) because some insurers/TPAs were routinely non-responsive and because a Circuit Court decision limited Medicare's ability to recover from TPAs. An employer is always responsible for the actions of any group health plan that it sponsors or to which it contributes.

Q7: **How can Medicare hold an employer that purchased insurance responsible for resolving the debt? Why doesn't Medicare go after the insurer?**

A7: An employer is always responsible for the conduct of any group health plan that it sponsors or to which it contributes. An employer cannot transfer legal obligations to a third party through a contract. This is explained in an enclosure to the initial recovery demand letter entitled, "Important Information for Employers".

An employer may direct its insurer to resolve the debt on the employer's behalf. However, if the insurer does not do so, the employer remains responsible for either paying the debt or documenting why it is not responsible.

Q8: **What documentation does Medicare consider sufficient to demonstrate that a group health plan-related MSP debt is not owed?**

A8: At the time the debt is being pursued, it has been reviewed several times to determine that it is valid. It is possible that the debtor has other information not available to Medicare that demonstrates that the debtor has no legal obligation to repay Medicare. Such information would include the following:

- The Medicare beneficiary was not covered by the group health plan or the group health plan was not obligated to be the primary payer when the services were provided (see prior question, "How do group health plan-related debts occur?");
- The services provided to the Medicare beneficiary were not covered under any circumstances by the group health plan;
- The group health plan had already made full primary payment to the provider of services or the Medicare beneficiary prior to the date of the initial recovery demand letter; and
- No entity responsible for payment under the plan had knowledge that the services had been provided to the Medicare beneficiary within the longer of the group health plan's timely filing requirements or the period during which the law authorizes Medicare to seek recovery.

These are explained below.

Q9: **When is a "Medicare beneficiary not covered by the group health plan or the group health plan was not obligated to be the primary payer when the services were provided"? What would be proper documentation of this defense?**

A9: It is possible that a beneficiary, entitled to Medicare on the basis of age or disability, did not have coverage under any employer plan based on their own or a spouse's or a family member's (for disability) current employment status at the time the services were provided, because the individual or his/her spouse or family member (for disability) had retired or left employment. Proper documentation would consist of all of the following:

1. A copy of the individual claim paid by Medicare and referenced in the original demand letter;
2. Date of Medicare's original demand letter containing the claim;
3. Associated reported identification numbers for that claim as provided in the demand letter;
4. Identification of the individual through whom the beneficiary had coverage; and
5. Certification of the date of retirement or termination of that individual.

Failure to provide all the above information could result in Medicare not accepting the documentation or not applying it properly.

In the case of a beneficiary entitled to Medicare on the basis of end-stage renal disease, the debt is still valid if the beneficiary had coverage under any group health plan on any basis.

Q10: What exactly does the "coverage limitation" defense encompass? What would be proper documentation of this defense?

A10: A beneficiary, who has employer plan coverage that is obligated to be a primary payer, may have had services not covered by the employer's plan. This would mean that the services are not the responsibility of the employer's plan. If properly documented, this would be a valid defense to the debt associated with those services. Proper documentation would consist of the following:

- A copy of the individual claim with the non-covered services annotated;
- Date of the original demand letter containing the claim;
- Associated report identification number; and
- Copy of plan documents (eg, Employee Services Handbook, Member Services Booklet, etc.) that establishes that the services are not covered under the plan with the applicable coverage terms annotated.

Q11: What should a responsible entity do if the group health plan paid primary for the services for which Medicare seeks to recover? What should a responsible entity do if the group health plan is an HMO and the services were covered by the HMO's capitation payment?

A11: It is possible that both Medicare and an employer plan made primary payment for the services identified on any unique MSP claim. If properly documented, an employer plan's full primary payment for the services on an MSP claim is a valid defense to the debt that had been associated with that claim. Proper documentation generally would consist of the following:

- A copy of the individual claim;
- Date of the original demand letter containing the claim;
- Associated report identification number for that claim as provided in the demand letter;
- Explanation of how the prior primary payment was determined; and
- Proof of payment (eg, copy of remittance advice).

If the employer plan is an HMO and the employer plan's full primary payment responsibility was resolved by a capitation payment to the provider, physician or other supplier that treated the Medicare beneficiary, proper documentation would consist of the following:

- A copy of the individual claim;
- Date of the original demand letter containing the claim;
- Associated report identification number for that claim as provided in the original demand letter;

- Copy of the relevant portions of the HMO contract with the provider, physician or other supplier stipulating that the only payment obligation of the HMO was payment of a capitated amount; and
- Proof that the capitated amount for the individual for the time period when the services were furnished was paid.

In these instances, Medicare will recover from the medical provider or supplier that received Medicare's payment.

Q12: **What is a group health plan's timely filing defense? When is Medicare not bound by a group health plan's timely filing requirements? What documentation is needed?**

A12: Most group health plans (GHPs) have established time limits during which claims must be submitted in order to qualify for payment. If a GHP or any entity responsible for payment under the plan (employer, insurer, third party administrator (TPA), or other plan sponsor ("responsible entities")) does not receive a claim within those time limits, the plan is not obligated to make payment (even if it would be obligated to make payment if the claim had been submitted prior to the expiration of the time limit). These time limits are typically called "timely filing" requirements. Applicable Federal law limits the ability of any responsible entity (including the employer/insurer/TPA/GHP/other plan sponsor) that received a demand letter to assert a timely filing defense to an MSP-based debt.

As a first point, the date of Medicare's original demand letter is the date applicable to any defense that the recipient of the demand letter, or any entity acting on its behalf, may have to the debt or any portion of the debt. This is true regardless of which of these entities the original demand letter is issued to, and regardless of whether or not the demand is immediately shared among these entities. For example, the insurer may not establish a timely filing defense on behalf of an employer based upon the date the insurer received the demand letter from the employer. The insurer may only establish a timely defense for the employer based upon the date of the demand letter to the employer.

Additionally, two different rules are applicable to the MSP claims that comprise the Medicare debts. These rules are explained below.

The first rule applies to all services, regardless of the date those services were provided. The recipient of the demand letter (regardless of whether it is the employer/insurer/TPA or other responsible entity) does not have a valid timely filing defense if either the employer, the insurer, the TPA, or other responsible entity had knowledge within the plan's timely filing period that the services were provided. This knowledge could come from a variety of sources, but is often due to the receipt of a claim from a provider, physician or other supplier (or the plan member), which included the services at issue.

The second rule applies to services provided on or after August 5, 1997, and further restricts the use of a timely filing defense. The Balanced Budget Act of 1997 eliminated timely filing defenses for at least 3 years from the date of the service. For services on or after August 5, 1997, there is no timely filing defense if Medicare's original demand letter is dated within 3 years of the date of the service. This rule applies even if the plan's timely filing period is less than 3 years. (If the services were on or after August 5, 1997, and Medicare's original demand letter is not dated within 3 years from the date of the service, then the first rule applies.)

Under the first rule, proper documentation of a timely filing defense would consist of the following:

- A copy of the individual Medicare claim supplied with the demand letter with the services for which the defense is offered annotated by the entity asserting the defense;
- The date of the original Medicare demand letter containing the claim (and the associated report identification number for Data Match recoveries);
- A copy of plan documents that establish the timely filing period with the applicable provisions annotated; and

- A written statement by or on behalf of the recipient of the demand letter that claims records of all responsible entities exist for the time period when the services were provided, were searched, and no record of the services being provided to the beneficiary were found.

Remember that if a demand letter is sent to an employer and another responsible entity such as an insurer or TPA responds, the responding entity is assumed to be acting as the agent of the employer. In this situation, the date of the original demand letter to the employer is the date applicable to any asserted timely filing defense.

Q13: **Is an employer still responsible for resolving a group health plan-related MSP debt if the employee became enrolled in a group health plan other than the one identified in the initial recovery demand letter?**

A13: The health plan information that Medicare provided in the original demand letter was, in almost all cases, provided by the employer in response to Internal Revenue Service (IRS)/Social Security Administration (SSA)/CMS Data Match questionnaires. In other cases, the health plan information was obtained from the beneficiary, the insurer, or the provider/physician/other supplier that furnished services to the beneficiary. Thus, the information is presumed to be accurate as of the time it was provided. Many employers offer employees the opportunity periodically to choose among several available group health plans. Because CMS was not advised of changes in employees' group health plan choices, the group health plan Medicare identified as providing the health insurance may not be correct as of the date particular services were provided to an identified beneficiary.

The MSP debt is still valid as long as the Medicare beneficiary, entitled to Medicare on the basis of age or disability, had coverage under any employer plan based on his/her own or a spouse's or family member's (for disability) current employment status. In the case of a beneficiary entitled to Medicare on the basis of ESRD, the debt is still valid if the beneficiary had coverage under any employer plan on any basis. If you are unclear about your responsibility relative to ESRD, please call the Medicare contractor.

Q14: **How does a responsible entity determine the proper amount to pay Medicare? How is interest determined? What documentation should be provided to assure proper crediting of the payment?**

A14: The original demand letters explain that interest is due on any debt that is not resolved timely (60 days from the date of the original demand letter) and includes the applicable interest rate. Interest applies from the date of the demand letter for each 30-day period that the debt is unresolved. (Periods of less than 30 days are treated as a full 30-day period.) Accordingly, to resolve any MSP claim for which payment is due, the responsible entity (group health plan, employer, insurer, third party administrator (TPA), or other plan sponsor) must pay both the principal due and the applicable interest. To assist the responsible entity in determining the amount due on any individual unresolved MSP debt, the responsible entity should contact the Medicare contractor who issued the demand letter.

The responsible entity (employer, insurer, third party administrator (TPA), group health plan, or other plan sponsor) should contact the Medicare contractor with any question on the exact amount the responsible entity owes.

Q15: **Can a responsible entity avoid the interest portion of the group health plan-related MSP debt by making a full primary payment to the provider of services following receipt of the original demand letter, Notice of Intent to Refer to Department of Treasury letter, or demand letter from the Department of Treasury or one of its collection agents?**

A15: No. The law requires that the responsible payer pay Medicare, not some other party. Medicare will continue to look to the responsible entity for payment of all interest accrued to the date of payment to the provider. Medicare will recover the principal from the party that the group health plan paid.

Q16: **Is a responsible entity required to repay Medicare for a group health plan-related debt if it no longer has the records necessary to prove it is not responsible?**

A16: Yes. A responsible entity's failure to maintain the records necessary to prove it is not responsible does not relieve the entity of responsibility to resolve the debt.

Q17: **How long can Medicare pursue recovery of an MSP debt?**

A17: The United States may undertake legal action to collect an MSP debt up to 6 years from the date of the original demand letter. In addition, these debts may be collected by offset of Federal government payments to the debtor for 10 years from the date of the original demand letter without undertaking legal action.

Q18: **With whom should a responsible entity deal in resolving a group health plan-related MSP debt?**

A18: Debtors should work with the entity that sent them the most recently dated recovery demand letter with respect to a particular debt. Prior to referral of a debt to the Department of Treasury, this would be the Medicare contractor. Once a debt has been referred to the Department of Treasury for collection action and a responsible entity has been contacted by either the Department of Treasury itself or a Treasury collection agent, the responsible entity should work with the Department of Treasury or its collection agent.

Q19: **Where is Medicare sending the original recovery demand letter and the Notice of Intent to Refer letter for group health plan-related debts? Employer representatives responsible for resolving such issues often first learn of the debt when a copy of the demand letter from the department of Treasury is forwarded to that official from elsewhere in the employer's organization.**

A19: The original recovery demand letter and the Notice of Intent to Refer letter are sent via certified mail/return receipt to the address of the employer provided in the employer's response to the IRS/SSA/CMS Data Match questionnaire or the entity that identified the employer as responsible. Employers are encouraged to advise all components of the company that demand letters involving Medicare should be forwarded to a particular unit (e.g., Benefits Management) if the employer wishes that unit to respond.

Q20: **What can an employer or other responsible entity do to minimize further collection activities related to group health plan MSP debts in the future?**

A20: Recovery actions will be minimized if Medicare is aware that another payer is primary to Medicare when claims are presented to Medicare for payment. If Medicare is aware that another payer is a primary payer to Medicare, Medicare advises the entity that submitted the claim to Medicare that it should bill the other payer. The best way for employers and/or insurers to be sure that Medicare has such knowledge is through quarterly Voluntary Data Sharing Agreements with Medicare. Interested parties may contact the Coordination of Benefits Contractor at 1-800-999-1118 for more information or visit their website at www.cms.gov/medicare/cob.

Q21: **Why are Medicare beneficiaries receiving a Notice of Medicare's Intent to Refer a debt to the Department of Treasury, as well as a recovery demand letter from Treasury?**

A21: Generally, these letters are related to unresolved MSP debts arising from the failure of a beneficiary to pay a Medicare recovery claim arising from a judgment, settlement or award a beneficiary received from workers' compensation, liability or no-fault insurance. If the Medicare beneficiary does not resolve the debt, the Department of Treasury may collect through offset of Federal payments to the beneficiary. This could include offsets against the beneficiary's Social Security retirement checks.

Q22: **What should a beneficiary do when in receipt of a Notice of Medicare's Intent to Refer letter?**

A22: It is important that the beneficiary respond in order to avoid collection from the beneficiary's Social Security retirement check. The original demand letter attached to the Notice of Intent to Refer letter explains the actions the beneficiary can take.

Q23: What is a Voluntary Data Sharing Agreement?

A23: As an alternative to completing the annual IRS/SSA/CMS Data Match questionnaires, these agreements allow employers/insurers to provide Plan coverage information to Medicare on a quarterly basis. CMS is able to update its internal records and immediately avoid making mistaken primary payments. In exchange, CMS provides the employer or insurer with Medicare eligibility information on employees who are no longer working. These are situations where Medicare is usually the primary payer. Savings to employers and insurers can be significant. Interested parties can contact the Coordination of Benefits Contractor at 1-800-999-1118 or visit their website at www.cms.gov/medicare/cob.

Q24: What is a Coordination of Benefits Contractor?

A24: The Coordination of Benefits (COB) program transferred claims crossover responsibility from individual Medicare contractors to a national claims crossover contractor, the Coordination of Benefits Contractor (COBC). It also established a nationally standard contract between CMS and other health insurance organizations that defines the criteria for transmitting enrollee eligibility data and Medicare adjudicated claim data. The new process includes the use of unique identifiers (COBA IDs) associated with each contract and makes use of a new national database for COBA information.

appendix

Medicare EDI Helplines

EDI Helpline is a regional telephone number Medicare customers can call to access information and material regarding electronic data interchange (EDI). The following lists provides states and/or regions and their appropriate EDI Helpline telephone numbers for Medicare Part B, Medicare Part B DMERC, and Medicare Part A.

MEDICARE PART B EDI HELPLINES

Alabama	205 220-6899
Alaska	800 967-7902
Arizona	800 967-7902
Arkansas	866 582-3247
California	530 879-2662 (N) or 213 593-6950 (S)
Colorado	800 967-7902
Connecticut	203 639-3160
Delaware	866 749-4302
District of Columbia	866 749-4302
Florida	904 791-8767
Georgia	912 921-3012
Hawaii	800 967-7902
Idaho	866 520-4022
Illinois	877 567-7261
Indiana	877 273-4334
Iowa	800 967-7902
Kansas	800 472-6481 or 785 291-7135
Kentucky	877 273-4334
Louisiana	866 582-3247
Maine	781 749-7745
Maryland	410 427-8712 or 410 427-8713
Massachusetts	781 749-7745
Michigan	877 567-7261
Minnesota	877 380-4742
Mississippi	205 220-2842
Missouri	866 582-3247
Montana	800 447-7828 Ext 8464
Nebraska	800 472-6481 or 784 291-7135
Nevada	800 967-7902
New Hampshire	781 749-7745
New Jersey	866 488-0546
New Mexico	866 582-3247
New York	866 889-7322
Upstate New York (BCBSWNY)	866 528-8097
New York (Queens)	646 458-6648

North Carolina	866 352-1608
North Dakota	800 967-7902
Ohio	866 308-5438
Oklahoma	866 582-3247
Oregon	800 967-7902
Pennsylvania	866 488-0546
Puerto Rico	787 749-4949 Ext 2381
Rhode Island	866 582-3247
South Carolina	866 749-4301
South Dakota	800 967-7902
Tennessee	866 520-4022
Texas	866 749-4302
Utah	801 333-2290
Vermont	781 749-7745
Virginia	866 749-4302
Washington	800 967-7902
West Virginia	866 308-5438
Wisconsin	877 567-7261
Wyoming	800 967-7902

MEDICARE PART B DMERC EDI HELPLINES

Region A	866 861-7348
Region B	877 273-4334
Region C	866 749-4301
Region D	866 224-3094

Note: For Medicare, Part B Railroad Retirement Board inquiries call 866 749-4301.

MEDICARE PART A EDI HELPLINES

Alabama	205 220-2545
Alaska	800 967-7902
Arizona	602 864-5259
Arkansas	866 582-3247
California	805 367-1170
Colorado	866 749-4302
Connecticut	866 889-7322
Delaware	866 889-7322
District of Columbia	410 561-4145 or 410 561-4299
Florida	904 791-8767
Georgia	888 883-2720
Hawaii	805 367-1170
Idaho	503 721-7033
Illinois	877 273-4334
Indiana	877 273-4334
Iowa	866 839-2441
Kansas	800 472-6481 or 785 291-7135
Kentucky	877 273-4334
Louisiana	877 635-7596 Ext 4995
Maine	888 476-7218 Option 5
Maryland	410 427-8712 or 410 427-8713
Massachusetts	888 476-7218 Option 5
Michigan	414 226-5999
Minnesota	800 967-7902

Mississippi	877 635-7596 Ext 4995
Missouri	877 635-7596 Ext 4995
Montana	800 447-7828 Ext 8464
Nebraska	888 233-8351
Nevada	805 367-1170
New Hampshire	888 476-7218 Option 5
New Jersey	877 296-6189 or 423 755-5717
New Mexico	866 749-4302
New York	866 889-7322
North Carolina	866 749-4301
North Dakota	800 967-7902
Ohio	877 273-4334
Oklahoma	918 560-2156
Oregon	503 721-7033
Pennsylvania	866 488-0546
Puerto Rico	787 758-9733 Ext 2580, Ext 2581, Ext 2582
Rhode Island	866 582-3247
South Carolina	866 749-4301
South Dakota	866 839-2441
Tennessee	423-535-5717
Texas	866 749-4302
Utah	503 721-7033
Vermont	888 476-7218 Option 5
Virginia	540 767-7020 or 540 767-7021
Washington	800 967-7902
West Virginia	540 767-7020 or 540 767-7020
Wisconsin	414 226-6032
Wyoming	307 432-2850
American Samoa	805 367-1170
Guam	805 367-1170
Northern Mariana Islands	805 367-1170

Note: For Mutual of Omaha EDI information and assistance call 866 734-6656. Mutual of Omaha does business in every state, except New York.

The National Fiscal Intermediary for Federally Qualified Health Centers (FQHC) is United Government Services LLC. The United Government Services telephone number for EDI information and assistance for FQHC facilities is 414 226-5999.

GLOSSARY

A

accreditation Certification that an organization meets the reviewing organization's standards. Examples include accreditation of health maintenance organizations by the NCQA or accreditation of preferred provider organizations by the American Accreditation Health Care Commission/URAC.

activities of daily living (ADLs) Measures, used in an index or scale, of an individual's degree of independence in bathing, dressing, using the toilet, eating, transferring (moving from a bed to a chair), and moving across a small room.

adjudicate To process an insurance claim for coverage determination by an insurance company or agent.

adjusted average per-capita cost (AAPCC) The estimated average fee-for-service cost of Medicare benefits for an individual by county of residence. It is based on the following factors: age, sex, institutional status, Medicaid, disability, and ESRD status. CMS uses the AAPCC as a basis for making monthly payments to managed care plans.

adjustments to payment rates Payment systems usually include adjustments to the base payment rates designed to allow for differences in providers' circumstances that are expected to affect their costs of furnishing care. Payment rates may be adjusted, for instance, to accommodate differences in local prices for inputs, which may account for more than 50% of the observed variation in providers' costs for a given product or service. Other adjustments may be made to reflect unusual circumstances, such as delivery of specialized types of care or atypical characteristics of beneficiaries.

allowable The fee (the "approved amount") the third-party payer decides the physician should be paid for the services provided to a patient. The amount is usually the same as or lower than the physician's fee and serves as a payment baseline for adjudicating the claim.

ambulatory payment classifications (APCs) Medicare's Outpatient Prospective Payment System for the vast majority of hospital outpatient services, effective August 1, 2000.

ancillary A term used to describe additional services performed related to care, such as lab work, X ray, and anesthesia.

appeal The request for review by a physician or other provider who questions the correctness of a health plan's reimbursement for services rendered. The physician usually appeals by sending additional information such as clinical or demographic information to clarify to the health plan and to receive appropriate reimbursement.

assignment An arrangement in which the policyholder designates that the physician receive the benefits (payment) for a claim. This differs from the usual procedure in which the person who has the insurance policy is the person who is to receive the benefits (payment) from that policy. Under assignment, in return for receiving direct payment from most third-party payers, the physician agrees to accept the third-party payer's allowable as the maximum amount that may be collected from the payer and patient for that claim.

B

balance bill The amount the physician collects from the patient, which is the difference between the physician's fee (the amount billed) for a service and the amount paid by a third-party payer. In some cases, the balance bill is limited to the difference between the third-party payer's allowable fee and the amount paid by the payer. If the physician accepts assignment of benefits, he or she may not bill the patient for the balance. Instead, the balance difference is not collected; the physician writes it off the books, and the patient is billed only for the amount of the copayment, deductible, or coinsurance, as applicable.

base payment amount In a payment system, the amount that a purchaser commits to pay providers for a standard unit of service or product furnished to a covered beneficiary. The base payment amount corresponds to a payment system's unit of payment, which may be individual services, bundles of services (such as hospital stays), episodes of care, or specified periods of time. Providers' payment rates for individual services or products are determined by applying two types of adjustments to the base payment amount. One is based on a relative weight designed to measure the expected relative costliness of each distinct service or product, compared with the cost of the average unit. The other type of adjustment is designed to reflect differences in providers' circumstances that are likely to affect their costs of furnishing care. The base payment amount (sometimes called a conversion factor) thus determines the level of the payment rates in the payment system.

beneficiary The person who "benefits" from having the insurance policy. Typically, this person is the patient, but it can also be a spouse or the parent or guardian of a child. Persons enrolled in the Medicare program are commonly referred to as beneficiaries.

beneficiary appeal A request by a Medicare beneficiary to have a health care decision altered or reversed.

benefits The amount payable by a plan to a provider, group, or hospital, as stated in the policy, toward the cost of a medical service.

benefits package A term informally used to refer to the employer's benefit plan or to the benefit plan options from which the employee can choose. A benefits *package* highlights the fact that a health benefits plan is a compilation of specific benefits.

board certified (boarded, diplomate) Designation given a physician who has passed a written and oral examination given by a medical specialty board and who has been certified as a specialist in that area.

bundling A payment method that combines minor medical services or surgeries and principal procedures when performed together or within a specific period of time. Some governmental programs and insurance plans "bundle" the payment of the lesser service into the payment for the principal procedure.

C

capitation A method of insurance reimbursement for professional services performed in which a provider is paid a fixed amount per patient for a defined time period (month or year) rather than a fee-for-service payment.

cap rate The fixed prepaid amount of payment under capitation. Also known as *capitation rate*.

case management A method of coordinating the services a patient receives to ensure the patient seeks and receives appropriate and necessary care to minimize duplication of services, tests, and costs.

case mix The mix of patients treated within a particular institutional setting such as a hospital or nursing home. Patient classification systems—such as DRGs and RUG-III—can be used to measure hospital and nursing home case mix, respectively.

case-mix index (CMI) A measure of the average expected relative costliness of the mix of services or products furnished by a provider or group of providers. The average is calculated by multiplying the number of units supplied in each classification category by the relative weight for the category, adding the results across all categories, and dividing by the total number of units across all categories.

Centers for Medicare and Medicaid Services (CMS) The US government organization that governs the financial affairs and operations of the Medicare and Medicaid systems for all health care providers.

certificate of coverage A description of the benefits included in an insurance plan. The certificate of coverage is required by state insurance laws and represents the coverage provided under the policy issued to the contract holder. The certificate is provided to subscribers via the certificate booklet.

CHAMPUS/CHAMPVA Acronym for the Civilian Health and Medical Programs of the Uniformed Services/Veterans Affairs. A government-sponsored health program for active-duty and retired personnel and their eligible dependents and for veterans. CHAMPUS is now known as TRICARE.

claim The request for payment of a health care provider's fees for services provided to patients.

classification system A system that provides the foundation for payment systems by identifying distinct services or products that will be priced separately because they are expected to require different amounts of providers' resources. Each payment system has a classification system that corresponds to the payment system's unit of payment (services, episodes of care, and so on). Examples include HCPCS used in the physician fee schedule and the DRG patient classification system used in the hospital inpatient prospective payment system.

Clinical Laboratory Improvement Act (CLIA) The act that regulates all laboratories that examine human specimens to provide information to assess, diagnose, prevent, or treat any disease or impairment. CLIA mandates that virtually all laboratories meet applicable federal requirements and have a CLIA certificate in order to receive reimbursement from federal programs.

coding The process of communicating to the third-party payers regarding the services performed (CPT) and the diagnostic conditions (ICD-9-CM) treated using a standardized listing of alphanumeric codes.

conditions of participation (COPs) The requirements that health care facilities and organizations must meet to be eligible to receive Medicare payments.

consultation A type of physician evaluation in which one physician requests the opinion and advice of another physician in diagnosing or treating a patient condition. The consulting physician must communicate his or her findings to the requesting or attending physician. CMS has established definitive criteria that define the parameters of a consultation.

contract capitation A per-member, monthly payment to a provider that covers contracted services and is paid in advance of the delivery of the service.

contractual disallowance The amount of a health care provider's charge that exceeds the contracted amount a health insurance plan has agreed to pay (allowance) and that must be contractually adjusted from the patient's financial responsibility.

conversion factor A dollar amount that is multiplied by a measure of relative resource use to determine a payment rate. Conversion factors, such as those used to pay physicians and hospitals (under DRGs and APCs), serve the same purpose as the base payment amounts in other payment systems.

coordination of benefits An insurance policy clause that defines how the plan will reimburse for services when more than one insurance plan is applied to the claim for physician services; the process of adjudicating claims between two or more health insurance plans.

coinsurance A type of cost sharing in which beneficiaries and insurers share liability in a specified ratio for the established payment to a provider for a covered service. For example, Medicare beneficiaries pay coinsurance equal to 20% of the program's physician fee schedule amount for physician's services.

copayment The fixed portion of a physician visit that the patient is responsible for paying to the physician or other provider for each service provided, commonly used in managed care plans. There may be a $5 to $35+ copayment for primary care visits, $10 to $50+ copayment for specialty visits, and a $5 to $35+ copayment for pharmacy, lab, or X-ray procedures. The copayment is a fixed fee per visit; the coinsurance varies with the cost of the procedure and is a percentage.

cost sharing Payments that health insurance enrollees make for covered services. Examples of cost sharing include coinsurance, copayments, deductibles, and premiums.

cost-based reimbursement The method Medicare initially used to pay health care facilities for services furnished to beneficiaries. Payment was based on providers' costs as reported on annual cost reports, which identified incurred costs by type of service, separated allowable costs reasonably related to the provision of patient care from those attributable to unrelated activities, and distinguished costs related to services furnished to Medicare patients from those incurred for others.

coverage The type and range of benefits—services, procedures, medical items, and so on—for which an insurance policy will pay. Coverage varies from payer to payer. It may include surgery or medical treatment of illnesses or injuries, emergency department care, and hospital services.

***Current Procedural Terminology* (CPT®)** A systematic listing and coding of procedures and services performed by physicians. Each procedure or service is identified with a five-digit code.

D

deductible The amount the patient must pay "out of pocket" before insurance reimbursement starts. Usually calculated on an annual basis, the deductible can range from $100 to $5000, depending on the insurance policy.

dependent A covered person's spouse, not legally separated from the insured, and unmarried child(ren) who meet eligibility requirements.

diagnosis The physician's classification of a patient's condition, sign, or symptom. Diagnoses are defined by the *International Classification of Diseases, Ninth Revision, Clinical Modification* (ICD-9-CM) coding system, volumes 1 and 2.

diagnosis-related groups (DRGs) A patient classification system used to identify distinct types of hospital inpatient cases that should be priced separately because they are expected to require different amounts or types of providers' resources. The DRGs are the foundation of Medicare's hospital inpatient prospective payment system. Each DRG is intended to distinguish patients with similar clinical conditions who are treated with common medical or surgical treatment strategies. For example, patients with blocked coronary arteries treated with coronary bypass surgery with cardiac catheterization are distinguished from those who do not have catheterization.

disallowance The amount of a health care provider's charge that exceeds a health insurance plan's maximum allowable payment (allowance) or contracted payment as a percentage of provider-billed amount. Also referred to as *disallowed amount*, *nonallowed amount*, or *contractual disallowance*.

drug formulary A listing of prescription medications that are approved for coverage by a payer. The list is subject to periodic review and modification by the payer.

durable medical equipment (DME) Medical equipment that has a long duration of usefulness. DME is covered under Medicare Part B and includes, but is not limited to, oxygen tents, hospital beds, and wheelchairs used in patients' homes.

E

eligibility Group policy or insurance contract provisions that state the requirements that applicants must satisfy to become insured with respect to themselves or their dependents.

emergency A condition of recent onset and sufficient severity including, but not limited to, severe pain that would lead a prudent layperson, possessing average knowledge of medicine and health, to believe that his or her condition, sickness, or injury is of such a nature that failure to obtain immediate medical care could result in one of the following:

- Placing the member's health in serious jeopardy
- Serious impairment to bodily functions
- Serious dysfunction of any bodily organ or part
- Other serious medical consequences

Such conditions include, but are *not* limited to, chest pain, stroke, poisoning, serious breathing difficulty, unconsciousness, severe burns or cuts, uncontrolled bleeding, or convulsions and other acute conditions.

employer group A group of eligible employees to whom health care benefits are extended through a benefits plan provider. The relationship is formalized through a contract. For the employer group to be recognized, a true employee-employer relationship must exist. Examples of groups that would not qualify include social clubs and independent contractors.

encounter form An itemized billing statement listing CPT and ICD-9-CM codes most often used by physicians to note diagnoses and treatment and related fees.

end-stage renal disease (ESRD) A medical condition in which a person's kidneys have stopped functioning on a permanent basis, leading to the need for long-term dialysis and other medical services. Medicare beneficiaries with ESRD are not allowed to join managed care plans. If a Medicare managed care plan member later develops ESRD, he or she is allowed to stay in the plan.

exclusive provider organization (EPO) A health insurance plan similar to an HMO but in which the member must stay within the provider network in order to receive benefits. EPOs are regulated under insurance statutes, not HMO legislation.

Employee Retirement Income Security Act (ERISA) An act that places regulations on employee benefit plans, including health insurance. One provision requires payers to send the member an explanation of benefits when a claim is denied. ERISA plan regulations supersede state plan regulations.

established patient A patient who has received professional services within the past three years from a physician or another physician of the same specialty (with the same billing number) who belongs to the same group practice.

exclusion A health insurance contract clause that defines conditions or treatments not covered by a health policy. Policy exclusions require practices to make patients aware of their financial responsibility for noncovered services through waiver of liability statements. Also called *exceptions*.

explanation of medical benefits (EOMB) The third-party payer report that explains the coverage and reimbursement determination for a claim or group of claims. Also referred to as an *EOB*.

F

Federal Medicaid Managed Care Waiver Program The process that states use to receive permission to implement managed care programs for their Medicaid or other categorically eligible beneficiaries.

federal qualification A status defined by the Tax Equity and Fiscal Responsibility Act, conferred by CMS after conducting an extensive evaluation of the managed care organization's structure and operations. An organization must be federally qualified or be designated as an HMO or a competitive medical plan to be eligible to participate in Medicare cost and risk contracts. Likewise, a managed care organization must be federally qualified or defined by state plan to participate in the Medicaid managed care program.

fee-for-service (FFS) A billing and reimbursement method in which physicians charge for each medical service or unit provided to a patient.

fee schedule A list of charges or payments coded by procedure. Physicians have internal practice charge fee schedules, while Medicare has a payment fee schedule.

fiscal soundness The requirement that managed care organizations have sufficient operating funds on hand or available in reserve to cover all expenses associated with services for which they have assumed financial risk.

flexible benefit option An option some Medicare managed care plans offer that allows members to select additional benefits with a different payment structure.

formulary A list of selected pharmaceuticals and their appropriate dosages. In some managed care plans, providers are required to prescribe only from the plan's formulary.

G

gatekeeper A primary care physician who serves as the patient's agent and arranges for and coordinates appropriate medical care and other necessary and appropriate referrals.

global period A defined period of time during which all medical services related to a similar condition or diagnosis are included in the payment for the initial surgery or treatment. Medicare sets global surgical periods from 0 to 90 days postoperatively.

graduate medical education The period of medical training that follows graduation from medical school; it is commonly referred to as internship, residency, or fellowship training. Medicare provides payments to hospitals to support its share of the direct costs related to these training programs and to support the higher patient care costs associated with the training of residents.

group health coverage A health benefits plan that covers a group of people as permitted by state and federal law.

group or network model A managed care organization model in which the managed care organization contracts with more than one physician group, and may contract with single and multispecialty groups that work out of their own office facility. The network may or may not provide care exclusively for the managed care organization's members.

H

Healthcare Common Procedure Coding System (HCPCS) A national coding system that provides a uniform method for health care providers to report professional services and supplies.

health insurance claim form The CMS-1500 form is the most commonly used claim form for processing physician service billing. UB-92 forms are used primarily by hospitals. These claim forms are accepted by most insurance plans for processing claims and include demographic patient information, coded clinical information, and charges.

health maintenance organization (HMO) A type of health insurance plan in which the physician is paid a capitated or fixed rate per month per patient enrolled in the practice. HMOs emphasize the provision of quality services while reducing utilization of specialists and increasing control of patient care by primary care gatekeepers.

Health Plan Employer Data and Information Set (HEDIS) A set of standardized measures of health plan performance. HEDIS allows comparisons among plans in terms of quality, access, and patient satisfaction; membership and use; financial information; and management. Employers, HMOs, and NCQA developed HEDIS.

health plan An organization that acts as insurer for an enrolled population.

Health Insurance Portability and Accountability Act (HIPAA) of 1996 An extensive law that provides funding and direction for investigations of fraud, abuse, and waste in the US health care system. HIPAA also mandates policies and protections for confidentiality of electronically transmitted medical information.

home health care Skilled nursing care, physical therapy, speech therapy, occupational therapy, medical social services, or home health aide services provided in Medicare beneficiaries' homes. The first 100 visits following an acute-care hospital stay or a skilled nursing facility stay are covered under Medicare Part A. Subsequent postacute visits and those not preceded by a hospitalization or a stay in a skilled nursing facility are covered under Medicare Part B. There is no beneficiary cost sharing for home health services.

hospice A medical and psychosocial program designed to provide for and relieve the suffering of terminally ill people. Medicare beneficiaries already enrolled in Medicare-certified hospice programs are not allowed to enroll in managed care plans. If a Medicare managed care plan member needs hospice care once enrolled, he or she will be allowed to stay in the plan.

I

indemnity plan A traditional health insurance plan that reimburses the policyholder a defined amount or percentage for expenses from illness or accident through fee for service. The most common indemnity plans pay 80% of total charges, leaving policyholders with a 20% coinsurance.

indirect medical education adjustment An adjustment applied to payments under the prospective payment system for hospitals that operate approved graduate medical education programs. For operating costs, the adjustment is based on the hospital's ratio of interns and residents to the number of beds. For capital costs, it is based on the hospital's ratio of interns and residents to average daily occupancy.

individual practice association (IPA) A type of health maintenance organization that provides services through an association of self-employed physicians or physician groups who provide services in their offices but negotiate contracts as a group of providers.

in-network Term used to describe when a patient sees a provider who has contracted with a managed care provider to participate in the network of physicians and hospitals.

inpatient A person admitted to the hospital as a bed patient for more than a specific number of hours.

instrumental activities of daily living (IADLs) Measures, used in an index or scale, of an individual's degree of independence in aspects of cognitive and social functioning, such as shopping, cooking, doing housework, managing money, and using the telephone. See *activities of daily living*.

insurance claim form A reprinted form filed with a health insurance carrier that details the services provided and other pertinent data to receive benefit (payment).

***International Classification of Diseases, Ninth Revision, Clinical Modification* (ICD-9-CM)** A system for classifying and coding diagnoses and procedures. This system is used to facilitate the collection of uniform and comparable health information. The ICD-9-CM coding system is maintained by the National Center on Vital and Health Statistics and CMS. It differentiates diagnostic conditions and reflects care practiced and is used by hospitals, governments, health insurance plans, and health care providers in the United States.

L

lifetime reserve days A benefit under which, if hospitalized more than 90 days for a single spell of illness, beneficiaries may draw upon a reserve of 60 days, which requires a daily copayment ($476 in 2006). Each lifetime reserve day used is nonrenewable.

limiting charge The maximum amount a nonparticipating physician can charge for services provided to a Medicare patient.

long-term care Services that support, treat, and physically rehabilitate people with functional limitations or chronic conditions who need ongoing health care or assistance with activities of daily living.

M

major teaching hospital A hospital with an approved graduate medical education program and a ratio of interns and residents to beds of 25% or greater.

managed care A controlled method of delivering health care services in the most appropriate and cost-effective way. All care, from managed indemnity to at-risk HMO care, is managed. The lower the premium, the more strictly the plan is managed. Many define this as PPO or HMO care. The purest definition is at-risk capitated care.

managed care organization (MCO) An entity that integrates financing and management with the delivery of health care services to an enrolled population. An MCO provides, offers, or arranges for coverage of designated health services needed by members for a fixed, prepaid amount. There are three basic models of MCOs: group or network model, individual practice association, and staff model.

management services organization (MSO) A management entity owned by a hospital-physician organization or third party. The MSO contracts with payers, hospitals, and physicians to provide services such as negotiating fee schedules, handling administrative functions, billing, and collections.

market basket index A price index designed to measure prices for the typical mix of goods and services providers purchase to produce a specific product or set of products relative to a base year. Generally, these indexes contain three elements: a set of input categories, such as labor, supplies, and purchased services; a set of price proxies representing the price levels for the input categories; and a fixed set of weights (proportions) representing the relative importance of each input category in providers' input expenditures for the base year. The actual or projected values of the price proxies for a year are multiplied by the category weights and summed to obtain the overall market basket index value for the year. The rate of change in input prices can be calculated by comparing index values over time. CMS computes separate market basket indexes for most facilities; it also calculates a similar measure, called the Medicare Economic Index, for physicians' office practices.

Medicaid A federal- and state-funded medical assistance program administered by each state that provides basic health benefits for persons who cannot pay for them or are otherwise indigent.

medical necessity A term of a contract under which payers pay only the cost of covered services considered medically necessary. Payers generally reserve the right to determine whether a service or supply is medically necessary. The fact that a physician has prescribed, ordered, recommended, or approved a service or supply does not, in itself, make it medically necessary and a covered service. A service is generally considered medically necessary if it is:

- Appropriate and consistent with the diagnosis and could not have been omitted without adversely affecting the patient's condition or the quality of medical care rendered
- Compatible with the standards of acceptable medical practice in the United States
- Provided not solely for a member's convenience or the convenience of the physician or hospital
- Not primarily custodial care
- The least costly level of service that can be safely provided; for example, a hospital stay is necessary when treatment cannot be safely provided on an outpatient basis

Medicare A federal health care program for people 65 years old or older and for people with conditions such as ESRD. Coverage includes Part A inpatient hospital and Part B outpatient physician services.

Medicare Part A Also called hospital insurance, the part of the Medicare program that covers the cost of hospital inpatient care and related posthospital services, including some care provided by SNFs and home health agencies. Eligibility is normally based on prior payment of payroll taxes. Beneficiaries are responsible for an initial hospital deductible per spell of illness and for copayments for some services.

Medicare Part B Also called supplementary medical insurance, the part of the Medicare program that covers the cost of physicians' services, outpatient laboratory and X-ray tests, durable medical equipment, outpatient hospital care, some home health care, and certain other services. The voluntary program requires payment of a monthly premium, which covers approximately 25% of program costs, with general tax revenues covering the rest. Beneficiaries are responsible for an annual deductible and coinsurance payments for most covered services.

Medicare carrier A health insurance company that has been awarded a contract to serve as the government's administrative contractor to process and adjudicate claims under the Medicare Part B outpatient health program for beneficiaries in a defined geographic location, usually by state.

Medicare HMO A managed care approach to Medicare. These plans use a limited network of health care providers and require prior approval from a primary care physician. When a person enrolls in a Medicare managed care plan, he or she selects a physician from the plan's list of primary care physicians. This primary care physician is then responsible for coordinating all of the beneficiary's health care needs.

Medicare intermediary A health insurance company that has been awarded a contract to serve as the government's administrative contractor to process and adjudicate claims under the Medicare Part A inpatient health program for beneficiaries in a defined geographic location, usually by state.

Medicare physician fee schedule The resource-based fee schedule Medicare uses to pay for physicians' services.

Medicare risk contract A contract between Medicare and a health plan under which the plan receives monthly capitated payments to provide Medicare-covered services for enrollees and thereby assumes insurance risk for those enrollees.

Medicare+Choice A program created by the Balanced Budget Act of 1997 to replace the methods Medicare previously used to pay HMOs. Beneficiaries have the choice to enroll in a Medicare+Choice plan or to remain in the traditional Medicare program. Medicare+Choice plans may include coordinated care plans (HMOs, PPOs, or plans offered by PSOs), private fee-for-service plans, or high-deductible plans with medical savings accounts.

Medigap insurance Privately purchased individual or group health insurance policies designed to supplement Medicare coverage. Benefits may include payment of Medicare deductibles and coinsurance as well as payment for services not covered by Medicare. Medigap insurance policies must conform to one of 10 federally standardized benefit packages.

modifier A two-digit alpha or numeric code used with procedure codes to provide additional clarification of the circumstances related to the provision of health care services. For example, CPT modifier 51, Multiple surgical procedure, is used with secondary surgical procedure codes to indicate that more than one procedure was performed by the same surgeon on the same day as another procedure.

N

National Committee for Quality Assurance (NCQA) A nonprofit organization that evaluates and accredits managed care plans. It is also responsible for implementing the HEDIS data reporting system, which provides standardized performance measures for managed care plans.

national provider identifier (NPI) Effective May 23, 2005, the NPI will serve as the standard unique health identifier for health care providers. The compliance date for all covered entities is May 23, 2007, except small health plans, which must comply by May 23, 2008. The NPI will be used to identify health care providers in all standard transactions. Legacy identification numbers such as UPIN, Blue Cross Blue Shield numbers, CHAMPUS numbers, or Medicaid numbers will not be permitted.

new patient A patient who has not received any professional services within the past three years from a physician or another physician of the specialty who belongs to the same group practice or uses the same billing number.

nonparticipating provider A physician, hospital, or other medical provider that has not entered into a service agreement with a particular payer to provide benefits upon certain terms including specified rates.

nursing facility (NF) An institution that provides skilled nursing care and rehabilitation services to injured, functionally disabled, or sick persons or regularly provides health-related services to individuals who, because of their mental or physical condition, require care and services that can be made available to them only through institutional facilities. In the past, certification distinctions were made between an SNF and an intermediate care facility (the latter was certified only to furnish less-intensive care to Medicaid recipients). The Omnibus Budget Reconciliation Act of 1987 eliminated that distinction by requiring all nursing facilities to meet SNF certification requirements for Medicare purposes.

O

open enrollment A period during which eligible persons can enroll in a health benefits plan.

other teaching hospital A hospital with an approved graduate medical education program and a ratio of interns and residents to beds of less than 25%.

outliers Cases that substantially differ from the rest of the population of cases. With regard to hospital payment, outliers are identified as cases with extremely high costs compared with the prospective payment rate in the diagnosis-related group. Hospitals receive additional payments for these cases under the PPS.

out-of-pocket expenses Costs borne by the member that are not covered by the health care plan.

outpatient A patient who visits a clinic or hospital to receive medical diagnosis or treatment but does not occupy a hospital bed for a specified minimum stay.

P

Part B premium A monthly premium paid (usually deducted from a person's Social Security check) to cover Part B services in fee-for-service Medicare. Members of Medicare managed care plans must also pay this premium to receive full coverage and be eligible to join and stay in a managed care plan.

participation A contract between a physician and a third-party payer under which the physician agrees to accept assignment on all claims submitted to that payer. Participation contracts are often for a limited period of time, such as a year.

peer review Evaluation of the quality of the total health care provided by plan providers by equivalently trained medical personnel.

peer review organization (PRO) CMS has replaced this term with quality improvement organization (QIO); however, the term PRO is still used in many publications and reference materials. See *quality improvement organization (QIO)*.

per diem reimbursement Reimbursement to an institution based on a fixed-rate-per-day rather than on a charge-by-charge basis. There may be separate categories of per diem, for example, medical, surgical, intensive care unit, each with a different reimbursement.

per member per month (PMPM) The unit of measure related to each effective member for each month the member was effective. The calculation is number of units divided by member months.

physician-hospital organization (PHO) Hospital and medical staff (or an independent practice organization) that provide services to patients and negotiate and obtain managed care contracts.

place of service code A series of standardized codes used by physicians to report the location where the health care services were provided (office, hospital, home, etc).

physician organization (PO) A group of physicians banded together, usually for the purpose of contracting with managed care entities or to represent the physician component in a physician-hospital organization.

point of service (POS) A plan in which members do not have to choose services (HMO vs traditional) until they need them.

preadmission certification A component of a utilization management program that reviews an inpatient hospital stay prospectively to determine coverage.

preauthorization A prospective process to verify coverage of proposed care, to establish covered length of stay, and to set a date for concurrent review.

precertification A method for preapproving all elective hospital admissions, surgeries, and other provider services as required by insurance carriers. Approval is essential before payment for services is received.

preexisting condition A physical condition that existed prior to the issuance of an insurance policy or enrollment in a managed care plan.

preferred provider organization (PPO) A managed care plan that contracts with networks or panels of providers to furnish services and be paid on a negotiated fee schedule. Enrollees are offered a financial incentive to use providers on the preferred list but may use non-network providers as well.

premium The periodic payment (usually monthly) made by a policyholder to an insurance company to subscribe to a health insurance plan.

preventive health care Health care that seeks to prevent the occurrence of conditions by fostering early detection of disease and morbidity and that focuses on keeping patients well in addition to healing them when they are sick.

primary care physician (PCP) The physician who serves as the initial contact between the member and the medical care system. The PCP is usually a physician, selected by the member upon enrollment, who is trained in one of the primary care specialties and who treats and is responsible for coordinating the treatment of members assigned to his or her panel.

primary carrier/payer The insurance carrier that pays benefits first when the patient has more than one insurance plan. The primary carrier is billed first.

principal inpatient diagnosis-diagnostic cost group (PIP-DCGs) A risk adjustment method that is the basis for the interim risk adjustment system for Medicare+Choice payment rates. Beneficiaries' relative health status is measured by means of the principal diagnoses of inpatient hospitalizations. The model is prospective, meaning that payments in a year are based on inpatient hospitalizations during the previous year.

prior authorization number The number assigned by a health insurance plan after the precertification approval process for treatment is completed.

private contracting A physician payment option created by the Balanced Budget Act of 1997. Under private contracts, beneficiaries agree to pay full charges directly to physicians and no bills are submitted to Medicare. Physicians who enter into these contracts cannot submit bills to Medicare for any patient for a period of two years.

productivity A measurement of the quantity of resources used to produce a unit of output. Productivity increases when an organization produces more output with the same resources or the same output with fewer resources.

prospective payment system (PPS) A system under which a provider's payment is based on predetermined rates and is unaffected by its incurred costs or posted charges. Examples of PPSs include the one Medicare uses to pay hospitals for inpatient care and the physician fee schedule.

provider The person or entity providing health care-related services, such as a physician or a hospital.

provider number A UPIN assigned to a health care provider by insurance carriers and the government for accounting and tracking purposes. The NPI will replace the UPIN as the standard unique health identifier for health care providers in 2005.

provider-sponsored organization (PSO) A Medicare+Choice organization that is a public or private entity and is established or organized and operated by a health care provider or group of affiliated health care providers.

Q

Qualified Medicare Beneficiary (QMB) Program A Medicaid program that pays for Medicare premiums, deductibles, and coinsurance for beneficiaries with incomes at or below the federal poverty level. Some beneficiaries may also qualify for full Medicaid benefits under state laws.

Quality Improvement System for Managed Care (QISMC) Health care quality measurement, reporting, and improvement requirements for health plans participating in Medicare+Choice.

quality assurance A process or system designed to identify problems in health care delivery, take action to address the problems, and assess the effectiveness of corrective actions.

quality improvement A process or system designed to improve the processes of delivering health care so as to increase the likelihood of achieving desired outcomes.

quality improvement organization (QIO) Under the direction of CMS, the QIO program consists of a national network of 53 QIOs responsible for each state, territory, and the District of Columbia. QIOs work with consumers, physicians, hospitals, and other caregivers to refine care delivery systems and ensure that patients receive proper care at the right time, particularly among underserved populations. The program also safeguards the integrity of the Medicare trust fund by ensuring payment is made only for medically necessary services and investigates beneficiary complaints about quality of care. QIO was formerly termed peer review organization (PRO).

R

referral The introduction or transfer of a patient's care from one physician to another or to another health care provider.

reimbursement Money paid by a third-party payer for a patient's medical bills.

reinsurance An insurance arrangement whereby the MCO or provider is reimbursed by a third party for costs exceeding a preset limit, usually an annual maximum. This is also called *stop-loss coverage*.

relative weights A value used with product classification systems in payment systems to adjust payment rates to reflect the expected relative costliness of each service or product, compared with the cost of the average service unit. Relative weights may be based on providers' national average charges or costs for cases in each product category. When charge or cost data are unavailable, weights may be based on judgments by clinicians or other experts, as are the relative values for the professional component of the Medicare physician fee schedule.

Resource Utilization Groups, Version III (RUG-III) A system for determining case mix in nursing facilities. The RUG-III system classifies patients on the basis of functional status (as measured by an index of ADLs) and the number and types of services used. Each RUG has a nursing index or weight indicating the average level of resources needed to provide nursing services to patients in the group. Rehabilitation RUGs also have indexes indicating the average levels of resources required to furnish therapy services.

risk adjustment A system of adjusting rates paid to managed care providers to account for differences in beneficiary demographics, such as age, gender, race, ethnicity, medical condition, geographic location, and at-risk populations (for example, homeless).

risk contract A contract payment methodology between CMS and an MCO (HMO or competitive medical plan). This requires the delivery of at least all Medicare-covered services to members, as medically necessary, in return for a fixed monthly payment from the government and sometimes an additional fee paid by the enrollee. The MCO is then liable for those contractually offered services without regard to cost. (Note: Medicaid beneficiaries enrolled in risk contracts are not required to pay premiums.) Risk contracts may occur between any insurer and provider group. The group at risk accepts prepayment and is responsible for all contracted care.

risk score A measure of the expected costliness of a beneficiary with specific characteristics, compared with the cost of caring for the average beneficiary. For example, if the average cost of caring for beneficiaries is represented by a risk score of 1, a beneficiary with a risk score of 1.2 would be expected to cost 20% more than average.

risk selection Any situation in which health plans differ in the average health risk associated with their enrollees because of enrollment choices made by the plans or enrollees. When risk selection occurs, health plans' expected costs differ because of underlying differences in their enrolled populations.

risk sharing A method of providing additional payment amounts for high-cost patients or to offset plan losses, for example, stop-loss policies that provide additional payments once a spending threshold has been reached.

S

secondary carrier/payer The insurance carrier that pays benefits after the primary insurance plan has paid first when a patient has more than one health plan.

skilled nursing facility (SNF) An institution that has a transfer agreement with at least one hospital that provides primarily inpatient skilled nursing care and rehabilitative services and that meets other specific certification requirements.

specialist physician A physician who is certified to practice in a specific field, other than general or family practice, for example, a cardiologist.

Specified Low-Income Medicare Beneficiary (SLMB) Program A Medicaid program that pays the Medicare Part B premium for Medicare beneficiaries with incomes between 100% and 120% of the federal poverty level.

staff model An MCO model that employs physicians to provide health care to its members. All premiums and other revenues accrue to the MCO, which compensates physicians by salary.

standardization A process of adjusting charges or costs for particular services or bundles of services to remove differences that result from geographic variation in price levels, demographic characteristics, beneficiary health risk, and other factors. Standardization is intended to make charges or costs more comparable among providers, plans, and geographic areas.

supplemental insurance Health insurance held by Medicare beneficiaries that covers part or all of the program's cost-sharing requirements and some services not covered by traditional Medicare. Beneficiaries may obtain these policies as a retirement benefit from a former employer or by individual purchase.

T

third-party payer An entity, such as an insurance company, that has agreed via a contract (that is, the insurance policy) to pay for medical care provided to the patient. *Third-party* refers to the involvement of another entity besides the two parties directly involved in medical care: the patient and the physician. The term *third-party payer* is frequently used interchangeably with *insurance company, insurer,* or *payer.*

TRICARE A health care program (formerly known as CHAMPUS) overseen by the Department of Defense in cooperation with regional civilian contractors. TRICARE began in March 1995 in Washington and Oregon and has expanded into all areas of the country. TRICARE provides three options to eligible beneficiaries: TRICARE Prime, similar to a health maintenance organization; TRICARE Extra, a preferred provider option that saves money for patients; and TRICARE Standard, a fee-for-service option, which is the same as the former CHAMPUS.

type of service code (TOS) A code to be entered in block 24C of the CMS-1500 form that defines the type of service provided (ie, medical care, surgery, etc).

U

UCR payment An abbreviation for *usual, customary, and reasonable payment,* an amount paid by a health plan based on a combination of the physician's usual fee, the customary fee charged by physicians in a specific locality, and the reasonable fee for the service.

uncompensated care Care provided by hospitals or other providers that is not paid for directly (by the patient or by a government or private insurance program). It includes charity care, which is furnished without the expectation of payment, and bad debts, for which the provider has made an unsuccessful effort to collect payment due.

unique physician identification number (UPIN) A number used by Medicare for accounting and tracking physician services. The UPIN was replaced by an NPI in 2005.

update A periodic adjustment (usually annual) designed to raise or lower a base payment amount to account for the effects of anticipated changes in factors that affect the costs that efficient providers would be expected to incur in providing care.

utilization management A process that measures the use of available resources to determine medical necessity, cost-effectiveness, and conformity to criteria for optimal use.

utilization review The process of examining health care services to measure medical necessity, quality of patient care, and the appropriateness of care to identify overuse or ineffective outcomes.

W

wellness programs A broad range of employer-sponsored facilities and activities designed to promote safety and good health among employees. Its purpose is to reduce the costs of accidents, sickness, absenteeism, lower productivity, and health care costs.

withhold incentive The percentage of payment held back by the insurer for a "risk account" in managed care HMO plans to cover unforeseen expenses. Withhold arrangements are used as an incentive for physicians to manage their utilization of higher-priced diagnostics and treatments with the potential for sharing profits (or losses).

INDEX

A

Abuse, E codes, 168
Accidental injury
   Blue Cross Blue Shield basic option benefits, *46*
   Blue Cross Blue Shield standard option benefits, *43*
Accounting controls, IBNR (incurred but not reported), 7
Accounts receivable, 237–238, 275–294
   process overview, *291*
Accreditation, definition of term, 409
Activities of daily living, 181, 409
Adjudicate, definition of term, 409
Adjusted average per capita cost, definition of term, 409
Adjustments to payment rates, definition of term, 409
ADLs, *See* Activities of daily living
Administrative law judges, 302
Adverse effects, E codes, 167–168
Air ambulances, 198
Alabama data, information, *See* State-by-state listings
Alaska data, information, *See* State-by-state listings
Allowable, definition of term, 409
AMA/Specialty Society RVS Update Committee, *See* RUC
Ambulance services, xi, 197–201
   fee schedule, *200, 201*
Ambulatory care, *See also* Physician services;
   Blue Cross Blue Shield basic option benefits, *45*
   Blue Cross Blue Shield standard option benefits, *43*
   Medicare deductibles and copayment, 61
   Medicare home health coverage, 196
Ambulatory payment classifications, definition of term, 409
Ambulatory surgery centers, *149–150*
American Medical Association
   electronic data interchange policies, 125–129
   Medicare payment cuts, 6
American Samoa, 172, 407
Ancillary, definition of term, 409
Ancillary services, xi, 171–207
   ambulances, 197–201
   dietary and nutritional services, 205–207
   durable medical equipment, 171–180, *172, 173–176*
   home health care, 190–196
   hospice care, 201–204
   nursing homes, long-term care, 180–190
Anesthesia
   CPT codes, 132
   CPT physical status modifiers, *149*
Anthrax, coding, 170, *170*
Appeals, 295–304
   definition of term, 409
   process, *288–289*
   sample letter requesting review, *296*
   statistics, *290–291*
Appointments, *See* Office operations
Arizona data, information, *See* State-by-state listings
Arkansas data, information, *See* State-by-state listings
Assignment, definition of term, 409

B

Bad debts, 260–266
Balance bill, definition of term, 409
Base payment amount, definition of term, 409
BCBS, *See* Blue Cross and Blue Shield plans
Beneficiary, definition of term, 409
Beneficiary appeal, definition of term, 409
Benefits, *See also* Insurance benefits; definition of term, 409
Benefits package, definition of term, 409
Billing, *See also* Claim preparation; errors, xi
   software, 121–122
   software, comparison of ICD-9-CM and CPT codes, inconsistencies, 153
   Web sites, 345–346
Biologicals, Medicare home health services not covered, 196
Blood transfusion, Medicare deductibles, 74–76, *76*
Blue Card Program, 46
Blue Cross and Blue Shield plans, 39–54
   accounts, 40–41
   basic option benefits, *44–46*
   Blue Card account, 46
   business accounts, 40
   customer service contacts, overseas and state information, *47–54*
   Federal Employee Program (FEP) 41, 46
   identification card, *40*
   local accounts, 40
   national accounts, 41
   PPO standard option benefits, *41–44*
   standard option benefits, *41–44*
   traditional insurance option, 54
Board certified, definition of term, 409
Boarded, definition of term, 409
Bone marrow measurement
   services covered under Medicare Part B, *58*
   services not covered under Medicare Part B, *57*
Breast examinations
   services covered under Medicare Part B, *58*
   services not covered under Medicare Part B, *57*
Bundling, definition of term, 410

C

California data, information, *See* State-by-state listings
Cancer, ICD-9-CM neoplasm table, 156
Cap rate, definition of term, 410
Capitation
   CPT codes, 169
   definition of term, 410
   description of, 7
Cardiovascular screening tests, services not covered under Medicare Part B, *57*
Case management, definition of term, 410
Case mix, definition of term, 410
Case-mix index, definition of term, 410
Catastrophic protection, Blue Cross Blue Shield standard option benefits, *44*
Centers for Medicare & Medicaid Services (CMS), 57
   coding guidelines, 135–144
   definition of term, 410
   observation services coding, 161–165
Certificate of coverage, definition of term, 410
CHAMPUS
   claim form, *91–94*
   definition of, 410
CHAMPVA (Civilian Health and Medical Program of the Department of Veterans Affairs), 104–106
   definition of, 410
   identification card, *105*
Charge tickets, *See* Encounter forms
Chemicals, ICD-9-CM table, 156
Child abuse, E codes, 168
Chiropractic care
   Blue Cross Blue Shield basic option benefits, *46*
   Blue Cross Blue Shield standard option benefits, *42*
Claim coding systems, *See* Claims coding systems
Claim, definition of term, 410
Claim filing, 237–238
Claim forms, 238–255, 413
   CHAMPUS, *91–94*
   CMS-1500 (universal claim form), 3, 238, 243–255
   copies of, 258
   UB-04 (uniform bill), 238–243
Claim preparation, 213–260
   CMS-1500 (universal claim form), 243–255
   patient information, 213
   UB-04 (uniform bill), 238–243
Claim processing, *See* Claims processing
Claims
   clean, state-by-state definitions, 12–18
   delays and denials, 18
   electronic, 8, 18–19, 115–130
   paper, 8–18
   paper, National Provider Identifier, *212*
   pended or delayed, 119–120, *120*

Claims coding systems, 131–170
  compliance programs, coding and billing, benchmarking, 314–316, *314–315*
  CPT, 132–151
  E codes, 165–169
  HCPCS procedure coding, 151, *152*
  HIPAA transactions and code sets, 335–340
  ICD-9-CM, 153–161
  observation services, 161–165
  V codes, 165, *166*
Claims processing, 8–19, 209–266; *See also* Claims processing, electronic; Medicare reimbursement; Payers; Reimbursement;
  actions following claim submission, 267–273
  appeals, *288–291*
  appeals and review, 295–304
  automatic adjudication, 119, *120*
  billing cycles, 255–256, 258
  clean claims, 12–18
  CMS-1500 form, *9–10*
  costs, 121, *121*
  delays and denials, 18
  error rates by category, *306, 307*
  filing explanation of benefits, 272–273
  fractional payment of allowed charges, 272
  HIPAA transactions, 337–339
  insurance claim forms, 238–255
  Medicaid claim submission, 83–84
  office operations and claim preparation, 213–260
  paper claims, 12–18
  paper vs. electronic, 118, *118*
  preposting actions, 270
  primary claims, 255–256
  sample encounter form (superbill), *11*
  sample letters, claim inquiries, *292–294*
  secondary claims, 256, 258
  telephone follow-up, 279–280
  tracer claims, 280
  unpaid claims follow-up, *277–279, 278–280*
  withhold adjustments, 272
Claims processing, electronic, 18–19, 115–130
  AMA electronic data interchange policies, 125–129
  automatic adjudication, 119, *120*
  costs, 121, *121*
  medical billing software, 121–122
  medical records privacy, 124
  paper vs., 118, *118*
  pre-claim submission operations, 123–124
  Provider Ownership Chain and Ownership System (PECOS), 129–130
  time to complete, 117–119, *117–119*
Classification system, definition of term, 410
Clearinghouses, national clearinghouse for health care claims, 126–127
Clinical Laboratory Improvement Act, definition of term, 410
CMS, *See* Centers for Medicare & Medicaid Services
CMS-1450, 238
CMS-1500 form, *9–10*, 238, 243–255
  AMA electronic data interchange policies, 128
  description of fields and instructions on completion, 244–255
Code on Dental Procedures and Nomenclature, HIPAA code sets, 337

Coding
  definition of term, 410
  Web sites, 345–346
Coding systems, *See* Claims coding systems
Coinsurance, 3, 267
  definition of term, 410
  TRICARE, 98, *99*, 100
Collection agencies, 261
Collection policies, 260–266, *262–263*
Colorado data, information, *See* State-by-state listings
Colorectal screening tests
  services covered under Medicare Part B, *58*
  services not covered under Medicare Part B, *57*
Compliance officers, 312, 313
Compliance programs, 305–320
  basic elements, 310–316
  coding and billing, 314–316, *314–315*
  internal control checklist, *319*
  Internet resources, Web sites, 346–347
  OIG guidance for individual and small group physician practices, 355–374
  OIG model program, 309
Complications, E codes, 169
Computerized claim processing, *See* Claims processing, electronic
Conditions of participation, definition of term, 410
Confidentiality
  HIPAA privacy rule, 323–330, 333
  medical records, 124
  patient registration confidentiality, 223–225, *224*
  privacy official, *326*
Connecticut data, information, *See* State-by-state listings
Consultation, definition of term, 410
Contract capitation, definition of term, 410
Contractual disallowance, definition of term, 410
Conversion factor, definition of term, 410
Coordination of benefits, definition of term, 410
Coordination of care, medical records, E/M documentation, 142
Copayment, 3
  definition of term, 410
  Medicare outpatient, 61
Cost-based reimbursement, definition of term, 410
Cost sharing, definition of term, 410
Costs, *See also* Expenditures;
  claims processing, 121, *121*
  Medicaid, 78, 80
  out-of-pocket, 4, 414
Counseling, medical records, E/M documentation, 142
Coverage, definition of term, 411
Covered entities, 322, 323, 332
Covered transactions, 322
CPT coding system, 132–151
  anesthesia codes, 132
  capitation, 169
  Category II and III codes, 133
  CMS coding guidelines, 135–144
  comprehensive, component and mutually exclusive codes, *137*

  definition of, 411
  E/M service codes, 132, 136–137, 138–144
  evaluation and management guidelines, 138–144
  evaluation codes, established patients, *143*, 144
  evaluation codes for new patients, *142*, 145
  format, 134
  HCPCS and, 151
  HIPAA code sets, 337
  index, 135
  level of care, 139
  medical nutrition therapy, 206
  medical service codes, 133
  modifiers, 146, 151, *147–150*
  National Correct Coding Initiative, 135–136
  1995, 1997 and draft E/M documentation compared, *143*
  notes, 135
  observation services and E/M codes, 162, 164
  pathology and laboratory medicine codes, 133
  radiology codes, 133
  selecting E/M services code, 144–145
  selecting procedure code, 144
  surgery codes, 133
  surgery coding, 145–146
  surgical package rules, 145–146
  symbols, 134–135
  translation of clinical and treatment information to appropriate codes, 236–237
Current Procedural Terminology, *See* CPT coding system

D

Decision making, medical records, E/M documentation, 141–142, *141*
Deductibles, 3
  definition of term, 411
  letters, 258, *260*
  Medicare outpatient, 61
  TRICARE, 98, *99*, 100
Defense Department, US, *See* Military personnel
Delaware data, information, *See* State-by-state listings
Dental care
  HIPAA code sets, 337
  national expenditure estimates and projections, *30*
Department of Health and Human Services, *See* Health and Human Services Department, US
Departmental Appeals Board, 302
Dependent, definition of term, 411
DHHS, *See* Health and Human Services Department, US
Diabetes outpatient self-management training, 205
Diabetes screening tests, services not covered under Medicare Part B, *57*
Diabetes self-management
  services covered under Medicare Part B, *58*
  services not covered under Medicare Part B, *57*
Diagnosis, definition of term, 411
Diagnosis-related groups, definition of term, 411

Dialysis, Medicare coverage, 69–71, *71*
Dietary services, xi, 205–207, *206, 207*
Diplomate, definition of term, 409
Disabilities
    Medicare coverage, 55–56
    workers' compensation, 112–113
Disallowance, definition of term, 411
Disaster recovery, 330
District of Columbia
    Blue Cross Blue Shield customer service contacts, *48*
    clean claim definitions, 13–14
    durable medical equipment regional carriers, *172*
    federal Medicaid assistance percentage, *79*
    Medicaid managed care enrollment, *87*
    Medicare EDI helplines, 405, 406
    TRICARE regions, 88
Documentation, general principles, 137–138
Drug formulary, definition of term, 411
Drugs
    Blue Cross Blue Shield basic option benefits, *45*
    Blue Cross Blue Shield standard option benefits, *42*
    HIPAA code sets, 337
    ICD-9-CM table, 156
    Medicare home health services not covered, 196
    Medicare prescription drug program, 375–381
    national expenditure estimates and projections, *33*
    OIG Medicare projects, *318*
Durable medical equipment, xi, 171–180, *172, 173–176*
    certificate of medical necessity, 178–179, *178–179*
    customized items, 177
    definition of term, 411
    disposal, and change in patient's status, 180
    Medicare coverage and noncoverage, *173–176*
    Medicare home health coverage, 196
    national expenditure estimates and projections, *37*
    OIG Medicare projects, *317*
    patient home use, 177
    regional carriers, *172*
    rental items, 177
    repairs, maintenance, replacement, delivery, 179–180
    supplies and accessories, 180

E

E codes, 165–169
E/M service codes, *See* Evaluation and management services (CPT coding system)
Electronic claims, *See* Claims
Electronic claims processing, *See* Claims processing, electronic
Electronic data interchange
    advantages, 116, *116*
    AMA policies, 125–129
    HIPAA, 322
    HIPAA regulations, 124–125

HIPAA transactions and code sets, 335–340
    medical billing software, 121–122
    medical practice installation, 121–125
    Medicare state helplines, 405–407
    shortcomings, 122–123
Eligibility, definition of term, 411
Emergency, definition of term, 411
Emergency medical technicians, 197
Employee Retirement Income Security Act, 111–112, 411
Employer group, definition of term, 411
Employer information, 218, *219*
Employer self-funded (ERISA) insurance plans, 111–112
Encounter form (superbill), *11*, 236–237, 411
End-stage renal disease
    definition of term, 411
    Medicare benefits, 69–71
Episode of care, 194
Equipment, durable medical, *See* Durable medical equipment
ERISA, *See* Employee Retirement Income Security Act
Established patient, definition of term, 411
Ethics, medical, Web sites, 348–349
Evaluation and management services (CPT coding system), 132, 136–137, 138–144
    1995, 1997 and draft E/M documentation compared, *143*
    observation services and, 162, 164
    selecting the E/M services code, 144
Evaluation services, Medicare home health services not covered, 196
Exclusion, definition of term, 411
Exclusive provider organization, definition of term, 411
Expenditures xi; *See also* Costs;
    estimates and projections, 21, *22–37*
    growth in spending, xi
    home health care, *191*
    national, xi
    per person, 21
    post-acute care, *182*
Explanation of medical benefits, *See also* Insurance benefits;
    definition of term, 411

F

Fair Credit Reporting Act, 264–266
Federal Employee Program, Blue Cross/Blue Shield account, 41, 46
Federal Medicaid Managed Care Waiver Program, definition of term, 411
Federal qualification, definition of term, 411–412
Federal Register, OIG compliance program for individual and small group physician practices, 355–374
Fee-for-service, definition of term, 412
Fee-for-service insurance, *See* Insurance, indemnity
Fee schedule, definition of term, 412
Fee schedule, Medicare, *See* Medicare reimbursement
Fees, usual, customary and reasonable reimbursement, 4–5

FEP, *See* Federal Employee Program
Fiscal soundness, definition of term, 412
Flexible benefit options, definition of term, 412
Florida data, information, *See* State-by-state listings
Formulary, definition of term, 412
Fraud, *See also* Compliance programs;
    OIG compliance program for individual and small group physician practices, 355–374
    qui tam lawsuits, 305–306, *308*

G

"Gatekeepers," 4
    definition of term, 412
Geographic practice cost index, *See* GPCI
Georgia data, information, *See* State-by-state listings
Glaucoma screening, services not covered under Medicare Part B, *57*
Global period, definition of term, 412
Global surgical period, 164
Glossary, 409–417
Government agencies, Web sites, 347–348
GPCI (geographic practice cost index), 5–6
    Medicare reimbursement, 57
Graduate medical education, definition of term, 412
Group health coverage, definition of term, 412
Group model, definition of term, 412
Group practice, Medicare definition, 210
Guam, 172, 407

H

Hawaii data, information, *See* State-by-state listings
HCPCS
    ambulance services, *197*
    CPT and, 151
    definition of term, 412
    HIPAA code sets, 337
    hospice care, *204*
    medical nutrition therapy, *206*
    procedure coding, 151, *152*
    translation of clinical and treatment information to appropriate codes, 236–237
Health and Human Services Department, US, 305
    OIG compliance program for individual and small group physician practices, 355–374
Health care expenditures, *See* Expenditures
Health care reform, state demonstrations, *84*
Health insurance, *See* Insurance
Health insurance claim form, definition of term, 412
Health Insurance Portability and Accountability Act (HIPAA), 124–125, 305, 321–343
    covered entities, 322, 323, 332
    covered transactions, 322
    definition of term, 412
    electronic data interchange, 322
    minimum necessary (need to know) 326
    National Provider Identifier standards, 340–341
    notice of privacy practices, 326–327

Health Insurance Portability and Accountability Act (HIPAA) (*continued*)
  privacy administrative tasks and how to do them, *328–329*
  privacy official, *326*
  privacy rule, 323–330, 333
  protected health information, 323–326
  safeguards, 327, *329*
  security rule, 330–335
  security safeguards, *334–335*
  standards, 322–323, *323*
  transactions, 322
  transactions and code sets, 335–340
Health maintenance organizations, 3, 107–109
  captive group model, 108
  "closed panel," 107
  definition of term, 412
  enrollment data, *109, 110*
  group model, 107–108, *109*
  independent group model, 108
  independent practice association model, 3, 108, *109*
  Medicare enrollment data, *110*
  network (direct contract) model, 108, *109*
  staff model, 3, 107, *109*
Health plan, definition of term, 412
Health Plan Employer Data and Information Set (HEDIS), definition of term, 412
Health practitioner, National Provider Identifier, 210
Healthcare Common Procedure Coding System, *See* HCPCS
HIPAA, *See* Health Insurance Portability and Accountability Act (HIPAA)
History-taking, *See* Medical records
HMOs, *See* Health maintenance organizations
Home health agencies, number of, *181*
Home health aides, 195
Home health care, xi, 181, 190–196
  changes with prospective payment system, 192, *193*
  definition of term, 412
  dialysis, *71*
  durable medical equipment, 177
  Medicare coverage, 194–196
  Medicare utilization data, *191*
  national expenditure estimates and projections, *32*
  OIG Medicare projects, *317*
  oxygen services, 177, 180
  services not covered by Medicare, 196
  spending, *191*
Home health spell illness, 194
Hospice, definition of term, 412
Hospice care, xi, 201–204
  finding Medicare-approved programs, 204
  OIG Medicare projects, *317*
Hospital care
  Blue Cross Blue Shield basic option benefits, *45*
  Blue Cross Blue Shield standard option benefits, *43*
  CPT modifiers for ambulatory surgery centers, outpatients, *149–150*
  long-term care, number of, *181*
  Medicare inpatient benefit days, *73*, 74

Medicare lifetime reserve days, *73, 74, 75*
Medicare Part A, 55–56
Medicare prior hospitalization requirement for skilled care, 185–186
national expenditure estimates and projections, *28*
observation services coding system, 161–165
OIG Medicare projects, *317*
outpatient services, HCPCS codes, *152*
rural, swing-bed facilities, 187
Hospital Insurance for the Aged and Disabled (Medicare Part A), 55–56
Hypertension, ICD-9-CM tables, 155–156

I

IADLs, *See* Instrumental activities of daily living
ICD-9-CM, 153–161
  definition of term, 413
  fourth- and fifth-digit codes, 157
  general coding guidelines, 156
  HIPAA code sets, 336–337
  medical necessity codes, 156–157
  NEC (not elsewhere classified) abbreviation, 154
  NOS (not otherwise specified, *eg,* unspecified), 154
  notes, 155
  symbols, abbreviations, notations, 153–154
  symptoms, signs, ill-defined conditions, 157–158
  tables, 155–156
  terrorism codes, 158, *159*
  translation of clinical and treatment information to appropriate codes, 236–237
ICD-10-CM, 158, 160–161, *160*
Idaho data, information, *See* State-by-state listings
Illinois data, information, *See* State-by-state listings
In-network, definition of term, 412
Indemnity insurance, *See* Insurance, indemnity
Indemnity plan, definition of term, 412
Independent practice associations, 3, 108
Indiana data, information, *See* State-by-state listings
Indirect medical education adjustment, definition of term, 412
Individual practice association, definition of term, 412
Informational software, 122
Injury, accidental
  Blue Cross Blue Shield basic option benefits, *46*
  Blue Cross Blue Shield standard option benefits, *43*
Injury coding, E codes, 165–166
Inpatient, definition of term, 412
Instrumental activities of daily living, 181
  definition of term, 413
Insurance, 1–19
  basic concepts, 1–19
  coinsurance, 3, 267, 410
  definition of term, 410
  copayments, 3, 61, 410

deductibles, 3, 61, 258, *260*, 411
employer self-funded (ERISA) plans, 111–112
fact sheet, 228, *231*
group, 2
individual, 2
point-of-service plans, 111
primary and secondary, 38–39
sources of payments to health care providers, *2*
statistics on uninsured Americans, xi
TRICARE coinsurance, deductibles, 98, *99*, 100
types of, 2–4
Insurance, automobile
  Medicare relationship to other insurance programs, 64
  primary and secondary insurers, 39
Insurance benefits
  assignment of benefits and payment to provider form, 225, *226*
  Blue Cross Blue Shield basic option, *44–46*
  Blue Cross Blue Shield standard option, *41–44*
  catastrophic care, *44, 46*
  coordination of, 38
  explanation of benefits (EOB), 256, *257*
  filing explanation of benefits, 272–273
  Medicaid coordination of benefits, 83
  primary and secondary coverage, 38
  TRICARE, 98, *99*, 100, 101, *102–104*
  TRICARE explanation of benefits (example), *271*
Insurance carriers, *See* Payers
Insurance claim form, definition of term, 413
Insurance claims, *See* Claim forms; Claim preparation; Claims; Claims processing
Insurance coverage
  advanced notice service waiver, *235*
  catastrophic care, *44, 46*
  primary and secondary, 38–39
  statistics, 1
  uninsured, sources of payments to health care providers, *2*
  verification, 217–223, *220*
Insurance, indemnity, 2–3
  "nondisclosed" payment allowance, 38
  usual, customary and reasonable reimbursement, 4–5
Insurance, liability, 5
Insurance payments, *See* Reimbursement
Insurance reimbursement, *See* Reimbursement
Interactive software, 122
Interest rates (time value of money), 276
International Classification of Diseases, *See* ICD-9-CM; ICD-10-CM
Internet resources, 345–354
  coding and billing Web sites, 345–346
  compliance program education and training, 312
  compliance-related Web sites, 346–347
  government agencies and Web sites, 347–348
  medical ethics Web sites, 348–349
  professional association and related Web sites, 349–352
  state medical board Web sites, 352–354

Iowa data, information, *See* State-by-state listings
IPAs, *See* Independent practice associations

K

Kansas data, information, *See* State-by-state listings
Kentucky data, information, *See* State-by-state listings
Kidney diseases Medicare benefits for end-stage renal disease, 69–71

L

Laboratory medicine
　CPT codes, 133
　OIG Medicare projects, *318*
Language pathology services, Medicare home health coverage, 195
Late effects, E codes, 168–169
Legislation
　Employee Retirement Income Security Act, 111–112
　Fair Credit Reporting Act, 264–266
　Health Insurance Portability and Accountability Act (HIPAA), 124–125, 305, 321–343
　Medicare Modernization Act of 2003, 375–381
　Medicare secondary payer guide, 383–395
　Personal Responsibility and Work Opportunity Reconciliation Act, 81
　prompt payment laws, 280, *280–287*, 288
Life support, ambulance services, 197–198
Lifetime reserve days, definition of term, 413
Limiting charge, definition of term, 413
Long-term care
　definition of term, 413
　description of, 181
　facilities, description of, 181
　hospitals, number of, *181*
　nursing home alternatives, 188–190
Louisiana data, information, *See* State-by-state listings

M

Maine data, information, *See* State-by-state listings
Major teaching hospital, definition of term, 413
Mammography screening
　services covered under Medicare Part B, *58*
　services not covered under Medicare Part B, *57*
Managed care, definition of term, 413
Managed care organizations, 3–4; *See also* Health maintenance organizations; Independent practice associations; Preferred provider organizations;
　capitated rates, 7
　contracted rates, 7
　definition of term, 413
　Medicaid, 84, *85, 86, 87–88*
　Medicare Advantage, 64–68, *65, 66, 67*
　OIG Medicare projects, *318*
　point-of-service plans, 111
　withhold adjustments, 272

Management services organization, definition of term, 413
Market basket index, definition of term, 413
Maryland data, information, *See* State-by-state listings
Massachusetts data, information, *See* State-by-state listings
Maternity care
　Blue Cross Blue Shield basic option benefits, *45*
　Blue Cross Blue Shield standard option benefits, *42*
McGraw-Hill Relative Values for Physicians, *See* RVP
Medicaid, 77–86, *87–88*
　claim submission, 83–84
　coordination of benefits, 83
　cost data, 78, 80
　coverage, scope of services, 82
　definition of term, 413
　eligibility, 77, 80–81
　federal assistance percentage by state, *79*
　home health coverage, 196
　managed care enrollment, state-by-state data, *87–88*
　managed care organizations, 84, *85, 86, 87–88*
　Medicare relationship to, 64, 84–86
　nursing home care, 188
　other insurance plans and, 83, 84–86
　Personal Responsibility and Work Opportunity Reconciliation Act, 81
　physician application and participation, 83
　primary and secondary coverage, 38
　sources of payments to health care providers, *2*
Medical billing, *See* Billing; Claim preparation; Claims processing; Claims processing, electronic
Medical equipment, durable, *See* Durable medical equipment
Medical ethics, Web sites, 348–349
Medical necessity, certificate of, *See* Durable medical equipment
Medical necessity codes, *See* ICD-9-CM
Medical necessity, definition of term, 413
Medical nutrition therapy, 205
Medical office staff, *See* Office staff
Medical products, national expenditure estimates and projections, *34*
Medical records
　coordination of care, 142
　counseling, 142
　decision-making, 141–142, *141*
　documentation principles, 137–138
　history-taking, 138, 139–140
　1995, 1997 and draft E/M documentation compared, *143*
　presenting illness, 138, 139, 142–143
　privacy and electronic claims processing, 124
　review of systems, 139–140
Medical services, *See* Physician services
Medical social services, Medicare home health coverage, 195
Medicare, 54–77; *See also* subheadings beginning with Medicare, *below*;
　Administrative law judges, 302
　advanced notice service waiver, *234*

Advantage, 64–68, *65, 66, 67*
advantages, disadvantages of participation, 59–60
claim assignment, 62
claim submission policies, 63
clean claims described, 12
CMS-1500 form only, for paper claims, 8, *9–10*
contractors, OIG projects, *319*
conversion factors, 6, *6*
coordination of benefits contractor, 403
costs per day, skilled nursing facilities, *184*
definition, description of, 413
electronic claims processing, 115–116
federal government's role, *72*
GPCI (geographic practice cost index), 5–6
group practice definition, 210
health insurance claim number suffixes, *63*
HMOs, 414
HMO enrollment data, *110*
home health care utilization, *191*
identification card, 62, *62, 63*
intermediary, 414
managed care, OIG projects, *318–319*
Medicaid relationship to, 84–86
Medical Savings Account, 65
Modernization Act of 2003, 375–381
nonparticipating physicians, 230
OIG projects, *316–319*
Part A, 55–56, 413
Part A EDI helplines, 406–407
Part B, 56–77, 414
Part B DMERC EDI helplines, 406
Part B EDI helplines, 405–406
Part D, OIG projects, *318*
participation, 59–60
patient charges, 62
physician fee schedule, 414
physicians defined, 56–58
prescription drug program, 375–381
primary and secondary coverage, 38
primary insurance claim, non-Medicare, 64
Program of All-Inclusive Care for the Elderly, 188, 189
required forms, 230
risk contract, 414
secondary claim filing, 64
secondary payers, recoveries and debt-related issues, 397–403
SELECT, 69
skilled nursing facility spending, 182, *183*
social managed care plans, 190
sources of payments to health care providers, *2*
state EDI helplines, 405–407
supplemental insurance policy letters, 258, *259*
TRICARE relationship to, 101–104
voluntary data sharing agreement, 403
Medicare Advantage, 64–68, *65, 66, 67*
Medicare benefits
　coordination (Medicare as secondary payer), 61–62
　coordination of benefits contractor, 403
　end-stage renal disease, 69–71
　explanation of benefits, 269
　filing explanation of benefits, 272–273

Medicare benefits *(continued)*
    hospice care, 202–203
    lifetime reserve days, *73*, 74, *75*
    prior hospitalization requirement for skilled care, 185–186
    secondary payer guide, 383–395
    skilled care, 184–185
Medicare billing, *See* Medicare reimbursement
Medicare carrier, definition of term, 413–414
Medicare+Choice, definition of term, 414
Medicare coverage
    durable medical equipment, covered and noncovered, *173–176*
    end-stage renal disease, 69–71
    home health care, 194–196
    managed care plan coverage of home health care, 196
    preventive services covered under Part B, *58*
    prior hospitalization requirement for skilled care, 185–186
    services not covered under Part B, *57*
    skilled care, 184–185
    supplemental insurance (Medigap), 68
Medicare Modernization Act of 2003, 375–381
Medicare+Choice, definition of term, 414
Medicare reimbursement, *See also* GPCI; Medicare benefits; Medicare coverage;
    ambulance services, 197–198
    appeal rights, Parts A and B, 297–303, *298–300*
    bill types, *77*
    billing procedures, 71–77
    blood transfusion deductibles, 74–76, *76*
    claim submission policies, 63–64
    coinsurance, *73*
    common working file, 72–77
    compliance issues concerning billing, 68
    conversion factors, 6, *6*
    Departmental Appeals Board, 302
    durable medical equipment, covered and noncovered, *173–176*
    electronic claims processing, 115–116
    examples of, 268–270
    fractional payment of allowed charges, 272
    GPCI, 57
    hospice care, *202*, 203–204, *204*
    hospital inpatient benefit days, *73*, 74
    ICD-9-CM use, 153
    lifetime reserve days, *73*, 74, *75*
    long-term care, nursing homes, 180–190
    National Provider Identifier requirement, *211–212*
    observation services coding system, 161–165
    payment cuts, 6
    physician fee schedule, 57–59, 414
    physician fee schedule updates, 6
    primary insurance claim, non-Medicare, 64
    prospective payment system and changes to home health care, 192, *193*
    RBRVS, 5–6, 57
    RVU updates, 6
    secondary claim filing, 64
    secondary payer guide, 383–395
    secondary payers, recoveries and debt-related issues, 397–403
    SNF care, *188*
Medicare SELECT, 69

Medigap insurance, 68, 414
Mental health, Blue Cross Blue Shield standard option benefits, *43–44*
Michigan data, information, *See* State-by-state listings
Military personnel
    Medicaid nonavailability statement, 78
    sources of payments to health care providers, 2
    TRICARE, 86–104
Minnesota data, information, *See* State-by-state listings
Misadventures, E codes, 169
Mississippi data, information, *See* State-by-state listings
Missouri data, information, *See* State-by-state listings
Modifier, definition of term, 414
Montana data, information, *See* State-by-state listings
Multiple causes, E codes, 168

N

National Center for Health Statistics, terrorism statistics, 158
National Committee for Quality Assurance, 414
National Correct Coding Initiative, 135–136
National Drug Codes, HIPAA code sets, 337
National Provider Identifier, 210–212
    definition of term, 414
    HIPAA standards, 340–341
National Uniform Claim Committee, 128
Nebraska data, information, *See* State-by-state listings
Needy family assistance, *See* Temporary Assistance for Needy Families
Neoplasms, *See* Cancer
Network model, definition of term, 412
Nevada data, information, *See* State-by-state listings
New Hampshire data, information, *See* State-by-state listings
New Jersey data, information, *See* State-by-state listings
New Mexico data, information, *See* State-by-state listings
New patient, definition of term, 414
New York data, information, *See* State-by-state listings
Niski, Michelle, xiv
Nonparticipating provider, definition of term, 414
North Carolina data, information, *See* State-by-state listings
North Dakota data, information, *See* State-by-state listings
Northern Mariana Islands, 172, 407
NPI, *See* National Provider Identifier
Nursing care, *See* Skilled care; Skilled nursing facilities
Nursing facility, definition of term, 414
Nursing homes, 180–190; *See also* Skilled nursing facilities
    alternatives to, 188–190
    national expenditure estimates and projections, *35*
    OIG Medicare projects, *317*
Nutritional services, 205–207, *206, 207*

O

Observation services
    coding system, 161–165
    CPT E/M codes and, 162, 164
Occupational therapy, Medicare home health coverage, 195
Office manager, *214*
Office of Inspector General
    compliance programs, 305–320
    Medicare projects, *316–319*
Office operations
    accounts receivable management, reports, 275–294
    actions following claim submission, 267–273
    appointments and preregistration, 213–217
    assignment of benefits and payment to provider form, 225, *226*
    authorization for release of medical-related information, 226, *227*
    bad debts, collection policies, 260–266
    capturing all billable services, 236–238
    claim appeals and review, 295–304
    claim preparation, 213–260
    CMS-1500 (universal claim form), 243–255
    compliance programs, 310–320
    disaster recovery, 330
    HIPAA compliance, 321–343
    HIPAA privacy administrative tasks and how to do them, *328–329*
    HIPAA security rule compliance, 330–335
    insurance coverage verification, 217–223, *220*
    internal control (compliance) checklist, *319*
    OIG compliance program for individual and small group physician practices, 355–374
    patient and insurance data entry, 230, 235–238
    patient registration confidentiality, 223–225, *224*
    patient sign-in sheet, *224*
    patient welcome letter, 228, *229*
    preposting actions, 270
    prioritizing accounts receivable, 276
    risk analysis, *331*
    sample letters, claim inquiries, *292–294*
    telephone follow-up on unpaid claims, 279–280
    translation of clinical and treatment information to appropriate codes, 236–237
    UB-04 (uniform bill), 238–243
    unpaid claim appeals, *288–291*
    unpaid claims follow-up, 277–279, 278–280
Office staff
    billing and collection staff job responsibilities, *215*
    compliance education and training, 311–312, *313*
    compliance officer, 311
    employee job description, 213
    HIPAA privacy official, *326*
    HIPAA training, 340
    improper, illegal activities, and disciplinary actions, 313
    manager's job responsibilities, *214*
    reception and patient registration job responsibilities, *215*
    sanctioning for noncompliance, 315–316

INDEX

Ohio data, information, *See* State-by-state listings
OIG, *See* Office of Inspector General
OIG Model Compliance Program Guidance for Individual and Small Group Physician Practices, 309
Oklahoma data, information, *See* State-by-state listings
Open enrollment, definition of term, 414
Oregon data, information, *See* State-by-state listings
Orthotics, 177
Other teaching hospital, definition of term, 414
Out-of-pocket expenses, 4, 414
Outliers, definition of term, 414
Outpatient, definition of term, 414
Outpatient care, *See* Ambulatory care
Oxygen
   equipment, 177
   home services, 177, 180

P

PACE, *See* Program of All-Inclusive Care for the Elderly
Pankau, Barbara, xiv
Pap smears
   services covered under Medicare Part B, *58*
   services not covered under Medicare Part B, *57*
Paper claims, *See* Claims
Paramedics, 198
Part B premium, definition of term, 414
Participation, definition of term, 414
Pathology, CPT codes, 133
Patients
   appointments and preregistration, 213–217
   assignment of benefits and payment to provider form, 225, *226*
   authorization for release of medical-related information, 226, *227*
   bad debts, 260–266
   complaints to state insurance commissioner, unpaid claims, *294*
   information, 213–260
   information forms, 214, *216*, 217
   medical cost estimate form, 228–229, *232*
   Medicare identification card, 62, *62, 63*
   new, information sheet, *216*, 225
   overdue letter, *264*
   registration confidentiality, 223–225, *224*
   registration, demographic and insurance coverage verification, 217–223, *219, 220*
   registration staff, *215*
   sign-in sheet, *224*
   signature-on-file form, 227, *227*
   welcome letter, 228, *229*
Payers, 21–113; *See also* Blue Cross and Blue Shield plans; CHAMPVA; Medicare; Medicaid; Reimbursement; TRICARE;
   Blue Cross and Blue Shield plans, 39–54
   commercial carriers, 21, 38–54
   Medicare coordination of benefits (Medicare as secondary payer), 61–62
   Medicare relationship to other insurance programs, 64
   Medicare secondary claim filing, 64

Medicare secondary payer guide, 383–395
Medicare secondary payers, recoveries and debt-related issues, 397–403
national expenditure estimates and projections, *25*
primary and secondary, 38–39
primary insurance claim, non-Medicare, 64
private, sources of payments to health care providers, *2*
prompt payment laws, 280, *280–287*, 288
sources of payments to health care providers, *2*
third-party, reimbursement, 267–269
TRICARE as secondary payer, 104
Payments, *See* Reimbursement
PECOS, *See* Provider Ownership Chain and Ownership System
Peer review, definition of term, 414
Peer review organization, definition of term, 414
Pelvic examinations
   services covered under Medicare Part B, *58*
   services not covered under Medicare Part B, *57*
Pennsylvania data, information, *See* State-by-state listings
Per diem reimbursement, definition of term, 415
Per member per month, 7, 415
Performance measurement, CPT Category II codes, 133
Personal care, 181
Personal Responsibility and Work Opportunity Reconciliation Act, 81
Physical examinations
   medical records, E/M documentation, 140–141
   Welcome to Medicare (services not covered under Part B), *57*
Physical therapy, Medicare home health coverage, 195
Physician-hospital organization, definition of term, 415
Physician networks ("in-network" physicians, PPOs), 4
Physician organization, definition of term, 415
Physician Payment Review Commission, 6
Physician services, *See also* Reimbursement;
   Blue Cross Blue Shield basic option benefits, *45*
   Blue Cross Blue Shield standard option benefits, *41–42*
   CPT codes, 133
   Medicare Part B, 56–77
   OIG Medicare projects, *316*
Physicians
   HIPAA National Provider Identifier standards, 340–341
   "in-network" (PPOs), 4
   Medicaid application and participation, 83
   Medicare definition, 56–58
   Medicare participation advantages, disadvantages, 59–60
   national health care expenditure estimates and projections, *29*
   National Provider Identifier, 210–212
   TRICARE participation, 98
Place of service code
   CMS-1500 form, 251, *252–253*
   definition of term, 415

PLI (professional liability insurance) RVUs, 5
Point of service, definition of term, 415
Poisoning, E codes, 165–166
Poverty, Temporary Assistance for Needy Families, 81–82
PPOs, *See* Preferred provider organizations
Practice management, *See* Office operations
Preadmission certification, definition of term, 415
Preauthorization, definition of term, 415
Precertification, definition of term, 415
Preexisting condition, definition of term, 415
Preferred provider organizations, 4, 109–111
   Blue Cross Blue Shield standard option benefits, *41–44*
   definition of term, 415
   eligible employees, *110*
   enrollment data, *109*
   "in-network" physicians, 4
   types of, *111*
Premium, definition of term, 415
Preregistration, *See* Office operations
Prescription drugs, *See* Drugs
Preventive health care
   Blue Cross Blue Shield basic option benefits, *44–45*
   Blue Cross Blue Shield standard option benefits, *41*
   definition of term, 415
   services covered under Medicare Part B, *58*
   services not covered under Medicare Part B, *57*
Primary care physician, definition of term, 415
Primary carrier, definition of term, 415
Primary payer, definition of term, 415
Principal inpatient diagnosis-diagnostic cost group, definition of term, 415
Prior authorization number, definition of term, 415
Privacy
   HIPAA rule, 323–330, 333
   medical records, 124
   patient registration confidentiality, 223–225, *224*
Privacy official, *326*
Private contracting, definition of term, 415
Productivity, definition of term, 415
Professional associations, related Web sites and resources, 349–352
Program of All-Inclusive Care for the Elderly, 188, *189*
Prompt-payment laws, *See* State laws
Proprietary software, 122
Prospective payment system
   changes to home health care, 192, *193*
   definition of term, 415
Prostate cancer screening
   services covered under Medicare Part B, *58*
   services not covered under Medicare Part B, *57*
Prosthetic devices, 177
Protected health information, 323–326
   electronic, HIPAA security rule, 330, *331*
   HIPAA security rule, 330–335
Provider, definition of term, 415
Provider number, definition of term, 415
Provider Ownership Chain and Ownership System (PECOS), 129–130

Provider-sponsored organizations, 112, 415
Puerto Rico
　Blue Cross Blue Shield customer service contacts, 47
　durable medical equipment regional carriers, 172
　Medicaid managed care enrollment, 87
　Medicare EDI helplines, 406, 407

Q

Qualified Medicare Beneficiary Program, definition of term, 415
Quality assurance, definition of term, 415
Quality improvement, definition of term, 415
Quality improvement organization, definition of term, 415–416
Quality Improvement System for Managed Care, definition of term, 415
Quality of care standard, 306–307, 309–310
Quality of health care, CPT Category II codes, 133
Qui tam lawsuits, 305–306, 308

R

Radiology, CPT codes, 133
Railroad retirement, prefixes, 63
RBRVS (Resource-based relative value scale), 5–6; *See also* RVUs;
　Medicare reimbursement, 57
　RVU totals for procedures, 5
Referral
　certification and authorization (HIPAA transactions), 339–340
　definition of term, 416
Rehabilitation facilities, number of, 181
Rehabilitation levels of care, 186–187
Reimbursement, *See also* Medicare reimbursement
　appeals, 288–291
　capitated rates, 7
　claim appeals and review, 295–304
　contractual adjustments, 270, 272
　definition of term, 416
　error rates (overpayment, underpayment), 306
　fractional payment of allowed charges, 272
　managed care methods, 7
　Medicaid claim submission, 83–84
　methods of, 4–7
　"nondisclosed" payment allowance, 38
　per-member, per-month, 7
　preposting actions, 270
　primary and secondary coverage, 38
　prompt payment and clean claims, 12–18
　prompt payment laws, 280, 280–287, 288
　RBRVS, 5–6
　relative value payment schedules, 5–7
　sources of payments to health care providers, 2
　third-party, 267–269
　usual, customary, reasonable, 4–5
　withhold adjustments, 272
Reinsurance, definition of term, 416
Relative value payment schedules 5–7
Relative value units, *See* RVUs
Relative weights, definition of term, 416
Renal disease, end-stage, *See* End-stage renal disease

Resource-based relative value scale, *See* RBRVS (Resource-based relative value scale)
Resource Utilization Groups, Version III, definition of term, 416
Rhode Island data, information, *See* State-by-state listings
Risk adjustment, definition of term, 416
Risk contract, definition of term, 416
Risk score, definition of term, 416
Risk selection, definition of term, 416
Risk sharing, 2, 416
RUC (AMA/Specialty Society RVS Update Committee), 5
　RVU update recommendations, 6
RVP (St. Anthony Relative Value for Physicians), 5, 6–7
RVUs (relative value units), 5
　malpractice costs (MP), 5
　practice expense (PE), 5
　updates, 6
　work (WK), 5

S

St. Anthony's Relative Value for Physicians, *See* RVP
SCHIP, *See* State Children's Health Insurance Program
Secondary carrier, definition of term, 416
Secondary payer, definition of term, 416
Security, HIPAA rule, 330–335
Skilled care, home health care, 193–194
Skilled nursing care, 181
Skilled nursing facilities, xi
　characteristics of, 184
　definition of term, 416
　levels of care, 186–187
　Medicare costs per day, 184
　Medicare covered benefits, 184–185
　Medicare spending, 182, 183
　number of, 181
　rural hospital swing-bed facilities, 187
SNFs, *See* Skilled nursing facilities
Social managed care plans, 190
Social Security, disability beneficiaries under Medicare, 55–56
Social services, Medicare home health coverage, 195
South Carolina data, information, *See* State-by-state listings
South Dakota data, information, *See* State-by-state listings
Specialist physician, definition of term, 416
Specified Low-Income Medicare Beneficiary Program, definition of term, 416
Speech language pathology services, Medicare home health coverage, 195
Spending, *See* Expenditures
St. Anthony's Relative Value for Physicians, *See* RVP
Staff model, definition of term, 416
Standardization, definition of term, 416
State-by-state listings
　Blue Cross Blue Shield customer service contacts, 47–54
　clean claim definitions, 12–18

　comprehensive health reform demonstrations (Medicaid), 84
　durable medical equipment regional carriers, 172
　federal Medicaid assistance percentage by state, 79
　Medicaid managed care enrollment, 87–88
　Medicare EDI helplines, 405–407
　prompt payment laws, 280, 280–287, 288
　TRICARE regions, 88–90
State Children's Health Insurance Program, 81–82
State laws, prompt-payment laws, 12
State medical boards, Web sites, 352–354
State Medicaid programs, 77–86
Substance abuse, Blue Cross Blue Shield standard option benefits, 43–44
Superbill (sample encounter form), 11
Supplemental insurance, definition of term, 416
Surgery
　CPT codes, 133, 145–146
　elective, 233
　global surgical period, 164–165
Swing-bed facilities, 187

T

Technology, emerging, CPT Category III codes, 133
Telephone
　follow-up, unpaid claims, 279–280
　Medicare EDI helplines, 405–407
Temporary Assistance for Needy Families, 81–82
Tennessee data, information, *See* State-by-state listings
Terminology
　glossary, 409–417
　long-term care, 181
Terrorism
　E codes, 169
　ICD-9-CM codes, 158, 159
Texas data, information, *See* State-by-state listings
Third-party payer, definition of term, 416
Transactions, HIPAA, 322, 335–340
TRICARE, 86–104
　benefits, deductibles, coinsurance, 98, 99, 100, 101, 102–104
　definition of term, 416
　eligibility, 95, 96
　explanation of benefits (example), 271
　Extra, 90, 99
　For Life, 100–101, 102–104
　Medicare relationship to, 101–104
　nonavailability statement, 98
　North region, 88–89
　participation, 98
　primary and secondary coverage, 38
　Prime, 90, 99
　Reserve Select, 95–96, 97
　South region, 89
　Standard, 95, 99
　West region, 89–90
Type of service code, definition of term, 417

INDEX

U

UB-04 form, 238–243
UB-92 form, 162, *163*, 238
UCR, *See* Usual, customary and reasonable reimbursement
Uncompensated care, definition of term, 417
Uniform bill form, *See* UB-04 form
Uninsured Americans, xi
Unique physician identification number (UPIN), definition of term, 417
Universal claim form, *See* CMS-1500 form
Update, definition of term, 417
UPIN, *See* Unique physician identification number (UPIN)
US armed forces, *See* Military personnel
US Centers for Medicare & Medicaid Services (CMS) see Centers for Medicare & Medicaid Services (CMS)
US Defense Department, *See* Military personnel
US Department of Health and Human Services, *See* Health and Human Services Department, US
US government agency Web sites, 347–348
US (HHS) Office of Inspector General, *See* Office of Inspector General
US Veterans Affairs Department, *See* Veterans Affairs Department, US
Usual, customary and reasonable reimbursement, 4–5, 270
  definition of term, 417
Utah data, information, *See* State-by-state listings
Utilization management, definition of term, 417
Utilization review, definition of term, 417

V

V codes, 165, *166*
  anthrax, 170, *170*
Vaccines, services not covered under Medicare Part B, 57
Veterans Affairs Department, US, CHAMPVA, 104–106
Veterans care, CHAMPVA, 104–106
Vermont data, information, *See* State-by-state listings
Virginia data, information, *See* State-by-state listings

W

Washington data, information, *See* State-by-state listings
Waters, Joanne M., xiii
Web sites, *See* Internet resources
Welcome letter, 228, *229*
Welfare reform, 81–82
Well child care, *See* Preventive care
Wellness programs, definition of term, 417
West Virginia data, information, *See* State-by-state listings
Wisconsin data, information, *See* State-by-state listings
Withhold incentive, definition of term, 417
Workers' compensation, 112–113
  Medicare relationship to other insurance programs, 64
  primary and secondary coverage, 39
World Health Organization, ICD-10-CM, 158
World Wide Web, *See* Internet resources
Wyoming data, information, *See* State-by-state listings

DATE DUE

Demco